The
Cognitive Bases
of
Human Learning

THE DORSEY SERIES IN PSYCHOLOGY

EDITOR   HOWARD F. HUNT   *Columbia University*

BARNETTE (ed.) *Readings in Psychological Tests and Measurements* rev. ed.

BARON & LIEBERT (eds.) *Human Social Behavior: A Contemporary View of Experimental Research*

BENNIS, SCHEIN, STEELE, & BERLEW (eds.) *Interpersonal Dynamics: Essays and Readings on Human Interaction* rev. ed.

COURTS *Psychological Statistics: An Introduction*

DENNY & RATNER *Comparative Psychology: Research in Animal Behavior* rev. ed.

DESLAURIERS & CARLSON *Your Child Is Asleep: Early Infantile Autism*

DEUTSCH & DEUTSCH *Physiological Psychology*

FISKE & MADDI *Functions of Varied Experience*

FITZGERALD & McKINNEY *Developmental Psychology: Studies in Human Development*

FLEISHMAN (ed.) *Studies in Personnel and Industrial Psychology* rev. ed.

FREEDMAN (ed.) *The Neuropsychology of Spatially Oriented Behavior*

HAMMER & KAPLAN *The Practice of Psychotherapy with Children*

HENDRY *Conditioned Reinforcement*

KLEINMUNTZ *Personality Measurement: An Introduction*

KOLSTOE *Introduction to Statistics for the Behavioral Sciences*

LIEBERT & SPIEGLER *Personality: An Introduction to Theory and Research*

MADDI *Personality Theories: A Comparative Analysis*

MARKEL *Psycholinguistics: An Introduction to the Study of Speech and Personality*

ROZEBOOM *Foundations of the Theory of Prediction*

SALTZ *The Cognitive Bases of Human Learning*

VON FIEANDT *The World of Perception*

The Cognitive Bases of Human Learning

ELI SALTZ
Wayne State University

1971
THE DORSEY PRESS   Homewood, Illinois   60430
Irwin-Dorsey Limited, Georgetown, Ontario

First Printing, May, 1971

Library of Congress Catalog Card No. 71–153172
Printed in the United States of America

To Rosalyn
Sharon, Joel, *and* David

Preface

BACKGROUND

After many years of very self-conscious empiricism, the psychology of human learning has begun to show signs of a vigorous interest in new (and often dramatic!) theoretical approaches. We find the postulation of multiple storage systems for memory; the distinction between learning systems and retrieval systems; the attempt to analyze "what is learned" into a complex system of interacting variables.

Further, there is evidence to suggest that psychologists in the area of human learning may have lost some of their fear of studying complex processes. There has developed a lively new interest in such issues as the nature of concept acquisition; the role of strategies in learning; and the more general question of the nature and function of variables like intention, meaning, and imagery. In short, there is a new interest in the role of the *cognitive,* information-processing variables in human learning.

To a great extent, the vitality and creative initiative that made animal learning a dynamic focus of interest in psychology between 1925 and 1950 seems to have reappeared, this time in the human learning area. How will the psychology of human learning look in the year 2000? Which of the theoretical approaches will prove valuable and which will be forgotten? Which processes will prove important to learning and which will turn out to have been largely inconsequential? In a sense, these are the questions that have motivated the present book.

The approach of the present book is directed largely toward examining the cognitive processes basic to human learning. The human organism processes information, attempts to relate the new information to previous information. We shall see that his success in this attempt will be an important factor in determining his ability to retain this new information (though the relationship is a complex one). The great importance of meaningfulness in learning is just one example of the operation of this process. People display a very powerful tendency to interpret the word in terms of previously developed concepts. In order to understand the learning process, *we* (as psychologists) must develop some conceptualizations about the manner in which the *human organism* represents concepts psychologically.

*From this point of view, some basic understanding of the nature and function of concepts must **precede** a consideration of the learning process in general.* For this reason, in the present volume we find an inversion of the usual order of chapters. Rather than trying to build up some simple notions of the learning processes and then applying these to concepts, the present book starts with a consideration of the nature of concepts and of psychological representation as exhibited in concepts, and attempts to build a picture of learning based on this.

Is this a description of a bootstrap operation? Clearly it is! One of the reasons for the slow development of some areas in psychology probably resides in the necessity for shifting back and forth between levels of analysis. A great deal of preliminary work was necessary before we knew enough about concepts to use them as a focus for further work on learning.

The primary objective of the present book is not that of detailing the facts of learning—though such detailing proved unavoidable in the service of the more primary objects. The primary objective of the book was to suggest the more promising directions in which psychologists are looking for the facts of learning, and for the theoretical principles which will organize these facts.

ADVICE TO THE READER

The reader is requested to work the short Demonstration Experiment at the beginning of a chapter before reading the chapter! Why were these experiments included in the book? One reason is that the experiments help make the topics less academic, more meaningful and concrete. A more important reason, however, is related to the nature of evidence and proof. It is possible to become involved in very abstract arguments when we try to discover the processes basic to a set of phenomena. Experiencing these phenomena can, at times, clear the air with regard to some of these arguments. Notions that may, at first, appear improbable may appear much more acceptable after having personally experienced the phenomena. For example, can learning occur without intention to learn? We can examine masses of data on such an issue and can become involved in very complex philosophical considerations. Before doing all this, the reader may benefit from placing himself in the relevant situation and experiencing it! Obviously, this type of experience is not necessarily scientific evidence in itself. However, it can provide a very salutary context against which to evaluate such evidence.

Please note that a short *precis* precedes each chapter. It is hoped that these will prove useful in assisting the reader to orient himself to the topics under consideration and to the direction which the discussions will take in the chapter.

ACKNOWLEDGMENTS

The writer is indebted to many people for their assistance in the preparation of the present manuscript. First among these is Professor Howard Hunt of Columbia University. As Psychology Editor for Dorsey Press, Professor Hunt showed great faith in the *content* of the book, despite the ponderous style of the early versions. Professor Hunt read the long first draft of the manuscript with great care. His detailed suggestions for a complete reorganization of the book (aimed at making it more comprehensible to the human mind) were painful but, in the end, produced a much better book.

Both Professor M. Ray Denny of Michigan State University and Professor Charles G. Stewart of Tulane University read the completed version of the entire manuscript and made many suggestions which were valuable in clarifying specific issues in the text. Since Professor Denny is an S-R theorist whose preferences for theoretical interpretations are often quite different from my own, his enthusiasm for the book was particularly gratifying.

In a much larger sense, the present book would never have been possible had it not been for Professor G. Robert Grice, now at the University of New Mexico. Bob Grice made learning theory a fascinating topic for me when I was a young graduate student in clinical psychology at the University of Illinois. But for his encouragement and personal interest, I might not have continued in psychology.

While our theoretical approaches have diverged over the years, my respect and affection for him have never wavered.

Finally, I wish to thank the numerous students at Wayne State University who read early versions of the book and made many helpful suggestions.

Detroit, Michigan   ELI SALTZ
April 1971

Contents

cubation of Anxiety. Overlearning: From Association to Structure? *A Model for Overlearning. Does the Model Fit the Data?* Short-Term Memory: *Are the Laws of Short-Term Memory Different from Those of Long-Term Memory? Are the Laws of Interference Applicable to Short-Term Memory? Is Extinction-Recovery Theory Applicable to Short-Term Memory? A Boundary Strength Interpretation of Short-Term Memory.* Conclusions.

PART I
NEW DIRECTIONS IN LEARNING AND THINKING

1 | Historical Perspectives

PRECIS

Before examining the present status of research and theory in the areas of learning and conceptual behavior, it is important to understand the historical context in which this work was performed. The present chapter considers two aspects of this context. The first aspect is the evolution of the conceptualization of the learning variable. Early work in learning was dominated by a global concept of "what is learned" that attempted to encompass processes such as thinking, motivation, incentive, and fatigue in a single learning variable. Later theorists differentiated the global variable into a *single* learning component and a *set* of performance variables. This development is traced through the theories of Guthrie, Tolman, and Hull.

The second aspect in the historical development to be examined is the de-emphasis, in recent years, of classical conditioning and instrumental learning. The theoretical basis for the early dominance of these techniques is discussed. It is shown that the basic assumptions of this theoretical position, with regard to the nature of the classical conditioning and instrumental learning techniques, proved to be unfounded.

Finally, the chapter suggests that recent evidence makes it reasonable to consider learning, *per se,* as a system of interrelated variables. The nature of the variables involved in this system is briefly outlined in this chapter. These variables are the focus of interest in Chapters 3, 4, 5, and 6.

DEMONSTRATION EXPERIMENT

The Problem

You are an anthropologist on a little-explored island and you hear a native use the word *orp*. Your native informant, Sam, tries to explain the meaning of the word, but, failing this, he says, "Watch, I show you orp." He points to three objects:

> A RED, TULIP-LIKE FLOWER;
> A RED, ROSE-LIKE FLOWER;
> A RED, PANSY-LIKE FLOWER.

Finally, with a great smile, Sam holds up a YELLOW FLOWER in his right hand and RED BEADS in his left hand and asks, "Which is orp?"

Without looking back at the story, first write down what you think an *orp* is; then write down the three objects that Sam showed you in trying to explain the meaning of *orp*.

Explanation of the Experiment

Did you learn anything in the story above? Clearly, this depends on what we mean by "learn." Most persons, shown the story, can with reasonable accuracy write down at least half the object pointed out by Sam. (How many did you recall?) Thus, they did learn something. They can remember the story, and this is one meaning we have for the word "learn." On the other hand, did you learn the meaning of the word *orp*? No! If forced to guess, you could expect to be correct only by chance.

We see from this demonstration that the word "learn" has at least two meanings. One meaning refers to a process which can produce *retention* of previously experienced stimuli or events. The second meaning refers to an *inferential* process that can determine subsequent decision behavior. In many learning tasks, we are concerned primarily with training for subsequent retention. However, tasks like discrimination learning and concept attainment demand inference in addition to retention. Shall both types of processes be considered "learning"? The answer to this question will depend on whether problem solving and learning for retention both are found to develop in the same way and to relate in the same manner to other variables. These issues will be explored in greater detail later in this chapter.

4

WHAT DO WE MEAN BY LEARNING?

Behavioral versus Situational Definitions

The most commonly encountered definitions of learning tend to be behavioral in nature. The "empirical" definition is a particularly popular example in this category. It states: *Learning is a relatively permanent change in behavior which occurs as a function of practice.*

At one time, many psychologists seemed to feel that such definitions, stated in terms of overt behavior, were the most desirable since they were objective and were not likely to lead to inferences about unverifiable internal processes. Unfortunately, it is often difficult to state such a definition in a manner which permits including all the phenomena which we usually consider relevant, and yet permits excluding phenomena which we consider irrelevant.

For example, consider the term "relatively permanent" which occurs in the empirical definition. A major difficulty in regard to this qualification arises from research in human short term memory. In Chapter 3 we shall see that if we show human subjects a very unfamiliar looking nonsense syllable and prevent them from rehearsing this syllable, their probability of correct recall after a three-second retention interval is approximately 90%. However, during the next 15 seconds, the probability of recalling the syllable drops to almost zero. It would be difficult to defend the proposition that this type of recall represents a "relatively permanent change in behavior." Yet, despite the fact that the item was lost over such a very short interval of time, we would hesitate to say that no learning had occurred.

Then can we strike the qualification "relatively permanent" from the definition? Why was it inserted in the first place? It was originally placed in the definition to handle factors which produce transient changes in behavior which we would normally *not* wish to consider changes due to learning. Fatigue and motivational level are two such factors. For example, increased motivation might increase correct performance for a period (e.g., while the boss is watching) ; once the motivational state returns to normal, the behavior will often drop to its former level.

Other areas of difficulty also exist in the empirical definition, but the example cited above should suffice to make the point: A given sort of behavior can often be produced by many different factors; it is often impossible, by observing the particular behavior, to determine how it was produced. Thus concepts which we defined in terms of behavior are frequently ambiguous.

SITUATIONAL DEFINITIONS OF LEARNING. Most of the major learning theorists have tended to define learning in terms of the situational factors which determine the changes in behavior rather than in terms of the behavior itself. The reason is simple. If a given situation results in learning, and if we know that the situation has occurred, we know that learning must also have occurred.

Let us consider some examples of situational definitions.

For E. R. Guthrie (1930, 1935), learning can be defined in the following manner: *If a response occurs in the presence of a stimulus, an association develops between this stimulus and this response.* Consider, for example, a person who touches a hot radiator and withdraws in pain. First the sight of the radiator and touching it occurred contiguously, and so this stimulus and response became associated. Next, however, the person withdrew in pain; at ths point, the sight of the radiator became associated with withdrawal. Since touching the radiator and withdrawing from it are incompatible responses, Guthrie assumes that the first of these two associations is obliterated in the competition. This leaves the radiator-withdrawal association intact.

Note that the paragraph above describes Guthrie's *definitional* specification of the conditions under which an association is formed. That is, he states that if these situational conditions were met (viz., a stimulus and a response occur together), he will *define* learning as having occurred. In order to be of use, however, such a definition must help us know how such learning will influence later behavior. Guthrie coordinates his definition of learning with later behavior by means of the following assumption: After learning occurs, if the *identical* stimulus reoccurs at a later time, that stimulus will elicit the *last* response associated to it. In the example above, the last response made to the radiator was withdrawal. Therefore, Guthrie would predict that the person will tend to withdraw from the radiator next time he encounters it.

At this level of discourse, the definition proposed by C. L. Hull (1943), within his theory of learning, is very similar to that of Guthrie. Hull states *that if a response occurs in the presence of a stimulus, and this response is followed by some type of reinforcement, an increment in association occurs between that stimulus and that response.* The greater the amount of reinforced practice, the greater the associative strength, and the greater the likelihood that subsequent appearance of the same stimulus will elicit the given response.

Let us consider the radiator situation from Hull's point of view. The response to the radiator that immediately preceded reduction in pain was the withdrawal response. Pain reduction is considered a reinforcer by Hull. Thus an increment in association developed between the sight of the radiator and withdrawal.

Finally, the operational definition of learning proposed by E. C. Tolman (1932, 1948) is also a situational definition, though it differs in important respects from those Guthrie and Hull. Tolman states that *if two events follow one another closely in time, the first event produces an expectation of the occurrence of the second event.* This expectation, which develops as a function of number of co-occurrences of the two events, constitutes the thing which is learned.

Returning one final time to the radiator example, for Tolman the sight of the radiator would be the first event, the pain upon touching it the second event. The acquired association would be the expectation of pain upon seeing the radiator.

Note that all three positions described above make learning virtually synonymous with the development of an association (though the things being associated are very different for Tolman as opposed to Guthrie and Hull). This is a very important point which we shall return to later.

Differentiation of Learning from Performance

One of the most important developments in learning theory over the past 30–40 years has been the gradual process of distinguishing *learning* from *performance*. What started out, conceptually, as a unitary, global variable has become differentiated into a number of separate, independent variables that are postulated as interacting to determine behavior. We shall examine this process by comparing the global notion of learning found in the theoretical position proposed by Guthrie (1930, 1935, 1938) with the successively more differentiated notions found in the theories of Tolman (1932, 1948) and Hull (1943, 1951, 1952).

GUTHRIE. We have already examined Guthrie's definition of learning in the previous section of this chapter. In what way is his concept of learning a global one? Primarily because variables like fatigue, motivation, incentive were seen as operating *as part of* the learning variable (i.e., as part of the stimulus-response association).

Let us consider motivation as an example. If the organism is hungry, the hunger will produce distinctive internal stimulation which will be part of the association. Further, if hunger is an innate stimulus to increased activity, the response which becomes associated with the stimulus will be a more vigorous one than if the animal were not hungry. Thus hunger may enter into the association at both the stimulus and the response; but it can affect performance only to the extent that *it is part of* the stimulus and/or response aspect of the association.

Fatigue operates in a similar fashion. The fatigued subject has a different stimulus condition than the nonfatigued. In addition, to the extent that fatigue leads to more lethargic behavior, the stimulus is attached to a slower response. But again, fatigue can operate only to the extent that it becomes a part of the stimulus-response association.

In effect, this is a one variable system, and that variable is the *S-R* association.

TOLMAN.   Tolman was probably the first of the major learning theorists to systematically distinguish between learning and performance variables. Tolman saw the organism as seeking and storing information. Under appropriate motivational or incentive conditions, this learned information may be put to use. Thus a rat may explore a complex maze, but exhibits no decrease in errors (i.e., no decrease in entering blind alleys) as long as he finds no food at the end of the maze. However, simply exploring is enough to develop the event-expectancy associations that constitute learning for Tolman: At each choice point in the maze, the rat learns to expect that if he turns in direction *A* he will find a blind alley, while if he turns in direction *B* he will find a path to the goal box. That such learning has indeed occurred during these early trials is indicated by the sharp drop in errors that occurs if the experimnter places food in the goal box at a later time.

For Tolman, variables like motivation, fatigue, and incentive are no longer part of the learning variable, *per se.* They are independent factors which interact with learning to determine when and if the organism will employ what he has already learned.

HULL.   Hull followed Tolman in elaborating on the distinction between learning and performance. In a sense, Hull gave us the first usable, multifactorial, structural analysis of behavior. He analyzed behavior into a set of component parts such as *learning* (which he called "habit strength" and symbolized by the letter *H*), drive *(D)*, amount of reinforcement *(K)*, and a fatiguelike inhibition factor

(*I*) resulting simply from the execution of a response. Performance, in the Hullian system, is an interaction between these elements:

$$\text{Performance} = f[\,(H \times D \times K) - I\,]$$

Note that Hull stated a multiplicative relationship between learning, drive, and amount of reinforcement so that if any one of these is zero no performance of the learned behavior can occur. Similarly, even if H, D, and K are greater than zero, inhibition (*I*) may be so great that it prevents performance.

Thus we see that, in Hull's behavior system, the elements were specified, operationally defined, and their functional interaction with one another was indicated. Hull's position can be contrasted with that of certain theorists (e.g., Crespi, 1944) who attempted to characterize certain *behavior* as essentially motivational (e.g., speed in running down a straight alley to food) and other *behavior* as essentially showing learning (e.g., choosing the correct side of a T-maze to run to in searching for food). Hull, on the other hand, posited a general structure of interrelationships between variables like learning and drive; and this structure was the same for all behavior. The specific associations that were learned might differ from situation to situation, the specific values of D, K, and I might change, but all these variables must be represented in the formulation in order to predict behavior.

It may seem strange today, but this crucial structural analysis, separating as it did the learning from the performance variables, was the aspect of Hull's system which created the greatest anguish among his fellow behaviorists of that time. Many of these earlier behaviorists felt that Hull was disregarding the principle of parsimony in removing motivation and fatigue from the associative variable and establishing them as independent variables that interact with association. The answer to this criticism was, of course, that the principle of parsimony demands that we construct a theory with the smallest number of variables *that will adequately predict behavior*. This principle certainly *can not* be interpreted as stating that a theory with few variables that predicts behavior poorly is to be preferred to a theory with many variables that predicts behavior very well!

Many Performance Variables but One Learning Variable

The distinction between learning and performance variables proved to be a tremendous stimulus to research, and its importance in no way should be minimized. However, it is clear that both

Tolman and Hull still conceptualized *learning* as a single, unitary factor, though both thought in terms of several different and distinct *performance* factors (e.g., drive, incentive, etc.) .

IS THERE AN ALTERNATIVE TO THE SINGLE-FACTOR APPROACH? In the preceding pages, we have examined the manner in which the global associative notion was differentiated into a number of independent variables. Extrapolating this tendency might lead us to anticipate that a corresponding differentiation process may be in store for the unitary-factor learning variable, *per se*. That is, we may anticipate seeing a number of different *learning* variables, in addition to the association. Eventually, behavior may be predicted on the basis of a formulation which involves a complex of performance variables interacting with a complex of learning variables.

Research over the past 20 years has already provided many indications concerning the form that the complex of learning variables will take. The last section of this chapter will outline a multifactor approach to the learning variable. In a sense, the remainder of the present book will be devoted to expanding on this outline.

Retention and Problem Solving

At the beginning of the present chapter, we asked the question, "What do we mean by learning?" Thus far we have analyzed the notion of learning from the standpoint of its definition, and we have examined the structure of the concept of learning as it has been differentiated from performance.

At this point, we shall look at two different types of learning situations and shall ask, "Do they obey the same laws?"

In the Demonstration Experiment, at the beginning of the present chapter, the reader was asked to participate in a learning experiment. What if someone had asked you, at the termination of that experiment, "Did you learn?" You would probably have answered, "What do you mean by learning?" If learning means solving the problem posed in the experiment, finding the correct answer concerning the meaning of the foreign word from the information provided by the native informant, the answer would have been, "No." On the other hand, if learning means the acquisition and storage of the information communicated by the informant, then certainly some learning occurred.

Clearly, in this very commonly encountered type of situation, the word "learning" has at least two meanings. Let us examine the characteristics of each of these.

LEARNING FOR RETENTION.   In many learning tasks, the critical product of learning is the ability to remember something. Memory can take any of several forms.

a) It can consist of an *image* (e.g., we picture an event just as it occurred).

b) It can take the form of the *repetition of an overt response* (e.g., we previously dialed a phone number correctly; we do it again).

c) Or, it can take the form of the *reaction to some remembered event* (e.g., we previously saw a man commit a crime; now we describe the man to the police).

PROBLEM SOLVING.   In problem solving, the person must *discover* the response (or pattern of responses) which will permit him to reach some particular goal in a consistent manner. Often this response is one which might not occur to him readily in the situation.

Problem solving (like memory, above) can take several forms. While the characterizations listed below are rough, they will give the reader an idea of the range of situations under consideration.

a) Response selection. (E.g., we have forgotten our house key and stand in front of the empty house in the cold and snow; we can break a window and enter; look for an open window to climb through; sit in the snow until someone with a key appears; go to a hotel, etc.)

b) Response patterning. (E.g., Köhler, 1925, reports a famous study in which a banana was suspended from the top of a chimpanzee's cage at a height greater than the animal's unaided reach. In the cage were two boxes which, if stacked one atop the other, would permit reaching the banana. Only one of the chimpanzees spontaneously stacked the two boxes and stood on them to obtain the banana, and even this animal did not arrive at the solution until he had spent many days trying other, unproductive solutions.)

c) Cue selection. (E.g., in the Demonstration Experiment, at the beginning of the present chapter, the anthropologist tried to discover if the foreign word "orp" should be used in reference to objects which are *red,* to *flowers,* or to *red flowers.*)

WHAT IS THE RELATIONSHIP BETWEEN LEARNING FOR RETENTION AND PROBLEM SOLVING?   The *distinction* between these two types of tasks can be stated as follows. In learning for retention, the person is *informed* what the correct response is, and must retain this; in problem solving, the person must *discover* what the correct response is.

In addition, learning for retention is typically a critical aspect of performing the problem-solving task. Both research and common sense indicate that problem solving is dependent on the memory of products of learning. If the person does not recall the outcome of his responses which were performed during previous practice on the problem, his performance must inevitably suffer. And, of course, once the person discovers the correct response, the task is converted from problem solving to the task of retention for use on the next occasion.

The description above indicates that problem solving can be considered as constituting a class of *transfer* tasks. That is, it typically involves using the products of prior experience *in a new stimulus situation*. It corresponds to the class of functions often referred to as *thinking*.

LEARNING THEORY AND THE TWO MEANINGS OF LEARNING.   Historically, a number of psychologists have treated these two meanings of learnings as though they were essentially different instances of the same basic process. Let us examine two classic experiments in the history of learning theory, and we shall see how some of the results might, conceivably, have been interpreted differently if the distinction between these processes had been made.

Thorndike (1898) pioneered in the field of learning with his studies of cats in a puzzle box. A cat was confined in a box from which it could escape by correctly manipulating a latch. Thorndike noted that, on early trials, the animals engaged in a great deal of "trial and error" behavior before finding the correct response. On these early trials, an animal might be in the box a long time before he made the critical response that opened the door. Gradually, over a large number of trials, the animal became faster at escaping from the box. The cat's behavior changed gradually as a function of practice.

Thorndike interpreted the gradual change in behavior as indicating that *learning* (i.e., for Thorndike, the *S-R* connection) increased in strength slightly on each reinforced trial.

If we examine the situation in an attempt to separate the effects of retention from those of problem solving, the interpretation appears somewhat different. Clearly, the prior experience of the cat has provided him with little relevant experience for solving the puzzle box. The cat is dealing with a transfer (or thinking) task involving inadequate prior retention from other tasks to determine the correct solution to the problem.

A study by Guthrie and Horton (1946) throws further light on the interaction between processes in the Thorndike-type of problem situation. The results of their study indicate transfer, or thinking, not memory, provides the greatest difficulty for cats in a puzzle box.

Guthrie and Horton used an apparatus very similar to the one employed by Thorndike; the door of the box could be opened by the cat if he pressed a lever that extended from the floor of the box. The results suggested that cats have a remarkably good memory. Once an animal hit upon a response that was adequate for opening the door, he repeated it in striking detail over a large number of subsequent trials. For example, if the cat accidently opened the door by backing into the lever, he was likely to repeat the identical response of backing into the lever again and again each time he was placed in the box. Clearly, learning for retention was very rapid following an initial success. Thus the slowness with which improvement occurred in the animals' speed-of-escape appears to have been due to a difficulty in transferring past learning to a novel situation, in other words, to problem solving or thinking.

IMPLICATIONS FOR LEARNING THEORIES. We have seen that there are important differences between learning for retention and problem solving. However, the existence of such differences does not *necessarily* imply that a different set of theoretical mechanisms must be postulated for determining each of these classes of processes. Indeed, in Chapters 2 and 3, we shall examine several theories that have attempted to account for both the human memory studies and the problem-solving aspects of concept formation with essentially the same mechanisms.

In this regard, it should be noted that the distinction between learning for retention and problem solving has taken on major theoretical significance in some of the more recent work on intellectual functioning and intellectual development. Jensen (1969), for example, has proposed that this distinction is the basis for specifying the difference between two types of intellectual abilities. In a very controversial paper, Jensen has presented data which suggest that some persons may have very excellent intellectual abilities based on learning for retention; but these persons may be poor at abilities based on problem solving or thinking. Others, on the other hand, may excel at problem-solving functions. Jensen has further suggested that the sort of educational system which is optimal for one of these types of persons may prove to be ineffective when applied to the other type. Thus, it can be seen that the issue has important implications not only for learning theory but also for educational practices.

HOW SHALL WE STUDY LEARNING?

The last 20 to 30 years have seen a marked increase in research on human learning, particularly verbal learning, memory, and concept attainment. Prior to this, many psychologists had expressed the opinion that it was premature to study these functions. While understanding these types of processes was often accepted as an *ultimate* goal, many psychologists felt that we must first discover the laws governing "simpler" types of situations and perhaps even "simpler" organisms (e.g., the albino rat or the chimpanzee). Even today, in many universities, it is traditional for the first course in learning to concern itself largely with classical conditioning and with animal-learning studies. It is often assumed that such a course will provide the student with knowledge concerning the basic mechanisms of learning which are essential to understand before human learning can be comprehended.

However, the insistence on the primacy of animal research and the study of "simple" experimental tasks is much less prevalent today than it was in previous years. We shall see that many of the psychologists working in the area of animal learning have been extremely articulate concerning the problems of developing the basic principles from research in this area. On the other hand, data coming from the research on complex human performance has been very suggestive for our understanding of both human and animal learning.

In the present selection we shall examine the arguments for considering classical conditioning and animal learning as providing the basic laws of learning. We shall also examine some of the problems which have arisen with regard to such an approach.

Evaluation of the Simple Learning Situation

Spence (1956) has cogently stated the argument for the traditional American concern with studying behavior in simple situations. He states that learning can best be investigated in situations that permit the study of the development of a single S-R association, free from interference produced by competing associations. If a learning situation involves many competing associations, Spence feels, then it will be difficult to distinguish processes involved in extinguishing the competing associations from those involved in strengthening the S-R association we wish to investigate.

With these considerations in mind, Spence suggests a hierarchy of tasks for studying learning, ranging from those involving the least-response competition (viz., the purest measures of growth in associative strength) to those involving the most-associative competition. Basically, Spence distinguishes three types of experimental situations in his hierarchy: classical conditioning, instrumental conditioning, and selective learning. Let us examine these three briefly.

1. CLASSICAL CONDITIONING.   Here, Spence feels, learning consists of the gradual development of habit strength, *de novo,* between a stimulus and a response. Prior to conditioning, the conditioned stimulus *(CS)* has no tendency to elicit the particular response being learned. Learning trials consist of pairing the *CS* with some unconditioned stimulus *(US)* which has a strong tendency to evoke some particular response (e.g., a puff of air to the eye has a strong tendency to evoke blinking, and thus can serve as a *US*). After pairing the *CS* and *US* for a number of trials, the *CS* gradually develops the ability to evoke a response that, typically, strongly resembles the response to the *US*.

Examples of classical conditioning can readily be cited. If a dim light is paired with a puff of air to the eye, the dim light gradually develops the ability to evoke an eye blink. Here the light is the *CS*, the puff the *US*. If a particular sound is paired with putting food in the subject's mouth, the sound gradually develops the ability to evoke a salivary response. Here the sound is the *CS*, food the *US*.

2. INSTRUMENTAL CONDITIONING.   Next in the hierarchy of complexity, Spence places instrumental conditioning. Instrumental conditioning is a situation in which (*a*) the subject is rewarded only if he performs the critical response which we are trying to teach him and (*b*) at the very beginning of the experiment, the correct response is already among the strongest in the subject's hierarchy of responses to the experimental stimuli. Learning consists of the further strengthening of this *S-R* connection with repeated reinforcements.

Examples are training an animal to run a straight alley for food at the other end or training an animal to press a bar to receive food.

Spence feels that classical conditioning is to be preferred, for the study of learning, over instrumental conditioning. While both are situations in which competing associations are minimal, classical conditioning traces the development of a new *S-R* association from zero strength, while instrumental conditioning intersects the learning curve at a fairly high level on the first trial.

3. SELECTIVE LEARNING.   This is the poorest of the situations for studying learning, according to Spence. In selective learning the subject has a number of possible choices, only one of which is correct; further, the correct response is initially relatively weak in the subject's hierarchy of responses to the experimental stimuli. Learning can not be directly observed, since early trials involve inhibition of incorrect responses before the correct response can be made and reinforced. If the subject does not respond on a given trial, we do not know if this is because the correct response is weak or if it is because some incorrect response is strong.

Examples are: multiple-unit mazes; discrimination tasks, particularly those involving many choices; and puzzle-box type problems.

Spence vigorously advocates classical and instrumental conditioning for studying the development of learning. This preference is based on the assumption that in these situations we have the least contamination by extraneous variables. Spence states (1956, pp. 36–37):

In contrast to the more complex selective learning situations, these classical and instrumental conditioning methods attempt to provide situations that permit the study of the acquisition of an S-R relation more or less in isolation from the weakening of other responses.

Complexities in the Simple Situations

Several issues are involved in evaluating the classical American preference for studying learning in simple situations. The first issue is: Are classical and instrumental conditioning really the simple situations assumed by writers like Spence? The second issue is: To what extent is it actually desirable to investigate learning in the absence of "the weakening of other responses"?

In the present section of this chapter we shall examine the first of these issues. We shall see that classical and instrumental conditioning are far from simple. Not only do they involve massive effects from competition, they also involve idiosyncratic technical problems which are probably irrelevant to the more general issues of learning. The second issue above will be examined in Chapter 3 where it will be suggested that much of our primary interest in learning usually revolves about the elimination of competing responses; acquisition in the absence of competition is probably a trivial issue of little concern either practically or theoretically.

Let us now turn to the evidence concerning the complexity of the conditioning situations.

CONTINUITY OF LEARNING ACROSS TRIALS. Lewin (1942) has questioned the meaningfulness of many learning curves on the grounds that they do not simply demonstrate an increase in response strength with increased practice. The actual response may be quite different at different levels of practice. Thus the curves often obscure qualitative changes in what has been learned by reporting learning as though it represented a change in the frequency of the same response. Logan's (1956) micromolar concept of learning is a more refined version of Lewin's criticism.

The problem of qualitative changes in the conditioned response is dramatically illustrated by Culler (1938, pp. 134–36) .

From training scores of dogs at Illinois we can predict, when shock is applied to a wholly naive animal, that its response will include many of these features: quick gasp or yelp, hasty withdrawal of foot, adduction of tail, then whining or barking, biting or snapping at nearby objects, twisting and jerking, occasional evacuation. . . . Now suppose a bell be rung just before the shock. After a few times, we witness a display of behavior . . . which seems to duplicate the actual *UR;* indeed, so realistic is the animal's performance that I have sometimes been misled into thinking that shock was being inadvertently applied along with bell. . . . In this initial stage, when *UR* is still tentative and diffuse, the *CR* may indeed give a photographic reproduction. Thereafter, the two diverge, *UR* and *CR,* each in accord to its own function. . . . This unlikeness of *CR* to *UR* has been emphasized by many writers; one example must suffice. Werner . . . complains of his fruitless quest for a real *CR* in rats. To shock (*US*) they would hop frantically about and breathe rapidly; to *CS* (bell) they would hold the breath and wait tensely.

Changes in the conditioned response can also occur because of changes in the unconditioned response. Culler (1938, p. 135) points out that:

Let us first be clear that the *UR* itself is not stable and definitive at the start. It alters and accommodates . . . after a dog is often shocked, the same shock applied in the same place no longer yields this loose and widespread activity. It yields rather a quick, effective removal of foot, which is then slowly replaced.

COMPETING STIMULI IN CLASSICAL AND INSTRUMENTAL CONDITIONING. A close examination of the data suggests that it would be difficult to defend the contention that competing stimuli are a minimal problem in classical and instrumental conditioning. Hilgard and Marquis (1940) , in their classic summary of conditioning phenomena, quote Mateer's (1918) description of her attempt to condition chewing and swallowing responses involved in eating, using children as subjects. Mateer stated: "I learned that even acceptance of a test posture, or entrance into the experimental laboratory, was a conditioning factor and that these and other casual environmental factors had to be unconditioned through disuse before any arbitrary conditioning factor might be used as predetermined in a planned procedure."

Apparently, under such circumstances, conditioning becomes a discrimination task of relatively uncontrolled type, since the negative stimuli which must be extinguished are not completely under the experimenter's control. Mowrer (1960, pp. 446–50) notes essentially the same effect. He presents data for a simple situation in which a buzzer and shock were paired and a white rat was trained to jump when the buzzer sounded. The animals appeared uncertain as to which aspect of the situation was the relevant stimulus, and initially jumping was more frequent in the interval between buzzer presentations than upon presentation of the buzzer. Mowrer points out that animals often learn to discriminate relevant from irrelevant stimuli only gradually in such situations.

Observations such as those of Mateer and Mowrer suggest that many stimuli, both internal and external, precede the unconditioned stimulus and become attached to the conditioned response. Since only some of these will *always* be followed by the unconditioned stimulus, the others will gradually be extinguished during the course of conditioning. Kimble (1961, pp. 364–69) summarizes a number of studies which clearly demonstrate that the process of extinguishing negative stimuli results in a generalized reduction of strength to the positive conditioned stimulus. Thus, even in classical conditioning, the acquisition curve often will not represent a pure function of increased learning. As shall be seen later, in Chapter 3, the results of studies such as that of Voeks (1954), who attempted to eliminate irrelevant stimulation prior to the unconditioned stimulus, have produced alterations in some of the classical concepts of learning.

RESPONSES TO THE CONDITIONED STIMULUS. It has been well known for many years that conditioned stimuli have responses attached to them before the subject enters the experimental situation. Osgood (1953, pp. 310–12) notes that the responses to the conditioned stimulus in salivary conditioning of the dog may include lifting the ears, barking, wagging the tail; in eyelid conditioning to light as the conditioned stimulus, dogs *open* their eyes to the light, humans *close* their eyes.

The alpha response to light is one of the better documented examples of the operation of competing stimuli in conditioning. Many eyelid conditioning studies have used a light as the conditioned stimulus, and a puff of air to the eye as the unconditioned stimulus. The alpha response is a relatively weak, *unconditioned* eyeblink which may occur to the *light*. Concern with the alpha response has been largely restricted to distinguishing it from the conditioned eyeblink in order to prevent inflation of conditioning rates. This distinction is possible because the alpha response has a latency of from 50 to 120 milliseconds while the conditioned response has a minimum latency of 250 milliseconds. On the other hand, an alpha response occurring within 120 milliseconds of a conditioned blink may modify the form of the conditioned response and, in extreme cases, prevent it from occurring. Grant and Adams (1944) show that the occurrence of an alpha response is not independent of the conditioning procedure. Comparing the alpha response following 40 conditioning trials in which light and puff were paired with the alpha response following 40 presentations of light alone, they report that the conditioning procedure keeps the alpha response at a relatively high level, where it can continue to interfere with performance.

INHIBITION OF THE UNCONDITIONED RESPONSE.   We have already observed (Grant and Adams, 1944) that the unconditioned stimulus can augment the natural response to the conditioned stimulus. The interaction between conditioned and unconditioned stimuli is more complex than this. Kimble and Ost (1961) demonstrate that the conditioned stimulus can *inhibit* the natural response to the unconditioned stimulus. Following 50 conditioning trials they found that the *unconditioned* response was markedly reduced in intensity. That this was not simply an adaptation effect was then shown by presenting the unconditioned stimulus without the conditioned stimulus. Withholding the conditioned stimulus resulted in a significant *increase in unconditioned response magnitude*. Kimble and Ost report that the inhibition of the unconditioned response by the conditioned stimulus had a detrimental effect on conditioning rate. The six subjects who showed the greatest amount of inhibition made *no* conditioned responses during the 50 conditioning trials.

THE ORIENTING RESPONSE.   In recent years, a number of psychologists, mostly Russian, have become concerned with the orienting response and its relation to conditioning. Writers such as Sokolov (1963) and Razran (1961) tend to treat it as the observable component of attention. The orienting response, as described by Sokolov and Razran, is a complex physiological reaction which can be elicited by many stimuli. When this response is very weak or absent to a conditioned stimulus, conditioning is typically very slow or totally absent. Moderate orienting responses to the conditioned stimulus appear to be optimal for conditioning, while very strong orienting responses again will be accompanied by weak conditioning. The finding that strong orienting responses to the conditioned stimulus are detrimental to conditioning suggests that these responses (or other internal responses which they index) compete with the conditioned responses and prevent its elicitation. These competing effects may be direct or they may be due to complex physiological interactions (e.g., aroused states of the sympathetic nervous system that prevent salivation).

Many conditioning studies begin with a series of conditioned stimulus presentations in an attempt to adapt out the potentially interfering natural responses to these stimuli. The effect of such a procedure is very little understood. Berlyne (1960, p. 69; 1963, pp. 330–31) summarizes Russian and American research which indicates that such adaptation may have a deleterious effect on subsequent conditioning, slowing it down greatly, or even, in extreme cases, preventing its occurrence. Berlyne seems to interpret this as an *extinction of the orienting response* to the stimulus and discusses the phenomenon in a section on attention (1960, p. 69). There may be several bases for the deleterious effect of extinction of the orienting response to a stimulus. It is possible that the subject simply ceases to react to the stimulus. This is certainly suggested by the physiological indices recorded during stimulus presentation. A second factor may be that, as the subject begins to reinstate his orienting response to an extinguished stimulus during subsequent conditioning, the orienting response (and corresponding stimulus properties of the response) changes qualitatively with trials. If this were the case, and the Russian literature suggests it is, the conditioned stimulus would be unstable in early trials. This too could impede conditioning.

CONCLUSIONS CONCERNING THE COMPLEXITY OF "SIMPLE" SITUATIONS. The utility of concentrating on "simple" situations for studying learning can be evaluated either in terms of the goals proposed by the proponents of such study or in terms of alternate goals which one may consider more desirable or more realistic. The writer wishes to emphasize that, *at this time,* the concern is with evaluating the utility of the "simple" situation in terms of the goals proposed by its proponents. The primary goal of such an emphasis, as clearly enunciated by Spence (1956), is to obtain a relatively pure index of growth in associative strength between a stimulus and response in the absence of competing systems. The data presented in the previous sections strongly suggest that these simple situations are much too complex for this goal.

As shall be seen in subsequent chapters, data from classical and instrumental conditioning are very valuable in our understanding of learning processes. Certain types of problems are best attacked by means of technologies of these tasks. However, these particular learning situations do not appear to occupy a status of *primacy* in the study of learning.

THE SHAPE OF THINGS TO COME

Differentiation of the Global Learning Variable

Earlier in this chapter, we examined certain historical changes in the conceptualization of the learning variable. We saw that around the first part of this century, many psychologists thought of learning as a very global variable. Since learning was defined in terms of a change in *behavior,* no systematic distinction was made between learning and performance variables. Not until the late 1920s and early 1930s did psychologists attempt a systematic differentiation of performance variables from the learning variable.

There is evidence for a continuation of this differentiation of the learning variable. However, instead of a differentiation between learning and performance, this has taken the form of distinguishing between a number of different *learning* factors. In this section we shall attempt to outline the general character of these multiple learning variables and to indicate how they interact. (Chapters 3 to 6 shall present the research basic to postulating these variables and shall discuss alternative theoretical positions in regard to these data.)

THE ASSOCIATION. The notion of an association has remained as a core feature in the complex of learning variables. We shall not state a technical definition of association at this time. In a nontechnical sense, the term refers to a hypothetical construct concerning a process which permits one "thing" to remind a person of an associated "thing." These "things" may take a number of different forms. For example, one word may remind a person of another word. A physical stimulus may remind a person to perform a motor act (e.g., when the light turns red, the person steps on the brakes and stops the car).

There is even research to suggest that one physical stimulus may remind the person of a second physical stimulus. (E.g., these are the so-called "sensory preconditioning" studies which will be discussed in Chapter 5. In these studies, an animal is presented with a light followed by a buzzer. The buzzer is then used as a stimulus to some act such as running to avoid shock. Later, when the light is presented again, it is found that animals often transfer the running response from the buzzer to the light, despite the fact that light has never been associated with shock directly. It is often assumed that this transfer occurs because the early pairing of light and buzzer led these two to become associated to one another. Thus light leads the animal to buzzer which leads him to make the response he had learned to buzzer, namely, run.)

Chapter 3 will examine the evidence with regard to the associative variable. There it will be seen that a considerable body of data supports the position that the association achieves maximum (or nearly maximum) strength during the first trial in which the subject *attends* to the two elements which are to be associated. (Chapter 10 will show that *attention* is crucial to formation of the association, but *intention to learn* is not.) It will be seen in Chapter 3 that the assumption of near maximal associative strength following the first presentation of elements can resolve a number of the paradoxes that have plagued concept attainment, among other areas.

STIMULUS DIFFERENTIATION. The work of E. J. Gibson strongly suggests the operation of a differentiation process which is independent of the associational processes. (This research will be analyzed in Chapter 4.) At this point we shall be concerned with only two issues: What do we mean by differentiation and why do we consider it a *learning* variable?

Evidence suggests that repeated attention to an unfamiliar stimulus reduces the tendency for this stimulus to be confused with other similar stimuli. Differentiation refers to this reduction in stimulus confusion. Why consider this as a learning variable? Because it is a systematic change that occurs as a function of practice. Differentiation of a stimulus does *not* appear to be dependent upon this stimulus being associated to any other element, either stimulus or response. Thus it is a nonassociative learning element.

Unlike the associative variable, differentiation appears to develop gradually as a function of practice.

RESPONSE DIFFERENTIATION. In Chapter 5, we shall see that responses appear to undergo a differentiation process that is very similar to that of stimulus differentiation. Indeed, we shall see that the distinction between stimulus and response is often primarily a matter of the arrangement of elements in a test situation. This point is most easily understood in the case where both stimulus and response are words. Here the subject is told that when he sees Word 1 (the stimulus) , he is to respond by saying Word 2 (the response) . The arbitrary nature of the situation can be seen by the fact that on the next trial the subject can be presented Word 2 as the *stimulus* and asked to emit Word 1 as the *response*. Kendler (1952) has distinguished between the *empirical* use of the distinction between stimulus and response, illustrated above, and the theoretical use. In the theoretical use, the theorist assumes that learning is betwen two theoretically different categories of elements, stimulus elements and response elements.

In our discussion of sensory preconditioning above, we saw a situation in which both the elements of an association were in the category of events usually referred to as stimuli; in other words, there appeared to be a stimulus-stimulus association, rather than a stimulus-response association. Such considerations lend further support to the possibility that we are dealing with a single variable of differentiation, rather than with separate variables of stimulus and response differention.

Like stimulus differentiation, response differentiation appears to develop gradually as a function of practice. Research to be analyzed later will suggest that until both stimulus and response differentiation have attained sufficient magnitude, association will not produce performance of the response upon presentation of the stimulus.

RESISTANCE TO INTERFERENCE.   Finally, even if the stimulus and a response item are both very well differentiated, and even though associative strength reaches nearly maximal strength upon the first presentation of the stimulus and response together, very often the subject will *not* be able to emit the response correctly upon presentation of the stimulus on Trial 2. Under what circumstances will this occur? It will occur if there is a great deal of interference from *other,* competing *S-R* systems. Chapter 6 shall present evidence which suggests that the *S-R* system must develop resistance to interference *as a unit,* and that this resistance can not simply be equated with increasing associative strength. In the present book we shall abbreviate the term "resistance to interference of the *S-R* system" to the shorter term *boundary strength.* This term implied that a system is bounded by the effects of practice from the interfering effects of other systems.

To eliminate any confusion, let us re-emphasize the distinction between the notion of boundary strength and that of differentiation. Boundary strength of an S-R system grows as a function of practicing the particular system as a unit. Differentiation of a stimulus or response, on the other hand, is not tied to the specific system in which the differentiation develops. It is a function of the total amount of practice on that stimulus or response element over all systems in which the element occurs.

THE INTERACTION BETWEEN LEARNING VARIABLES. The evidence to be examined suggests that the variables described above are not simply a set of isolated factors, one of which may be relevant to performance in one situation while a second is relevant in another situation. Instead we are dealing with a system of interacting variables, each of which must be represented in some specific quantity before learning can become transformed into performance.

We shall see that there are a great many unanswered questions about the nature of the interaction between these variables. One issue, for example, is: Can associations develop when the stimulus is so weakly differentiated that the S-R system can not support correct performance? The results of several studies suggest that the answer to this question may be *yes*. In other words, the results suggest that "latent associations" may develop under such circumstances. In these studies, subjects typically could not recall the correct response to the stimulus on a test trial administered immediately after the first pairing of the stimulus and response. However, additional practice involving presentation of the *stimulus alone* (i.e., the correct response for this stimulus was *not* indicated to the subjects during this practice) appears to have strengthened stimulus differentiation sufficiently to permit subsequent correct performance of the latent association. To date, while the evidence for the existence of latent associations is relatively strong, we know little about the conditions under which such associations develop, or fail to develop.

WHAT IS LEARNED? Based on the variables described above, we can now define the product of learning as a bounded system of two or more differentiated elements which are associated to one another.

Conditions Necessary for Learning

In the previous section we characterized the content of Chapters 3 to 6 as being concerned with describing, "what is learned." Chapters 7 to 12, in contrast, can best be described as emphasizing "the conditions necessary for learning." Here we shall consider the role of variables like *intention to learn, strategies of learning,* and *stress.* A question that shall recur in these chapters will be: Does the variable in question have a differential effect on the various factors of the learning complex (viz., the association, the differentiation, and the boundary strength) ?

Turning to the distinction between learning for retention and problem solving, we shall find that these are often differentially affected by the variables under consideration. Reinforcement, for example, will be found to have a relatively negligible effect on retention but a more pronounced effect on problem solving.

2 | Introduction to Concept-Development and Inferential Behavior

PRECIS

The emphasis in the present chapter is on the nature and structure of concepts and the manner in which concept structure influences inferential behavior. The various dimensions (e.g., sensory, evaluative, motor) which constitute the basis for responding to a stimulus (e.g., person or event) can be thought of as determining an n-dimensional cognitive space. A concept consists of a region in this space. Systematic developmental changes occur in such concept regions and these changes are related to developmental changes in inferential behavior. Piaget's work on conservation is considered in this context. Finally, the two major approaches to concept learning (discrimination learning models versus growth models) are contrasted and evaluated against the criterion of relevance to real-world concepts.

DEMONSTRATION EXPERIMENT

The Problem

Answer each of the following questions.

1. A father goes to work where he is a doctor. He makes sick people well by examining them and giving them medicine. Is he still a father?
2. A father goes to work. On the way home from work in the evening he stops at a bar to have a drink. His friends there are drunkards and he becomes a drunkard too. Is he still a father?
3. A boy is a very good baseball player. He hits well and fields well. He becomes a liar and cheats on his tests in school. Is he still a good baseball player? Can he still hit well? Can he still field well?
4. A man is a doctor. He knows how to fix broken bones. He knows how to make sick people well. However, he goes into debt and owes a great deal of money, so he robs a bank and is a thief. Is he still a doctor? Does he still know how to fix broken bones? Does he still know how to make people well? If you were sick, would you go to him to make you well?
5. A tree in the back yard begins to talk. He has many wonderful stories to tell about the people who lived in this house before you did. It develops that he can even walk a little. Is he still a tree?
6. The prince suddenly turned into a frog and went jumping and croaking into the lily pond. Is he still a prince? Shall he be treated royally?

Explanation

In the present chapter we shall see that the *definitional* attributes of a concept are not necessarily the *psychological* attributes of the concept. Further, the psychological structure of the human organism appears to develop with age, permitting the psychological representation of concepts to change and expand.

We shall see that the young child has very narrow, constricted concepts. At the age of five, a father who is a doctor is no longer a father. In short, the typical five-year-old answers, "No," to the first question above. By eight years of age, the typical eight-year-old no longer has difficulty with the first question. However, this does not mean that his concept of father is fully developed; at this age, a father must be *good,* and if he is not good then he can no longer be considered an instance of the concept. Thus the average child at eight insists that the drunkard is no longer a father, in question two.

Not only will the child refuse to use a particular *label* for an instance of a concept, he may insist that the instance has lost critical attributes of the concept, under conditions of relatively modest alteration of attributes which seem, by adult standards, to be superficial to the concept. For example, children between five and eight years of age may insist that a boy is no longer a good baseball player if that boy lies and cheats in school. They will deny that he can still hit and that he can still field. Clearly, the child acts as though there were certain dependencies between attribute dimensions that we, as adults, do not see.

On the other hand, we shall see that under certain circumstances adults will show residuals of the same tendency to behave as though certain attribute dimensions were correlated. For example, later in the chapter, we shall see liberals who refuse to accept the possibility that a liberal can be an assassin; presented with evidence that the liberal was, indeed, an assassin, they shall insist that he was framed.

Consider also questions five and six above. Many adults behave on these as though *shape* were the critical attributes of trees and princes. If it *looks* like a tree, it is a tree; if it *looks* like a frog, it can not be a prince.

FOCUS OF THE CHAPTER

Concept formation and concept utilization are among the most important aspects of higher mental processes. As we shall see in the present chapter, the manner in which a person reasons and engages in inferential behavior is largely based on the nature and structure of his concepts.

Concept formation is extremely complex because it involves learning that a great many disparate objects or events belong together in a single category. For example, some mothers are tall, some are short; some are beautiful, some are ugly; some are gentle, some are aggressive. Despite these differences, all are mothers. Since the end product of concept learning is the ability to deal with novel stimuli (e.g., a mother we have never seen before) in terms of our past experiences (e.g., we know a great deal about the general characteristics of mothers) , concept learning is an aspect of learning to think inferentially. Once the concept has been learned, it becomes a powerful tool which can facilitate thinking. On the other hand, it can also lead to grossly erroneous inferences, as we shall see.

The present chapter will introduce the topic of concepts. The nature of concepts will be discussed. It will be seen that systematic developmental changes occur in concept structure as a function of age. These changes are critical to the types of inferential behavior that can occur. Further, we shall see that opinions and attitudes concerning social and political events are a closely related set of phenomena. (Other, more specialized topics concerning aspects of concept acquisition in the *laboratory* will be discussed in later chapters, particularly Chapters 3, 7, 8, 9, 11, and 12.)

Many books on learning place a chapter on concepts somewhere near the end of the volume. The goal, in many of these, is to use the constructs developed for simple learning in an attempt to explain the phenomenon of concept acquisition. From such a point of view, concepts are usually dealt with as a sort of complex discrimination learning task.

In the present book, on the other hand, the situation is somewhat reversed. The analysis of conceptual behavior undertaken in the present chapter will prove to have broad implications for the simpler learning situations. Conceptual behavior displays in a fairly clear manner the complex organization of psychological variables which is often only obliquely intersected by simpler learning situations. Thus, while this organization of variables is crucial to the simpler learning situations, these simpler learning situations may not be optimal instruments for discovering the structure of intellectual processes.

WHAT IS A CONCEPT?

Cultural Determinants

A formal definition of the term *concept* will be presented in a later section of this chapter. First, an attempt will be made to analyze the characteristics that constitute real concepts as they exist outside of the laboratory.

In a complex and changing environment, there are many sets of features which tend to vary together in a fairly consistent way. It is often advantageous for an organism to differentiate such sets of features and respond to them as entities. This is particularly true when (as often happens) there are restricted classes of instrumental responses which are appropriate and adaptive if they can be correlated with these sets of features. For example, if a particular set of features can be identified as a "dog" (as opposed, perhaps, to a "wild animal"), there are a particular set of responses which can adaptively be made. *Thus, one characteristic of a concept is that it is a bounded set of attributes that is reacted to as an entity* (see definition of "bounded" in Chapter 1). The problem of boundedness is crucial, since a particular attribute in combination with one set of other attributes can constitute one concept, while in combination with another set of attributes can constitute a completely different concept. For example, a woman with her baby is a *mother;* flying an airplane, the same woman is a *pilot.* In short, it is the particular *organization* of attributes that, typically, constitutes a concept.

To a great extent, pressures of the environment make it useful for people to bound certain organizations of features rather than others. Consequently, it is not surprising to find that divergent cultures may differ considerably in some of their concepts. For example, Hockett (1954) reports that in Mandarin Chinese dialect, *fruit* and *nuts* are placed together into a single concept; within this concept, the major subconcepts revolve about the attribute dimension of wet-dry, so that wet fruits and nuts are in one subconcept, dry are in another. An even more dramatic example comes from the Hopi Indians. C. M. Solley (personal communication) reports that the concept of living, or animate, is based on two attributes. One attribute is concerned with movement and the other is concerned with a quasi reproductive function. A cloud is referred to as belonging in this concept because it moves and can break into several clouds. A horse is also included as an instance since it can move and can reproduce. On the other hand, a mule is *not* an instance of this concept since it can not reproduce.

From this point of view, concepts are largely definitional in nature: A particular set of attributes may be organized by a person (or culture) as a concept so that certain instances which appear to possess these attributes can be reacted to in a similar manner. If someone cuts the attribute pie differently, he may emerge with a different set of concepts. In this sense, one concept is as "true" as another.

Definitional versus Correlated Attributes

Certain attributes of concepts are *definitional* from the point of view of a culture. These are crucial attributes of the concept, as far as the culture is concerned. Consider the concept of *father.* From the point of view of the defining culture, only two attributes are crucial: *male* and *parent.* Yet other attributes, such as *good,* have become associated with the concept. As shall be seen later in this chapter, eight-year-old children often deny that an instance is a father, if the instance does not have the attribute of goodness (Saltz and Hamilton, 1968). Correlated attributes appear to increase in number with age. When asked to describe the concept of father, Kantrowitz (1969) found that five-year-old children gave an average of four attributes; seven-year-old children gave an average of eight attributes. Osgood, Suci, and Tannenbaum (1957) indicate that college students produce complex and reliable patterns of traits for such a concept on the Semantic Differential. A typical Semantic Differential pattern for father includes attributes such as *strong, good, warm.* These are clearly not definitional.

Conceivably, correlated attributes could be found, for some concepts, which occurred with 100% probability. However, even if all fire engines in the world were painted red, red would not be a definitional attribute of fire engines. Many of the correlated attributes of a concept may occur with probabilities of less than 100%. This is the basis of what has in the laboratory been called *probabilistic* concepts. Such concepts shall be considered in greater detail in a subsequent section of this chapter.

Often people respond to concepts primarily in terms of their correlated attributes and may even insist that these are the definitional attributes. The concepts of *beauty* and *justice* provide interesting examples of this confusion between definitional and correlated attributes. The definitional attributes of beauty are a particular set of internal emotional responses. Many varieties of stimuli—musical, visual, etc.—may evoke these responses. From generation to generation, the specific external stimuli which evoke such responses change. One has only to compare either the paintings of the 19th century with modern art or the beauty queens of the 1920s with those of the 1960s to see this. New fashions in women's clothing may appear grotesque until they have been correlated with otherwise pleasing feminine appearances. Yet, in any generation, people are quite prone to attempt definitions of beauty in terms of these correlated attributes. For example, many art critics at the turn of the century assumed that degree of representation of reality was a definitional attribute of beauty in painting. When the early cubistic art appeared, lack of representation was considered a *definitional* deficit.

Justice provides another example of this same problem. Each culture has a set of values which it defends by means of institutional commandments and injunctions. The definitional attributes of justice involve evaluating given sets of behavior against the baseline of the values of the particular culture. This aspect of the concept of justice is cross-cultural. However, the same *overt* behavior may be dealt with quite differently from one culture to another, if the *values* of these cultures are different. Thus each culture will have its own set of correlated attributes for justice. Because of the difference in values, judgments which are clearly instances of justice in one culture may be reacted to violently as barbaric injustices by another culture.

Attributes as Dimensions in Cognitive Space

Concepts have been characterized as bounded sets of attributes. The present section shall attempt to specify the nature of such attributes. In general, attributes are stimulus characteristics of the internal and external environment. Often, attributes are sensory in nature. For example, the attributes of *banana* include ranges of values along a number of visual dimensions: a range of *colors* from green to yellow to black; a fairly restricted range of *sizes* that usually does not exceed a foot in length; a crescent shape. In addition, bananas have a range of values along taste and tactile dimensions. In order to learn the concept of banana, one must learn that the specified values along these dimensions "go together" as an entity.

At this point, let us define the notion of *cognitive space*. By the term cognitive space we shall mean the characteristics of the *set of dimensions* on which a person can react to the stimuli (both internal and external) of his environment. From this perspective, concepts are *regions in multidimensional space* formed by the intersection of the relevant attribute dimensions. Concepts are described as regions, rather than points, because a concept may have a number of different attribute values on a given dimension (e.g., bananas may be green, yellow, or black; they occupy a range of values on the length dimension).

While we have used sensory attributes as examples, it has probably already occurred to the reader that many attributes are not primarily sensory in nature. We often make judgments concerning goodness and evil, beauty or ugliness, intelligence or stupidity in relation to a person, object, or event. These are certainly not sensory dimensions; they are evaluative in nature. Similarly, in Chapter 5, when we discuss the phenomena related to sensory-preconditioning, it will prove heuristically advantageous to consider *motoric* dimensions as part of the cognitive space. This means that the cognitive space must consist of a number of types of dimensions in addition to the sensory.

One must be careful not to adopt too simplistic a view concerning the nature of attribute dimensions. Many attributes are complex concepts in their own right. The concept *father*, for example, can be described in terms of two definitional attributes, male and parent; in addition, we shall see later in this chapter that the correlated attribute of goodness can be a crucial aspect of father for young children. At one level, we can classify a person as a father on the grounds that he falls on the male side of the sexuality dimension and, in addition. we know that he has a child. This should not obscure the fact that both maleness and parenthood are complex concepts which can be defined in terms of attribute dimensions. Despite being complex, the state of affairs appears to be extremely orderly in a hierarchial sense. Note that every addition of an attribute, or attribute set, further delimits a concept in cognitive space. For example, parent can refer to either father or mother; the addition of the attribute of maleness restricts the concept to fathers.

The cognitive space notion will prove useful in a number of contexts in subsequent chapters. In the second half of the present chapter, it will be seen that this formulation clarifies many of the interesting issues which arise in concept development in children.

Definition of Concept and of Concept Learning

Based on the discussion thus far in the present chapter, the following definition of the term *concept* can be offered. *A concept is a bounded region in the cognitive space which is reacted to as an entity.*

A corresponding definition of concept learning can also be offered. *Concept learning is the associating and bounding of the set of attributes.*

Much of our inferential behavior can be seen as determined by the nature of our concepts. For example, if I react to an object as though it has the attributes of an eatable fruit, I may appease my hunger; if, on the other hand, I decide it has the attributes of a wax fruit, I will look further for food. Again, if a man kills someone and we decide that the event has the attributes of honor, justice, and bravery (as may happen in war) , we will give the killer a medal; if we decide the event has the attribute of murder, we will hang the killer. In order to make this type of inferential use of a concept, we must be able to discriminate the instances of the concept from noninstances with some reasonable degree of success. Discrimination processes are therefore very important for the *use* of concepts in inferential behavior.

Response Definitions of Concepts and Concept Learning

The position outlined above must be contrasted to the frequently used definition of a concept as a *common response (or basis for classification) for dissimilar stimuli* (see T. Kendler, 1961; Hunt, 1962; Archer, 1964). The corresponding definition of concept learning is the acquisition of a common response for dissimilar stimuli.

How do the response definitions differ from the bounded-attributes definitions proposed in the present chapter? The primary difference is in the locus of the similarity that unites a group of instances as belonging to a common concept. The bounded-attributes definitions are in terms of both the stimuli which constitute the concept *and* the responses to these stimuli. The response definitions place this locus in the responses made to the stimulus instances. The stimuli are specified only as being *dissimilar*. Thus the instances could have absolutely nothing in common except for the fact that the person makes the same responses to them. And, indeed, the *exclusive-disjunctive* concepts, to be described later in this chapter, involve just this state of affairs. For example, a subject may be told he is correct if he selects a square that is any color but red or a red object as long as it is not a square; but if he selects a red square he is told he is incorrect. In such a study, the experimenter has arbitrarily defined as a single concept, "red-if-not-square plus square-if-not-red."

It is the writer's contention that this type of response definition of concepts is not consistent with the nature of concepts in the real world. This will be seen more clearly when we examine the characteristics of exclusive-disjunctive concepts later in the chapter. At present a simple example will suffice. The word "bear" has several meanings. One meaning refers to a particular species of mammal; another refers to carrying a burden. Despite the fact that the identical response, "bear," can be made to instances of both these meanings, this does not combine the species of mammal and the bearing of a burden into a single concept. A careful reading of the concept-learning literature will show that the writer has not created a straw man by giving this type of example.

Is it possible to save the "common-response" definition of concepts by use of a more complex notion of response? For example, Osgood

(1952, 1953) has defined the *meaning* of a word in terms of the totality of internal responses stimulated by the word. (These internal responses were measured by means of a test which he called the Semantic Differential. This test is a set of rating scales for bipolar dimensions such as *good-bad, active-passive, strong-weak*.)

The writer does not believe that patterns of responses will prove more helpful than single overt responses for defining concepts. It is true that the pattern of responses for *bear* (the animal) will differ from the pattern for *bear* (as in carry). However, *different instances within each concept will also show different patterns*. When the instance of *bear* is a frolicking cub, the pattern of responses will be quite different from the pattern when the instance is a charging grizzly bear. In fact, the bear cub could conceivably produce a pattern much more similar to certain instances of *bear* as carry (e.g., a mother carrying her baby) than to the instance of the angry grizzly.

The problem of the common-response definition for concepts is part of the more general problem of defining psychological variables in terms of the behavior they produce. We have previously encountered this issue in Chapter 1 when we discussed the empirical definition of learning. As we saw at that time, the use of behavior as a criterion for the occurrence of a variable tends to be ambiguous since often a given response may be produced by several *different* variables.

Levels of Abstraction

Another commonly found definition of concepts is that they are the abstraction of common properties from a number of specific instances. For some psychologists, the terms *abstraction* and *concept* appear to be virtually synonymous. Many laboratory studies of concepts fit the abstraction notion very well. For example, a subject may be shown figures such as triangles and squares. These figures may be large or small, red or green. If triangle is chosen by the experimenter as the concept to be identified, the subject presumably ignores size and color and abstracts the attribute of triangle as the criterion for response. Like the response definitions, this position also appears to overemphasize a restricted aspect of concepts. The abstraction notion stresses the fact that, often, instances of a concept may have values on some dimensions which are not crucial to the concept (e.g., are not in the region of the cognitive space which constitute the concept).

The discussion in this section permits a theoretical distinction between the classical notion of abstraction and the cognitive space notion. Let us consider the concept of *fruit* as a convenient example. The concept of fruit is presumably an abstraction of the attributes that are shared by specific instances of fruit; one must abstract certain attributes that are common to both bananas and oranges, for example, to arrive at the more abstract concept of fruit. Note that of the total set of attributes that define a specific instance, such as banana, only a small subset are relevant to defining fruit. Not all fruit are crescent-shaped or have the consistency or taste of the banana. In set theory terms, the concept as an abstraction is the intersection of the attributes of the instances that determine the concept.

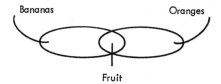

Fruit

This raises some interesting problems. For example, the taste of a banana is different from that of an orange. This distinctive taste is not within the intersection and thus is not an attribute of the concept fruit.

From a cognitive space point of view, the more abstract concept includes the entire set of attributes of its constituents. In terms of set theory, the concept is the *union* of sets. Thus the attributes of bananas and of oranges are also the attributes of fruit. The more abstract concept occupies a larger region of the cognitive space than the more concrete concept. Along the taste dimensions, for example, fruit occupies both the regions which characterize bananas and the regions which characterize oranges. This produces several interesting states of affairs. The defining attributes of bananas are obviously defining characteristics of fruit. (If a stimulus has the defining set of attributes characteristic of bananas, it is a fruit.) On the other hand, these attributes do not occur with 100% probability in fruit, since not all fruit are bananas.

It should be noted that concepts may be organized hierarchically in terms of level of abstraction. For example, the concept of fruit is considered more abstract than concepts such as bananas or oranges, because both bananas and oranges are instances of fruit.

The ability to attain abstract concepts is often considered an indication of intelligence. The Similarities test of the Wechsler Intelligence Scale (1944) measures just this type of ability. Subjects are given pairs of items, such as banana and orange, and are asked how these are alike. Fruit is considered a good answer to this item. Successive generations of students, when first introduced to the Similarities test, have been puzzled by the relationships between level of abstraction and adequacy of response to such items. If ability to respond in terms of higher levels of abstraction is a sign of intelligence, why is food not a better (i.e., more intelligent) answer than fruit, since it is more abstract. And, of course, "thing" is more abstract than either fruit *or* food.

Abstractness is, clearly, not a virtue in its own right. Concepts have utility to the extent that they permit restricting particular types of responses to some set of instances as opposed to some other set. Thus the most adequate level of abstraction is the one that permits the greatest degree of discrimination between the relevant set of instances and all other possible sets. Contrary to common belief, lower levels of abstraction typically provide the most adequate basis for response since they are more precise in locating a concept in cognitive space. Consider the example of the definition of *oranges*. Given three possible answers—something to eat, fruit, and citrus fruit—the least abstract is citrus fruit, and most people would agree that it is the most adequate of these responses.

Truth and Falsity in Concept Identification

It has been seen that concepts may differ among cultures. Similarly, even within a culture, people may not agree on the meaning of common concepts. Some psychologists have pointed to such lack of agreement as evidence for the position that each individual has his own idiosyncratic conceptual system. If a child called his baby-sitter, "mother," these psychologists would insist that the response is not false; instead, this child's concept of mother is simply different from that of most adults in the cuture. This is, of course, a defensible point of view.

In what sense, then, can one refer to the "truth" or "falsity" of a conceptual response? Three types of issues arise in this connection. The most obvious sense in which the term "false" can occur is in regard to the relationship between the cultural use of a concept and the person's attempt to behave in accordance with the cultural use. A person may not know the critical attributes of a concept as used in his culture and may react to stimuli inappropriately from this point of view. The small child whose concept of "mother" is "a woman who takes care of me and loves me" may call a baby sitter "mother." Most laboratory studies of concepts have been concerned with specific issues revolving about this latter meaning of the "truth" of a concept. The experimenter constructs an artificial concept by arbitrarily specifying a set of attributes (e.g., red and triangle) as defining the concept. The subject is rewarded if he picks the "correct" instances and is not rewarded if he picks "incorrect" instances.

A second sense in which a conceptual response may be false occurs when a person is mistaken in thinking that a particular instance contains the crucial attributes of a concept. For example, a wax apple may look so real that the person attempts to eat it. In this case, he reacts to a stimulus as though it has attributes which, in fact, it does not have.

In addition to these two meanings of the "truth" of a concept, a somewhat different (and less frequently considered) type of issue also can arise. Since the stimuli of our world are often very complex, one can encounter a stimulus which contains many of the attributes of a concept *plus* some attributes which have, in the past, been negatively correlated with the concept. The person who must act on the basis of this stimulus has a problem. For example, Saltz and Wickey (1965) studied the problems in inferential behavior encountered by liberals who were confronted with a stimulus person who had attributes of both *liberal* and *assassin* simultaneously. Some of these liberals reacted by saying the stimulus person was only pretending to be a liberal, while really being a paid agent of reactionary forces. Others denied that he was an assassin. These liberals claimed the stimulus person was really "framed." It can be seen that the resolution of this conflict could have important consequences for behavior.

Part of the problem, in the conflict situation, refers back to the second meaning of the truth of a concept. Some liberal subjects in the Saltz and Wickey study were questioning whether the relevant attributes of the concept "liberal" were really present in the stimulus person. The reason they questioned this is an interesting problem that can be related to the cognitive space notion of concepts outlined previously in this chapter. If liberals conceive of the concept of liberal as having the attribute of "good" while the concept of assassin has the attribute of "bad," then these two concepts occupy different ranges of values on the evaluation dimension. For persons with this type of cognitive structure, liberal and assassin occupy different and incompatible regions in the cognitive space so that an instance which falls in one of these regions cannot fall in the other. This issue has been considered by social psychologists in terms of balance theory. For the most part, the issue has been ignored within the more traditional approaches to concept structure.

TYPES OF CONCEPT

The vast majority of experiments on concepts have been concerned with some form of concept learning. Typically, the experiment is essentially one in which subjects are presented arrays of stimuli (e.g., colors, forms, etc.) and the subjects must indicate whether a given stimulus is or is not an instance of the concept. The subjects must test various possibilities and determine which the experimenter is consistently calling correct.

Certainly in the real world, and sometimes in the laboratory, concepts have complex organizations of attributes. The types of organization classically considered by psychologists are *simple, conjunctive, disjunctive,* and *probabilistic.*

Simple (Prebounded) Concepts

Simple concepts are usually defined as those in which only a single attribute operationally defines the concept. If this attribute is present, the concept is present. If the attribute is absent, the concept is absent. All other attributes which are present serve only as distractors which make the task more difficult. Many of the early classic studies were concerned with such operationally simple concepts. Hull's (1920) pioneering work on concept learning was clearly of this type. In this study, a single perceptual stimulus, such as a checklike mark, was embedded in a number of complex figures that resembled Chinese ideographs. Subjects were to give a particular nonsense response when the checklike figure was present in the complex, but not when this critical cue was absent. Here the critical attribute itself remains constant while the environment of surrounding attributes changes.

A closer examination of simple concepts used in many studies indicates that the characterization presented above may be misleading and certainly ignores a factor that is often crucial. Often the crucial attribute is in reality a complex set of attributes which constitute a very familiar, coded concept. For example, an experimenter may specify *triangle* (or triangularity) as the crucial feature to which the subject must respond, disregarding other attributes (e.g., color, size). *Triangle* is a set of attributes which the subject has learned to treat as a single entity before entering the experimental situation. His task in the laboratory becomes that of discovering which of his already extant concepts is now being reinforced by the experimenter. In other words, the crucial stimulus is a precoded conjunction of a number of attributes which have developed boundary strength or *resistance to interference* through previous experience. Many conjunctions of attributes which adults take for granted as simple, unitary stimuli were initially quite difficult to bound. This is indicated by research on development of visual perception in persons who were blind until they were adults (von Senden, 1960). Months were required to learn the visual concept of *triangle* when the subjects were not permitted to use their previously learned, sightless cue for this concept (e.g., were not permitted to trace the figure with a finger). Clearly, then, it would be more accurate to refer to most simple concepts as *prebounded conjunctive* concepts.

Many studies have involved a single value of a single attribute dimension as the stimulus to be identified. For example, the subject might be told that he is correct only when he chooses a *red* figure. Thus the subject might learn to classify together an apple, a fire engine, and a red bandana. (Underwood and Richardson, 1956a, have developed a corresponding concept task in which *words* such as apple, fire engine, etc., were to be responded to by naming a sensory property, such as red, which was an association common to all these words.) The word *red* refers to a restricted range of values on a single dimension of color. From this point of view, red is an attribute of several concepts, and the experimental task is one of attribute identification rather than concept learning. Such studies were considered concept learning because they fit the "common-response" definition of concept learning; a subject could learn to give a common response, red, to dissimilar stimuli.

Unbounded Conjunctive Concepts

If the so-called "simple" concepts are typically prebounded conjunctive concepts, the type of concepts usually called conjunctive, in laboratory studies, are unbounded conjunctions of attributes. In the laboratory, the conjunctive concept is operationally defined in terms of two or more previously unrelated attributes which must be present simultaneously. For example, the experimenter may invent the concept "red and triangle." Each card shown the subject may contain a circle, a square, or a triangle; and the figure may be red, green, or blue. The subject is reinforced (told he is correct) only when he selects cards having the attributes *red* and *triangle* simultaneously. Contrary to the case of simple concepts, the conjunctive nature of the attributes is not precoded. Such attribute combinations are usually quite arbitrary. The relationship between attributes exists only in the laboratory, and the subject can only engage in rather arbitrary combinatory behavior in trying to reason the basis of solution. (Strategies used by subjects in such situations have been studied by a number of experimenters, e.g., Bruner, Goodnow, and Austin, 1956.)

Historically, the type of concepts which Smoke (1932) referred to as "relational" appear to be, essentially, unbounded conjunctive concepts of the type described above. For example, Smoke used as a concept a circle with one dot inside the circle and one dot outside the circle.

Not too surprisingly, laboratory studies indicate that unbounded conjunctive concepts are more difficult to learn than simple (bounded conjunctive) concepts. There are several reasons for this. First, since the relevant conjunctive attributes are already well bounded in the simple concept, they are already treated as a single stimulus. An important consequence of this is: If the subject guesses correctly the relevant stimulus in learning a simple concept and if he continues to respond on the basis of this guess, he need make no more errors. However, in an unbounded conjunctive concept this is not necessarily the case. If the correct attributes are red-plus-triangle and the subject notes only red, he may respond to a red square as the concept and be told he is incorrect. If this response leads to extinction of the response to red, concept attainment will be impeded. Under most conditions, the greater the number of attributes to be bounded into a single concept, the more difficult the learning becomes (e.g., Bulgarella and Archer, 1962; Walker and Bourne, 1961).

If one accepts the characterization of a concept as a bounded set of attributes, the learning of a conjunctive concept becomes prototypic of learning concepts in general. The problem with laboratory studies of conjunctive concepts is that they typically demand a reorganiza-

tion of existing concepts. In this sense, there is heavy proactive interference in acquisition.

Disjunctive Concepts

The disjunctive concept, as studied in the laboratory, is at odds
with the definition of a concept suggested earlier in this chapter. It
will be seen that this discrepancy appears to arise from the fact that
the laboratory studies do not adequately represent the structure of
real world disjunctive concepts.

Laboratory studies of disjunctive concepts, like conjunctive concepts, involve two or more attributes. However, the two attributes
need not occur simultaneously to define the concept. Two types of
disjunctive concepts are often distinguished, the inclusive and the
exclusive. A disjunctive concept is inclusive if the two or more attributes are permitted to occur simultaneously. For example, *red*, or
circle, or *red-plus-circle* could all be instances of a concept. Or, from
the real world again, a psychotic may be defined as a person having
hallucinations, or delusions, or both.

Disjunctive concepts are called *exclusive* if they exclude the joint
occurrence of attributes from the concept. This leads to rather arbitrary and difficult concepts in laboratory situations. For example, the
experimenter may tell a subject that he is correct if he selects a red
card or if he selects a card with a circle as an instance of the concept;
however, if the subject selects a card which is both red and contains a
circle, he is told that he is incorrect. This differs from most real
world exclusive disjunctive concepts in that, in the real world, the
joint occurrence does not ordinarily occur. For example, "citizens of
the United States" is often cited as an exclusive disjunctive concept
on the grounds that it involves two criterial attributes that are
mutually exclusive. These attributes are "born in the United States"
and "naturalized." A person is a citizen for one of these two reasons,
but not both, because if a person were born in the United States, it
would ordinarily be unnecessary for him to be naturalized. If, indeed, someone *were* both born in the country and then naturalized,
the two attributes would not cancel each other.

From the subjects' point of view, disjunctive concepts used in the
laboratory have several disquieting characteristics. If the concept is
defined by red and/or circle, the subject is sometimes rewarded when
he responds to a card which does not contain a circle. Therefore, he
concludes, circle is irrelevant. In effect, the subject must simultane-

ously learn two separate and discrete invariances (i.e., two simple concepts) red is one, circle the other. If the subjects are set to learn one concept, this state of affairs can be very confusing. The only characteristic of the situation which ties various stimuli together as a single concept is that the subjects' act of selecting either one will lead to reinforcement. Presumably, the laboratory interest in this type of concept stems from the fact that it represents a variety of concepts found in the real world. The writer feels that this laboratory task is a misinterpretation of reality.

Examination of a real-world disjunctive concept can help to re-solve some of the problems which have been raised. The concept "United States citizen" can be defined by one of two exclusive attributes—born in the United States or naturalized. If this were all there were to the concept, it could be analyzed as two distinct concepts tied together by a single selection response, in this case the shared label *citizen*. Actually, however, the concept consists of a much larger set of attributes including the rights to vote and to protection when traveling in foreign countries. It is these that tie the exclusive disjunctive attributes into a single concept. In the general terms in which cognitive systems have been discussed in this chapter, the concept can be analyzed as two overlapping systems in which x and y are the disjunctive aspects and a, b, c are conjunctive attributes.

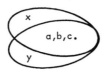

In the figure as drawn above, there is no overlap between x and y *per se* and so there exists an exclusive disjunction between these attri-butes. If there had been partial overlap between x and y, these attributes would constitute an inclusive disjunctive subsystem.

Clearly, x and y are considered to be in a single concept because of the overlap (i.e., invariance) between the *other* elements of their two systems. The two systems are considered to be a single concept *despite* not *because* of their disjunctive elements. Yet most laboratory studies involving the learning of disjunctive concepts take exactly the opposite point of view and attempt to define the concepts in terms of the disjunctive elements. Little is known concerning how

much and what types of disjunction people will tolerate in considering two systems as the same concept. Most of the work relevant to
this issue has been done in the area of social psychology under the
topic of balance theory and has not been properly evaluated by
experimental psychologists with respect to the present set of problems.

It is interesting to note that operational definitions of "concept"
and "concept learning" appear to have been devised to accommodate
the very aspects of the laboratory tasks which the present section calls
into question. For example, Tracy Kendler (1961) defines concept
learning in terms of the acquisition or utilization of a common
response to dissimilar stimuli. Thus using the label "DAX" for both
red stimuli which are *not* circles and for circles which are *not* red
would permit considering these two discrete and otherwise unrelated
attributes as a single concept. Similarly, Bourne (1966, p. 1) states
that a concept exists whenever two or more distinguishable objects or
events have been grouped or classified together and set apart from
other objects on the basis of some common feature or characteristic
of each. Bourne considers disjunctives like *red-or-circle* as a concept,
presumably because a common label can be used for both.

Some writers have, indeed, defined concepts primarily in terms of
a common verbal label to diverse stimuli (see Archer, 1964). This is
essentially an extreme interpretation of the position taken by writers
like Kendler and Bourne. A simple example developed previously in
this chapter will show that a common label does not insure a single
concept. The word "bear" can be used to label either an animal or
the act of carrying a heavy burden. Despite this common label, these
are not considered a single concept, since the label can have more
than one meaning.

Of the types of concepts described, most laboratory studies find
disjunctive concepts to be the most difficult to learn. This appears to
be a consequence of the characteristic which the present section has
attempted to elucidate: Disjunctive concepts in the laboratory are
misrepresentations of real concepts. If the subject tries to discover a
single concept, he will look for characteristics not to be found in the
laboratory materials. An important study by Wells and Defanbacher
(1967) is relevant to this issue. These experimenters compared
efficiency of solution for conjunctive and disjunctive concepts using
human subjects and monkeys. For the human subjects, the disjunctive concepts proved significantly more difficult than the conjunctive.
The monkeys solved both types of problems equally readily. Not set

to seek a common concept, the monkeys simply solved the disjunctive concept in terms of two simple cues, either one of which could lead to reinforcement.

Probabilistic Concepts

The typical definition of probabilistic concepts states that these are concepts for which there are no fully valid cues. Thus it is impossible to predict with certainty from knowledge of the relevant attributes. Several probabilistic concept tasks have simulate natural concepts. R. E. Goodnow (1954) had subjects identify silhouettes of airplanes as either Type X or Type Not-X on the basis of combinations of three attributes. One attribute (wing shape) was a 100% predictive cue. Planes of Type X all had one shape; planes of Not-X had a different shape. The other two attributes were not fully predictive. For example, straight tail was found on 67% of Type X planes but also on 33% of Type Not-X. Subjects, on certain trials, were required to classify on the basis of only the partially predictive attributes.

Several points must be considered. First, this is an interesting study, from the point of view of the present discussion, since the distinction between defining and correlated attributes can be made. The tail shape is clearly a correlated attribute, occurring on most, but not all, Type X planes. On the other hand, is wing shape a defining attribute because a given shape occurs on 100% of Type X planes and on 0% of Type Not-X? For purposes of the particular study performed by Goodnow, it appears safe enough to consider 100% predictive cues as defining attributes. If this were a real concept, however, there would be insufficient knowledge to decide. The defining attribute might be "enemy plane." In this case, a Type Not-X plane would become a Type X plane, if it were known that an enemy pilot had captured it.

It should, at this point, be fairly clear that probabilistic concepts must have defining attributes—otherwise they could not be concepts. It also follows that, if these defining attributes were available, they would be 100% predictive. However, *the statement that a concept is probabilistic immediately indicates that the defining attributes are either completely unavailable or are available only for some instances of the concept. At least some of the instances must be judged from correlated attributes.*

CONCEPTS WITH INACCESSIBLE DEFINING ATTRIBUTES. An extremely important study by Solley and Messick (1957) demonstrates a situation in which the defining attributes are completely inaccessible. Subjects were shown pictures of stickmen who represented members of a fictitious tribe. Two of the four attribute-characteristics of one tribe are summarized in Table 2–1.

TABLE 2–1. Percentage of Occurrence of Attributes of Stickmen in Tribe A

	Tall	Short	Totals
Fat	15%	5%	20%
Skinny	60%	20%	80%
Totals	75%	25%	100%

From Solley and Messick, 1957. Reproduced with permission of the *American Journal of Psychology*.

As can be seen in Table 2–1, no single attribute or combination of attributes is perfectly predictive. In fact, whereas most (60%) of the tribesmen are tall and skinny, some (5%) are just the opposite, short and fat. The defining attributes for belonging to the tribe (e.g., blood relationships, living in same village, etc.) are unavailable to the subject. What type of concept can be learned in this sort of situation? Subjects in the Solley and Messick study learned the *statistical distribution* of the correlated attributes. After successively viewing 80 stickmen of Tribe *A*, subjects were able to answer a set of Semantic Differential items in a way which mirrored the marginal frequencies extremely close.

MISINFORMATION INTERPRETATION OF PROBABILISTIC CONCEPTS. If one were to ask a subject to describe Tribe *A*, and the subject said that a small number were short and fat, while most were tall and thin, this would be a veridical statement. It could be concluded that the subject had learned something about Tribe *A*. If, on the other hand, the subject reported that all the members of Tribe *A* were tall and thin, one would conclude that the subject had missed something. From this point of view, it is interesting to note that the more traditional probabilistic concept studies have viewed the low probability alternative of a correlated attribute as providing misinformation. For example, Bourne (1966) describes a concept identification task in which response to red is usually rewarded and response to green is not rewarded. On some trials, however, the subject is told that the green stimulus is the instance of the concept. This is considered misinformation, rather than as teaching that the concept is usually red, but sometimes green.

The measure of concept learning usually employed also has some interesting characteristics. Subjects are required to classify each instance presented to them, after which they are informed if the response was correct. Goodnow and Postman (1955) and Pishkin (1960) report that subjects tend to match probabilities in this type of situation. For example, consider the situation in which all dimensions but *color* are rewarded on a purely chance basis. For color, the experimenter responds to the subjects' choices as though red were correct on 70% of the trials and as though green were correct on the remaining 30%. Subjects tend to respond to these colors at these ratios: On 70% of the trials they chose green, on 30% they chose red. Bourne (1963), however, finds that this is a transitory effect, and if subjects are given a large enough number of trials, they will respond to the more frequently reinforced stimulus attribute on virtually 100% of the trials. These situations indicate something about the subjects' attempt to *maximize reinforcement,* but the significance of the data for the subjects' *idea of the concept* is not clear. Does it mean that at intermediate trials they felt the concept (i.e., the unmentioned and unavailable set of defining attributes) was red 70% of the time and green 30% of the time, but after many more trials they decided it was really always red? Or did the subjects really abandon the task of attempting to determine the attributes of the concept, and fall back on maximizing reinforcement?

It has yet to be demonstrated, in probabilistic concept learning, that the standard concept formation methodology gives an adequate picture of the concept which is learned. The standard procedure involves the subject classifying a given stimulus as an instance or noninstance. As was indicated above, this measure is difficult to interpret. A 100% choice of a given probabilistic attribute could represent an attempt to maximize reinforcement; the subject may know that the concept is only *usually* red, not always red. On the other hand, 100% choice of red might indicate the subject thought the concept was always red. On this issue, the Solley and Messick (1957) methodology appears to be much superior to the standard procedures.

RULE LEARNING VERSUS CONCEPT LEARNING. Much of the theorizing on probabilistic concepts is more concerned with decision-making processes *based* on the concepts than with learning the concepts. Bruner, Goodnow, and Austin (1956), for example, discuss a situation in which a soldier must decide whether to act as though a bomb were a dud or not. Bruner et al. point out that if 30% of the bombs were duds, and the soldier knew this, he might still act as though none were duds, since to guess that a bomb is a dud could lead to death if the guess is wrong. Research manipulating payoff matrices associated with various decisions has been informative concerning the effect of payoff on decision making; whether there are accompanying changes in the subjects' knowledge of the concepts basic to the decisions is less clear. The subject who always decides the bomb is not a dud may really believe few bombs are duds; he may believe 70% are duds, but is protecting himself from the lethal 30% which are alive.

Both the study by Goodnow (1954) and by Solley and Messsick (1957) discussed above provide a basis to the subject for rationalizing the existence of critical defining attributes which could underlay the correlated attributes actually manipulated. Thus, in Goodnow's study, subjects could conceive of a Type X plane which always has a delta wing and usually has a straight tail. The other studies cited appear to leave no basis for an underlying defining set of attributes. Subjects can, at best, try to develop rules for reinforcement.

Conclusions concerning Types of Concepts

The four types of concepts examined have in common the basic characteristic of all concepts; they each consist of a bounded set of attributes that can, under certain conditions, be reacted to as a single entity. In the simple concept condition, the set of attributes selected by the experimenter are *already* reacted to as an entity (e.g., triangles) , and the experimenter makes no systematic attempt to break up this set of attributes and present some of them, without others, as noninstances of the concept. In the conjunctive concept studies, on the other hand, the experimenter typically takes several unrelated concepts and combines these in a new, arbitrary concept (e.g., red triangle) . Here the individual components of the new concept may, indeed, be presented independently as noninstances. In principle, at least, learning conjunctive concepts comes closer to concept *formation* than does learning simple concepts.

The disjunctive concept, as it exists in the real world, is a concept which includes two types of attributes: (1) those definitional attributes which must always be present if the concept is to be present; and (2) some attributes which overlap with the definitional attributes, but not with each other. In the most frequently cited disjunctive concepts, at least one attribute of the latter type must be present—for the concept to be present, but it is immaterial *which* of these is present (i.e., they are functionally equivalent attributes). From the point of view of the cognitive space model, the absence of all attributes of the latter type throws a stimulus into a region of the cognitive space that does not involve the concept.

The typical disjunctive concept learning task, as employed in the laboratory, appears to be a misrepresentation of disjunctive concepts as they exist in the world. As typically employed, such tasks involve the simultaneous acquisition of two simple concepts.

Finally, except for a small number of exceptions (e .g., Goodnow, 1954; Solley and Messick, 1957), most of the studies of probabilistic concepts reported in the literature appear to treat such concepts as examples of misinformation. Instead, studies of probabilistic concepts indicates modes of information processing when the definitional attributes are either wholly or partially unavailable, and the subject must rely on correlated attributes for information.

In short, these four types represent variations of a common basic concept structure.

CONCEPT LEARNING: THE DISCRIMINATION MODEL

Two types of theoretical models for concept learning shall be distinguished in the present chapter: the discrimination model and the concept growth model. The former will be discussed in the present section, the latter in the next section of the chapter.

The discrimination model is a natural outgrowth of the definition which states that a concept is a common response to a set of dissimilar stimuli. From this point of view, concept learning is usually seen as a complex form of discrimination learning. Writers like Hunt (1962) and H. H. Kendler (1968) are explicit on this. It is implicit in the procedure employed by almost all the concept learning studies in the experimental literature. The discrimination model assumes that the subject learns a concept by emitting the critical response to successive stimuli, sometimes correctly and sometimes incorrectly. Eventually he learns to restrict the response to only the correct set of stimuli. In most versions of the discrimination model, the incorrect responses carry the burden of producing correct conceptualization. Restle (1962), followed by Bower and Trabasso (1963) states explicitly that learning occurs only after an error. The rationale for this position is that a subject may be correct in giving the concept response to a given stimulus, yet his *reason* for giving the response may be wrong (e.g., he picks a red triangle as an instance of the concept because he thinks red is the crucial attribute; actually, triangle is crucial). According to Restle, the subject learns nothing from such a trial. Only after an error will he change his conceptualization. (The evidence on this issue will be reviewed in Chapter 3; in general the evidence appears to throw considerable doubt on this formulation of concept learning.)

Another type of discrimination model stems from the early work of Hull (1920) and is represented by Gibson (1940) and by Kendler and Kendler (1962). From this position, the subject is reinforced for responding to the correct stimulus, and the tendency to make this response is strengthened. By stimulus generalization, the response now tends to be evoked by erroneous stimuli that resemble the correct stimulus. Concept learning is largely a matter of *extinguishing* the generalized response to these incorrect stimuli, while maintaining the response to the correct stimulus.

The procedures, followed in most laboratory studies of concept learning, are based on some version of the discrimination model. For the most part, the laboratory studies involve discovery tasks. The experimenter selects some stimulus attribute, or set of stimulus attributes, as the concept and embeds this in a number of irrelevant stimuli. The subject must decide upon presentation of a stimulus whether or not it contains the crucial set that defines that concept. Early in the series of trials the subject can only guess, then note whether the experimenter tells him he was correct. This procedure is followed because it is often assumed that natural concepts, in the culture, are learned in this manner. In short, natural concept learning is thought of as a complex trial and error problem, and so complex trial and error is studied in the laboratory. The critical issues that result from this point of view are those arising from trial-and-error problem solving, such as (1) the types of hypothesis testing procedures used by subjects; (2) whether reinforcement automatically leads to selection of the reinforced stimuli or whether awareness is crucial to repeated selections (the topic of awareness in concept learning will be dealt with at length in Chapter 11); and (3) the role of negative information (e.g., if told that a stimulus complex does *not* contain the concept, can the subject eliminate classes of stimuli as being relevant to the concept).

The Role of Negative Instances

Since the discrimination models place so much weight on the processing of negative instances, it appears reasonable to assume, on the basis of these models, that prior experience in concept learning outside the laboratory should prepare people to be reasonably adept at such information processing. In general, the experimental evidence is quite contrary to such an assumption. Hovland and Weiss (1953) developed a task in which, on purely logical grounds, the amount of information in positive and negative instances was equated. Despite this, the number of subjects who solved the task was greatest when all the instances were positive. The smallest number of solvers occurred when all instances were negative. When some instances were positive and others negative, number of solvers was intermediate between the other two conditions. In other words, subjects in the Hovland and Weiss study tended not to be able to process negative information efficiently.

Freibergs and Tulvig (1961) examined the ability of subjects to *learn* how to process negative information by presenting them with 20 different problems. Time to solution improved relatively steadily over the 20 problems so that, while negative instances resulted in much slower learning than positive instances over the first ten problems, by the twentieth problem there was little difference.

The results of these studies are very provocative. The fact that subjects are so poor at processing negative information relative to positive information on early problems, coupled with the virtual disappearance of this disparity after 20 problems, suggests that they have not had much practice at this type of information processing outside of the laboratory. To this extent, the laboratory problems appear to be nonrepresentative of the processes involved in learning natural concepts. Another, and more basic, suggestion also arises from these data. If subjects have not, in fact, had much experience with negative instances outside of the laboratory, this would suggest that natural concept learning is not, in essence, a trial-and-error discriminative task of the sort that characterizes concept learning tasks employed within the laboratory.

Concept Learning as an Intellectual Task

Studies based on the discrimination model provide little support for the opinion, shared by many psychologists, that concept learning is a higher order intellectual activity. Certainly the type of trial-and-error concept learning, described above, does not relate well to the indices of intelligence that have been most useful in other situations. The present section will review the evidence on this topic. All the studies reviewed will involve the procedure in which the subject must identify which of a number of different stimulus attributes the experimenter has chosen as the correct concept.

One of the most dramatic pieces of evidence on this topic is provided in a study reported by Hoffman (1955). In this study, a number of different concept tasks were learned by subjects of subnormal intelligence, subjects of normal intelligence, and subjects of superior intelligence. Subjects of subnormal and normal intelligence were able to learn some concepts as readily as subjects of superior intelligence. Overall, there was little evidence that higher intelligence was an advantage in the solution of such problems.

Saltz and Hamilton (1969) found that, for those children who solved a concept problem, there was no relationship between number of errors and intelligence. Children with I.Q.'s of around 80 averaged as few errors as those with I.Q.'s above 130. On the other hand, there was a relationship, though an extremely weak one, between intelligence and number of children who solved the concept problems.

The theoretical position proposed by Osler assumed that intelligence is an important variable in determining the type of process by which concepts are learned. High I.Q. children, she suggested, learn by hypothesis testing which leads to an all-or-none type of acquisition function; children with normal I.Q., on the other hand, learn by gradual increments in S-R strength for the correct set of stimuli.

Osler and Fivel (1961) tested this theory by comparing the relative learning rates for high I.Q. and normal children and found only marginal support for Osler's position. Statistical significance was attained only when five of the most gradual learners were arbitrarily reclassified as sudden learners. Saltz and Hamilton (1969), in a more precisely analyzed study, found no evidence for differences in learning rate prior to concept solution. Both higher and lower I.Q. children, in this study, solved in an all-or-none fashion.

The Osler and Trautman (1961) study tested an indirect deduction from the Osler theory. They proposed that if the task involves few possible hypotheses which can be tested, the higher I.Q. children should exceed the lower, since hypothesis testing would be efficient. However, if the task materials permitted many possible bases for hypotheses, then higher I.Q. children would no longer have an advantage since the various hypotheses would conflict, and it would also be laborious to test them all. While the data reported by Osler and Trautman support this prediction, Wolff (1967) could not replicate these results.

In short, there is little support for the position that high and low I.Q. children use different mechanisms for concept learning.

An extremely important study of the relationship between intelligence and concept learning was reported by Whitman (1966). Whitman suggested that the cognitive styles variable developed by Sigel (see Kagan, Moss, and Sigel, 1963) might be a critical link relating intelligence and concept learning. Sigel has suggested that there are individual differences in the way people process information, with some people tending to respond to the descriptive aspects of stimuli and other people tending to respond to the categorical aspects. For example, given a picture of an orange as a stimulus, descriptive subjects might classify it with balls and circles on the basis of its shape, categorical subjects might classify it with pears and bananas on the basis of the more abstract fact that all can be categorized as fruit.

Whitman extended Sigel's position by pointing out that concepts, as well as personal styles, can be classified as descriptive or categorical. For example, within the context of the typical concept learning study, *stripes* could be a descriptive concept. If a stimulus contains stripes (e.g., a barber pole, an American flag, a zebra), it could be considered an instance of the rewarded concept by the experimenter. An example of a categorical concept would be *containers* (e.g., a pot, a boat, an envelope). Whitman reasoned that concept learning should be easiest when the subject's cognitive style was consistent with the style of the concept which was to be learned. He further reasoned that intelligence is a type of flexibility in the face of information which is inconsistent with the subject's cognitive style. This led to several hypotheses. (1) Concept learning should be easier when cognitive style and concept style are consistent than when these are inconsistent. (2) Intelligence should be unrelated to concept learning when cognitive style and concept style are consistent. (3) When cognitive style is inconsistent with concept style, intelligence should be related to ease of concept learning.

Whitman tested these hypotheses on a group of eight-year-old children whose I.Q.'s ranged from 84 to 143. The three hypotheses were all supported by the data. When cognitive style and concept style were compatible (i.e., descriptive subjects learned the concept "stripes," categorical subjects learned the concept "containers"),

I.Q. was unrelated to number of errors for either type of concept. However, when cognitive style and concept style were incompatible (i.e., descriptive subjects learned the concept "containers," categorical subjects learned the concept "stripes"), the higher I.Q. subjects learned much more rapidly than the lower I.Q. subjects, with the difference highly significant statistically.

Analyses of strategies used by subjects in laboratory studies of concept learning appear to be consistent with the position that much of the behavior involved in concept learning is not highly intelligent. Bruner, Goodnow, and Austin (1956) have conducted one of the most comprehensive studies of strategies. They found that even among a highly selected group of Harvard and Wellesley undergraduates who were instructed concerning the meaning of postive and negative instances, many subjects had great difficulty maintaining a consistent strategy. In addition, if intelligent strategies were extremely effective in solving concept problems, one would expect that subjects would be most effective if they could select or generate the crucial instances which would test their hypotheses, as opposed to merely receiving instances in a random fashion. A number of studies indicate that such generation or selection of instances is not very helpful. Huttenlocher (1962) found that children actually were hindered in solution by being permitted to generate their own instances. Schwartz (1966a) compared generation, selection, and random presentation for simple, conjunctive, and disjunctive concepts and found no significant differences in percentage solution due to type of instance presentation. In a second study, Schwartz (1966b) had college students learn either conjunctive or disjunctive concepts. Subjects in one group, under each concept type, were permitted to select their own order of instances to test. Each subject in a control group was yoked to a subject in the selection group so that the yoked subject received the same order of instances as that selected by one member of the selection condition. Finally, a third group, under each concept type, received the instances in a random order. Overall, random presentation was not significantly worse than selection. For the conjunctive concept, a high correlation was found between performance of the yoked pairs of subjects. Some yoked subjects "inherited" efficient orders of stimuli from the selection subjects; others were yoked to poor solvers and this affected performance of the yoked subjects. Thus order presentation was a relevant variable in solution. However, the selection group was not particularly effective in choosing an optional strategy. For the disjunctive concept (which was considerably more difficult than the conjunctive concept), the correlation between yoked subjects and their mates in the selection group failed to be significant.

In conclusion, it appears that intelligence is not strongly related to those concept learning tasks that are based on the discrimination models. It shall be seen that other types of concept learning tasks are more relevant to intellectual performance. Apparently, psychologists who wish to develop a theory of intelligence based on conceptual behavior must look beyond the discrimination models to find an adequate characterization of concepts.

CONCEPT LEARNING: THE GROWTH MODEL

The concept growth position holds that a person's first exposure to a concept is typically a positive instance of the concept (e.g., "that is a dog"). The person then tends to restrict his use of the concept to new instances which are extremely similar to the original exposure. Only gradually does he expand his use of the concept as he learns that dogs may vary over a fairly wide range on the size and shape dimensions. From this point of view, people are much *more likely to err by failing to use a concept* when it is appropriate than by using the concept in a negative instance. This type of mechanism is adaptive, since it will assure that if a real world concept is used, it will probably be used correctly. This is quite different, of course, from the situation which obtains in the laboratory studies which use concept tasks based on a discrimination model; these studies force subjects to use the concept at a high emission rate and force errors of commission.

The concept growth model is consistent with data such as Hovland and Weiss (1953) and Freibergs and Tulvig (1961) which indicate that information from negative instances is extremely difficult for subjects to process unless they have had a great deal of laboratory experience with such material. In the real world, communications would be very confusing if people emitted concept responses to inappropriate stimuli with any degree of frequency.

Learning from Context

An eight-year-old child, asked by the writer how he had learned the meaning of a concept, answered, "Somebody told me." Indeed, this appears to be the basis for much of our knowledge of concept meaning. A term is used in a given context (e.g., "Look at the cow"). Evidence to date (e.g., Saltz and Sigel, 1967) suggests that the young child tends not to emit concept responses to inappropriate stimuli (i.e., he does not overgeneralize). Instead, it is only gradually that he learns to extend a concept to the broad class of objects included by adults. I. E. Sigel (personal communication) reports that for five-year-olds, the term *animal* is restricted to four legged mammals. Not until eight or nine years of age are snakes and birds systematically included in the concept. This is quite a different picture of concept learning from the one presented by the typical laboratory study.

A technique has been developed by Werner and Kaplan (1950) for studying the development of meaning from context. This technique appears to capture the real-world concept-learning situation in a realistic manner and has been modified for use in a number of recent studies. In the original Werner and Kaplan study, children were asked to determine the meaning of a nonsense word on the basis of the context provided by a set of sentences, each containing the nonsense word. This technique was used by Deese (1967) in one of the most promising programmatic approaches to concept learning to be reported in recent years. Instead of using completely arbitrary combinations of stimuli as concepts, Deese employed natural concepts which do not have familiar labels (e.g., things to sit on, things carried by hand). For each concept which was to be learned, subjects were presented ten sentences which coded the concept by means of a nonsense word. The subjects were asked to define the concept, then to invent ten new sentences using the nonsense word as defined. The definitions task proved to be very difficult and many subjects provided inadequate definitions. However, even when the definitions were not adequate, the subjects often invented new sentences that were quite acceptable in terms of the original concept to be learned. For example, based on sentences in which the concept to be learned was *man-made objects*, one subject gave the definition *anything that is hard to the touch*. A new sentence invented by this subject was, "All X's will eventually disintegrate" (Deese, 1967, p. 649). The sentence is at least as adequate for the original concept as it is for the subject's definition.

Clearly, context is not perfect as a method of *exact* information transmittal. On the other hand, it provides a basis for subjects to use concepts in an approximate fashion before the laborious process of exact learning has been completed. A child, for example, can be given a concept name and can use it reasonably adequately for a long period of time without realizing the definitional attributes of the concept. Only in restricted situations does one find, to his surprise, that many of the child's concepts are quite bizarre (e.g., Saltz and Hamilton, 1968, find that many children deny that a bad man can be a father). The traditional laboratory studies of concept learning leave one unprepared for such findings, since these studies are so arranged that incorrect hypotheses will typically lead to massive errors.

The study described above suggests that man's inefficiency as an information processor may be an adaptive characteristic. This is also suggested in another of the studies described by Deese (1967). This study mirrors the real problems encountered by learning concepts from context, where the person transmitting the information is not a perfect transmitter. Deese used a technique whereby one subject was taught a concept, then this subject would teach it to another subject. At times the first subject would learn the concept only roughly and would make errors in presenting instances to the second subject. Despite these errors in transmission, the second subject often learned the concept. Deese reports questioning subjects on how they could reconcile their definition with particular erroneously presented instances. Subjects gave answers like, "I didn't think that counted," or, "The teacher made a mistake," or, "I just didn't think about it, I guess." (Deese, 1967, p. 648.) The picture is quite different from that of many of the recent mathematical models of concept learning, in which the subject is seen as an efficient information-processing machine whose main problem is his short memory for results of his previous hypothesis testing. On the other hand, Deese's results are quite consistent with those of Amster (1966), who also used a form of the Werner-Kaplan technique. Amster found that a correct meaning does not, apparently, develop gradually over a number of sentences containing a nonsense word. Instead, some one single sentence provides an optimal context for discovering the meaning and this sentence determines learning.

An aspect of Deese's (1967) research on serial reproduction suggests the operation of boundary strength in concept stability. Deese gave the first subject a definition of a nonsense word and had him invent ten sentences using the word as defined; these ten sentences were presented to a second subject who guessed at the definition, then used his guess to invent ten additional sentences which were presented to a third subject, etc. Some groups were given definitions which were already coded with familiar names; others were given straightforward concepts in the language which were not so coded (e.g., things to sit on). The interesting characteristic of the uncoded concepts is that they overlap a number of more familiar concepts (e.g., *things to sit on* overlaps chairs, stools, couches, tree stumps, etc.). As would be expected from the present analysis, Deese found that the successive definitions of the coded concepts remained at a high level of accuracy across reproductions while the definitions of the uncoded concepts dropped rapidly to an unacceptable level of accuracy.

Hooper (1964) employed a variant of the Werner-Kaplan task in a study designed to investigate the mechanisms of general intelligence. He noted that vocabulary size is one of the best predictors of general intelligence. It appeared, therefore, that a better understanding of intelligence might be obtained if it were possible to determine the psychological variables involved in vocabulary. Hooper reasoned that much of vocabulary is acquired from the contexts in which words are used. It seemed reasonable to hypothesize, on this basis, that one aspect of vocabulary size should be the ability to reason from context. This study found a relatively high correlation between performance on the modified Werner-Kaplan test and the vocabulary subtest of several intelligence scales. It should be recalled that the more traditional trial-and-error concept learning tasks do not relate well to measures of intelligence.

Concept Conservation

Most of the studies reported above have studied concept acquisition. In the succeeding sections, a number of studies will be reported that use a technique based on the work of Piaget (1950), which shall be called concept conservation. It is therefore desirable to distinguish between acquisition and conservation at this point.

In the typical *concept learning* study, the subject is presented with arrays of stimuli and must discover which subset of these the experimenter wishes him to respond to. The discovery phase is crucial. Once the particular subset is found by the subject, the identification of further instances is trivial. For example, given complex stimulus arrays, the experimenter may wish to have the subject select only those stimuli which contain a triangle. Depending on the manner in which the stimulus arrays are constructed, this basis of solution may be easy or difficult to discover. Once discovered, however, the subject has little difficulty identifying subsequent stimuli as either having or not having a triangle.

The *concept conservation* studies, on the other hand, start by telling the subject what the relevant concept is. The subject is then presented with new stimuli and must decide if they are instances of the concept. Here the discovery phase is trivial and the identification of new instances is a problem. Put somewhat differently, concept learning is concerned with discovering a concept in the face of stimulus variability. Both are concerned with the utilization of past experiences in dealing with novel stimuli.

It should be noted that the conservation task can be used as an indication of the concept structure for a given person. For example, the child who says that a drunkard can not be a father has a different attribute structure for father than the college student who says a drunkard *can* be a father. Since changes in concept structure are part of the process of concept learning, the conversation task can be used to study concept learning.

Development of Concept Structure in Children

The assumption is frequently made that children tend to overgeneralize concepts (viz., infer that too many stimuli belong to a concept) , and only as they grow older do they learn to restrict their concepts to the appropriate stimulus instances. This assumption is consistent with the discrimination models of concept learning and is often offered as evidence for such models. However, despite the widespread acceptance of this proposition, most of the evidence for it is anecdotal. For example, young children are said to call all men, "father."

One of the few experimental studies indicating evidence for the overgeneralization tendency in young children was reported by Gibson and Gibson (1955) . The study was based on E. J. Gibson's (1940) theory of stimulus differentiation, which will be reviewed extensively in Chapter 4. In terms of this theory, the Gibsons assume that concepts are very undifferentiated for young children. Differentiation, which increases with age, is assumed by this theory to consist of a decrease in the slope of generalization gradients about the concept. The study by the Gibsons involved presenting a nonsense stimulus to a child as a standard stimulus. The standard was then removed, and the child was successively presented with 30 stimuli. The child was asked to indicate whether each stimulus, in turn, was the same as, or different from, the standard. The results indicated that young children were very likely to say that a stimulus was the same as the standard when in fact it was not. With increased age, the frequency of this type of error decreased.

Several problems arise in attempting to evaluate this experiment reported by Gibson and Gibson (1955). First, of the 30 test stimuli, 29 were actually different from the standard. Thus, there were 29 possibilities for overgeneralization, but only one case in which an overdiscrimination error could occur. To the extent that younger children tend to be less accurate (e.g., more distractable) than older children, the younger children would appear to show greater overgeneralization since most of their errors would, of necessity, be scored as overgeneralizations. Second, it is known that memory improves with age. In the Gibson and Gibson study, memory played a large role since the standard was removed before the test stimuli were presented. Consequently, it is possible that the greater number of errors made by younger children (and scored as overgeneralization) largely reflected their poorer memory, rather than a tendency toward overgeneralization.

Saltz and Sigel (1967) attempted to examine the overgeneralization issue in an experiment that controlled for some of the problems found in the Gibson and Gibson study. First, for half the test stimuli, "same" was correct; for half, "different" was correct. Second, the standard and the test stimuli were presented simultaneously. Saltz and Sigel (1967) presented subjects with pairs of photographs, each photograph showing the face of a young boy (viz., about five years old). Some pairs were pictures of the same boy (though in somewhat different poses) and some pairs were pictures of two different children. The subjects were asked, "Are these the same boy?" The crucial issue was: Would types of errors change with age? They did. Six-year-old children tended to err by claiming that two pictures were of *different* boys, when actually they were of the same boy. By 19 or 20 years of age, the direction of error reversed somewhat, and subjects were more likely to claim two pictures were of the same boy when actually they were of different boys.

In short, rather than overgeneralization, the Saltz and Sigel study found overdiscrimination in young children. These results suggest that young children have fairly restricted concepts containing relatively few attributes. In terms of the cognitive space model of concepts, the young child's concept occupies a very restricted region on the relevant attribute dimensions. Small differences between the standard and a test stimulus project the latter into a region of the cognitive space not occupied by the concept standard, and lead the young child to deny that the concept is still appropriate.

Studies of social concepts indicate the same general pattern of differences across ages. Sigel, Saltz and Roskind (1967) asked six-, seven-, and eight-year-old children whether a father who goes to work, where he is a doctor, is still a father. Only 40% of the six-year-olds were willing to say that the doctor was still a father. About 80% of the eight-year-olds were able to conserve the concept of father under the conditions of being of doctor. This study also indicated that the conservation of the concept was related to *degree* of stimulus change. For example, increased variation in time perspective led to poorer conservation. Significantly more children conserved when told the father *is* a doctor than when told that the father *studied and became* a doctor. Similarly, the addition of actual changes in physical location of the father decreased conservation. If the children were shown four stickmen which were identified as fathers, and four which were identified as doctors, and if one of the stickmen from the father group was physically moved to the doctor group, all three age groups were less likely to conserve the concept of father.

The restricted nature of concepts in children is even more dramatically illustrated in a study by Saltz and Hamilton (1968). Eight-year-old children were used as subjects, since the Sigel, Saltz, and Roskind (1967) study had indicated that children at this age conserve the concept of father fairly well in the father-doctor type situation. Saltz and Hamilton presented the children with a problem involving a father who becomes a *drunkard*. While approximately 80% of these children could conserve the concept of father in a father-doctor transformation, only 40% could conserve the father concept in a father-drunkard transformation. In a modification of the semantic differential, it turned out that both father and doctor were rated as approximately equally "good," while drunkard was rated as very "bad."

The basis of the lack of conservation in the father-drunkard problem appears to lie in the inability of these children to incorporate the "bad" attributes of drunkard into the concept of father. In terms of the cognitive space model, father occupies a region that intersects the evaluative dimension at the "good" end; an instance, such as drunkard, that falls at the "bad" end of the evaluative dimension is outside of the region that constitutes the concept for many of the younger children. "Good" is clearly a correlated (rather than definitional) attribute, and with experience the concept will expand to occupy a larger range of values on the evaluative dimension. An interesting verification of this suggested mechanism was found in examining conservation of the concept *brother* when the transformation brother-bully was used. Saltz and Hamilton found that bully was rated as being as bad as drunkard; on the other hand, brother was rated as much less good than father. As might be expected from these differences in the ratings, the eight-year-olds were much more able to conserve the concept brother when brother was a bully, than to conserve the concept father when father was a drunkard.

Modigliani (1969), in a comprehensive study of concept structure, further explored the relationship between concept conservation and the location of a stimulus instance on a *dimension crucial to the concept*. Subjects first learned to sort drawings of potted plants into two categories, *A* or *B,* on the basis of the shape of the leaf on the plant. Learning was carried to 32 errorless trials to assure that subjects were responding systematically to the correct cues. Then the subjects were shown a pot with *two* leaves; one was the Category *A* leaf, while the other was a new shape, quite different from either of the two previously seen. In terms of the cognitive space model, the new instance occupied two distinct points on the definitional attribute dimension. Only one of these points was within the region of the Category *A* concept. In this situation, over 90% of the subjects chose the alternative that the instance belonged in neither Category *A* nor *B*. This response was relatively constant between children 6 years of age and young adults around 20 years of age. Apparently, when a new instance occupies too large a region in cognitive space on the *definitional* dimension, relative to the instances on which the concept was learned, the concept ceases to be conserved.

Modigliani's data appeared to constitute a particularly severe problem for the level-of-abstraction position concerning the nature of concepts. It will be recalled that this position views a concept as the abstraction of the relevant attributes of the instances from which the concept was attained (i.e., the concept is the interection of the attribute sets). Therefore, a subject should identify a new (unfamiliar) stimulus as an instance of a concept if this new stimulus contains the abstracted set of attributes which are characteristic of the concept. Modigliani has identified a situation in which this type of conceptual response to the abstraction does not occur. Similar problems will be seen to arise in other experimental situations to be described below.

Role of "Irrelevant" Dimensions

Dimensions may be irrelevant to a concept in several different senses of the term irrelevant. (1) *Correlated but not definitional.* Examples of this type of dimension were seen in the preceding section (e.g., father is considered to be on the good end of the evaluative dimension). (2) *Uncorrelated but necessary.* A given irrelevant dimension may be necessary for a particular concept, though no specific attribute values on this dimension are crucial (e.g., a father who has no value on a height dimension is difficult to picture). (3) *Uncorrelated and dispensable.* Dimensions may be dispensable due to the fact that several concepts often occur together in compound stimulus instances. For example, a flower and a flower pot may occur together in a single stimulus instance, yet either may occur alone. Thus the attributes relevant to flower, such as color of the flower, will be absent when the pot is presented empty.

Modigliani (1969), in another portion of the study previously cited, examined the characteristics of uncorrelated and dispensable attribute dimensions and found that *children appear to incorporate these into their structure of a concept.* In this study, subjects learned to categorize drawings of potted plants in terms of one characteristic of the instances (e.g., shape of the flower pot). Thus pots of one shape were called Category *A* and pots of a second shape were Category *B*. Each pot always contained a flower (sometimes a daisy, sometimes a tulip) and a leaf (sometimes broad, sometimes narrow). After each subject reached a criterion of 32 successive errorless trials, Modigliani presented a Category *A* pot alone, without flower or leaf. Thus a number of irrelevant dimensions were completely dispensed with. The six-year-old children proved to be most restricted to the stimulus context in which the instances were learned; 88% failed to conserve the concept (i.e., chose the alternative that the pot fell into neither the *A* nor the *B* category). At 12 years of age, 56% of the children failed to conserve. Even in the college group, 20% failed to conserve. The performance of the 12-year-olds and college students is particularly interesting, since these must have had previous experience with empty flower pots.

One can conceive of a situation in which each instance in which a concept occurs is treated as a separate concept. For example, a child reinforced for choosing tulips might think of tulip in a narrow pot as a different concept from tulip in a wide pot. This would represent an extremely restricted concept (or set of concepts) for tulip, where each subconcept would be a point rather than a region in the cognitive space. Suppes and Ginsberg (1963) have presented data which indicate that young children may acquire a concept in the laboratory by learning which specific stimuli are instances of the concept and which are not, rather than learning, the general structure of the concept. Suppes and Ginsberg interpreted these data as suggesting that the children "learned by rote" and did not acquire the concept. The formulation in the present chapter suggests, instead, that the children learned multiple, restricted concepts.

Development of the Ability to Differentiate Dimensions

A study by Ervin and Foster (1960) points up an interesting problem that may be very important for the understanding of concept development in children. This study suggests that some stimulus dimensions may be sufficiently correlated in the child's early experience that he is not capable of responding independently to each of them.

Ervin and Foster presented children with a series of problems illustrated by the following example. First a child was shown two balls, one larger than the other, and was asked to indicate the larger ball. The child was then asked to indicate if one of these balls was *stronger* than the other. The correlation between attributes like *large* and *strong* proved to be very great for young children (about six years old) and decreased with age. In the realm of physical dimensions, the six-year-old children also showed a moderate tendency toward correlating *big* with *heavy*, and *strong* with *heavy*. By 12 years of age, the tendency to correlate these attributes was markedly reduced.

Ervin and Foster (1960) also examined certain evaluative attribute dimensions: clean-dirty, happy-sad, pretty-ugly, good-bad. Children were shown pairs of drawings of a girl's face. For example, one drawing might be smiling, the other not. First the children were asked which face was happier, then they were asked which face was more good. Of the six-year-olds, 62% were found to use happy, good, and pretty as synonymous attributes. Again, as in the physical dimensions, this tendency dropped markedly between 6 and 12 years of age. However, even at 12 years the tendency toward correlation among these terms was still relatively high.

These findings are reminiscent of the data reported by Saltz and

Wickey (1965), cited earlier in this chapter. Saltz and Wickey found evidence that suggested "good" and "liberal" were correlated dimensions for some adults. Given a stimulus person who was liberal, these adults denied that he could be an assassin, since an assassin is bad.

Clearly, the greater the degree of correlation between attribute dimensions for a given person, the fewer the number of distinctions he can make and the more impoverished his cognitive space. Potentially, the issues raised by Ervin and Foster are therefore of great importance. Unfortunately, little systematic research has followed from this study. However, the basic notion of gradual differentiation of attribute dimensions with age will prove useful in the succeeding section of this chapter.

PIAGETIAN CONSERVATION

Piaget (1950, 1957) has been concerned with conservation of concepts such as weight, mass, volume, and number. The writer believes that the issues here are essentially the same as those in the conservation studies cited above. A typical task employed by Piaget to measure the child's ability to conserve mass can be described as follows. A child is shown two identical beakers, *A* and *B,* filled to the same degree with water. The child agrees that the two beakers contain *the same amount of water.* The child then watches while the water in one of these beakers is poured into a third beaker, *C,* which is taller and thinner than the other two. Next the child is asked whether the amount of water in *C* is the same as the amount in beaker *A.* Young children typically say *no,* the two beakers do not contain the same amount of water. Clearly, the child is not saying that the water *per se* has changed. He is saying that a property of the water, its amount, has changed.

This is the same problem which is encountered in concept conservation (e.g., the father-doctor problem). The child does not claim that the man who is a doctor is not the same as the man who was a father. He is saying that a property (fatherliness) has changed. (It is possible, of course, that extremely young children may not even conserve the person. However, in the writer's experience, by five years of age failure of conservation extended only to the property of the person, not the person *per se.*) Thus in both quantity conservation and concept conservation, some property of an object must be conserved despite transformations of the object.

There is evidence to suggest that in quantity conservation, as in concept conservation, greater discrepancy between the standard and its transform, along some dimension, is likely to produce reduced conservation. For example, Bruner (1964) reports a study in which children were first shown the two identical beakers containing the water and also were shown the taller, thinner beaker into which the water was to be poured. The tall, thin beaker was then placed behind a screen so that, while the children could see the water being poured, they could not see the level which the water reached in the tall beaker. With the perceptual discrepancy between the standard and the transform thus obscured, children were found to increase their conservation significantly.

A similar effect was reported by Piaget and Inhelder (1962), using a ball of clay as the standard. When the clay was flattened into a pancake shape, young children insisted that the amount of clay in the transform (i.e., the pancake) was greater than the amount in the standard (i.e., the ball). At an age where children were beginning to conserve on this problem, making the clay pancake even flatter led to a loss of conservation.

On the basis of such studies, Bruner (1964) has suggested that loss of conservation is produced by *perceptual conflict* between the standard and its transform. The writer would agree with this interpretation for the class of studies in which the transformation is along a perceptual dimension. However, studies such as those of Sigel, Saltz, and Roskind (1967), and Saltz and Hamilton (1968) indicate that degree of change along nonperceptual dimensions will have a similar effect. In short, cognitive discrepancy is the crucial factor, with perceptual discrepancy simply one type of cognitive discrepancy.

It should be noted that some studies have failed to find a relationship between tendency to conserve and *degree* of discrepancy between the standard and the transform. For example, Hooper (1967) examined conservation of mass by pouring tiny beads from a short, wide beaker into taller, thinner beakers. He used two sizes of transform beakers, both having the same volume, but one taller and thinner than the other. The standard beaker was two inches high, the shorter transform beaker was four inches high, and the taller transform was eight inches high. He found no difference in tendency to conserve between the shorter and taller transforms. At present, the best interpretation of such results appears to be that loss of conservation was asympototic at the level of discrepancy represented by the shorter (four-inch) beaker.

Another aspect of the issue of degree of discrepancy between standard and transform was also investigated by Hooper. Hooper tested the distinction made by Elkind (1967) between equivalence and identity. In the example from Hooper's work, cited above, beakers A and B were equivalent; the contents of B were poured into C, and so the final comparison was between the two physically present containers, A and C. The question asked the child was whether the amount in C was the same as the amount in A. If the child said *no*, he was not directly stating that the amount had changed in the process of transferring the beads from one container to another. The change was implied indirectly by the fact that he had previously stated that A and B contained equal amounts. In the identity condition, on the other hand, Hooper used only two beakers, the standard, A, and a transform, C. The contents of A were poured into C, and the child was asked whether C contained as many beads as A had previously contained. Now if the child said *no*, this directly implied a change in quantity. While Piaget appears to have considered equivalence and identity as essentially the same process, Hooper found significantly more conservation under identity conditions than under equivalence.

Several possible bases exist for the difference between identity and equivalence conditions. One is memory as a factor in the degree of discrepancy. In equivalence, the perceptual discrepancy between the level of beads in A and C is immediately present—the child has both A and C before him, both filled, and the level of beads in A is perceptually below that of C, since A is wider than C. In the identity condition, the child must remember the level in A in order to react to the discrepancy between A and C. There is some basis for believing that this memory factor is not crucial. Hooper compared degree of conservation when C was physically present with degree of conservation when, after the pouring operation, C was hidden behind a screen. There was no difference in conservation between these conditions.

A second basis of difference between equivalence and identity resides in the ability of children, at this age, to make inferences. In the identity condition, when the child fails to conserve, he is stating fairly directly that the quantity has changed as a function of the operation of pouring into a taller beaker. This is clearly less true in the equivalence condition. It is only by inference from the equality between A and B that the child is committing himself to a change in quantity.

Interpretation of Quantity Conservation

To most normal adults, the solutions to quantity conservation problems appear obvious. They are shocked to find that young children make errors on such problems. For example, to most adults it appears obvious that if a clay ball is pressed into the shape of a pancake, the pancake contains the same amount of clay as was present in the original ball. In fact, quantity conservation is not a purely logical problem for the child. Logically, a physical theory could easily be invented that did not imply conservation of mass with changes in shape. However, such a theory would not fit the empirical facts of present day physics. It is necessary for a child to learn that, given a particular piece of clay, dimensions such as length and width are irrelevant to its mass. This is difficult to learn because, in common experience, longer pieces of a thing often have greater mass than shorter pieces of the same thing.

Apparently, the independence between dimensions must be learned separately for dimensions such as mass, weight, and volume. At age nine, for example, almost all children can conserve mass (e.g., they recognize that changing the *shape* of a ball of clay does not alter the *amount* of clay); however, almost none can conserve volume (Elkind, 1961). In terms of common experience, it is not surprising that volume conservation should be difficult to learn. There are many common situations in which changing the shape of an object does indeed change its volume. For example, many people have had the experience of emptying food from a can and stepping on the can to flatten it; in this condition the volume of the can is reduced virtually to zero. Only restricted classes of physical transformations will result in unaltered volume. In order to conserve volume correctly, the child must learn which classes of transformations have the required properties.

A startling example of the importance of irrelevant dimensions in failure to conserve was reported by Wohlwill and Lowe (1962). The study was concerned with conservation of number, using length as the irrelevant dimension. Kindergarten children were presented two parallel rows of seven chips each. One of the rows of chips was then extended in both directions to a length twice that of the other row. The children were then asked which row had more chips. Of the nonconservers (i.e., children who claimed that the longer row had more chips), 23 were asked to count the number of chips in each row. After counting correctly, 19 of the 23 persisted in not conserving. Apparently, the meaning of "more chips" was not restricted to number for these children, but was also largely influenced by length.

CONSERVATION AND DIFFERENTIATION OF RELEVANT DIMENSIONS. The findings described above appear to be very consistent with Ervin and Foster's (1960) conclusion that young children have not yet completely differentiated certain physical dimensions (e.g., size and weight). From this point of view, if two dimensions are undifferentiated, a change along one of the dimensions will be interpreted as involving a corresponding change in the other dimension. For example, if the dimension of number of objects is not well differentiated from the dimension of the ordinal length occupied by these objects when arrayed in a line, the child will tend to interpret an increase in the length of a row of chips as indicating a corresponding increase in number of chips.

Recently, Mehler and Bever (1967, 1968) have suggested an even more radical position with regard to differentiation of attribute dimensions. These writers have suggested that attribute dimensions such as length and number are initially differentiated in the extremely young child. However, this differentiation gradually breaks down between the ages of two and four years as the child encounters the fact that *many* items usually occupy more space than *few* items. In other words, the child learns to correlate the dimensions. After four years of age, the differentiation between dimensions re-establishes itself. This position is based on data from studies in which children were asked which of two rows of clay pellets contained "more." In some cases, the short row contained more, in some cases the long row. The two year old children were almost perfect in picking the short row when it contained more pellets. Percentage correct in this condition dropped with age to about four years, then rose again. It should be noted that the data reported by Mehler and Bever, as well as their interpretations of these data, have been questioned on a number of grounds by both Beilin (1968a and 1968b) and Piaget (1968). While the issues involved are interesting, they are beyond the scope of the present book.

LACK OF CONSERVATION AS FAILURE IN COMMUNICATION. The position on conservation taken by Braine and Shanks (1965) offers an interesting contrast to the positions outlined above. Braine and Shanks have suggested that the basis for nonconservation may be a misunderstanding, by the child, of the experimenter's question concerning conservation. More specifically, they suggest that a child may actually be aware that qualities such as mass, etc., are conserved; however, the child answers the conservation question incorrectly, because he interprets the experimenter's question incorrectly. The child, they suggest, believes that the experimenter is asking if the transformed stimuli *look different* (e.g., look bigger, look as though there were more water in the taller container, etc.) .

In a sense, the Braine and Shanks hypothesis reflects the incredulity of the sophisticated adult when he finds that the child does not understand something which, to the adult, appears logically self-evident. Several lines of evidence appear to be inconsistent with the Braine and Shanks hypothesis. In their own study, attempting to stress the distinction between "really bigger" and "looks bigger" did not have the dramatic effect one might have hoped for on the basis of the hypothesis. In addition, the hypothesis is most relevant for perceptual stimuli and does not appear appropriate for the more general, cognitive nonconservation found in studies such as Sigel, Saltz, and Roskind (1967) , and in Saltz and Hamilton (1968) .

PIAGET'S INTERPRETATION OF CONSERVATION. The position proposed by Piaget can only be indicated in a relatively sketchy manner in this book. A more detailed account can be found in Piaget (1950, 1957) and in Inhelder and Piaget (1958) . In essence, Piaget suggests that a number of logical operations must be available to the child before the child can think intelligently. The operation of logical multiplication is one which is necessary for conservation. In order to conserve mass, for instance, the child must be able to logically multiply the dimensions of length and thickness, so that he realizes that a long, thin piece of clay is equivalent to a short, fat (spherical) piece. While the notion of logical operations is very appealing, evidence concerning these operations is difficult to come by. In order to show the dependence of conservation on logical multiplication, it is first necessary to show that some behavior, which can be identified as logical multiplication, precedes conservation. This is not, however, sufficient. Since various types of behavior differ in difficulty, logical multiplication may occur before conservation because it is easier, rather than because it is causally necessary to conservation. In short, evidence that these behaviors emerge in a developmental order is necessary but not sufficient to confirm the Piagetian interpretation. In an important study, Shantz and Sigel (1967) have failed to find this necessary developmental order. Shantz and Sigel tested children separately on both conservation and on tasks which more directly tapped logical multiplication. The test of logical multiplication required that children fill one empty cell of a 2 × 2 matrix with a picture that represented the logical intersection of two dimensions. For example, in a matrix formed by a color dimension and a size dimension, children were shown a large yellow clock, a small yellow clock, and a large green clock. The child was considered to have performed the logical multiplication successfully if he chose a small green clock to place in the empty cell of the matrix. While a positive correlation was found between success in conservation and success in logical multiplication, this correlation was relatively small. The Shantz and Sigel study certainly can not be considered the final word on the relationship between logical multiplication and conservation. However, their data clearly pose a problem for the Piagetian position.

Learning to Conserve

The position taken in this chapter is that one learns empirically which properties are conserved during certain classes of transformations and which transformations do not conserve these properties. On the other hand, it seems likely that more than the absolute amount of experience is relevent to profiting from experience. If a younger child has more restricted concept structures than an older child, the younger child may structure his experiences into a larger number of isolated concepts. In other words, he will not react to all his experiences as though they are related to the same concept. Instead, he may conserve over some ranges of standards (e.g., small clay balls), transformed over restricted ranges of transformations (e.g., shaped into footballs, but not shaped into sausages). From this it follows that conservation learning should be facilitated if concept structures could somehow be enlarged, or if the correlations between independent dimensions within a concept (e.g., length and amount) could be reduced.

To date there is little conclusive empirical evidence concerning types of training which might produce conservation learning. In a previously cited study, Wohlwill and Lowe (1962) attempted to extinguish the correlation between length and number in attempting to teach children to conserve number. Their experimental group improved in ability to conserve, but no more so than a control group which was untrained. However, only one relatively brief training session was employed.

Shantz and Siegl (1967) point out that for every study that has succeessfully trained children to conserve, some other investigator has failed to obtain results using approximately the same procedure. For example, teaching verbal rules was effective in a study by Beilin (1965), but not in a study by Mermelstein, Carr, Mills, and Schwartz (1967); reversibility training was found to be useful in a study by Wallach and Sprott (1964), but not by Sonstroem (1966).

Shantz and Sigel (1967) investigated two types of training which are particularly interesting because the training tasks were not directly related to conservation. In one, children were trained to analyze and label the multiple attributes of familiar objects. The second procedure was aimed at training children to remember a sequence of actions, to visually analyze pictures for details, and to increase their ability to verbally express ideas. From the point of view of the present chapter, these techniques appear to be training in enlarging the number of attributes in a concept. While both procedures were followed by significant increments in conservation, unfortunately no control group was employed against which to evaluate the procedures.

CONCLUSIONS

In this country, research on concepts has been largely dominated by the issue of concept *learning*. Consequently, the emphasis has been on variables related to acquisition rate, rather than an attempt to formulate a theory concerning the nature and structure of concepts. Almost no heed has been paid to the question of how concepts are used, once they have been acquired, and how they influence future thinking and behavior. (There are, of course, important exceptions to this generalization, e.g., Kendler and Kendler, 1962; Ervin and Foster, 1960.) Further, the most commonly employed models of concept learning have tended to reduce research to an investigation of complex discrimination learning. These models envision concept learning as involving extensive trial-and-error behavior, with massive tendencies toward emission of incorrect responses. Reduction in these tendencies toward incorrect emissions is often seen as a major component in acquiring the concept.

Considering first the issue of concept learning, an examination of responses to real-world concepts suggests that people learn these largely on the basis of positive instances. Early concept responses stay very close to the context in which the concept was initially encountered. For this reason, people will only infrequently use a concept response incorrectly; errors, in other words, are likely to be of omission rather than commission. Such findings are at odds, of course, with the discrimination models of concept learning cited above.

Issues concerned with the manner in which concepts are used, once they have been acquired, have been investigated by means of concept-conservation tasks. Developmental studies of conservation indicate that young children have very restricted concepts involving narrow ranges of values on relevant stimulus dimensions. In addition, the number of independent dimensions available to the young child is also restricted, since he appears unable to differentiate a number of important dimensions from one another. For example, the liberal adult learns to differentiate the dimensions of liberal-conservative and good-bad so that he can accept the notion that there are situations in which a liberal may commit a bad act or a conservative may have his moments of goodness. From this perspective, intellectual development involves increased differentiation of dimensions and an ability to form more abstract concepts which consist of broad regions of values on relevant dimensions, rather than restricted sets of points on these dimensions. It is interesting to note that this view of concepts permits accommodation of the broad range of issues treated by social psychologists under the topic of balance-theory. The notion of concept structure thus becomes very valuable in fostering understanding of a number of previously unrelated phenomena.

PART II | WHAT IS LEARNED?

3 | Learning as Resistance to Forgetting

PRECIS

Recent findings in both human and animal studies suggest a radical revision of our notions concerning the nature of learning. These studies suggest that, in most situations, subjects will learn almost perfectly after a single trial. Their great problem is the rapidity with which they then forget. This chapter will consider the position that much of which we previously considered to be learning can be viewed, instead, as resistance to forgetting. Since forgetting is largely attributable to competing cognitive elements that interfere with the material which we want to remember, the crucial factors in learning appear to involve the increase in *resistance to interference.*

Stated somewhat more technically, learning can at this point be partitioned into two categories of variables: the associative variable on the one hand and the variables related to resistance to interference on the other hand. The former, it will be seen, appears to reach very high levels of strength upon the first trial; the latter appear to increase in strength more slowly. In the present chapter, resistance to interference will be dealt with as though it were a single factor. Chapters 4, 5, and 6 will analyze this factor in its component variables.

DEMONSTRATION EXPERIMENT

The Problem

If you turn to the next page, you will find a word enclosed in a box. Read the word (it should not take more than a second to do so) then turn back to this page. Do it now!

As you have just seen, a single meaningful stimulus can be perceived and processed very rapidly. Now, count by threes (3, 6, 9 . . .) as rapidly as possible until you reach the number 66, being sure to make no errors—then return to this page and continue reading.

Have you counted successfully to 66? (If not, then please do so, now!) What is the word in the box on the next page? _____

Explanation

Almost everyone will have remembered the single word on the next page. In the present chapter, we shall see that such associations are acquired at virtually maximum strength upon a single presentation. Indeed, we shall see that this is true for most human learning—often even when the material involved is nonsense rather than a meaningful word. Then why do learning curves often rise so slowly? Why do we often perform poorly when tested on a chapter we have read? We shall see that the major problem for the human mind (and perhaps also the animal mind) in such situations is *forgetting* produced by interference from erroneous materials, rather than the development of an association.

In the present demonstration, you were shown a single item under conditions of minimal interference. You then engaged in 30 to 60 seconds of irrelevant reading and counting that (presumably) kept you from rehearsing. The test then showed that most of you had indeed learned in a single trial.

HUMAN MEMORY AND CONCEPT LEARNING

Short-Term Memory

Some of the most dramatic evidence for the rapid development of associative strength comes from studies of short-term memory using a technique devised by Peterson and Peterson (1959). The objective of this technique is to minimize rehearsal of the material during the retention interval. Following the presentation of an item (e.g., a real word or a nonsense word), subjects are required to count backwards by threes or fours, at a fixed rate, from an arbitrarily chosen number. Upon a signal, the subjects attempt to recall the item.

Typical data collected using this technique indicate that, if subjects are shown a single word for a second or more and the word is then removed, the retention immediately after removal (viz., the 0-second retention interval) is virtually perfect. This is true if the item is a real word or a three-consonant nonsense word. Figure 3–1 presents some illustrative data on this point. Note the extremely high percentage of recall at 0-seconds for all three studies illustrated.

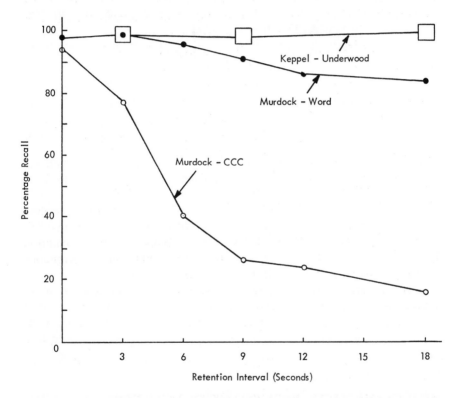

FIGURE 3–1. Short-Term Retention of the First Nonsense Syllable Learned (Keppel and Underwood); of Nonsense Syllables after Many Other Syllables Have Been Learned (Murdock-CCC); and of Real Words, after Many Other Real Words Have Been Learned (Murdock-Word). See text for discussion. (Figure adapted from Murdock, 1961; and from Keppel and Underwood, 1962a. Reproduced with permission of the American Psychological Association and the Academic Press.)

Let us now examine the individual curves more closely.

THE MURDOCK-CCC DATA. These data, taken from Murdock (1961), involved short-term retention of nonsense word (viz., consonant triads) using the Peterson and Peterson (1959) technique. Each subject was well practiced in the technique, having been presented with many items to recall. The data represent the average percentage recall over all items presented to the subjects.

Clearly, at 0-seconds the subjects showed that they had acquired the appropriate associations. However, approximately 80% of the items were forgotten if the retention test was delayed by 18 seconds. A number of other studies have reported essentially the same type of data in the retention of nonsense words (e.g., Melton, 1963) : almost perfect retention immediately after removal of the item, and a sharp drop in recall within 18 seconds.

THE KEPPEL AND UNDERWOOD CURVE. Keppel and Underwood (1962a) suggested that the rapid forgetting, in studies such as those cited above, is due to the large number of items to be learned by each subject. Earlier items exist as a potential source of interference which could disrupt the retention of later items. If this were the case, there should be very little forgetting of the first items learned, and extremely rapid forgetting of later items. Any such effect would have been obscured in previous studies, since these pooled over all items learned to obtain an average retention measure.

To test their hypothesis, Keppel and Underwood examined the retention of the *first* nonsense word shown to each subject, using the Peterson and Peterson technique to prevent rehearsal. Their results (labelled "Keppel-Underwood" in Figure 3–1) are consistent with the hypothesis. When the subjects had seen no previous items, retention was almost perfect over a 30-second interval. Similar results have been reported by other investigators (Loess, 1964; H. Paul, 1966; Wickens, Born, and Allen, 1963) . Examination of retention errors also supports this hypothesis. For example, both Loess (1964) and H. Paul (1966) report that about 80% of all errors, in the retention of nonsense syllables, involved intrusions of letters from the immediately preceding several items. (The mechanisms involved in this type of interference will be considered in Chapter 6.)

MURDOCK-WORD CURVE.   Finally, in Figure 3–1, note the curve labelled "Murdock-Word." These data, from Murdock (1961), show the retention of a single real word under conditions paralleling those of the "Murdock-CCC" data for three-letter nonsense syllables. Even after a large number of previous words had been learned and tested for retention, there was almost no forgetting of a single real word during an 18-second retention interval. Apparently, well-integrated materials show great ability to resist interference from proactive competition in this type of situation.

CONCLUSIONS FROM FIGURE 3–1.   The short-term memory studies cited above display an important common characteristic. A test which follows immediately upon removal of the visual stimulus (i.e., the 0-second retention interval of Figure 3–1) shows that an extremely high degree of learning has occurred. Almost all items are perfectly recalled, whether three-letter nonsense syllables, single meaningful words, or three unrelated words. A number of writers (Saltz, 1961b; Peterson, Saltzman, Hilner, and Land, 1962; Murdock, 1963; Melton, 1963) have been struck by the fact that learning not only occurs following a single presentation trial, but that the strength of this learning is usually superthreshold immediately following the single trial. These writers all make the point that the theoretical issue appears to be that of accounting for forgetting, rather than accounting for learning. This orientation is quite different, of course, from the point of view in the maze-oriented theories proposed by Guthrie, Hull, Tolman, and others. In Hull, for example, a stimulus will not regularly elicit a given learned response until the number of reinforced trials has raised the associative strength of the S-R pair above threshold, after which it will regularly do so.

EFFECT OF PRACTICE ON SHORT-TERM MEMORY.   If, as the studies cited above indicate, a great deal of the learning has occurred on the first trial, what is the function of practice? A study by Hellyer (1962) suggests that the primary effect of practice is to reduce forgetting. Using three-letter nonsense material, Hellyer presented each item 1, 2, 4, or 8 times in immediate succession. A variation of the Peterson and Peterson technique was used to prevent rehearsal during the retention intervals. The data, summarized in Figure 3–2, show that at a three-second retention interval there is very little difference in memory between one and eight trials. The effect of increased practice comes into play at the longer retention intervals. Since studies such as Keppel and Underwood (1962a) suggest that

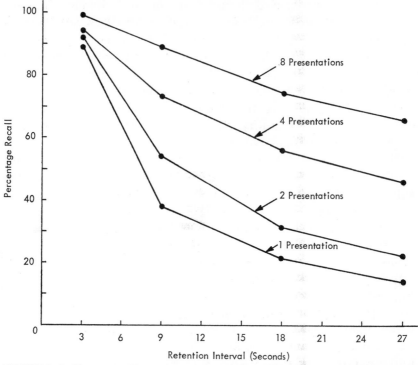

FIGURE 3–2. Short-term Memory for a Nonsense Syllable (CCC) as a Function of Number of Successive Presentations of the Syllable before the Retention Interval. (Adapted from Hellyer, 1962. Reproduced with permission of the American Psychological Association.)

interference is the primary cause of forgetting in the short-term memory situation, it seems reasonable to interpret Hellyer's data as indicating that practice increases resistance to interference. (This will be discussed in Chapter 6.)

CONCLUSIONS. It can be seen that, had short-term memory rather than maze learning and conditioning been the reference experiments for learning, our basic conceptions concerning the learning process might be very different today. Interestingly, a great deal of recent data from the older, more traditional areas of human and animal learning appear to be converging toward the same theoretical conclusions which have arisen in short-term memory.

Verbal Learning

The critical importance of interference processes is extremely evident in studies of human verbal learning. In a typical verbal-learning study, a subject is shown ten pairs of words. The subject is told to learn these so that when he is next shown the first word of each pair, he will be able to say the second word. Trials are repeated until the subject can perform at some pre-established criterion level, such as recalling all the responses correctly in a single test.

But why use ten pairs of words? The obvious reason is that the learning of a single pair would be too rapid. Most verbal-learning studies are concerned with factors that increase or decrease the rate of learning. The influence of such factors would be untestable if, in the extreme case, learning was perfect after a simple trial. Clearly, the limiting situation for verbal learning is the short-term memory situation.

What processes are we referring to when we speak of "learning" in the typical verbal-learning study? If our "list" of pairs consisted of learning a single real word as a response, learning would be perfect after one or two trials. As more pairs are added to the list, the percentage of correct responses on the first test trial would drop. Does this mean that the associative strength of each pair decreases as list-length increases? Or does it mean that correct recall has been impaired by increasing amounts of interference? Similarly, a list of ten pairs can be constructed so that the ten stimulus items are very similar to one another or the list can be constructed so as to minimize similarity. In the former case, subjects may remember only one or two responses to their appropriate stimuli. In the latter case, four or five responses may be remembered correctly. Again, the difference in the "learning" curve does not represent a difference in associative strengths for the two lists; it represents a difference in degree of interference between pairs.

Essentially, then, studies of the acquisition of paired associates lists are studies of factors influencing interference between items in the list, and not simply indices of the growth of associative strength between a stimulus and response. The characteristic paired-associates learning curves (indicating, as they do, the number of responses recalled correctly after various amounts of practice) could readily be interpreted as representing an index of the number of systems which have developed sufficient resistance to escape from the massive interference produced by the other items.

A study by Jung (1964) is interesting in relation to this issue. His data suggest that, *once a system has developed some degree of resistance to interference, a reduction occurs in the disruptive effect produced by the addition of new, competing material.* Jung explored a "cumulative," technique for presenting paired associates in which he first presented a small subset of pairs for several trials, then gradually increased the number of pairs over successive trials. Over the several experiments reported by Jung (1964), this technique never led to significantly poorer performance than that obtained using the standard paired-associate procedure. In some cases it resulted in significantly better performance than that of the standard procedure. This is true despite the fact that, in the Jung technique, the items introduced into the list on later trials were presented (and practiced) less frequently than the same items in the standard procedure. Jung presents data which indicate that the good performance found using his cumulative technique is largely a function of superior performance on the small subset of items presented early in learning. As would be anticipated, performance was not as good for items introduced on later trials.

It might be noted that a number of investigators have suggested that subjects use a strategy for learning that consists of acquiring several items at a time, then going on to the next subset. In effect, then, Jung's procedure could be thought of as having organized the subject's learning in a manner which roughly corresponded to what the subjects would have done for themselves in the standard learning procedure. This may be the case. However, saying that a subject has such a strategy does not indicate the process of learning, it merely indicates the order in which the process occurs. A "pure" strategy theory, for example, implies a relatively linear learning curve, with each subset of items learned as easily as any other. Actually, verbal-learning curves usually are negatively accelerated, with the greatest number of items learned on early trials and the remainder of the trials necessary to master a small residual subset. Similarly, in Jung's experiment an unadorned strategy position would have some difficulty accounting for the disproportionate slowness involved in acquiring the later items added to the list. The strategy notion appears to require the additional proposition that retention of successive subsets will be more difficult when all this material must be retained simultaneously. This proposition brings us back, again, to the competition and interference conclusion.

Concept Learning

To a great extent, the position developed in the present chapter has been building up to the consideration of concept learning. It is here that some of the older, single-unit positions have their greatest problems. It is here that a multifactor approach, which assumes virtually maximum association on the first trial, plus the development of resistance to interference, becomes extremely important.

Concept learning is, in the terms of Chapter 1, primarily a "thinking" task. The subject is presented with a stimulus array and is told to indicate whether or not it represents an instance of the concept which the experimenter is trying to teach. Often, the subject has little or no idea concerning which aspect or aspects of the stimulus are relevant. For example, the experimenter may show the subject a set of cards which vary in shape (e.g., either circle or square), in color (e.g., either red or green), and in size (e.g., either large or small). Further, the experimenter may decide that red is correct. If the experimenter shows the subject a card containing a large red square, and tells the subject that this is an instance of the concept, the subject does not know if this is an instance because it is red, because it is large, because it is square, or because of some combination of these attributes.

The subject's problem is apparently one of competing cognitive systems.

From one point of view, learning may be perfect. If the card is removed, the subject may remember in great detail the set of attributes presented to him. (After several cards have been presented, each varying along the several attribute dimensions, sufficient interference may, of course, develop so that the subject no longer remembers the first card.) If on the other hand, by "learning" we mean that the subject knows after seeing the first card which attribute is uniquely correct, little "learning" has taken place. As shall be seen in the succeeding section, this ambiguity in the use of the term "learning" has created great confusion.

The writer has proposed, earlier in this chapter, that associations are near maximal strength after the first attention to the relevant material. Subsequent retention will be determined by the amount of interference present and by the ability of the learned material to resist this interference. The importance of this approach becomes clear when we examine concept learning. Let us consider the simple concept-learning task described above, in which the experimenter systematically rewards *red* as the correct concept, with form and size as irrelevant dimensions. From a position that assumes gradual increments in associative strength as a function of practice, correct solution of the problem can not occur until the response *red* has accrued a sizable amount of associative strength to the stimulus complexes. Contrary to this assumption, there is a great deal of evidence to suggest that a number of subjects will make *no* errors in such a task. They will respond correctly on the first trial and continue to respond correctly. If the first stimulus shown the subject is a large red square and his hypothesis is *red,* he will say the card is an instance of the concept and he will be told he is correct. Even if both irrelevant dimensions change on the next trial (i.e., he is shown a small red circle), there is great likelihood that he will again say the stimulus is an instance of the concept. Similarly, if the stimulus on the second trial is *green* rather than *red,* the subject is unlikely to call the stimulus an instance of the concept even if the values of the irrelevant dimensions remain the same as on the first trial.

Such data are reminiscent of the short-term memory data. Given a single meaningful stimulus, the hypothesis red, the subject can recall it with little memory loss over relatively long periods of time. A study reported by Haygood and Bourne (1965) is very interesting from this point of view. Their data suggest that in many concept-learning tasks, the major problem for the subjects appears to be related to problem solving or *thinking* rather than *learning* (as these terms were defined in Chapter 1).

Subjects were given concept problems involving four dimensions: color, size, form, and number (e.g., three large red triangles). Each dimension had three possible values (e.g., the forms on a stimulus card might be red, or green, or blue). The simplest problem employed by Haygood and Bourne involved conjunctive concepts. That is to say, a concept consisted of one value from each of two dimensions (e.g., red circle). The study was complex, involving a number of experimental conditions. For our present purposes, we shall consider the condition in which the experimenters described the four dimensions to the subjects, but did not indicate that the concept was a conjunction, and did not indicate which values of the four dimensions were relevant to solution.

Subjects were successively presented with five different concepts to solve. On the first concept, the subjects made an average of 3.6 errors prior to solution. By the fifth concept, average errors reduced to 2.0. The latter is very close to the theoretical minimum for a perfect problem solver with complete memory for all his prior choices. In this type of situation, the performance of the well-practiced subject who understands the structure of the problem (i.e., has discovered that all previous problems have been simple conjunctions) appears to be governed by the constraints imposed through lack of sufficient information.

An example of a strategy which could produce results such as those of Haygood and Bourne, cited above, is the wholist strategy described by Bruner, Goodnow, and Austin (1956). This strategy involves taking the first positive instance *in toto* as the initial hypothesis. As new positive instances are encountered, the subject modifies his hypothesis to include only these attributes which are common to both the new instances and his preceding hypothesis. This type of strategy reduces the subject's memory load tremendously. For example, since Haygood and Bourne employed four dimensions with three values on each dimension, 81 different combinations of stimulus values are possible. However, if the subject takes the first positive instance as his initial hypothesis, he reduces his memory load to four values, one for each of the dimensions. With subsequent positive instances, he can ignore some of these values, reducing his memory load even more.

If interference is increased, forgetting will, of course, occur. This is shown in studies that have increased the number of irrelevant dimensions in the concept task. Also, Erickson and Zajkowski (1967) increased interference by having subjects learn three concepts concurrently. Under these conditions, subjects showed strong signs of retesting hypotheses which they had previously found to be incorrect. In other words, memory was greatly disrupted by interference. On the other hand, when the subjects learned one concept at a time before going on to the next concept, this tendency toward disruption of memory was sharply reduced.

In summary, the concept-learning experiments appear to support our conclusions, based on the short-term memory studies, concerning the development of associative strength. In the absence of strong interference processes, association of a well-differentiated response (e.g., *"red* is the correct concept," or *"triangle* is the correct concept") occurs at very great strength on the first trial. From this point of view, it is not relevant that such an association may be "wrong" in terms of later information to be provided the subject.

As in short-term memory studies, we see that the presentation of subsequent material can strongly disrupt early associations. Similarly, when the subject is required to learn several concepts concurrently, we have a situation much like that of the verbal-learning studies. The mass of material to be acquired produces great interference and the subject behaves as though previously acquired associations had never been acquired.

All-or-None Hypothesis: Verbal Learning

In considering the laws determining formation of associations, it should be noted that some writers have proposed all-or-none hypotheses for associative development that are incompatible with the analysis outlined above. Such hypotheses have been proposed by Rock (1957) and Estes (1960) in the area of verbal learning, and by Restle (1962) and Bower and Trabasso (1964) in the area of concept learning.

Let us first consider the hypotheses as they relate to verbal learning. The all-or-none positions appear to stem from the observations that very few subsequent errors occur for any given pair, after the first time that pair has been responded to correctly. While these theories differ in some details, the following assumptions appear to be common to all of them: No associative strength develops between a stimulus and response during the trials in which the response is not correctly anticipated. Once the association has formed, it is at full strength as far as learning is concerned, though presumably additional trials may implement later memory for the association.

Such theories are inconsistent with the conclusion, reached earlier in this chapter, that associations reach a high level of strength upon the first presentation of a pair under instructions to learn. It is therefore important to examine the evidence in regard to the all-or-none positions.

Rock's (1957) all-or-none position started with the following assumption: If a subject is tested on a previously presented S-R pair and he can not remember the correct response even with unlimited time for recall, the subject has not learned anything about the relevant association. Therefore, if that particular S-R pair is now discarded from the paired-associates list and a new pair substituted for it, rate of learning should not be impaired. Rock tested this hypothesis using, as a control group, a condition in which pairs were retained in the list even if responded to erroneously. His results were consistent with the all-or-none hypothesis: Number of trials required to reach a criterion of perfect performance on all pairs was virtually identical for both the experimental and control groups. Thus he concluded that no learning occurred for an S-R pair prior to the first correct response on the pair. Similar results were obtained by Clark, Lansford, and Dallenbach (1960) in a replication of this design.

Rock's original report of his study indicates that the experimental and control groups were given somewhat different instructions. The experimental group appears to have been instructed to "learn" the items of each pair, while the control group was instructed to "associate" them. Reed and Riach (1960) tested the effect of this discrepancy in instructions in a 2 × 2 design, with half the experimental subjects and half the control subjects told to associate, while the other halves were instructed to learn. They found that, with instructions held constant, the control groups did significantly better than the experimental. On the other hand, the experimental group told to learn performed as well as the control group told to associate. They concluded that when instructions are held constant, trials on a pair prior to the first correct anticipation facilitate learning.

In addition, Underwood, Rehula, and Keppel (1962) have thrown considerable doubt on the extent to which Rock was able to control the difficulty of his lists when he substituted new pairs in place of those not correctly anticipated. Underwood *et al.* demonstrated that the original list learned by the control group was likely to be harder than the list finally learned by the experimental group. This is because the pairs missed and subsequently excluded from the list tended to be more difficult than the pairs correctly anticipated and retained in the list. Postman (1962a) found essentially the same results.

The problem of control over list difficulty was solved in an ingenious fashion by Martin (1965) in a study whose results were contrary to Rock's all-or-none position. Martin developed a technique whereby the identical final list was learned by both the experimental and the control group. The procedure was as follows. The initial list learned by the experimental and control groups involved nine pairs of words which were in common and three pairs (the most difficult in each list) which were different. In these three critical pairs, the same stimulus and response terms were used in the two lists, but they were *paired* differently. After two trials, the three critical pairs in the experimental list were changed so as to be identical with the corresponding three pair in the control list. Since these three were the most difficult pairs, almost no subjects in either group recalled the correct responses in the first two trials, despite being permitted unlimited time for response. The few subjects in either group who did respond correctly to any of the three critical pairs during the first two trials were dropped from the study. Martin found that the control group learned the critical three pairs significantly more quickly than the experimental group. Thus, contrary to the Rock's all-or-none position, something was learned about the correct associations during the first two trials despite the fact that no correct responses were made.

THE ESTES' LEARNING-TEST TEST STUDIES. Estes (1960) and Estes, Hopkins, and Crothers (1960) attacked the issue of all-or-none learning from a somewhat different methodological point of view. Consider the situation in which a subject is given a paired-associates learning trial followed by two successive test trials. From the all-or-none position, Estes reasoned that if the subject failed to respond correctly to a given stimulus on the first test trial, this indicated that no learning of the particular association had occurred. Therefore (if no learning trials intervened), there should be virtually no correct responses to the item on a second test trial that followed immediately after the first test. This prediction was borne out by the results reported by Estes and his colleagues. However, Underwood and Keppel (1962) and Wollen (1962) have pointed out that these results indicate little about an all-or-none associative theory. Even if associative strength had been developed on the learning trial, if learning (e.g., in our terms, resistance to interference) were not sufficient to produce a correct response by the first test trial, most theorists would not predict that the response would be correctly emitted on an immediately succeeding test with no additional learning trials intervening.

ANALYSIS OF PRECRITERION PERFORMANCE. A third type of test for the Rock hypothesis of all-or-none trial learning has been proposed by Bower (1962). He reasoned that, if a subject responds correctly on a given trial, this may indicate learning or a chance guess. On the other hand, if he is given unlimited time to respond but does not respond correctly, a one-trial position indicates that no learning has occurred up to this point. Thus, for items to which a subject responds incorrectly on trial N, the subject's condition is the same as on the trial 1. From this it follows that the average number of errors between any given trial and criterion—the items incorrect on trial N—should be equal to the average number of errors between any other trial (M) and criterion—the items incorrect on trial M. On the other hand, if learning occurred even during the sequence in which the subjects were responding incorrectly, the average number of errors, following an error on a given trial, should decrease as a function of succeeding trials. Bower reports that errors are constant over trials and he interprets these results as supporting a one trial position.

First, it should be pointed out that Bower's reasoning is not completely consistent. Assuming a perfect one-trial learner who makes no correct responses for a long sequence of trials, then makes only correct responses, the number of errors following any given incorrect trial must be less than on the previous incorrect trial. Then why does Bower obtain results indicating a constant number of errors across trials? Probably because he pools across items and subjects, assuming that all items are equal in difficulty and all subjects are equal in learning ability. On early trials, with almost no correct responses occurring as yet, all subjects are represented on most items. This will tend to reduce the average of subsequent trials before criterion, since the average includes fast learners who make few errors and easy items on which few errors occur. On the other hand, since Bower deals only with number of trials to criterion following erroneous responses on any given trial, the fast learners and easy items drop out by later trials. This keeps the average number of errors from dropping.

Suppes and Ginsberg (1963) and Saltz (1964) have pointed out that Vincentizing the precriterion trials provides a more defensible test of the all-or-none hypothesis. This procedure consists of dividing the total number of precriterion trials on each item into equal blocks of trials. Thus, if a subject requires 15 trials to reach criterion on a given item, these 15 trials can be divided into 3 blocks of 5 trials each. If the same subject requires 12 trials to reach criterion on a second item, the 12 precriterion trials can be divided into 3 blocks of 4 trials each. It then becomes possible to determine if number of correct responses increases across blocks of trials. Each subject and each item is represented at each successive block of trials, using this Vincentization technique. Both Suppes and Ginsberg (1963) and Saltz (1964) report a significant increase in percentage of correct responses as a function of precriterion trials. It should be emphasized that these results indicate an increase in frequency of correct response *for an individual item* prior to the onset of the criterion block of trials for that item. These results must be considered inconsistent with the all-or-none hypothesis.

CONCLUSIONS CONCERNING THE ROCK HYPOTHESIS. The evidence to date must be interpreted as indicating that learning beings prior to the trial in which the response occurs correctly for the first time. The Martin (1965) study, in addition, indicates that strong determiners of learning are involved in the first few presentations of verbal material, despite the absence of overt correct responses during this period. These data are consistent with the position that strong associations form on the first trial, but that the great degrees of interference, produced by the large numbers of items to be learned simultaneously, prevents correct performance.

All-or-None Hypotheses: Concept Learning

In concept learning, the all-or-none hypothesis is primarily concerned with the attainment of the correct solution to the concept problem. Much of the theoretical development on this topic is based on the pioneering work by Restle (1962). Restle described several strategies that a subject may employ in attempting to solve a concept problem. Basic to all of them is the assumption that the subject samples from a pool of hypotheses. If the subject calls a stimulus an instance of a concept and is told he is incorrect, he discards the hypothesis and selects another. The discarded hypothesis then returns to the pool and may be resampled at a later trial; in effect, the subject has no memory for his discarded hypotheses. Essentially the same position is taken by Bower and Trabasso (1964).

Note that a subject may be *correct* in identifying a stimulus as an instance of the concept, *and yet have the wrong hypothesis.* (E.g., he thinks the concept is red, so he chooses the red triangle as correct; actually, triangle is the concept, so his selection is correct for the wrong reason.) Restle and also Bower and Trabasso assume that no learning occurs on trials in which the subject responds correctly. Learning (i.e., change of hypotheses) occurs only after an incorrect response.

WHAT IS LEARNED?   While these writers state that learning does not occur until the subject samples the correct hypothesis, it is clear that by "learning" they are referring to correct solution of the concept problem, not to the formation of associations. Bower and Trabasso (1964) appear to argue that these two meanings of the term "learning" are the same; but from the position taken in the present book, this is not tenable. Consider, for example, a subject who is shown a large red circle and is told this is an instance of the concept. If the subject hypothesizes that *circle* is the concept and is next shown a small green circle, the well-practiced subject will usually respond to the new stimulus by calling it an instance of the concept. Clearly an association has been formed and there is little or no forgetting over the relatively short intervals involved. The association may not produce the correct response to the concept problem (i.e., the experimenter may have decided that *red* is the correct concept) . This is irrelevant to the present issue.

Obviously, then, the Restle model has, implicit within itself, the position taken in this book that associations form with great strength on the first presentation.

A second crucial issue now arises. When told that a large red circle is an instance of the concept, if the subject hypothesizes that *circle* is the concept, what happens to the other stimulus components? The Restle model implies that these acquire *no* associative strength. Actually, the subject may be capable of describing all the stimulus components (i.e., may be able to state that the stimulus was a large red circle) , even after the stimulus was removed. Whether he could do so or not would depend on the number of components. If the number were very great, he might not attend to all the components, or if he did attend, interference processes might produce forgetting.

SAMPLING WITH REPLACEMENT.   Thirdly, the Restle model implies complete obliteration of earlier associations upon presentation of subsequent trials. This implication arises from his assumption of "sampling with replacement." In brief, the assumption states a subject randomly selects a hypothesis from the pool of possible hypotheses. If his subsequent responses based on this hypothesis are correct, the subject will retain the hypothesis. If, on the other hand, these subsequent responses are incorrect, the subject discards the hypothesis and it is replaced in the pool of possible hypotheses from which it may be selected again on a later trial. Restle assumes that its probability of being resampled is unaffected by the fact that it was previously found to be incorrect.

The issue of complete obliteration is an interesting one and has stimulated a great deal of research. Before examining the data, it should be noted that the issue has been subject to some ambiguous interpretation. Some writers have interpreted the issue as asking whether any "learning" has occurred prior to the selection of the correct hypothesis. As we have seen, the problem here is the ambiguous meaning of the term "learning" in this context.

STUDIES OF SAMPLING WITH REPLACEMENT.   In general, the data suggest that while a great deal of forgetting occurs, under most conditions this forgetting is not complete. Levine (1962) and Holstein and Premack (1965) both presented subjects with a block of trials involving *random reinforcement* prior to systematically reinforcing a particular attribute. If complete obliteration had occurred for the memory of hypotheses tested during the block of random reinforcements, these randomly reinforced trials should not have affected the subsequent concept learning. Thus no difference in trials to solution should have been found between the control group and the group receiving the block of randomly reinforced trials. Contrary to this hypothesis based on the memory obliteration notion, both studies found that an initial block of randomly reinforced trials impeded solution of the concept problem.

Levine (1966) examined in detail the performance of subjects engaged in a concept-learning task. He found that if the subjects' first hypothesis proved to be incorrect, the subjects were significantly less likely to test this hypothesis on the following trial than would be expected if the subjects replaced the hypothesis in the pool and resampled randomly. Further, if the subjects' second hypothesis was also incorrect, their third hypothesis tended to be different from either of the first two hypotheses. Again this tendency was significantly different from the expectation based on the assumption that the subjects replaced their hypotheses in the pool and resampled randomly.

Further, Levine found that the more often his subjects were correct in responding to the stimuli, the more likely they were to select the only hypothesis consistent with all the previous information. In other words, subjects were able to make use of previous information from positive instances of the concept, even though their hypothesis may have been incorrect on these previous trials.

Levine concluded that subjects not only used the outcomes of their responses to reject incorrect hypotheses, but they rejected more incorrect hypotheses in trials in which they responded *correctly* than in trials in which they responded *incorrectly*. Similar findings are reported by Richter (1965). This is clearly contrary to the assumption made by Restle and by Bower and Trabasso that subjects learn only from their own errors. Such results show that subjects remember a fair amount from previous trials. Also, clearly, correct responses do more than increase the probability of a repetition of the response to the components of the stimuli.

Another approach to the question of whether prior hypotheses are obliterated is represented by the research of Trabasso and Bower (1966). In this study, the concept being reinforced was shifted after every second error by a subject. If the subject has forgotten all his previous hypotheses, these shifts should not disrupt the concept solution process. Trabasso and Bower found that such a shift resulted in slower concept attainment than found for control subjects. Thus memory for previous incorrect hypotheses is again indicated. This study is particularly worth examining in detail by persons interested in the phenomena under consideration, since Trabasso and Bower carefully discuss all the methodological pitfalls involved in shifting concepts (including methodological errors in their own previous studies).

The data from the concept solution problems are consistent with those of short-term memory. Subjects can remember an immediately preceding meaningful verbal response (e.g., hypothesis) extremely well. As new verbal responses occur, these produce interference which reduces memory for the early responses.

CLASSICAL CONDITIONING AND INSTRUMENTAL LEARNING

In the areas of human memory and concept learning, we have seen that there is a great deal of evidence to support the position that the initial attention to material produces extremely strong associations. Subsequent trials are necessary to decrease interference from competing material. In the present sections, we shall see a corresponding line of evidence in conditioning and in instrumental learning.

In Chapter 1 we saw that the processes related to interference are much more prevalent, in instrumental and classical conditioning, than is commonly admitted. These are extremely complex learning situations that involve a great many complications. They are not, as is sometimes assumed, relatively pure situations in which to measure the development of associative strength. In the present chapter, we shall see that when interference effects are reduced, instrumental learning and classical conditioning display extremely rapid development of associative strength. It will be seen that the data from instrumental and classical conditioning closely parallel those of human verbal memory and concept attainment, though the magnitude of the effect may not be as great. There is some indication that species of subject may be an important consideration. Human subjects, even in classical conditioning, appear to show the effect quite strongly; the effect may be somewhat weaker in the white rat.

Classical Conditioning

THE VOEKS STUDY. One of the few attempts to control interfering effects due to competing stimuli in *conditioning* is reported in a set of important papers by Voeks (1954, 1955). The study was designed to examine the course of eyelid conditioning under conditions in which internal and external stimulus conditions were kept as constant as possible during the presentation of the conditioned stimulus. Fluctuations in external stimuli were minimized by training subjects in a soundproof room. Internal stimuli associated with the conditioned-unconditioned stimulus sequence were isolated from the irrelevant intertrial stimuli by engaging the subjects in the following rigorous behavior routine. At a signal indicating the onset of a trial, a subject began a regime of rhythmical breathing until the experimenter said, "hold," at which point the subject inhaled deeply and held his breathe until the end of the trial. On being told to "hold," the subject depressed two telegraph keys, one with each hand. The springs in the keys are described as sufficiently strong to involve arm and shoulder muscles. Depression of the keys activated the conditioned stimulus (a buzzer) and in .45 seconds later the puff to the eye. Upon termination of the buzzer, the subject released the keys and resumed normal breathing. This regime, rehearsed before the onset of the actual conditioned trials, was designed to increase the similarity of on-trial stimuli and also served to discriminate them from between-trial stimuli.

Voeks reports that half of her subjects invariably made the conditioned response after once doing so. Most of the other subjects also had relatively flat learning curves with only one or two failures of response. Dividing the number of trials following the first occurrence of the conditioned response (but not including it) into quartiles, she found that only 21.8% of the subjects made more responses in the fourth quartile than in the first; while in 78.13% of the cases, the number of responses in the first quartile was equal to or greater than that of the fourth quartile.

Accepted at face value, this portion of Voeks' data suggests that conditioning occurs on one trial if competing stimuli can be eliminated. However, there is an aspect of the data which produces difficulties for this interpretation: Of the 16 subjects who jumped from 0 to 100% performance in one trial, approximately half required six trials before emitting the first conditioned response, and some required as many as 12 trials (see Voeks, 1954, Figure 3). If learning occurs in one trial, why not the first trial? There are several possible explanations for this reluctant type of behavior.

THE SPENCE EXPLANATION OF VOEKS' DATA. Spence (1956) has proposed an interesting modification of Hullian behavior theory in an attempt to explain the Voeks' data. Hull (1943) had assumed that learning increased gradually as a function of practice. Since the conditioned response usually does not occur on the first few trials of conditioning, Hull also assumed that a minimum, threshold value of learning must be reached before the correct response can be made. However, this left the problem that once the threshold amount of learning had been attained, the response would be suprathreshold on all subsequent trials; therefore, the response should occur with 100% probability on all these subsequent trials. Since most conditioning data at that time indicated gradual increases in probability of response, Hull made the further assumption that performance oscillates in a random fashion from trial to trial within restricted limits. Thus the response might be above threshold on one trial, but below threshold on the next. As learning grows in strength with practice, only extreme degrees of oscillation can drive performance below threshold. Eventually, learning becomes so great that performance remains suprathreshold no matter how much oscillation occurs.

For Hull, oscillation was an intraorganismic variable, unrelated to stimulus conditions. The modification proposed by Spence was that oscillation is a function of amount of stimulus variablility. Thus, when stimulus variability is present, as in most studies prior to Voeks, oscillation will occur and performance will improve gradually. In studies such as Voeks' which prevent stimulus variability, oscillation will not occur and performance will jump from 0% to 100% correct responses in one trial, once learning has reached suprathreshold levels of strength. This modification of Hull accounts for much of the data.

However, what are the consequences of this modification for Spence's general position? It appears to have serious implications for both his theoretical and methodological approaches to conditioning. As to *theory*, this position now implies that competing responses and their elimination are an important problem in conditioning, and that conditioning, as usually studied, is a process of differential development of a particular bond as opposed to irrelevant bonds. Thus, conditioning becomes quite similar to selective learning in the Spence system. This new interpretation of the conditioning situation has serious *methodological* significance. Conditioning no longer has the status of a "pure" learning situation in which the development of associative strength can be studied uncontaminated by the unlearning and spontaneous recovery of other connections. If all the other competing responses were eliminated, performance should jump to 100% in a single trial and no indication of the underlying associative strength could be obtained.

ORIENTING RESPONSE EXPLANATION FOR VOEK'S DATA.   Another possible explanation of the delayed onset of 100% learning in Voeks' study is based on the orienting response. This is based on the fact that Voeks presented the conditioned stimulus a number of times before the onset of the conditioning procedure. This was done in an attempt to detect subjects with strong alpha responses as well as to provide practice in the experimental regime of breathing and key pressing. It has already been indicated in this chapter that such adaptation to the conditioned stimulus may produce what the Russians have spoken of as extinction of the orienting response and may hinder subsequent conditioning.

THE KIMBLE "PSEUDOCONDITIONING" STUDIES.   Another related phenomenon, of great potential importance, has been reported by Kimble and his associates (Kimble, Mann, and Dufort, 1955; Kimble and Dufort, 1956; Dufort and Kimble, 1958). These results suggest that conditioning occurs in relatively few trials and that subsequent increases in performance are not due to increments in associative strength. The general type of phenomenon obtained in these studies is perhaps best illustrated by Experiment IV in Kimble, Mann, and Dufort (1955). An experimental group was first presented with 20 eyelid conditioning trials—conditioned stimulus being a dim light; unconditioned stimulus, a puff of air to the eye. On trials 21 to 40, the light was withheld and only the puff was presented. During trials 41 to 60, conditioning was reinstituted with light and puff again paired. Finally, 30 extinction trials were administered. Despite the fact that no conditioning could have occurred on trials 21–40 (since only the puff was presented), the percentage of correct responses was significantly greater than during trials 1–20 and was at least as great as that found in a control group which received continuous conditioning during all 60 trials. In addition, the experimental group made significantly more conditioned responses during extinction than the control group. It was possible, of course, that the improvement in performance by the experimental group following puff alone in trials 21–40 was a function of some type of reminiscence. To investigate this, a second control group received neither light nor puff during a time span equivalent to trials 21–40 in the other groups. Following this treatment, this control group performed significantly more poorly than either of the other two groups.

Kimble interprets these results as indicating that the associative phase in conditioning is completed rapidly and that additional conditioning trials serve merely to increase drive level. Within Kimble's framework, the data reported in Kimble and Dufort (1956) suggest that, though rapid, conditioning does not occur in one trial. Level of performance after the puff-alone trials proved to be a function of the number of trials that precede puff-alone. On the other hand, Kimble and Dufort employed a ten trial conditioned stimulus adaptation procedure to extinguish alpha responses prior to the onset of conditioning. Since this procedure may result in a gradual change in the stimulus properties of the conditioned stimulus over the early conditioning trials, it is difficult to evaluate this component of the data. It should also be noted that a series of puff-alone trials which *preceded* the first conditioning trials were found to depress conditioning in a manner similar to that found in other studies of adaption of the uncondition stimulus prior to conditioning (e.g., McDonald, 1946).

Final evaluation of the phenomenon reported by Kimble is in doubt since Goodrich, Ross, and Wagner (1957, 1959) did not succeed in replicating these results. The procedural variables which are responsible for the failure of Goodrich *et al.* to obtain the effect are at present unknown.

Instrumental Learning

COMPETITION AND ACQUISITION. Evidence in the area of instrumental learning places an even greater strain on some of our concepts of the process of learning and the nature of what is learned than the evidence from conditioning.

THE SALTZ, WHITMAN, PAUL STUDY. As might be expected, if classical conditioning fails to provide a learning situation completely free from competing systems, the problem is even more severe in instrumental learning. For example, Saltz, Whitman, and Paul (1963) have reasoned that a multitude of competing responses are present in the simple runway situation. The omnipresence of exploratory behavior is one indication of this. Another type of competition that is subject to greater possible manipulation is that based on the difference in behavior necessary in the alley as opposed to the goal box. In the alley, the animal runs. In the goal box, he stops running and eats. To the extent that the *S-R* systems in the alley overlap with the goal box systems, running in the alley should be impeded. While this problem has usually been ignored, serious difficulties would appear to arise in conceptualizations of runway behavior, if one did *not* assume that the animals differentiated runway from goal box. The last response made by the animal prior to reinforcement is stopping running. Consequently, cessation of running should increase in strength as a function of trials, according to the reinforcement theory. In place of the empirically obtained increments in speed as a function of trials, classical reinforcement theory appears to predict a consistent decrement in speed.

The study designed to test the differentiation proposition was extremely simple. White rats were run in a situation in which alley and goal box were the same color (both white or both black) or in which they were different colors (one white, the other black). The goal box was screened by a cloth which was the same color as the alley, so that any effects of the stimulus characteristics of the goal box were likely to be cognitive, as opposed to sensory. In this experiment, the results clearly demonstrated that system competition plays an important role even in runway behavior. Animals running in a white alley to a black goal box were superior in performance to animals running in a white alley to a white goal box. Similarly, animals running in a black alley to a white goal box were superior to those running in a black alley to a black goal box.

It is instructive to compare a competing systems approach to a more classically Hullian approach to the problem outlined above. Amsel (1958) has assumed that similarity between alley and goal box should *facilitate* performance. This assumption was based on the following reasoning. Food in the goal box produces conditioned anticipatory eating responses. These anticipatory responses are assumed to have motivational properties. If goal box and alley cues are similar, these motivational properties should generalize to the alley and the animals should show superior performance.

THE COOPER STUDY. The Saltz, Whitman, and Paul study certainly manipulated only a small portion of the cue population relevant to the differentiation of the competing systems. The greater the degree of such differentiation, the faster the system being acquired should be expected to extricate itself from the matrix of interfering systems. A provocative study by Cooper (1963) attempted to differentiate stimuli in three sensory modalities simultaneously. The response being trained was that of crossing a hurdle. Seven groups of animals learned to make this response to a stimulus consisting of a light, a buzzer, vibration of the apparatus, or some combination of these. The results are presented in Table 3–1. Performance is clearly related to stimulus complexity. It is also clear that when all three stimuli were presented simultaneously, asymptotic performance must have been reached in very few trials. The standard deviation data presented by Cooper are particularly interesting. Variability of performance drops sharply as a function of stimulus complexity. Cooper reports that the correlation between mean and standard deviation of latency is .92. Thus there is relatively little intrusion of interfering responses, such as stopping responses, when all three stimuli are presented simultaneously.

TABLE 3–1. The Effects of Stimulus Complexity on Performance: Means and Standard Deviations of Time Required for Response by Each Experimental Group over All Trials

Experimental Stimulus Conditions	Mean Time Required for Response	Standard Deviation
Vibration alone	43.25	19.67
Light alone	31.09	18.65
Buzzer alone	28.02	17.26
Buzzer + Vibration	15.77	12.95
Light + Vibration	12.72	12.14
Light + Buzzer	7.51	7.70
Light + Buzzer + Vibration	5.27	4.77

From Cooper, 1963. Reproduced with permission of the American Psychological Association.

Cooper points out that in his study it is possible that increased stimulus complexity may produce its effect by increasing drive level, and that further studies are required to distinguish complexity from drive. On the other hand, it is possible that similar mechanisms are involved in complexity and drive manipulation. Drive increase may act to narrow the range of effective stimulation (e.g., Easterbrook, 1959) .

OVERT COMPETING RESPONSES IN LEARNING. From the position taken by Saltz, Whitman, and Paul (1963) , it would follow that practice should increase the differentiation between alley and goal box. Such differentiation should lead to faster running in the alley, since it should reduce interference from the competing response appropriate to the goal box. Other sources of interference are also active and may, at times, produce overt responses that compete with running in the alley. Animals may stop running and groom themselves, or may initiate exploratory behavior such as smelling the corners of the alley, or may try to climb the walls. Cicala (1961) has shown that such overt competing responses tend to decline systematically in frequency as a function of number of reinforced trials. Clearly, if an animal stops to groom himself, it will take him longer to run the alley. Since running time is the typical measure of learning in such studies, the elimination of overt competing responses could sharply alter the shape of the learning curve.

THE PEREBOOM AND CRAWFORD STUDY.   Of the studies which attempted to eliminate the effects of *overt* competing responses, the most dramatic results are those reported by Pereboom and Crawford (1958). Pereboom and Crawford reasoned that running time, as usually measured, is based on two components. The first is related to the actual speed with which the animals move while running in the alley. The second is the amount of time the animals spent in the alley *not running*. If speed measures are based only on total time between opening of the start box door and the entering of the goal box, these two components are confounded. In their study, Pere-

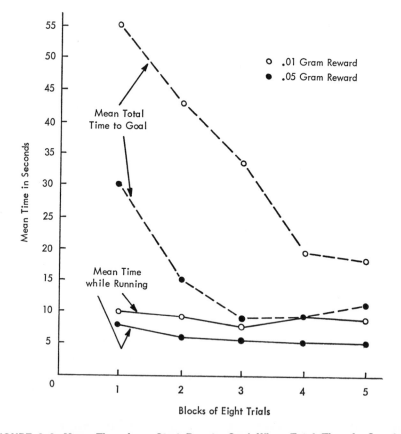

FIGURE 3–3. Mean Time from Start Box to Goal When Total Time Is Counted (including time involved in competing responses), and When Only Time in Motion Is Counted (excluding time involved in competing responses). Subjects received either .01 or .05 grams of food as a reward for running. (From Pereboom and Crawford, 1963. Reproduced with permission of the American Psychological Association.)

boom and Crawford measured these two components separately, obtaining both total time to traverse the alley and also time while actually running. In addition, the tendency toward competing responses was reduced by subjecting the animals to a pretraining regime which consisted of placing the animals in the middle of the alley and permitting them to explore freely. This type of preliminary free exploration is known to reduce the likelihood of competing exploratory tendencies during early learning trials.

Figure 3–3 summarizes the Pereboom and Crawford (1958) results.

Note the learning curves based on only the time involved in actual running. These curves represent learning under conditions of reduced competition. Observe that under these conditions, performance reached extremely high levels after the first trial. Further practice produced little additional improvement in performance. These data are, of course, a far cry from the typical runway learning data that show great changes in performance with practice. On the other hand, more typical learning curves were obtained when the learning scores did *not* exclude competing responses. This can be seen in the curves for *total* running time which are shown in Figure 3–3.

If one accepts the assumption that changes in running speed as a function of practice are an index of learning, the Pereboom and Crawford data suggest that, in the absence of competing responses, learning is near maximum after the first trial.

Studies related to Pereboom and Crawford. At least three other studies have examined learning under conditions involving elimination of overt competing responses. None has found results as dramatic as those of Pereboom and Crawford. For example, Marx and Brownstein (1963) and King (1967) used some version of the Pereboom and Crawford technique. In both these studies, actual time running was distinguished from time engaged in other activities. Marx and Brownstein found somewhat flatter curves for actual time running than for total time from start box to goal. However, the difference appears to have been small, with both types of scores reaching asymptote in very few trials. King (1967) found parallel curves for actual running time and for time scores that included overt competing responses. Cicala (1961) employed a somewhat different procedure for eliminating the effects of overt competition. This procedure, adapted from an earlier study by Cotton (1953), consisted of dropping from consideration any trial on which a competing response occurred. Learning curves based only on competition free trials appear to have reached asymptotic speeds in fewer trials than curves based on all trials. However, the competition free trials are far from flat.

In general, these results suggest that competing response tendencies are not restricted to overt competing responses. From this point of view it should be noted that, of the studies which controlled for overt competing responses, only Pereboom and Crawford permitted free exploration prior to learning. Possibly, elimination of overt competing responses is most effective if prior exploratory opportunities have led to extinction of a portion of the covert competing response tendency.

Competition and Motivation

In the previous sections of this chapter we have seen that one can focus on learning processes from two alternative points of view: Learning can be seen either as a process of developing associative strength or as a process involving reduction of competing response tendencies. These same points of view clash again in considering the effects of motivational variables on performance.

The associative approach can be characterized by Hull's (1943) theory. From this theory, correct responses (e.g., running directly from the start box to the goal) and incorrect responses (e.g., the competing behavior which interferes with such running) are both represented as habit tendencies in the alley. Drive multiplies all habit tendencies, whether these are correct or incorrect. In terms of the habit strength variable, probability of response is related to the absolute difference between the habit strength of the correct response (H_c) and the strength of the incorrect response (H_i). This is formalized as $H_c - H_i$. The effect of drive becomes $D\ (H_c - H_i)$. In other words, if no competing habits are operating (i.e., $H_i = 0$), changes in D will have a relatively great effect on performance. As H_i increases in value so as to approach H_c, the difference $H_c - H_i$ moves closer to zero, and changes in drive have a reduced effect on behavior, since $D \times 0 = 0$ no matter what the value of D. Similarly, if the associative values of the incorrect responses (H_i) are stronger than those for the correct responses (H_c), then increased drive will be *detrimental* to performance of the correct response, and again the facilitating effect of drive on performance will be obscured. This latter point is spelled out in great detail by Spence (1956). In short, from this point of view, drive should have its greater facilitating effect on the correct response when competing responses are eliminated.

On the other hand, an alternative position can be taken which states that drive acts primarily to reduce the effects of competition. For example, it might be assumed that increased drive level acts to increase the ability of rewarded S-R systems to resist interference. From the point of view of adaptation, this point of view states that a hungry animal is more likely to ignore stimuli that are irrelevant to food than is a sated animal.

First, it should be noted that both positions predict a decrease in the probability of competing responses as a function of increased drive level. Data reported by Cicala (1961) support this prediction.

THE COTTON STUDY.   Several studies have investigated the effects of motivational variables on runway performance under conditions in which overt competing responses were *eliminated*. For example, Cotton (1953) investigated the effects of hunger motivation on runway speed. Motivation was defined in terms of hours of food deprivation. Specifically, he was testing the Hullian (1943) formulation that drive multiplies existing habits and increases response strength. If competing response tendencies are multiplied, the resulting curve of performance as a function of drive level should be flatter than the curve obtained in the pure case of no competing responses.

Cotton itemized six types of competing responses that rats can make in learning to traverse a straight alley for food: (*a*) retracing, (*b*) facewashing, (*c*) touching the cover of the runway, (*d*) exploring the windows through which a photocell beam of light passed, (*e*) scratching self, and (*f*) biting self. If any of these responses occurred during a trial, this trial was excluded from the calculations of "competition-free" behavior.

In Cotton's study, each animal was first trained under several drive levels before measuring the effects of drive. Each animal was then tested under all the drive levels. The major effect of increased drive in this study was to reduce the occurrence of competing responses. When all trials were considered, including those in which competing responses occurred, Cotton's data showed a sizable relationship between hours of deprivation and running speed. However, when the trials involving competing responses are omitted from the data, the curve becomes much flatter.

THE KING STUDY.   King (1959, 1967) reports very similar data. His study differed from Cotton's in that each animal was trained and tested under only one drive level. Under these conditions, the functional relationship between speed and drive level, after elimination of time involved in making overt competing responses, was not quite as flat as that obtained by Cotton. On the other hand, contrary to the Hullian prediction, this curve was flatter than the curve obtained when trials involving competing responses were included in the data.

THE CICALA STUDY. Finally, a series of studies by Cicala (1961) employed both the Cotton procedure of testing each animal at each drive level and also the King procedure of testing a different group at each drive level. When each animal was tested at each drive level, the data were extremely similar to those of Cotton. Drive level affected performance only when overt competing responses trials were included in the data. When overt competing responses were eliminated, drive had little effect on runway speed. The Cicala study that involved a different group of animals at each drive level obtained essentially parallel curves when competing responses were included and when they were excluded from the data. Thus these data were not consistent with those reported by King. In no case, however, was the effect of drive greater when overt competing responses were eliminated.

STUDIES OF MAGNITUDE OF REINFORCEMENT. Studies by Pereboom and Crawford (1958) and by Marx and Brownstein (1963) on magnitude of reinforcement closely parallel those by Cotton (1953), and King (1959) and Cicala (1961) on drive level. Previous studies (e.g., Crespi, 1942) have demonstrated that time involved in running the alley decreases as magnitude of reward becomes greater. However, as previously noted, Pereboom and Crawford reasoned that such measures of running time include time involved in performing competing responses, such as exploration and grooming. When time involved in performing competing responses was eliminated, the Pereboom and Crawford data indicate that running speed *per se* is very little affected by magnitude of reward. As can be seen in Figure 3–3, most of the variance involved in performance for different magnitudes of reward is a function of the degree to which competing, nonrunning behavior interferes with running.

MARX AND BROWNSTEIN. A study by Marx and Brownstein (1963) largely supports the Pereboom and Crawford data in regard to the effect of magnitude of reinforcement. Marx and Brownstein utilized sucrose concentrations of 8%, 16%, 32%, and 64% as rewards for running down an alley. They employed two types of measures to control for competing responses. One measure was very similar to that of Pereboom and Crawford, consisting of total time in forward motion required to traverse the alley. The other measure was similar to Cotton's and involved calculating the data only for those trials in which the animals made no stopping responses. The results for these two types of control measures were equivalent. The only significant effect of reinforcement magnitude was attributable to somewhat slower performance by the animals trained under 8% sucrose concentration. The other groups were relatively unsystematic with regard to magnitude of reinforcement, the 16% concentration subjects often running faster than those with 64% sucrose concentration. Again it appears that the primary effect of reinforcement magnitude is to reduce the interference produced by competing systems. Unfortunately, however, Marx and Brownstein do not present the complete data for speed when competing responses are not eliminated from the performance measure.

CONCLUSIONS CONCERNING MOTIVATIONAL VARIABLES. It might be noted that manipulating magnitude of reward produces a set of circumstances very similar to those investigated by Saltz, Whitman, and Paul (1963), namely an increased differentiation between alley and goal-box cues. As magnitude of reward is increased, this *decreases the similarity between alley and goal box.* As one would expect from the Saltz, Whitman, and Paul study, such decreases in similarity result in faster running in the alley. This is not to suggest that magnitude of reinforcement has no motivational properties in addition to the differentiation function. The writer is simply pointing out the potential differentiation characteristics which are manipulated when amount of reinforcement is increased.

The data obtained by Cotton, King, and by Cicala relating drive to runway performance, and the data of Pereboom and Crawford, and of Marx and Brownstein relating magnitude of reinforcement to runway performance, suggest that it may be necessary to revise our conceptualizations concerning the influence of motivating variables. Instead of increasing the response strength of all ongoing behavior, these variables appear to increase the ability of dominant response systems to resist interference from competing systems. As will be shown in Chapter 12, similar effects are found in evaluating the effects of stress on behavior. Stress, however, can be shown to break down response systems, with the degree of breakdown being inversely related to the strength of the response system. Thus very strong systems show almost no deterioration with stress while very weak systems may be totally annihilated. It is possible that similar mechanisms operate in regard to motivational variables. The running response, being very strong, may be unaffected by increased motivation while weaker systems are made even weaker.

On the other hand, the mechanisms of stress and motivation may be quite dissimilar. As suggested above, motivational variables may act directly to increase the resistance to interference of a system in a manner more like that of increased practice. To date there is insufficient evidence to distinguish between these possibilities. This is particularly true since the studies of drive and magnitude of reward cited above can not be assumed to have eliminated all competing systems effects. Competing systems could obviously interfere with running behavior without producing a complete cessation of such running.

SELECTIVE LEARNING

In many ways, selective learning forms the prototype of the more complex learning and problem-solving behavior. Because of its complex nature, it has often been passed over in the search for basic laws. What are some of the complexities involved in selective learning?

1. Spence (1956) has pointed out that in selective learning, the correct response is usually low in the hierachy of reactions to the stimulus situation. Strong competing responses may impede the development of selective learning.

2. In selective learning, incorrect responses are often reinforced. This can be seen in a typical black-white discrimination problem. For example, black, as the correct stimulus, will be alternated randomly between right and left in the apparatus, to insure that the animal really learns to respond to the black rather than to a simple position cue. However, every time the black is on the right, and the animal responds correctly, the tendency to respond to the right is reinforced. The inadvertent strengthening of incorrect associations provides another source of competition.

3. The animal may not be aware of the appropriate stimulus dimension. He may not perform the appropriate orienting responses to the relevant stimuli until quite late in the experiment.

Yet all these complications are problems of degree, rather than problems of kind in comparing selective learning with classical and instrumental conditioning. This fact has been documented throughout the present chapter. In attempting to control these factors, one runs the danger of controlling out the critical variables that are of greatest interest. And, to the extent that these variables are thought to be eliminated when they are still operative, one runs the even greater danger of totally misinterpreting even the data from classical and instrumental conditioning. Indeed, as the writer has suggested, there is strong evidence to suggest that the latter has actually occurred.

All-or-None Learning in the Rat

Earlier in this chapter, we examined the all-or-none hypothesis in relation to human verbal learning and concept solution. In terms of the parallels we have seen between the verbal areas and instrumental learning, it is interesting to note that the all-or-none hypothesis is closely related to the noncontinuity theories which created considerable controversy in the area of animal discrimination learning during the 1930s.

THE LASHLEY-KRECHEVSKY POSITION.   Lashley (1929), on the basis of observations made during such discrimination learning, noted that the performance curves tended to remain at a chance level for a long period, then tended to raise rapidly. He suggested that no learning was occurring during the initial period of chance performance. This position was systematized in a more formal manner by Krechevsky (1932, 1938) who suggested that animals perform systematically to various cues in the environment and learn nothing about the appropriateness of a cue dimension until they begin to behave systematically toward it. He referred to these systematic behaviors as "hypotheses."

THE REVERSAL SHIFT TEST.   McCulloch and Pratt (1934) tested this position, developing the experimental design later used by Martin (1965) in testing the more recent all-or-none formulations of Rock (1957) and others. Animals were trained to discriminate two stimuli (i.e., heavy versus light). One of these stimuli was consistently reinforced, the other never reinforced. While the animals were still responding at a chance level, the reinforcement was switched so that response to the previously reinforced stimulus now resulted in failure of reinforcement, response to the previously nonreinforced stimulus now resulted in reinforcement. If the noncontinuity position was tenable, this reversal should have no effect on subsequent rate of learning. McCulloch and Pratt found that the experimental group, in which reversal of reinforcement occurred, learned significantly more slowly than the control group, in which reinforcement had been consistently associated with the same stimulus throughout the entire experiment. Spence (1945) obtained essentially the same results in a discrimination study in which black versus white were the relevant cues. In such studies it is clear that learning had started to develop early, during the period when the animals exhibited no sign of such learning. Thus, these animal data are quite consistent with the later work in the human learning realm.

ATTENTIONAL FACTORS AND ALL-OR-NONE LEARNING. It should be noted that the studies of both McCulloch and Pratt and of Spence employed discriminations in which the perceptual differences between the positive and negative stimuli were extremely salient. In the McCulloch and Pratt study, the rats pulled one of two trays into the cage to obtain food, the weight of the trays being the crucial cues. Spence's *discriminanda,* white versus black, are known to be readily distinguishable in the rat. This feature of the experiments was quite intentional, of course. As Spence (1940) clearly indicates, one could hardly expect discrimination learning to occur if the subjects were not attending to the relevant cues.

Krechevsky (1938) developed a discrimination task in which the relevant cues were placed in such a position that the rats did not, at first, orient themselves so as to perceive them. The initial phase of learning in this situation involved the development of the appropriate orienting responses to permit reception of the critical stimulus aspects. Under these circumstances, of course, a reversal in positive and negative stimuli, prior to the development of the appropriate orienting responses, had little effect on learning rate. Ehrenfreund (1948) demonstrated the same effect most clearly in a subsequent, well-controlled study.

These results, obvious though they are, point up an important factor. A great deal of learning, in some situations, had nothing directly to do with the association between the relevant stimulus and response. The subject must first learn to react to the appropriate aspects of the stimulus situation. In human learning, this type of variable is most often found in concept formation and problem solving and constitutes one of the major differences between these studies and the so-called "rote" learning studies. In rote learning, the discovery phase is minimized.

CONCLUSIONS

The present chapter has taken a very general look at the problems of competing systems as they appear in verbal learning, concept solution, classical conditioning, and instrumental conditioning. It has been shown that a distinction between associative strength and resistance to interference can reasonably be made in all three of these areas. With appropriate control for competing responses, associative strength can be shown to reach asymptotic strength in relatively few trials: The writer believes that it is probably not crucial whether the number of trials to asymptote is 1 trial or somewhat greater than 1. In fact, it will probably be impossible to control all other factors to the extent that an exact determination is empirically possible. In the end, the assumption that proves most convenient theoretically will no doubt prevail.

Evidence presented in this chapter strongly suggests that classical and instrumental conditioning do not have a unique position in learning research with respect to uncovering the exact functions of learning. Competition between systems appears to play as large a role in these experimental situations as in supposedly more complex learning. Where competition has been largely controlled in classical or instrumental conditioning, performance curves rise so sharply that the question of learning equations seems inappropriate. It is probably not too extreme to state that the classical concern with learning has really implied a concern with the factors involved in resistance to competition rather than with the growth of an associative factor.

It also seems likely that the primary effect on the cognitive elements of such noncognitive factors as drive and magnitude of reinforcement is to modify the relationships between competing systems.

The writer has, obviously, made the common assumption that the same basic laws are continuous through all forms of learning. This does not mean that the same gross empirical laws will always obtain. Kimble (1961, pp. 78–106) has, for example, compared the phenomena of classical conditioning and instrumental learning, showing that many of their laws are similar, but some are not. Similarly, the laws determining the development of associative strength may be the same for the rat in a discrimination apparatus and the college student at a memory drum. However, it is possible to instruct the human to attend to specific relevant cues and thus produce very rapid development of associations. The rat may require 40 trials in which no relevant associations develop because he has not isolated the relevant cues for attention (Krechevsky, 1938; Ehrenfreund, 1948).

With the tremendous increase in research in specialized areas such as verbal learning and instrumental learning, it is not surprising that psychologists have tended to restrict their interests to particular types of data collected under particular conditions and employing particular species of subjects. This is probably as unfortunate as it is inevitable. It has led to essentially the same sort of phenomena being conceptualized in completely incompatible ways in each restricted domain.

4 | Stimulus Differentiation

PRECIS

E. J. Gibson made a major contribution to learning theory when she proposed that stimulus differentiation, as well as the bond between the stimulus and a response, is a learned aspect of the *S-R* system. The present chapter evaluates this suggestion and compares it to the alternative position, taken by psychologists such as Neal Miller, Dollard, Goss, and others, that the phenomena of stimulus differentiation can be explained within the formulation which holds that learning consists of only a *single* variable, namely, the *association*. The data to date support Gibson's general multivariable position concerning the nature of learning; however, the specific mechanisms which she proposes require some modification. The function of stimulus differentiation appears to be that of preventing interference from competing systems.

DEMONSTRATION EXPERIMENT

The Problem

Below you will see 18 words, 9 of them real words in the language and the other 9 nonsense words. You will read each of the words once and go on to the next word. After you have read the entire list over once, you will be given a recognition test on these items. Remember, read each word to yourself once, then go on to the next word.

LAW	BUG	TEN	DIY	LER	GAC	JAB	PET	MUD
BEJ	TUZ	MOF	CUT	HAS	SIP	POB	FEH	HAX

Now cover the words above so that you can not see them, and let us find out how many you can recognize below. In the recognition test below you will find pairs of words that are identical except for one letter. One of the words in each pair will be a word that you saw above. Check the correct word in each pair.

BAG	LOW	JAB	MAF	DIY	TAZ	TEN	CUT	MAD
BUG	LAW	JOB	MOF	DUY	TUZ	TIN	COT	MUD
BEJ	POB	LIR	HAS	SAP	POT	FAH	HAX	GAC
BIJ	PEB	LER	HIS	SIP	PET	FEH	HOX	GIC

Explanation

Most people have much more difficulty recognizing unfamiliar stimuli, upon seeing them for a second time in a test like the one above, than recognizing familiar stimuli. The unfamiliar stimuli seem to be more easily confused with one another. Familiarity appears to increase the discriminability of stimuli.

THE CONCEPT OF STIMULUS DIFFERENTIATION

In Chapter 3, we analyzed the structure of a cognitive system into two components: (1) the associative component, and (2) the ability of the system as a whole to resist interference from other systems. In Chapters 4 to 6, we shall analyze this resistance to interference into its component elements. The first of these elements to be considered is the differentiation of the stimulus.

What Is Stimulus Differentiation?

The theoretical position formulated by E. J. Gibson (1940) is one of the important landmarks in the history of learning theory. This theory challenged the single variable, associative formulation concerning the nature of learning and initiated one of the most intensive controversies in the history of the field. The influence of this formulation has extended from studies of human learning to studies of animal learning, from motor learning to concept acquisition, and from studies of child development to studies of adult functioning.

THE GIBSON THEORY.   On the surface, Gibson's (1940) theory appeared to be simply an ingenious application of classical conditioning principles to the area of verbal learning. Her differentiation notion appeared to refer to differential reinforcement: reinforcement of the correct response and extinction of incorrect, competing responses. However, Gibson hypothesized that differentiation, once acquired, becomes a characteristic of the stimulus for the subject and will affect future learning involving this stimulus. Thus emphasis is no longer only on the bond *per se*, but includes the acquired characteristics of the stimulus.

In order to understand the mechanics of Gibson's theory, we must first define the concept of *stimulus generalization*. Stimulus generalization can be defined in the following manner. If two stimuli are similar, a response learned to one of these stimuli (Stimulus A) tends to be elicited, to some extent, by the other stimulus (Stimulus B). The greater the similarity between these stimuli the greater the tendency for the second stimulus to elicit the response learned to the first stimulus.

Gibson theorized that, *as a function of differential reinforcement, the generalization gradient of a stimulus becomes steeper.* This represents a decrease in the likelihood that a Stimulus B will elicit a *new* response learned to Stimulus A. Such a reduction in generalization facilitates new learning since it produces a decrease in interstimulus competition.

Let us consider an example of the way this mechanism might function. Assume that a subject learns two different tasks, one following the other, and both involving the same stimuli. In Task 1, assume that the subject learns a motor response (R_A) to a circle (S_A) and a second, different motor response (R_B) to a triangle (S_B). Since there is some similarity between the appearance of a circle and a triangle, the subject will have some tendency to emit R_A when he sees S_B, and R_B when he sees S_A. This state of affairs is illustrated in Figure 4–1. These incorrect response tendencies produced by stimulus generalization will impede learning. Note that, according to Gibson's theory, this training on Task 1 should reduce the generali-

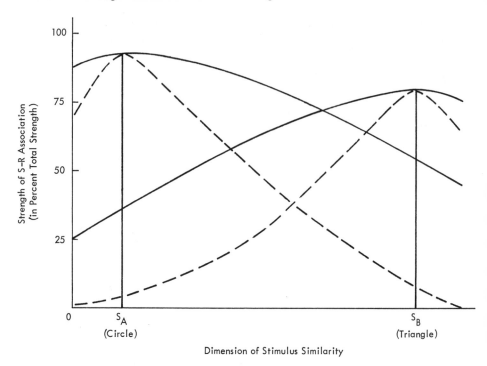

FIGURE 4–1. Hypothetical Illustration of Gibson's Model. The state of affairs at the beginning of Task 1 (when the subject first encounters the relevant stimuli) is illustrated by the solid lines. These lines represents the amount of generalized tendency to emit the response learned to Stimulus *A* (the circle) when shown Stimulus *B* (the triangle), and *vice versa*. The dashed lines represent the new generalization gradients found in Task 2. After Task 1 experience with the stimuli, the generalization gradients drop so that neither stimulus has much tendency to evoke a response which is being newly learned to the other stimulus.

zation between S_A and S_B. This means that if the same subject now learns a Task 2 in which *new responses* (e.g., verbal responses) are learned to S_A and S_B, Task 2 will involve *less stimulus generalization* between S_A and S_B than had existed in Task 1. Therefore there will be less interstimulus competition and (other factors remaining equal) *faster learning.*

Subsequent data caused Gibson to revise her theory somewhat. By 1956 (e.g., Gibson & Walk, 1956), differential reinforcement was no longer considered crucial to stimulus differentiation. For example, prolonged observation of a stimulus, even in the absence of reinforcement, was found to produce a differentiation effect.

GIBSON CONTRASTED WITH *S-R* THEORIES OF 1940. Today, whether one agrees with it or not, Gibson's theory appears relatively easy for most psychologists to understand. Surprisingly, this was not the case when the theory was first published. The early incomprehensibility of the theory appears to be largely attributable to the dominance of a very simple, single variable *S-R* theory. This theory was so strongly accepted that it was not even thought of as a theory; it was thought of as a metatheory, a necessary way of looking at nature *prior* to developing specific theories. This simple *S-R* theory took the position that facilitation of one task by another could only occur through the instrumentality of the *S-R* association. Let us consider a hypothetical example of transfer based on the associative mechanism. A rat in a T-maze learns that in the presence of the stimuli of a choice point (S_1), he will be reinforced with food if he turns right (R_1). In Task 2, the rat must learn to perform the sequence learned in Task 1 (i.e., turn right to S_1) and then turn left (R_2) at the next choice point (S_2) before he will be reinforced. Thus in Task 2 the complete sequence leading to food becomes:

$$S_1 - R_1 - S_2 - R_2.$$

Clearly an animal that has first learned Task 1 $(S_1 - R_1)$ will later be able to learn Task 2 more quickly than an animal that must learn the entire Task 2 sequence without already knowing Task 1. Facilitation of Task 2 occurs because the *association* between stimulus and response learned in Task 1 is relevant and appropriate to Task 2.

In a second type of associative transfer, a subject learns a response to a particular stimulus in Task 1. In Task 2, the same response is appropriate, and the stimulus is *similar* (but not identical) to the stimulus of Task 1. Due to stimulus generalization, there will be a tendency for the stimulus of Task 2 to elicit the response of Task 1. Again, the similarity of association between the two tasks is a crucial aspect of the transfer phenomenon.

Gibson's theory, on the other hand, posited a class of transfer phenomena in which between-task similarity of the *association* was not a necessary factor. To better understand this distinction, let us consider in some detail one of the first tests of Gibson's differentiation notion. This study, by Gagne and Baker (1950), manipulated stimulus differentiation in a two-stage design. During the first stage, subjects learned a different letter of the alphabet to each of four light patterns. In the second phase of the study, the subjects learned a motor response, pressing a different toggle switch, for each of these lights. The letters which served as responses in phase 1 were chosen to be as meaningless as possible in relation to the positions of the switches in the critical second phase motor task. Four groups of subjects differed in the number of light-letter presentations during phase 1. Subjects were presented with each light-letter pair either 0, 2, 4, or 8 times. The results indicated a systematic decrease in phase 2 errors as a function of amount of practice during phase 1. In other words, practice in learning a specific response to each of a set of stimuli facilitated the subsequent learning of new responses to these stimuli despite the fact that transfer could not be mediated by any similarity between the responses of the two phases.

To the single-variable associative psychologists of that time, the Gagne and Baker results could make sense only if it could be demonstrated that the letter which served as a response to a particular stimulus in phase 1 was, in some way, a prior associate of the motor act that served as the response to the same stimulus during phase 2. Since such associations could not be demonstrated in any unambiguous fashion, the results were considered somehow queer and difficult to understand.

CONTROLLING FOR "LEARNING-TO-LEARN" EFFECTS.   One obvious problem arising in a study such as that of Gagne and Baker is the influence of "learning to learn" or, in other words, those ill understood, general factors that often operate to facilitate performance simply as a consequence of prior experience on similar types of tasks. Most of the more recent studies of stimulus differentiation have controlled such factors and report results confirming those of Gagne and Baker. One example should suffice. G. N. Cantor (1955) taught preschool children the names "Jean" and "Peg" for the pictures of two female faces, during phase 1. A control group was given similar phase 1 training; but instead of the two "female" faces, the control group was presented with two male faces and learned to name one face "Jack" and the other face "Pete." Phase 2 was identical for both experimental and control groups. Here the children were shown two wooden cars, each having one of the female faces on its side. The subjects were instructed to roll a car down a track and were told that, if the car hit a button on the bottom of the track, a light would go on and this would result in a reward. Actually, the light was under the experimenter's control, and he turned it on (and administered the reward) on the basis of which of the cars the child chose to roll down the track. For each child, the experimenter arbitrarily designated one of the two cars as correct. In 30 trials, the mean number of correct responses was approximately 22.7 for the experimental group and 16.8 for the control. This difference was highly significant. Thus facilitation of performance in phase 2 was specifically attributable to experience with the relevant stimuli during phase 1 and not simply to general "learning to learn" during the initial phase.

Some of the other studies, using irrelevant stimuli during phase 1 for the control group, which have found a stimulus differentiation effect include Attneave (1957), J. H. Cantor (1955), Katz (1963), Kurtz (1955), and Martin (1965).

It will be noted that some of these studies involved relatively pure learning tasks. Subjects were explicitly instructed concerning which stimuli were to be associated with each response. Other studies (e.g., G. N. Cantor, 1955; Katz, 1963; Kurtz, 1955) potentially involved a sizable thinking component; these studies involved discovering the basis for reinforcement, sometimes in a concept-learning context. As shall be seen later, evidence suggests that stimulus differentiation facilitates both the learning and the thinking processes independently.

ENVIRONMENTAL ENRICHMENT AS A FACTOR IN THE DEVELOPMENT OF STIMULUS DIFFERENTIATION. Some of the most provocative evidence concerning stimulus differentiation comes from research on early experience in the rat. This research has broadened the scope of the differentiation phenomenon so as to relate it to the problems of cultural enrichment and cultural deprivation. In addition, it has provided evidence for the contention that reinforcement is not a necessary factor in the production of differentiation.

Gibson and Walk (1956) reported the first of the studies concerned with environmental enrichment. In this study, animals were raised from birth to approximately 90 days in one of two types of environment. The experimental groups were raised in cages surrounded by white cardboard walls several inches from the wire mesh of the cages on three sides. Four black metal forms (two triangles and two circles) were hung against the white cardboard. The placements of these forms on the walls were changed from time to time to assure a random relationship to food and water. No forms were hung on the white cardboard surrounding the cages of the control animals.

When the animals were approximately 90 days old, they were trained to discriminate between a circle and triangle identical to those hung on the walls surrounding the experimental group, with food as the reinforcement. For half the animals the circle was positive and the triangle negative; for the other half, this was reversed. The results showed a clear-cut and dramatic superiority in discrimination learning for the animals with the "enriched" early experience. In this study, stimulus differentiation apparently occurred despite the lack of differential reinforcement to the two types of stimuli during the early development of the animals.

The effect of early experience does not appear to be restricted to stimuli identical to those involved in the early experience. In a study similar to the one cited above, Gibson, Walk, Pick, and Tighe (1958) raised animals with equilateral triangles or circles hung on the wall and tested subsequent discrimination learning with either stimuli identical to those on which they were raised or with similar but not identical stimuli: ellipse versus isosceles triangle. There was no significant difference between these groups, though both were superior to a group which was raised without forms hung around the cage.

Apparently, this facilitation of subsequent discrimination learning is not mediated by the animals relating the forms to one another during the early experience. In a third study, Walk, Gibson, Pick, and Tighe (1958) raised their experimental subjects with only a single metal pattern on the wall. In subsequent discrimination learning between a triangle and circle, the pattern which had been hung on the wall during infancy was the positive stimulus for one group and the negative stimulus for another. Both experimental conditions learned the discrimination more rapidly than the "deprived" control group—with the group having the initial stimulus negative during discrimination learning performing better than the group which had had it positive.

Interestingly, the use of patterns *painted* on the walls surrounding the cages did not facilitate later discrimination learning (Walk, Gibson, Pick, and Tighe, 1959). Only when the stimuli were pieces of metal hung from the wall did the effect occur.

Meier and McGee (1959) report a set of related phenomena. In this study, animals were raised from birth in one of the three different environments. A motor visual group was raised with various geometric objects, some placed inside the living area and some separated from the living area by glass walls. These objects, all three-dimensional, included square blocks, rectangular blocks, crosses, circles, and half circles. A visual group had the same objects present, but all were separated from the animals by a glass wall. Finally, a minimum exposure group had none of these objects. Between 155–162 days of age, the animals were trained to discriminate a three-dimensional cross versus a three-dimensional triangle. The performance of the motor-visual group was superior to that of the visual group, which in turn was superior to that of the minimal stimulation group.

Kimble (1961, pp. 222–23), in referring to these studies (and particularly that of Gibson and Walk, 1956), states:

"From the S-R point of view the problem posed by these results is that it is difficult to see how overt, molar responses, even if they were conditioned to the stimulus, could be of much help in mastering the discrimination problem. Such responses transferred to the learning situation would be of no particular use, because the stimuli were shifted from side to side. Moreover, for half the animals, the circle was positive; and for the other half, the triangle was positive. Thus, to maintain the S-R position, it is necessary to say that some subtler form of behavior such as, perhaps, Wyckoff's (1952) observing responses were strengthened during the first part of the experiment; thus the experimental animals would be better prepared to "pay attention" to the relevant cues than the animals in the control group. Another S-R explanation might hold that perceptions have response properties and, like other responses, can be modified by learning."

Alternatives to Gibson's Theory

THE MILLER-DOLLARD-GOSS ACQUIRED-COMPOUND THEORY. The position taken by Miller and Dollard (1941), and elaborated by Goss (1955), attempts to restate the stimulus differentiation problem in a form more compatible with the position that only *associations* are learned—i.e., a single element S-R theory.

This position attempts to account for the predifferentiation data by positing a new, compound stimulus which consists of several S-R units which have been linked together. If successful, this type of theory would make it unnecessary to assume any learning factors except for the S-R bond, and would preserve the single element position.

Stated simply, the Miller-Dollard-Goss position holds that an organism experiences some sensory feedback (symbolized as s_1) from any response (R_1) that he makes. If this response is learned to an external stimulus (S_A), then this external stimulus plus the feedback stimulus form a new compound stimulus mediated by the response:

$$S_A - R_1 \cdot s_1$$

Applied to the Gagne and Baker study, for example, the acquired-compound stimulus would be formed in the following way. A stimulus (light pattern S_A) becomes associated to a verbal response (alphabet letter R_1), and this response produces a sensory feedback (s_1). When the subject, in phase 2 of the experiment, learns to press a toggle switch to the light, he will of course cease omitting R_1 overtly. However, the response will still occur covertly (r_1) and will still elicit the sensory feedback. Thus the new compound stimulus can be symbolized as $S_A - r_1 \cdot s_1$.

Let us now consider how these notions are used to predict facilitation in subsequent learning. Assume that the subject must first learn a letter (R_1) to one stimulus, and a second letter (R_2) to a second stimulus (S_B). The following illustrates the theoretical state of affairs for these two systems when the subject must now use S_A and S_B as stimuli for two different toggle switch responses (R_{T1} and R_{T2}).

$$S_A - r_1 \cdot s_1 - R_{T1}$$
$$S_B - r_2 \cdot s_2 - R_{T2}$$

(Let us call the new compound stimuli $S_A \cdot s_1$ and $S_B \cdot s_2$).

The crucial assumption of the theory states that: If the similarity between s_1 and s_2 is *less* than the similarity between S_A and S_B, then the similarity between the new compound stimuli, $S_A \cdot s_1$ and $S_B \cdot s_2$, will be less than the similarity between the external stimuli S_A and S_B *per se*. Therefore there will be less stimulus generalization between the compound stimuli than between the external stimuli, and the learning of new responses to these compounds should be easier than if the acquired compounds had not been learned.

A second aspect of this theory has provided the principal basis for testing it against Gibson's theory. Goss (1955) points out that the similarity between s_1 and s_2 may be *greater* than that between S_A and S_B. In this case, the new stimulus compounds resulting from learning will be more similar to one another than were the external stimuli, S_A and S_B. Goss refers to this second case as *acquired equivalence* of cues, and the effect of such acquired equivalence will be to *increase* generalization between the two stimulus complexes. Attaching new responses to the stimulus compounds should, because of the increased generalization, be more difficult than attaching them to the original S_A and S_B stimuli. (A similar position is outlined by Mandler, 1954.) Gibson's theory provides no basis for predifferentiation to produce decrements in later learning, as long as the responses of the original task do not compete with the responses of the later task.

ATTENTION TO CUES. A second alternative to Gibson's differentiation theory has been called *attention to cues* by such writers as Arnoult (1957). This position has several versions. Perhaps the most sophisticated form of the theory was advanced by Lawrence (1949) who states that there is a hierarchy of stimulus dimensions to which the subject will attend in any situation. With differential reinforcement, the priority of the dimensions will change so that initially disregarded stimulus dimensions may become salient while initially salient dimensions may become disregarded. Wyckoff (1952) states a very similar position. Hake and Eriksen (1955) state that subjects learn to attend to those aspects of the relevant stimuli that are critical to distinguishing them from one another. While these positions appear to be very similar, we shall see that they produce somewhat different predictions in specific studies.

Unlike the Miller-Dollard-Goss position, the attention-to-cues formulation was not, apparently, developed in an attempt to defend the single variable approach to learning. Its relevance to the single variable *S-R* approach hinges on the issue of whether or not attention can be considered a response comparable to leg flexion, salivation, and verbalization. Psychologists in the area of perception hold quite diverse points of view on this issue, and the arguments are beyond the scope of interest of the present book.

RESISTANCE TO INTERFERENCE FROM OTHER STIMULI. The pages following will review the literature to date on the relative merits of the various theoretical positions. By way of preview, it will be noted at this point that the general position taken by Gibson tends to be supported: The single variable *S-R* approach appears to be inadequate to handle the data, and a second variable is required. However, the specifics of Gibson's differentiation mechanism require some modification. In a sense, the data suggest a mechanism that is the inverse of the one proposed by Gibson. In effect, Gibson posited that prior experience reduces the tendency of the experienced stimulus to interfere with *other* stimuli. (This can be thought of as "the altruistic stimulus" position.) For example, if a rat is trained to approach a circle but not a triangle, Gibson's position states that prior experience with the circle *decreases the tendency to approach the triangle*. This would, of course, facilitate discrimination learning. The inverse position states that prior experience with a stimulus *permits that stimulus to resist interference from other stimuli* (i.e., produces stimulus isolation). The specifics of this position will be detailed toward the end of the present chapter, after we have examined the relevant empirical data.

EMPIRICAL EVALUATION OF THE THEORIES

Acquired-Compound Stimuli

Evidence concerning the acquired-compound stimulus theory of Miller and Dollard (1941) and Goss (1955) has, to a great extent, been concerned with the issue of acquired equivalence. This is largely due to the fact that the prediction of acquired equivalence represents a crucial test between the position of Miller-Dollard-Goss as opposed to that of Gibson. From the Miller-Dollard-Goss position, two stimuli becomes less differentiated and more similar if the external stimuli are relatively different from one another, while the responses trained to them have internal (within the subject) stimulus consequences which are relatively similar to one another. From Gibson's position, on the other hand, there is no basis for predicting stimulus equivalence; the type of training just described should produce differentiation training between the two stimuli. Consequently, evidence for an acquired equivalence effect would suggest that the class of phenomena, described in this chapter, might be more adequately explained by a single factor S-R model than by postulating a second factor of stimulus differentiation.

Strong versus weak versions of acquired equivalence. In examining the data, it is crucial to distinguish between a "strong" and a "weak" form of acquired equivalence. As proposed by Goss, the theory predicts that learning new responses to the external stimuli should be more difficult for subjects who had acquired equivalence to these external stimuli than for subjects who had never before seen the stimuli. This is the strong version of theory, and this is the version which must be satisfied if the theory is to support a single factor S-R position.

A weak equivalence effect is one in which only *relative* decrements occur due to response similarity. For example, from the acquired-compound stimulus position, we would expect poorer phase 2 learning as a function of increased similarity between responses in phase 1. However, such results will be considered a weak equivalence effect unless accompanied by an *absolute decrement* in phase 2: The pretrained subjects must perform more poorly during phase 2 than subjects with no pretraining on the relevant external stimuli.

Studies involving a common response to discriminable stimuli. The most frequently used design to test acquired equivalence has involved the very reasonable assumption that a response (and its stimulus consequence) is likely to be more similar to itself than any two different external stimuli are similar to each other. Thus Robinson (1955), for example, used a phase 1 condition in which five different fingerprints were associated with a common response, "cops"; and another five were associated with a second common response, "robbers." The assignment of stimuli to each response was arbitrary. A second group learned a distinctive, different name to each of the ten stimuli. In the former group, by definition, the five stimuli associated with a common response should become more equivalent than the same five stimuli in the latter group, where each stimulus is associated with a different response. The number of trials during phase 1 was kept roughly the same for the two groups. The phase 2 test involved testing for discrimination of the fingerprints. A stimulus from phase 1 was presented as a standard followed by ten other stimuli, five of which were identical to the standard. Subjects were to respond "same" or "different." No evidence for acquired equivalence was obtained in this study. The two groups described above did equally well on the phase 2 test; and both performed significantly better than a control group with no phase 1 training.

De Rivera (1959) obtained results which tended to indicate a weak equivalence effect. De Rivera reasoned that in Robinson's study, subjects who associated one response to half the stimuli and a second response to the other half might operate on one of two bases. They might seek a single characteristic for all the stimuli attached to a single response (converting the problem into one of concept attainment). Or, they could search for a unique characteristic for each separate stimulus and attach the response to this. If the subjects employed the concept attainment strategy, they would, in effect, be disregarding distinguishing characteristics of the several stimuli being attached to a given response. To test this, De Rivera utilized ten fingerprints similar to those used by Robinson. In phase 1, one group learned a *different* verbal response to each stimulus. Two groups learned one response to half the stimuli, a second response to the other half. One of these groups was told that the stimuli attached to a given response had *no* characteristics in common, and that learning would be fastest by choosing some aspect of each stimulus and attaching the response to it. Thus subjects were encouraged to develop their own distinctive responses to each stimulus. The other group was given concept attainment instructions: These subjects were told to find a *common characteristic* for all the stimuli attached to the same response. This group was the true equivalence condition. All groups were given eight trials of phase 1 training. Phase 2 consisted of learning a new set of ten responses (numbers from 1 to 10) to the stimuli.

Results indicated that *all three types of pretraining on the relevant stimuli produced significant facilitation of phase 2 learning* as compared to a control condition. Thus the evidence was contrary to a strong equivalence position. The strong equivalence position required that the control group learn faster than the equivalence group during phase 2.

There was some evidence for a weak equivalence effect. This is indicated by the fact that phase 2 performance was somewhat poorer for the group with concept instructions in phase 1 than for the group which in phase 1 learned a different response to each stimulus. This difference was of borderline significance (about .04 level of confidence if a single-tailed test is used) .

Hake and Eriksen (1955) used a design which is very similar to Robinson's. Stimuli were 16 patterns of lights. Subjects learned either 2, 4, or 8 different verbal responses to these stimuli in phase 1 (i.e., one response common to 8, 4, or 2 different stimuli) . Each S-R pair was presented ten times in a randomly alternating order. In phase 2, subjects learned new verbal responses to these stimuli. As in Robinson's study, no acquired equivalence effect was observed. Subjects who associated a common response to many stimuli in phase 1 learned phase 2 as rapidly as subjects who learned different responses to these stimuli.

Finally, in this set of studies which manipulated number of stimuli associated to a single response, we have an experiment by Katz (1963) . This study is particularly important since it has been interpreted as supporting the Miller-Dollard-Goss equivalence theory. As we shall see, however, this interpretation is tenuous due to an inappropriate control condition.

The stimuli used by Katz were four relatively meaningless abstract shapes. The subjects were children in the first, second, and fourth grades in elementary school. During phase 1, a distinctive-label group learned a different verbal response (viz., a nonsense syllable) , to each stimulus. A common-label group learned one verbal response to two of the stimuli and a different verbal response to the other two stimuli. The control group saw the four stimuli, during phase 1, for as many trials as the other two groups, but, instead of learning labels to the stimuli, were instructed to count them. Two criterion tasks were administered successively as phase 2. In the first, a test of perceptual discrimination, the stimuli were presented in pairs (2 seconds per pair) and subjects were instructed to respond "same" if they thought the stimuli in the pair were identical, "different" if they thought the stimuli in a pair were not identical. In the second criterion task, subjects were presented three of the four stimuli in a discrimination learning task. In the perceptual discrimination task, all groups were equally accurate when the two stimuli in a pair were identical. However, for the stimuli which had been associated with the same response in the common-label group, the common-label group had a relatively strong tendency to erroneously state they were the same stimulus; the distinctive-label group performed best on this task; and the control group was intermediate in success. Similar results were obtained in the discrimination learning task. Here the correct stimulus and one of the two irrelevant stimuli had both been associated with the same response, in phase 1, by the common-label group. The common-label group learned most slowly, the distinctive-label group most rapidly, and the control group was again intermediate.

While the results are clearly consistent with the weak equivalence position, the control group is inappropriate for testing the strong form of the theory since the control subjects received training on the relevant stimuli during phase 1. Several studies, to be discussed in a later section of this chapter, demonstrate that instruction to merely look at the stimuli will facilitate subsequent phase 2 performance. (This is, of course, consistent with Gibson's animal studies of enriched environment, described previously.) Thus, it is impossible in this study to determine if the poorer performance by the common-label group represents an absolute negative transfer (i.e., a strong equivalence effect), as required by the acquired-compound stimulus position, or if transfer by this group is actually positive but less sizable than in the other groups (i.e., a weak equivalence effect).

MANIPULATION OF RESPONSE SIMILARITY. Gerjuoy (1953) reports a study in which a *different* response was associated to each stimulus in phase 1. For one group, these different responses were similar to one another. In a second group the responses were not similar. No difference in phase 2 learning was found for these groups. Thus this study provides no indication of either a strong or a weak equivalence effect.

TEST OF THE SIMILARITY-AVERAGING ASSUMPTION. The Miller-Dollard-Goss theory makes the assumption that the distinctiveness of a compound stimulus is determined by the *average* of the distinctiveness of the components of the compound. This averaging assumption is, of course, the basis of the strong equivalence prediction. Data by Saltz (1963) suggest that this basic assumption is incorrect. In this study compound stimuli were words plus colors. Evidence from control groups that learned the responses to either the words or the colors alone indicated that the color stimuli were less discriminable than the words. The compound word-color stimuli produced better learning than either words or colors alone. With this type of material, at least, cue compounding produced a total increase in stimulus differentiation, rather than an averaging effect between the discriminability of the two components of the compound. Recent papers by Saltz and Wickey (1967) and Saltz and Ager (1968) indicate that increased differentiation due to compounding is the most likely explanation for these data. It should be noted that an animal study by Cooper (1963) produced similar data.

In short, the studies summarized above show no evidence for a strong equivalence effect. Consequently, they must be interpreted as inconsistent with the Miller-Dollard-Goss theory of acquired compound stimuli as the basis for the stimulus differentiation phenomena.

PRETRAINING ON A SINGLE STIMULUS. A study by Attneave (1957) also provides problems for the Miller-Dollard-Goss theory. Attneave trained subjects to reproduce *a single pattern in phase 1.* Phase 2 consisted of learning a different verbal response to each of *ten variations on the original pattern.* Phase 2 performances proved to be significantly superior for this group as compared to a control group that practiced reproducing an irrelevant pattern in phase 1. For the Miller-Dollard-Goss theory, facilitation of phase 2 learning should occur only if distinctive responses had been learned to the phase 2 stimuli during phase 1. None of these phase 2 stimuli were present in phase 1. In fact, the Miller-Dollard-Goss position would appear to interpret this study as one of acquired equivalence. Since the phase 2 stimuli resembled the single stimulus of phase 1, the learned response to the phase 1 stimulus should have generalized to the stimuli of phase 2. Thus all the phase 2 stimuli should be compounded with the same generalized response, and this should have increased the similarity between these stimuli, producing a phase 2 decrement in performance.

EVIDENCE FOR WEAK EQUIVALENCE. Let us now turn to evidence in regard to the weak equivalence effect. Evidence for the weak effect would indicate that some compounds are more facilitating than others, but would not provide support for the total Miller-Dollard-Goss theory. In general, there is a fair amount of data for a weak equivalence effect under at least restricted experimental conditions. De Rivera (1959), cited above, found evidence for a weak equivalence when subjects learned a common response to sets of five stimuli in phase 1; however, the weak effect occurred only when subjects were told that each set of five stimuli had a common feature. Without such special instructions, a common response to sets of five stimuli in phase 1 facilitated phase 2 as much as learning a different response to each stimulus in phase 1. De Rivera interprets these equivalence results as being due to attentional factors rather than to a compounding of external stimuli and response-produced stimuli. The Katz (1963) study, also previously cited, provides further support for a weak effect.

Ellis, Bessemer, Devine, and Trafton (1962) also find evidence for a weak effect. In this study, subjects could not see the stimuli and were forced to use tactile cues. One group learned a different response to each of eight stimuli, but these responses were relevant to the tactile cues. A second group learned the response "wide" to the four wide stimuli, "narrow" to the four narrow stimuli. The phase 2 task involved recognition of the 8 phase 1 stimuli from among 16 stimuli. The group which learned a different response to each stimulus performed significantly better on phase 2 recognition than the group with only one response for each subset of four stimuli. These writers did not include a control group without phase 1 training on the stimuli. Consequently the data are not relevant to the strong equivalence issue.

Newman and Saltz (1960) found that increased similarity of acquired stimuli produced relative decrements in verbal paired associates learning. However, appropriate controls for determining absolute decrements were absent.

Several studies report no evidence of either a strong or a weak equivalence effect. These include Gerjuoy (1953), Robinson (1955), and Hake and Eriksen (1955), cited above. Thus even the weak effect is not always obtained.

CONCLUSIONS CONCERNING THE MILLER-DOLLARD-GOSS THEORY. In summary, there is no clear-cut evidence for an absolute loss in differentiation between stimuli as a function of similarity between the responses learned to those stimuli in a phase 1. Thus these data do not support the acquired stimulus theory of Miller, Dollard, and

Goss. In those studies in which a group that had no phase 1 training on the stimuli is included as a control in phase 2, the presumed stimulus equivalence group is uniformly superior to this control group in phase 2. This finding supports Gibson's position that experience with stimuli produces differentiation.

Attention to Cues

The evidence suggests that some version of an attention-to-cues theory is necessary to account for certain aspects of the differentiation phenomenon. To date, however, most of the conceptualizations concerning attention to cues have lacked sufficient detail to be useful. One of the problems with attention-to-cues theories is that they have often been dealt with as though they were empirical facts rather than theories. One cannot simply stop after saying that phase 1 affords the opportunity to examine the stimuli. Under what conditions will the attention take place? Is there a unitary attention factor, or are there several such factors? What is the consequence of such attention? All these, and other problems, must be handled in some types of formulation. The problem is dramatically evident in comparing the study by Hake and Eriksen (1955) with that of De Rivera (1959). Both interpret their data as supporting an attention-to-cues position, yet their theoretical analyses come close to being inconsistent with one another.

Hake and Eriksen (1955), in a study described earlier in this chapter, found no difference in phase 2 performance between subjects who learned a common response to sets of stimuli in phase 1 and subjects who learned a different response to each of these stimuli in phase 1. Phase 2 involved learning a new response to each of the phase 1 stimuli. Thus the results provided negative evidence in regard to the acquired stimulus equivalence theory of Miller-Dollard-Goss; the writers interpreted their data as suggesting that phase 1 merely provided subjects with an opportunity to attend to cues and to discover the differences between the stimuli.

However, what interpretation could have been given the data had the results been different, and the common-response subjects of phase 1 had performed more poorly on phase 2 than the subjects who had learned a different response to each of the stimuli during phase 1? Unfortunately, the results could again have been interpreted as supporting the attention-to-cues position. This is seen in the De Rivera (1959) study. De Rivera conducted a study, similar to that of

Hake and Eriksen, and he found a small tendency for one of his common-response conditions to perform more poorly on phase 2 than the condition that, during phase 1, learned a different response to each stimulus. De Rivera interpreted these results as follows: The subjects in the common-response condition attempted to discover the common aspects of the stimuli which were associated to a single response; thus the subjects restricted their attention, during phase 1, and ignored cues which could be relevant to phase 2 performance.

Lack of an equivalence effect in Hake and Eriksen (1955) and the presence of an equivalence effect in De Rivera (1959) have both been offered as evidence for an attention-to-cues position. It appears that the attention-to-cues position, when left at the intuitive level, is too imprecise and permits ambiguity of predictions.

LAWRENCE'S THEORY OF ACQUIRED DISTINCTIVENESS.   The theory advanced by Lawrence (1949, 1950) is a more precisely stated formulation of an attention-to-cues position. Lawrence was concerned with the hierarchy of cues to which an organism will attend. He hypothesized that the reinforcement of cues raises the stimulus dimension of these cues in the organism's hierarchy of dimensions attended to. If one dimension rises in the hierarchy, it is assumed that this is at the expense of other dimensions. For example, if the organism initially attended to color cues but now form cues were relevant for reinforcement, the organism would learn to attend to form and would tend to ignore color.

Lawrence tested his theory using white rats as subjects. The initial, critical experimental problem encountered by Lawrence was that of developing a task in which stimulus transfer could occur, between phase 1 and phase 2, without the benefit of mediation by instrumental responses. This problem was solved in an ingenious manner. Phase 1 consisted of a simultaneous discrimination task, while phase 2 consisted of a successive discrimination task. Simultaneous discrimination refers to a situation in which the two cues to be discriminated are presented simultaneously, and the organism must choose between them. For example, assume that black-white is the relevant discrimination; in simultaneous discrimination, one alley in a T-maze is painted white, the other alley is black, and the animal must decide which of these two alleys to enter. When he enters one of these alleys (e.g., black), he is rewarded; when he enters the other alley (e.g., white), he is not rewarded. Black will typically be on the right side of the maze half the time and on the left side half the time, so the animal does not specifically learn to run right or to run left but learns to approach the black and avoid the white.

In successive discrimination, on the other hand, only one of the relevant cues is presented on any given trial and the animal learns to make some specific response to each cue. For example, the maze might be all black on one trial, all white on the next. In the presence of the black, the animal might be rewarded if he ran to the alley on the right but not if he ran to the alley on the left; conversely, in the presence of the white, he might be rewarded if he ran to the left but not if he ran to the right.

If phase 1 involves simultaneous discrimination of black-white, while phase 2 involved successive discrimination of black-white, then it can be seen that the same cue dimension would be relevant for both phases, but the specific responses which led to reward in phase 1 would no longer be relevant in phase 2.

Two crucial predictions were tested in Lawrence's (1949) first study. The first prediction was that when the same cue dimension (e.g., black-white) was relevant in both phases, phase 2 learning would be facilitated. (The control group, used as a basis of comparison, was one in which the rewarded dimension of phase 1 was absent in phase 2.) The results were strongly in support of this prediction.

The second prediction was that when the rewarded dimension of phase 1 was present during phase 2, but was not the basis of reinforcement, a negative transfer effect would occur. For example, black-white might be the relevant dimension in phase 1, while wide-narrow was relevant in phase 2 (e.g., if the alley is wide, turn right; if narrow, turn left). If black-white were an irrelevant dimension in phase 2 (e.g., the wide alley might be black half the time and white half the time), Lawrence reasoned that the animals would attend to the black-white dimension (since it had been raised in the animals' hierarchy during phase 1); thus the discovery of the correct dimension would be delayed. Contrary to the prediction from the theory, no negative transfer occurred when the phase 1 relevant cue dimension varied randomly in phase 2.

The absence of a negative transfer effect in these data is a serious problem for Lawrence. If attentional hierarchies are the main variable operating, elevating a stimulus dimension in the hierarchy in phase 1 should result in response to this dimension at the expense of other dimensions in phase 2. Positive results in this study can be accounted for as easily by Gibson as by Lawrence, and so do not constitute a critical test of Lawrence's position. On the other hand,

Gibson's theory does not imply that the presence of a differentiated irrelevant stimuli will interfere with learning to respond to relevant stimuli. This is particularly true for Gibson if the instrumental responses to the irrelevant differentiated stimuli are also irrelevant. It is not certain that the positive transfer would be predicted by the acquired-compound stimulus theory of Miller-Dollard-Goss, since prediction would depend on whether the response consequences of approach to the positive stimulus and avoidance to the negative were more dissimilar to each other than the positive stimulus was different from the negative. This would appear to be difficult to determine.

A second study by Lawrence (1950) provides dramatic evidence for the potency of differentiation; it also suggests that subjects may learn to *disregard* classes of stimuli. Phase 1 of this study involved training animals on a successive discrimination problem. Half the animals were trained to turn in one direction on trials in which the maze was all black, in the other direction on trials in which the maze was all white. Presence or absence of a chain curtain was an irrelevant cue sometimes associated with turning in one direction, sometimes associated with turning in the other. The other half of the subjects were trained, in a successive discrimination, to respond to the presence or absence of the chained curtain with black-white as irrelevant. In phase 2, subjects learned a simultaneous discrimination in which *both* the black-white dimension *and* the presence or absence of chained curtains were relevant; for example, the chain curtains were always on the side in which the goal box was black, while the other side of the apparatus, which was white, never had the chain curtain.

After this discrimination had been learned, the two stimulus dimensions were set in opposition and simultaneous discrimination training was continued. The relevant dimension of phase 1 proved dominant in this situation. The extent of this dominance is indicated by the performance of a subset of animals for whom the relevant cues of phase 2 were *reversed* during the post-phase 2 test trials. Reversal learning was faster for the relevant dimension of phase 1 than for the irrelevant. Thus, not even the negative transfer of the instrumental responses, during reversal, could override the differentiation effect.

If phase 2 had merely resulted in better instrumental learning to the phase 1 relevant cues than to the phase 1 irrelevant, one would expect that reversal of the phase 2 cues would produce greater negative transfer of instrumental responses for the phase 1 relevant cues and superiority for the phase 1 irrelevant cues. The fact that the opposite actually occurred strongly suggests that, during phase 1, subjects actually learned to *ignore* the irrelevant cues.

The finding, in Lawrence's (1950) study, that animals learn to ignore cues from nonrewarded stimulus dimension was supported in a later study by Bensberg (1958). This study is important since it employed human subjects. In Bensberg's study, an irrelevant dimension of phase 1 was made the relevant dimension in phase 2. Subjects in this condition performed more poorly in phase 2 than did subjects in a control group for whom none of the phase 1 dimensions were present during phase 2.

The acquired ignoring of stimuli does not appear to be an invariable consequence of irrelevance. In the Gibson *et al.* series of studies on early experience, the forms hung about the walls of the cage were irrelevant and yet facilitation of subsequent performance to these forms occurred. The same is true in the large number of studies which have demonstrated incidental and latent learning. Perhaps the critical variable for acquiring the tendency to ignore stimuli is that an instrumental response must be attached erroneously to the stimulus (due to partial reinforcement occurring on those trials in which the stimulus, by chance, covaries with the positive stimulus), followed by extinction on subsequent trials. At any rate, there is obviously a great deal yet to be learned about this phenomenon.

EVIDENCE FOR A TWO FACTOR THEORY OF DIFFERENTIATION. A study by Kurtz (1955) appears to be particularly important because it strongly suggests that differentiation and attention to cues may be two independent variables.

The study was specifically designed to manipulate attention to cues. In phase 1, subjects learned to discriminate between stimuli (viz., line drawings) that were so similar to one another that, on casual inspection, they might be thought identical. For example, one set of stimuli consisted of two faces that differed only in the angle of the eyebrows; another set consisted of two kites that differed only in angle of inclination. In order to perform these phase 1 discriminations, it was necessary for subjects to carefully examine the similar sets for differences.

The effect of phase 1 experience with these stimuli was evaluated in phase 2 by means of a paired-associates learning task with verbal responses. Each of the subjects was presented with eight such pairs in phase 2; the stimuli of six of these pairs were the same as, or similar to, stimuli seen in phase 1. The stimuli of the remaining two pair were the control items against which phase 1 experience was evaluated; these were new stimuli, similar to each other but not to the stimuli of phase 1.

Kurtz found that phase 1 experience facilitated learning in phase 2 under the following conditions. (a) Two of the stimuli of phase 2 were similar patterns which the subjects had learned to discriminate from each other in phase 1. Responses were learned to these significantly more rapidly than to the control stimuli. (b) Two of the phase 2 stimuli closely resembled a discriminated set from phase 1, and differed in the *same* aspect as the original phase 1 stimuli. Again, responses were learned to these stimuli significantly more rapidly than to the control stimuli.

Phase 1 experience led to decrements in phase 2 learning under the following condition. (c) One of the stimuli was from a set in phase 1, another was a new stimulus that was similar to it. However, these two stimuli were *identical* in the aspect which served as the basis of discrimination in phase 1 and different in a new aspect. Responses were learned to these stimuli significantly more *slowly* than to the control stimuli. Kurtz interprets this as indicating that for these c items, subjects had to extinguish the attention response acquired in phase 1 before acquiring the correct basis for discrimination. These results strongly support an attention-to-cues position.

Another aspect of Kurtz's data, however, suggests a type of differentiation effect in addition to that produced by attention to cues. Here Kurtz analyzed each set of two similar stimuli as though they were one item. In this analysis, a response appropriate to one of the two items in a pair is not considered incorrect if elicited by the other item of the pair. Now Kurtz found that the c items were learned significantly more rapidly than the control items and as rapidly as the items in the a and b sets. In other words, subjects quickly learned that a response was appropriate to a particular set of stimuli if these stimuli had been experienced in phase 1 (or were similar to stimuli that had been experienced in phase 1), even though they had difficulty discriminating between the two stimuli in the set.

The relative superiority of learning new responses to old stimuli, as opposed to learning them to unfamiliar stimuli, does not in this case appear to be attributable to acquired attention to cues during phase 1. While the two stimuli *within* each set were very similar and required training before the relevant cues could be ascertained, the various sets were extremely dissimilar from one another. For example, one of Kurtz's sets contained two faces that differed only in the angle of the eyebrows, while another set contained two kite-shaped figures that differed only in angle of inclination on the page. Distinguishing *between sets* did not therefore require practice.

Gibson's Differentiation Theory

STRENGTHS OF THE THEORY.   Up to a point, the Gibsonian notion of reduction in generalization fits the data well. This position is certainly consistent with the basic differentiation effect, as displayed in studies such as Gagne and Baker (1950) and G. Cantor (1955). These studies show that experience with a set of stimuli in one situation will facilitate later learning of new responses to these stimuli.

To a great extent, it is also consistent with studies in which only a *single* stimulus is involved in the pretraining during phase 1 (e.g., Walk, Gibson, Pick, and Tighe, 1958). Here, let us assume that generalization is reduced for the single stimulus presented in phase 1. If, in the subsequent phase 2 discrimination learning, this stimulus is positive and some new stimulus is negative, the reinforced responses of approaching this pretrained stimulus will not generalize to the new stimulus; thus there will be little incorrect tendency to approach the new, incorrect stimulus. As we have seen, the data are in good agreement with this prediction.

The theory also has the advantage that it does *not* predict the strong acquired equivalence effect, since the evidence for such an effect is virtually nonexistent.

WEAKNESSES OF THE THEORY.   The greatest problems for Gibson's theory arise from the studies by Kurtz (1955), Attneave (1957), and Murdock (1958c). These studies have in common the fact that they employed a *within-subject* design during phase 2 for the evaluation of stimulus pretraining. In these studies, phase 2 consisted of presenting a subject with some stimuli which had been differentiated in phase 1, plus some new stimuli which served as the control items.

A careful examination of the Gibson theory shows that, in such situations, *the theory predicts better learning for the new, undifferentiated stimuli than for the stimuli that had been differentiated in phase 1.* This prediction can be easily demonstrated. Gibson states that prior experience with a stimulus reduces the generalization gradient *of this stimulus* so that its response *is not so readily evoked as an incorrect response by other stimuli.* (This is the "altruistic" differentiation effect noted earlier in the chapter.) Therefore, in phase 2, the responses being learned to the pretrained stimuli should *not* interfere with the learning of responses to the unfamiliar, control stimuli. Learning responses to the control stimuli should therefore be relatively rapid. On the other hand, since the generalization gradients of the control stimuli have not been reduced in phase 1, the responses to the control stimuli should interfere with the learning of the responses to the pretrained stimuli during phase 2. Contrary to the prediction, evidence indicates that the phase 2 learning is superior for the pretrained stimuli as compared to the control stimuli.

Since this prediction from Gibson's theory is so important, let us take a more concrete example of the relevant mechanics of the theory in the within-subject situation. Murdock (1958c) pretrained subjects on four stimuli during phase 1. In phase 2, these four stimuli, plus four new stimuli, were associated each to a different response. First let us consider the amount of interference operating upon one of the pretrained stimuli, during phase 2. Since the other three pretrained stimuli have reduced generalization gradients, they will interfere very little with this fourth pretrained stimulus. However, all four of the control stimuli will still generalize their responses to a great extent. Thus all four control stimuli serve as a powerful source of interference with the learning of a response to any of the pretrained stimuli. Turning now to the acquisition of a response by one of the control stimuli, we again find little interference being generated by the four pretrained stimuli. The major source of interference must be from the other three control stimuli.

Thus the learning of a response to any of the pretrained stimuli encounters interference from all *four* control stimuli; the learning of a response to any of the control stimuli encounters interference from only the remaining *three* control stimuli. Clearly, there is less interference to the learning of a response to a control stimulus than to a pretrained stimulus, during phase 2.

In all three studies cited above, just the opposite occurred. Learning was superior for the pretrained stimuli as compared to the control stimuli. These results appear to require a revision of the Gibson formulation.

It should be noted that the necessity for revision of Gibson's theory was not obvious in the past because most studies have employed independent experimental and control groups. If all the stimuli in a list have been differentiated, then the facilitation in learning any given S-R pair could be attributed to reduction in generalization from *other* differentiated stimuli in the list.

Stimulus Isolation Theory

A review of the data presented in the present chapter suggests a revision of the Gibson theory. For convenience, we shall refer to this revision as a stimulus isolation theory.

The stimulus isolation theory states that experience with a stimulus produces functional isolation of the stimulus from interference by other stimuli. Thus, if all the phase 2 stimuli were differentiated in phase 1, there would be a reduction in interference between these stimuli and phase 2 learning would be facilitated. If only some of the phase 2 stimuli were differentiated in phase 1, these differentiated stimuli would resist interference; thus responses to the differentiated stimuli would be acquired more readily than responses to the new, undifferentiated stimuli. The stimulus isolation position (like the Gibson theory which suggested it) posits a form of learning (viz., stimulus isolation) which influences the formation of associations, but is not in itself an association. It represents a type of pure stimulus learning.

There are, of course, many alternative ways of conceptualizing the specific mechanisms involved in stimulus isolation. One is suggested by the cognitive space model outlined in Chapter 2. Consider each stimulus as a point in multidimensional cognitive space. The differentiation of a stimulus can be conceptualized as expansion of the cognitive space in the region of the stimulus, increasing the distance between all the points in the region. The expansion would be greatest near the differentiated stimulus and would decrease as we move away from this stimulus. In effect, this would be the equivalent of multiplying the vectors in a matrix (where each vector represents a multidimensional stimulus) by a factor which is proportional to the distance between a given vector and the vector representing the differentiated stimulus. Thus the expansion of the cognitive space in a particular region should effect all the stimuli in this region. This type of conceptualization would provide a basis for explaining the Attneave (1957) data. Attneave, it will be recalled, found that pretraining on a single stimulus facilitated later discrimination of a new set of stimuli which were similar to the pretrained stimulus.

From this point of view, attention to cues could represent moving stimuli out along new orthogonal dimensions on which the stimuli did not previously differ. This position could also explain the facilitative effects of cue compounding found even when the new elements of the compound are more similar to each other than the original stimuli (i.e., the weak equivalence effect). Figure 4–2 suggests how this might occur, using the stimuli of the Saltz (1963) study as an example. In this study, each verbal stimulus in a paired-

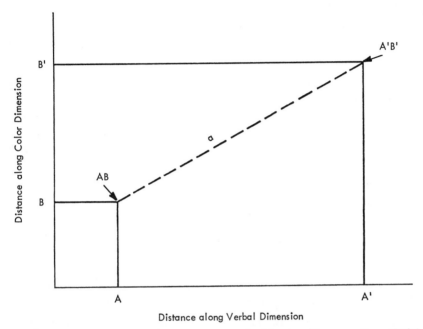

FIGURE 4–2. Hypothetical Illustration of Saltz's Stimulus Compounding Model. (See text for explanation.)

associates list was presented on a different colored background. The hypothetical distance between two such verbal stimuli (A and A^1) is indicated on the abscissa. The distance between the colors (B and B^1), on which the verbal stimuli are presented, is indicated on the ordinate. Since color and verbal dimension are assumed to be orthogonal dimensions, the distance between the stimulus compounds (AB and A^1B^1), as measured by the line a, will be greater than the distance between either A and A^1 or B and B^1 alone.

A clarification of the relationship between differentiation and stimulus similarity is in order at this point. Since differentiation involves a reduction in interference between similar stimuli, some writers have assumed that the effect of prior training should be greater for a very similar stimuli than for less similar stimuli. This may prove to be true. However, it is not a logical consequence of the differentiation concept. It is logically possible, for example, that interference tendencies are so great, between very similar stimuli, that large amounts of pretraining are necessary to produce an effect on phase 2; for stimuli of only moderate similarity, small amounts of pretraining may produce stimulus isolation. The issue is an empirical one, at least for the present. Surprising little work has been done relating differentiation effects to stimulus similarity. One of the experiments reported in Murdock (1958c) finds a significant facilitation of phase 2 performance only for stimuli that are very similar. This is a within groups effect in which, for each subject, half the stimuli in phase 2 were experienced in phase 1, half were not. The percentages of facilitation were 18.0%, 3.4%, and 8.8% for the high, medium, and low degrees of similarity respectively, with only the 18.0% significantly different from zero ($t = 4.18$, $p. < .01$). On the other hand, the difference between 18.0, 3.4, and 8.8 (a between groups comparison) was not significant. Consequently, the issue cannot be considered clearly resolved by these data.

Concluding Remarks Concerning Evaluation of Differentiation Theories

It should come as no great surprise to find that theories formulated two decades ago have been shown to be inadequate by subsequent research. None of the theories for stimulus differentiation has come through completely unscathed, though some have weathered better than others.

In some ways the acquired-compound stimulus theory has been hardest hit. The issue of acquired equivalence of cues is perhaps more critical for this position than for any of the others. As has been seen, there is a remarkable lack of evidence for acquired equivalence in the conditions relevant to the acquired stimulus position. While some of the studies at issue can, perhaps, be attacked on procedural grounds, the consistent failure of the phenomenon to appear is very impressive.

Studies such as those of Attneave (1957) and Walk, Gibson, Pick, and Tighe (1958) in which phase 2 performance was facilitated by the presentation of a *single* stimulus during phase 1 are also difficult for the acquired-compound stimulus formulation to assimilate. Finally, as far as negative evidence is concerned, the acquired stimulus theory has difficulty making any sort of prediction in many situations in which a differentiation effect has been demonstrated.

For example, in the Lawrence (1949) study, the responses to the relevant stimuli of phase 1 are approach to one stimulus (e.g., the black goal box) and avoidance of another (e.g., the white goal box). For the acquired stimulus position to make a prediction here, it would be necessary to demonstrate that the stimulus consequences of approach and avoidance are more dissimilar from one another than black is dissimilar from white. If such a psychophysical determination were feasible, it would be necessary to engage in such an exercise prior to many of the differentiation studies discussed, in order to make a defensible prediction. Obviously, a theory which does not pose this type of requirement is preferable.

There is a great deal of evidence favorable to *some* type of attention-to-cues position. Unfortunately, except for Lawrence (1949, 1950) and perhaps Wyckoff (1952), these positions are too vaguely stated. Lawrence's particular version of the attention-to-cues position is troubled by his inability to demonstrate negative transfer in the situation where the cue dimension which was relevant in phase 1 appears as an irrelevant dimension in phase 2. While the rest of his data are consistent with his position, they are also consistent with a generalization reduction theory.

The study by Kurtz (1955) appears to provide the most unambiguous evidence for a type of attention-to-cues effect. In addition, a whole tradition of research including the work of Ehrenfreund (1948) and also the Russian work on the orienting response, discussed in the previous chapter, make attention-to-cues a reasonable process.

In addition to attention-to-cues, however, a second process also appears to be operating. This is indicated by the fact that differentiation effects occur in situations that are not easily interpreted by means of attention-to-cues. The studies by Attneave (1957) and by Walk, Gibson, Pick, and Tighe (1958) are in this category. Here, only a single stimulus was presented during phase 1, yet phase 2 facilitation occurred. Kurtz's (1955) data also suggests the operation of an additional differentiation factor in a situation where attention-to-cues seems inapplicable.

What are the characteristics of this second process? Up to a point, the Gibsonian notion of generalization reduction fits the data well. However, as has been pointed out in previous sections of this chapter, serious problems for Gibson's theory arise from the studies of Kurtz (1955), Attneave (1957), and Murdock (1958a). In these studies, phase 2 consisted of presenting a subject with some stimuli which had been differentiated in phase 1, plus some new stimuli. The Gibson position predicts better learning for the new undifferentiated stimuli, than for the stimuli which had been differentiated in phase 1. The data are contrary to this prediction.

The *stimulus isolation* position, suggested in this chapter, appears to be more successful than Gibson's original theory in fitting the differentiation data. This position states that experience with a stimulus tends to isolate this stimulus from other stimuli, reducing the effects of interstimulus interference. As distinguished from Gibson's theory, this position states that stimulus differentiation increases the extent to which the differentiated stimulus becomes isolated from interference produced by *other* stimuli.

Variables Influencing the Differentiation Effect

We have already examined a number of variables related to differentiation. For the most part, these have been variables relevant to the evaluation of the theories under consideration. Having formulated some idea about the mechanisms producing the differentiation effect, it is now of interest to examine several other important, related variables.

NUMBER OF PHASE 1 TRIALS.   Most of the evidence concerning number of trials indicates that the degree of phase 2 facilitation increases as a function of the number of phase 1 trials (e.g., Gagne and Baker, 1950; Rossman and Goss, 1951; J. H. Cantor, 1955; Arnoult, 1956). Unfortunately, few of these studies employed sufficient variation in phase 1 trials to permit a more specific statement of the relationship. Consequently, many potentially important issues remain unspoiled by empirical evidence. There is no indication at this time, for example, whether more trials are required in phase 1 when a greater number of stimuli are involved; nor is there sufficient evidence concerning the relationship between trials and various types of phase 2 tasks. Arnoult (1956) reports that five trials during phase 1 are as effective as 25 trials when phase 2 is a recognition task. The other studies, employing perceptual-motor learning in phase 2, appear to require many more than five trials for phase 1. Gagne and Baker (1950) and Rossman and Goss (1951) find very little effect with only four phase 1 trials. In Gagne and Baker's study, a sharp increment occurs with eight trials, which is the greatest number of trials they employed. Rossman and Goss jump from four trials on phase 1 in one group to approximately 20 trials in another, and find a sizable phase 2 difference in facilitation between these points. Unfortunately, these studies vary in so many ways that comparisons are hazardous.

We have previously suggested, in this chapter, that stimulus isolation appears to correspond to the resistence to interference mechanisms, as described in Chapters 2 and 3. Attention to cues, on the other hand, appears to correspond to the concept identification processes cited in those chapters. In other words, attention to cues appears to involve discovering relevant differences between similar stimuli. To the extent that this position is reasonable, we would expect different functional relations to phase 1 trials for these two aspects of differentiation. Locating the *correct* concept appears to follow all-or-none laws. Thus we would expect to find that differentiation based on attention to cues should also follow such laws. On the other hand, short-term retention data such as that of Hellyer (1962) suggests that resistance to interference develops gradually. Therefore, stimulus isolation might be expected to develop gradually as a function of phase 1 trials. There are no relevant data on these issues. However, it is hoped that the present re-examination of the issues will lead to renewed interest in research on such topics.

Several writers (e.g., Gagne and Baker, 1950; Rossman and Goss, 1951; Murdock, 1958b) were specifically concerned with Gibson's (1940) assumption that stimulus generalization first increases then decreases as a function of phase 1 practice. No evidence for the initial increase in generalization (which would be marked by an initial decrement in phase 2 performance) was observed.

TYPE OF PHASE 1 TASK. To a great extent, the interest in type of phase 1 task has been related to the issue of whether phase 1 must involve associating specific responses to the relevant stimuli. The acquired-compound stimulus theory suggests that such associations are crucial to differentiation. The alternatives to this have involved simply exposing subjects to the stimuli, instructing subjects to examine the stimuli, or requiring subjects to perform psychophysical judgments concerning the stimuli.

The studies by Gibson and her co-workers, manipulating early exposure of rats to stimuli, obtained subsequent facilitation in discrimination learning to these stimuli despite the fact that specific responses to the stimuli were not required during the early exposure period.

Robinson (1955) had subjects state whether each stimulus being presented was the same-as or different-from the immediately preceding stimulus. This led to as much phase 2 facilitation as was found for a group that learned a different verbal response to each stimulus in phase 1. Both groups were superior to a control group that had no phase 1 experience.

G. N. Cantor (1955) employed a group that merely examined the stimuli (pictures of two female faces) during phase 1. While this group did not perform as well, on phase 2, as a group which learned names for each stimulus, performance on phase 2 was superior to that of a control group whose phase 1 experience involved learning names for irrelevant stimuli. Similar results were obtained by Goss (1953) using light intensities as stimuli.

Pfafflin (1960) found that instructions to observe the stimuli during phase 1 produced somewhat better phase 2 discriminations than assigning labels to the stimuli. This effect interacted with stimulus meaningfulness, being very strong for highly meaningful stimuli and slightly reversed for stimuli of very low meaningfulness. The stimuli in this study were silhouettes. Somewhat similar results are reported by Ellis and Muller (1964), who found that instructions to observe were superior for forms of low complexity, while labels were superior for highly complex abstract stimuli.

Overall, it appears that phase 2 facilitation can occur even in the absence of specific responses associated to each stimulus in phase 1. In defense of the compound stimulus theory, some writers have hypothesized that subjects may develop specific associations (e.g., labelling) even in the absence of instructions to do so. Convincing controls against such hypothesized self-instructions appear difficult to design. To further complicate this issue, superiority of phase 2 performance in groups which learned to make specific responses to each stimulus during phase 1 can be rationalized in a very reasonable fashion from an attention-to-cues position: If a subject must make a specific response to each stimulus, he will be forced to seek different, distinguishing aspects for each stimulus. Furthermore, if he fails to find these distinguishing cues on early trials, this failure will be brought to his attention since it will lead to incorrect responses during phase 1. Such forced attention-to-cues would no doubt be more important when stimuli are difficult to discriminate, whereas simple observing might be adequate for more meaningful material or material that is readily discriminable for some other reason.

STIMULUS MEANINGFULNESS. The effect of phase 1 practice appears to decrease as a function of the meaningfulness of the stimuli. Pfafflin (1960) investigated this problem using shapes that varied from silhouettes of common objects (e.g., car, house) to forms on whose meaning there was almost no agreement in a pretest. For the highly meaningful stimuli, only subjects who were merely instructed to observe during phase 1 showed phase 2 facilitation. Groups which learned verbal responses to the meaningful stimuli during phase 1 actually performed somewhat more poorly, on phase 2, than a control group with no phase 1 practice. On the other hand, she obtained a marked degree of phase 2 facilitation for all experimental groups when the stimuli were meaningless forms.

EARLY STUDIES FAILED TO FIND DIFFERENTIATION OF VERBAL MATERIALS. The stimulus differentiation of verbal materials is extremely difficult to show under usual procedures. Underwood and Schulz (1960) report several studies in which phase 1 training produced either no effect on phase 2 or was detrimental to phase 2 paired-associates learning. In one study, phase 1 consisted of training subjects to integrate nonsense syllables. This consisted of presenting the syllables intact, followed by a test in which the subjects were required to fill in a missing letter in each syllable. In another study, phase 1 consisted of pairing verbal materials with nonsense forms, the forms serving as stimuli and the verbal materials as responses. Subsequent phase 2 paired-associates learning, in which the verbal materials served as stimuli, yielded no evidence for facilitation; in some cases, negative transfer effects were obtained.

Battig and Williams (1962) also were unable to demonstrate stimulus differentiation with verbal materials. Using low association nonsense syllables, phase 1 consisted of a verbal discrimination task in which the subjects were presented pairs of stimuli and were required to learn which item of each pair had been arbitrarily designated as correct by the experimenter. In subsequent paired-associates learning, using these syllables as stimuli, no facilitation was demonstrated.

DEVELOPMENT OF VERBAL DIFFERENTIATION IN CHILDREN. Some writers have interpreted this type of data as indicating that stimulus differentiation is not a relevant variable for verbal learning. Presumably this amounts to saying that verbal materials, even nonsense syllables, are already close to asymptote in stimulus differentiation due to the great familiarity of such material. A study by Staats, Staats, and Schutz (1962) is of particular interest from this point of view since it examined the effect of stimulus pretraining on children of kindergarten age (about five years old). These children could not read and were apparently relatively unfamiliar with the appearance of typed words. Phase 1 consisted of showing the children cards on which three words were typed; two of the words were identical, one was different. Subjects were to indicate the word that "doesn't belong." Phase 2 was a paired-associates task in which the children were taught to pronounce four of the words from phase 1. In this study, where the typed words were unfamiliar to the children (though the oral responses were familiar words), differentiation produced facilitation of phase 2 performance.

Saltz, Metzen, and Ernstein (1961) report data which indicate that the results obtained by Staats *et al.* are not a function of subject age, *per se,* but a function of stimulus meaningfulness. In this study, two groups of children were employed; one group was approximately 6 years of age, and other approximately 11. The stimuli were silhouettes of common objects that children could readily name. Consequently, the material was in essence highly meaningful and verbal in nature. In phase 1, the subjects learned to make a distinctive motor response to each stimulus. In phase 2, they learned a letter of the alphabet as a response to each stimulus. With each subject as his own control, phase 2 learning was no better for silhouettes which had been presented on phase 1 than for new silhouettes. This failure to find phase 2 facilitation was consistent at both age levels.

The two studies cited above combine to indicate that, before children can read, the typed appearance of words is simply a complex perceptual stimulus of a relatively undifferentiated nature.

POSSIBLE ARTIFACTS MASKING VERBAL DIFFERENTIATION. Turning to the differentiation of nonsense syllables in adults, there is reason to doubt the early evidence which suggested that the stimulus differentiation of such material is virtually asymptotic. An important artifact appears to have obscured the effect of pretraining in these early studies. The artifact is related to a phenomenon called "stimulus selection" by Underwood (1963). Prior to differentiation training, nonsense syllables tend to be seen as unintegrated sets of letters. Given a set of such nonsense syllables as nominal stimuli, Underwood reports, subjects will often select a single letter of each syllable (usually the first letter) as the functional stimulus. A single letter of the alphabet is, of course, a very well differentiated item. There is a good deal of evidence to suggest that utilization of a single letter facilitates learning (e.g., Newman, 1963; Horowitz, Lipman, Norman, and McConkie, 1964). These facts could strongly influence the effects of stimulus pretraining on subsequent phase 2 learning. To the extent that predifferentiation leads to integration of the syllable, the subject will respond to the syllable as a whole rather than select a single letter. Non-pretrained subjects, on the other hand, would tend to select a single letter of the syllable as the functional stimulus. This difference in functional stimuli for pretrained versus non-pretrained subjects could obscure the differentiation of the total syllable as measured by phase 2 learning.

A study by Gannon and Noble (1961) suggests the operation of the artifact described above. During phase 1, the subjects pronounced each of the verbal items (disyllabic nonsense words); each item was presented 20 times. In phase 2, subjects associated these as stimuli to other disyllabic nonsense words. The critical aspect of this study was that the subjects were required to pronounce each stimulus as it appeared, during paired-associates learning, prior to anticipating the response term. Thus subjects were required to respond to the total stimulus, whether or not they had been pretrained on it. Under these conditions, stimulus pretraining led to facilitation of phase 2 paired-associates learning.

Schulz and Tucker (1962*b*) replicated the Gannon and Noble design but also included a group which was not required to pronounce the stimuli during phase 2. The group which articulated the stimulus prior to anticipating the response, in phase 2, showed the facilitation reported by Gannon and Noble. On the other hand, the group which did *not* pronounce the stimuli during phase 2 showed an *inverse* relationship between amount of pretraining and subsequent phase 2 learning. These data are extremely consistent with the operation of the stimulus selection artifact, as described.

However, in a second study, Schulz and Tucker (1962*a*) found that these relationships disappeared upon increasing the anticipation interval from 2 seconds (the interval used both by Gannon and Noble and by Schulz and Tucker, 1962*b*) to 4 seconds. Under the 4-seconds condition, pretraining produced a nonsignificant facilitation of phase 2 performance for both the group that pronounced the stimuli in phase 2 and for the group which did not pronounce in phase 2. Schulz and Tucker interpret their data as indicating that pretraining may increase the speed with which the stimuli can be pronounced, permitting pretrained subjects more time to emit the response. With a 4-second anticipation interval, they reasoned, the increase in pronunciation speed would be less effective. This interpretation does not explain why the *decrement,* as a function of pretraining, found in the group which did not pronounce during phase 2, should also disappear at the 4-second anticipation interval.

Alternative explanations for the disappearance of the stimulus pretraining effect in the 4-second condition are possible. For example, there is some evidence (which will be presented in Chapter 5) that differentiation increases as a function of the amount of time available for the subject to examine the stimulus. Were this the case, increasing the anticipation interval to 4 seconds could increase the stimulus differentiation for both pretrained and non-pretrained subjects.

A study by Martin (1965) avoided some of the methodological problems involved in the Gannon-Noble technique, since he did not require articulation of the stimulus. His procedure made it likely that the pretrained and non-pretrained subjects were making the same *type* of response to the paired-associates stimuli by carrying out the equivalent of pretraining within the context of the criterion paired-associates task. After two trials of paired-associates learning, Martin removed the three most difficult stimuli for one group and substituted three new stimuli, keeping the original responses. In a second group, the responses to the three critical stimuli were reassigned so that, while both the original stimuli and responses were retained in the list, the pairings were different. Despite the negative transfer effects inherent in re-pairing *S-R* terms, learning was superior for this group as opposed to the group which was presented with three new stimuli. Thus stimulus differentiation acquired on the first two trials was sufficient to facilitate performance.

In the Martin study, since pretraining was in the context of the learning task, subjects could stabilize the same type of response to each stimulus that they would use in paired-associates learning. Consequently, if subjects had a tendency toward a relatively efficient mode of responding to nonsense stimuli (e.g., using the first letter of each syllable as the functional stimulus), pretraining was relatively unlikely to disrupt this. This is clearly different from a pretraining task such as pronouncing each item, which trains the subjects to make a restricted mode of response that may reduce the relative efficiency of subsequent paired-associates learning.

Can a Response Become Associated to an Undifferentiated Stimulus?

Some writers (e.g., Lawrence, 1949) have suggested a two phase learning process in which stimulus differentiation must precede the associative phase. An alternative to the Lawrence position is one which assumes the existence of "latent" associations: Such an assumption states that an undifferentiated stimulus may form an association with a response, but the subject is not capable of emitting the response correctly until the subject develops further differentiation to the stimulus. There is evidence from a number of studies which suggests that this type of latent association may indeed be formed (e.g., Estes, Hopkins, & Crothers, 1960; Greenbloom & Kimble, 1965; Butler & Petersen, 1965). In these studies, subjects were first shown pairs of verbal items which they were to associate. Next they were given a series of *test* trials in which the stimuli were presented *without the responses*. These studies found that the subjects *improved steadily*, over these test trials, in the number of correct responses they could recall to the stimuli, despite the fact that the responses were never shown to them during this series of test trials.

It seems reasonable to interpret these data as indicating that the associations were formed during the initial paired presentations, but that the correct responses were not emitted during the early test trials because the stimuli were insufficiently differentiated. Successive presentations of the stimuli without the responses resulted in an increased stimulus differentiation. When this differentiation reached appropriate levels, the latent associations could manifest themselves in correct responses to the stimuli. Thus it appears that the formation of associations does not necessarily depend on the prior development of stimulus differentiation. An exception to this is found when the differentiation process involved is that of attention-to-cues. Ehrenfreund (1948) finds that *appropriate* associations are not developed when the subject has failed to notice the relevant stimulus dimension. This is, of course, what one would expect.

CONCLUSIONS

The present chapter presents evidence which indicates that stimulus differentiation, in addition to the bond between the stimulus and a response, is a learned aspect of the S-R system. The function of stimulus differentiation appears to be that of preserving the integrity of the system by preventing the interference from competing systems. In subsequent chapters we shall see that stimulus differentiation is only one of the aspects of a cognitive system that serves this function.

When the stimuli involved in a particular learning situation are very familiar, much of the differentiation has probably already been acquired and brought into the situation by the subject. Verbal materials, even nonsense syllables, appear to be near asymptotic levels of differentiation for adult subjects. Familiar objects appear to have reached close to asymptotic differentiation by the age of six.

A problem which has yet to be studied adequately is the relationship between extinction of the orienting response, as described in Chapter 3, and the development of stimulus differentiation in experiments like those of Gibson, Walk, and their colleagues on exposure to stimuli during infancy. Since, in the latter set of experiments the stimuli were merely static aspects of the environment, it is not clear why the orienting responses to these stimuli did not extinguish, leading to depression of subsequent discrimination between these stimuli. Instead, of course, discrimination proved to be facilitated.

Conceivably, the answer to this problem may lie in the distinction between attention-to-cues as one process, and stimulus isolation as another process in differentiation. Extinction of the orienting response may primarily affect attention to cues. The mechanisms may be related to those described, for example, by Broadbent (1958) in his discussion of filtering in attention. However, if extinction of the orienting response occurs, it appears to be accompanied by differentiation of the stimuli, which presumably continues until the extinction reaches such a level that the stimuli are no longer attended to. Subsequent presentation of the stimuli in a new context for discrimination learning might then produce disinhibition of the extinguished orienting responses. This differs, of course, from the procedure in the conditioning studies where extinction of the orienting response to a stimulus and subsequent attempts to condition a response to the stimulus occur in the same context situation.

In the previous chapters, evidence has been presented which suggests that associations may be formed at very high strength on the first trial. Learning of stimulus differentiation appears to be a slower process. It is therefore suggested that one of the reasons that learning curves rise relatively slowly as a function of trials is that stimulus differentiation, rather than associative strength, grows slowly with practice.

5 | Response Factors in Cognitive Systems: Availability and Differentiation

PRECIS

The distinction between stimulus and response has been challenged on a number of grounds in recent years. The present chapter examines this issue. The ambiguity of the distinction is clearest in verbal learning; here a person can be presented two words and either one can later be presented as the stimulus and the person asked to recall the other word as the response. However, even nonverbal, external physical stimuli (such as lights and tones) can be shown to have response properties. Also, responses appear to develop differentiation of a sort that is very comparable to the stimulus differentiation examined in Chapter 4. The relationship between response differentiation and response availability is considered. Prevalent theories of response availability are seen to be extensions of the single variable S-R position and must be evaluated from this point of view.

DEMONSTRATION EXPERIMENT

The Problem

A. Backward Associations. First let us examine your ability at backward associations. For each of the items below, give the item that should *precede* it; that is to say, give the item that would normally be the *stimulus* to the item you are looking at.

1. _____, D. C.
2. _____, C, D, E, F
3. _____ Doodle
4. _____ hold these truths to be self evident, that all men were created equal . . .
5. _____ or not to be, that is the question.
6. _____, 157, 158, 159

B. Images. Next let us examine your ability to imagine various visual, auditory, and olfactory stimuli.

1. Picture a tree, blooming in summer. Picture the green leaves, the tall branches. Can you picture this very vividly, almost as though it were really present before you? Some people can, can you?
2. Imagine the sound of chalk or a fingernail scratching across a blackboard. Many people can imagine this so vividly that their spines tingle. Can you?
3. Picture freshly baked bread. Imagine the pleasant aroma arise from the bread. Some people can imagine it so vividly that their mouths water at the thought. Can you?
4. Picture a cat sitting on your lap. It is a big, white, furry cat, purring contentedly while lying on your lap. Picture the cat as vividly as you can. Can you almost feel his soft fur?
5. Imagine a record playing "White Christmas." Imagine it as vividly as you can.

Explanation

Most readers will have little difficulty with the backward associations above. The correct answers were: Washington, B, Yankee, We, To be, and 156 for questions 1 to 6 respectively.

Clearly, in verbal associations the distinction between stimuli and responses is arbitrary: A word looks the same and sounds the same whether it functions as a stimulus or a response. Further, as we saw above, once the association is formed, it is often possible to present the subject with the item that functioned as the response and have him emit the item that had previously functioned as stimulus.

152

Is this a peculiarity of verbal associations? Or do all associations have this reversible quality to some degree? This question is more complex than it at first appears, as we shall see when we consider the research that has been attempted. However, at one level at least, it is often possible to *emit an image* of a stimulus *as a response.* Many people report that they can accomplish this with great vividness. We can not look into their minds and determine how accurate they are; however, we can attempt to emit such images ourselves and judge our own vividness. Section *B* above involved just such an introspective response. Could *you* emit images of stimuli?

THE DISTINCTION BETWEEN STIMULUS AND RESPONSE

Chapters 3 and 4 have been concerned with associative and stimulus factors in learning. The present chapter will examine response factors. Recent research has revolutionized our conceptions of the role of the response in learning and has required a radical revision of many theories. Concepts that were considered almost self-evident truisms have, in the past few years, been thrown into extreme doubt. To a great extent, the inadequacies of the past seem to have arisen because of a problem we have already observed in this work: Too literal an interpretation of animal research, accompanied by the attitude that instrumental and classical conditioning were somehow basic in determining the concepts and laws of more complex processes. For example, theorists like Guthrie (1935) and Hull (1943) defined stimuli as types of physical energy which produce sensory-receptor events; they defined responses as motor or glandular events. Clearly, they were thinking in terms of the conditioning and instrumental learning situations in which one presents a physical stimulus and observes some motor or glandular reaction. And clearly, from this approach, one would not think in terms of initiating the response to see if the physical stimulus would appear.

Recent research in a number of areas has suggested that it may prove desirable to reconceptualize our notions of stimulus and response. In the Demonstration Experiment above, we examined one such area. For example, a subject may be shown two verbal items (e.g., DOG–HAT) and with the instructions to learn these so that when later *shown the first item,* he can *emit the second item.* The first item is called the stimulus, the second is called the response. However, it is then possible to present the second item as the stimulus and request that the subject emit the first item as the response. Under proper experimental conditions, it can be demonstrated that the association is symmetrical, or nearly so, despite the fact that the subject's original learning involved the first item as the nominal stimulus. Asch has gone so far as to suggest that the distinction between stimulus and response is an arbitrary convention (e.g., Asch and Ebenholtz, 1962*a*, 1962*b*; Asch and Lidner, 1963). His position is that at best we may designate a *functional* stimulus and a *functional* response.

How general is this state of affairs? Does it appear in other realms besides that of verbal learning? In conditioning, for example, a subject may learn to salivate to a bell. Can a bell *response* be elicited by a salivary stimulus? Very little is known about this problem. Obviously, a distinction between bell-salivation and word-word associations is that both the stimulus and the response words have overt, measurable response functions. Such functions are less apparent for stimuli such as a bell.

Two approaches can be taken to the issue of the arbitrary nature of the distinction between stimulus and response. One approach is to look for nonobvious, measurable response categories for stimuli such as bells, tones, etc., and determine if these can be elicited as forward or backward associations to other stimuli. *Images* are one such response category (e.g., does the subject have an image of a ringing bell when he salivates).

The second approach is more abstract. One can conceptualize points (or regions), in a cognitive space, such that some points have stimulus properties only (i.e., values on stimulus dimensions) while some have both stimulus and response properties. It can further be assumed that associations form between such elements. From this point of view, response functions are not critical to the formation of an association. Thus any two elements, such as a bell and a light, could be associated. Such associations could be examined empirically by later attaching a new element, which possesses response functions, to one of the previous elements (e.g., the bell) and testing for transfer to the other (e.g., the light). The reader may recognize that, in effect, we have described the sensory preconditioning studies.

In the following two sections we shall examine evidence in regard to both of the approaches discussed above.

Images as Responses

The use of images as an index of the response properties of stimuli is a relatively undeveloped area. However, some of the studies are provocative, despite their lack of complete experimental rigor. Among these studies, those of Leuba are particularly challenging.

In Leuba's studies, subjects were hypnotized and simultaneously presented with two stimuli. They were then given instructions for posthypnotic amnesia of the events which occurred during hypnosis and were awakened. Presentation of one of the stimuli, during the posthypnotic period, almost invariably led to an *image* of the other stimulus. For example, one of the subjects was given seven simultaneous presentations of a snapping sound and the smell of creosote during the hypnotic state. Upon awaking, he was presented with the snapping sound; at this the subject said, "creosote," wrinkled his nose, and turned his head away. Another subject was shown a drawing of a cube while moving his arm. Leuba reports that upon making this movement after waking, the subject clearly saw the drawing as an image. Visual, olfactory, and tactile images were all reported by Leuba (1940). Leuba and Dunlap (1951) reported similar results when subjects were requested to imagine a response which had been paired with a stimulus during hypnosis. Again, under those conditions the subjects reported images of the original stimuli.

Ellson (1941) reported similar results in a somewhat more orthodox experiment not involving hypnosis. During initial training, subjects were presented with a light followed by a tone. The tone rose in volume from below threshold to threshold in several seconds after onset of the light. Subjects were instructed to signal when they heard the tone. In test trials, the tone onset did not commence until 15–30 seconds after the light. Responses prior to tone onset were considered as indicating the occurrence of a tonal image. A control group which received the test trials without the original pairing of light and tone indicated significantly fewer images than the experimental group.

Hefferline and Perera (1963) found data that were very consistent with those of Ellson. In this study, subjects were instructed to press a key when the experimenters sounded a tone. Unknown to the subjects, the tone was presented only when the subjects emitted a minimal intensity finger twitch. The twitch, recorded electrically, was so slight that the subjects were unaware that they were producing the response. The tone was gradually diminished in intensity, over trials, and finally completely eliminated. At this point, when the subjects spontaneously emitted the twitch response, *they reported hearing the tone.* Thus *an image was elicited by a response* made by the subject.

On the other hand, several studies have failed to find these types of effects. Kelley (1934), for example, paired tone with color for many trials. No subject reported a color when the tone was presented alone.

THE EFFECTS OF SUGGESTIBILITY ON REPORTS OF IMAGES.   The reader may wonder whether some of the positive effects obtained in the above studies may have been produced by the suggestibility of the subjects. Just the opposite is indicated by data from a study by Barber and Calverley (1964). Subjects who were asked to produce either auditory or visual images *had a great tendency to suppress these images* unless reassured that such images did not represent manifestations of abnormal behavior.

More specifically, for the auditory image, the subjects were told to close their eyes and imagine a record playing "White Christmas." For the visual image, the subjects were told to imagine a cat sitting on their laps. Subjects then rated the vividness of their images. Under these conditions, the average rating was of a vague impression of the music or of the cat. Subjects were then told to imagine "Jingle Bells" or to imagine a dog. This was preceded by informing the subjects that such images could commonly occur in very strong form. Under these conditions, subjects reported very vivid auditory and visual images. Murphy and Myers (1962) also report that subjects indicate strong images (in this case hallucinations) under proper suggestive instructions. The major problem which arises, in interpreting these data, is whether the instructions actually strengthened the images or whether they merely resulted in cooperative verbal behavior from subjects who either wished to please the experimenter or who wished to appear capable of "normal" behavior. At any rate, these studies raise the possibility that subjects may suppress either the image or the report of the image unless reassured that such images are not pathological.

On the other hand, while the conditions and limits governing image responses are not known, we typically do not go through life to the accompaniment of nonexistent bells, sights, and pinpricks.

Sensory Preconditioning

If the distinction between stimulus and response is arbitrary, it should be possible to associate a light to a tone, despite the fact that there is no specific, overt "light" response or "tone" response, and despite the fact that the subject may not report that the light elicits the image of the tone. This could be a pure association in the cognitive space with no motoric repercussions. The sensory preconditioning studies are relevant to this issue. It is well known that if two stimuli, such as light and tone, are presented simultaneously (or with relatively little time between them), and one of these stimuli is then conditioned to some overt response, the other stimulus will now also be capable of eliciting the same response.

Several studies have investigated directionality in such sensory preconditioning studies. For example, Silver and Meyers (1954) paired a light and buzzer during preconditioning albino rats. For some animals the light *preceded* the buzzer, for some the light *followed* the buzzer, and for some the two occurred simultaneously. Animals were then trained to run upon presentation of the buzzer. (The experiment was, of course, counterbalanced with regard to training stimuli.) Finally, they were tested on transfer of the running response to the light.

All the preconditioned groups produced significantly more transfer to the light than their relevant nonpreconditioned controls. These results suggest that the pairing of two sensory events is capable of producing some sort of equivalence relationship between the two. In addition, further analysis of the data revealed that the sequential order of the two stimuli, during the original preconditioning, influence the extent of this equivalence relationship. Let us examine the various sequential effects more closely, and see which were most effective in producing transfer.

The greatest transfer occurred when the light preceded the buzzer in preconditioning. This sequence was interpreted as the *forward direction* in preconditioning. Let us see why. The forward preconditioning can be illustrated as follows:

1. Preconditioning phase: LIGHT—BUZZER
2. *S-R* phase: BUZZER—RUNNING
3. Transfer-test phase: LIGHT— (Will the animal run?).

Silver and Meyers assume that in phase 3, running occurs because the external stimulus, the light, produces a buzzer response in the animal; the buzzer response then produces the running, since the animal learned to run to the buzzer in phase 2. Thus phase 3 could be illustrated as follows:

3. LIGHT— (Buzzer response) —RUNNING

The preconditioning group in which light *followed* buzzer in phase 1 was interpreted as a backward association between stimuli. The basis for this can be illustrated as follows:

1. Preconditioning phase: BUZZER—LIGHT
2. *S-R* phase: BUZZER—RUNNING
3. Transfer-test phase: LIGHT—

For light to produce a buzzer response, in phase 3, would represent a backward association from this point of view, since the buzzer preceded the light in the preconditioning phase. It should be noted that, empirically, backward preconditioning and simultaneous preconditioning (light and buzzer presented simultaneously during phase 1) produced equal amounts of transfer.

A study by Coppock (1958) found similar results, though the transfer due to simple backward associations in pretraining did not reach significance. The interesting aspect of this study is the inclusion of an "inverted pre-extinction" condition. In pretraining, this condition involved ten trials of forward associations (tone followed by light) followed by ten trials of backward associations (light followed by tone). Coppock reasoned that if only forward associations are formed, the ten backward association trials should constitute extinction of the tone-light association, since tone would not be followed by light on these trials. A *GSR* response was then conditioned to the light, and transfer to the tone was tested. The inverted pre-extinction condition showed the *greatest* amount of transfer, exceeding that of the simple forward preconditioning subjects. In short, the additional preconditioning trials given the inverted pre-extinction group appeared to strengthen the tone-light system despite the fact that these additional trials involved backward associations. In support of this interpretation are the data from Coppock's "simple pre-extinction" condition. In this condition, the ten tone-light preconditioning trials were followed by ten trials on tone alone. Coppock reasoned that these latter trials should produce extinction of the tone-light association. Consistent with this reasoning, the simple pre-extinction group showed less transfer of the *GSR* response to the tone than was found in the simple preconditioning subjects.

The studies by Silver and Meyers (1954) and by Coppock (1958) support the notion that elements in cognitive space become associated. Some of these elements may have response functions, but it has not been demonstrated that such response functions are necessary for association. In this sense, it is arbitrary to distinguish stimulus and response elements in forming an association. These studies also suggest that such associations are bidirectional, though not necessarily symmetrical.

Role of the Response in Learning

S-R theorists such as Guthrie (1935) and Hull (1943) have assumed that learning is an association between a stimulus and a response. This represents the classical theoretical position in American psychology. A number of writers have tried to accommodate the sensory preconditioning data to this position by means of a mediation position that preserves the integrity of the distinction between stimuli and responses (e.g., see Kimble, 1961, pp. 216–18). This mediation position is interesting and deserves to be examined in some detail.

First, the mediation position assumes that the stimuli involved in the preconditioning each has a distinction response associated to it. If the two stimuli were light and buzzer, the light might have a minimal blink response associated to it; the buzzer might produce a slight tendency toward startle. Let us assume that the sequence of presentation is LIGHT–BUZZER during the phase 1 preconditioning. After a number of such LIGHT–BUZZER pairings, the laws of classical conditioning might come into play so that the light would take the role of the CS and would begin to evoke the startle response as a conditioned response. This state of affairs could be diagrammed as follows. At the onset of the preconditioning phase we would find

LIGHT (CS) –
BUZZER (UCS) –STARTLE (UCR).

By the end of the preconditioning phase, once conditioning has occurred, we would find

LIGHT (CS) –STARTLE (CR).

Turning to phase 2, in which the buzzer is associated to a running response, the mediation position now assumes that internal, non-observable feedback stimuli from the startle response become associated to the running. This can also be diagrammed.

BUZZER–STARTLE . . . (s) –RUNNING

Finally we come to the critical phase 3, the test for transfer, in which the light is presented without the buzzer and we observe whether the animal runs, despite the fact that he has never been specifically trained to run to the light. The light, it will be recalled, was conditioned to produce the startle response in phase 1. In phase 2, the startle response was attached to the running response by way of the feedback stimuli, (s). Now phase 3 can be diagrammed as

LIGHT—STARTLE . . . (s) —RUNNING

The animal runs to the light!

This theoretical explanation of the transfer effect found in phase 3 is not, of course, presumed to be subject to direct test. For example, it is irrelevant whether or not we actually find a distinctive response, such as the minimal startle to the buzzer, which can become associated to both light and running and thus mediate between them. The distinctive response is a theoretical construct, invented for the purpose of explaining the particular set of data. How, then, are we to evaluate this explanation? It must be evaluated against the context of empirical evidence concerning the reasonableness of the critical assumptions.

CURARE STUDIES.   A great deal of evidence from several areas suggests the inadequacy of such dependence on the role of the reponse, *per se*, in learning. The studies involving derivatives of curare are relevant here. These drugs produce paralysis which prevents the occurrence of skeletal responses (and also, therefore, prevent the extroceptive or proprioceptive stimulus feedbacks which are crucial to the mediation position). In general, these studies involve training subjects while they are under the influence of the drug, and therefore can not respond overtly, and testing for the effects of this training when the drug effects are removed.

Early curare studies (e.g., Harlow and Stagner, 1933) used a form of the drug which had anesthetic properties. These studies typically failed to find postdrug evidence of learning. More recently, forms of curare have been developed which produce paralysis but do not impair sensory reception. Using these derivatives of curare, postdrug tests have found strong evidence for learning. Beck and Doty (1957) paired tone and shock to the leg of cats while the animals were drugged. Despite the fact that no perceptible leg movements were observed during training, leg flexion to the tone under postdrug conditions was equivalent to that obtained in control animals trained under normal conditions. To unequivocally eliminate the possibility of imperceptible limb movement during training, a hind limb was de-efferentiated, in another group of subjects, by crushing ventral roots L_3 to S_4 inclusive, followed by training under drugged conditions. When tested in the normal state after reinnervation, clear evidence of learning occurred in two of the three cats. Thus the study shows strong evidence that learning can occur if the subject can receive the relevant pair of stimuli, even if he can not emit the relevant response.

Similarly, Black (1958) showed that extinction of an instrumental response could occur under the curare derivative, despite the fact that the subjects did not make the relevant response. First, dogs were trained under nondrugged conditions by pairing a tone and shock. The shock continued until the animal made a head movement. Following learning, all the dogs were drugged and the experimental group was presented the tone for 55 trials without shock. In a post-drug test, the experimental animals extinguished significantly more rapidly than the control.

Solomon and Turner (1962) showed that an instrumental discrimination could be learned, in the absence of overt responses, under a curare derivative. Dogs were trained to press a panel to avoid shock upon presentation of a light, S^0. When animals reached criterion on this task, they were drugged and on some trials received a new light, S^+, followed by shock; on other trials they received a light, S^-, which was not followed by shock. After recovery from the drug, the dogs were tested on all three lights. The avoidance response to S^+ was typically equal in magnitude to that of S^0, while the response to S^- was weak, absent, or extinguished quickly. Solomon and Turner conclude that types of transfer can occur in the absence of mediation by peripheral skeletal responses and their feedback stimuli.

CS-UCS INTERVAL. Another line of evidence which suggests that the response function is not crucial to the association between cognitive elements comes from the research on the optimal CS-UCS interval for conditioning. The optimal interval has been found to be about .450 milliseconds both for muscular responses such as the eyelid response and for autonomic responses such as the GSR. This would be unexpected if the association were between CS and the *response*, since the latency of muscular responses is well under one second, while the latency of the autonomic responses is between two and five times greater than this. Thus the interval between the two stimuli, CS and UCS, appears to be crucial, rather than the interval between CS and response, as would be expected from the classical S-R frameworks. Indeed, White and Schlosberg (1952) have cited this type of evidence as supporting the view that associations form between the internal representations of stimulus events.

Consistent with the general position taken above are the results reported by Mowrer and his associates (e.g., Davitz, 1955) and by Wegner and Zeaman (1958). These studies are very consistent in showing that the critical CS-UCS interval is between CS and *onset* of UCS.

Lest there be any misunderstanding on the issue, it must be stressed that the response functions of a stimulus are extremely important, even if the point is accepted that the association is not between stimulus and response, but is between cognitive elements which may have response functions. First of all, our knowledge of the existence of an association depends upon being able to measure some response function related to this association. In addition to this, operation of response functions *per se* is an important problem.

Backward Conditioning

If two stimuli can become associated into a bidirectional cognitive system, as suggested above, one would expect to find that classical conditioning should also exhibit bidirectionality. That is to say, if food preceded a tone during training, one should expect to find that later presentation of the tone should elicit salivation. Consistent with the sensory preconditioning data, there is indeed a fair amount of evidence supporting bidirectionality and indicating that backward associations are weaker than forward. Razran (1956), in his review of backward conditioning, reports that many of the Russian studies found such results. Particularly in aversive conditioning, Razran reports that the phenomenon is unlikely to occur if the UCS is extremely intense. He interprets this as indicating that intense noxious stimulation may interfere with perception of the CS. Another possibility may be suggested. If the UCS element elicits the association to the CS element, this association may be subject to interference from the strong sensory aftereffects of an intense, noxious UCS. Consistent with this interpretation is the fact that the optimal UCS-CS interval is longer than the optimal CS-UCS interval.

Another interesting characteristic of backward associations is that they sometimes show a nonmonotonic function with trials, first increasing in strength, then vanishing. Jones (1962) suggests that the reinforcing properties of the UCS may be crucial here. This suggestion is reminiscent of the distinction between learning and performance made by writers such as Hull and Tolman. While the backward association may have been formed, reinforcement conditions may not be appropriate for performance.

Bidirectionality in Verbal Learning

Let us return to the distinction between stimulus and response properties in verbal learning, where both the functional stimulus and the functional response typically have overt, measurable response functions. A number of psychologists have assumed that such associations are unidirectional. Hull (1935a), for example, assumed that only forward associations develop in verbal serial learning, and this assumption was preserved in his later elaboration of this theory (Hull, Hovland, Ross, Hall, Perkins, and Fitch, 1940). This assumption stemmed largely from the early conditioning studies in which backward conditioning was extremely difficult to demonstrate. If verbal learning is interpreted as a conditioning type of process, the first item of a pair is usually thought of as the conditioned stimulus and the second item as the unconditioned: With training, the subject learns to anticipate the response of the second item upon presentation of the first. Since, in classical conditioning, presentation of the UCS *prior* to presentation of the CS does not lead to conditioning, it seemed reasonable to assume that a subject would not learn backward verbal associations either. Evidence to the contrary (e.g., McGeoch, 1936a) had to be explained as due to other factors such as stimulus generalization. For example, if $A—B—C$ are three items in a serial list, a subject might emit response B upon presentation of stimulus C because stimulus C resembles stimulus A.

Recently, a large number of studies have investigated the issue of backward associations and have found that it exists in sizable degrees. The initial reaction of at least some psychologists to such data was to assume that forward and backward associations between two items represent two different associations, independently formed. From this point of view, Feldman and Underwood (1957) suggested that backward associations represent an example of incidental learning.

To a great extent, Asch's formulations have been central to both the increased theoretical interest in the problem of directionality and to the great surge of research on the topic. As was stated earlier in this chapter, Asch suggested that the distinction between stimulus and response is an arbitrary one, reflecting the technical practices of teaching and testing in the laboratory rather than any realistic appraisal of psychological processes. From this it follows, Asch stated, that the association between these two items is not only bidirectional, it is *symmetrical!*

How do we test for bidirectionality and symmetry of associations? Three different techniques have been used. Unfortunately, these are not really equivalent, and there are serious problems which surround the most frequently used of these. First, let us describe the three techniques; then we shall analyze some of their characteristics. The techniques are: (1) *B-A recall.* After subjects have learned pairs in the *A-B* direction, they are then shown the *B* terms and are asked to recall the appropriate *A*'s. (2) *Comparison of learning rates under unidirectional versus bidirectional conditions.* Some subjects learn the pairs in only one direction, while other subjects are presented with *A-B* pairing on some trials and *B-A* pairing of the same items on other trials. (3) *Transfer tests of directionality.* For example, in a retroactive inhibition study, if subjects first learn *A-B,* degree of interference can be compared between conditions in which the second list is *A-C* versus *B-C* as the second list.

Let us now turn to the ways in which these techniques were used to investigate the relevant theoretical issues.

B-A RECALL.   Asch has proposed that an association between two items is symmetrical. Therefore, if both items are *equally available* as responses, Asch hypothesized that a subject's ability to give *B as a response to A* will be as great as his ability to give *A as a response to B.*

Note that even if Asch is correct about the theoretical symmetry between items, the likelihood of sustaining this particular experimental hypothesis is extremely small. The basic problem is a methodological one. Consider how one would go about testing this hypothesis. Let us assume that *A* and *B* are two maximally available, familiar words. First the subject is taught the *A-B* association so that whenever he sees *A,* he says *B.* Next we have the test for symmetry: We show the subject *B* and ask him to tell us the word that went with it in the learning phase. What serious problem have we introduced? We have *changed the testing conditions* between the two phases of the experiment. It is well known that people are very sensitive to alterations in external conditions between learning and test phases. Keeping the material constant but moving the subject from one room to another will produce decrements in retention (Bilodeau & Schlosberg, 1951) !

Surprisingly enough, despite the methodological problem raised above, some studies have found no discernible difference between

B-A and *A-B* recall after the initial learning of *A-B;* and, in most of the studies in which availability of *A* and *B* was equated, while significant differences in recall were found between *B-A* and *A-B,* these differences were relatively small in magnitude.

Asch, in his own research (Asch and Ebenholtz, 1962*a*) attempted to equate the response-availability of stimulus and response terms by free recall training of all items prior to pairing the items. In two of the three relevant experiments reported, *A-B* recall exceeded *B-A* despite the pre-familiarization. Asch and Ebenholtz interpreted their data as indicating that the paired-associates phase re-established the superior availability of the response term. Some evidence supporting this latter possibility is reported by Merryman and Merryman (1968). Here subjects were pretrained on free recall of all items (nonsense syllables). These items were then paired and learned as a paired-associates list. Finally, subjects were again asked to recall all items. Significantly more recall occurred for the items that had been responses in the paired-associates phase than for the items which had functioned as stimuli.

Horowitz, Brown, and Weissbluth (1964) found evidence supporting the Asch and Ebenholtz prediction of symmetry under conditions of equal availability in a study involving an ingenious design, illustrated in Figure 5–1. Subjects learned paired associates

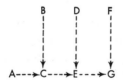

FIGURE 5–1. Pattern of Associations Employed by Horowitz, Brown, and Weissassociates lists. (Reproduced by permission of the American Psychological Association.)

such that some items served as the stimulus in one pair and the response in another. Other items served only as stimuli. Thus the stimuli of certain pair were practiced as responses in other pair and were in this way made available. Subsequently, the subjects were presented with the items and asked to emit the first two words that came to mind for each. Results indicated that backward and forward associations were equally likely if the backward association involved an item that had been a response in some other pair. For example, item E was as likely to evoke C, its stimulus in one pair, as G, its response in another pair. However, there was relatively little likelihood that E would evoke D. Item D had, of course, also served as a stimulus to E, but had never been a response in original paired-associates learning. In this type of situation, availability training for the stimulus items is built into the paired-associates phase, eliminating the problems which arise when availability of A and B terms are produced prior to paired-associates learning.

On the other hand, Battig and Koppenaal (1965) found A-B recall to be superior to B-A recall in a study similar to that of Horowitz *et al.* In this study, *each* term functioned as the stimulus in one pair and the response in another (e.g., A-B, B-C, D-A, C-D). Following paired-associates learning, subjects were given each item either in the form A ——— or ——— A. In the former case they were asked to write the appropriate response term; in the latter case they were asked to write the appropriate stimulus term. Since only a single response was expected for each item and the instructions were written (many subjects were tested simultaneously), it is of course possible that some subjects merely interpreted the task as a continuation of the paired-associates phase and gave the response which would have been appropriate in paired associates.

An even greater problem for Asch's position arises from the studies by Newman and Gray (1964) and Gray and Newman (1966). In both these studies, the degree of pronounceability of nonsense syllables, used as stimuli in paired-associates learning, proved to be unrelated to the degree of superiority of subsequent A-B versus B-A recall. Since pronounceability is related to availability, one would have expected a greater tendency toward symmetry with highly pronounceable syllables.

UNIDIRECTIONAL VERSUS BIDIRECTIONAL LEARNING. A number of studies have tested the symmetry position by making the assumption that if associations are symmetrical, learning should be equally fast if the pairs were presented in the same direction on every trial (e.g., always A-B) or if the pairs were reversed in direction on alternate trials (e.g., A-B on one trial, B-A on the next).

As was true of the B-A recall studies, methodological considerations make this outcome relatively unlikely. Again we are comparing a situation in which conditions are extremely stable (viz., the conditions in which the subject sees A-B on every trial) to a situation with conditions in which there is great instability and change from trial to trial. Given such methodological problems, it is again surprising to note how small the obtained differences often prove to be between unidirectional and bidirectional learning conditions; and, indeed, several studies could find no significant differences.

Results from these studies employing nonsense syllables are less relevant than those employing real words. As we saw in Chapter 4, there is a tendency for subjects to use only a portion of a nonsense syllable as the functional stimulus and this tendency facilitates learning. If given a pair in both directions, A-B and B-A, the subject will tend to use the entire A item as the functional stimulus and this should impede learning.

Consistent with the analysis above, there appears to be a greater tendency toward asymmetry when nonsense syllables are used (e.g., Voss, 1965; Schild and Battig, 1966) than when real words are used (e.g., Underwood and Keppel, 1963a; Schild and Battig, 1966; Segal and Mandler, 1967). The Schild and Battig (1966) study is particularly interesting from this point of view since both types of materials were employed. While unidirectional learning was significantly faster than bidirectional for nonsense materials, these writers found no difference for meaningful words.

Underwood and Keppel (1963a) used adjectives in paired associates and found a small advantage for unidirectional learning. While the difference did not approach significance for trials to criterion, the probability of a correct response following the first correct response was significantly greater for unidirectional learning than for bidirectional.

Segal and Mandler (1967) used high frequency nouns and found an advantage for unidirectional presentation. This study is interesting in that it indicates the importance of position cues in such learning situations. Following paired-associates training, subjects were presented 16 trials of free-recall learning. For some subjects, the A items constituted the items in the free-recall list, for others the B items, and for others a mixed set of A and B items. Free-recall learning was best when all items were A items or B items, compared with the mixed list. Segal and Mandler interpret these data as indicating that position as first or second item of a pair serves as an additional cue for retrieval.

NEGATIVE TRANSFER. A number of studies have demonstrated that backward associations may interfere with the formation of forward associations. For example, Umemoto and Hilgard (1961) have shown a strong interfering effect when the same item is used as a stimulus for one pair and a response for another pair (i.e., each item served a double function in the list). Presumably, in this type of situation, if the subject learns a pair, *A-B*, and another pair, *B-C*, in the same list, *B* would evoke *C* because of the forward association, and would evoke *A* through the action of the backward association. This response competition then results in interference and impedes learning.

Ekstrand (1966) points out that if associations were completely symmetrical, double function lists such as those used by Umemoto and Hilgard should be impossible to learn. Given *B* as a stimulus, subjects should be equally likely to emit *A* and *C* as the response. Such lists are indeed very difficult but they can be learned (e.g., see Primoff, 1938; Young, 1961; Newman, 1964). If associations are bidirectional, additional cues must exist which permit us to determine, given *B*, whether *A* or *C* is the appropriate response. This is clearly indicated in the Battig and Koppenaal (1966) study previously cited. While this study did not find complete symmetry in a double function list, it showed that if a subject was asked to give the stimulus to an item he was very likely to do so correctly. Position cues such as those suggested by Segal and Mandler (1967) may be crucial here.

TRANSFER TESTS OF DIRECTIONALITY. Murdock (1958*a*) has suggested one of the more ingenious tests of the symmetry hypothesis. This test minimizes the major problem found in the previously cited tests, the stability of conditions for the unidirectional subjects as opposed to the subjects being tested for bidirectionality. Further, the technique suggested by Murdock is not as dependent as the other techniques on the stimulus being available as a response. In fact, the stimulus can even be completely nonavailable as a response (e.g., a nonsense form or meaningless sound).

Let us examine the basis for Murdock's technique. In the standard pro-active interference design, subjects learn a paired-associates list, *A-B*, followed by a second list, *A-C*. Since the stimuli are the same in the two lists, acquisition of the second list should be impeded by competition from the first list responses.

Murdock reasoned that, if backward associations are formed (i.e., if the association is symmetrical) in the learning of the first list, then, in addition to the forward *A-B* association, *B-A* will also be formed. If this is the case, then a second list of *B-C* items should also produce negative transfer. A comparison of the degree of negative transfer in these two situations (*A-B, A-C* as opposed to *A-B, B-C*) will yield an index of the relative strengths of the forward and backward associations acquired in List 1.

Note that List 2 involves the same degree of absolute alteration in experimental conditions for the tests of both forward and backward associations. In the test of forward associations, List 2 involves one item that is the same as in List 1 (viz., the stimulus) and one that is altered (viz., the response). In the test of backward associations, List 2 involves one item that is the same as in List 1 (viz., the List 1 response item) and one item that is altered (viz., the List 1 stimulus item).

Murdock (1958a) reports that both types of designs produced negative transfers and that the degree of this transfer was equal for the two types of situations. Thus forward and backward associations appear to have been equally strong.

As was noted earlier in this chapter, the type of design employed here by Murdock is particularly interesting because *it does not require that the stimulus of original learning be an available, verbalizable response in order to evaluate the strength of backward associations.* In Murdock's study, it is likely that many of these stimuli were *not* very available. Both stimuli and responses were 100% association level nonsense syllables from the Glaze norms and subjects were not required to verbalize the stimuli during learning. Thus the study suggests that symmetry of associative strength may occur even in the absence of overt response availability for the stimulus member of the association, if the appropriate design for measuring such symmetry is employed. This last issue cannot, however, be considered conclusively settled by the Murdock study. The fact that the two experimental conditions produced equal amounts of negative transfer might merely reflect lack of sensitivity in measurement (e.g., too few subjects).

INTER-TRIAL REHEARSAL AS A BASIS FOR BACKWARD ASSOCIATIONS. Some writers have examined the possibility that backward associations in verbal learning are really forward associations produced by rehearsal. For example, if the subject rehearses a pair several times in succession (e.g., A-B, A-B) the backward sequence B-A will occur. Wollen and Gallup (1968) tested this by presenting material at half-second rate to preclude such rehearsals. In the control groups, no pair was followed by itself, while in the experimental groups there were three successive repetitions of each pair. The experimental groups produced significantly better B-A recall than the control in a test following paired-associates training. However, the amount of B-A recall in the control was very sizable. Katz and Greenbaum (1968), on the other hand, found no increase in B-A associations as a consequence of telling subjects to rehearse each pair by repeating it.

The control group was prevented from rehearsing by counting backwards after each presentation of a pair.

ARE VERBAL ASSOCIATIONS SYMMETRICAL?   The research evidence exhibits a really surprising amount of strength for backward verbal associations. In many of the studies which we have examined, there was no systematic advantage in favor of the forward associations; when forward associations were stronger than backward, the difference was often smaller. And all this occurred despite the fact that many of the experimental techniques involved procedural biases that were likely to result in relatively greater strength for the forward than for the backward associations.

The issue of symmetry is a theoretical one. We can not directly observe symmetry. However, to the extent that equal strength of forward and backward associations is a critical deduction from this theoretical position, the data to date must certainly be considered encouraging for the notion of symmetry and for the even more basic notion of the arbitrariness of the distinction between stimulus and response in verbal associations.

Résumé: Is the Distinction between Stimulus and Response an Arbitrary One?

In the sensory preconditioning studies and in verbal learning we have seen that, to a great extent, the distinction between stimulus and response may be arbitrary. In terms of the cognitive space notions outlined in Chapter 2, we can see that the elements involved in association are such that several radically different states of affairs may exist with regard to the composition of the functional stimulus and the functional response. For example, both the functional stimulus and the functional response may have values primarily on *sensory* attribute dimensions, as in the sensory preconditioning studies. In that case, we may not be aware that an association has even been formed unless we examine the relevant transfer situations. In other cases, both the functional stimulus and the functional response have values on both sensory and motor dimensions, as in verbal learning studies.

The evidence for bidirectionality of association is extremely strong in most of the types of situations examined. Is this bidirectionality symmetrical? This issue has yet to be settled. In verbal learning the evidence suggests that, if there is a difference in strength between forward and backward associations, this difference is not great. In sensory preconditioning, on the other hand, direction appears to be somewhat more important.

It should be noted that symmetry, while an important issue, is not a crucial one for the notion of the arbitrary nature of the distinction between stimulus and response. Clearly, the distinction could be arbitrary even if the association were stronger in one direction than another. In Chapter 7 we shall consider the problem of cognitive integration, and we shall see that bidirectionality can disappear almost completely under certain conditions. We shall see examples in which, given the last three letters of a common four-letter word, many subjects are unable to supply the correct first letter and identify the word. Apparently, the mind is capable of integrating sequential inputs in such a manner that these can be reacted to as entities rather than as bidirectional sets of elements. True, at some earlier stage in the person's history these were not yet entities, but were bidirectional sets of elements. However, once integration has occurred (e.g., a sequence of letters has been integrated into a word), these sequences as a whole can take on the properties of either functional stimuli or functional responses, in a fairly arbitrary fashion, depending on the requirements of the situation.

RESPONSE DIFFERENTIATION

There is sufficient evidence for some type of equivalence between stimuli and responses that it should not prove surprising to find a response differentiation effect similar to the differentiation observed for stimuli. A number of studies report such a phenomenon. As we shall see, however, some psychologists have invoked a type of theoretical explanation for the response phenomenon which is completely unrelated to the stimulus phenomenon. Despite the great similarities between these phenomena, this group of psychologists has attempted to develop two different sets of theoretical mechanisms— one for stimulus pretraining, the other for response pretraining. The present chapter will evaluate the competing theories offered for the response pretraining effects.

The Effects of Response Pretraining

A study by Underwood, Runquist, and Schulz (1959) is typical of the many experiments reported on the effects of response pretraining. In this study, subjects were first presented with a list of ten words for five trials and were required to free recall the words after each trial. In the second phase of this experiment, these words were used as the response items in a paired-associates learning task. The results indicated that subjects with this type of response pretraining learned the paired associates faster than subjects with no prior free recall training or with irrelevant words in the free-recall phase. Later, Underwood and Schulz (1960) demonstrated the same effect using a variety of tasks for response pretraining.

However, Underwood and his co-workers did not attribute the effect to response differentiation. Instead, they suggested a process of response availability. Paired-associates learning, they proposed, is a two stage process. The first stage is one of making the responses available. This stage, they hypothesized, must necessarily precede the association between the stimulus and the response.

It should be recognized that the two stage theory is within the tradition which attempts to conceptualize learning in terms of a single learning element, the association. In stage 1, the subject associates the responses to the general set of environmental stimuli that surround him (e.g., the room, the memory drum, the sight and sounds of the experimenter). At this point the subject simply learns to emit the appropriate *set* of responses to a global stimulus complex; during this stage, no one response in the set is more correct than another. How can we know if the responses are available to the subject? One way would be to ask him to tell us all the responses from the list that he can recall. If he can recall all the response items then we can assume that the subject has completed the relevant set of global associations required in stage 1, and he is now ready to undertake stage 2. In stage 2, the subject learns to associate the responses to *specific* stimuli. Of the set of responses which were made available in stage 1, only one response is appropriate to a given stimulus in stage 2; a second response of the set is appropriate to a second specific stimulus; and so forth.

It can be seen from the discussion above that the basic construct at each of the two stages is the *S-R* association. All that changes as one moves from stage to stage is the specification of what constitutes the stimulus (in stage 1 the stimulus is the general environment; in stage 2 it is some specific cue, such as a given word or nonsense syllable) and what constitutes the response (in stage 1 the response is the *set* of responses to be learned in the general situation; in stage 2 it is the specific response that is appropriate to a specific stimulus).

RESPONSE DIFFERENTIATION AND RESPONSE AVAILABILITY CON-
TRASTED. In the previous section we examined some data which
indicate a rough parallel between the effects of stimulus and response
pretraining on subsequent associative learning. The response differentiation position holds that basically the same mechanisms are
operating in the stimulus and in the response situation—both are
instances of the differentiation of a cognitive element in the cognitive space. The response availability position, on the other hand,
postulates that two different mechanisms are involved.

The results of several studies throw considerable doubt on the
availability formulation. For the most part, these studies involve the
evaluation of the effects of response pretraining on subsequent learning under conditions in which all the relevant responses were made
available to both pretrained and non-pretrained subjects. A study by
Runquist and Freeman (1960) provides a good example of this type
of procedure. Phase 1 of this study involved familiarizing subjects
with a set of words. During phase 2, subjects were presented with a
"verbal discrimination" task. Here, sets of two words were shown
simultaneously; the experimenter arbitrarily designated one word of
each set as "correct" and instructed the subject to remember which
word this was so that when he next saw a set he could indicate which
word was correct. This procedure, in effect, made all responses
available whether previously presented in phase 1 or not. In the first
study in this series, one of the words in each set was a pretrained item
from phase 1, the other word was not. For half the sets the pretrained
item was designated as correct, for the other half the new word was
correct. The results indicated that subjects with relevant pretraining
on phase 1 learned the phase 2 verbal discriminations more readily
than a control group without pretraining.

These results are not readily interpretable from an availability
position, since both pretrained and non-pretrained items were
equally available to all subjects: Both types of items were physically
present in front of the subjects during the test for retention. Thus
the availability mechanism provides no simple manner in which
pretraining could have facilitated memory for the correct item. The
differentiation mechanism does provide such a basis for superior
recall. Differentiation, it will be recalled from the previous chapter,
is assumed to involve a functional isolation of the item from other
items, reducing the effect of interference upon the item. Thus, if a
subject says to himself, "Word A is correct," or, "Word A is wrong,"

he is more likely to remember this if word A had been differentiated by means of pretraining in phase 1.

In a second study in the series reported by Runquist and Freeman (1960), pretraining had no significant effect on verbal discrimination. In this study, both items in a set had previously been pretrained for the experimental group, while the control group had no relevant pretraining.

Saltz (1961a) also found a significant effect of response pretraining on later memory in a situation involving response availability for both pretrained and non-pretrained subjects during the memory test. This study essentially replicated the Underwood, Runquist, and Schulz (1959) procedure with one critical difference. During phase 2 paired-associates learning, all subjects were shown cards containing all the response terms and the subjects were forced to use the cards. To insure that the cards were used, each response on a card was numbered, and the subjects were required to say the number corresponding to the response they considered correct. The cards were changed on every trial, so that a given word was coded by a different number on each trial. Thus it was necessary for the subjects to scan the card on each trial in order to find the word and its appropriate number. Despite this forced availability, subjects who had been trained on the responses alone during phase 1 learned the paired-associates phase more rapidly than the control subjects without phase 1 training.

THE INTERACTION BETWEEN DIFFERENTIATION, TIME, AND MEANINGFULNESS. In most paired-associates learning experiments, the subjects are permitted very little time in which to think of the correct response and tell it to the experimenter. Often, if the subject does not recall the response within two seconds, he is told what the response should have been and is tested for the next item in the list. In short, the response must be very ready to be emitted. However, several studies have permitted the subject to pace himself in deciding how long he needs to recall the response, or in deciding that he simply does not remember and might as well proceed to the next item. These studies have produced some very provocative results.

Let us first consider those studies that have used real words as responses. With real words as responses, *response pretraining ceases to be a relevant factor in paired-associates learning* under conditions of self-pacing. This has been found by Runquist and English (1964), Saltz and Felton (1968a) and Barnes and Saltz (1970). Runquist and English suggested that the disappearance of the pretraining effect in their study might have been due to their use of a forced availability procedure during the paired-associates phase. However, this now seems unlikely since the effect also vanished in the Barnes and Saltz study which did not involve forced availability.

Turning to the studies which used nonsense materials as responses, we find a quite different pattern of results. Here the pretraining effect is found even under conditions of self-pacing, and appears even when forced availability is used in the paired-associates test situations. For example, Horowitz and Larsen (1963) used Japanese words, transliterated into the English alphabet, as responses. In the phase 2 test of paired associates, these experimenters used a matching test: The subject was shown all the stimuli and given a pack of cards containing the correct responses; and he was required to match a response to each stimulus. This is clearly a forced availability technique. The results were extremely clear-cut. Compared to subjects who were pretrained on irrelevant responses, those subjects who learned the transliterated Japanese words in phase 1 required few trials in order to learn these words as responses to stimuli in phase 2.

The Saltz and Felton (1968a) study also involved a set of conditions in which nonsense materials were pretrained in phase 1 and used as the response items during phase 2 paired-associates learning. Phase 2 involved the forced availability technique developed by Saltz (1961). Again, as in Horowitz and Larsen, response pretraining led to facilitation of phase 2 learning despite the fact that subjects were permitted to pace themselves.

Two fairly clear conclusions arise from the Horowitz and Larsen (1963) and the Saltz and Felton (1968a) studies. First, the results of these studies are inconsistent with the response availability theory: During phase 2, subjects who received response pretraining learned faster than those who did not, *despite the fact that the correct responses were available to all subjects during phase 2,* whether or not they had been pretrained on the relevant responses. Second, these studies show that the response pretraining effect *per se* is *not dependent on rapid pacing* of subjects during the test for paired-associates learning.

The question which arises at this point is: Why does the effect of pretraining vanish under conditions of self-pacing when real words are used as responses, but not when nonsense syllables are employed? In a very general way, the answer must reside in the fact that real words are, by their very nature, already highly differentiated, while nonsense words are not. Apparently, additional differentiation of real words, in the form of predifferentiation training, is capable of facilitating subsequent associations only if time pressure is put on the subject. Weakly differentiated nonsense words, on the other hand, are more capable of benefiting from pretraining even in the absence of such time pressures.

What do these considerations suggest about the characteristics of elements in cognitive space? First, they suggest that differentiation can be thought of as consisting of two components, one long term and the other more transitory. Thus experience, whether recent or long past, can be assumed to have laid down a permanent differentiation of the relevant region. However, recent experience has an additional differentiating capacity that decays with time. The latency of a response, from this point of view, is related to the degree of differentiation of the region, and so real words which have been recently pretrained will have an advantage over other words under conditions of time pressure on responding.

But what occurs when the subject can pace himself during the phase 2 test of associative learning? There is some evidence to suggest that the answer to this question may reside in the types of processes engaged in by subjects in attempting to recall a response. Often, when a subject can not recall a response immediately upon presentation of a stimulus, the subject reports recalling a piece of the response. (E.g., "It starts with a 'b'.") If the response is highly differentiated (as most real words are) , this may be sufficient to reinstate the entire response. Thus pretraining may become largely irrelevant to the correct retention of real words under conditions of self-pacing. On the other hand, when we turn to nonsense words, only the pretrained words may be sufficiently differentiated to benefit from such partial cues.

EXPERIMENTAL ARTIFACTS IN STUDYING RESPONSE PRETRAINING.   In discussing stimulus pretraining in Chapter 4, we saw that certain experimental artifacts may obscure the appearance of the differentiation phenomenon. The same artifacts may occur in studies of response pretraining and therefore the issue will be re-examined at this point. In Chapter 4 we saw that, when nonsense syllables are used as the nominal stimuli, subjects may attempt to use a single letter of the nonsense syllable as the functional stimulus. Under appropriate conditions, the use of this strategy may prove very effective and may obscure stimulus differentiation effects. Saltz and Felton (1968a) report that a similar strategy must be guarded against in studies of response pretraining. Since the forced availability technique involves displaying the responses, the subjects may learn to associate the stimulus to a single letter of the appropriate response. When he finds this letter on the display, he can identify the response.

To eliminate this possibility, Saltz and Felton used two letter nonsense words such as *KV, KG, MV, MG,* where no single letter uniquely identified a given response. Horowitz and Larsen (1963) used transliterated Japanese words as response; as in Saltz and Felton, there was great repetition of letters and letter sequences between responses. The importance of this type of control can be seen in a study by Kuiken and Schulz (1968) who used *CVC* type nonsense syllables as responses with minimal overlap between syllables. No facilitation due to response pretraining was found by Kuiken and Schulz using a forced availability technique and a relatively short (2 seconds) time for response.

Interaction between Association and Response Differentiation

It has been suggested, in this book, that in the typical paired-associates learning situation the association between a stimulus and response is extremely strong after the first presentation. Subsequent increments in performance as a function of practice are attributed to increases in stimulus and response differentiation, and to increments in "boundary strength" of the system, a concept which will be considered in the next chapter. Another possibility is that associative strength at any given moment is limited by the degree of stimulus and response differentiation already developed. Evidence provided by Estes, Hopkins, and Crothers (1960) suggests that associative strength is not limited by stimulus differentiation. In this study, the stimulus and response terms were presented simultaneously, followed by several successive test trials in which only the stimuli were presented. Despite the fact that the responses appropriate to each of the stimuli were not indicated after the simultaneous presentation on the first trial, performance increased steadily during successive test trials. These results were interpreted as indicating that strong associations were developed on the first trial, but that performance lagged until sufficient stimulus differentiation developed.

Do similar processes operate in response differentiation? Results reported by Saltz and Youssef (1964) appear relevant to this problem. During initial training subjects were shown the list of *S-R* pairs four times; after each of these presentations of the list, the subject was shown only the stimulus terms and was asked to recall the appropriate response for each. Thus, in stage 1 of this study, all subjects had a minimum of four exposures to each response, and in individual cases as many as eight exposures to some responses were possible if a subject recalled appropriately on each test trial. Next, in stage 2 of the experiment, the subjects in the experimental group were given five presentations of the response terms without the stimuli. The control group rested during this stage. Finally, in the third stage of the study, all subjects returned to the original paired-associates task. Results indicated no difference between experimental and control groups in stage 3 performance.

Two alternative interpretations of these data are possible. One interpretation is that the data are counterindicative with regard to the hypothesis that latent associations form but are not manifest in performance until sufficient response differentiation develops. The other possible interpretation is that response differentiation had already reached asymptote during stage 1, and no further differentiation was possible during stage 2. Certainly Noble's (1955) data suggest a very rapid rise in response differentiation as a function of response exposures.

Evidence suggesting the possibility of latent associations is reported by Horowitz, Day, Light, and White (1968) in the context of a study investigating backward associations. Subjects learned *A-B* associations in phase 1. Phase 2 for the experimental group involved presentation of the *A* item without the corresponding *B* terms. The control group was presented irrelevant items in phase 2. During phase 3, subjects were shown the *B* terms and requested to recall the relevant *A* associates. The mean number of correct backward associations was greater for the experimental than for the control group. Apparently the *A-B* associations had been formed in phase 1, but differentiation of the *A* terms was inadequate, at that point, to produce a sizable amount of correct recall. Additional differentiation in phase 2 permitted the latent associations to appear. On the other hand, it should be noted that the *A* terms were nonsense words. It is possible that during phase 1, when these terms were the stimulus items, subjects merely selected partial cues arising from the *A* terms. Such partial cues might have been inadequate to evoke the *A* terms in recall without further exposure to these terms.

It is clear that the present data on the issue of interaction between association and response differentiation is inadequate to provide a suitable basis for evaluating this issue.

Interaction between Response Pretraining and Response Similarity

Two of the studies discussed above (Underwood, Runquist, and Schulz 1959; and Saltz, 1961a) employed response terms of high similarity in one set of conditions (i.e., the response terms were synonyms) low similarity in another set of conditions. Response pretraining did not interact with similarity in either study. By the end of the training period, both the pretrained and the non-pretrained groups which learned the highly similar responses were performing more poorly than the corresponding groups with low similarity between responses. However, the degree of facilitation produced by response pretraining was approximately equal for these two types of materials.

Underwood, Runquist, and Schulz argue that the absence of an interaction between similarity and pretraining is counterindicative for a response differentiation position. Their conclusion is apparently based on the assumption that, since differentiation should reduce similarity, and since similarity is already relatively low for the low similarity items, a differentiation position would predict relatively greater effect for the pretraining of highly similar items. As was suggested in the previous chapter, this type of reasoning is not implicit in the differentiation position. Consider the assumption that differentiation increases the ability of an item to resist interference from competing items by increasing the distance in cognitive space between this item and the competing items. In the condition involving dissimilar responses, the item under consideration is already relatively far, in cognitive space, from the competing items. Thus very few trials, during pretraining, might be sufficient to almost completely eliminate interference during the paired-associates learning of phase 2. On the other, in the condition involving similar responses, the item under consideration may be so close to the other, competing items, that a large number of pretraining trials are required to reduce interference by any substantial extent. It should be clear at this point that the exact relationship between similarity and degree of pretraining required to produce a given reduction in interference is an empirical, not a logical, issue.

Indeed, at this time the small amount of evidence available suggests that a few trials of predifferentiation is more likely to be effective for dissimilar than for similar materials. Under conditions of low response similarity the effect of prior response learning was clearly evident by the second trial of paired-associates learning in Saltz's study. For highly similar responses, on the other hand, it is not until the fifth trial that the response pretrained conditions begins to excel. Similar trends appear in the Underwood, Runquist, and Schulz data.

Expansion of the Cognitive Space as a Function of Differentiation

In the area of stimulus differentiation, studies like that of Attneave (1957) suggested that if a stimulus is differentiated, this effect spreads to similar stimuli so that they also become more readily discriminated. This effect was interpreted as suggesting that differentiation resulted in an expansion of the cognitive space in the vicinity of the differentiated stimulus. An analogous effect has been observed by Horowitz and Larsen (1963) for generalization of response differentiation. The response terms were either Japanese or Russian words, transliterated into the Roman alphabet. The Japanese words were all structurally highly similar and were quite different from the Russian words. For the American subjects of this experiment, both Japanese and Russian words of this type were the equivalent of nonsense materials. One group learned to recall one set of Japanese words, a second group learned the other set of Japanese words, and the third group learned a set of Russian words. All subjects then learned the same paired-associates list, with English words as the stimuli and one of the sets of Japanese words as the response items.

In one condition of the Horowitz and Larsen study, a matching test, described earlier, was used to test learning of the paired associates. This was a forced availability condition in which all the responses were presented to the subjects and they were required to match each of these with its appropriate stimulus. Subjects who had originally been pretrained on the Russian words performed most poorly on the phase 2 paired-associates task. Subjects who had originally learned Japanese words that were similar to those of the paired-associates phase performed almost as well on the paired associates as the subjects for whom the items of phase 1 were identical with the responses of the subsequent paired-associates task. These results strongly suggest that response differentiation generalizes to responses similar to those originally differentiated.

Can these results be attributed to a mediated association process of the type posited by Barnes and Underwood (1959)? For the critical generalization group, such a process would presumably function as follows: During phase 1, the Japanese words which were similar (but not identical) to those of phase 2, become associated to the general situational stimuli. Since the Japanese terms of phase 1 are similar to those of phase 2, they would serve as mediating stimuli in eliciting the latter, facilitating paired-associates learning.

The data of a second condition of the Horowitz and Larsen study seem to be inconsistent with such a mediation formulation and suggest that mediating associations are actually working in opposition to generalization of differentiation. Phase 1 of this condition was identical to phase 1 described above. In phase 2, however, subject learned the paired associates under standard anticipation conditions. Each stimulus was presented, and the subjects were required to emit the appropriate response from memory, without the benefit of a printed list of the responses. In this condition, subjects who had *originally learned Russian words, in phase 1, learned the paired associates more rapidly than subjects who had originally learned Japanese words different from those of phase 2.* Apparently then, if the subjects must rely on general situational stimuli for evocation of the response terms, similarity of responses between phases 1 and 2 will produce massive associative interference. The matching test for paired associates appears to break up this interference by providing strong stimuli for the new response (i.e., the response items, printed on cards). Since these responses enjoy generalized differentiation, paired-associates learning is then facilitated, despite the interference from pretrained responses.

It should be noted that Horowitz and Larsen found very little occurrence of inappropriate phase 1 intrusion errors in phase 2. While the occurrence of such intrusions would have been of interest, their absence is hardly surprising. Subjects typically are very effective in censoring between list intrusions, and these are most frequently evidenced in blocking and omission of response during phase 2 performance.

RESPONSE AVAILABILITY

Empirically, at least, response availability appears to refer to how readily a response can be emitted. Asch and Ebenholtz (1962a, 1962b), for example distinguish between the learning of a response as opposed to learning the specific occasion upon which to emit this response. This is similar to Skinner's (1938) discussion of the operant in instrumental conditioning. Mandler (1954) is concerned with a related problem when he discusses response integration. Presumably, a response must be integrated into some sort of unit before it can be attached to stimuli.

The present section will be concerned with conditions producing availability and the role of availability in associative learning. These issues assume some importance since the concept of availability has been used to explain phenomena in a number of different learning areas in recent years.

We have already considered the role of availability in situations involving response pretraining. In these situations there is little evidence to suggest that facilitated phase 2 learning is a function of availability *per se,* since the facilitation occurs even if a forced availability technique is used in phase 2. In fact, the writer (Saltz, 1961a) has suggested that response availability may be a secondary phenomenon based on response differentiation. In the present section we shall see that response availability will characteristically increase in situations that increase differentiation, and will tend to decrease in situations which reduce differentiation.

Frequency and Availability

Most of the writers who have used the availability concept appear to regard frequency of usage as one of the prime determinants of availability. Certainly the relationship between frequency and readiness of response emission is an impressive one. Both Johnson (1956) and Howes (1957) have examined the relationship between the frequency with which words appear as responses on the Kent-Rosanoff free-association test and the frequency with which these words appear in the Thorndike-Lorge (1944) frequency count of words appearing in standard reading matter. Quite different types of analyses are used by these writers, but both report high relationships.

Goldiamond and Hawkins (1958) report a particularly provocative experiment on the relationship between frequency of experience with items and the emission rate of these items. Low meaningful nonsense syllables were presented to subjects during a phase 1 period with frequencies of 25, 10, 5, 2, or 1 presentation. Subjects spelled and pronounced each as it appeared. Next subjects were told that they were to participate in a recognition test involving the words they had pronounced in phase 1. When a word was flashed in the window, they were to guess which word had been presented, even if they were not sure, since this was a test of subliminal perception.

Actually, *no words were flashed on the window*. This situation is particularly interesting because it permitted the measurement of emission rate in the absence of relevant stimuli. Goldiamond and Hawkins found that average response frequency for the items was a linear function of the log frequency of phase 1 occurrence. Apparently, at an empirical level at least, one can describe a response hierarchy in which the strength of each response is related to its previous frequency; in the absence of specific stimuli which would evoke specific responses from this hierarchy (or, at least, would bias the emission rate), free response probability will be proportional to response strength in this hierarchy.

A number of studies have suggested that frequency of experience with items will influence perceptual threshold for these items: More frequently experienced words will be perceived more readily at faster tachistoscopic presentation rates (e.g., Howes and Solomon, 1951; Solomon and Postman, 1952; Zajonc and Nieuwenhuyse, 1964). While these results may be inflated to some extent by the emission rate phenomenon described by Goldiamond and Hawkins (1958), Zajonc and Nieuwenhuyse (1964) show that the effect cannot be completely accounted for in these terms.

What mechanisms account for the availability effect? In many of the studies cited above, frequency was manipulated in a manner almost identical with that in the studies of the relationship between response pretraining and subsequent paired-associates learning. In these studies it was also shown that such pretraining facilitated subsequent performance. Yet availability, in the sense of knowing which responses were relevant to the learning phase, was not a crucial factor. To extend the response differentiation position suggested for the associative learning studies to the present availability studies, the following type of mechanism can be suggested. Greater experience with a given response increases the ability of the response to resist interference from other responses. The greater the tendency of other responses to interfere with a given response, the less the likelihood that this given response will be emitted. This suggests that more differentiated responses are more likely to be emitted than less differentiated responses.

Von Restorff Effect

Some evidence supporting the relationship between response differentiation and availability is to be found in studies of the Von Restorff isolation effect. Von Restorff (1933) demonstrated that, if most of the items of a list are relatively similar but several items are relatively different (e.g., several isolated nonsense syllables are interspersed in a list of meaningful words), the isolated items will be learned relatively more rapidly than the homogeneous, nonisolated items.

In the serial learning area this phenomenon has been frequently misinterpreted, until recent years, in a most instructive fashion. Gibson (1940), in her theory of paired-associates learning, proposed that the Von Restorff effect was an instance of the operation of stimulus generalization. If most of the stimuli in a paired-associates list are relatively similar to one another, Gibson argued, there will be a great deal of stimulus generalization between these. Thus each of these stimuli will tend to elicit the responses of the other stimuli, and these incorrect elicitations will compete with elicitation of the correct response, impeding learning. On the other hand, if one of the stimuli is different from the other, it will not tend to elicit as many of the responses appropriate to the other stimuli and learning of the correct response to this isolated stimulus will be relatively rapid. Many subsequent writers, working on the phenomenon in the serial learning area, interpreted their data as consistent with Gibson's position. Yet, as Newman and Saltz (1958) point out, almost invariably, these writers did not find a stimulus effect but found a response effect instead. In serial learning, the most conspicuous effect of inserting an isolated item into an otherwise homogeneous list is to *increase the rate with which the isolated item is learned as a response* to its appropriate stimulus (e.g., Jones and Jones, 1942; Smith and Stearns, 1949; Kimble and Dufort, 1955). Facilitation of the tendency for the isolated term to elicit its appropriate response (viz., the prediction stemming from Gibson's theory) does at times occur. However, this effect is usually quite weak (e.g., Jones and Jones, 1942; Smith and Stearns, 1949; Newman and Saltz, 1958). This misinterpretation of the facts of isolation appears to be part of the general bias in favor of stimulus effects that was so prevalent until recent years.

The facts of the isolation phenomenon, particularly as observed in serial learning and in free recall, appear to sustain the response differentiation interpretation of availability. Both Newman and Saltz (1958) and Saltz and Newman (1959) report that a nonsense word, inserted as an isolated term in a list of meaningful words, tends to be emitted as an intrusion error to other words in the list. This intrusion tendency is significantly greater than that for a meaningful word, in the same serial position, learned by a control group. Early in learning, the isolation effect appears to be primarily one of increased response availability, with little evidence for increased associative strength. Saltz and Newman, for example, presented a serial list for one trial, instructing subjects to learn the serial associations between the items. Following this single presentation, subjects were shown each item in turn and asked to give the first word from the list that came to mind for each. The experimental groups did *not* emit the islated item to its *appropriate* stimulus more frequently than the control groups emitted the nonisolated control item to its stimulus. However, the increased tendency to emit the isolated item to *inappropriate* stimuli was significant.

The tendency to emit an isolated item to inappropriate stimuli suggests that differentiated items have a tendency to intrude on less differentiated systems. In addition, it suggests that strongly differentiated items may be less bound to their specific stimuli than are poorly differentiated items. A second part of the Saltz and Newman (1959) study supports the latter possibility. Here the subjects were shown a list of words once and then were asked for free recall of the words in the list. (Viz., "Tell me as many of the words from the list as you can remember.") Measurement of the degree of stimulus control over the emission of a response was based on the assumption that each item in the original list served as at least a partial stimulus to the item that followed it in the list. Suppose, then, that a subject recalls a given word, "X," from the list; our best guess as to the next word he will recall is the word which followed "X" in the original list. The data showed that recall of the isolated item was much less influenced by the recall of its stimulus than was true for the control item.

These data can readily be interpreted in terms of the position that increased differentiation (produced by decreasing similarity) results in greater response emission. This is consistent with the resistance-to-interference theory proposed in the previous chapter. Differentiation represents a decrease in the tendency of other items to generalize their responses to the differentiated item. The classical generalization formulation, on the other hand, has greater difficulty with such data. Gibson (1940), it will be recalled, suggested that differentiation represents a decrease in the tendency of the differentiated item to generalize *its* response to *other* items. Were this the case, we would expect to find that the differentiated, isolated response should occur *less* frequently as an intrusion than does a nonisolated control item.

Further evidence in favor of the response differentiation position is found in a study by Rosen, Richardson, and Saltz (1962). It has been suggested above that generalization can be reduced by decreasing the sensory similarity between items or by increasing the amount of experience with the items. An isolated item should be readily emitted because sensory differentiation reduces intrusions from other items. Since the other items in the list are relatively weakly differentiated, the isolated item will predominate. However, if all the items in the list are strongly differentiated, by virtue of being highly practiced, the relative superiority of the isolated item should be reduced. In the Rosen, Richardson, and Saltz study, degree of previous experience with the verbal material was manipulated by having some groups learn serial lists of meaningful words, while other groups learned lists of pseudowords. Isolation was produced by typing one word in a list in red, while all the other words were typed in black. Consistent with the response differentiation position, the isolation effect was significantly stronger for the low meaningful list than for the high meaningful. More directly pertinent to the response availability issue, isolation of a pseudoword in the low meaningful list resulted in a significant increase in the extent to which this pseudoword was emitted as an intrusion error to other items in the list. No such increase in emission rate occurred for the isolated word in the list of highly meaningful material.

Two conclusions concerning response availability are suggested by the studies of the Von Restorff effect. First, reducing the extent to which an item is similar to the rest of the items in a list increases the response availability of this item. If this manipulation is conceptualized as reducing the extent to which other items can intrude on the isolated item, this effect can be conceptualized as indicating that the degree of response availability of an item is directly related to its degree of differentiation. Secondly, *differentiation produced by directly manipulating similarity appears to act in a manner very similar to that of differentiation produced by manipulating frequency of exposure* of a response.

Similarity and Availability in Free Recall

Some of the evidence from studies of the effects of response similarity on free recall are, on the surface at least, inconsistent with the conclusions concerning response similarity and response differentiation drawn from the Von Restorff effect data. For example,

Underwood, Runquist, and Schulz (1959) and Ekstrand and Underwood (1963) report that free recall for a list of synonyms is better than for a list of words having no obvious relationship. However, as we shall see, this relationship is by no means as clear-cut as it may at first appear. First, it must be noted that synonyms are words which have acquired, inter-item associations. Thus, in addition to the general situational cues for recall, the synonyms tended to cue each other. The effect of such inter-item associations is demonstrated in studies such as those of Bousfield, Whitmarsh, and Berkowitz (1960). These writers report that when words are presented in random order to subjects, the subjects tend to recall the words in clusters of items that are associated to one another. Rothkopf and Coke (1961) also find that probability of recall for a word in a list can be predicted on the basis of the inter-item associations between the words in the list. A word which, in a free association test, occurs frequently as a response to other items in the list, tends to be recalled readily in a free-recall situation.

If inter-item associations are the basis for the increased recall as a function of similarity, cited above, increasing similarity *in the absence* of such associations should lead to decrements in recall. Underwood, Ekstrand, and Keppel (1964) report precisely such a finding. The items to be recalled were six nonsense syllables. For the low similarity condition there was little overlap in letters of the alphabet between the syllables. For the high similarity conditions, all six syllables were constructed using just five letters, producing great overlap between syllables. In this study, the free recall of the high similarity material was extremely more difficult than for the low. It should be noted that Horowitz (1961) found results that were, over the first five trials of free-recall learning, opposite to those of Underwood, Ekstrand, and Keppel (1964). However, as the latter writers pointed out, Horowitz used only four letters to construct twelve syllables in his high similarity condition. This produced a situation in which, of the 24 possible syllables which could be constructed with four letters, 12 were correct in the list. Subjects who learned the set of four letters could therefore guess with 50% chance of success.

Despite the facilitory effects of guessing in Horowitz's high similarity condition, and of inter-item associations when synonyms are used, there is evidence even in these types of studies that high similarity impedes free-call acquisition. In Horowitz's study, superior recall of the similar list disappeared by the sixth trial. From trials 6 to 10, free recall was superior for the low similarity condition. The present writer, in an unpublished study, obtained results quite comparable to those of Horowitz. Here subjects learned lists of 14 meaningful words. For one set of groups, these words were similar in the sense of being synonyms. For a second set of groups, the words in each list were relatively unrelated. As in both the Horowitz study and the study by the Underwood, Runquist and Schulz, the similar items were better recalled, in early tests of free recall, than the nonsimilar items. As in the Horowitz study, this tendency was reversed by the seventh or eighth trial, and the non-similar lists were significantly better recalled than the similar from this point to the fifteenth and last trial. While Underwood, Runquist, and Schulz did not find a reversal effect, this can probably be attributed to two methodological factors. First, these writers presented the lists for only five trials. The reversal had not yet occurred, in either the Horowitz study or that of the present writer, by the fifth trial. Second, Underwood, Runquist, and Schulz used relatively short lists (ten items) which were almost completely learned by the fifth trial of their study.

The initial superiority of recall for similar lists, found by Underwood, Runquist, and Schulz (1959) by Horowitz (1961) and by the present writer, can be attributed to the fact that the greatest effect of cueing produced by previous associations is most likely to occur on the first trial. Data presented by Saltz (1961a) suggest that development of response differentiation requires more trials when the items are similar than when they are low in similarity. In subsequent free recall trials after the first, response differentiation should then proceed more rapidly for the nonsimilar list, leading to the eventual reversal effect. When similarity was manipulated in a way that did not increase inter-item associations (e.g., Underwood, Ekstrand, and Keppel, 1964) superior recall was found for the less similar list. This produced a situation more like that of the Von Restorff studies since, in the latter, associative structure was typically not manipulated. For example, in the Rosen, Richardson, and Saltz study, the subjects in the experimental and control groups learned the same words. Similarity was manipulated by typing one of those words in red for the experimental groups, while all the words were typed in black for the control groups.

Similarity and Availability in Associative Learning

In the preceding section we saw that free recall is greater, on early trials at least, when the responses are synonyms or are from the same conceptual category. Thus we find greater response availability due to inter-item cueing in a situation which also *decreases* item differentiation. *This situation provides an interesting opportunity to examine the effects of availability* per se *on associative learning, where any facilitory effects can not be attributed to increased differentiation.* A number of studies have shown that paired-associates learning is significantly poorer when responses are synonyms than when they are unrelated words. Underwood, Runquist, and Schulz (1959) find this using the standard anticipation method in paired associates; Saltz (1961a) and Saltz and Felton (1968a) have shown this using the forced availability technique during paired associates. Underwood, Runquist, and Schulz attributed this effect to competing associations. (The issue of competing associations is discussed more fully in Chapter 6.) It is therefore clear that response availability certainly does not overcome *all* the detrimental effects produced by inter-item competition and the reduction in item differentiation.

On the other hand, the crucial problem for response availability is, does it reduce *any* of the detrimental effects produced by inter-item competition and decreased differentiation? In other words, if availability is increased without a corresponding increase in differentiation, will availability still facilitate associative learning? Underwood, Ekstrand, and Keppel (1965) suggest it does, but the evidence is not completely convincing. These writers test this issue by assuming that *stimulus* similarity produces only the detrimental effects due to inter-item competition; *response* similarity, on the other hand, produces not only the inter-item competition, but also increased response availability. Therefore, they reason, the effects of increased *response* similarity should be less damaging to associative learning than the effects of increased *stimulus* similarity.

Reasonably enough, to test their contentions these writers conducted a series of studies comparing the effects of stimulus similarity with those of response similarity. In these studies, similarity was operationalized as nouns from the same concept category. Thus, if all the stimuli (or responses) were animal names, the list was considered to be one of high stimulus (or response) similarity. If the items came from a number of different concept categories, the list was considered to be one of low similarity.

In Experiment I of this series, both high frequency and low frequency words were examined. *For high frequency words,* low similarity produced faster learning than high similarity, and *the magnitude of this difference was equal for stimulus and response similarity.*

On the other hand, *for low frequency words, increased response similarity led to a facilitation of paired-associates learning,* while increased *stimulus* similarity led to a *decrement*.

While the latter results suggest that availability overcame competition effects in the low frequency material, *this finding could not be replicated in Experiment II.* Here the low frequency lists of Experiment I were again used, in addition to a set of new lists of low frequency. For both the new lists and the old, the results of Experiment II showed that *increased response similarity produced decrements in learning, and these decrements were again equal to the effects of stimulus similarity found in Experiment I.* It appears that the low frequency results of Experiment I were simply due to sampling error.

Perhaps the most unexpected aspect of the Underwood, Ekstrand, and Keppel (1965) data is in their Experiment V. Here they varied number of concepts in a list, using 1, 2, 3, 6, or 12 concepts. In the 1-concept lists, all items in the list were, of course, from the same concept. In the 12-concept list, each word was from a different concept. They report a systematic decrease in correct responses, during learning, as list similarity increased (i.e., as number of concepts decreased) for the stimulus similarity condition. On the response side, however, there were no effects on learning due to increasing response similarity. Since these results are inconsistent with those of previous studies (e.g., Underwood, Runquist, and Schulz, 1959; Saltz, 1961a; Underwood, Ekstrand, and Keppel, 1965, Experiments I and II), they must be examined more closely. First, it should be noted that when words were used as stimuli, letters of the alphabet were used as responses; when words were used as responses, letters of the alphabet were used as stimuli. Consistently through these studies, use of letters as responses produced better learning than the use of words. In Experiment V, a fair amount of learning occurred in all the conditions involving similar stimuli and letters as the responses. However, in the response similarity conditions, with words as responses, very little learning occurred in any condition, whether high or low response similarity. It appears that the response similarity material was too difficult to produce differences between experimentally manipulated degrees of similarity.

Future better-controlled studies may yet show that response availability influences learning in the absence of increased differentiation. For the present, however, the evidence supporting this proposition appears very tenuous.

Stimulus Problem in Availability

If response differentiation increases the emission rate of a response, does this imply that there is no stimulus control over the responses? In the Howes (1957) and Johnson (1957) studies, this conclusion is obviously unfounded. While more frequently experienced words occurred most readily as responses on the Kent-Rosanoff word association test, these words were appropriate responses to their test stimuli. The stimulus word *table* evoked the response *chair,* rather than any number of other common words which occurred as frequently as *chair* in subjects' reading experience. In the Goldiamond and Hawkins (1958) study, however, such obvious stimulus control was missing. The subjects were led to believe that a word was flashed in a window when actually no word was presented. The frequency with which a word was guessed, in this situation, was proportional to the frequency with which this word had been experienced by the subjects.

Bilodeau and Schlosberg (1951) have demonstrated that the overt environment can exhibit some degree of stimulus control over verbal responses. They showed that subjects remembered more of an original list when tested in the same room as that of original learning as opposed to a different room. Still, retention is known to occur despite radical alteration of the environment. Many of the stimuli for recall appear to be internal, within the subjects, though their nature is far from understood today.

While responses may start out attached to the general internal and external environment in the relatively free, probablistic manner seen in the Goldiamond and Hawkins study, a fairly rapid narrowing of stimulus control seems to set in relatively soon. This is seen in the Saltz and Youssef study (1964). Here free recall of the response items of a paired-associates list was tested after 4, 15, or 20 paired-associates trials. After four trials, the number of responses which could be free-recalled was approximately equal to the number of correct responses to the stimuli of the paired associates. After 15 and 20 trials, the verbal stimuli actually elicited more correct responses than the number of these responses the subjects could freely recall when simply asked to tell all the responses from the list that they could remember. It appears, then, that it is erroneous to assume (as Underwood and Schulz, 1960, appear to) that response availability, in the sense of being able to recall the relevant responses, must be present as a prior condition of associative learning.

The general conclusion which must be drawn, at this time, is that response availability *per se* has probably been overemphasized as a factor in associative learning. Response differentiation appears to be the basic variable, with availability simply an aspect of differentiation.

CONCLUSIONS

Psychologists have often thought of associations as developing between a sensory input and some motor or glandular response made by the organism. The evidence examined in the present chapter strongly suggests that this may not be the most useful way of conceptualizing the situation. Instead, the evidence appears more consistent with a position that states that associations develop between points in the person's cognitive space; such points may have values on *only* stimulus dimensions or on both stimulus *and* response dimensions. In the sensory preconditioning studies we have examples of situations in which the associated elements have values primarily on stimulus dimensions, with little or no response properties. The very existence of such associations was relatively difficult to discover, since we typically became aware of an association only when it results in some observable behavior. Only by ingenious experimentation did psychologists demonstrate the possibility of "responseless" associations.

In verbal paired-associates learning, on the other hand, we find situations in which each of the elements in an association has values on *both stimulus and response* dimensions. Finally, in Chapter 7 we shall discuss response integration and serial learning, and there we will encounter evidence for elements whose functional values are almost exclusively on response dimensions.

It follows from the conclusions stated above that the designation of a cognitive element as either a stimulus or a response is often determined by the particular context in which the element appears (i.e., the same element may *function* as a stimulus in one situation and as a response in a second situation). From this perspective, it is not surprising to find that differentiation is not only a characteristic of stimuli; it is also a characteristic of responses. In other words, differentiation is a characteristic of a cognitive element, whether this element functions as a stimulus or a response.

Strong evidence has been found for the hypothesis that differentiation of the response element is one of the factors protecting an *S-R* system from intrusion by other systems. Unlike associative strength, such differentiation appears to develop gradually as a function of practice. Also, response differentiation appears to be the basis for the commonly reported phenomenon of response availability.

As in stimulus differentiation, two factors appear to be relevant to response differentiation. These are (*a*) similarity between responses and (*b*) degree of prior practice on the response. Both these factors appear to have parallel effects not only in reducing intrusions from other responses, but also in increasing the availability of the differentiated response.

These parallels between stimulus and response differentiation strengthen the case for reconceptualizing cognitive systems as differentiated points (or, at times, regions) associated in cognitive space, with the terms "stimulus" and "response" serving to designate the *function* of one of these points in a given situation.

6 | Memory and the Resistance to Interference between Cognitive Systems

PRECIS

Even if both stimulus and response elements are well differentiated separately, the cognitive system consisting of the two elements together must acquire resistance to interference from competing systems before recall can occur reliably. The resistance to interference of a *system* will be referred to as its *boundary strength* to distinguish it from stimulus and response differentiation. The present chapter will examine the variables determining boundary strength.

Also, it will be seen that the amount of boundary strength which a cognitive system must develop, before recall can occur reliably, is a function of a number of different variables relating that system to the competing systems which interfere with retention. Such variables will be specified, and theories relating these variables to both long- and short-term memory will be evaluated. The extinction-recovery formulation, once widely accepted as a mechanism for interference between systems, will be shown to be inconsistent with the existing data. A boundary strength formulation will be developed to account for the effects of proactive interference and of proactive and retroactive inhibition.

DEMONSTRATION EXPERIMENT

The Problem

You are a messenger in a department store and must deliver messages to people working in the various clothing departments. First your boss asks you to locate SAM and JIM. You will quickly find each name on the directory, glance at each location for only a second, and never look back. Now, turn the page, find out where SAM and JIM are, then turn back to this page. *Do it now!*

Now write the correct location for each:

SAM:

JIM:

That was very easy, wasn't it?

Now the boss has a message for each of the six employees. Again quickly find each name, in turn, on the directory; glance at each location for only a second before going on to the next name; and never look back. Turn the page, read the six names and locations, then turn back to this page.

Now write the correct location after each name.

FRED: BOB:

SAM: JIM:

DAVE: HANK:

Explanation of the Experiment

How many did you get right when you were given only two names? How many when you were given all six? Most people remember the two with little difficulty. Most people have a great deal of difficulty with the six.

Note that the difficulty with the six locations occurred despite the fact that both stimuli and responses were familiar, well differentiated items! Clearly, under conditions of great interference, differentiation of the individual items is not sufficient to guarantee retention of associations. Yet, note that retention was good when only *two* people were to be found on the directory; thus the correct associations were *learned,* and the problem encountered was with *retention.* This issue was discussed at length in Chapter 3.

Take a piece of paper and jot down the items that you think should have been easiest to remember, and why you think this should be the case.

Now let us compare notes on *your* opinions concerning the relative difficulty of the items and the findings of *previous* experiments. First, Sam and Jim should accrue some advantage in retention, since they have been practiced more than the other items. We shall see, in this chapter, that practice is a crucial factor in enabling a system to resist interference from competing systems. (Despite this, many people will still forget one or both of these.)

Second, note that every name but one, in the directory, is followed by the name of a variety of clothing. Dave is "absent." In terms of the cognitive space notions of the present book, the system involving Dave is distinct from the other systems. How should this effect the ability of the Dave-system to resist interference from the other systems that have been learned?

Third, note that two of the men are in the same department. In other words, the memory systems involving these men are extremely close, completely overlapping at one point. How should this affect retention of these two systems?

PRACTICE AND BOUNDARY STRENGTH

Thus far, the examination of the learning process suggests the following conclusions.

1. When there is little or no interference from competing systems, memory for the learned response to a stimulus reaches very high levels in very few trials—often after a single trial.

2. When several systems are in competition, increased differentiation of the stimulus and response members of a particular system will aid in the ability of this system to resist interference from competing systems.

3. However, even if both stimulus and response are well differentiated, subjects may require many trials to establish a new system under conditions of great interference.

These effects are seen in both animal and human learning.

The Effects of Practice

Under conditions of great interference we often find the following pattern of results. If recall is demanded immediately after the first presentation of the material which is being learned, recall is near perfect. This can be interpreted as indicating that the *association* reaches great strength after the first trial. On the other hand, massive forgetting occurs if the material has been presented only once and the demand for recall is delayed. Practice has its greatest effects *on the delayed retention.* The "learning curve" rises gradually with practice because *practice gradually decreases the amount of forgetting that occurs in the delay interval.* From this point of view, a new

```
┌─────────────────────────────────────────────┐
│                                             │
│         DEPARTMENT STORE DIRECTORY          │
│                                             │
│         Name            Department          │
│                                             │
│         SAM             HATS                │
│                                             │
│         DAVE            Absent              │
│                                             │
│         JIM             GLOVES             │
│                                             │
│         BOB             HATS                │
│                                             │
│         HANK            SHOES               │
│                                             │
│         FRED            COATS               │
│                                             │
└─────────────────────────────────────────────┘
```

factor must be introduced in addition to the association. This factor is required to account for the increase in probability of recall as a function of practice under conditions of interference.

In the present book, the term *boundary strength* will be used to designate this particular source of resistance to interference.

ANIMAL STUDIES. Several of the animal studies described in Chapter 3 support the position that practice acts to decrease the intrusive effects of competing systems. One of these is a study by Pereboom and Crawford (1958). In this study, animals were trained to run a straight alley, with running speed used as an index of learning. The traditional measure of speed is based on *total* time to traverse the alley, including the time involved in competing responses such as stopping, grooming, and scratching. Using this measure, Pereboom and Crawford obtained the usual results: Speed increased markedly as a function of practice. However, they also calculated speed on the basis of actual time in motion—the time involved in making the competing responses was eliminated from the calculation of speed. Using this measure, little increase in speed occurred as a function of practice. The Pereboom and Crawford study suggests that when competing responses are not acting, practice has little effect on performance; the primary effect of practice, in the type of situation cited, is to reduce the interference from competing systems.

A study by Cicala (1961) is also relevant. Cicala directly measured the frequency of competing responses made by white rats in learning to run down a straight alley to obtain food. Again, as in the Pereboom and Crawford study, the competing responses were stopping, grooming, scratching, and so forth. Cicala found that the frequency with which such responses occurred decreased in a regular fashion with increased trials.

HUMAN STUDIES: PRACTICE AND RETENTION. It is reasonable to expect that the boundary strength (i.e., resistance to interference), developed in acquiring an S-R system, will serve to protect that system from interference over time. Therefore, retention should be related to the degree of resistance to interference acquired in original learning.

A classic demonstration of this relationship can be found in a study reported by Krueger (1929). Using monosyllabic nouns as material, Krueger tested retention after three degrees of learning. The base line for determining degree of learning was the number of trials required by a subject to respond perfectly on a single trial (100% condition). The second degree of learning consisted of giving subjects half-again as many trials as those required to reach the base line (150% condition). The greatest degree of learning consisted of giving subjects twice the number of trials required to reach base line (200% condition). Retention was tested either 1, 2, 4, 7, 14, or 28 days after acquisition. A counterbalanced design was used in which each subject learned a number of different lists. Consequently, a great deal of interference operated to increase forgetting. Krueger obtained a negatively accelerated curve for retention as a function of number of acquisition trials, with a greater difference between the 100% and 150% conditions than between the 150% and the 200% conditions. However, the 200% condition still resulted in sizably more retention than the 150% condition. It appears that the ability of a system to resist interference continues to develop at a negatively accelerated rate with increased practice even beyond the level of practice necessary to produce perfect performance. The most striking effect of increased practice is at long retention intervals. After 28 days there was almost no recall at any practice level. However, when retention was measured by means of percentage of saving in relearning (i.e., percentage *fewer* trials required for relearning than for original learning), a 25% saving occurred in the 200% practice condition, while virtually no saving occurred at the 100% practice condition.

As might be expected, the effect of level of practice has a sizable influence on retention at lower levels of practice than those examined by Krueger. Ekstrand and Underwood (1965) had naive subjects recall both letter sequences and word pairs after reaching performance levels of approximately six correct of a nine item list during the last practice trial. Test for recall after 24 hours indicated a retention drop of over 40%. This is to be compared to the 15% recall typically obtained with naive subjects brought to a criterion of one perfect trial. Ekstrand and Underwood (1965) plotted percentage recalled as a function of number of reinforcements for both a modified free-recall task and a paired-associates task and found a rising curve for both. With one reinforcement, only 12% to 25% recall occurred after 24 hours. Three to five reinforcements were required to bring recall to the 50% level.

The effect of acquisition level on retention is so great, that no comparison can be made of the effects of other variables on retention without somehow taking this factor into account. Underwood (1964) indicates that many of the experiments performed in previous years are uninterpretable for this reason.

HUMAN STUDIES: PRACTICE AND RETROACTIVE INHIBITION. Studies of retroactive inhibition also support the position that practice increases the boundary strength of a system. Such studies are of particular interest since the ability to resist interference is observable in a relatively direct way. In studies of retroactive inhibition, subjects learn two lists successively. They are then tested for recall of the first of these. The degree to which the first list is forgotten, due to the learning of the second list, is called the degree of retroactive inhibition. Clearly, the degree of first list recall is an index of *the ability of the first list to resist interference from the second list.*

Before examining some representative data, let us first outline the general procedure employed in the typical study of retroactive inhibition. This will make the meaning of the data somewhat clearer. In the typical experiment, the experimental group learns List 1, then learns List 2, and finally attempts to recall the responses of List 1 again. However, how could we interpret such data if we found that a great deal of List 1 forgetting occurred? This forgetting could be due to List 2 interference; on the other hand, it could be due to interference from material learned yesterday, last week, or last year. In short, we must have a control group that provides a base line of the degree of List 1 forgetting that would have occurred even if no List 2 interference were present. The most commonly used control group is one that learns List 1, then rests (or engages in some neutral activity, such as cancelling numbers or rating cartoons for their amusement value) for the amount of time required by the experimental group to learn List 2; finally, the control group attempts to recall List 1. The degree of forgetting attributable to retroactive inhibition is calculated by determining the difference in recall of List 1 for the experimental and control groups. The formula used most frequently to calculate the percentage of retroactive inhibition is,

$$\% \ R.I. = \frac{\text{Control Recall} - \text{Experimental Recall}}{\text{Control Recall}} \times 100.$$

The resulting quotient indicates the percentage forgotten by the experimental group, compared to the control group.

The data have been very consistent concerning retroactive inhibition as a function of number of List 1 trials. Therefore, only two studies will be cited. McGeoch (1929) reports one of the earliest experiments on this topic. With only six trials on List 1, McGeoch found 83% forgetting attributable to retroactive inhibition. With 26 trials on List 1, retroactive inhibition dropped to 45%.

Briggs (1957), in a carefully controlled study, compared percentage forgetting between 2 and 20 trials on List 1. Using the formula presented above, at 2 trials on List 1, forgetting was 63%; forgetting dropped in a regular fashion with increased practice on List 1 so that after 20 trials forgetting was only 38%.

In brief, practice on a system increases the ability of that system to resist interference from subsequently learned materials.

Factors Determining the Amount of Interference

The amount of boundary strength required to insure adequate performance on a given *S-R* system is not constant. Instead, it depends on the degree of interference to which the system is subjected. As we saw in the Demonstration Experiment that opened the present chapter, a single practice trial may produce sufficient boundary strength to insure recovery of the correct response if only a minimal amount of interference is operative. On the other hand, sizable amounts of practice may be required under conditions of extreme interference.

The present section will examine the factors that are known to influence the degree of interference. The succeeding section will examine some of the theories that have been proposed to account for the manner in which these factors operate.

Before considering the factors related to interference in detail, we shall briefly characterize them.

1. RECENCY. *When two competing systems are learned sequentially, the organism is constructed so as to assume that the last one learned is the one to be given priority in retention.* With the passage of time, this advantage tends to disappear; if two competing systems are learned at about the same time, the advantage in retention of the more recent system will usually not persist longer than about 48 hours.

2. DISTANCE. *If two systems are in competition, interference between the systems will be greatest when the systems are close to one another in the cognitive space.* For example, if two competing systems have a common stimulus, the systems are clearly quite close; if the two systems have stimuli that are synonymous words, the distance is increased and interference is decreased; if the two systems have stimuli that are unrelated words, the distance is increased even more; and, if one of the systems has a word as a stimulus while the other has a number or color as the stimulus, the distance is even further increased.

An interesting question which arises is, under what conditions are two systems in competition? Systems are obviously in competition if they involve learning different responses to the same or similar stimuli. For example, we know that a green traffic light is a signal to "go." If we were in a foreign country in which a green traffic signal meant "stop," we would have a decision problem upon seeing the green signal, and the possibility of an incorrect response would be increased.

On the other hand, what if the two systems overlapped at their responses? The issue of interference would be related to the task requirements. If any light meant "go," then the problem of competition would be negligible; the same response would be appropriate to either a red or a green signal. However, under different task requirements, identical responses to different stimuli could lead to interference. For example, the response that moves the gear shift into reverse on a standard American automobile will put the car in low-forward in some foreign automobiles. Here the external stimuli relevant to going forward and the external stimuli relevant to going backward, in two consecutively learned systems, may be associated to the identical response, and this produces interference. Later in this chapter we shall see that experimental data support the contention that response overlap produces interference. Thus, the data are consistent with the suggestion made in Chapter 5 that the distinction between stimulus and response may be arbitrary; *interference is a function of system overlap,* whether the locus of overlap is at the stimulus or the response elements of the systems.

3. SYSTEM FREQUENCY.   In the first section of this chapter we saw that the ability of a system to *resist* interference is a function of the amount of practice on that system. Corresponding to this, the ability of a system to *produce* interference onto another system is a function of the frequency of practice on the interfering system. If we think of practice on a system as affecting a boundary strength variable, the two processes described in this paragraph may resolve to the same basic process. Consider the situation in which two systems are learned consecutively, first *A-B,* then *A-C;* both systems share a common stimulus term. Practice on *A-B* develops resistance to interference for this system; the greater the practice, the greater the resistance to interference. The subsequent presentation of *A-C* represents an intrusion on the *A-B* system. In order to learn *A-C,* the tendency to give *A-B* must be weakened. Thus greater resistance to interference of *A-B* must interfere with the learning or recall of *A-C.* In other words, *increased boundary strength for one system must produce increased interference with the retention of competing systems.*

4. NUMBER OF COMPETING SYSTEMS.   *The amount of boundary strength which must be acquired before a given system can be recalled with reliability is related to the number of competing systems, as well as the frequency of competing systems.* This has been studied primarily in the case where all competing systems involve the same stimulus term; in other words, distance between the competing systems has been kept constant at the stimulus side of the systems. A given amount of practice can be concentrated in one competing system; or the same amount of practice can be dispersed among a number of different competing systems. Keeping both degree of practice on the competing systems and the distance between competing systems constant in this manner, amount of practice required to retain a given system in the face of such competition can be investigated. The results have been both complex and intriguing, for such studies. If a new system is presented and the test for retention is relatively immediate (within a minute or two), retention of the new system is better when practice on competing systems has been dispersed among a large number of different competing systems. It is as though the organism has been constructed to assume that, if all the competition to a new system is concentrated in very few systems, these must be important to protect against new learning; on the other hand, if the competition has been dispersed among many

systems, none of these can be too important, and a new system can be acquired with ease. After a lapse of time, however, the advantage due to recency dissipates for the newly acquired system and it becomes just another of a large number of competing systems sharing a common stimulus. At this point, interference is greater when it is dispersed among a large number of different competing systems.

5. TIME.   One of the most interesting variables related to interference is the time between presentation of materials and the test for retention. In Chapter 3 we saw that there is virtually no measurable interference acting on a nonsense item immediately after its presentation; within 18 seconds, however, this interference can build up to the point where there is virtually no recall of the item, despite the fact that the subject may be engaged in what appears to be neutral, noninterfering activity during the 18 seconds. *The potential for interference was clearly present immediately after presentation of the item, but time is required before this interference can make itself felt.*

A similar state of affairs will be found in long-term retention. If a subject first learns system *A-B,* then learns system *A-C* (a relatively large amount of practice involved in the acquisition of each of these systems), retention of *A-C* will be virtually unaffected by interference from *A-B* for at least ten minutes after *A-C* was practiced. *After about ten minutes, however, interference from* A-B *will slowly begin to manifest itself, growing stronger with time.*

How Is Interference Studied?

Before considering the theories of interference which are most currently being actively proposed and tested, it is necessary to examine the research techniques which are relevant to the evaluation of these theories.

Most studies of interference are some variation of one of the following three experimental paradigms: (*a*) proactive interference, (*b*) proactive inhibition, or (*c*) retroactive inhibition. Let us consider these in turn.

PROACTIVE INTERFERENCE.   Often we are interested in the effect of interference on *learning* new materials. To this end, we may have a subject learn two (or more) systems consecutively, and we examine the effects of the earlier of these systems on the amount of practice required to learn the latest of the systems.

We have already stressed, earlier in this book, that we have no direct access to measure of learning *per se;* we must study the *memory* traces that result from such learning. This is certainly pertinent to our consideration of proactive interference. The crucial last set of materials, whose learning we wish to study, is presented to the subject; the subject is then tested for retention of this material a short time later (within a minute, usually). Thus the critical measure of the effects of interference is a variety of short-term memory test. Successive presentations and memory tests are then administered, sometimes for a fixed number of trials and sometimes until the subject reaches some performance criterion.

The proactive interference experiment can be diagrammed as:

LEARN *A* . . . LEARN *B*.

Since our major concern is the discovery of the variables that influence interference, we are primarily interested in the conditions of Task *A* that will increase or decrease the rate of learning Task *B*. Thus, with Task *B* held constant, we may have one group learn *A* to a high criterion while another learns *A* to a low criterion, in order to assess the effect of Task *A* practice on the interference produced on Task *B*. Or Task *A* may vary in similarity to Task *B*.

Finally, we often need a control group to assure that Task *A* is really producing interference in the learning of Task *B*. For example, without such a control group someone might interpret our data as indicating that a small amount of practice on Task *A* produced a great deal of facilitation in the learning of Task *B,* while a great deal of practice on *A* produced a reduced amount of Task *B* facilitation. A typical control condition is:

(REST) . . . LEARN *B*.

If the control group learns *B* more readily than the group that first learned *A,* we interpret Task *A* as one that produced interference on the learning of Task *B*. However, we saw in Chapter 4 that this type of control condition is not always adequate. For example, Tasks *A* and *B* may involve the same stimuli being learned to different responses. This state of affairs is one that is known to yield interference. Yet, if the subject has never engaged in this type of task before, "learning to learn" may be produced by Task *A,* and so Task *B* could actually be *easier* to learn under some circumstances. As we saw in Chapter 4, a solution to this problem can consist of having a control group learn, as a control Task *A,* some completely neutral task that is unrelated to Task *B* on the critical dimensions being studied.

PROACTIVE INHIBITION. Operationally, proactive inhibition differs from proactive interference in that it is concerned with the later *retention* of Task *B*, following the learning of some Task *A*. In other words, the subject learns Task *A*, then learns Task *B*, and, after an interval of time, attempts to recall Task *B*. The *experimental* condition, in proactive inhibition, can be diagrammed as:

LEARN *A* . . . LEARN *B* . . . RECALL *B*.

As in proactive interference, one type of control group can be diagrammed:

(REST) . . . LEARN *B* . . . *RECALL B.*

Again, as in proactive interference, a control for nonspecific variables, such as learning to learn, is often desirable. For this type of control, an initial Task *A* is used which is neutral with respect to the critical variable in Task *A* of the experimental group. For example, if we are concerned with whether stimulus identity between Tasks *A* and *B* is a factor in proactive inhibition, the control condition could involve a Task *A* in which the stimuli and responses are completely different from those of Task *B*.

RETROACTIVE INHIBITION. We have already discussed retroactive inhibition in some detail earlier in this chapter. In brief, here we are concerned with the extent to which a Task *B* interferes with the retention of a previously learned Task *A*. The experimental condition can be diagrammed as:

LEARN *A* . . . LEARN *B* . . . RECALL *A*.

Again, two types of controls are possible. The first is:

LEARN *A* . . . (REST) . . . RECALL *A*.

The second is:

LEARN *A* . . . LEARN *B* . . . RECALL *A*

where Task *B* is neutral with regard to the critical dimension being varied in the experimental group.

THE EXTINCTION-RECOVERY THEORY OF INTERFERENCE

A number of writers have attempted to borrow the concepts of experimental extinction and spontaneous recovery from conditioning as explanatory mechanisms to account for the phenomena of interference in verbal learning. This position has been popular for several reasons. First, it is parsimonious, since it uses a common set of mechanisms for conditioning and for verbal learning. Second, as shall be seen, it provides a very simple theory to account for the phenomena of proactive inhibition as well as for some of the phenomena of retroactive inhibition and proactive interference. Unfortunately, some serious problems have arisen in regard to the operation of several of the processes that are crucial to the theory. Despite this, it has remained relatively popular.

To understand the theory, let us take a simple example in which a subject learns two sets of materials successively, Task *A* and Task *B*. In this example, the stimuli of Task *A* are identical to those of Task B. If we apply the laws of classical conditioning to this situation, we would assume that in learning Task *B* the presentation of a stimulus would tend to elicit the response which had been learned during Task *A*. The occurrence of this response would, of course, impede the learning of the new, Task *B* response to that stimulus. Consistent with such an expectation from conditioning theory, proactive interference is indeed found under the general circumstances outlined above.

Further, in our example of the operation of conditioning theory, when the Task *A* responses are elicited erroneously during the learning of Task *B*, these responses will not be reinforced. In classical conditioning, when a conditioned stimulus elicits a conditioned response and no reinforcement ensues, the connection between this stimulus and response is weakened; this weakening is called the extinction of the conditioned response. This extinction means that the Task *A* response no longer tends to be elicited by the stimulus. Such a notion of extinction is consistent with the phenomenon of retroactive inhibition: When a subject learns Task *A* followed by Task *B*, the stimuli of *A* being identical to those of *B*, later recall of the Task *A* responses to their appropriate stimuli is impeded.

At this point we introduce the concept of spontaneous recovery. In classical conditioning, when a conditioned response is extinguished, the response will typically recover strength if the subject is permitted to leave the situation for an interval of time, and is then tested later. This is referred to as "spontaneous" recovery since no training is required to produce it. Applying the notion of spontaneous recovery to the verbal learning situation, which we have been using as an example in the previous paragraphs, leads to the following expectation. If the subject learns Task *A* followed by Task *B*, the learning of

Task *B* will produce extinction of the Task *A* responses. With the passage of time, these Task *A* responses will recover in strength spontaneously, resulting in competition between the Task *A* and Task *B* responses to the same stimuli. This competition will reduce the tendency of the stimuli to to elicit the *B* responses. In short, it will produce *proactive inhibition* of the Task *B* responses.

As was seen above, there is a good general agreement between many of the interference phenomena found in verbal learning and the expectations based on the laws of classical conditioning. In the next section we shall examine the data more closely to see if this agreement is consistent in a fine grain analysis of the verbal learning phenomena or if it is essentially superficial in nature.

The Evidence Concerning Extinction

MELTON'S UNLEARNING HYPOTHESIS. The impetus to the extinction-recovery position came from a provocative study by Melton and Irwin (1940). These investigators had subjects learn two successive lists and tested for the retention of List 1. Earlier in this chapter, in indicating the factors that lead to interference, we noted that increased practice on competing materials is an important source of interference. This relationship was clearly found in the Melton and Irwin study. List 1 retention *decreased* in relatively regular fashion as number of learning trials on List 2 increased. *However,* they felt that this decrease in List 1 retention could not be completely accounted for by increased competition from List 2 responses. If response competition were the primary factor in preventing recall of List 1, then overt intrusions from List 2 should increase as number of List 2 practice trials increased, Melton and Irwin suggested. Instead, intrusions from List 2, during the recall of List 1, were at a maximum for subjects who had received relatively low levels of List 2 practice and dropped in a regular manner for subjects who received greater amounts of practice on List 2. It appeared that the List 1 responses had simply been unlearned. Melton and Irwin consequently postulated that in addition to competition, *per se,* it was necessary to postulate a second variable which they called "factor *x*."

While the Melton and Irwin (1940) study was conducted using serial lists, a number of later studies showed essentially the same results using paired-associates materials in which List 1 (*A-B*) and List 2 (*A-C*) used the same stimuli but different responses (e.g.,

Thune and Underwood, 1943; Briggs, 1957; Barnes and Underwood, 1959) . Here the theoretical extinction mechanism appeared directly applicable: During the learning of List 2, *A-C*, the stimulus could evoke the incorrect List 1 response, *B*, which would not be reinforced; this would result in the extinction of the *A-B* association.

CAN PROACTIVE EXTINCTION OCCUR? Probably the first serious difficulty in interpreting unlearning as an extinction process came from research on proactive inhibition. Atwater (1953) , for example, reported that greater amounts of List 1 practice produced increased proactive inhibition of List 2. *However,* List 1 intrusions, during the test for proactive inhibition of List 2, increased and then decreased as a function of amount of List 1 practice. It appears, then, that intrusions from List 1 are not sufficient to account for the relationship between amount of List 1 practice and the degree of proactive inhibition of List 2. But this is exactly the state of affairs that led Melton and Irwin (1940) to postulate an unlearning factor in *retroactive* inhibition. To be consistent, one must now postulate an unlearning of List 2 as a function of trials on List 1. It would be difficult, however, to rationalize this unlearning factor as the extinction variable conceptualized in instrumental learning and conditioning. To do so would necessitate assuming that *the second list responses occurred* and were not reinforced *during the learning of the first list.*

IS UNLEARNING A FUNCTION OF INCORRECT RESPONSES? We have seen that the extinction mechanism, as conceptualized in conditioning, is tied to the notion that the stimulus elicits a response which is then not reinforced. In verbal learning this is thought to correspond to the elicitation of an incorrect response; the bond between the stimulus and the incorrect response is then weakened by the extinction mechanism.

A number of studies have taken this general position as a point of departure in studying the utility of the extinction notion. For the most part these studies have manipulated variables which the experimenters felt should increase the amount of List 1 intrusion during the learning of List 2; from the extinction notion, it was then anticipated that such an increase in intrusions should lead to poorer retention of List 1 (i.e., greater retroactive inhibition on List 1) .

Let us first consider those studies that were successful in increasing the intrusions of List 1 during List 2 acquisition. Keppel and Rauch (1966) increased such intrusions by means of instructions to guess. While these instructions increased the emission of List 1 responses as intrusions during the learning of List 2, this increase was *not* accompanied by an increase in retroactive inhibition of List 1.

Paul and Silverstein (1968) employed an ingenious procedure for increasing intrusions. In most studies, subjects are aware of the shift from List 1 to List 2 and know that the List 1 responses are no longer appropriate during List 2. Thus the intrusion rate is usually relatively small. Paul and Silverstein were able to increase the intrusion rate by using a number of the List 1 items in List 2. This produced enough uncertainty about which responses were appropriate to List 2, that subjects increased their emission rate for all List 1 responses. The critical analysis was over those items for which the stimuli were identical in Lists 1 and 2, but the responses were different. Increased intrusion rate was accompanied by a *decrease* in retroactive inhibition. These results are clearly completely opposite from the expectations emerging from extinction theory.

Another attempt to manipulate intrusion rate is found in a set of studies by Postman (1965) and Goggin (1968). Postman assumed that the likelihood of List 1 intrusions should be a function of the degree of dominance attained by the subsequently learned materials; if this dominance is great, little intrusion of List 1 can occur. In order to reduce the dominance of the List 2 materials, Postman used *several different* lists between the learning and recall of List 1; presumably, if a subject learned several different lists after List 1, none of these would attain great strength and the likelihood of List 1 intrusions during the learning of these several lists would be increased. While Postman *does not* report greater intrusions during the learning of several lists as opposed to the learning of a single List 2, the several-lists condition *does* produce greater retroactive inhibition of the List 1 recall, and this is consistent with the extinction interpretation.

Goggin (1968), however, was uneasy about the Postman (1965) study on the grounds that it did not clearly show that increased intrusions was the basic factor producing increased retroactive inhibition in the several-lists condition. When interference is produced by a number of lists that intervene between the learning and the recall of List 1, clearly there is greater potential interference at work and an increase in retroactive inhibition of List 1 would be of little surprise from the point of view of a number of different theories. Therefore, in order to test the Postman notion that decreased List 2 dominance would increase intrusions from List 1 and thus would increase retroactive inhibition of List 1, Goggins attempted to decrease the dominance of the interfering materials in a somewhat different manner. All subjects learned *two different lists after List 1;* the dominance of these two lists was manipulated by varying the pattern of their presentation. For example, one group received eight trials on List 2 followed by eight trials on List 3; in this condition, the dominance of the List 2 responses was assumed to be fairly high. In a second group, the pattern was four trials on List 2, four trials on List 3, then another four trials on List 2 and another four trials on List 3; this alternation between Lists 2 and 3, Goggin reasoned, would reduce the dominance of their respective responses and would make intrusions from List 1 more likely.

While the experimental manipulation did affect the number of List 1 intrusions that occurred during the learning of Lists 2 and 3, greater number of intrusions did not systematically lead to greater retroactive inhibition of List 1, as the extinction notion demanded. The two conditions that produced the largest and the smallest number of intrusions, respectively, were about equal in degree of retroactive inhibition of List 1. Two other conditions produced very sizable degrees of intrusions and very little retroactive inhibition. Thus Goggin's data provided no support for the extinction interpretation of unlearning.

Finally, several studies have been reported that manipulated variables which, supposedly, should influence rate of List 1 intrusions during learning of List 2, but no such elevated intrusion tendency could be shown in the data. These studies include Goggin (1967), and Postman, Keppel, and Stark (1965). While the conditions which should have produced an elevated intrusion rate actually resulted in an increase in retroactive inhibition, the absence of an increase in intrusions in these conditions makes the data somewhat difficult to interpret. In these studies, the experimenters usually have assumed that the expected increase in intrusions actually occurred, but the intrusions were *covert.* On the other hand, a number of potential sources of retroactive inhibition exist in these studies and the positing of an extinction variable is not necessary to account for the results.

In short, an increase in List 1 intrusions, during the learning of List 2, has *not* been found to produce a consistent tendency toward extinction of the List 1 associations. Some studies found *no* effect due to increased intrusion rate (e.g., Keppel and Rauch, 1966), one study found that increased List 1 intrusions during List 2 learning actually *decreased* retroactive inhibition of List 1 (Paul and Silverstein, 1968), and another study found large variations in intrusion rate and large variations in retroactive inhibition, but these were uncorrelated (Goggin, 1968).

In this section, we have considered only studies in which the stimuli of List 1 are identical to the stimuli of List 2, but the responses of the two lists are unrelated. Some studies have examined the condition of identical stimuli and *related* responses. Such studies often report increased intrusion rate but decreased retroactive inhibition as response similarity between lists increases. However, these are more complex situations in which a number of variables are operative in addition to any presumed extinction variable.

EXTINCTION AND THE SIMILARITY BETWEEN COMPETING SYSTEMS. It is well known that proactive interference, proactive inhibition, and retroactive inhibition all tend to increase as a function of increased similarity between the stimuli of Lists 1 and 2. This is certainly consistent with the extinction position. If the stimuli of the two lists are *identical,* then intrusions of a List 1 response during the learning of List 2 should reduce the tendency of that List 1 response to be emitted during the later recall of List 1. (Viz., if List 1 is *A-B,* and List 2 is *A-C,* intrusion of the *B* response to stimulus *A* during the learning of List 2 should result in some extinction of *A-B,* and this should make recall of *A-B* more difficult.) On the other hand, if the stimuli of Lists 1 and 2 are *similar, but not identical,* there should be less tendency for List 2 to elicit the responses of List 1. In addition, if such elicitation does occur (due to stimulus generalization), the extinction of the List 1 associations should be weak, since it is a *generalized* extinction tendency (in the conditioning use of the term "generalization"). Thus, as far as stimulus similarity is concerned, extinction theory is consistent with the generalization made earlier in this chapter: If two systems are in competition, interference between the systems will be greater when the systems are close to one another in the cognitive space.

But what if the stimuli of two systems are unrelated but the responses are identical? The absolute distance in the cognitive space is identical to that discussed above, but the *locus* of similarity is moved from the stimulus to the response side of the systems. A number of studies have examined this issue: Bugelski and Cadwallader (1956), Twedt and Underwood (1959), Dallett (1962), Jung (1962), Keppel and Underwood (1962*b*), Postman (1962*b*, 1962*e*), and Mc-Govern (1964). All the studies cited, except for Bugelski and Caldwallader, report interference effects as a result of this design, though the magnitude of this interference is uniformly smaller than that obtained when stimulus distance is manipulated. The reduced interference could be due to the fact that this design produces greater opportunity for response differentiation, and we saw in Chapter 5 that response differentiation continues to be a factor in learning at levels of practice that produce asymptotic stimulus differentiation.

It should be noted that interference attributable to interlist response similarity has been found in proactive interference (Twedt and Underwood, 1959), proactive inhibition (Dallett, 1962), and retroactive inhibition (McGovern, 1964).

An ingenious application of extinction theory has been suggested to account for these data. Assume that the first list is B-A and the second list is C-A. Keppel and Underwood (1962b) have suggested that during the learning of List 2, the response A elicits the stimulus B as a backward association. Since the backward association A-B is not reinforced, it is extinguished. This would, presumably, lead to extinction of the tendency for the forward association. In addition, spontaneous recovery of the B-A association would lead to later proactive inhibition of C-A.

How reasonable is the notion of extinction of backward associations? To a great extent this depends on the place of the notion in the matrix of other information we have on response similarity. A study by Postman, Keppel, and Stark (1965) is relevant here. This study examined similarity of *response class* between Lists 1 and 2. The stimuli of the two lists were identical, while the responses were different. However, for some subjects the responses in the two lists were in the same response class (either letters were used as responses in both lists, or adjectives in both lists); for other subjects the responses were in different response classes (e.g., adjectives in List 1, letters in List 2). The results indicated greater retroactive inhibition when the responses in the two lists were from the same response class than when they were from different response classes.

Clearly, the Postman, Keppel, and Stark (1965) data are consistent with the general statement of the relationship between interference and distance between competing systems in cognitive space. Do these data also fit into the general matrix of events that can be handled by extinction theory? Postman *et al.* have suggested an extinction interpretation of their data. They suggest that if the responses of two lists are from the same response class, subjects are more likely to emit List 1 responses as intrusions during List 2 acquisition. This should result in extinction of these responses to their List 1 stimuli and thus should yield increased retroactive inhibition. However, no evidence for such an increase in intrusions was found in the study.

It appears, then, that it is possible to find some potential source of increased intrusions for the various situations in which response similarity is manipulated; however, the source of such intrusions must be discovered in a fairly *ad hoc* manner for each situation, and the evidence that such intrusions do indeed occur is not always readily available.

EXTINCTION AND AMOUNT OF PRACTICE ON THE INTERFERING SYSTEMS. The evidence from retroactive inhibition, concerning the relationship between recall and amount of practice on the interfering systems, is certainly consistent with the extinction notion. Most of the studies show that the first few trials of List 2 produce the greatest effect on List 1 retention, with further List 2 practice producing successively smaller decrements. Representative studies are those of Thune and Underwood (1943), Underwood (1945), and Briggs (1957).

Extinction theory would anticipate that List 1 intrusions during List 2 acquisition would be greatest on the first few trials of List 2, producing the greatest amount of extinction at this point. As the extinction of List 1 responses develops, less subsequent tendency toward intrusions exists, and thus extinction would develop more gradually.

Perhaps the greatest difficulty for extinction theory, as related to amount of practice on the interfering materials, comes from proactive inhibition. Here we find almost the same relationship between amount of practice on the interfering materials and retention as was found in retroactive inhibition (e.g., Atwater, 1953). This presents a problem for extinction theory since *in proactive inhibition the interference arises from List 1.* It does not appear reasonable to assume that increased practice on List 1 provided a greater opportunity for List 2 intrusions to occur during the learning of List 1, with greater consequent extinction of the List 2 responses.

The problem that arises for extinction theory is simply this: The relationship between retention and amount of practice on the interfering materials is the same for proactive and retroactive inhibition. Yet, while an extinction theory is consistent with this relationship in retroactive inhibition, it appears inapplicable to proactive inhibition. At this point we must ask: Is it necessary to posit two different mechanisms to explain the same general effect, one mechanism for retroactive inhibition (viz., extinction) and a different mechanism for proactive inhibition?

EXTINCTION AND THE NUMBER OF COMPETING SYSTEMS. Earlier in this chapter it was noted that retroactive inhibition is greater when a given amount of practice on competing materials is dispersed among several competing systems than when it is concentrated in one system. In other words, a subject who learns Lists 2, 3, and 4 for five trials each will recall less of List 1 than a subject whose 15 trials were all concentrated in one of these competing lists.

Postman (1965) has proposed an extinction interpretation of this phenomenon. If the subject receives a small number of trials on each of several lists, the responses of these lists do not develop great dominance, and thus the intrusions from List 1 are more likely to occur. Such intrusions produce extinction of the List 1 responses and more retroactive inhibition of List 1.

The results of a study by Goggin (1968), cited above, are not consistent with the Postman hypothesis. Goggin, it will be recalled, manipulated the dominance of Lists 2 and 3 by altering their pattern of presentation. She found that decreased dominance of the responses to the interpolated lists did, indeed, produce greater numbers of List 1 intrusions during the learning of Lists 2 and 3, but that this did not result in greater retroactive inhibition of List 1. Some characteristic of multiple interfering systems results in increased retroactive inhibition; however, this characteristic is not the encouragement of greater List 1 intrusions during the learning of the multiple competing systems.

Here again we find a situation where a given variable has the same effect on proactive and retroactive inhibition. Underwood (1945) reports that if, instead of a single List 1, subjects learn several preliminary lists, proactive inhibition is increased for the last list learned. (Number of trials on the interfering materials was kept constant, of course, for subjects who learned one competing list and those who learned several competing lists.) Again it would be desirable if a common mechanism could be found to explain both proactive and retroactive inhibition in a situation where both appear to be affected in the same way by a given independent variable.

CONCLUSIONS CONCERNING THE EXTINCTION THEORY. We have seen that the evidence concerning the utility of the extinction notion in verbal learning is extremely mixed. The direct tests of this notion have involved setting up situations in which the frequency of intrusion errors was increased and examining the consequence of this increase for retroactive inhibition. *Rather uniformly, such increases had no effect on retroactive inhibition.* In some of these studies, the experimenters have argued that increasing the frequency of *overt* intrusions was no guarantee that *total* number of intrusions was increased; in conditions producing few overt intrusions, the covert intrusions could, perhaps, have been very frequent. While this argument can be made for certain of the studies (e.g., Keppel and Rauch, 1966), the designs of other studies make this very implausible (e.g., Paul and Silverstein, 1968).

Several studies reported an increase in retroactive inhibition under conditions which, on theoretical grounds, were expected to produce an increase in intrusion rate; however, the increase in intrusions was not demonstrable in these studies and the writers typically were content to assume that a covert increase had occurred. Such results are difficult to interpret. This is particularly true since, in most of these studies, the manipulation that was thought to produce increased intrusions could also be thought of as increasing the amount of interference between the competing systems. This latter, rather than an increase in extinction due to intrusions, could have been sufficient to cause the reported increases in retroactive inhibition.

It appears that at present the evidence identifying unlearning, in verbal learning, with the concept of extinction as developed in conditioning is extremely weak.

Spontaneous Recovery

Conditioning studies report that an extinguished response tends to recover strength spontaneously over time. As we saw earlier in this chapter, this type of recovery has played an important role in certain theoretical explanations of proactive inhibition. It is assumed, in these explanations, that if a subject learns List 1, followed by List 2, and if the two lists have the same stimuli but different responses, the learning of List 2 will lead to the extinction of List 1. With time, however, the extinguished List 1 responses spontaneously recover their strength, leading to an increased interference with (and forgetting of) List 2.

Unfortunately, from the point of view of this theory, there is little good evidence for spontaneous recovery of List 1 over the time intervals crucial to account for proactive inhibition.

What are the critical time relations necessary to account for proactive inhibition? First, it should be noted that there is very little good evidence of any effective proactive inhibition within 10 minutes after the end of learning List 2. (We are referring, here, to studies involving a number of trials in the acquisition of a list of materials, and not to the short term memory situations described in Chapter 3.) Some evidence of proactive inhibition can be found 20 minutes after List 2 acquisition, but the effect is relatively unstable at this point and is easily lost (e.g., Underwood, 1949, 1950a; Atwater, 1953). There is evidence to suggest that proactive inhibition does not grow very rapidly within the first 75 minutes after learning (Underwood, 1949). In some studies, a strong effect has not been found until the retention interval has reached six hours (Koppenaal, 1963). A very sizable effect is found within a 24-hour retention interval, and this increases further in magnitude to 48 hours (Underwood, 1948a). It should be noted that these studies involved identical stimuli between Lists 1 and 2, the optimal condition for producing List 1 extinction.

Let us now turn to the studies that have examined spontaneous recovery of List 1 responses over time. Unless otherwise noted, all these studies involved paired-associates list in which the stimuli of List 1 were identical to those of List 2, while the responses were different between the two lists.

EARLY STUDIES. The study cited most frequently in support of spontaneous recovery in verbal learning is that of Briggs (1954). At various time intervals after the learning of the two lists, the subjects were shown the stimulus items and were asked to emit the first response from either list that came to mind. Number of List 1 responses increased over the first 24 hours after learning, then remained approximately constant between 24 and 72 hours. On the other hand, Briggs, Thompson, and Brogden (1954) failed to find the increase in frequency of List 1 responses over time, again using the controlled associations technique. Similarly, Underwood (1948b), using the same technique, found no significant change in frequency of List 1 responses at test intervals of 1 minute, 5, 24, and 48 hours after learning.

Turning to the more orthodox retention test for List 1 (viz., requesting subjects to give the List 1 response appropriate to each stimulus), neither Briggs (1954) nor Deese and Marder (1957) found any tendency for number of List 1 responses to increase over time.

LATER STUDIES: USE OF A CONTROL GROUP. The proponderance of evidence cited above suggests no *absolute* increase in List 1 recall as a function of time. However, some writers (e.g., Underwood, 1948*b*) have pointed out that List 1 recall drops more slowly than List 2 recall, over time. This, they suggested, could indicate a *relative* recovery of List 1 which works counter to the "normal" process of forgetting. This suggestion could be evaluated only by comparing recall of List 1 following the learning of List 2 (viz., the extinction condition) with the recall of List 1 when no subsequent List 2 was learned (viz., a no-extinction condition). Here the spontaneous recovery position would predict that recall of List 1 would drop more slowly over time in the extinction condition (since extinction would dissipate with time) than in the no-extinction condition.

None of the studies designed to test for the relative recovery of List 1 has reported evidence supporting the spontaneous recovery theory of proactive inhibition.

Early studies using this design were reported by Koppenaal (1963), Ceraso and Henderson (1965), and Houston (1966), all of whom used the so-called *MMFR* technique: Subjects were instructed to recall *both* the List 1 and the List 2 response to each stimulus. None of these studies found an absolute recovery of List 1 associations. Koppenaal found a relative recovery of List 1 responses at 6-hour recall, but this disappeared by 24 hours. The other studies did not find even a relative recovery. Abra (1968) reported a study involving the *MMFR* technique that differed somewhat from the others cited. Here both stimuli and responses were identical between Lists 1 and 2; however, the pairings were different. This is a situation that produces great interlist interference and a very sizable tendency toward List 1 intrusions during the learning of List 2. In this study there was neither absolute nor relative recovery of List 1 over a 24-hour retention interval, compared to a control group which did not learn a List 2.

Dallett (1964) and Houston (1966) employed the more orthodox retention test of asking subjects to give List 1 responses to each stimulus. Again, neither absolute nor relative recovery of List 1 responses was found. The measured retention interval was 48 hours in the former study and one week in the latter.

SPONTANEOUS RECOVERY OVER VERY SHORT RETENTION INTERVALS. The studies cited above looked for spontaneous recovery within the time intervals most relevant to the proactive inhibition phenomena and failed to find evidence for such recovery. However, Postman and his co-workers (Postman, Stark, and Fraser, 1968; Postman, Stark, and Henschel, 1969) did succeed in finding evidence for spontaneous recovery of List 1 within 20 minutes after it was acquired. Thus it appears that mechanisms similar to those found in conditioning can be found in verbal learning. However, they appear to be largely irrelevant to the major issues of proactive inhibition. It will be recalled that relatively little proactive inhibition is typically found at 20 minutes.

SPONTANEOUS RECOVERY AND SIMILAR STIMULI.   Within the extinction-recovery theory, extinction should be greatest when the stimuli of List 1 are identical to those of List 2; and, presumably, recovery from extinction should also be greatest when there is more extinction to recover from. Surprisingly, then, the strongest evidence for List 1 recovery has not been found in studies employing identical List 1 and List 2 stimuli, but in studies employing *similar* stimuli between lists. Rothkopf (1957) was the first to report this. He found greater List 1 recall 21 hours after learning than immediately after learning under conditions in which the stimuli of Lists 1 and 2 were similar but not identical. In other words, he found an *absolute* recovery of List 1. It is important to note that this increase in List 1 recall was *not* accompanied by a decrease in List 2 recall. Thus, the study did not support the extinction-recovery hypothesis that increased proactive inhibition of List 2 occurs as a function of the recovery of List 1 strength with time.

The Rothkopf effect was examined more closely by Saltz and Hamilton (1967). Again an absolute recovery of List 1 was found. This recovery reached its peak within one hour after learning and remained constant between 1 and 24 hours. A parallel curve of List 1 recall was found between 1 and 24 hours in a control group. Thus no further relative recovery was demonstrable after the initial jump that occurred within the first hour.

Clearly, even in the condition of similar stimuli, where recovery *has* been found, the interval of time in which such recovery occurs is relatively restricted.

THE NEWTON AND WICKENS STUDY.   Newton and Wickens (1956) have reported a study that is very interesting for several reasons. First, the data are particularly damaging to the extinction-recovery theory. Second, the data suggest the operation of certain mechanisms which may prove important in our understanding of the manner in which interference functions.

In the Newton and Wickens study, the interval between acquisition and recall of List 1 was 48 hours for all subjects. Groups differed in the interval between acquisition of List 1 (*A-B*) and List 2 (*A-C*).

This interval was 0, 24, or 47 hours in duration. From the extinction-recovery position, the greatest opportunity for recovery of List 1 should occur in the 0-interval condition, since here List 1 has 47 hours to recover in strength prior to the test for recall. In the 24-hour condition, List 1 has only 24 hours in which to recover; in the condition involving the 47-hour interval between acquisition of the two lists, List 1 has virtually no time for recovery and so recall should be poorest.

A little thought will indicate some of the advantages of the Newton and Wickens design over most of the others described above. Since the interval between acquisition and recall of List 1 is constant for all subjects, the question can not arise: Is it possible that the recall after 48 hours is really facilitated by a recovery process, compared to 0-hour recall, but that the facilitation is obscured by the "normal" operation of forgetting? In the Newton and Wickens study, we do not have the problem of a constantly shifting base line, in terms of normal forgetting over time, and we can concentrate on the interference processes.

The Newton and Wickens data actually were contrary to the predictions based on the extinction-recovery theory. Compared to a control group in which both the stimuli and the responses of List 2 were dissimilar to those of List 1, the recall of List 1 *dropped,* rather than increasing, with increases in the potential recovery interval between List 2 acquisition and recall of List 1.

The Newton and Wickens data suggest the possibility that, the longer two competing systems coexist in the cognitive space, the more they will produce a mutual breakdown in resistance to interference. This hypothesis will be examined in greater detail later in the present chapter.

CONCLUSIONS CONCERNING THE RECOVERY MECHANISM. The evidence concerning the spontaneous recovery mechanism is even more negative than concerning extinction. While some evidence for spontaneous recovery has been found, this phenomenon appears to be of such a nature that it could not produce the type of effects necessary to support the extinction-recovery theory in its broad generality. For example, most of the evidence indicates that List 1 recovery, when it occurs, is asymptotic within 20 minutes to an hour after List 2 acquisition. Thus it could not easily be made to account for the occurrence of proactive inhibition; the latter is extremely weak at 20 minutes and continues to grow up to at least 48 hours after List 2 acquisition. Second, when recovery, of List 1 is found, it does not necessarily seem to be accompanied by an immediate decrease in List

2 recall. Again, this finding is not consistent with the assumptions of the extinction-recovery theory. Finally, the strongest occurrences of recovery have been found in situations involving *similar* rather than *identical* stimuli between the competing systems. This does not fit the typical assumptions about the operation of extinction-recovery, and suggests that the phenomenon, even when it occurs, is more complex than is assumed in the attempts to use conditioning as a basis for the laws of verbal learning.

Extra-Experimental Sources of Interference

Before leaving the topic of the extinction-recovery theory, one final area of research will be considered. Underwood and Postman (1960) have proposed a theory relating the sources of interference in retention to the variables that constitute meaningfulness in verbal learning. The extinction-recovery mechanisms provide the primary source of predictions in this theory. Since the theory has been widely cited, it deserves some consideration at this point.

The theory takes as its point of origin the demonstration by Underwood (1957) that proactive inhibition can have a powerful influence on retention. From this point of view, the prior, "extra-experimental" associations which the subject brings into the laboratory should be expected to influence *retention* of new associations which he acquires in the laboratory.

Underwood and Postman distinguish two varieties of situations: Those in which the letter sequences are the crucial unit of analysis and those in which word sequences are the crucial unit.

LETTER SEQUENCE HYPOTHESIS. Let us first consider the letter sequence hypothesis. Sequential probabilities between letters vary considerably. In English q-u is a high probability sequence. If the subject is required to learn q-b, it is assumed that he must first extinguish the u response to q. With the passage of time after acquisition of q-b, u should spontaneously recover and interfere with the retention of q-b. On the other hand, if the letter sequence which is to be learned is already well integrated, very little extinction of prior letter contingencies is involved. If little extinction of prior letter contingencies occurs, there is little likelihood of spontaneous recovery of prior letter sequences which could interfere with retention. The letter sequence hypothesis therefore predicts that forgetting will be greater for low meaningful, unintegrated units than for more meaningful, well integrated units.

THE WORD SEQUENCE HYPOTHESIS. The prediction for word sequence units is based on the same mechanism, but the specific prediction is somewhat different. If a word is meaningful (e.g., frequent in the language), it should have strong associates which must be extinguished before the word can be associated to a new response. Spontaneous recovery of the prior associate should lead to forgetting of the new association. On the other hand, a less meaningful word should have weaker associations to prior words. Thus little extinction and spontaneous recovery of such prior words should occur to produce forgetting. The prediction for word sequences is that more forgetting will occur for highly meaningful words than for low meaningful words.

THE EVIDENCE. Results of a number of studies are consistent in providing scant support for the Underwood and Postman position. Postman (1961) constructed serial lists of words which had Thorndike-Lorge values of either 1–3 or 1000–3300 occurrences per 4.5 million words in the language. All subjects were brought to a criterion of one perfect trial. Meaningfulness, as indexed by Thorndike-Lorge frequency, had no significant effect on recall at either 2- or 7-days after learning. In a second serial learning study, Postman (1962d) taught subjects three lists and tested for retention of the third list after 30 seconds, 30 minutes, and 7 days. He found no significant difference in the retention of high versus low frequency lists. Postman (1962c), in a study cited previously, also tested for retention of paired associates in which stimuli and responses were independently varied in Thorndike-Lorge frequency. For the groups which were tested 7 days after learning, the high and medium frequency stimuli were equally effective in eliciting their correct responses and were significantly superior to the low frequency stimuli. These differences are opposite in direction from those predicted by the extinction-recovery theory. It should be noted that, since learning was slower for the low stimulus frequency material than for the material of higher stimulus frequency, some overlearning of items no doubt occurred in the low frequency condition. However, such overlearning should act primarily to increase retention of the low frequency material, and so the comparison made is actually a conservative one.

Ekstrand and Underwood (1965) tested the word unit hypothesis in a free learning situation. Subjects were presented word pairs and were tested on trials in which the pairs were to be recalled in any order. For one group, both words in each pair were high frequency on the Thorndike-Lorge scale, for another group both words were low frequency. The two words in each pair were unrelated. Subjects were trained to approximately six correct of nine pairs. Retention was analyzed in a manner which corrected for differences in learning rates between materials. As was true in the Postman studies, no evidence for differential forgetting between high and low frequency material was found.

The results of tests for letter sequence effects have been equally discouraging for the theory. The paper in which the theory was originally proposed (Underwood and Postman, 1960) presented some tentative data which, for the most part, showed no differences in retention of well-integrated versus less-integrated materials. A more definitive study is reported by Underwood and Keppel (1963c). Paired associates consisting of single letter stimuli and single letter responses were employed. For one group the pre-experimental association between the two letters was high, for another group the pre-experimental association was low. The letter sequence prediction was that retention would be better for the pre-experimentally integrated sequences. No differences in 1- or 7-day retention were found for the two types of materials. Ekstrand and Underwood (1965) tested the letter sequence hypothesis in a free-learning, free-recall situation in which subjects were presented items consisting of two letters, and were required to recall both letters of each item in free recall. Again, no difference in 24-hour retention occurred between initially well integrated sequences and initially poorly integrated sequences when degree of learning, prior to the retention interval, was equated for these materials.

Underwood and Keppel (1963c) conclude that there is no evidence for either the word sequence or the letter sequence hypothesis. Since these hypotheses were based on the extinction-recovery mechanism, this conclusion is not too surprising, when we consider the negative nature of the evidence, summarized earlier in this chapter, concerning the relevance of extinction and spontaneous recovery for the major issues of interference and retention in the area of verbal learning.

UNLEARNING AND ASSOCIATIVE COMPETITION

In the preceding sections it was seen that extinction mechanisms have severe problems in accounting for unlearning. Similarly, a single factor competition position (McGeoch, 1936b; Wendt, 1936) is difficult to defend. Such a position would hold that if a subject learned two systems involving identical stimuli but different responses (system *A-B* followed by system *A-C*), subsequent presentation of the stimulus would lead to a situation in which the two responses would compete for elicitation. Further, the relative strengths of the *A-B* versus the *A-C* associations would determine which of the two responses would be emitted. Presumably, from this point of view, if the two systems were equal in strength, response conflict might result in neither response being given.

Several lines of evidence suggest that this view is too simple and that other processes must be involved. One source of difficulty for the single variable, response interference position comes from studies of the relative strength of List 1 versus List 2 systems immediately after List 2 acquisition (in other words, studies of retroactive inhibition). These studies indicate that recall of List 1 is typically much lower than that of List 2, even if both have been equally practiced. Briggs (1957) for example had subjects learn two lists successively, then presented each stimulus and requested subjects to give whichever response, the one from List 1 or the one from List 2, that came to mind first. With five learning trials on each list, subjects emitted a mean of 2.25 List 1 responses, 3.5 List 2 responses. With 10 learning trials on each list, the respective means were 2.06 and 6.5 responses. With 20 learning trials on each, the respective means were 2.25 and 6.44. Only in the condition in which only two learning trials had been given to each list were the number of emissions approximately equal for List 1 and List 2 responses.

Another source of difficulty for the simple competition notion comes from studies such as Koppenaal (1963), reviewed earlier in this chapter, on the temporal course of retroactive and proactive inhibition. These studies indicate that if subjects learn two lists successively, recall of List 1 drops very gradually with time, while recall of List 2 drops much more sharply. In short, order of acquisition is a factor in the interaction between two *S-R* systems.

The pattern of recall over time when the stimuli of the two lists are *similar*, but not identical, is even more damaging to the simple competition notion. Here an actual *rise* occurs in List 1 recall in the hour following List 2 acquisition (Rothkopf, 1957; Saltz and Hamilton, 1967). From the point of view of a simple associative competition notion, this could occur only if the competing List 2 associations dropped in strength over the interval. Rothkopf, however, found no such drop in List 2 recall.

THE GUTHRIE ASSUMPTION. Guthrie (1935) has proposed a variation of the competition position. Instead of assuming that *A-B* and

A-C are two coexisting *S-R* systems whose associations compete, Guthrie assumed that the learning of a new response to a stimulus breaks the previously learned associations. This position could account for the superior recall of List 2 responses after List 2 acquisition in the studies by Briggs (1957) and others. However, it does not appear capable of handling the temporal changes in recall, particularly in the studies involving similar but not identical stimuli between lists.

Nor does the Guthrie assumption appear capable of explaining the great instability of both proactive and retroactive inhibition. Both types of inhibition disappear very quickly during relearning, their effects being restricted largely to the first recall trial (e.g., Thune and Underwood, 1943, for retroactive inhibition; Atwater, 1953, for proactive inhibition). Such results make it difficult to defend the position that learning List 2 (*A-C*) destroys the previously acquired List 1 associations (*A-B*).

It is interesting to note that the instability of unlearning is also a characteristic of instrumental learning in the white rat. The phenomenon of spontaneous recovery is one example of such instability. Also, after the extinction of a response, the reintroduction of reinforcement often leads to relearning in many fewer trials than were necessary for original learning.

UNLEARNING AS A BREAKDOWN
IN BOUNDARY STRENGTH

In this chapter, we have reviewed a great deal of evidence concerning the laws of interference between competing systems, and we have examined some of the theories which have attempted to account for these laws. As we have seen, these theories are not well supported by the data. At this point we shall try to re-evaluate the data, and shall attempt to determine more adequate directions for future theories.

Reciprocal Breakdown of Two Competing Systems

Earlier in this chapter it was suggested that learning trials operate to increase the ability of an *S-R* system to resist interference from competing systems (i.e., practice increases the boundary strength of an *S-R* system). From this point of view, the unlearning data suggest that if two competing systems are acquired successively, the second system breaks down the boundary strength of the first. Further, we shall see later in this chapter that this tendency for one system to break down the boundary strength of another is a reciprocal one; the first learned system also shows a tendency to break down the boundary strength of the second system. The mechanics of the breakdown notion can be described in the following general manner. If an *S-R* system is inserted into the cognitive space close to a competing system, the insertion of this new system will lead to a breakdown in the boundary strength of earlier system. The amount of this breakdown will be a function of (*a*) the distance in the cognitive space between the two competing systems, with greater breakdown accompanying smaller distances; (*b*) the initial boundary strength of the first system before the introduction of the second system, with stronger systems more resistant to interference from new systems; (*c*) the degree of boundary strength of the new, competing system, with greater boundary strength of the new system leading to greater breakdown in the old system.

The initial impact produced by the introduction of a new system into the cognitive space is a relatively sharp breakdown of the older systems in the space, with little immediate detrimental effect on the new system. However, evidence to be presented shortly will show that this particular relationship between the strengths of old and the new systems is a temporary one; the interaction between systems in cognitive space is not static over time.

THE SIGNIFICANCE OF LIST 2 INTRUSIONS DURING THE RECALL OF LIST 1. If unlearning represents a breakdown in resistance to interference, one would expect that an increase in practice on List 2 (*A-C*) should be accompanied by two simultaneous effects: Recall of List 1 (*A-B*) should *decrease;* List 2 intrusions during the recall of List 1 should *increase.* As we have seen, the systematic increase in intrusions does not occur. Indeed, it was the failure of this increase to be found in studies such as Melton and Irwin (1940) that originally led to the positing of an extinction mechanism. The data clearly show that the greatest tendency toward List 2 intrusions occurs at intermediate levels of List 2 strength. When List 2 has been greatly practiced, *recall* of List 1 is minimal; however, List 2 *intrusions* during the recall of List 1 *are also minimal.*

Underwood (1949, 1950*b*) has proposed a "list differentiation" notion that seems adequate to account for the drop in List 2 intrusions at high levels of List 2 practice. It is well known that subjects can suppress strong competing responses which they know to be incorrect. In List 2 (*A-C*) learning, for example, it is rare to find any List 1 (*A-B*) intrusions, even on the first trial. Thus, as number of List 2 trials increases, subjects should be better able to differentiate the responses appropriate to List 2 from the responses appropriate to List 1, and to suppress the former in recalling the latter.

Time: The Dynamic Interaction between Competing Systems

There is evidence to suggest that a spread of responses may occur between two competing systems as a function of time—a process similar to the osmotic process found between living cells. This process appears to operate so as to break down the boundary strengths of *both* competing systems. As shall be seen, this process shows promise for explaining the increase in proactive inhibition that occurs with the passage of time.

The first evidence for such an osmotic function comes from a study by Newton and Wickens (1956) cited earlier in this chapter. A somewhat similar study by Postman, Stark, and Henschel (1969) supports the conclusions to be drawn from Newton and Wickens. Additional evidence comes from a study by Saltz and Asdourian (1963) which will be described in the next section of this chapter.

OSMOTIC EFFECTS IN RETROACTIVE INHIBITION. The Newton and Wickens (1956) study examined retroactive inhibition as a function of the length of time in which competing systems coexisted in the cognitive space. They found that, compared to a control condition, List 1 recall was systematically poorer, the longer the List 1 and List 2 systems coexisted in cognitive space.

The Postman, Stark, and Henschel (1969) data support the conclusion which we have drawn from the Newton and Wickens (1956) study. This is particularly interesting since the Postman *et al.* study involved testing for List 1 recall only 20 minutes after acquisition of List 2—an interval that produces spontaneous recovery of List 1. As in the Newton and Wickens study, Postman and his co-workers employed an *A-B, D-C* group (i.e., Lists 1 and 2 were dissimilar in both stimulus and response terms) which we can use as a base line against which to evaluate the effects of time in the *A-B, A-C* experimental conditions. The short period of coexistence was about 2 minutes, the long period was about 18 minutes.

Let us first consider the conditions in which *List 1 was learned to a relatively low criterion*. Here it was found that increased interval of coexistence between Lists 1 and 2 led to a relative drop in List 1 recall for the *A-B, A-C* condition as compared to the *A-B, D-C* condition. More specifically, after the short interval of coexistence (viz., 2 minutes), the amount of recall was relatively similar for the *A-B, A-C* condition and the *A-B, D-C* condition; at the longer interval

(18 minutes), the List 1 recall was superior in the *A-B, D-C* condition. This relationship was found in two experiments reported by Postman *et al.* (1969).

In two other experiments, reported in the same paper, *List 1 was learned to a relatively high criterion.* (I.e., the boundary strength of the List 1 systems was greater in these experiments than in the ones cited earlier.) In these experiments the relative drop in List 1 recall, as a function of increased period of coexistence, did not occur.

Thus, the Postman, Stark, and Henschel (1969) data indicate that *osmosis between competing systems,* as a function of duration of coexistence, *is related to the amount of boundary strength of the systems.* Apparently, introduction of a competing system into the cognitive space produces a sharp breakdown in boundary strength; however, if this breakdown is not asymptotic, a further deterioration in boundary strength can occur over time through the operation of the osmotic-like process.

OSMOTIC EFFECTS IN PROACTIVE INHIBITION.   An osmotic, spread-of-response notion is consistent with the phenomena of proactive inhibition. As a function of time, responses from a List 1 set of systems intrude onto the List 2 systems, producing a breakdown in the boundary strength of the List 2 systems and weakening their likelihood of recall. From this position we would expect proactive inhibition to be great when List 1 has been well practiced, and to be small when List 2 is well practiced. The data reviewed earlier in this chapter support these expectations.

Another advantage of the notion of an osmotic spread over time is that it does not assume the spontaneous recovery of List 1 responses over time. Thus the failure of spontaneous recovery to occur in many proactive inhibition situations is not relevant to the notion of an osmotic spread. On the other hand, while the notion fits the proactive inhibition data very well, it is largely *post hoc* with regard to these data. For this reason, evidence relevant to the osmotic mechanism was sought in the area of retroactive inhibition earlier in this chapter; and, in the succeeding section evidence will be sought in the area of anxiety provoked behavior.

Osmotic Spread versus Incubation of Anxiety

Saltz and Asdourian (1963) report an attempt to investigate the osmotic spread mechanism in a situation as removed from paired-associates human learning as possible. An examination of the literature suggested that the osmotic spread mechanism might be the basis of an effect called "incubation" by Diven (1937). Thus, it was in the context of the incubation effect that the Saltz and Asdourian study was undertaken.

Diven (1937) reported that a *GSR*, conditioned to a verbal stimulus, tended to increase in intensity as a function of time after conditioning. Presentations of the stimulus 1 hour, 24 hours, and 48 hours after conditioning tended to elicit progressively stronger *GSR*'s. Diven suggested that the anxiety response to the verbal stimulus incubated and grew with time—hence the "incubation effect." Evidence interpreted as supporting the Diven incubation explanation has been reported by Bindra and Cameron (1953), Mednick (1957), and Golin (1961). However, Saltz and Asdourian noted that the reported increases in anxiety with time occurred only in situations where careful controls were absent for distinguishing between an *increase in the intensity* of the response, as opposed to an osmotic *spread* of the response from one cognitive system to another. In Diven's study, for example, subjects were presented with verbal stimuli (i.e., meaningful words) and instructed to free associate to each of these words. Subjects were shocked 12 seconds after the presentation of a key word. Since 12 seconds between *CS* and shock is known to be too long an interval for good anxiety conditioning, it appears reasonable to assume that the real conditioned stimulus was not the key word presented by Diven; instead, it was the free association emitted by the subject immediately prior to shock. Since the free associates were in a chain initiated by the key word, they should in most cases have overlapped with this word in similarity. Consequently, the possibility existed that the increase in *GSR* to the presented stimulus, as a function of time, represented a spread of response from the "real" *CS* (viz., the free association emitted by the subject immediately before shock) to the originally presented stimulus. The same interpretation is applicable to the Bindra and Cameron (1953) and Golin (1961) studies, both of which employed a 15 second *CS-UCS* interval with subjects emitting responses during the interval. This interpretation is consistent with Mednick's (1957) results. She also employed *GSR* conditioning, but used a more adequate three-second *CS-UCS* interval. Mednick found no increase in *GSR* intensity to the training words, with time following conditioning. However, she did find a significant incubation to stimuli *similar to* the training *CS*.

Saltz and Asdourian (1963) reasoned that if the incubation effect represents a spread of response between *S-R* systems as function of time, no such effect should be observed if only a simple *S-R* system were involved—i.e., if the response were first acquired and then tested in the same stimulus situation. On the other hand, if the training and test stimuli were similar (i.e., close in cognitive space), a spread of response from one system to another could occur with the passage of time. To test this formulation, white rats were pretrained to run a straight alley for food. After reaching asymptotic speeds, the animals were placed directly into either the original goal box or a goal box which differed from the original only in color, and a strong electric shock was administered. The animals were then tested for avoidance behavior in the original alley, either 1- or 22-hours after shock.

The results were consistent with a spread of response formulation. For animals which were shocked and tested in the same apparatus, there was no difference in performance between the groups tested 1- and 22-hours after shock. Both groups exhibited massive avoidance behavior. However, when the shock apparatus was different from the subsequent test apparatus (though similar to it) the group tested 22 hours after shock displayed significantly more avoidance of the goal box than the group tested one hour after shock.

A second aspect of the Saltz and Asdourian data was even more dramatic. Subjects can be assumed to exhibit consistent individual differences in boundary strength. It follows from this that subjects who form strong boundaries should show less spread of response than subjects who form weaker boundaries. An index of boundary strength could be found in the Saltz and Asdourian study, based on the rationale of the previously cited study (see Chapter 3) by Saltz, Whitman, and Paul (1963). In the latter study, it was shown that performance in a runway involves the differentiation between two *S-R* systems: In the alley the animal must run, but in the goal box he must stop running. The greater the interference from the goal box responses, the slower the animal will run in the alley. Consequently, asymptotic runway speeds prior to shock should serve as an index of boundary strength. As a test of the effect of individual differences, animals in the groups tested 1- and 22-hours after shock were matched on asymptotic runway speeds. Consistent with the individual differences formulation, the greatest difference in avoidance behavior between 1- and 22-hour groups appeared in animals whose preshock asymptotic speeds were slowest. For the matched subjects, the correlation between the preshock index of boundary strength and the difference in avoidance between the 1- and 22-hour subjects was —.69, a highly significant relationship.

Support for the conceptualization of the incubation effect as a spread of response occurring during the passage of time is found in a study by McAllister and McAllister (1962). Animals in this study were first given a series of shocks in one box, then placed in a similar box from which they could escape by jumping a hurdle. The animals were never shocked in this second box, and so avoidance tendencies shown here must represent transfer from the original apparatus. When tested in the hurdle-jumping apparatus on the same day in which they had been shocked, the experimental group jumped the hurdle no sooner than a control group. However, if placed in the hurdle apparatus the day after shock, the experimental group jumped the hurdle to escape from the box much more readily than the control group.

The studies cited above uniformly utilized an anxiety response of some sort. However, data reported by Perkins and Weyant (1958) indicate that the spread of response from one system to another is not restricted to anxiety responses. Perkins and Weyant trained animals to run for food in an alley painted one color (e.g., white); the animals were then tested either in the same alley or in one painted a different color (e.g., black). Nonreinforced test trials began immediately after training for half the subjects, a week after training for the remaining subjects. Results indicated that, when tested immediately after training, running speed was significantly faster for subjects trained and tested on the same color alley than for subjects trained on one color and tested on another. For subjects tested a week after training, no such decrement occurred as a function of stimulus change. Even more crucial, subjects tested in an altered alley a week after original training performed *better* than subjects tested in the altered alley immediately after training.

Perkins and Weyant interpret their data as indicating that generalization increases as a function of time. Operationally, of course, this is equivalent to saying that responses spread from one system to another as a function of time. At present, at least, a conceptualization of this phenomenon in terms of boundary strength seems preferable to a generalization formulation, since the boundary strength notion can account for the individual differences data reported by Saltz and Asdourian (1963), as well as providing a basis for explaining proactive inhibition in verbal learning.

It might be noted that the osmotic spread between systems bares certain similarities to an often observed clinical phenomenon. In a fairly large percentage of cases, phobic reactions, which were originally fairly circumscribed, gradually spread to more and more situations until the patients' anxiety-free sphere is extremely limited. The extent to which the basic mechanisms in such cases are related to the mechanisms under discussion in the present section is, of course, not known. However, it is interesting to speculate that the tendency for such spread in phobic anxiety is related to the individual differences in boundary strength found in the Saltz and Asdourian study.

OVERLEARNING: FROM ASSOCIATION TO STRUCTURE?

It has been seen, in this chapter, that with increased practice a system tends to exhibit greater ability to resist interference from competing systems. A related issue has arisen in the literature. Will a strongly acquired system tend *not* to interfere with *other* systems close to it in the cognitive space? Several studies have suggested the operation of such a mechanism. These are primarily animal studies involving reversal shifts—e.g., in a black-white discrimination task, animals are first rewarded for approaching *white,* then the reward is shifted to the *black.* Reid (1953) and Pubols (1956) are two examples of such studies. Up to a point, increased trials on the original discrimination led to greater difficulty in learning the reversal. With extreme overlearning of the original task, however, the reversal problem became easier and easier to the point where there was either no interference from the original task, or, at times a facilitory effect was found on the reversal.

Mandler (1962, 1965) has suggested that overlearning on the original task permits the organism to shift from an associative basis of response to the relevant stimuli to what he refers to as a structural basis. He assumes that the associative laws are not necessarily the same as the laws of structure. The latter permit more flexibility in combining stimuli and responses, and are related, by Mandler, to "thinking." Association permits the acquisition of functional units which may then become available as the basis of new behavior.

Before turning to a new basis of behavioral laws, the present discussion will consider the possibility that the overlearning phenomena may be explicable in terms of the interaction between the basic processes already described in this book.

A Model for Overlearning

Practice on Task 1 can initiate two antagonistic processes, with regard to transfer to a reversal task. First, the present chapter has shown that practice increases the ability of the practiced system to resist interference. This resistance to interference, produced by overlearning the Task 1 system, should deter the reversal learning involved in Task 2. This can be illustrated simply. Consider the situation where an animal first learns *A-B* as Task 1 (e.g., the stimulus is a choice point in a T-maze, one alley of the choice point white and the other alley black; the animal is rewarded for entering the white, rather than the black alley). As *A-B* increases in boundary strength with practice, it is capable of greater resistance to interference from the reversal system, *A-C* (e.g., at the same stimulus choice point, make a new response: Approach the *black* alley). Despite the fact that the experimenter is now rewarding the new, *A-C* system, the old *A-B* system will resist interference from the new system.

On the other hand, increased practice leads to greater stimulus and response differentiation, as was seen in Chapters 4 and 5. Since Tasks 1 and 2, as illustrated above, involve the same stimulus, this stimulus should be well differentiated after overlearning on Task 1. This differentiation should permit *faster* learning of the new *A-C* system.

From this point of view, the crucial factor in determining the effects of *A-B* overlearning will be the relative number of trials required before boundary strength becomes asymptotic versus the number of trials required before differentiation becomes asymptotic. If the boundary strength of *A-B* reaches a maximum in fewer trials than are required for differentiation to reach a maximum, overlearning will have relatively little effect on boundary strength while it continues to increase stimulus differentiation; in that case, overlearning should facilitate *A-C* reversal learning. On the other hand, in situations where the stimulus is already well differentiated before the onset of Task 1, differentiation should reach a maximum before boundary strength; here overlearning *A-B* should interfere with reversal learning of *A-C*.

At this point, a first approximation will be presented to a model relating the interference effects of *A-B* boundary strength and the facilitory effects of differentiation. This model will be stated more precisely in Chapter 9, where it will be evaluated in detail. The model is concerned with Task 2 performance as a function of experience on Task 1.

$$P = C - aB + bD$$

Here, P is the probability of a correct response to A-C, the reversal Task 2; C is the boundary strength of A-C; aB is a function of the boundary strength of A-B, the Task 1 system which is competing with A-C; and bD is a function of the stimulus differentiation of the choice point. Operationally, B is a function of the number of trials involved in practicing A-B; D is a function of the total amount of experience with the stimulus, both in the context of learning A-B and in the other situations in which the stimulus was encountered.

Does the Model Fit the Data?

The position outlined above is consistent with several aspects of the overlearning data. Reid (1953) points out that in transfer to the reversal task, the overlearned group persists in the Task 1 response longer than the control group, following cessation of the reinforcement for that response, before making the first Task 2 response. However, once the Task 2 response has been made and reinforced, the control group shows a significantly greater tendency to revert to the old Task 1 system. In short, the Task 2 system is less able to resist interference from Task 1 in the control than in the overlearning group.

Another aspect of the overlearning effect is consistent with the position outlined above. If one set of stimuli (e.g., black-white) is relevant to reinforcement, while a second set of stimuli in the situation (e.g., left-right) is irrelevant, we have seen in Chapter 4 that differentiation occurs primarily for the relevant stimuli. If this is the case, then overlearning on the relevant cues should not facilitate later performance if the irrelevant cues of Task 1 are made the relevant cues of Task 2. This deduction is supported by data from Brookshire, Warren, and Ball (1961). In this study, half the animals learned a brightness discrimination in a T-maze; the other half learned a position response in the maze. Animals which overlearned on Task 1 (whether brightness or position discrimination) *reversed* more quickly than their controls. In the reversal, of course, the relevant cues of Task 1 are still relevant in Task 2, but a new response is required to these cues. However, animals which over-learned on one set of cues during Task 1 and were then switched to the other set of cues in Task 2 (e.g., black-white relevant on Task 1, left-right relevant on Task 2) did no better than their nonover-learned controls on Task 2.

Paul (1965), in his review of the overlearning research, points out that a number of studies have failed to find faster reversal learning following overlearning. From the position outlined above, such failure would be expected if the stimuli were already well differenti-ated prior to the overlearning trials, so that the asymptote of differ-entiation would be reached before boundary strength reached asymptote. None of the animal studies has systematically examined this issue.

It is interesting to note that there is relatively little evidence for an overlearning effect in human verbal learning. In Chapter 5 it was pointed out that verbal *stimuli* are usually near asymptote on differ-entiation prior to the onset of the experiments; the same verbal materials, when used as responses in learning, are not yet at asymp-tote on differentiation. (This discrepancy between stimulus and response differentiation, it will be recalled, appears to be due to the fact that the stimuli are physically present for the subject, while the responses are carried as traces in the mind.) From this fact, one would expect to find that overlearning facilitates transfer primarily in situations where the *response* items are identical between tasks (e.g., List *A-B* followed by List *C-B;* or the *A-B, A-B_r* situation in which List 2 consists of the same stimuli and responses as List 1, but the pairing is altered). Overlearning should have less of a facilitory effect when the *stimuli* of the successive tasks are identical. The data are, by and large, consistent with these expectations. A study by Mandler and Heinemann (1956) provides an example. Overlearn-ing of an *A-B* list facilitated subsequent learning of both *A-B_r* and *C-B* lists; however, no significant facilitation of *A-C* lists was found. (The stimuli in these lists were single digit numbers; the responses were triads of consonants, such as *LFH.*)

While such data are consistent with the model outlined above, they are not consistent with those positions that hold that overlearn-ing of an *S-R* system somehow transforms the nature of this system so that it no longer interferes with other systems.

A more detailed discussion of overlearning in verbal learning is to be found in Mandler (1962, 1965) and in Jung (1965).

SHORT-TERM MEMORY

Are the Laws of Short-Term Memory Different from Those of Long-Term Memory?

A number of writers have suggested that short-term memory involves a set of processes that are completely different from those of long-term memory. For example, some have suggested that *trace decay* is the basic process of forgetting in short-term memory, while *interference* is the basic process in long-term memory. The present section of this chapter will consider this general problem.

WHAT IS SHORT-TERM MEMORY? The topic of short-term memory was introduced in Chapter 3. The technique developed by Peterson and Peterson (1959) illustrates a typical procedure. Here an item (e.g., a three-consonant nonsense syllable) is presented to a subject for a limited period of observation (e.g., one second). The item is then removed and the subject engages in some relatively unrelated activity which is designed to prevent rehearsal (e.g., counting backwards by fours from some number given by the experimenter). At a signal, the subject attempts to recall the item. In this type of experiment, the retention interval usually varies between 0 to 18 seconds from presentation of the item to the test for recall.

In a sense it is misleading to label such experiments as studies of short-term memory; crucial characteristics of such studies include factors in addition to the fact that memory is tested after 18 seconds, rather than after 24 hours. Other crucial characteristics include the fact that these studies usually investigate memory for a *single system* under conditions of *minimal practice*. Under such conditions, particularly when nonsense syllables or sets of unrelated words are used as the material to be remembered, almost complete forgetting occurs within 18 seconds. Consequently, tests of long-term retention would be futile. These are short-term memory studies in the sense that they study conditions in which, typically, very rapid forgetting occurs.

THE TRACE DECAY NOTION. Brown (1958) has proposed a trace decay theory to account for short-term retention. This position appears to have been accepted, with modifications, by Broadbent (1958) and Peterson (1966) among others. Briefly, Brown suggests that after an item is received by a subject, it forms a trace which decays rapidly. However, if decay has not proceeded too far, rehearsal can restore the trace to its original strength. If rehearsal can be prevented, forgetting will be a function of time. However, as long as the subject can rehearse, time alone will not be a critical factor in retention. Brown supports this position with data which indicate that *amount of material* preventing rehearsal is the important variable in forgetting, not time between presentation and recall of an item.

Similar results were reported by Murdock (1961). Here subjects were instructed to remember the first word of a series. The rate of presentation of succeeding words varied between a word every half-second to a word every two seconds. Thus time between presentation and recall was fourfold as great for some series as for others. Holding number of words in the series constant, time had no effect on retention. These data present some obvious difficulties for the trace notion. If the intervening items prevented rehearsal, trace theory states that longer intervals between presentation and test should yield greater forgetting. This did not occur.

It should be noted, incidentally, that the Murdock (1961) data are consistent with a retroactive inhibition position as outlined in the earlier sections of this chapter: *The number of items intervening between the presentation and test for recall was the critical variable in forgetting, rather than time* per se.

We shall see that several different theories have incorporated the trace decay notion into a more complex formulation in attempting to explain the phenomena of short-term retention. However, without such modifications, the simple trace decay position appears susceptible to several lines of attack. Peterson and Peterson (1959) plotted the latency of response for subjects who were signalled to recall three seconds after presentation of a consonant triad. Within 2 seconds of the signal, subjects averaged only 30% correct responses; an additional 40% were emitted between 2 and 4 seconds after the signal. On the basis of a trace concept, one would normally expect most of the correct responses to occur immediately after the signal, with a rapid drop as the trace decay progresses.

Murdock (1961) compared the retention of nonsense consonant triads with that of meaningful words, using the Peterson and Peterson technique of having subjects count backwards from an arbitrarily chosen number. He found that retention of meaningful words was much superior to that of nonsense syllables. A simple trace decay position would have difficulty accounting for such a difference.

Hellyer (1962) investigated the effect of repeated presentations on short-term memory. Each item was presented 1, 2, 4, or 8 times in immediate succession. If rehearsal merely prevented the *onset* of decay, recall should be equal for all presentation conditions after a given retention interval in which rehearsal was prevented. Instead, using a variation of the Peterson and Peterson technique, Hellyer found that greater numbers of presentations markedly reduced forgetting.

THE TWO-STORAGE-SYSTEMS MODELS OF RETENTION. A number of writers have suggested models that involve the notion of two storage systems: one storage system for short-term memory and a second for long-term memory. These include Broadbent (1958), Waugh and Norman (1965), and Atkinson and Shiffrin (1968).

Broadbent (1958) has modified Brown's position in a manner which could account for Hellyer's data as well as the Murdock (1961) data for meaningful words. Broadbent assumes that there is an immediate storage and a permanent storage system, and that repetition leads to material being transferred from the immediate to the permanent storage system. Thus repeated items (Hellyer) and familiar items (Murdock) are assumed to be in the permanent storage system. Loss of material in the immediate storage system would be primarily due to decay, while loss of material in the permanent storage system would be due to interference.

In general, the dual storage models take the position that the capacity of the short term storage is extremely limited, and that new items displace old items in this storage.

WHY DO WE NEED A DUAL STORAGE NOTION? Both intuitive (anecdotal) and experimental evidence has been presented in defense of the necessity for a dual storage notion. Anecdotally, it is pointed out that stimuli, such as an unfamiliar telephone number, often must be repeated over and over again or they will be forgotten; any interruption may disrupt retention. After examining the stimulus and, perhaps, recoding it in some more meaningful fashion, the stimulus can be retrieved despite a lengthy delay.

Writers such as Broadbent (1963) have argued that the data relating stimulus similarity to retention make the dual storage notion valuable. They have contended that similarity between items being retained will affect material in the long-term store, but not in the short-term store. If true, this would support the conclusion that two different sets of laws are required for material being retained under the different sets of conditions. However, recent data have indicated that both semantic similarity between items and acoustic or articulatory similarity can affect retention in typical short-term memory studies. The effects of semantic similarity are indicated by Murdock and vom Seal (1967) and in a series of experiments conducted by Wickens (1970). Studies indicating effects of acoustic or articulatory similarity include Murray (1965, 1967), Hintzman (1967), and Levy and Murdock (1968).

Supporters of the dual storage notion can argue (and actually have done so) that the occurrence of similarity effects in retention can be used as an index which indicates that we are dealing with the long-term, rather than the short-term, storage system. Unless this argument can be stated in a more precise fashion, however, it leaves us in the position of categorizing behavior, after the fact, rather than permitting us to use the notion of dual storage as a means of predicting retention.

Another phenomenon which has been cited as indicating the need for a notion of dual storage comes from the literature on brain lesions. A number of writers in the short-term memory area have been struck by the dramatic effects of hippocampal lesions on retention. Patients appear capable of perceiving stimuli and retaining them over extremely short periods of time, as indicated by the fact that digit span appears to be unaffected. Further, memory for pre-operative events appears to be intact, indicating very little if any deficit in long-term memory. However, memory for ongoing events will be completely lost if the patients are distracted after perceiving the events, or if rehearsal is prevented. (See Milner, 1966, for a review of the literature concerning this phenomenon.)

While the data concerning effects of hippocampal lesions are consistent with the dual storage notion, they are certainly not conclusive on the topic, since a number of other mechanisms could be suggested which would also be consistent with these data. For example, it could be suggested that the hippocampus is instrumental in the *forming* of boundary strength, but once formed, lesions will no longer be relevant in the maintenance of the boundary strength.

THE HEBB-MELTON STUDIES. One of the more telling types of evidence against the dual storage notion comes from experiments by Hebb (1961) and Melton (1963). These studies suggest that trace decay of short-term memories does not occur; thus they undercut the contention that different laws are necessary to account for long- and short-term memory.

Hebb was one of the early proponents of a trace decay theory. He argued that if a single presentation of an unfamiliar item (viz., a random number sequence) decayed completely during the subsequent learning of similar items, there should be no facilitation in the recall of this item following a later presentation. Data presented by both Hebb (1961) and Melton (1963) are contrary to this prediction. Cumulative effects of practice were found despite the intervention of large numbers of other items between presentations of such random sequences of numbers. Thus the distinction between a temporary short-term storage and a permanent long-term storage appears difficult to maintain.

Are the Laws of Interference Applicable to Short-Term Memory?

The first part of the present chapter was concerned with an examination of the general characteristics of interference and boundary strength, particularly in the contexts of proactive and retroactive inhibition. We shall now consider the extent to which the laws found in those contexts are relevant to the short-term memory situation.

Clearly, the very procedures employed in many short-term memory tasks preclude the operation of some of the variables of long-term retention. For example, osmotic spread over a 48-hour period can not be studied in situations where the interval between presentation and test for retention is 18 seconds—and where, indeed, there is often virtually no measurable recall after 18 seconds. Despite some of the great differences in procedure, however, we shall find a sizable communality in laws between the long- and the short-term situations.

PROACTIVE FACTORS IN SHORT-TERM MEMORY. Evidence to date indicates that proactive inhibition is the primary source of forgetting in the Peterson and Peterson (1959) type of short-term memory situation. The classic study on this issue is that of Keppel and Underwood (1962a), a study that was described previously in Chapter 3. Studies previous to Keppel and Underwood had attempted to secure more stable estimates of retention by pooling each subject's performance over many trials. Keppel and Underwood were the first to systematically examine the retention of *each* of the first few items presented to their subjects. Contrary to the data reported when recall was pooled over all items shown, Keppel and Underwood found that subjects *could* retain a three-consonant nonsense syllable, with almost no loss in retention, over an 18-second interval; however, this was true only for the first such item learned. By the third or fourth item, retention dropped rapidly to the levels described by the earlier studies which pooled over all items.

In other words, in the absence of proactive sources of interference (viz., previously learned material which was close to the just-learned item in the cognitive space) there was little or no loss of retention using the Peterson and Peterson technique. However, proactive interference built up very rapidly, in this situation, reaching a maximum after only two or three items. A number of subsequent studies substantiated the Keppel and Underwood discovery (e.g., Wickens, Born, and Allen, 1963; Loess, 1964; H. Paul, 1966).

PROACTIVE INTRUSIONS. Further support for the importance of proactive interference in the Peterson and Peterson type of short-term memory situation comes from the fact that the great majority of errors in this situation appear to stem from intrusions arising from the immediately preceding items. Loess (1964) reported that 70% of the errors in his study were overt intrusions of this sort. H. Paul (1966) reported that about 80% of the errors in her study arose as intrusions from the immediately preceding items. See also Melton (1963) for a summary of the intrusion data from some of the earlier studies.

INTERFERENCE AS A FUNCTION OF DISTANCE IN THE COGNITIVE SPACE. We saw, earlier in this chapter, that for well-practiced systems which were to be retained over long periods of time, interference was a function of the distance in cognitive space between competing systems. This relationship between distance and retention is also found in short-term memory, but with some interesting modifications. In the short-term memory studies, systems appear to be much less resistant to interference than in the multitrial systems examined earlier in the chapter. Interference appears to be effective across much larger distances in the cognitive space when we deal with the short-term memory systems of weak boundary strength.

Wickens, Born, and Allen (1963) reported some of the earliest data on this topic. This study manipulated inter-item similarity between triads of consonants. Subjects first learned syllables composed of the same letters as found in the subsequent test items or syllables different from those on which they were later to be tested. Letter overlap between prior items and test items had no effect on retention of the test items. Very similar results were obtained in a study by H. Paul (1966). Massive forgetting of the test items occurred in both studies; in both studies, this forgetting was clearly attributable to proactive interference; and in both studies, amount of forgetting was approximately the same whether or not the previously learned items overlapped in letter content with the test items. In short, simply being in the region of the cognitive space occupied by other sets of letter combinations was sufficient to produce maximal interference; letter duplication added nothing to this.

On the other hand, interference could be reduced by moving out of the region occupied by letter sets to a region occupied by numbers. Wickens, Born, and Allen (1963) presented subjects with a series of nonsense syllables, followed by an item that consisted of a triad of numbers. Proactive inhibition built up very quickly over the set of syllables so that recall was extremely poor after the third or fourth syllable. Introduction of the number triad at this point led to a "release" from proactive inhibition; the number triad was as easily recalled as the first syllable had been. Corresponding results were obtained when the subjects were first shown a series of number triads, followed by a nonsense syllable; the nonsense syllable was recalled as easily as the first of the number triads.

Wickens and Clark (1968) report a similar release from proactive inhibition upon extreme shifts in *semantic meaning*. For example, subjects were first presented a series of word triads in which all the words were evaluatively positive (e.g., success, nice, enjoy), followed by a triad in which the words were evaluatively negative (e.g., kill, danger, worry). Proactive inhibition built up across the series of positively evaluated triads: While recall of the first of these triads was virtually 100% (over a 20-second retention interval), recall of the fourth such triad was down to about 60%. Introduction of the negatively evaluated triad, at this point, led to jump in recall to about 80%. Thus, as we saw in Chapter 2, distance along meaning dimensions can influence cognitive functioning.

Thus we see that short-term memory is affected by distance along dimensions of formal similarity (e.g., distance between letter triads and number triads) and by distance along dimensions of semantic similarity.

RETROACTIVE INTERFERENCE. The studies considered in this section, thus far, employed a technique that prevented the occurrence of retroactive inhibition. These studies forced the subjects to engage in an activity, between presentation and test of an item, that was very dissimilar from the material being retained. Consequently, no sources of retroactive interference were present. When the retention interval is filled with items similar to those of the test item, however, we find that massive retroactive interference does occur.

In fact, it appears that a given amount of competing material will produce much more interference if it operates retroactively than if it operates proactively. This can be seen in a study reported by Murdock (1963). Subjects were presented with series of paired words. After the presentation of a series, subjects were shown the first word of one of the pairs and were asked to recall the word that had been paired with it. Various series differed in length. Thus proactive interference could be evaluated by comparing retention of pairs having the *same* number of items *following* them in the series, but *different* numbers of items *preceding* them. Similarly, retroactive effects could be evaluated by comparing retention of pairs having the same number of items preceding them, but different numbers of items following. While proactive effects were found in this study, they were relatively small compared to the retroactive effects. For example, if eight items *preceded* the word to be recalled, and no items followed it, retention was approximately 89%. Thus there was very little loss in retention when only proactive interference was operating. However, when *no items preceded* the word to be recalled and *three items followed it,* retention dropped to 40%.

Strong retroactive effects on short-term retention are also reported by Tulvig and Arbuckle (1963), and by Peterson, Saltzman, Hilner, and Land (1962), among others. Thus the sequence effects noted early in this chapter are clearly seen in short-term retention. The last item learned has priority in retention.

Is Extinction-Recovery Theory Applicable to Short-Term Memory?

We have seen that short-term memory is heavily influenced by interference. The theorists who have advocated an extinction-recovery theory for interference effects in long-term retention have attempted to think in terms of a parallel theory for short-term memory. In the present section we shall see if such a formulation fares better in the area of short-term retention than it did in long-term retention.

EXTINCTION OF LETTER SEQUENCE HABITS. How might the extinction-recovery theory operate in short-term retention? The letter-habit hypothesis, proposed by Underwood and Postman (1960), appears to have been designed with the Peterson and Peterson type experiment in mind. The Underwood and Postman theory assumes that in learning real words we develop strong associations between letter combinations. When we then enter the laboratory and are shown a new combination of these letters in the form of a nonsense syllable, we must first extinguish the previously learned associations between letters before we can learn the new, nonsense associations.

For example, if the first two letters of a nonsense syllable are *h-b* and if *h-a* is a strong letter habit from previous experience, the old *a* response must be extinguished in learning the new *b* response. With time, spontaneous recovery of *a* occurs; this interferes with the newly learned *b* response and leads to forgetting *b*.

Several problems arise in attempting to apply the letter sequence formulation to short-term memory. The first problem arises is that, as we have seen earlier in this chapter, there is almost no evidence for *extra-experimental* sources of interference in letter sequence habits. However, if we *did* accept the possibility of extra-experimental sources of interference, a second problem would arise: If the major source of forgetting in short-term memory studies were extra-experimental sources of interference, why should such interference be strongest on the third or fourth item learned rather than on the first item? In other words, this mechanism can not explain the fact that the first item learned in the typical short-term memory study is extremely well retained, and it is only in the later items that we begin to see evidence for massive interference.

A second problem for the extra-experimental sources of interference comes from the studies which directly examined extinction of previously acquired materials. Saltz (1965), for example, attempted to extinguish letter sequence habits by asking subjects to respond to two-letter sequences which have a strong third-letter response in the language (e.g., DO-typically evoked the response G, as in DOG, or C, as in DOC). The subjects were asked to emit the first response that came to mind for such two-letter sequences and were told that they were incorrect on some of these. While extinction of letter sequences was found in this study, it developed slowly over a great number of trials. Similarly, Peak and Deese (1937) report that extinction of an entire nonsense syllable is extremely slow. Consequently, it appears uncertain that sufficient letter sequence extinction for the sequences of real language could be developed in a single presentation of a nonsense syllable to produce the typical short-term memory effect.

Could we assume that the letter sequences which are extinguished are those that arise within the experimental situation rather than extra-experimentally? Such an assumption could account for the fact that proactive effects build up rapidly over the first few items learned in the short-term memory situation. On the other hand, such an assumption would have difficulty with the finding that such an increase in proactive effects occurs *even in studies which involve no letter duplication between the successive items being learned.* Thus. the letter habits which must be extinguished can not have arisen within the experimental situation, *per se.*

It appears that the letter sequence habit, as a basis for forgetting, fares no better in short-term memory than it did in long-term memory.

CONTEXT STIMULI AND THE WHOLE RESPONSE AS THE BASIS FOR EX-TINCTION-RECOVERY. A second mechanism, derived from the extinction-recovery position, would identify the general context of the experiment as the stimulus for each item to be remembered; further, the learned response would be the whole nonsense word. For this point of view, the preceding items must be extinguished when the new item is associated with the context. Spontaneous recovery of the extinguished item would produce interference with, and forgetting of, the new item. Here it could be assumed that the strength of the association of an item to the context, developed in a single presentation, is weak. Thus the successive presentation of one or two other items in the context might be sufficient to produce extinction, and subsequent recovery, of the first item, as demanded by the data of Keppel and Underwood (1962a), Wickens *et al.* (1963), and Paul (1966). Note that recovery must be assumed to occur very rapidly.

Actually, too little is known about the extinction and recovery of minimal association to adequately evaluate this mechanism. The small amount of existing evidence appears to be incompatible with this hypothesized mechanism. For example, a deduction from this position would indicate that if two items were presented, one after the other, the learning of the second item should tend to extinguish the first item. As a function of time after the acquisition of the second item, the first should spontaneously recover in strength. One might expect, then, that the strength of the first item should at first be weak, but should then increase as a function of time after the presentation of the second item. Data reported by Peterson and Peterson (1962) are relevant to this prediction. Sets of two items were presented in succession, followed by an interval of counting backwards. Some of the sets were followed by a retention test for the first item, some by a test for the second item. The tests occurred 4, 8, or 16 seconds after the presentation of the item to be recalled. Not until the moment of the test were subjects told which item was to be recalled. In this study, there was no evidence for spontaneous recovery of the first item as a function of retention interval. The second item was better recalled than the first at all retention intervals. If anything, this superiority of the second item increased, rather than decreased, with longer retention intervals.

In short, present versions of the extinction-recovery theory appear inadequate to account for the facts of short-term memory.

A Boundary Strength Interpretation of Short-Term Memory

In this section, we shall attempt to integrate the data of short-term memory from the point of view of the general formulation presented in the present book.

ACQUISITION.   In Chapter 3 it was suggested that associations develop with great strength on the first presentation and that subsequent practice serves to develop the ability of the learned system to resist interference from competing systems. From this point of view, the Peterson and Peterson type study represents a situation in which systems of minimum boundary strength and low differentiation are successively learned. (They are minimum in boundary strength because they have been presented only once in the context situation; they are low in differentiation because the individual items, *per se,* are unfamiliar, poorly integrated sequences.)

When the subject learns a single, meaningful word, the boundary strength is still weak, but the item to be retained is well differentiated, and thus is better able to resist interference. On the other hand, repeated presentation of a nonsense syllable, as in Hellyer (1962), increases both boundary strength and differentiation.

RETENTION.   It appears, from the data, that cognitive systems of combined low boundary strength and low differentiation are extremely susceptible in interference. Can simple response competition accommodate the retention data? Can we assume that newly acquired responses become associated to stimuli which are similar to those of previous responses, and that the competition between the two sets of responses to a common stimulus produces forgetting of the most recently acquired response? Apparently not. Such an explanation does not take into account the fact that the interference with such later material *does not occur immediately.* Instead, the operation of interference develops with time after the new material has been learned.

The position was taken, in this chapter, that proactive inhibition in long-term retention is mediated by an osmotic spread between system as a function of time. This position appears to be applicable to short-term memory as well. However, since the resistance to interference of the systems learned in the short-term situation is characteristically very weak, the spread occurs in a matter of seconds, as opposed to the longer periods required in long-term retention. When, indeed, the successive items are single, well differentiated words, the spread again requires a longer period of time before it is manifested in performance. Since each system is susceptible to massive interference and weakening in a short period of time, it is not surprising that studies such as Loess (1964) and H. Paul (1966) find that most intrusions are from the immediately preceding items. The fact that an asymptote for forgetting occurs after very few prior items is also consistent with the findings concerning the locus of intrusion errors.

A study by Corman and Wickens (1968) lends some support to the osmotic response-spread notion in short-term memory. Subjects were required to remember triads of letters. The 10-second retention interval was filled with *both* numbers and interfering letters. In one condition the interfering letters were presented late in the interval. Note that this is a *retroactive* interference paradigm rather than proactive. Despite the fact that retroactive effects are massive in this type of situation, some difference in retention was found between these two conditions. Consistent with the osmotic spread notion, a tendency toward more errors occurred when the interfering material was presented early in the retention interval (permitting a longer period of coexistence of the two systems) though this effect was not significant statistically. Also consistent with the osmotic spread notion, more intrusions from the interpolated material occurred when the interfering material was presented early in the retention interval. This effect was statistically significant. A more direct test of the notion would be one in which the interval between two items was manipulated, with retention of the *second* item tested at a constant interval after presentation.

RETENTION OF REAL WORDS: IS IT A FACTOR OF LEARNING OR OF MEMORY? Underwood (1964) has suggested that the superior short-term retention of real words (compared to nonsense syllables) is not a memory factor but is a function of the superior learning of the integrated word prior to the retention interval. This type of distinction between learning and memory is less critical, from the point of view of the present book, than it is for Underwood. Here we have assumed that the associative phase is virtually at asymptote upon reception of the material by the subject, and that subsequent differences in memory reflect differential ability of well differentiated and poorly differentiated system to resist interference. Underwood, on the other hand, suggests that if a well differentiated and a poorly differentiated response are both recalled perfectly, immediately after presentation, the single presentation may represent overlearning for the well differentiated item. He specifies that this can only be tested if both items are equally well retained at a level substantially below perfect retention, followed by a comparison of retention for the items at a longer time interval. It should be noted that this position is clearly parallel to the one taken by Underwood for the evaluation of variables hypothesized as affecting long-term retention.

Houston (1965) has attempted to examine the issues raised by Underwood. By presenting six word items for 2.5 seconds, as opposed to five word items for 1.5 seconds, he was able to produce 80% retention of both lengths at 0 seconds after presentation. He then tested for retention at intervals between 1.5 and 6 seconds after presentation. Retention of the six word items was successively poorer than for the five word items at the longer retention intervals. Thus, even within the conditions specified, above, by Underwood, material which is easier to integrate appears to be more resistant to interference.

DOES OVERLEARNING REDUCE THE TENDENCY OF AN ITEM TO INTRUDE ON OTHER ITEMS? This issue of overlearning in long-term retention has already been discussed in this chapter, with special reference to the animal work on reversal shift. The issue arises again in a somewhat different context in connection with short-term memory.

We have seen that a single presentation of a nonsense item is sufficient to produce extensive proactive interference onto a succeeding item. What would happen if the first of these items were well practiced before the second item was presented? Would the interference effects onto the second item be increased (since the boundary strength of the first item would be greater than that of the second)? The evidence indicates quite the opposite: Overlearning of the first nonsense item leads to a *decrease* in the amount of proactive interference that operates onto a second item (Scott, Whimbey, and Dunning, 1967a, 1967b). Let us consider how such an effect could occur.

In Chapter 4, the suggestion was made that differentiation appears to enlarge the distances in the cognitive space defining the differentiated item. Such an enlargement of the cognitive space would have two consequences. First, it would move the differentiated item away from other items that might interfere with the retention of the differentiated item. Second, if the differentiated item is farther from other items, it must also interfere less with *their* retention.

Under what conditions will overlearning interfere with later items and under what conditions will it lead to a reduction in such interference? The greater the differentiation of an item before overlearning, the more we would expect overlearning to produce greater interference, since at this point boundary strength would be more likely to increase at a faster rate than differentiation. Further, the less the initial difference between the two competing items, the greater the likelihood that overlearning of the first item will still be accompanied by some degree of interference upon the second item. These hypotheses have yet to be tested.

At any rate, it is important to note that overlearning has been found to have at least partially parallel consequences for short-term memory and for aspects of long-term memory.

CONCLUSIONS

Studies of retention indicate the operation of the basic variables as outlined in the previous chapters of this book. There is evidence to suggest that both boundary strength of a system, and differentiation of the elements in the system, play important roles in long- and short-term memory.

Both long- and short-term memory studies are consistent in displaying the operation of proactive and retroactive inhibition. They are also consistent in that a number of specific variables show parallel effects in long- and short-term memory; these include the effects of amount of practice, similarity between material to be retained and the interfering material, and the operation of unlearning. Evidence for an osmotic spread as a factor in interference is also found in both long- and short-term memory.

Turning to the theoretical formulations which have been proposed to account for interference, both long- and short-term memory are consistent in providing little support for the extinction-recovery formulation. Looking first at the extinction aspect of this formulation, the evidence equating extinction and unlearning is very weak. For example, if unlearning were really extinction, it would develop only upon the unreinforced occurrence of List 1 responses during the acquisition of List 2 (or the unreinforced occurrence of system 1 responses during the learning of system 2 in short term memory). Evidence relating intrusions errors of this type to unlearning is extremely negative. Other evidence is similarly unpromising with regard to this issue.

Comparable problems arise with regard to the recovery aspect of the extinction-recovery formulation. While spontaneous recovery is, at times, observed, it occurs at intervals after learning which are inappropriate to account for the proactive inhibition phenomena; since the initial development of the extinction-recovery formulation was designed with the view of explaining proactive inhibition, this poses a serious problem for the utility of the notion. Further, the greatest evidence for recovery is found in situations where the stimuli of the competing systems are *similar,* but not identical. Thus the recovery which does occur is not that which is predicted from the extinction-recovery formulation.

An alternative theoretical approach is suggested in this chapter. This approach identifies unlearning with a breakdown in boundary strength, and proposes an osmotic spread of interference between coexisting cognitive systems that are close to one another in the cognitive space.

PART III | CONDITIONS NECESSARY FOR LEARNING

7 | The Integration of Cognitive Units: Sensory Integration and Serial Learning

PRECIS

Unfamiliar cognitive complexes (both stimuli and responses) often require a great deal of integration before they can be dealt with as coherent units. Consequently, this chapter is an extension of Chapters 4 and 5 which treated stimulus and response differentiation, respectively. Since integration must occur before meanings can be reliably assigned to stimuli, the present chapter is a prelude to Chapters 8 and 9 which will consider meaning and meaningfulness.

The present chapter describes sensory integration and compares it to some of the known phenomena related to the integration of words as meaningful units. Striking parallels are noted between these areas. Finally, it is suggested that the laws of serial learning may prove to be the laws of integration. Data from the area of serial learning are analyzed from this perspective.

DEMONSTRATION EXPERIMENT

The Problem

Examine Figure 7–1. What do you see:

FIGURE 7–1. Wife or Mother-in-Law? See text for explanation.

Explanation

Figure 7–1 is the famous "Wife and Mother-in-law" picture. It is an ambiguous picture that can be seen either as a lovely young woman (the "wife") or as a not-too-handsome older woman (the "mother-in-law"), and it represents a classical illustration of the integration of cognitive systems. Many of the elements in this picture are interpretable as two completely different things, dependent on which of the two faces is being attended to. The line that represents the chin of the wife becomes a nose when one sees the mother-in-law; the wife's ear is the mother-in-law's eye. In short, these are two competing, bounded systems of the type described in Chapter 2. They represent two different ways of integrating a set of visual stimuli.

Previous experience can play a very powerful role in determining how we integrate a set of attributes such as those in Figure 7–1. Leeper (1935), for example, modified the figure in two different ways. One modification eliminated some of the attributes that are important to identifying the figure as the mother-in-law (e.g., the mother-in-law's eye). The other modification eliminated attributes important to identifying the picture as the wife. Some subjects were first shown the modification that looks unam-

254

biguously like the wife, and then were shown Figure 7–1. All of these interpreted the ambiguous figure as the wife. Other subjects were first shown the picture that looks unambiguous like the mother-in-law, and then Figure 7–1. Of these, 95 percent saw Figure 7–1 as the mother-in-law.

SENSORY INTEGRATION

Sensory Integration as a Product of Experience

THE VON SENDEN STUDIES. Most of the visual stimuli around us appear compellingly real, more like objects than percepts. Intuitively, it seems that we must always have been able to see things essentially in the same ways that we see them now. How could this chair, for example, look any different to an infant than it looks to us? The evidence, however, is dramatically contrary to such intuitions.

The classic work of von Senden (1960) provides a clear demonstration of the importance of learning to sensory integration. Von Senden studied form perception in congenitally blind persons who gained sight after the removal of cataracts. These persons knew what triangles and circles were, for example, and could not only describe them verbally but could also identify them tactually. Despite this, months of practice were required before they could recognize some of these simple figures. Von Senden's description of the difficulties in training for triangle recognition are particularly interesting. After a lengthy training sequence, in which the subjects always saw the triangle with its base down, the subjects finally learned to recognize this figure as a triangle. At this point, von Senden presented the triangle upside down (with the base up), and it was no longer recognized.

The von Senden studies show that unfamiliar stimulus complexes are often extremely difficult to perceive.

THE IVO KOHLER STUDIES. The studies reported by Ivo Kohler (1963) are even more dramatic than those of von Senden. Kohler fit his subjects with special glasses that inverted the visual field so that the world looked upside down. After wearing these glasses for a week or more, the subjects *began to see the world rightside up again*. This process occurred gradually. At first, shown two pictures, one rightside-up and the other upside-down, the subjects reported that the rightside-up picture looked upside down, while the upside-down picture looked rightside up. At an intermediate stage, *both* pictures looked rightside up, though "differently" rightside up in some manner that was difficult to specify. At this stage, external cues often led to an inversion of the percepts. For example, a cigarette was seen as upside down until lit; at this point the direction of the smoke drifting from the cigarette led the subject to see the cigarette in its correct orientation. In the final stage the subjects saw the world as rightside up again. At this point, when the glasses were removed, *the world suddenly turned upside down again.*

Some of the issues involved in the integration of sensory stimuli are most clearly displayed in the intermediate stage of the Kohler studies, when integration is only partially accomplished. In this stage a subject may see a face as upside down, but then note that the *lips* appear to be rightside up. At this point, the face is not yet perceived in an integrated fashion; part is seen in one orientation, part in another.

The results of a second study are no less important for an investigation of sensory integration. In this second study, subjects wore glasses in which the bottom was a clear, nondistorting glass, while the top of the lens produced an angular distortion ranging between 10–30 degrees for various subjects. Learning to perceive veridically thus required more than a complete inversion of the entire stimulus field; it involved integrating two halves of the field into one unitary percept. Yet, *with time this was accomplished* by Kohler's subjects.

Kohler's findings indicate a degree of experiential control over perception that was never suspected by most of us. These results suggest that the integration of sensory stimuli into percepts is a complex variety of learning.

THE STABILITY OF INTEGRATED PERCEPTS. Earlier in this chapter, integrated stimuli were described as bounded systems. This is most clearly seen in Figure 7–1 where many people have great difficulty seeing the wife and the mother-in-law simultaneously. Each organization of the attributes resists interference from the alternative organization. An interesting aspect of this demonstration is that the two faces require completely different integrations of subcomponents of the picture. As was noted earlier, the line that constitutes the wife's jaw must be reintegrated into a nose in order to see the mother-in-law. Thus a particular integration of an entire stimulus complex (e.g., seeing the figure as the wife) will preclude the perception of certain subcomponents (e.g., the mother-in-law's nose) .

The stability of integrated percepts is, of course, a well-known phenomenon. The classic work of Gottschaldt (1926) on embedded figures is particularly relevant to the issues being considered in the present chapter. Gottschaldt found that previous experience with a figure did not facilitate finding this figure when it was integrated into a more complex figure. In the next section of this chapter it will be seen that words, as integrated linguistic units, display exactly the same characteristic. This is particularly important because we are often concerned with relating various phenomena to the frequency of exposure to the relevant stimuli. Clearly, frequency of a stimulus may be quite irrelevant to behavior if that stimulus has always, in the past, been encountered only as an aspect of a larger, integrated stimulus.

INTEGRATION OF WORDS

Language learning provides another example of the difficulty in perceiving unfamiliar stimuli. A person learning a foreign language may find the sound patterns so unfamiliar that he has difficulty distinguishing one word from another. Further, on encountering a word for the second time, he may not recognize ever having heard it before. The patterns do not appear to "hang-together." Corresponding problems may occur in attempting to pronounce the words. In short, unfamiliar verbal complexes often require a great deal of integration before they can be dealt with as coherent units.

DEMONSTRATION EXPERIMENT

The Problem

Below are the last three or four letters of six common words. In every case, the first letter is missing. Can you tell, by looking, what these six common words are?

1. -E-N-Y	4. -W-I-C-E
2. -A-C-H	5. -A-K-S
3. -S-E-D	6. -O-T-O-R

(Turn the page for the correct answers.)

Explanation

Most people can not identify the words in the puzzle without first going through the alphabet, systematically, trying each letter in turn.

The first of these words is so difficult that some persons can not identify it even after applying the entire alphabet to the last three letters; they try the correct letter, then reject it as incorrect and continue trying other solutions to the word. Yet this is a common English word that every literate person has encountered often.

Answers:

1. D-E-N-Y	4. T-W-I-C-E
2. E-A-C-H	5. O-A-K-S
3. U-S-E-D	6. M-O-T-O-R

Why is this puzzle so difficult? Because each of these sequences of letters tends to evoke an integrated response, and this response is different from the one required to pronounce the correct word. These common words, in short, are integrated sequences, and these sequences are not compatible with the integration which is evoked by subsequences of the words. The phenomenon is one often noted by the Gestalt psychologists (though by no means their exclusive property): The whole is different from the enumeration of its parts.

Research on the Integrated Nature of Words

The available research supports the suggestion that we react to words as integrated sequences, rather than as sets of letters which must be made into words. Horowitz (1969) summarizes a number of studies that make this point. He notes, for example, that if a person is given the sequence "exp-ct," he will usually be able to say the correct word more quickly than he can say which letter is missing. Indeed, some studies indicate that reading words and finding individual letters in these words are two distinct psychological processes.

EMBEDDED VERBAL UNITS.   The evidence which we have been considering in the present section is consistent with the results found earlier in this chapter concerning sensory integration. There it was seen that integration may produce a state of affairs in which individual subunits are no longer responded to as such. At this point the reader may wonder about the generality of such a phenomenon in verbal materials. Are the examples we have discussed "freaks" which, while dramatic, are characteristic of very few real words? Data reported by Underwood and Schulz (1960) inadvertently support the generality of the evidence from sensory integration studies.

The Underwood and Schulz studies were designed to examine the relationship between frequency of experience with a verbal item and the ease of learning this item as a response in paired associates. As shall be seen in the next chapter, a number of studies have found that such learning is easier for more frequent responses when *real words* are used as the responses. Underwood and Schulz were concerned with whether this effect reflected an underlying substratum of the frequency with which individual letters occurred together in the language. To determine this, they first examined thousands of English words to calculate the extent to which various letter combinations occurred. For example, it was found that GHT occurs with relatively high frequency in printed English: KBR occurs relatively infrequently. Using triads of letters as the responses in paired-associates learning, Underwood and Schulz found that the correlation between rate of learning and the frequency of triad occurrence in the language was zero. On the other hand, they found that, when single letters of the alphabet were used as responses in learning, letter-frequency in the language correlated moderately with learning.

In short, frequency is related to learning for integrated response units (viz., words and single letters) but not for compound segments taken from larger integrated units. The individual subunits are often no longer responded to as such, when they occur in the context of larger, integrated units.

SERIAL FACTORS IN WORD RECOGNITION. There is a striking resemblance between the typical serial learning curve and the curve relating word recognition to the serial order of letters in the word. In serial learning, the first items in a list are typically learned most rapidly, the middle items most slowly, and the end items at some intermediate rate. This function mirrors closely the results of a number of studies which investigated the importance of letters, in different positions in a word, for recognition of the word. Miller and Friedman (1957) found that subjects were best at reconstructing a word when a letter in the middle of the word was deleted. Performance deteriorated as the deletion was moved toward either end of the word. Bruner and O'Dowd (1958) presented words tachistoscopically with an error at the beginning, middle, or end of the words. Consistent with Miller and Friedman, errors at the beginning of words proved most disruptive, errors in the middle least disruptive. Similar results have been reported by Marchbanks and Levin (1965) and by Horowitz, White, and Atwood (1968).

Clearly there is a resemblance between serial positions which are learned most rapidly and serial positions that are most crucial for word recognition. Is this a coincidence? Perhaps. However, we shall see that serial learning appears to be an integrative process that may in general mirror word integration.

SERIAL LEARNING AS SERIAL INTEGRATION

THE LASHLEY HYPOTHESIS. Lashley (1951) was one of the first psychologists to emphasize the integrated nature of well learned sequential behavior. He pointed out that many sequences run off so quickly that, physiologically, it is difficult to defend the proposition that the immediately preceding response element could have served as a stimulus (i.e., could have fired an affector discharge in sufficient time to elicit the succeeding element).

Motor responses such as those involved in playing the violin are cited, by Lashley, as examples of integrated responses which occur too rapidly to be conceptualized as a long string of minute S-R connections. The well-trained rat in a multiple-unit maze exhibits a highly integrated and stable series of responses, with little obvious delay in making decisions at successive choice points.

Again, as in Chapter 5, we see the close parallel between phenomena that are characteristic of stimulus processes (viz., stimulus integration) and those characteristic of response processes (viz., response integration). In verbal serial learning, the two are difficult to separate. Is a word an integrated stimulus sequence, an integrated response sequence, or both? The notion was proposed in Chapter 5 that cognitive elements could be conceptualized as involving values on stimulus dimensions, response dimensions, or both. This point of view seems particularly appropriate for the type of processes under consideration at this time.

SERIAL LEARNING AND COGNITIVE INTEGRATION.   Both Youssef (1964, 1967) and Jensen and Rohwer (1965) have suggested that the laws of serial learning are essentially those of cognitive integration. From this point of view, knowledge of the development of serial learning would provide a more adequate understanding of the integration processes. Evidence to be presented in this chapter supports this position. The subsequent discussion of serial learning will be organized largely around Youssef's position, since it is somewhat more specific than that of Jensen and Rohwer; however, it must be understood that these two are very similar in their general outlines.

Before presenting Youssef's hypothesis in more detail, let us first examine the general nature of serial learning and the S-R position that has classically been applied to it. In serial learning, the subject is typically presented a list of items (e.g., words or nonsense syllables) in a constant order. Upon presentation of each word in the list, the subject attempts to anticipate the next word. Many writers have assumed that the basic processes of serial learning are identical to those of paired-associates learning (e.g., Gibson, 1940). Consider A-B-C-D as a four-item serial list. If learning is essentially the same as in paired associates, the pairs to be learned could be conceptualized as *A-B, B-C, C-D*.

DIFFICULTIES WITH *S-R* INTERPRETATION. Difficulties in interpreting serial learning as a chaining of paired associates first arose from the work of Primoff (1938) and Young (1961, 1962). In these studies, subjects first learned a serial list, then learned a paired-associates list in which the pairs were adjacent items from the serial list. If *S-R* connections are formed between adjacent serial items, it was reasoned, positive transfer should occur between the serial and paired-associates lists. No such transfer was obtained. Young (1962) and Young and Clark (1964) hypothesized that the lack of positive transfer might be because the functional stimulus to a response, in a serial list, is not just the immediately preceding item, but instead might be the compound of the two or three immediately preceding items. A test of this hypothesis also failed to produce positive transfer from serial to paired-associates lists.

Relatively few studies have found any sizable transfer from serial to paired-associates learning. One of these few is a study by Horowitz and Izawa (1963). However, as Young and Casey (1964) point out, this study suffered from a methodological difficulty. The experimental groups first learned a serial list, then a paired-associate list derived from the serial list. Positive transfer was found in comparing the experimental and control groups on the paired-associate material. However, this transfer could be the result of learning to learn, since the experimental groups had learned a previous list while the control groups had not. When Young and Casey controlled for this factor, no positive transfer occurred.

Studies by Postman and Stark (1967) and Stark (1968), on the other hand, found evidence for positive transfer even with the learning-to-learn factor controlled. The Postman and Stark study was particularly well controlled since it involved a group that learned, as paired associates, words that were nonadjacent in the phase 1 serial list. Thus this group had differentiation training on the items of the serial list, yet learned them in an order that should produce negative transfer in paired associates. The negative transfer condition produced small but significant decrements in performance compared to a control group which learned irrelevant items in the phase 1 serial list. It should be pointed out that phase 1 serial learning involved relatively few trials in both the Postman and Stark (1967) and Stark (1968) studies. This is an important factor from the point of view of Youssef's (1964, 1967) theory.

The results of the studies cited above suggest that relatively little positive transfer occurs when adjacent items in a serial list are learned as paired associates.

While associations built up in prior serial learning produce little transfer to a subsequent paired-associates task, transfer in the opposite direction has been noted frequently. Young (1959), for example, found positive transfer to a serial learning list after first having subjects learn a paired-associates list. In this study, the *S-R* terms of the paired-associates list were made the adjacent items in the serial list. As we shall see, this asymmetry has important theoretical implications.

THE YOUSSEF THEORY. On the basis of evidence such as that outlined above, Youssef (1964, 1967) has proposed a two stage theory of serial integration. The first stage involves the development of adjacent associations. This is suggested by data, such as those of Young (1959), which indicate that paired-associates learning can facilitate subsequent serial learning. However, repeated practice on the list initiates the second stage in which the items in the list run off as a single, integrated unit; as such, an item no longer acts as the functional stimulus for the item that follows it in the list.

Indeed, examination of the studies which failed to find transfer from serial to paired-associate learning shows that they typically involve a high degree of learning of the serial list prior to the test for transfer. Youssef employed five levels of serial learning (0, 7, 14, 21, and 28 trials) prior to the test for transfer. In accordance with his prediction, he found that practice produced a U-shaped transfer effect. No transfer to the paired-associate list was found with 0 or 28 trials on the serial list (i.e., the smallest and largest number of trials, respectively). *Between* these points, transfer first increased, then decreased.

On the basis of Youssef's theory, one would expect to find marked evidence of transfer from the serial learning phase to the paired-associates phase under conditions which *disrupted* the integration of the serial list. One such condition has been reported in the literature. Shuell and Keppel (1967) varied the starting point of the serial list on each trial. Thus the list could not be learned as a single integrated response, and subjects could not move from the paired-association stage to the integration stage. And, indeed, sizable positive transfer to phase 2 paired-associates phase was found, compared to a control group. A second experimental group which learned the phase 1 serial list with the same starting point on each trial showed no such positive transfer.

Remote Associations

The analysis proposed by Youssef makes more comprehensible recent findings in several sub-areas of verbal learning. Remote associations is one of these sub-areas. In 1885, Ebbinghaus (1913) suggested that memorizing a serial list leads to the development of associations between each item and every other item in the list. In addition, the strength of an association between any two items was assumed to be greater, the closer the two items were to each other in the list. This position is incompatible with Youssef's, who states that in the process of integrating a list into a single unit, the individual items lose their stimulus properties for eliciting one another.

Let us examine the evidence relevant to the remote association hypothesis. Over the years, two principal types of studies were used to test the hypothesis: The derived lists experiments, developed by Ebbinghaus, and the association experiments, of which McGeoch's (1936a) is the most often cited.

DERIVED LISTS DATA. The derived lists technique involves reorganizing a previously learned serial list so that formerly distant items would now be adjacent. The remote association hypothesis predicts that the speed of learning the derived list will be directly related to the nearness of the now adjacent items to one another in the originally learned list. For example, if 1, 2, 3, 4, 5, 6, 7, 8, was the sequence of items in the original list, a first order derived list might be 1, 3, 5, 7, 2, 4, 6, 8. Here a systematic pattern is used in which every other item is skipped. A second order derived list might be 1, 4, 7, 2, 5, 8, 3, 6. Here the pattern consists of skipping two items. From the Ebbinghaus position, it would follow that the second order derived list should be more difficult to learn than the first order derived list. Using himself as his only subject, Ebbinghaus presents data in support of this prediction.

Slamecka (1964) suggests that these results could have been due to the fact that Ebbinghaus was aware of the principle by which the derived lists were constructed. Slamecka tested this possibility in a well-controlled series of experiments. His results showed that, if subjects were not informed about the relationship between Lists 1 and 2, there was no superiority in learning a first order derived List 2 over a List 2 which consisted of a random rearrangement of the items from List 1. These results are consistent with those of a previous study by Goldstein (1950). However, when subjects were informed of the relationship between Lists 1 and 2, Slamecka found that subjects learned a first order derived list faster than a randomly rearranged derived list. Slamecka interprets these results as indicating that remote associations are not formed. Facilitation in learning a derived list may occur, he suggests, if the subjects are aware of the pattern used in constructing the derived list and use the omitted items as mediators.

In a similar type of study, Hakes, James, and Young (1964) also failed to obtain evidence for the existence of remote associations in serial learning. The control group in this study learned two lists of completely different items. The experimental groups learned second lists that were first, second, or third order derived lists. Simultaneous comparisons over the four types of material indicated no significant differences. However, comparing the first order derived list with the control, where the Ebbinghaus position would predict the greatest facilitation, this study found a significant negative transfer effect. The derived list was learned significantly more slowly than the control list.

DATA FROM THE ASSOCIATION TECHNIQUE. The association technique for measuring remote associations consists of first having subjects learn a serial list to criterion. Each item of the list is then presented separately and in a random order; subjects are instructed to give the first response that comes to mind upon seeing each of these stimuli. McGeoch (1936a) reports a systematic decrease in the probability of a response being elicited by a stimulus the greater the remoteness between the stimulus and the response in the original serial list.

Raskin and Cook (1937) point out that systematic gradients such as those reported by McGeoch can be artifactual. For example, in a ten item list, nine items can be responded to with adjacent items. On the other hand, only the first item can produce a forward remote association nine items removed from the stimulus; both the first and second items can produce forward remote association eight items removed, etc. When Raskin and Cook correct their data for opportunity for occurrence of each degree of remoteness, they obtain a U-shaped curve in which very near and very remote associates are relatively probable, while associates of middle-degree remoteness are least likely.

This relationship is a difficult one to understand and Slamecka (1964) suggests that it is also not free of artifacts. In learning a serial list, Slamecka notes, items in the middle of the list are most difficult to learn and are consequently not emitted correctly as frequently as items from the two ends of the list. Since later recall has been shown to be related to frequency of emission during learning, the Raskin and Cook data may reflect differences in frequency of emission during learning. Preliminary evidence indicating that this may be the case was provided by Slamecka. He was able to reproduce the Raskin and Cook U-shaped curve in a situation in which no serial learning occurred, but the subjects merely responded to each item a different number of times prior to the association test.

CONCLUSIONS CONCERNING REMOTE ASSOCIATIONS. Clearly, then, recent evidence from both derived list and association studies are counterindicative to the position that serial learning results in functional remote associations between items in the list. This is consistent with Youssef's notion that the product of serial learning is an integrated unit in which the stimulus properties of each item for eliciting subsequent items is lost.

It should be pointed out that this position does not deny the possibility that remote associations may develop and function in the preintegration phase of serial learning, where the paired-associates paradigm is presumed to be operative. Some evidence to this effect is found in studies, such as Bugelski (1950), which plotted anticipatory errors during the course of serial learning. Bugelski finds a gradient of forward remote associations, even after a Raskin and Cook type correction for opportunity to give associations at various degrees of remoteness.

This type of data must be treated somewhat cautiously in light of recent observations by Peterson, Brewer, and Bertucco (1963). These writers point out that subjects may utilize guessing strategies, during serial learning, such that they guess responses which have not yet occurred on a given trial. This would result in very few backward associations. In addition, toward the end of the list there would be a pile-up of remote associations with very short distances from the stimulus item.

While a careful examination of Bugelski's data suggests some such mechanisms to be at work, a gradient of remote associations still is discernible. For example, if guessing were the only factor involved, then for any given stimulus item all the forward remote associations should be equally probable, and a gradient of remote associations should occur only upon pooling stimuli. This does not occur. A gradient of remote associations during anticipation learning is evident for each individual stimulus in Bugelski's data. Guessing strategy alone appears to be incapable of accounting for this fact, and it must be concluded that a gradient of remote associations is formed, at least on early preintegration trials of serial learning.

Further evidence for remote associations in the absence of list integration is found in a paired-associates study by Martin and Saltz (1963). Since list integration is not a factor in paired associates, remote associations should be demonstrable in this type of study. Martin and Saltz had subjects learn a paired-associates list in which the pairs were always presented in the same order. After 12 paired-associates trials, the subjects learned the response terms of the pairs as a serial list. When the order of the items in the serial list corresponded to the order of items in the paired-associates list, serial learning was significantly facilitated. This design is fairly close to the derived lists design of Ebbinghaus. Such evidence suggests that it may be premature to discard theories, such as that of Bugelski (1950), which use the concept of remote associations to account for phenomena occurring *during the process* of serial learning.

Stimulus Isolation in Serial Learning

It has already been pointed out, in Chapter 5, that studies of the von Restorff effect in serial learning indicate relatively little facilitation of the tendency for the isolated item to elicit its appropriate response. Instead, the effect consists primarily of facilitation of the tendency for the isolated item to occur as a *response* (Newman and Saltz, 1958). On the other hand, in paired associates, isolation of a stimulus term produces at least as much effect as isolation of a response term. This difference between stimulus effects in serial versus paired-associates learning become more comprehensible if we assume that individual items lose their stimulus properties during the course of serial learning.

Isolation of an item appears to increase the availability of the item (by means, presumably, of increasing its differentiation). This, in turn, appears to facilitate the integration of the item into the final unit response. Evidence for this comes from the Saltz and Newman (1959) data which indicate that isolation does *not* seem to affect the order of emission of responses. In Saltz and Newman, subjects were instructed to learn a list of words in serial order, but the list was presented only once. Following this single presentation, the subjects were asked to recall as many items from the list as possible. The seventh item in the experimental list was an isolated item. In the control list, the seventh item was not isolated. Otherwise the two lists were identical. For those subjects recalling the isolated item, on the average it was the 4.6th item to be recalled; for subjects recalling the control item, on the average it was the 4.8th item to be recalled. Thus order of emission was virtually unaffected for the isolated word. Of course, more subjects recalled the isolated term than the control term. Thus *isolating an item in a serial list appears to be primarily effective in increasing the rate at which this item is integrated* into the unit response that is learned.

Length of List

Integration should become more difficult as list length increases. While very few studies have manipulated list length in a fashion which provides analytic information on this problem, several recent reports by Italian investigators provide stimulating data. Battachi (1958) systematically varied list length, using lists as long as 24 items. Plotting errors against serial position, he obained the usual bowed-shape curve for short lists: fewest errors on early and late items, with items from the middle of the list proving the most difficult to learn. However, with very long lists, Battachi found a marked tendency for the errors to break into two bowed-shape curves. Apparently the long lists were being learned as two units. Interestingly enough, these units were not of equal length. The break in the error curve typically fell much closer to the end of the list than to the beginning.

Giovanelli and Tampiere (1964), using 12 item lists, found that normal subjects tended to give the classical bowed-shape error curve, while brain-damaged subjects tended to give bimodal curves more similar to those obtained by Battachi for very long lists. Apparently, subject-capacity variables influence the size of the unit which will be integrated.

Serial Position Curve

While the evidence seems rather strong that the product of serial learning is an integrated unit (or, perhaps, several such units if the list is sufficiently long), the process of integration is not well understood. If the initial stage of serial learning is a paired-associate task for adjacent items, why should the serial position error curve have the characteristic bowed form? A number of different theories have been proposed to account for this phenomenon (see McGeoch and

Irion, 1952). Most of these are response competition theories in one form or another. For example, Hull, Hovland et al. (1940) and Bugelski (1950) suggest that remote forward associations form between items of a list; inhibition of delay then develops to prevent the premature emission of these forward associations. This inhibition, spanning the items in the middle of the list, inhibits their correct elicitation.

McGeoch (1942) implies that the difficulty in learning items in the middle of the list is due to interference from remote forward and backward associations. The assumptions of this theory are as follows: (1) The greater the strength of remote forward and backward associations to any item in a list, the more these associations will interfere with elicitation of the correct response to the item. (2) The greater the distance between two items in a list, the weaker the association between them.

Table 7–1 shows that the average distance between an item and its

TABLE 7–1. Degree of Forward and Backward Remoteness between Items in a Serial List (as indexed by number of items between each stimulus of the list and its incorrect associations).

Stimuli	Responses					Average Distance
	A	B	C	D	E	
A	—	CR	1	2	3	2.0
B	0	—	CR	1	2	1.0
C	1	0	—	CR	1	.7
D	2	1	0	—	CR	1.0

CR—Correct Response.

interfering remote associations is much less for items near the middle of a list than for items near the end of the list. The table indicates the number of items intervening between any two given items in a serial list. If *A-B-C-D-E* represent the five words in a serial list, it can be seen in Table 7–1 that *C*, the middle word, is separated by only one word, at the most, from any other item in the list. On the other hand, an end item like *A* is separated by three other items (viz., *B-C-D*) from the word at the opposite end of the list. From McGeoch's position, it then follows that remote associations will interfere more with the learning of *C-D* than with the learning of *A-B*. This is because *C* will have a strong tendency to elicit *E*, *B*, and *A* as incorrect responses which could compete with the correct *C-D* association. In contrast, for stimulus *A*, response *C* is the closest incorrect, competing response in the list; both D and E are much more remote than any of the potentially competing responses to C.

Several pieces of data appear difficult to account for by means of such formulations. Battachi's (1958) data indicate that, when lists are very long, the serial position curve breaks into two bow-shaped curves. Such a relationship would not be anticipated on the basis of the theories outlined above. A study by Lippman and Denny (1964) also presents some problems for the remote association positions cited. In this study it was found that factors which interfere with the integration of the list into a single, discrete response unit distort the classical bowed-shaped curve. One group, for example, learned a serial list in which inter-trial interval (i.e., the time between the presentation of the last item in the list and the next presentation of the first item) was equal to the inter-stimulus interval (i.e., time between presentations of successive items of the list). This produced a marked flattening of the curve. (It should be noted that Glanzer and Peters, 1962, report similar results.) However, if the curve was replotted by considering the "first" item to be that item most frequently anticipated correctly, the resultant serial position curve very closely approximated the classical one. Lippman and Denny appear to suggest that, when the list does not objectively have a beginning and end, the subjects develop their own anchor points. The problem presented to remote association theories is clear. Such theories could accommodate the aspect of Lippman and Denny's study which shows a flattening of the serial position curve when the list has no distinct beginning or end. However, these theories do not easily provide a mechanism by which subjects can alter the degree of remote association by providing their own anchor points.

It appears that list integration may be an important factor influencing the order in which items are acquired, but the mechanisms basic to this order are still not well understood.

CONCLUSIONS

Often a great deal of experience with a stimulus (or response) complex is required before this complex can be dealt with in a consistent manner as a single unitary event. This is seen dramatically in the studies of sensory integration, where unfamiliar stimuli are often extremely difficult to perceive, or to recognize when encountered again at a later time. The studies of Ivo Kohler are particularly dramatic, since they demonstrate that we are capable of completely re-integrating common visual percepts after they have been subjected to extreme degrees of distortion; with experience, the distortion disappears and the stimuli look completely veridical!

The relationship between the embedding phenomenon as found in sensory stimuli and in linguistic units suggests that similar processes of integration are involved in these types of cognitive events. Further, the manner in which visual and auditory complexes develop into integrated units suggests that integration may be one of the mechanisms which relates frequency to differentiation (where differentiation refers to the ability of an element to resist confusion with other elements).

What is suggested above is an hierarchical arrangement in which the first level consists of the differentiation of elementary sensory inputs. These can then be combined to form a new percept. (E.g., individual letters of the alphabet must be differentiated before they can be reacted to in a stable fashion. Once they have been differentiated, the person can learn to assemble them into words. Each such word must be differentiated in turn.) The interesting speculation, at this point, is that differentiation of associational groupings may involve the same principles regardless of their level of complexity or molarity.

The serial learning research suggests that such learning may represent a form of serial integration. The theory proposed by Youssef is relevant to this issue and appears capable of accommodating a relatively wide range of the serial learning data.

8 | Meaning and Mediation: The Relationship between Concepts

PRECIS

The present chapter will distinguish between meaning and meaningfulness and will discuss the impact of meaning on learning. Meaningfulness will be considered in the subsequent chapter.

With the discussion of meaning, we return again to the issues relating concepts to learning. The meaning of a word (or picture, or object) can be related back to the attribute dimensions that constitute the cognitive space.

New experiences involve the projecting of concept-meanings onto a pre-existing organization of these concepts. Despite the fact that it has become a cliché to say that new experiences with concepts are reorganized to conform to our pre-existing organization of these concepts, we know relatively little about the mechanics of such effects, to say nothing of the manner or degree to which they will manifest themselves. In the present chapter, some of the known information in this area is discussed.

Mediation studies, particularly those involving natural-language associations, are clearly concerned with the organization of concepts and the manner in which this organization affects subsequent learning. In the present chapter we shall see that mediational structures function in ways that are quite unexpected from the point of view of mediation as a chain of associations. The entire mediational system appears to be bounded as a single entity, so that the strength of the relationship between individual pairs of items becomes a negligible factor in transfer.

The meaning of more complex units, such as sentences, can be analyzed into two components: (a) *The individual concepts that constitute the sentence.* A sentence may lose meaning if its component concepts lose meaning. For example, the phrase *pink accidents* involves a loss of meaning because the modifier (pink) of the concept (accidents) is not appropriate to the attribute space that defines the concept. (b) *The relationship between the concepts in the sentence.* This is the aspect of the sentence referred to as "knowledge" or "principles" by Gagne. For example, the clause *the grass ate the lions* would be considered anomalous because most persons would not believe this piece of knowledge.

271

DEMONSTRATION EXPERIMENT

The Problem

Read the following description of a Saturday afternoon with the Jones, and answer the matching test based on this.

Saturday Afternoon with the Jones

Father repaired an old bicycle. John, the 12-year-old son, went fishing. Mother drove to town to do the shopping. Susan, the 16-year-old daughter, shortened an old dress on the sewing machine.

Matching Test

Match the words in columns *A* and *B.* You may look back at the story while matching.

A	*B*
Boy _____	a) Station wagon
Father _____	b) Trout
Mother _____	c) Needle
Sister _____	d) Toy

Explanation

None of the words in column *B* appeared in the story, "Saturday Afternoon with the Jones." Nor did two of the words in column *A*. Despite this, there is great agreement among people performing this task. This agreement occurs because we enter the situation with a great deal of prior cognitive programming. "Trout" is part of the concept of "fishing." "Bicycle" is part of the concept "toy." And so forth.

Note that the matching could not have been done in the same manner without the story. For example, persons who had not read the story, when asked to match columns *A* and *B,* often paired "boy" with "toy," and "father" with "station wagon."

What are the processes involved in the demonstration above? There are several. First, as was noted earlier, elements of the story are parts of concept structures that the reader possesses before entering the present experimental situation. Second, the story relates these conceptual elements to various members of the Jones family—in other words, one set of concept elements is related to another set of elements. Third, given the various members of the family, the reader can now draw on the entire set of attributes belonging to the concept to which the family member was associated in the story.

The situation can be diagrammed in the following manner.

Stage 1. *The preprogrammed conceptual structures* (e.g., "bicycle" is a region of the larger cognitive region that defines "toy"). Call such a structure *A-B* (e.g., *A* corresponds to "bicycle," *B* to "toy").

Stage 2. *The story as a context for relating concepts* (e.g., "father" is related to "bicycle"). Call this *A-C* (e.g., *A* still corresponds to "bicycle," *C* to "father").

Stage 3. *The transfer situation,* using the elements developed in the first two stages (e.g., given "father," will the reader think of "toy"). Call this *C-B,* a relationship which never occurred before in a direct fashion, but is mediated by *A,* as *C-A-B.*

Note that in order to give the appropriate "toy" response to "father," the reader must resist interference from the prior relationship between "father" and "station wagon."

MEANING AND MEDIATION

The Distinction between Meaning and Meaningfulness

MEANING. The notion of *meaning* must be distinguished from that of *meaningfulness,* since both of these have been investigated to some extent in learning research. The meaning of a word is the set of referents of that word. When dealing with words that denote concrete objects, instances of such referents can often be pointed to or described in physical terms. Referents of abstract terms are often sets of behaviors or sets of feelings, or combinations of these. For example, as we saw in Chapter 2, a word like "beauty" may refer to a set of physical objects which evoke a particular pleasurable reaction. When a learning study is concerned with the effects of *specific referents* of a word on learning, the issue is one of meaning.

For example, a number of studies have examined the acquisition of association between two words under conditions in which these two words share a common set of referents. Such studies are often called studies of mediated transfer. Other experiments have examined questions related to *partially shared* referents: If two words are from the same concept (e.g., horse and cow) and therefore share certain referents (e.g., both are animals, both have four legs, etc.) will interference result if we try to learn a different response to each of these?

In Chapter 2 we conceptualized the psychological representation of a concept in terms of bounded regions in the cognitive space. From this point of view, the referents of a word (or picture, or other type of sign or symbol) can be represented in terms of relevant psychological dimensions and their intersection. This may prove to be a valuable consideration. Deese (1968), for example, has raised the question of how we are to account for the frequently encountered phenomenon of *paraphrasing*. He notes that for any sequence of words, a completely different sequence can be found which will have the same meaning. Further, it is common to have a person hear an event described in one sequence of words and then have him recall it at a later date in a paraphrased form. This indicates, Deese suggests, that the basic units with which we are dealing are *not* associations between words. If this is the case, then what are these basic units? Archer (1964) refers to such units as "ideas." However, this leaves us with the problem of characterizing the notion of the "idea" in some relatively rigorous fashion. It shall be seen in the present chapter that the dimensional representation in cognitive space may serve the needed requirements for a way in which to characterize the "idea."

These issues will be examined in greater detail when we discuss the notions of synonymity and mediation, later in this chapter.

MEANINGFULNESS.   Chapter 9 will consider the notion of meaningfulness in a more comprehensive fashion. At this point our concern is with distinguishing it from the notion of meaning. Meaningfulness is concerned with the *extent* to which a word or nonsense syllable has meaning, as opposed to a concern for the *specific meaning* of the word. Intuitively, we may feel that it is reasonable to say that some words have more meaning than others. However, if we are dealing with real words, and if we can define each of these, in what sense can we say that one is more meaningful than another?

We shall see, in the next chapter, that words can be distinguished in terms of a number of variables in addition to their specific referents. Some words are more familiar than others. (We have seen in earlier chapters that frequency of prior experience is related to both the differentiation and the boundary strength variables.) Words also differ in the extent to which they can elicit relevant images. Finally, words differ in the extent to which they evoke other words as associations. We shall see that all these factors are extremely important to an understanding of the role of meaningfulness in learning.

It should be noted, at this point, that the original use of nonsense syllables by Ebbinghaus (1913) and Glaze (1928) was designed primarily to control *meaning* rather than *meaningfulness*. These investigators felt that real words often have prior associations to one another, or share common referents. In such cases, learning to associate one of these words with another would not represent new learning, but would constitute strengthening of previous learning. To avoid these problems, nonsense syllables were used which had few or no referents. We shall see that the use of such materials tended to complicate, rather than to simplify, the study of learning processes.

The Mind as an Organizer of Experience

The representational regions of the cognitive space *do not exist in an unorganized fashion such that they can be aroused in any arbitrary, random manner* that an experimenter may invent. Instead, there appear to be a number of organizing factors at work. Some of these were explored in Chapter 7; there we saw that isolated stimulus sequences are often completely obscured because the mind integrates them into larger units. The discovery by Bartlett (1932) concerning the distorted recall of culturally unfamiliar material is also related to the issues under discussion. Bartlett's British subjects, when presented a story involving a war between ghosts, altered the supernatural aspects of the story so as to make it conform to Western expectations.

SERIAL ORGANIZATION OF EXPERIENCE. We know very little, thus far, about the organizational properties of the mind. Several extremely provocative entries into this area have been reported, but these have involved extremely simple types of organizations. An early study is that of DeSoto and Bosley (1962) who examined certain aspects of serial organization. A number of classes of materials which we encounter in our daily lives are ordered in serial fashions. The number series is one example; the alphabet is another. DeSoto and Bosley used the sequence *freshman, sophomore, junior, senior.* These were used as the response terms in a 16-item paired-associates lists; each of these responses was associated to four different stimulus words. The entire list was presented in several random orders. The learning data followed the typical bowed-shaped serial-learning curve described in Chapter 7: The pairs involving the response *freshman* were the easiest to learn; next came the pairs involving the response *senior;* the most difficult pairs were those involving the responses *sophomore* and *junior.*

In other words, *the psychological organization of the responses* determined the learning rates for these pairs. These words had been originally learned as a sequentially organized set; this fact predominated over the random order of presentation employed in the experiment. This was true despite the fact that the prior organization of the words was irrelevant to the objective requirements of the task.

Pollio and Draper (1966) report essentially the same type of organizational influence when they used the numbers 1, 2, 3, 4, 5 as response terms in paired-associates learning. As in DeSoto and Bosley (1962), Pollio and Draper obtained the bowed-shaped serial-learning curve when trials to learn were plotted against the numerical sequence of the response items; again, this was true despite the fact that the pairs had been presented in random order during learning. Ebenholtz (1966) extended this finding by first having subjects learn a set of nonsense syllables in a serial order, then using these same nonsense syllables as stimuli in a paired-associates task. The prior serial order of the nonsense syllables determined the ease with which they were learned.

DIMENSIONAL SEQUENCES AS DETERMINERS OF COGNITIVE ORGANIZATION. The studies described above involved materials which had *previously been learned in serial sequence.* Even more frequently, we deal with material that can be ordered in terms of psychological dimensions, even though we have not learned this ordering as a serial sequence in the past. Pollio (1968) discusses an experiment involving several such dimensions. One of these was the dimension: *beautiful, pretty, fair, homely,* and *ugly.* Another was: *cold, cool, mild, warm,* and *hot.* Using these words as responses in paired associates, Pollio reports that ease of learning distributed itself along these dimensions as though they were serially ordered. In other words, those pairs involving adjectives from the end points of the dimensions were most easily learned; those pairs involving adjectives arising from the middle of the dimensions were most difficult to learn.

Such results suggest that the ordering of elements along cognitive dimensions taps viable psychological processes and does not simply represent an *ad hoc* exercise in logic. The mind appears to organize incoming stimuli in terms of previously acquired cognitive structures.

Finally, it should be noted that the type of phenomena described above are not restricted to the organization of purely verbal dimensions. A study by Blockovich (1969) used circles of various sizes or lines at various angles of inclination, as stimuli in paired associates. Despite the fact that the pairs were presented in various random orders, ease of learning distributed itself in a bowed serial curve along these physical dimensions. Pairs involving the largest and smallest circles were learned relatively easily; ease of learning fell off in a regular fashion as a function of approach to the middle-sized circle. A corresponding curve was obtained for the dimension of angles. Again we find that the mind processes incoming information in terms of pre-existing cognitive organizations.

MEDIATIONAL PROCESSES IN LEARNING AND THINKING

The demonstration Experiment at the beginning of the present chapter provided an example of mediational processes in operation. After reading the story, in that example, most people can match *mother* with *station wagon,* despite the fact that the term station wagon never appeared in the story. Why? Because the story tells us that mother drove to town to do the shopping. The crucial factor that permits the matching of mother with station wagon is the relationship between the words *drove* and *station wagon.* These are both aspects of the same concept. Psychologists in this area of research would call the word *drove* a mediator: It mediates the matching of the terms *mother* and *station wagon* in this example.

A great many studies have been conducted in the area of mediational processes. As can be seen in the *mother, station wagon* example, most of these studies have been concerned with developing sequential structures of associations and with demonstrating that such structures can influence subsequent processing of information in learning and thinking. We shall see that such structures appear to involve the formation of higher order cognitive units in which the simple associations, between *paired* words or symbols, drop out as functional units.

Mediation: The Basis of Thought?

Early studies of mediation were designed to suggest mechanisms which might explain how humans and lower animals combine cognitive or behavioral units to produce behavior that could be described as showing foresight or reasoning. Pioneering studies by Shipley (1933) and Lumsdaine (1939) were concerned with mediation in simple chains of associations. The chain was constructed in the following manner. First, a light was used as a conditioned stimulus to develop a conditioned eyeblink response; the unconditioned stimulus was a sudden tap on the cheek. Next, the tap on the cheek was used as a *conditioned stimulus* to finger withdrawal; here, a shock to the finger was the unconditioned stimulus. The question was now asked: If the light had been conditioned to evoke the eyeblink, and if the eyeblink had been part of the stimulus to finger withdrawal, would the light elicit the finger withdrawal even though light and finger withdrawal had never been paired directly? The results of both studies showed that such mediation could occur.

The chain of forward associations described above can be schematized in the following way:

Stage 1. *A-B* (where *A* is light, *B* is tap-eyeblink)
Stage 2. *B-C* (where *B* is tap, *C* is finger withdrawal)
Stage 3. *A-* (*B*) *-C* (will presentation of *A* elicit *B-C?*)

In Chapter 1 we characterized thinking as the utilization of prior learning in a new situation. From that perspective, we can see that the Shipley-Lumsdaine paradigm represents a mechanism for thinking. Hull (1935*b*) has proposed detailed mediational mechanisms in an attempt to explain several types of reasoning behavior from a purely behavioristic point of view. More recently, Osgood (1953) and Maltzman (1955) have spelled out comprehensive theories of thinking that have employed the mediation process as a basic assumption. An example from Osgood will give some flavor of these theories. Consider a situation, Osgood suggests, in which you need a fire in order to survive, but you do not have kindling wood for a fire. Equivalent to *B-C* above, you have the association *wood-fire*. In your pocket you find a pencil. Equivalent to *A-B* above, you have the association *pencil-wood*. The two associative segments, *A-B* and *B-C*, can now be run off as a unit upon seeing the pencil: pencil-wood-fire. You use the pencil as kindling and are saved.

Varieties of Mediational Paradigms: Do They Function Differently?

The Shipley-Lumsdaine paradigm is a three-stage chain in which all the associations are in the forward direction. If one changes the order of the elements in the three stages, eight different possible mediational paradigms can be specified. For example, in place of the *B-C* forward association of Stage 2 we might have a *C-B* backward association. One might anticipate that backward associations should provide poorer mediational support to Stage 3 than would forward associations. Table 8–1 outlines the eight possible three-stage paradigms.

TABLE 8–1. Types of Three-Stage Mediation

Forward Chain $(A \rightarrow B \rightarrow C)$	Stage 1: Learn Stage 2: Learn Stage 3: Test	*A-B* *B-C* *A-C*	*B-C* *A-B* *A-C*
Backward Chain $(A \leftarrow B \leftarrow C)$	Stage 1: Learn Stage 2: Learn Stage 3: Test	*B-A* *C-B* *A-C*	*C-B* *B-A* *A-C*
Stimulus Equivalence $(A \rightarrow B \leftarrow C)$	Stage 1: Learn Stage 2: Learn Stage 3: Test	*A-B* *C-B* *A-C*	*C-B* *A-B* *A-C*
Response Equivalence $(A \leftarrow B \rightarrow C)$	Stage 1: Learn Stage 2: Learn Stage 3: Test	*B-A* *B-C* *A-C*	*B-C* *B-A* *A-C*

A comprehensive study by Horton and Kjeldergaard (1961) examined all eight of these three-stage paradigms, and found that all eight led to a facilitation of Stage 3 performance, compared to a control group in which Stage 3 was unrelated to the initial stages. Further, these researchers were unable to find a significant difference in the *degree* of facilitation among the various paradigms.

This study suggests that, once the appropriate cognitive structures are formed, the original direction of the associations becomes irrelevant to the subjects' ability to use the structures. Such conclusions are very consistent with the evidence, which we examined in Chapter 5, concerning the arbitrary nature of the distinction between stimulus and response, particularly in the area of verbal associations.

Horton and Hartman (1963), concerned about the implications of associative symmetry in the Horton and Kjeldergaard (1961) study, attempt to assess this in a study aimed primarily at the issue of the relative strengths of forward versus backward mediation. In contrast to the Horton and Kjeldergaard study, which compared all possible forward association paradigms with all possible backward association paradigms, Horton and Hartman considered only one example of each. The forward association, mediational paradigm examined was *A-B, B-C, A-C;* the backward was *A-B, B-C, C-A.* Unfortunately, the materials used were very low frequency words which were, for the most part, the equivalent of nonsense materials for most of the subjects involved (e.g., nilum). Thus it can not be assumed that the *A* stimuli, as encountered in the Stage 1 *A-C* pairs, were as available *as responses* as were the *C* responses in these pairs. From this it follows that the Stage 3 *C-A* pairs (viz., the backward associations) would be at a disadvantage compared to the Stage 3 *A-C* pairs (viz., the forward associations).

While the Horton and Hartman (1963) study found a significant advantage in the mediational effect for the forward associations as opposed to the backward, the implication of this difference is not clear since the conditions of response availability were not constant for the two paradigms.

Finally, a study by Cramer and Cofer (1960) investigated the eight, three-stage mediation paradigms using natural language associations and found essentially the same results as Horton and Kjeldergaard (1961). The distinction between these two studies is interesting and should be pointed out. The Horton and Kjeldergaard study involved the development of the appropriate associations between arbitrarily selected nonsense syllables at each of the three stages. Thus the associative history of the various stages was determined in the laboratory.

In contrast to this, Cramer and Cofer (1960) took advantage of the fact that sizable associations between words develop naturally in the language. As an example of the use of natural language associations, consider a simple *A-B, B-C, A-C* forward chain mediational paradigm. Here, the *A-B* association might be a natural language association, acquired many years prior to the experiment, such as the pair *table-chair*. The first list encountered by the subject in the laboratory might then be *B-C*—e.g., *chair-dax*. The Stage 3 test, *A-C*, would then involve learning *table-dax*. If mediation were successful in Stage 3, then *table* would remind the subject of *chair*, which in turn would remind him of *dax*, and he could respond correctly, giving *dax* to *table*.

The Cramer and Cofer (1960) study indicates that the relative equivalence of effectiveness for the eight mediational structures of the three-stage paradigms is a general and replicable phenomenon across both natural associations and associative structures developed in the laboratory.

FOUR-STAGE MEDIATIONAL STRUCTURES. In the preceding paragraphs we have concentrated on the three-stage mediational paradigms and have found that the mediation effect is consistently obtained. As the number of stages involved in the mediation process increases, the number of elements which mediate the critical test association also increases. Let us consider a simple four-stage paradigm in which all the associations are in the forward direction: viz., a four-stage chain:

Stage 1. *A-B*   Stage 3. *C-D*
Stage 2. *B-C*   Stage 4. *A-(B-C)-D*

In Stage 4 we test for the existence of the mediational structure. Presumably, if this structure was developed during the first three stages, the subject should learn the *A-D* association very readily during Stage 4 test performance. Presentation of *A* should evoke *B,* due to Stage 1 practice; *B* in turn should evoke *C,* due to practice in Stage 2; and *C* is already associated to *D* as a consequence of Stage 3 training. Thus, all the requisite associations are already developed for *A* to elicit *D* before the first trial of Stage 4 training.

Note that in the four-stage paradigm, two elements, *B* and *C,* are required to mediate the *A-D* association. On the other hand, in the three-stage paradigms described in the earlier sections, only a single element is required to serve as mediator, e.g., *A-(B)-C.* It is not surprising, perhaps, that this increase in the number of elements involved in the mediational structure results in a great deal of instability in the four-stage structures as compared to the three-stage, so that the four-stage is often difficult to establish. Some studies have reported evidence for four-stage mediational structures, particularly when natural language materials were used (e.g., Russell and Storms, 1955; Cofer and Yarczower, 1957; McGehee and Schulz, 1961) . Even in these studies, the effects are often weak. The Martin, Oliver, Hom, and Heaslet (1963) study provides an interesting example of the way in which the four-stage effects may suddenly disappear after the investigators had thought they had developed a procedure adequate to produce the mediational phenomenon.

Of particular interest is a large scale study reported by Jenkins (1963) in which he attempted to evaluate the relative effectiveness of 16 different four-stage mediation paradigms. This investigation was designed to parallel that of Horton and Kjeldergaard (1961) in which the eight possible three-stage paradigms had been compared. Like Horton and Kjeldergaard before him, Jenkins shunned the use of natural language associations; instead, he attempted to develop new associations between pairs of nonsense syllables at each of the stages in the paradigms. In this study, Jenkins failed to find evidence for mediation in any of the 16 four-stage paradigms!

As shall be seen in the next section of this chapter, there is evidence to suggest that the set of associations which constitute a mediational structure can be conceptualized as *a single, integrated unit with its own boundary strength.* As we have seen in Chapters 2 and 7, a greater amount of boundary strength is required to protect the integrity of a cognitive system when that system includes a larger number of elements. Thus the instability of the four-stage paradigms, as opposed to the relative stability of the three-stage paradigms, can be accounted for by the fact that the former involve a greater number of elements to be bounded than the latter.

Does the Mediational Structure Constitute an Integrated Cognitive System?

Research concerned with the associative strength of individual S-R units in the mediational chain has produced some of the most provocative data in the literature on mediational phenomena. Since early theories of mediation conceptualized the process as a chaining of individual S-R units, the associative strengths of these individual units was considered a crucial factor in the success of the mediation. For example, let us conisder the simple three-stage mediation paradigm, A-(B)-C, formed by forward associations. In Stage 3, the subject is likely to emit the C response to the A stimulus because prior to this stage he had already learned A-B and B-C. However, what if the A-B connection were very weak? In that case, the likelihood of A eliciting B would be reduced, and if B were not elicited by A, how could B perform its mediating function and elicit C? Clearly, it could not. Thus the greater the associative strength between A-B (or between B-C), the greater the likelihood that the mediation will be successful, and that in the Stage 3 test, A will elicit C.

This prediction from association theory has failed to be sustained either when A-B was a prior association in the English language or when A-B was learned in the laboratory.

STUDIES INVOLVING NATURAL LANGUAGE ASSOCIATES. A study by Kincaid, Bousfield, and Whitmarsh (1962) will serve to illustrate a number of similar experiments from Bousfield's laboratory on this topic. As A-B they used pairs of words which had been found to be associates on the Russell and Jenkins (1954) version of the Kent-Rosanoff word association test. The assumption was made that the frequency with which a word, A, elicited a second word, B, in the word association norms, is an index of the associative strength of the A-B connection. The subjects were taught B-C in the laboratory, then tested for the mediated A-C. While a strong mediation effect was found in this study, this effect was *unrelated to the strength of the A-B associations* in the Russell-Jenkins norms. Extremely weak

A-B associations in the Russell-Jenkins norms produced as much mediation as extremely strong associations.

Jenkins (1963) reports an unpublished dissertation by one of his students, Carlin (1958), which obtained essentially the same results as Kincaid, Bousfield, and Whitmarsh (1962).

Corroborating data are reported by Peterson and Blattner (1963) in a study involving an *A-B, B-C, A-C* chain; here *B-C* was a prior association in the natural language, taken from the Russell-Jenkins norms. The strong associations, in this study, were those that occurred with between 35% to 85% frequency in the norms, while the weak associations were those that occurred with between 1% and 3% frequency. (*Heavy-light* is an example of a strong association; *heavy-lead* is an example of a weak association.) Subjects were taught *A-B* and then tested on *A-C*. Both strong and weak *B-C* associations produced sizable mediation effects and were equally effective in producing these effects.

STUDIES INVOLVING ASSOCIATIONS DEVELOPED IN THE LABORATORY. Several studies have investigated the effect of associative strength on subsequent mediational behavior in situations where all the relevant associations were developed in the laboratory, rather than using natural language associations. These include: Horton and Hartman (1963), Peterson and Blattner (1963), Peterson (1964), Schwenn and Underwood (1965), Schulz and Weaver (1968), and Weaver, Hopkins, and Schulz (1968). All of these studies manipulated the associative strength of *A-B, B-C,* or both *A-B* and *B-C* by varying either (*a*) the number of training trials or (*b*) the number of correct responses during learning.

All of these studies found significant mediational effects. However, only the Weaver, Hopkins, and Schulz (1968) study found any evidence indicating that this effect was related to the *strength* of the *A-B* or *B-C* association.

In a related study, Horton and Wiley (1967*a*) manipulated strength of the *A-B* and *B-C* associations by varying the *time* between acquisition of Stages 1 and 2 and the test for Stage 3 mediation. Stage 3 occurred 0, 1, 3, 5, or 10 days after the acquisition of Stages 1 (viz., *A-B*) and 2 (viz., *B-C*). In this study, there was no drop in the mediation effect across the 10-day interval, as measured by rate of *A-C* acquisition. If anything, there appeared to be a slight *increase* in mediation across this interval, but this was not significant. In other words, diminution of *A-B* and *B-C* strength with time did not reduce their ability to mediate the *A-C* response.

WHAT ARE THE IMPLICATIONS OF THE STRENGTH-OF-ASSOCIATION STUDIES? In the Demonstration Experiment at the beginning of the present chapter we read a story in which, "Father repaired an old bicycle . . . Mother drove to town." In the subsequent matching test, this story was sufficient to permit the matching of *father* to *toy* rather than to *station wagon;* and it permitted the matching of *mother* to *station wagon*. This demonstration is pertinent to the data we have been reviewing, in the last few pages, for several reasons. First, the dominant association to *father,* within the matching task, for people who had *not* read the story, was *station wagon*. Before reading the story, no one matched *father* and *toy*. Yet reading the story was sufficient to establish a *local context* in which father and toy appeared to "go together" for virtually all subjects. And this happened despite the fact that the word *toy* did not appear in the story! (Incidentally, such results would probably *not* occur in a culture which employed bicycles as an important means of transportation.)

A second point to be made, in regard to the Demonstration Experiment, is that the frequency of association between words like *drove* and *station wagon* is not extremely great. Yet, *drove* was easily capable of serving as the mediator to *station wagon* for virtually all subjects.

Clearly, then, it appears to have been the *relationship between concepts,* established in the story, that permitted the facile mediation between words in the matching test, not the prior frequency of association between words. Local context proved sufficient to permit the establishment of relationships between concepts, and these relationships proved sufficient to permit the mediation effects to occur. This conclusion appears to be consistent with the empirical data, presented in the immediately previous sections, concerned with the relationship between associative strength and the probability of obtaining a mediation effect. Associative strength does not appear to be a critical factor in mediation.

WHAT IS MEDIATIONAL STRUCTURE? An even more radical suggestion appears to emerge very strongly from the strength of association studies. The studies described above suggest that the development of a mediational structure involves the organization of a new, multi-element system in which the boundary strengths of individual pairs of elements are no longer crucial. Instead, the entire set of elements (e.g., *A-B-C* in the simple three-stage paradigm) behaves like a single, bounded system.

Let us trace the development of a three-stage, forward association chain (viz., *A-B, B-C, A-C*) through Stages 2 and 3.

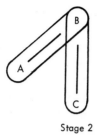

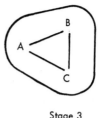

Stage 2

Stage 3

At Stage 2, the subject has learned two competing systems, *A-B* and
B-C. We have encountered this particular type of competition previously in this book (see Chapters 5 and 6), and know it produces
massive interference: Acquisition of *A-B* leads to proactive interference in the subsequent acquisition of *B-C*, while the learning of *B-C*
leads to retroactive inhibition in the recall of *A-B* (e.g., Murdock,
1958a; Mandler and Earhard, 1964; Goulet and Postman, 1966;
Horton and Wiley, 1967a). At this point we enter Stage 3. Note that
entering Stage 3 represents, essentially, an *altered state of mind on
the part of the subject*. In Stage 3, he is shown a Stage 1 stimulus
(viz., *A*) and is asked to give the appropriate Stage 2 response (viz.,
C), despite the fact that he has never before seen *A* and *C* together in
this task. Several studies have shown that subjects can often give the
correct *A-C* response without a single trial of *A-C* training! The
subject can merely be told to give the response, from the previously
learned list, which he thinks is most likely to be correct for each of
the *A* stimuli. This is sufficient to bring the subject into Stage 3, and
to largely dissipate the competition between *A-B* and *B-C* that was
observed in Stage 2.

The mediational structure can be conceptualized as a closed, three-
element system in which all the elements are interconnected. The
studies concerned with strength of associations in mediational systems suggest that, once such a unitary mediational system is developed, the crucial issue is not the boundary strengths of the individual
subsystems, but the boundary strength of the total three-element
system.

A study by Weaver and Schulz (1968) appears to be consistent
with the type of interpretation offered above. In this study, recall of
A-B was tested following varying numbers of *A-C* trials. For subjects
in the mediation condition (viz., *A-B, B-C, A-C*), recall of *A-B* remained *constant* whether *A-C* had been learned to 0, 3, 7, or 15
trials. For nonmediation subjects, on the other hand (viz., those who

learned *A-B, D-C, A-C*), acquisition of *A-C led to interference* with *A-B* recall.

We have already seen that such closed, mediational systems are difficult to establish when more than three elements are involved (Jenkins, 1963). This is, of course, consistent with the fact that, the greater the number of elements in a system, the greater the amount of boundary strength which is required to permit the system to resist interference.

While systems which have four or more elements are apparently very unstable, even the three-element system is not completely stable and may break down, with time, into competing subsystems. Dallett (1964), for example, found some degree of both proactive and retroactive inhibition in the three-element paradigm after 48 hours. These effects were due to competition between the simple associations comprising the mediational system.

The Role of Awareness in Mediation

Early behaviorists developed the mediational notions in an attempt to account for *thinking* in objective, behavioral terms. If anything, the mediational mechanism was to account for the phenomena which the layman had associated with awareness; the use of awareness as a mechanism in accounting for mediation would have been considered self-defeating. Yet time has led to just such a state of affairs; researchers who had spent years studying the phenomena surrounding the mediational mechanisms found the data extremely complex and some (see particularly Jenkins, 1963) have turned to a notion of awareness in an attempt to explain aspects of the data involved in mediation. A more general discussion of the notion of awareness must be postponed until Chapter 11, which will be devoted to examining awareness and verbal control of behavior. However, the topic must be introduced here in connection with mediation.

Let us consider an example in which experimenters might be sorely tempted to speak of subjects consciously using the existence of mediators to facilitate their performance. In the Barnes and Underwood (1959) study, subjects first learned *A-B,* then learned *A-C* in a situation in which *B* and *C* were synonyms. In other words, we are dealing with a three-stage paradigm in which the first stage, *B-C,* is a natural association in the language. Once the subjects had learned the *A-B* list (e.g., *A-happy*), it was possible for them to learn the *A-C* list (e.g., *A-cheerful*) after a *single presentation,* and with almost no errors. The subjects' behavior could be described as *using* the *B* response to elicit *C*.

Why refer to the subjects *using B* rather than merely invoke the running off of the mediational chain? The primary reason is that we must specify the functioning of some type of operator mechanism that permits the subject to *suppress* the *B* response after a single exposure to *A-C* and to *select* the appropriate *C* response. The importance of such an operator becomes particularly clear when we note that the mediator, *B,* is typically strongly bounded to a *number of different words* (e.g., *happy* could serve as a mediator for *cheerful, gay, joyful,* etc.) and the facilitation effect in the *A-C* test would be approximately as great whichever of these had arbitrarily been selected to serve as *C*.

The importance of an awareness notion is indicated by comparing those studies in which the entire test list involved a single mediational principle with studies using mixed lists in the test stage, some pairs in the test list having mediators in the prior list, some not. In the mixed list studies, the relationship between the stages of the experiment is not as obvious to the subjects. Some may not notice the existence of mediators. Even when the existence of mediators is noted, the subjects are not always sure which items involve mediators and which do not. As we might expect from the assumption of an awareness mechanism, the mediation effect is much weaker in studies employing a mixed list design (e.g., Ryan, 1960; Bastian, 1961; Postman, 1962*e*) than in studies in which the entire list involves the Stage 3 mediational test (e.g., Barnes and Underwood, 1959) .

AWARENESS AND THE FAILURE TO FIND FOUR-STAGE MEDIATION. We noted earlier in this chapter that Jenkins (1963) and his students engaged in a large-scale attempt to develop 16 of the 32 possible four-stage mediation paradigms in the laboratory, and that they failed to find evidence for mediation in any of these paradigms. Further, it should be noted that some of these paradigms had previously been found to produce a mediation effect when natural language associations had been employed.

Why had the four-stage paradigms proved unsuccessful when Jenkins had attempted to develop the four stages in the laboratory? In attempting to explain this failure, Jenkins (1963) suggested a set of considerations very closely related to the awareness processes discussed above. Let us examine Jenkins' argument in terms of one of the four-stage paradigms he studied. In his experiment the successive stimuli and responses were all verbal elements (words and nonsense syllables). In the following enumeration of the stages, the letters in parenthesis represent the presumed mediators.

Stage 1. Learn A-B.
Stage 2. Learn C-B.
Stage 3. Learn A- $(B$-$C)$ -D.
Stage 4. Test C-D.

The crucial connection between C and D should have been acquired in Stage 3, when the subject learned A-D; note, however, that this connection, if it developed, must be developed in a covert fashion since the subject did not overtly emit B-C during Stage 3. The critical test for the operation of a mediation mechanism occurred at Stage 4. Only if Stage 4 learning is facilitated, as opposed to the performance of a control group, do we know that a mediational structure has been established, in these studies.

When Jenkins (1963) failed to find any evidence for facilitation of Stage 4 learning, he asked: Is it possible that subjects must actually *emit* the mediational B-C responses in Stage 3, even if only covertly, in order to form the C-D association at Stage 3? Further, is it possible that the requirements of the task, during Stage 3, actually discourage such covert emission of B-C? In Stage 3, the subject is *instructed* to learn A-D, a verbal association; it is possible that the covert emission of B-C as verbal responses to A might interfere with A-D acquisition; this might lead subjects to suppress the B-C responses to A during Stage 3.

In support of this possibility, Jenkins (1963) points out that at least two studies have succeeded in finding a mediation effect using the four-stage paradigm outlined above (Shipley, 1935; Wickens and Briggs, 1951) and that in these studies the mediating responses were less likely to interfere with the acquisition of subsequent associations than in the purely verbal learning situations characteristic of the Jenkins' laboratory. Consider Wickens and Briggs (1951) as an example. Here subjects learned to make the same verbal responses to two different stimuli, a light and a tone. Thus Stages 1 and 2 consisted of the associations light-word and tone-word. In Stage 3 the tone was associated with a shock so that tone elicited a *GSR*. Since the verbal response to the tone and the *GSR* to the tone are not incompatible responses, suppression of the tone-word association would not be necessary in order to learn tone-*GSR*. Stage 4 results were consistent with this interpretation: The *light* was found to elicit the *GSR* despite the fact that light and shock had not been paired. Presumably this was produced by the mediated association: light- (word) -*GSR*.

While Jenkins' (1963) argument is plausible, a note of caution must be introduced. In the three-stage paradigm, similar problems of suppression of potential mediators also may arise. For example, consider the paradigm:

Stage 1. Learn *A-B*.
Stage 2. Learn *A-C*.
Stage 3. Test *B*- (*A*) -*C*.

Here we would expect massive unlearning of the *A-B* association during Stage 2, and the unavailability of the mediator, *A*, in Stage 3. Instead, both the Horton and Kjeldergaard (1961) and the Cramer and Cofer (1960) studies indicate the mediation is as strong in this paradigm as in any of the other three-stage designs investigated.

CONCEPT-UTILIZATION IN THE FOUR-STAGE PARADIGMS. In discussing the four-stage paradigms, earlier in this chapter, it was noted that the most successful studies involving such paradigms have been those that used natural language associations. We may now ask why this should be the case. At one time it was assumed that the reason for this was that natural language associations are extremely strong as compared to laboratory developed associations. The more recent evidence relating strength of association to mediation indicates that this type of explanation is inadequate. The best evidence to date suggests that there is some small minimum degree of associative experience which is necessary for each pair at each stage of the mediation paradigm in order to produce a mediation effect; anything above this small minimum appears to be irrelevant. This evidence has been reviewed in an earlier section of the present chapter.

Examination of a four-stage paradigm, involving natural language associations, which was successful in finding a mediation effect, will prove informative. Below is a mediational structure taken from the classic study by Russell and Storms (1955). Stages 1 and 2 were assumed to exist in the subjects as natural language associations, since these were associations found in the Russell-Jenkins word association norms. Therefore, only Stages 3 and 4 were learned in the laboratory.

Stage 1. *A-B:* Soldier-Sailor (Assumed) .
Stage 2. *B-C:* Sailor-Navy (Assumed) .
Stage 3. *D-A:* zug-Soldier (Learned) .
Stage 4. *D*- (*A-B*) -*C:* zug- (Soldier-Sailor) -Navy (Learned) .

Since *Navy* was not found as an associate to *Soldier,* in the Russell-Jenkins norms, but *Sailor* was, it was assumed that the *Soldier-Navy* association must be mediated by the term *Sailor.* Thus the *zug-Navy* association must be mediated by the chain *Soldier-Sailor.*

Note, however, that *Soldier* and *Navy* are both members of a larger concept of *military.* Thus *zug-Soldier* and *zug-Navy* both involve associations between *zug* and a common region of the cognitive space determined by the attributes of the concept *military.* What the writer is suggesting is that such natural language mediation may not represent a four-element chain of associations between words. Instead, the word *Soldier* may activate the entire relevant region in the cognitive space, and this may mediate the correct response in Stage 4: *zug-* (military concept) *-Navy.*

The question raised here is not whether chains of associations can be developed. We saw in Chapter 7 when we discussed serial learning that they certainly can be formed. The question being raised is whether such chains are the actual basis of fairly complex mediational sequences which have been studied. Since the difficulty in establishing four-stage chains can not be attributed to weakness of the associative strengths in the individual stages of the paradigms, it seems reasonable to look for the difference between natural language mediators and laboratory-developed mediators *within the basic structure* of our conception of the mediator.

When Mediation Is Detrimental (or Irrelevant)

For the most part, in the studies discussed above the mediators facilitated the performance of some response which the subjects were instructed to make. In other words, the mediators were consistent with the subjects' task requirements. We shall see that this need not be true; under certain circumstances, the occurrence of mediation could be detrimental (or at best irrelevant) to the task requirements.

MEDIATED INTERFERENCE. Let us first consider the situation in which the development of a mediating structure should, within the usual assumptions of chaining theory, lead to interference with subsequent learning. We shall see that the evidence for this type of effect is not extremely strong and that the data again suggest that the chaining notions require modification.

The following three-stage paradigm should, presumably, lead to interference: A-B, B-C_r, A-C. Here, the B element in Stage 2 is associated to a C which will be the appropriate response to *some* A element in Stage 3, but not to the A which was associated to B in Stage 1. The Stage 3 mediation situation will, there, be A-$(B$-$C_r)$-C, with C and C_r competing responses. The reader will recognize that, if the hypothesized B-C_r mediation actually occurred, this would be equivalent to the A-B, A-B_r interference paradigm discussed in Chapter 6 and found to be the most disruptive for learning of all the paradigms examined.

Three studies have reported data on the mediated interference paradigm in recent years. The strongest evidence for the existence of mediated interference comes from Horton and Wiley (1967b). This study examined both mediated interference and mediated facilitation as compared to a control condition. The facilitation effect proved to be massive, but the corresponding interference effect was of borderline significance: Number of correct responses in the first five trials of Stage 3 learning indicated a barely significant advantage to the control group over the interference group; number of trials to criterion in Stage 3 did not produce a significant difference between the interference and the control groups.

Hopkins and Schulz (1967), using materials and procedures that had, in the past, produced sizable facilitation effects in the A-B, B-C, A-C paradigm could not find a significant interference effect when they used an A-B, B-C_r, A-C paradigm. A small amount of interference was obtained, but it failed to reach statistical significance.

Perhaps the most important of these studies, in terms of its potential implications, is that of Earhard and Mandler (1965). As in the other two studies, the A-B, B-C_r, A-C paradigm was used; however, these writers compared two different types of instructions. One group was informed of the mediation hypothesis and were given examples of the manner in which mediated chains develop. The second experimental group was given no such instructions. Earhard and Mandler found a small tendency toward interference in the instructed subjects; this effect was not significant when evaluated against a nonmediation control group and was of approximately the same magnitude as the effect found in the two previously cited studies. The noninstructed experimental group, trained in the mediated interference paradigm, actually showed some facilitation in Stage 3 learning, as compared to the nonmediation control group. This facilitation was a borderline effect, significant for trials to criterion but not for number of correct responses during the first six trials. On the other hand, the difference between the two *experimental* groups was clearly statistically significant.

The Earhard and Mandler (1965) study suggests that even the small amount of mediated interference reported in other studies may be the result of the subjects consciously *trying* to use the mediators.

Note, incidentally, that the mediated interference paradigm does *not* produce the closed three-element system described earlier in this chapter as characteristic of three-stage facilitation paradigms.

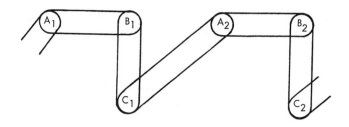

In the interference paradigm, A_1-B_1 and A_2-B_2 are developed in Stage 1; B_1-C_1 and B_2-C_2 are developed in Stage 2; but the Stage 3 connections, such as A_2-C_1, do not permit the integration of the three-element systems. At this point it is interesting to speculate that the *automatic* operation of the mediational system occurs only in cases of integrated systems in which the individual subsystems (e.g., *A-B, B-C*) have lost their boundary strengths in the process of developing into a superordinate three-element system. If the mediational circuit is not complete, the subject may still attempt to chain his associations, but this will lead to the phenomenon of mediated interference.

MEDIATED GENERALIZATION. Like the mediated interference situation, mediated generalization is a condition in which the mediators are typically either contrary, in their effects, to the subjects' task requirements, or at best are neutral. As in the interference studies, we shall see that mediated generalization may *fail to occur* if its effect would disrupt correct performance, as the subject interprets the situation.

First, let us examine the meaning of the term "mediated generalization" before we turn to the relevant data. Consider a situation in which neither Stimulus 1 nor Stimulus 2 is initially capable of eliciting a given response; we say that stimulus generalization between Stimulus 1 and Stimulus 2 has occurred if, after we have trained a subject to emit the given response to Stimulus 1, we find that he also has a tendency to emit the response to Stimulus 2. Such stimulus generalization can occur for many reasons. For example, the two stimuli may be so similar, physically, that the subject has difficulty distinguishing one from the other.

Another possible reason for stimulus generalization is the mediational process. In the forward chain, A-B, B-C, A-C, for example, neither A nor B had a tendency to elicit C prior to Stage 2. However, after B-C has been acquired, we now find that A-C also has some strength.

Clearly, then, the mediation situations which we have discussed at length in previous sections of this chapter can all be characterized as examples of mediated generalization. In what sense are we distinguishing this term, then, in the present section? The distinction, as found in the studies that use this term, is based on *the instructions to the subject* during the test for the mediation effect. In Stage 3 of the mediated *facilitation* studies, described in the previous sections, the subject is told to learn A-C, or is given A and is asked what response he believes would be appropriate. In the mediated *generalization* studies, on the other hand, the subject is presented with A, after learning B-C, and the experimenter watches to see if the subject behaves as though he had been shown B again.

An experiment by Mink (1957, 1963) provides an interesting example of a mediated generalization situation in which the mediational effects act in a manner *contrary* to the subjects' task instructions. First subjects were trained to press a lever upon presentation of each word in a list. Next they were shown a second list which contained three different types of words: (*a*) words from the first list; (*b*) associates of words from the first list: (*c*) control words unrelated to the first list. The instructions were to *press the lever upon seeing a word that had appeared in the first list*. In this case, responding to an *associate* of a word that had appeared in the first list would constitute a mediated generalization; it would also represent an error, or deviation from instructions.

One of the paradigms examined by Mink (1963) was the three-stage forward association chain, A-B, B-C, A-C, which we have seen produces consistent mediated facilitation of A-C learning. No tendency toward a mediated generalization effect was found for this paradigm. (It should be noted that this failure to obtain mediated generalization with the forward chain has been substantiated in a number of replications of the Mink study; see Jenkins, 1963.) Recall that this paradigm also failed to produce a consistent mediated interference effect in the studies reviewed on that topic. These data suggest that subjects may be able to control the initiation of the forward chain, using it only when it facilitates performance.

On the other hand, Mink did find a mediated generalization effect when he employed a paradigm in which the Stage 3 mediational chain involved reversing the direction of the Stage 1 association. The paradigm had the form: *A-B, A-C, B-(A)-C*. Here, the link between the stimulus *B* and the mediator *A*, in Stage 3, is the backward association of Stage 1, *A-B*. During the test for mediated generalization, in this paradigm, subjects tended to press the lever to the *B* stimuli despite their instructions to press only to the stimuli which they had seen in the previous list, namely the *A* stimuli.

A study by Razran (1949) on mediated generalization of the conditioned salivary response contrasts in some very interesting ways with that of Mink. Razran employed both of the paradigms later to be used by Mink (1957, 1963), the forward chain and the backward mediator. Let us consider an example, from Razran, of each of these.

	Forward Chain	Backward Mediator
Stage 1.	Yankee-Doodle	Yankee-Doodle
Stage 2.	Doodle-Salivate	Yankee-Salivate
Stage 3.	Yankee-(Doodle)-Salivate	Doodle-(Yankee)-Salivate

Razran found much greater tendency toward mediated salivation in the forward chain than in the backward mediation paradigm. This is exactly the reverse of the difference obtained by Mink, of course.

Jenkins (1963) has attempted to explain the discrepancy between the Mink and the Razran data by suggesting that the subject must actually emit the critical mediating response (even if only covertly), either in Stage 2 or 3, if mediated generalization is to occur. If, in Stage 2 of the forward chain, the subject emits the response *Yankee* to the stimulus *Doodle,* then *Yankee* will become directly associated to salivation by conditioning, and will of course elicit it during Stage 3. And, of course, if *Yankee* does not elicit the implicit *Doodle* response in Stage 3 of the forward chain, no mediated generalization should occur. Corresponding analyses can, of course, be made for the backward mediation paradigm.

Then Jenkins (1963) proceeded to analyze the experimental procedures employed by Mink and by Razran and concluded that Mink's procedure made it likely that subjects would give the associate to the presented stimulus during Stage 2, but not Stage 3. Since the Stage 2 stimulus in the forward chain (e.g., Doodle) does not strongly elicit the Stage 3 stimulus (e.g., Yankee) as a response, the Stage 3 stimulus will not become directly associated to the salivary response in Stage 2. Thus the forward chain will be ineffective in eliciting the mediated generalization. On the other hand, in the backward mediation paradigm, the Stage 2 stimulus (e.g., Yankee) will have a strong tendency to elicit the stage 3 stimulus (e.g., Doodle), and thus the latter will become a conditioned stimulus to salivation, and we shall find a strong mediated generalization effect in the backward paradigm.

The Razran procedure, Jenkins went on to speculate, discouraged Stage 2 associations to the presented stimulus, but encouraged associations in Stage 3. Since the Stage 3 stimulus in the forward chain (e.g., Yankee) was likely to elicit the crucial mediator (e.g., Doodle), mediated generalization occurred here. However, the Stage 3 stimulus in the backward paradigm (e.g., Doodle) was less likely to elicit the crucial mediator (e.g., Yankee) since this is a backward association.

While an explanation such as Jenkins' (1963) is plausible, the writer has some reservations on the grounds that studies of mediated facilitation have consistently found mediation effects in both of the paradigms described above.

Several points should be noted in comparing the Mink and the Razran data. First, while Razran found a larger effect for the forward than for the backward paradigm, a sizable amount of mediated generalization *was* found for the backward paradigm. (It may be noted that the example cited by Razran for the natural language association of Stage 1, namely *Yankee-Doodle,* was probably not the best example possible. Yankee-Doodle tends to be an integrated unit of the type discussed in Chapter 7. Indeed, when used as a single word by itself, Doodle has a distinctly different meaning from that which it has in the sequence Yankee-Doodle.)

Second, while the mediated salivary response was not one which the subject interpreted as correct in the situation, neither was it an incorrect response. In the Mink study, on the other hand, the mediated generalization tended to elicit a response which the subject had been instructed not to make; it was a response to be suppressed.

These considerations lead to an interpretation of the mediated generalization studies cited above which is somewhat different from that proposed by Jenkins (1963). The data suggest that the forward chain is under greater subject control than the backward paradigm, and that the subject is thus better able to suppress the mediated generalization in the forward chain.

When Will Mediation Occur?

On the basis of the studies on mediated facilitation and mediated interference, the writer would like to suggest the following hypothesis. *Mediation is most likely to influence behavior when the subjects seek such mediation in an attempt to facilitate their performance.*

SYNONYMITY

It would have been difficult to consider the notion of synonymity without having first examined the processes of mediation. On the other hand, we shall see that an understanding of synonymity will broaden our understanding of the mediational processes.

Let us begin with a rather superficial definition of synonymity: Two words are synonymous if they have the same meaning. An important problem with this definition, as we shall see, is that words can become synonyms in very different ways, and that each way represents a somewhat different cognitive structure; there are, therefore, several different types of synonym relationships.

CONTEXTUAL SYNONYMITY.   Two words may become synonymous because they occur interchangeably in the same contexts. From the point of view of our discussion of meaning as a region in the cognitive space, this type of synonymity represents a structure in which each of the two words activates exactly the same region in the cognitive space. Conversely, if the external stimulus conditions activate this region directly (viz., the context occurs in the absence of the words), the region may activate either of the synonyms. Note that the latter condition, in which the context activates the verbal responses, corresponds to the phenomenon of paraphrasing discussed by Deese (1968).

We can diagram the structure for contextual synonymity as Case 1, below.

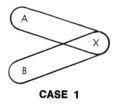

CASE 1

Here we need not assume any direct association between the two synonyms, *A* and *B;* both are diverse phonemic values in the cognitive space which are associated to a common region, *X,* in this space.

The notion of synonymity can be redefined for Case 1: Two words are synonymous if they both activate the same region in the cognitive space with the exception of the phonemic dimensions relevant to the words themselves.

The Case 1 structure can lead to either mediated facilitation or to interference in later learning. Mediated facilitation will occur under the following circumstances. Any item associated to one of the synonyms will be very quickly learned as an associate to the other synonym. For example, if a subject first learned *A-C,* the later learning of *B-C* would be very rapid due to the action of the mediation process. The mediated system involved in the rapid learning of *B-C* would be: *B-(X-A)-C.* This can be diagrammed as Case 1 *(M)*. Here we have four elements bounded into a single system, with one of the elements, *X,* representing an entire region of the cognitive space.

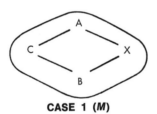

CASE 1 (M)

Interference would tend to occur if one of the synonyms were associated to one item (e.g., *A-C*), while the other synonym was associated to a different item (e.g., *B-D*). This can be diagrammed as Case 1 *(I)*.

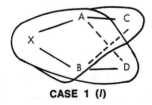

CASE 1 (I)

This is an interference paradigm because the mediational process will lead to a tendency for *C* to occur as an intrusion to *B* (by way of the mediational system $B\text{-}(X\text{-}A)\text{-}C)$, and for D to occur as an intrusion to A (by way of $A\text{-}(X\text{-}B)\text{-}D)$. Note that the mediation is relatively indirect, involving a four-element mediational system; this will prove to be an important point in evaluating several studies of mediated learning.

ASSIGNED SYNONYMITY.   A child hears a word for the first time and asks his father what the word means. The father tells the child that the word has the same meaning as some other word that the child already knows (e.g., "Sad means unhappy."). Let us assume that A is the new word and B is the word that the child already knows. The child forms the direct association $A\text{-}B$. The meaning of the new word is assigned and does not have to be acquired from the context in which it is used.

Thus, Case 2, assigned synonymity, originates as the chain: $A\text{-}B\text{-}X$ (where X is again the region in the cognitive space that represents the meaning of B and A). While it seems reasonable to assume that the uses of synonym A in its relevant meaning contexts will eventually lead to a direct $A\text{-}X$ system, such an assumption is not critical to the present discussion.

As in Case 1, the Case 2 structure can lead to either mediated facilitation or interference in later learning. Facilitation will occur if the subject first learns an item as an associate to one of the synonyms, then learns the same item as an associate to the other synonym (e.g., $A\text{-}C$ followed by $B\text{-}C$). In this case the second association with C will be learned very rapidly. This can be diagrammed as Case 2 (M).

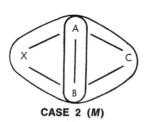

CASE 2 (M)

Note that the mediational system $B\text{-}(A)\text{-}C$ can bypass the "meaning," X, of the synonyms A and B. Thus we may have a three-element mediational system in Case 2 (M), as opposed to the four-element mediational system in Case 1 (M).

As in Case 1 (I), interference would occur if one of the synonyms were associated to one item (e.g., $A\text{-}C$), while the other synonym were associated to a different item (*B-D*). However the structure of the Case 2 (*I*) interference paradigm is different from that of Case 1 (*I*).

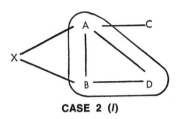

CASE 2 (*I*)

In Case 2 (*I*) the mediated interference system contains only three elements (e.g., *A*-(*B*)-*D*) in place of the four elements in Case 1 (*I*).

While Case 2 has been discussed as a paradigm for synonymity, it should be evident that the identical set of system relationships would obtain if *A-B* were *any* prior bounded association. Several writers (e.g., McClelland and Heath, 1943; Ryan, 1960; Jenkins, 1963) have suggested that the association between synonyms, rather than the similarity in meaning, may be the crucial factor in producing the typically obtained retroactive inhibition and transfer effects found when List 1 and List 2 have similar stimuli or responses.

EVIDENCE CONCERNING THE UTILITY OF THE DISTINCTION BETWEEN CASE 1 AND 2. Several studies suggest that the distinction, made in the previous sections, between Case 1 structures and Case 2 structures is relevant to the degree of mediation that will occur.

In an early study of verbal mediation, Bastian (1956, 1961) compared the amount of positive transfer that was obtained under three different conditions: (*a*) List 2 responses were associates of List 1 responses, and both lists involved identical stimuli; in other words, a Case 2 (*M*) paradigm. (*b*) List 2 responses were similar *in meaning* to List 1 responses, but association norms indicated little or no tendency for one of these words to elicit the other directly; again both lists employed identical stimuli, making for a Case 1 (*M*) paradigm. (*c*) Finally we have the control group of items in which the List 1 and List 2 responses were neither associates nor similar in meaning.

Bastian (1961) found that both Case 1 (*M*) and 2 (*M*) produced significantly faster List 2 learning than the control condition. Comparing Case 1 (*M*) with 2 (*M*), would we expect to find that these different structures would have differential effects on mediation? The analysis above suggests that they should. Case 1 (M), contextual synonymity, involves a four-element mediational structure. Case 2 (M), on the other hand, involves a three-element structure. We have seen that three-stage structures are more stable than four-stage structures. It therefore would be predicted that Case 2 (M), direct association between List 1 and List 2 responses, should produce faster List 2 learning than should Case 1 (M). This is precisely what Bastian (1961) found.

Ryan (1960) used essentially the same procedure and materials as Bastian, but reversed the stimulus-response relationships such that the *stimuli* of Lists 1 and 2 were: associated words, words similar in meaning but not associated, or unrelated control words. The responses of the two lists were identical (whereas in Bastian's study it was the stimuli that were identical). The pattern of results was identical to that found by Bastian. Both Case 1 and Case 2 structures produced faster List 2 learning than the unrelated control items. Again, as predicted from our structural analysis, Case 2 (M), in which the stimuli of Lists 1 and 2 were directly associated, produced better mediation of List 2 acquisition than did Case 1 (M), in which the stimuli of Lists 1 and 2 were similar in meaning but were not associates of each other.

It is interesting to note that Ryan (1960), Osgood (1961), and Jenkins (1963) interpret the data of the Bastian (1956, 1961) and Ryan (1960) studies as indicating two different types of processes. Transfer due to similarity in meaning is considered a different process from transfer due to association between the items of the two lists. Only the latter is considered a mediation effect. Within the framework suggested in the present chapter, on the other hand, the two cases are both instances of multi-element, bounded systems; the primary difference between the two cases appears to be in the *structure* of the bounded systems.

STRUCTURE VERSUS ASSOCIATIVE STRENGTH. Earlier, in our discussion of mediation mechanisms *per se,* we found a great deal of evidence to the effect that *mediational facilitation of later learning is not influenced by the degree of associative strength between individual elements in the mediational system.* (This was shown by the studies, previously cited by Kincaid, Bousfield, and Whitmarsh, 1962; Schulz and Weaver, 1968; and many others.)

On the other hand, the evidence of the immediately preceding section indicates that *mediation is influenced by the structure of the mediational system* as represented in the cognitive space.

THE INTERFERENCE PARADIGMS FOR SYNONYMITY. Cases 1 (I) and 2 (I) above were specified as situations in which synonymity could produce interference, rather than facilitation of new learning. A great number of verbal learning studies have been conducted in which stimulus or response similarity *between simultaneously acquired* paired associates was induced by using synonymous terms, or terms from the same conceptual category, as the learning materials. These are studies of *within list* similarity. (Chapter 5 analyzes many such experiments.) The mechanisms which produce similarity and, consequently, interference in these studies are the mechanisms of the two Cases diagrammed in this chapter.

At this point, the reader may recall that our examination of mediated interference, *per se*, suggested that such a phenomenon is either extremely weak, or in some cases nonexistent. This suggests that interference based on similarity due to synonymity should also be a relatively weak effect. A careful examination of the data relevant to this point indicates that this deduction is correct!

Contrary to popular belief among many verbal learning psychologists, similarity due to synonymity produces relatively little interference unless the subject is deluged with relatively large numbers of very synonymous items. This can be seen clearly in the early studies by Underwood (1953a, 1953b). Rather than having all the stimuli or all the responses in a list synonymous, Underwood used several sets of synonyms, so that no more than three or four words were members of the same synonym cluster. This set of experiments found very little interference in learning which could be attributed to synonymity. The present-day conviction concerning the interference properties of synonymity is based on later studies in which subjects were confronted with 10 or 12 synonymous stimuli or responses to be sorted out in a single list.

In short, the synonymity data support the conclusions suggested in the previous section on mediated interference: Mediated interference is a weak effect compared to mediated facilitation.

THE ROLE OF CONCEPT STRUCTURE IN LEARNING

We have already touched upon the role of concept structure in learning when we discussed synonymity and mediation. The region in the cognitive space corresponding to the concept was symbolized as X in the previously outlined mediational structures.

In the studies already examined, we have seen that, if one associate of a concept becomes associated to a new item, other associates of the concept are often capable of eliciting this new item, too, despite the fact that these other associates were never directly connected to the new item. The studies to be considered at this point were designed to explore new aspects of the role of concept structure in learning.

Learning a Response to Several Instances of a Concept

Several studies have attempted to attach a new response to the *meaning* of a concept, rather than to a single instance of the concept. How can this be done? One way is to have the subject learn the response to several instances of the concept.

Cerekwicki, Grant, and Porter (1968) report an eyelid discrimination conditioning study that used this technique. Words were used as stimuli. The positive stimuli consisted of 1, 2, 3, or 4 different instances of one concept, while the negative stimuli consisted of a corresponding number of instances from a different concept. For example, the positive stimuli might be the names of three different flowers, while the negative stimuli were the names of three different animals; on each trial a different flower name or animal name would be presented, so that at least six trials would be necessary before a subject saw all three positive and all three negative instances.

Cerekwicki, Grant, and Porter were particularly interested in the learning exhibited by subjects showing "voluntary" conditioning patterns (i.e., subjects who showed very rapid eyelid responses of a type which are probably not being mediated by the autonomic nervous system but are probably products of the central nervous system). The present discussion will concentrate on the performance of these subjects. In this study, the effect of number of different concept-instances varied with stage of training. On the first block of trials, discrimination performance was better for the 1-instance than for the 4-instance conditions. However, by the final block of trials (trials 70–80), performance was a regular, increasing function of the number of instances used as stimuli. Apparently, the stimulus variability of the 4-instance condition led to early decrements in performance; however, by the end of the experiment this was more than compensated for by other factors related to learning the discrimination to the concepts rather than to an instance from a concept.

Corresponding results are reported by Saltz and Modigliani (1968) in a paired-associates verbal learning study. In this study, one group of subjects learned a response to a single instance of a concept (e.g., the word "foggy") ; a second group learned the response to three instances of the concept (e.g., on Trial 1 the stimulus might be "foggy," on Trial 2 "hazy," and on Trial 3 "misty") . As in Cerekwicki, Grant, and Porter, learning was somewhat slower in the 3-instance group than in the 1-instance group during the early trials. All subjects were brought to approximately the same criterion of learning, and memory was tested either 24 hours later or 7 days later. Significantly less forgetting occurred in the 3-instance condition than in the 1-instance condition, and this effect was relatively constant over the two time intervals.

The effects reported above can not simply be attributed to stimulus variability, since stimulus variability leads to decrements in learning. In the Cerekwicki, Grant, and Porter (1968) study, for example, four *unrelated* stimuli as the cue to eyelid closure led to virtually no discrimination learning. Clearly, the interrelatedness of the words constituting the positive or negative stimuli was crucial to the phenomenon.

The results summarized above suggest the proposition that: Learning and memory are facilitated if a response is associated to the *meaning* of a concept rather than to an *instance* of the concept.

The two studies, above, involved manipulating the conceptual characteristics of stimulus items. A study by Bevan, Duke, and Avant (1966) reports a set of experiments concerned with response characteristics. This study was concerned with the free recall of words and pictures. Subjects were shown either an identical stimulus on each of several trials or a somewhat different version of the stimulus could be presented on each trial. (For example, a subject might see the same picture of an apple on each of four trials; or he could be shown a different apple in each picture for four trials, so that the color and shape might vary somewhat from trial to trial.) Again, multiple instances were facilitating. Subsequent recall of material was better when subjects were presented several variations on a concept. The results were consistant for verbal and for pictorial materials.

POSSIBLE EXPLANATIONS FOR THE EFFECTS.   What mechanisms could account for the results cited above? Several can be suggested; at present there is insufficient evidence for choosing between them.

One such mechanism is based on the fact that multiple instances typically specify a concept more precisely than a single instance might. For example, the word "bear" could refer to an animal or could refer to the verb meaning "to carry." But in the context: bear, lion, . . . it is clear that we are referring to an animal. Similarly, "foggy" could refer to a state of mind or to an atmospheric condition; again, in the context: foggy, hazy, misty, . . . it is clear that we are referring to atmospheric conditions.

Such specificity insures that a restricted region of the cognitive space is the relevant stimulus. This interpretation is consistent with the data examined in Chapters 3 and 4 which indicated that learning was facilitated when the stimulus was specified on a greater number of dimensions. It is also consistent with the conclusions in Chapter 2 concerning concrete and abstract concepts.

A second interpretation, proposed originally by Saltz and Modigliani (1968), is related to the issue of the reduction of interference. According to this interpretation, if a single instance of a concept is learned as a stimulus to a response, over time the other instances of the concept could arise as responses which interfere with new learning. However, if these other instances of the concept were also associated to the new response, interference produced by the other concept instances would simply serve as additional cues to the newly learned response.

Finally, Bevan, Duke, and Avant (1966) suggest a motivational basis for the effect of multiple instances of a concept on learning. Multiple instances, they suggest, could keep the subjects from becoming bored.

Concepts as Storage Units

Mandler (1967) has recently summarized the results of a series of experiments which he and his students have conducted over the past few years. These studies appear to have important implications for our understanding of the role of concepts in memory.

Mandler finds that the recall of a set of words is related to the extent with which subjects can categorize these words into different conceptual categories. Specifically, subjects were presented with a deck of cards, each card having a different word on it. The subjects were requested to sort these cards into categories, with the restriction that no fewer than two nor more than seven categories be used. Results indicated that within the limits of 2 to 7 categories, number of words subsequently recalled was a linear function of the number of categories which the subjects had used in sorting these words. Unfortunately, there is little evidence concerning the use of more than seven categories. In one of the experiments in this series, Mandler placed no restriction on the number of categories the subjects might use; the data suggest that facilitation increased through 11 categories, though the curve relating recall to number of categories seemed to be leveling sharply. However, very few subjects in this experiment used more than seven categories, and the function is extremely unstable for greater numbers of categories.

As would be expected, the number of words that a subject sorted into a particular conceptual category during the sorting phase of the experiment is related to the number of words subsequently recalled from that category. With less than five words in a category, almost no forgetting occurred. Beyond this, percentage recall dropped in a regular fashion with increased number of words in the category.

Mandler interprets his data in terms of hierarchies of associations. He suggests that the human memory span is about 5 ± 2 items. Assume, then, that one layer in the hierarchy is the concept names; the subject in the experiment should be able to recall 5 ± 2 of these concept names. Each concept name, in turn, should then be capable of producing a memory span of 5 ± 2 *of the words in each of the concepts* which is recalled. From this it follows that, the greater the number of concepts (between two and seven concepts) into which the items are categorized, the better should be the recall.

Such cueing functions are, of course, quite reasonable. Tulvig and Pearlstone (1966), for example, tested for recall under conditions in which subjects either were, or were not, given the names of the various categories into which the words of a list could be organized. If the names were given to the subjects, this was done after the learning session and just prior to recall so that the category names could not influence original learning; the crucial issue, in other words, was whether this type of organizational factor could facilitate *memory*. The manipulation proved extremely effective. Much more retention was found when subjects were given cues to categories of responses in the list. Tulvig and Pearlstone (1966) interpret their data as indicating that the material was in storage in the subjects' memory; the categorical cues helped retrieve the material from storage.

SOME DIFFICULTIES FOR THE ASSOCIATIVE HIERARCHY NOTION. While the notions proposed by Mandler (1967) and by Tulvig (1968), relative to the associational hierarchy, are interesting and provocative, some problems arise in these formulations when we consider them against the context of issues raised in the present volume. First, let us examine the range of organization that can be found in a set of materials. At one end of the dimension we have no organization—each word is in a different conceptual category from every other word in the list. At the other end of the dimension we have complete organization so that *all* the items in the list are in the *same* conceptual category. Clearly, the case considered by both Mandler and Tulvig is somewhere between these extremes on the dimension. Note that, simply in terms of the 5 ± 2 notion of memory span, the two extremes on this dimension (viz., each item in a separate concept and all items in the same concept) should be equivalent in amount recalled. If all items are independent, there are no supra-ordinate cues and the subjects should recall 3–7 items; if all items are in the same concept, there is one supra-ordinate cue, and it will lead to the recall of 3–7 items. The fact that these two conditions are not, empirically, found to be equivalent in the amount of recall that they induce must be accounted for by means of other, additional mechanisms.

What does happen to free recall at the extremes of the dimension discussed above? In Chapter 5 we saw that free recall is *facilitated, on early trials,* if all the items in the list belong to the *same concept class;* however, on *later trials* this condition becomes *inferior* to the one in which each item belongs to a different concept.

There is some evidence to suggest that number of trials may have essentially the same effect, as that indicated above, in the Mandler type of situation. For example, Dallett (1964, in his Experiments IV and V) permitted subjects only one trial before recall; he found a *decrease* in recall as a function of number of concepts represented in the list. Mandler (1967), on the other hand, found that increased number of concepts led to *greater* recall; in this study, subjects were given a series of trials before the recall test. It is not clear, from Mandler's associative hierarchy notion, why an increase in the number of conceptual categories in a list should facilitate recall after several prectice trials, but should be detrimental to recall after a single practice trial.

While Mandler's theory is primarily focused on the free-recall situation, some interesting parallels can be seen between his data and those of paired-associates learning. Paired-associates learning is slower if all the responses are in the same category than if each response is in a different conceptual category. Yet this cannot be explained as being due to facilitated retrieval produced by the cue value of the concepts. This effect occurs even when the memory for the responses, *per se,* is not a factor, and so retrieval cannot be a relevant issue (e.g., Saltz and Felton, 1968*a,* in which the response terms were presented in a modified *S-R* matching technique during the test trials). To be consistent, *Mandler must, apparently, assume two different mechanisms, one for free recall and a different one for paired associates, to explain why the same variable (number of concepts) has the same effect in these two different learning situations.*

An alternative explanation for aspects of the Mandler data. In the present book, the position has been taken that concepts are bounded systems that resist interference from other systems (e.g., Chapters 2 and 6). Mandler's data appear to be consistent with this position. From this point of view, if words can be placed in different concepts by a subject, there should be less interference between these words. This position suggests that much of the interference leading to forgetting is likely to be *intraconcept* interference. Thus, an increase in the number of words in any single concept, above some threshold number, should lead to increased intraconcept interference that would offset the facilitation produced by the fact that the words in a single concept are likely to be highly associated to one another, and therefore likely to evoke one another as responses.

Why, then, do we find the interaction between amount of practice and number of conceptual categories used by subjects, as these two variables influence recall? Why is recall superior, after very few trials, when the material can be classified into only one or two conceptual categories (as opposed to six or seven categories)? And why does the six or seven category situation later produce superior recall as number of practice trials increases? While no conclusive answers can be given to these questions, some possibilities can be suggested.

When all the items in a list are related to one or two concepts, the amount of inter-item association (either direct or mediated) between the items of the list is usually quite high; thus the items will tend to evoke each other. However, further improvement with practice will be relatively slow, since there is little protection against intraconcept interference.

Turning to the situation where the list is categorized into a larger number of concepts, the position taken by Tulvig (1968) appears very persuasive. After one or two trials the subject has a *retrieval* problem: He may recall a relatively high percentage of the items in the few categories that he can remember; however, since the concept categories are unrelated, and since he has had only a few trials on the material, he may remember relatively few categories, and each of these tends to evoke the items that are members of the concept class.

If we add to the Tulvig position the notion that a concept protects its members from interference produced by members of other concepts, we see that recall should be much greater, after a great deal of practice, when the items to be recalled are members of a number of different concept classes.

ORGANIZATIONAL FACTORS IN KNOWLEDGE AND PRINCIPLES

For the most part, the discussion of meaning in this chapter has centered on the organizational properties of concepts and of associative networks. Relatively little work has been done on the organization of concepts into larger functional units. However, this area has received renewed interest in recent years largely due to the research on language, on the one hand, and due to the work of Gagne (1965) and his co-workers on the learning of principles, on the other hand. As we shall see, these two approaches tend to converge.

For Gagne, knowledge involves a sequence of concepts. For example, a sentence like, "Flowers bloom in spring," involves the coordination of three concepts: (a) flowers, (b) bloom, (c) spring. Before one can understand the sentence, it is necessary to understand the referents of the three concept names. Then one must coordinate these referents in relation to one another. Gagne refers to such chains of concepts as *principles* and points out that principles often have an hierarchical organization.

In order to understand the notion of hierarchical organization of principles, let us consider the research conducted by Gagne on the teaching of mathematics (e.g., Gagne and Paradise, 1961; Gagne, 1962; Gagne, Mayor, Garstens, and Paradise, 1962). Ability to multiply requires the prior learning of both addition and subtraction. Before a child can learn to divide, he must be able to perform the operations of multiplication; this means, of course, that he must be capable of addition and subtraction, too. Thus we have an hierarchy with addition and subtraction as the base.

Gagne (1965) believes that much of our knowledge is organized in just this sort of hierarchical fashion and that the failure of children to learn in school may often be due to the teachers' failure to appreciate this fact.

Organizational factors in knowledge and in principles are among the most complex issues in psychology; consequently, they are among the least understood. At present we can only wait to see the directions taken by future research on these topics.

Syntax as an Organizational Factor

No consideration of the organization factors of the mind would be complete without at least a reference to the role of syntactic organizers.

Prior experience has programmed the mind so that it can process and store information that arrives in syntactically orderly units. A study by Marks and Miller (1964) provides an interesting example of this sort of processing ability. Subjects learned verbal sequences like—*Pink accidents cause sleeping storms*—which have an orderly syntactic form, though their meaning is anomalous; or they learned the same words in a random sequence, such as—*Accidents pink storms sleeping cause*. Learning was more rapid for the syntactically orderly sequences.

There is even a tendency for sequences of nonsense syllables to be more easily learned if they inflected in a syntactically orderly manner (Epstein, 1961, 1962), though these effects are not large. Johnson (1968), in a review of the literature on this topic, reports that such effects are relatively unstable, and cites several unpublished studies that have failed to obtain such results.

Brent (1965) reports that syntactically organized sequences of words are not only learned faster than disarrayed orders of the same words, but they are also better able to resist proactive interference. In addition, Brent found that syntactically orderly sentences produced virtually *no retroactive inhibition* onto a previously learned random serial order of the same words, while a second random order produced massive retroactive inhibition onto the original, previously learned random order of words. These results dramatically point up the fact that syntactic sequences are processed in a very different fashion from nonsense sequences.

While the role of syntax, *per se,* is extremely interesting, this fact should not cause us to disregard the even more important role played by the meaningfulness of the verbal sequence. Johnson (1968) points out that *ungrammatical but meaningful* sentences are much easier to learn than anomalous sequences which are grammatically correct. On the other hand, while grammatical sequences are somewhat easier to learn than ungrammatical when both types are meaningful, this difference is relatively small.

At this point it seems reasonable to ask, what do we mean when we refer to a sequence as having meaning? There are at least two aspects to this issue. One is related to the congruence of the concepts and their *modifiers,* in a sentence. The second is related to the organization of the concepts, *vis-à-vis* each other. In the discussion below, we shall use the anomalous sentence from Marks and Miller (1964) to illustrate these two aspects of meaning: Pink accidents cause sleeping storms.

Turning first to the congruence of concepts with their modifiers, let us consider the phrase *pink accidents.* This phrase suggests that the concept of accidents has some range of values on the color dimensions. Since this concept does not have color attributes, the phrase has no literal meaning. Similarly, the attribute dimension of waking-sleeping is not relevant to storms (except metaphorically).

Next let us turn to the organization of the concepts in the sentence. Stripped of its adjectival modifiers, the sentence becomes: Accidents cause storms. In Gagne's terms, this statement is a principle. However, in our culture we do not accept this particular principle as correct. The problem here is analogous to the one in Chapter 2, where we saw that eight-year-old children can not accept the concept of a father who is a drunkard, except that in the present example, the relationship between the two concepts in the sentences is one of causality, rather than of identity.

CONCLUSIONS

We have seen in the present chapter that the meaning of a word can be related to the notions of concepts and the attribute dimensions of cognitive space, as these were discussed earlier in Chapter 2. Incoming information is projected onto this network of pre-existing concepts; the structure of this network certainly influences retention, and probably also influences comprehension. Despite the dramatic quality of the research which has led to these conclusions, little further research has been undertaken in this area.

Mediation, we have seen, consists of a particular organization of concepts in which each concept is capable of reminding the subject of every other concept in the set. One of the most striking findings in this area is that the set of concepts in a mediational system appear to become bounded as a single system in which the strength of the relationship between individual pairs of concepts in the system loses its importance in determining the mediational effect. There is even the suggestion (based on a study by Martin, Oliver, Hom, and Heaslet, 1963) that, if one of the individual pairs of concepts becomes too strongly interrelated, this could weaken the tendency for the larger set of concepts to become adequately bounded.

One set of factors determining the effectiveness of a mediational system appears to be the subject's awareness that the system exists and his ability to control the system. Again we encounter an area where very little actual research has been conducted, despite the potential importance of the phenomena under consideration. Here the problem appears to be simply, that many psychologists are uncomfortable with variables such as awareness, and avoid them when possible.

Synonymity, we have seen, is again an issue of concepts in an attribute space. Two words are synonymous, we saw, if they occupy exactly the same region in the cognitive space. Many of the issues involved in the effect of synonymity on learning prove to be mediational in nature. They resolve themselves into situations in which some new stimulus becomes associated with one word; later, the new stimulus is required to evoke the synonym of the word in order to produce a positive transfer (or the stimulus evokes the synonym unintentionally, to produce interference). An analysis of the synonym situations is very instructive, since it suggests several different structures which can produce mediational effects. We find that the different structures differ in the extent to which they permit mediational facilitation of new learning. Thus, while strength of relationship between pairs of concepts in a mediational system *was not* relevant to the degree of mediation obtained, the structure of the relationship between the concepts in the system *was* relevant to the degree of mediation.

Since this chapter has been concerned with the organization of concepts into larger inter-concept systems, it is interesting to note that the sentence is one of the most frequently encountered illustrations of the occurrence of such systems. While an attempt was made to characterize sentences in terms of the notions cognitive space and concept interaction already discussed in this book, the writer realizes the magnitude of a comprehensive attack on the issues of the sentence; the comments in the present chapter, on this topic, were intended as directional signals more than anything else.

9 | Meaningfulness and Learning

PRECIS

In the previous chapter we saw that the specific meaning of a word can influence new learning and transfer. In the present chapter we shall consider the variable of meaningfulness. Here we are no longer concerned with the specific meaning of a word; we are concerned, instead with the *extent* to which the word has meaning.

A model for meaningfulness is presented which considers the effects of two variables on the ease with which a word enters into new associations: (*a*) The tendency of the person to conserve old, important meanings of the word, and (*b*) the degree of differentiation of the word. The role of level of abstraction and imagery is also analyzed.

Finally, the meaningfulness of nonsense syllables is examined. We shall see that this issue is even more complex than that of the meaningfulness of real words. An important reason for this is that most persons tend to respond to a real word in approximately the same way. Nonsense syllables, on the other hand, evoke a tremendous heterogeneity of encoding responses. The evidence is very strong that use of nonsense syllables *does not* permit us to examine learning in the absence of meaning; instead, it forces us to examine learning in the absence of any *control* over meaning. For the most part, research employing nonsense syllables has not been concerned with the *development* of meaningfulness; it has been concerned, instead, with relating learning to the extent with which nonsense syllables elicit, resemble, or remind subjects of real words.

DEMONSTRATION EXPERIMENT

The Problem

Do you know the *meaning* of each of the words listed below?

TOGA	ROLLS ROYCE	BOLSHEVIK
COAT	FORD	DEMOCRAT

Write each of the words on a piece of paper. After each word, *estimate the frequency* with which you have encountered this word on a scale from 1 to 7. (Rate the word as 1 if you have encountered it very seldom, 7 if you have encountered it very frequently; use the numbers between 1 and 7 for intermediate frequencies.)

Now try to picture the referent to each of these words. Rate the vividness of the image on a scale from 1 to 7. (Rate the word as 1 if you have no clear image of the referent, 7 if you have an extremely clear image; use numbers between 1 and 7 for words having images of intermediate degrees of clarity and specificity.)

Finally, let us measure the number of different associations each word brings to your mind. Do this in the following manner. Place a watch or clock with a second hand in front of yourself. For each word in turn, give as many different associations as you can think of in 30 seconds. Don't chain associate—for example it would be a chain association if, to the stimulus word *tall,* you first said, "Short," then said, "Midget." This would be considered a chain association since your second response, "Midget," was elicited by *your own prior response,* "Short," *rather than by the stimulus word,* "Tall."

Explanation

Note that all six of the words above *have meaning* in the sense that these all are real words whose referents you know. Note also that each of these words has a referent that is distinctly different from any of the other five words (though pairs of words have referents which are in the same concept class). In what sense can we compare the meanings of words when these meanings consist of distinctly different referents? In the demonstration above, we have explored three different ways in which such meanings can be compared and contrasted. First, words may seem more or less *familiar.* Second, referents may be more or less easily *imagined.* Finally, some words may evoke long, complex sets of associations, while other words may be extremely impoverished in this respect.

Let us briefly examine some of the relationships between the three aspects of meaning. A number of studies have found that more familiar words (e.g., words that occur more frequently in the language) tend to evoke greater numbers of associations than do less familiar words. The

314

examples chosen above *do not* conform to this generalization. Most of you will have given more associations to *Rolls Royce* than to *Ford*, to *Bolshevik* than to *Democrat.* Can you see any characteristics of the less familiar words in these sets that could account for this inversion of the usual relationship? Do these characteristics suggest anything about the basis for the more typical relationship between familiarity and number of associations? Evidence in relation to these issues will be presented later in this chapter.

THEORIES OF MEANINGFULNESS

Meaningfulness is concerned with the *extent* to which a word or nonsense syllable has meaning, as opposed to a concern with the *specific* meaning of the word. Let us start by acknowledging the fact that the question of the effect of meaningfulness on learning is a question of the manner in which past experience with a word influences subsequent learning involving this word. From this perspective, we can, perhaps, avoid some of the philosophic disagreements of the past concerning the "real" meaning of meaningfulness. The issue becomes, what aspects of past experience with a word can influence future learning.

Single-Factor Associative Theories

A single-factor associative theory permits consideration of only a single factor from past experience—the associations to the word. The works of Noble (1952), Underwood and Schulz (1960), and Postman (1962c) probably reflect well the status of the single factor theory in regard to meaningfulness. Noble's operational definition of the meaningfulness of a word is the *number of different associations* emitted to the word in a 60-second period. Noble calls this construct m. If a word has many associates, according to this criterion, it is a highly meaningful word. If it has few associates, it is a less meaningful word. The critical effect, then, of past experience with a word is to increase the number of associates to that word, according to this position.

Both Underwood and Schulz (1960) and Postman (1962c) point out that the m value of words is correlated with the frequency with which these words occur in the language, and they suggest that frequency may be the basic mechanism behind m. Frequent words, they argue, occur in many contexts, and consequently these words become associated to many other words, producing high m.

But how is m relevant to new learning? On the stimulus side,

Underwood and Schulz (1960) and Postman (1962c) suggest that the m value of a *stimulus* word influences learning by means of a mediation mechanism. If a word has many associates (i.e., is high m), these writers suggest, the probability is increased that the word is associated to some mediator which is, in turn, associated to the new response. Thus facilitation of learning should occur. However, Postman (1962c) goes on to point out, the associations which determine m must also compete with the new response being learned. The resultant effect should depend on the degree of competition relative to the degree of mediation.

On the response side, Underwood and Schulz (1960) suggest that the m value of the response term may only be an *index* of the ease of learning, rather than a determining factor; frequency of occurrence of the word in the language may be the critical variable. Increased frequency, they argue, leads to increased response availability. As we saw in Chapter 5, these writers assume that response availability facilitates learning. According to this position, response m is related to learning only because high frequency words tend also to be high in m value.

A Multifactor Theory of Meaningfulness

A somewhat different analysis arises on the basis of the multifactor position described in the present book. We have seen that previous experience with verbal material increases the differentiation of this material (Chapters 4 and 5). We have also seen that previous experience with an *S-R system* increases the ability of this system to resist interference (Chapter 6). Saltz and Modigliani (1967) have proposed a model based on the joint effect of these variables.

CONSERVATION OF MEANING. Let us first consider the issue of resistance to interference. Important concepts (i.e., concepts which occur frequently in a person's history) can be assumed to have acquired resistance to interference which protects the meaning of the concept from disruption by casual new associations. Thus, the greater the past frequency for a given meaning of a word, the more difficult it should be for a person to acquire new associations to the word. Of course, any given word typically has several meanings and enters into an even greater number of other cognitive systems. The *average* resistance to interference of these cognitive systems can be written as F/M, where F is the past frequency of the word and M is the number of systems in which the word is involved. (We shall see that Noble's m can be used as a rough index of M.) Keeping M

constant, new learning should be inversely related to F; keeping F constant, new learning should be facilitated by increasing M.

THE DIFFERENTIATION OF WORDS AS A FACTOR IN MEANINGFULNESS. Turning to the differentiation variable, increased frequency of a word should lead to greater differentiation. This, in turn, should result in facilitation of new learning.

A MODEL FOR MEANINGFULNESS. Saltz and Modigliani (1967) have suggested the following type of model to predict learning.

$$\text{Correct } R = C - (aF/M - bF) \qquad (1)$$

where C is the resistance to interference of the S-R system being learned; aF/M is the conservation of previous meanings of the word against new learning; bF is the differentiation of the word; a and b are the functions relating conservation of previous meanings and differentiation, respectively, to new learning.

This equation can be simplified as follows:

$$\text{Correct } R = C - F(a/M - b) \qquad (2)$$

From this it can be seen that the *effect* of M will decrease as F decreases. In addition, at the value of M at which $a/M = b$, it can be seen that $a/M - b = 0$; thus at this value of M, F will have no effect on new learning. Empirical data relevant to these implications will be examined in subsequent sections of this chapter.

Before going on to examine the research on meaningfulness, it should be noted that the equations presented above are very similar to the equation suggested for the overlearning-shift phenomena summarized in Chapter 6. The primary difference is in the fact that the procedure of the overlearning-shift studies produced a situation in which $M = 1$. In other words, subjects in those studies learned only one previous response to the relevant stimuli before the shift to a new response was introduced. Because of this, the equation for predicting the probability of the correct, postshift response could be collapsed to have the form: $C - (aF - bF)$.

LEARNING AND THE MEANINGFULNESS OF REAL WORDS: THE DATA

The Correlation between Frequency and m

We have seen that both Underwood and Schulz (1960) and Postman (1962c) assume that m and the frequency of occurrence of a word in the language are both indices of the same basic meaningfulness variable. On the other hand, the position taken by Saltz and Modigliani (1967) suggests that, in some situations at least, frequency and m will have opposite effects on learning—in short, they are not indices of the same basic variable. The discrepancy between these two positions can only be answered conclusively by relating both variables, independently, to learning. However, the existence of an extremely high correlation between m and frequency would support the notion that these are essentially the same variable; a very low correlation would pose problems for the Postman and Underwood-Schulz position.

Two studies have examined the correlation between m and frequency, Winnick and Kressel (1965) and Saltz (1967a). Both studies found the correlations to be between .3 and .4, using Pearson r. Saltz (1967a) also calculated an *eta* correlation which corrects for the fact that the relationship between the two variables may not be perfectly linear; an *eta* of about .45 was obtained. Thus, while there is a relationship between the two measures, it tends to be moderate to low.

Stimulus Meaningfulness

There is surprisingly little evidence concerning the effects of stimulus meaningfulness on learning when real words are used as stimuli. In studies examining m, for example, one typically finds that the lowest m items are nonsense words while the highest m items are real words. While stimulus m is related to speed of learning in these studies, it is difficult to evaluate the extent to which such effects may merely indicate that nonsense words are more difficult to learn than real words. Several studies (e.g., Kimble and Dufort, 1955; Noble and McNeely, 1957) varied stimulus and response m in a correlated fashion so that it is impossible to know if the effects on learning were related to the stimulus or the response member of the S-R system. Finally, very few studies have controlled frequency when examining the effects of m (and vice versa).

THE EFFECT OF STIMULUS m ON LEARNING. As would be expected from both the mediation theory and from the model proposed by Saltz and Modigliani (1967), it appears that high m stimuli lead to somewhat faster learning than low m stimuli. Studies by Cieutat, Stockwell, and Noble (1958) and Hunt (1959) show trends in this direction, though this is statistically significant only in the former study. Both studies appear to involve nonsense words as low m materials and real words as high m. Saltz (1967a) reports results from three separate experiments, all of which involved only real words. In these studies, frequency was held constant in evaluating m. It should be noted that the range of m values among real words is relatively restricted. However, within this restricted range, all three studies found better learning for the highest m stimuli than for the lowest, though the effects were small in magnitude and significant in only two of the three experiments. A study by Modigliani and Saltz (1969) also used only real words and controlled for frequency. Again there was a small tendency toward better learning of high m stimuli, but here the effect was not significant.

THE EFFECT OF STIMULUS FREQUENCY ON LEARNING.   In general, the evidence appears to be contrary to Postman's (1962c) assumption that word frequency influences learning only to the extent that frequency is related to m—i.e., that m provides the basic mechanism while frequency is only a vehicle for increasing m. In his own study, Postman (1962c) found that learning was nonmonotonically related to frequency. Moderate stimulus frequency led to better learning than either high *or* low stimulus frequency. As we have seen, there is no evidence for such a nonmonotonic effect with m. The discrepancy between the effects of stimulus m and stimulus frequency suggests that these two variables may have quite different effects on learning, and that this difference may be obscured by the positive correlation between them.

Studies by Saltz (1967a) and by Modigliani and Saltz (1969) indicate that this is indeed the case. In these studies (as is true for all studies reported in this chapter) the Thorndike-Lorge (1944) word count was used as the index for word frequency. Since Noble's (1952) original list contained a disproportionate number of very frequent words, Saltz (1967a) scaled 100 words for m using words which varied widely in frequency. Using this material, it was possible to construct lists that varied in stimulus frequency but not in m, or that varied in m but not in frequency. Both the Saltz and the Modigliani and Saltz studies were consistent in showing that *increased stimulus frequency resulted in slower learning* when m was controlled.

INTERACTION BETWEEN m AND FREQUENCY VALUES OF STIMULI. The evidence indicates, then, that under controlled conditions, increasing stimulus m *facilitates* learning, but increasing stimulus frequency is *detrimental* to learning. These results are, of course, consistent with Equation 2 of the Saltz and Modigliani model. It should also be noted that Equation 2 states that variation in m (which constitutes the operational definition of M) will have its greatest effect on learning when frequency is high, and this effect will shrink as frequency becomes lower. Both the Saltz (1967a) and the Modigliani and Saltz (1969) data are consistent with this, the interaction between m and frequency being significant in the Saltz study.

Modigliani and Saltz (1969) attempted to fit their data and the earlier data reported by Saltz (1967a) to Equation 2 with very interesting consequences. The two studies were similar except that in Saltz (1967a) the stimuli and responses were unrelated terms while in the Modigliani and Saltz (1969) study each response was an *associate* to its relevant stimulus. Learning was, of course, much faster in the latter study than in the former. Despite this, the primary difference between parameters for the two studies was in C, which we have identified as the resistance to interference of the new system being learned. The values of a and b were extremely similar for the two studies, indicating that the contribution of aF/M and of bF, in the equation, tend to be constant over relatively wide variations in difficulty. As one would guess from the fact that increased frequency led to decrements in learning rate, the value of the a parameter was greater than the value of the b parameter.

Response Meaningfulness

Evidence concerning the effect of response meaningfulness on learning comes from studies of free recall and from paired associates. Again, as in studies of stimulus meaningfulness, relatively few experiments have studied learning of *real words* as a function of response meaningfulness. And, for the most part, frequency and m effects have been dealt with as though they were a unitary variable.

FREE RECALL. Turning first to studies of free recall, results have been fairly consistent in indicating that increased word frequency is related to better recall. On the other hand, the effect is typically quite small. For example, Hall (1954) investigated free recall as a function of Thorndike-Lorge frequency. He constructed 4 lists of 20 words each, with all the words in a given list at the same Thorndike-Lorge frequency. The range of frequencies was between one per million words for the list of least frequent words to 50–100 per million for the list of most frequent words. Subjects were presented a list for five trials at a 5-seconds per word rate. After the fifth trial, the subjects were permitted five minutes to recall as many words as they could. Increased frequency resulted in greater number of words recalled. The relationship was monotonic and statistically significant, though the absolute differences in amount recalled at the various levels of frequency was small, ranging from 12.04 correct for the lowest frequency list to 15.04 correct for the highest.

In a similar study, Bousfield and Cohen (1955) also found a significant tendency for free recall to be greater when lists were of higher Thorndike-Lorge frequency. In this study, only two levels of frequency were employed, 2.6 per million and 24 per million. Each list consisted of 60 words, with only one presentation prior to recall. Again the differences were relatively small, 22.18 correct for the low frequency material, 25.55 correct for the high frequency material. Similar results were reported by Bousfield, Cohen, and Whitmarsh (1958).

Murdock (1960) described free recall in terms of the equation $R = C\ (1 - e^{bN})$, where R is the number of items recalled after each presentation, N is the number of presentations, C the asymptote of correct recall, and b is the slope of the curve. Murdock reports that b is a linear function of the log of the Thorndike-Lorge frequency of the words to be recalled.

Several studies have failed to obtain a relationship between Thorndike-Lorge frequency and amount of recall (Peters, 1936; Winnick and Kressel, 1965). The Winnick and Kressel study is particularly interesting since these writers controlled for the abstractness versus concreteness of their words. Concrete words proved to be much easier to recall than abstract, while frequency *per se* was unrelated to recall. Since more frequent words tend to be more concrete, the question arises as to whether the abstractness variable may underlie some of the frequency results reported in other studies. On the other hand, Winnick and Kressel used relatively short lists (16 words per list) in a mixed list design so that only half the words in a list were high frequency items, and half were low frequency. In addition, of their eight high frequency words, only four were in the range of 100 or more occurrences per million words, while four were in the range 19 to 45 per million. The range for the low frequency words was 7 to 14 per million. Their analysis consisted of comparing the mean recall for the eight high frequency words with the mean for the eight low frequency words. It is possible that their test was not adequately sensitive, since it has been shown that the effect of frequency on recall is only moderate.

RESPONSE FREQUENCY AND PAIRED-ASSOCIATES LEARNING.   Paired-associates studies also indicate a positive relationship between learning and the Thorndike-Lorge frequency of the response items of the list. Jacobs (1955) employed a paired-associates list in which the stimuli were nonsense syllables, all of approximately the same association level, while the responses were real words which covered the entire range of Thorndike-Lorge frequencies. The correlation was .74 between number of correct responses per pair and the Thorndike-Lorge frequency of the response member of the pair. Postman (1962c) used a 3 × 3 factorial design in which he manipulated the Thorndike-Lorge frequency of stimuli and responses independently. Response frequency was significantly related to learning at all levels of stimulus meaningfulness.

Winnick and Kressel (1965) investigated the effect of Thorndike-Lorge frequencies of response terms in a paired-associates study using nonsense syllables as stimuli. High frequency responses were learned significantly more rapidly than low. It is interesting to note that the response terms used were identical to those employed by these writers in their study of free recall, previously described. In free recall, frequency proved unrelated to learning. Apparently, the effect of Thorndike-Lorge frequencies is more pronounced in paired associates than in free recall. This could be due to the relatively great speed with which any real words are learned in free recall.

RESPONSE m AND PAIRED-ASSOCIATES LEARNING.   Studies such as Cieutat, Stockwell, and Noble (1958) and Hunt (1959), cited in the section on stimulus meaningfulness, manipulated response m over the entire range of Noble's m scale. Thus their low m items are primarily nonsense words. These studies indicate that high m words are learned faster than low m words, and that a given variation in response m has a more pronounced effect on learning than the same degree of variation when the words are used as stimuli.

INTERACTION BETWEEN FREQUENCY AND m VALUES OF RESPONSES. It should be noted once more that the studies, summarized in this section on response meaningfulness, have not controlled for m when studying frequency, nor have they controlled for frequency in studying m. Since frequency and m are positively correlated, and yet have inverse relationships with learning on the stimulus side, there is some ambiguity in interpreting these results. In addition, it should be noted that the response m studies cited above all draw their response items from the same pool of 100 words scaled for m by Noble (1952). The frequencies of the words in their list are profoundly skewed, with a preponderance of high frequency words. As we saw in Equation 2, m effects should be maximal at the highest frequency level.

Only one study, Saltz and Modigliani (1967), examined m and frequency of response terms as separate variables. As anticipated on the basis of Equation 2, m and frequency interacted strongly in their effect on learning. At m of 6, variations in frequency (from 1 occurrence per 4.5 million words to 2000 occurrences per 4.5 million words) had no effect on learning. A moderate effect of increased frequency was found at m of 7, and an ever more sizable effect was observed at m of 8. Earlier, when we discussed Equation 2, we saw that some level of M must exist at which $a/M - b = 0$. At this level of M, the equation collapses to $C - F(0)$; in other words, F will cease to have an effect on learning at this value of M, since $F \times 0 = 0$, no matter how large the value of F. The Saltz and Modigliani (1967) data on *response* meaningfulness indicate that, if m is used as an index of M, $a/M - b = 0$ at approximately $m = 6$, since at this value of m, differences in F are unrelated to learning. Note that for stimuli, the value of m at which $a/M - b = 0$ proved to be over $m = 9$. This discrepancy is due to the fact that for stmuli $a > b$, while for responses $b > a$.

Modigliani and Saltz (1969) have shown that Equation 2 fits both the stimulus meaningfulness data and the response meaningfulness data. Thus the general form of the relationship between F and M remains the same in both situations. However, for stimulus meaningfulness the value of the a parameter is larger than the value of the b parameter, while the opposite is true for response meaningfulness. Thus it is the relative contributions of the differentative variable and the conservation of meaning variables which changes as a word is changed from stimulus to response.

Is m AN INDEX OF NUMBER OF DIFFERENT MEANINGS FOR A WORD? Some interesting data concerning the interpretation of m also arose from the Saltz and Modigliani study. Some writers have suggested that m is an index of the number of different meanings for a word. To examine this issue, the number of different dictionary meanings (dm) was obtained for a sample of 100 words, omitting meanings listed as archaic or obscure. Correlations between dm and m were approximately zero. On the other hand, dm correlated about .60 with frequency. Response dm was significantly related to learning when frequency was controlled. At least a part of the basis for the lack of relationship between m and dm is suggested by an examination of the actual associations obtained in scaling m. Often the associations tend to exhaust a *single* meaning of a word. If this single meaning is rich in connotations, a large m value results.

The learning data suggest that dm may prove to be another relevant dimension in assessing meaningfulness. At this point it seems reasonable to speculate that M, in Equation 2, may consist of a combination of the m and dm variables.

Response Availability

In Chapter 5 we saw a fair amount of evidence which indicated that response availability, *per se,* is not a crucial variable in learning. In that chapter we examined studies in which word frequency was manipulated in the laboratory. Similar evidence is found when we examine meaningfulness as it develops in natural language. The evidence here comes primarily from the work of Epstein (1963) and of Runquist and Freeman (1960) .

Epstein pretrained his subjects on all responses so that his subjects could recall both high and low m responses perfectly before the paired-associates phase of the experiment. Despite this equalization of availability, lists containing high m responses were learned faster than lists containing low m responses. These results are contrary to expectations from an availability position for the effects of response m. They are consistent with Equation 2, which states that m functions to modulate the effect of frequency. Note, however, that Epstein's results might also be interpreted as consistent with a mediation position. Greater m would presumably increase the likelihood that some mediator exists between the response and its stimulus in the list.

The Runquist and Freeman (1960) study on the other hand, presents difficulties for both a pure availability hypothesis and a mediation hypothesis. In this study, subjects were presented with pairs of words and were told that one word of each pair was correct. In other words, the task was one of verbal discrimination. Learning was faster when the two words to be discriminated were both high frequency than when they were both low frequency. Since the two words in a pair were both presented to the subjects, no response recall was required and superior ability to recall more frequent words (i.e., superior response availability) was an irrelevant factor. In addition, subjects were not required to associate each response to a specific stimulus; thus the mediation processes also appear to be irrelevant. Subjects *were* required to discriminate between the two words in order to choose the correct one. Thus response differentiation (*bF* of Equation 2) remains as a relevant mechanism in accounting for the results.

Imagery and Level of Abstraction

While frequency and *m* have been the most systematically investigated dimensions of meaningfulness, a great deal of extremely interesting work has developed, in recent years, concerned with the level of abstraction of words and the degree to which words evoke images. The abstraction dimension runs from extremely concrete words which refer to objective, external stimuli (e.g., apple, chair) through objective but less specific stimuli (e.g., love, justice, order). Paivio (1965) has suggested that imagery is the major psychological attribute underlying the dimension of abstraction level. Images, he suggests, serve as mediators or "conceptual pegs" which permit a word to be firmly attached, as a stimulus, to some response. In a recent factor analysis, Paivio (1968) found data to support this position, since imagery and level of abstraction both had their primary loadings on the same factor.

In general, studies find superior learning when concrete words are used as stimuli, as compared to abstract words (e.g., Paivio, 1965; Yarmey and Paivio, 1965). However, the effects may become small, or disappear entirely, when these items are used as responses.

Studies such as Paivio (1965) report a high correlation between *m* and abstractness-concreteness, with concrete nouns eliciting a much higher *m* value than abstract nouns. Thus, in many of the learning studies reported, it is difficult to determine the extent to which the obtained relationships are due to an interaction between these variables. Yarmey and Paivio (1965), however, equated concrete and abstract nouns for *m* and again found the same relationship: Concrete stimuli lead to faster paired-associates learning than abstract stimuli, but concrete and abstract response terms did not differ in their effects upon learning.

In another study, Paivio and Madigan (1968) employed an imagery scale in place of the scale for abstraction, since these two scales correlate extremely highly ($r = .83$). Again mean *m* and mean frequency were equated for words of high and low imagery. In their study, imagery was a significant variable on both the stimulus and response side of paired associates, though the differences in *stimulus* imagery had more effect on learning than the differences in response imagery.

INSTRUCTIONS TO IMAGINE.   In the studies we have examined thus far, subjects were presented with words that differed in the extent to which they could evoke images; however, the subjects were *not* given special instructions to use this characteristic of the words during the learning sessions. There is little evidence concerning how many (if any!) subjects actually tried to use the images as aids to learning. A set of experiments reported by Bower (1970) throws important light on the role of imagery, since Bower actually instructed his subjects to use the images. The effects of these instructions were singularly impressive. Bower claims that the subjects who were told to use images recalled one-and-a-half to three times the amount of material recalled by control subjects. It appears, then, that images, *per se,* are a very potent factor in learning. The question which remains to be answered is—how do images produce this effect?

HOW DO IMAGES WORK?   We have seen that Paivio (1965) has suggested a "conceptual peg" notion to explain the effects of imagery. Bower (1970) appears to support a very similar notion.

However, alternative possibilities are suggested by our earlier discussions of stimulus differentiation and the role of conceptual representation in learning. In Chapter 4 we examined evidence which indicated that retention could be facilitated by increasing the cognitive dimensionality of the items involved in the memory systems. Specifically, studies like those of Saltz (1963) showed that human subjects learned more rapidly when stimuli were word-color compounds than when they were either words or colors alone. Cooper (1963) demonstrated a related phenomenon in animal subjects. A model was presented in Chapter 4 which related this increase in dimensionality to an increase in the distance between elements in the cognitive space (see Figure 4.2).

In effect, the writer is suggesting the possibility that a word, plus the image that it evokes, constitute a compound simulus. Further, since words and images are on different cognitive dimensions, the compounding could produce an increase in dimensionality which would increase the representational distinctiveness of the compound from other compounds.

This type of interpretation is supported by data from a related area in the learning literature. A number of studies have shown that (particularly for children) three dimensional representations of objects are learned faster and retained better than two dimensional representations of the same objects! (E.g., Semler & Iscoe, 1963; Iscoe

& Semler, 1964.) This effect is difficult to understand in terms of conceptual pegs. Why should a three dimensional object serve as a better peg than a two dimensional object? On the other hand, the data are very consistent with the position on representational dimensionality.

ABSTRACTION AND LEARNING. In the preceding sections we discussed the specific role of imagery in learning. At this point, let us examine the more general question of how abstraction influences learning.

The issue of characterizing *abstraction* was first explored in Chapter 2. We saw there that the notion of level of abstraction could be conceptualized in terms of the specificity of a concept in the cognitive space. Consider, for example, the concepts *apple* and *fruit*. Fruit is more abstract than apple, of course. In terms of the cognitive space, we noted in Chapter 2, fruit occupies a much broader region on the various, relevant attribute dimensions than does apple. Fruits can be as large as watermellons or as small as cherries, as sweet as melons or as tart as lemons. Our notions of apples, on the other hand, are much more restricted on these dimensions. It follows that, if we are asked to *imagine* an apple, this will be easier to do than if we are asked to imagine a fruit. In fact, if asked to imagine a fruit, we are likely to imagine a *particular* fruit, such as an apple!

The Demonstration Experiment, at the beginning of the present chapter, provides several interesting examples of the relationship between imagery and specificity of a concept. Despite the fact that Ford is a much more frequent stimulus than Rolls Royce, the imagery associated with the latter was much greater than that associated with the former. An examination of the subjects' associations to each word gave a clear indication of the reason for this. Rolls Royce reminded subjects of wealth, jewels, fur coats; they could picture a specific car, since the Rolls Royce has remained similar in appearance over many years. On the other hand, the Ford is driven by rich and poor, has changed its appearance often over the years—subjects have few specific images (or associations) in connection with the Ford. Thus both m and imagery ratings are higher for the Rolls Royce than for the Ford. (This example also suggests why m and imagery have been found to be so highly intercorrelated.)

From this point of view, the data relating imagery-abstraction to learning can be interpreted as stating: *The smaller the region in the cognitive space that constitutes a bounded cognitive system, the faster will be the acquisition of this bounded system.*

A number of issues remain unresolved, with regard to the mechanisms of imagery-abstraction. It is not clear why this variable should have a greater effect on stimuli than on responses. The inconsistent findings with regard to level of abstraction of response terms suggests that, as in the relationship between m and frequency in Equation 2, some other variable may be serving as a moderator on abstraction. It is possible that the inconsistent response-abstraction results may reflect too tight control over response m in the vicinity of $m = 5$ to 6; this is the region in which $a/M\text{-}b = 0$, and variations in other variables may wash out. On the stimulus side, $a/M\text{-}b = 0$ occurs at m values of 9 to 11, which are beyond the range of most English words used in these studies.

The Role of Concept Meaningfulness

A given meaning may be carried by a number of different words, some of which may occur much more frequently in the language than others. Consequently, in considering the meaningfulness of a word, it is probable that one should take into account the meaningfulness of the entire concept in which the word is lodged. For example, if an infrequent word sets off a frequent meaning, it is likely to excite the entire network of associations to the frequent meaning. Thus, if two *words* are equally frequent in the language but their *meanings* differ in frequency, one would expect a corresponding discrepancy in the m for these words. Similarly, if two words had identical m values but one came from a more common meaning than the other, one would expect the word from the more common meaning to be *lower* in frequency of occurrence in the language.

Almost no research has been reported which relates the meaningfulness of a word to the meaningfulness of its concept. An unpublished study performed in our laboratory examined this issue in an exploratory fashion. Paired-associates lists were constructed in which the response terms were equal in frequency. However, the frequency of their meanings varied over a large range. A strong tendency was found for more rapid acquisition of the responses which came from more frequent concepts. The problems involved in determining concept frequency, in this study, probably reflect one of the reasons so little research has been attempted in this area. Each concept was identified in Roget's *Thesaurus,* and the frequencies of all words in this concept class were then obtained from the Thorndike-Lorge tables. Severe problems arose, however, since many words have several meanings, some of which are relevant to the concept, some not. For example, under the concept *happy* one finds the word *sunny*. Clearly the frequency of the word *sunny* must be partitioned between the meaning *happy* and the meaning referring to weather conditions. Lorge (1949) has made a valuable start in this area by classifying the various meanings of a sample of very frequent words, and by partitioning the total frequency of each word among its various meanings.

MEANINGFULNESS OF NONSENSE WORDS

One can consider two different types of issues in reference to the meaningfulness of nonsense words. First, one can be concerned with the effect of various types of experimental manipulations on nonsense words in relation to subsequent behavior toward these nonsense words. For example, in Chapters 4 and 5 we examined learning as a function of pretraining on nonsense words. The issue here is the manner in which stimuli acquire meaningfulness. The second issue is that of measuring the meaningfulness of nonsense words prior to the subjects' experience with such words. Since most subjects have had little contact with such material prior to the laboratory situation, the issue becomes one of *derived* meaningfulness—the extent that a nonsense word has meaningfulness because it *resembles* a real word. This issue appears to have little importance except for methodological problems such as making sure that all nonsense words in a given study are homogeneous with respect to their resemblance to real words. It is unfortunate, therefore, that this issue has been the one most intensively studied.

Development of Meaningfulness

In Equations 1 and 2, presented earlier in this chapter, the frequency of a word in the conservation-of-meaning variable (aF/M) was considered to be identical to the frequency of the same word in the differentiation variable (bF). This is a reasonable assumption, since real words occur in context. Thus, each time a word occurs (increasing differentiation) it occurs in association with other material (increasing the resistance to interference of some S-R system). These variables can, to some extent, be separated in dealing with nonsense words. One can present a nonsense word alone, as in free recall studies, so that associations are less likely to be formed. From this point of view, Equation 1 can be rewritten

$$R = C - [a\,Fa/M - b\,(Fa + Fi)]\tag{3}$$

where Fa is the frequency with which the word occurs in an association, Fi is the frequency of individual presentation of the word when it does not enter into an association. This equation can be rewritten to correspond more closely to Equation 2.

$$R = C - Fa\,(a/M - b) + b\,Fi\tag{4}$$

Most of the pretraining studies described in Chapters 4 and 5 involved manipulating Fi rather than Fa. Since Fi enters only into the differentiation term of Equation 4, we would expect such pretraining to be largely facilitative. As we saw in Chapter 4, stimulus pretraining can, indeed facilitate subsequent paired-associates learning under the properly controlled conditions. This was particularly true for nonverbal material, but some nonsense syllable studies also showed a facilitative effect (e.g. Gannon and Noble, 1961; Martin, 1965). Pretraining of nonsense items that are to be used as *responses* in subsequent learning results in an extremely consistent facilitation of subsequent paired-associates learning (e.g., Saltz and Felton, 1968a), as we saw in Chapter 5.

In Chapter 6, we examined evidence related to conservation of past associations (aFa/M). Within broad limits, we found that increased number of trials on list 1 resulted in poorer learning of list 2 in the *A-B, A-C* paradigm. A similar effect appears to occur in the *A-B, C-B* paradigm if B is an already well differentiated term. A study by Underwood (1945) is particularly interesting since it involved manipulation of M with Fa held constant. Using nonsense syllable stimuli, Underwood kept the number of occurrences of each stimulus constant, but manipulated the number of different responses attached to each stimulus. Subsequent learning of a new response to a stimulus proved to be easier, under these conditions, when a number of different responses had previously been attached to the stimulus.

Derived Meaningfulness

Early investigators in this area, such as Glaze (1928), were interested in the problem of scaling presumed nonsense material to determine which items already had meaning in the sense that they reminded a subject of a real word. In modern parlance, Glaze was examining the *encodability* of nonsense words into real words. The problem appeared relatively straightforward when Glaze undertook his now classic normative study of the derived meaningfulness of nonsense syllables. Glaze presented 2019 three-letter nonsense syllables (each syllable consisted of a consonant-vowel-consonant combination) one syllable at a time, to 15 subjects. The subjects were to indicate, in one or two words, what, if anything, each syllable meant to them. The value assigned to each syllable was the percentage of subjects indicating that the syllable meant something to them. For example, all of Glaze's subjects indicated that BEL meant something to them, and so this syllable was assigned a value of 100%. None of his subjects reported anything for LAJ, and so this syllable was assigned a value of 0%.

Up to this point the issues involved in the scaling are relatively clear. However, the interpretation of a scale value becomes more uncertain for values between 0% and 100%. If a given item has a scale value of 67%, does this mean that the item is at 100% meaningful for 67% of the subjects and at 0% for the remaining 33%? Or does it mean that the item can be considered as intermediate in meaningfulness for all subjects, with a mean of 67% and some dispersion about this mean? In fact, almost all researchers using the Glaze scale (or the scales developed by Krueger, 1934; or Archer, 1960, which are very similar to Glaze's) appear to have made the latter assumption. Only inferential evidence exists on this issue.

Noble (1961) attempted to extend the Glaze procedure in a very provocative manner. He reasoned that an all-or-none scale lost a great deal of sensitivity. Consequently, he asked subjects to rate 2100 consonant-vowel-consonant syllables (*CVC's*), on a 1 to 5 scale, for the *number* of things each syllable brought to mind. The scale ran from *None* to *Very Many*. As Noble points out, the percentage of subjects rating greater than *None* for a given syllable corresponds to the Glaze, Krueger, Archer all-or-none scaling. Noble's use of an average rating obviously implies the assumption that the scale is psychologically a continuous function. This is certainly reasonable for the common meaningful words which are included in his scale (e.g., *man, hat*). The situation is less clear for the nonsense items. Certainly the correlation between Noble's continuous function and the all-or-none Glaze-type scale is extremely high (e.g., Noble reports $r = .928$ between his scale and Archer's 1960 revision of the Glaze norms).

Learning and Meaningfulness

An analysis of the psychological characteristics of nonsense syllables can best be made against the context of information concerning the relationships found between learning and indices of nonsense syllable meaningfulness.

NONSENSE SYLLABLES VERSUS WORDS. First, it is rather uniformly found that learning is better for real words than for nonsense syllables. Cason (1933) used a paired-associates procedure in which he compared four types of pairs: word-word, word-nonword, nonword-word, nonword-nonword. A single list consisted of 16 pairs, 4 of each type. Word-word pairs were learned best; word-nonword and nonword-word pairs were learned equally well; nonword-nonword pairs were most poorly learned.

In a similar study, Sheffield (1946) also found that word-word pairs were easiest to learn and nonword-nonword pairs most difficult. In this study, words proved more effective as responses than as stimuli (viz., nonword-word pairs were easier to learn than word-nonword pairs).

Underwood and Schulz (1960) in Experiment 7 equated words and nonsense syllables for frequency of occurrence in the English language. They also found that, when these items were responses in paired associates (using numbers as stimuli) the words were more readily learned than the nonsense syllables.

The distinction between learning words and learning nonwords is not complete and sharp. Lindley (1960), in a serial learning study, found that for most subjects, syllables that were very meaningful on the Glaze norms were as easy to learn as real words. This was particularly true if the nonsense syllables occur as the first three letters of common English words.

LEARNING AND NONSENSE SYLLABLE MEANINGFULNESS. Learning of nonsense syllables is related to Glaze-type association level of syllables. In serial learning studies, McGeoch (1930) and Sisson (1938), among many others, report that learning is faster for high meaningful items than for items of low meaningfulness. The McGeoch study is particularly interesting in that he used a wide range of Glaze values: 0, 20, 46, 53, 73, and 100. Two lists of ten items each were constructed for each Glaze value. The same 36 subjects learned all lists, though the order differed from subject to subject. The data indicated a relatively linear increase in number of correct responses as a function of increased Glaze-meaningfulness. The same design was then repeated using 31 of the original 36 subjects. In this second study, the relationship between learning and Glaze values was much more irregular, reaching an asymptote at around 46% Glaze value. It is interesting to note that a reduction in relationship between meaningfulness and learning occurred after the subjects had acquired experience in learning nonsense lists. We shall return to this issue later in the chapter.

As in the predifferentiation studies examined in Chapters 4 and 5, response manipulation has a greater effect on performance than stimulus manipulation. L'Abate (1959), in a 2 × 2 design, compared the effect of high versus low Glaze-value stimuli and high versus low Glaze-value responses. He found that differences in response meaningfulness had a greater effect on paired-associates performance than differences in stimulus meaningfulness. Similar results were obtained by Cieutat, Stockwell, and Noble (1958). While both stimulus and response effects were significant in this study, differences in response meaningfulness produced greater differences in learning rate than did differences in stimulus meaningfulness. The studies reported above used the standard anticipation test for learning, in which subjects were required to *recall* the correct response upon *presentation* of a stimulus.

It is interesting to note that Cieutat (1961) found a greater difference due to variations in stimulus meaningfulness than due to response meaningfulness when *the test was by means of a modified recognition technique.* Here the response items were physically present, and the subjects were required to select the response that was appropriate for each stimulus. It has been suggested previously in this book that items which are physically present before a subject are more differentiated than items which are internal traces in memory. Thus the relatively small effect on learning produced by varying stimulus meaningfulness, in the standard anticipation study, would be interpreted as due to the fact that even low meaningful stimuli would be moderately differentiated as a consequence of their physical presence. The finding that variations in response meaningfulness cease to have a greater impact on learning than variations in stimulus meaningfulness, when a recognition technique is used, appears to support this position. Unfortunately, the Cieutat data must be considered merely suggestive, since this study involved an extremely unusual procedure in addition to the recognition test, and the characteristics of this procedure are not at present understood.

Pronunciability and Meaningfulness

The data summarized above clearly show that the Glaze-type meaningfulness of a nonsense syllable is directly related to the ease with which it is learned. The succeeding sections are concerned with the mechanisms producing this relationship.

Underwood and Schulz (1960) have developed an index of the pronunciability of nonsense syllables which they have found to be correlated .67 with Glaze association values. Because of the extent of this correlation, it is not surprising that the relationship between learning and pronunciability parallels the results reported for Glaze values. Increased pronunciability of either stimuli or responses facilitates learning, with the effect of response pronunciability exceeding that of stimulus pronunciability. Underwood and Schulz have suggested that pronunciability is an index of the integration of a nonsense syllable. They have also suggested that pronunciability may be the more fundamental of the two measures, since they found that when the two were highly correlated in a list, both correlated well with learning; however, when pronunciability and Glaze values were uncorrelated in a list, pronunciability predicted learning but Glaze values did not.

Saltz and Ager (1962), however, have shown that the Underwood and Schulz conclusions may have been based on inadequacies within Glaze's norms. The original Glaze values have several deficiencies. They are over 30 years old, and many changes have occurred in the language over this period. In addition, these norms were based on only 15 subjects. Using the more recent and better standardized norms compiled by Noble (1961) as a basis for reanalyzing the Underwood and Schulz data, Saltz and Ager found that pronunciability and the revised Glaze-type values correlate to approximately the same extent with learning.

Data reported by Lindley (1963) are even more damaging to the pronunciability position. Lindley constructed four serial lists, systematically varying pronunciability, meaningfulness (combining the Noble, 1961; and Archer, 1960, revision of Glaze norms to assess this variable), and frequency of nonsense syllables. The experimental design for this study is indicated on Table 9–1. If Lists 1 and 2 differ in rate of learning, the effect can be attributed to pronunciability. If Lists 2 and 4 differ, the effect can be attributed to Glaze-type meaningfulness. And if Lists 3 and 4 differ, the effect can be attributed to frequency. The only significant difference in learning ob-

TABLE 9–1. Experimental Design Employed by Lindley (1963) Comparing the Effects of Meaningfulness, Pronunciability, and Frequency of Nonsense Syllables on Serial Learning

	Materials		
Lists	Glaze-type Meaningfulness	Pronunciability	Frequency
1	low	hard	low
2	low	easy	low
3	high	easy	high
4	high	easy	low

tained in this study was between Lists 2 and 4, suggesting that Glaze-type meaningfulness (i.e., the extent to which a syllable reminded subjects of real words) was the critical variable, rather than pronunciability or frequency.

Frequency and Learning

Superficially, at least, it would seem reasonable to assume that items having higher Glaze-type meaningfulness should be those which the subjects have experienced more frequently. Therefore, compared to items of low Glaze value, these should be more integrated and differentiated, using these concepts as they were developed in Chapters 4 and 5. On the response side, this would be consistent with the data obtained using both real words and nonsense syllables. On the stimulus side, it would seem reasonable to expect the effect of differentiation to be relatively more pronounced for nonsense syllables than for words, since all familiar words are already at a fairly high level of differentiation. Consequently, the facilitory effects of differentiation should be more observable for nonsense syllables than for real words.

A careful examination of the data suggests that this position, while perhaps not completely inadequate, is at least an oversimplification. Frequency of occurrence in the language can refer to two very different sorts of things when we deal with nonsense syllables. It could refer to the frequency with which the syllable, *per se,* occurs in the language. Or it could refer to the frequency with which the subjects' responses to the syllable occur in the language. The distinction being made here is between the *nominal* item (i.e., the syllable as presented by the experimenter) and the *functional* item (i.e., the syllable as encoded by the subject). There is strong evidence to suggest that these are not necessarily the same.

THE NOMINAL SYLLABLE.   Let us first look at the issue of the frequency of the nominal syllable. Underwood and Schulz (1960) report data which show that low meaningful CVC's contain more of the infrequently used letters of the alphabet, while high meaningful CVC's are made up of more frequently used letters. In addition, they examined the likelihood that CVC's at various levels of meaningfulness occur as units in English words. A relatively linear relationship was found, using various counts of the language as a basis for judgment. Of the Glaze items having 0% scale scores, only 4% occur as units in English words. Of the Glaze items having 100% scale scores, 92% occur as such units. Such data indicate that *a very large percentage of the Glaze items almost never occur as sequences in English words.* Even of the 100% Glaze-value items, 8% actually do not occur as letter sequences in the Underwood and Schulz data. While Underwood and Schulz used only a *sample* of English words, the sample was relatively large compared to the average subject's vocabulary, and was weighted toward the more common words. It seems safe to say that 8% of the high Glaze level items either do not occur at all or are very rare sequences in English. Obviously, then, while frequency of occurrence in the language is correlated with Glaze value, it is not the basic variable which determines Glaze value. And, indeed, Underwood and Schulz (1960) and Lindley (1963) find no relationship between learning and the frequency of occurrence of CVC's in the language.

One problem with frequency of letter sequence occurrence is that letter sequences will often be hidden within integrated words. As was seen in Chapter 7, small response sequences within larger integrated responses tend to lose their stimulus characteristics. The CVC ZED, for example, is relatively low in the Glaze scale (27% level). Yet it occurs in such familiar words as *amazed, dazed,* and *grazed.*

A study by Lindley (1960) supports the position that the lack of relationship between learning and CVC frequency may be partially due to the hiddenness of the CVC's in real words. The CVC's are less likely to be hidden if they are the first three letters of a word. Lindley found that, equating for Glaze level, CVC's which are the first three letters of common words were easier to learn in a serial list than CVC's which are never found as the first three letters of common words. In this study, Lindley utilized an all-or-none measure of frequency. There is no information at present to indicate whether, among CVC's that occur as the first three letters of words, greater frequency of such occurrence is related to learning.

Another problem, which the reader has no doubt already recognized from the ZED example, above, is that the pronunciation of the isolated *CVC* is likely to be quite different from the pronunciation of the identical letter sequence in a real word. Thus the frequency of the sound sequence is likely to be very different from the frequency of the letter sequence. In any case, however, hidden sequences cannot be the complete answer to the problem of the relationship between Glaze level and learning. Too many *CVC*'s at various levels on Glaze-type scales do not occur at all in English words.

THE FUNCTIONAL SYLLABLE.   This brings us to the issue of the *functional* item. If the letter sequence *LUV* is pronounced like the word *love* by a subject, it is clear that the nominal letter sequence is not identical to the functional item. In such a situation, it might not be relevant whether or not the letter sequence LUV occurred frequently in English words. In fact, we have seen that of the *CVC*'s at the 100% association level in Glaze's scale, 8% actually do not occur as letter sequences in English words, according to the Underwood and Schulz data. The problem becomes even more severe when one considers that certain infrequent letter sequences may be pronounced in various ways, some of which will be closer to spoken words than others. *X A B,* for example, may be pronounced as *cab* by one subject and as *zab* by another.

Stability of Encoding Nonsense Syllables

Saltz and Felton (1968*b*) have suggested that *stability* of encoding a nonsense syllable to a real word may be an important factor in learning. This was based on an analysis of the responses given by subjects to nonsense syllables when the subjects were operating under the Glaze-type instructions to write down the word or idea suggested by each of 50 nonsense syllables. First, it was found that the structural characteristics of the more highly meaningful syllables were more closely related to the subjects' responses than was true of low meaningful syllables. For extremely high meaningful syllables, the responses were very likely to involve the actual three letters of the syllable as the first three letters of the response. This tendency dropped sharply as a function of reduced Glaze values. Responses to syllables of moderate meaningfulness were fairly well determined by the first letter or first two letters of the syllable, or by a simple transformation of the syllable. Low meaningful items were least capable of being related to their responses. Further, degree of intersubject agreement on responses to a syllable was markedly related to meaningfulness value. Here, percentage of *different responses* given to a syllable ranged from 77% for lowest meaningful syllables to 33% for highest meaningful. As can be seen, there is a fair degree of response variability between subjects even for the most meaningful syllables. In general, then, it appears that lower meaningful syllables are more arbitrary, less tied to stimulus characteristics than is true for higher meaningful syllables.

Finally, immediately after responding to the 50 syllables, the subjects were presented the identical syllables in the same order, and were asked to *recall* the response they had just given to each syllable. Despite the fact that their original responses presumably represented the word or idea suggested by each syllable, subjects forgot 27% of their responses to the lowest meaningful syllables, and 5.6% of their responses to the highest meaningful syllables.

It appears reasonable to assume that uncertainty of response to a nonsense syllable is a crucial factor in the relationship between Glaze-type meaningfulness and learning. If the subject's response to a syllable is unstable, learning will be impeded. In comparing familiar real words with nonsense syllables, it is clear that the characteristics of subjects' responses to real words are better understood and are more predictable. Subjects may or may not be able to encode a nonsense syllable, and they may respond to the entire syllable or to only a small portion of it.

It has been seen that nonsense syllable meaningfulness is more important for response terms than for stimulus terms. This is certainly reasonable. If a subject has difficulty remembering his encoded response to a syllable when it is directly before him, this difficulty must be compounded if the syllable must be remembered. Underwood (1963) has shown that when a stimulus is a low meaningful nonsense syllable, subjects will often use just a single letter of the nonsense syllable as the functional stimulus. This is not as easily done when the nonsense syllable is the response in paired-associates learning, nor in serial learning or free recall, where the subject must emit the entire response.

Similarity and Meaningfulness

It is tempting to hypothesize that the stability of response to an item is an aspect of the differentiation of the item. (This sort of assumption has been suggested by other writers, such as Sheffield,

1946.) If items tend to be reacted to differently from trial to trial, it is not unreasonable to assume that the confusion between items might be great. In such a situation, the ability of an item to resist interference from other items might be expected to be low. This is certainly suggested by the fact that item recognition is inversely related to meaningfulness. Not only are low Glaze items difficult to attach to one another, but subjects have difficulty recognizing that these were the same items they saw on the previous trial. Further evidence supporting this position is found in research relating learning to item similarity at various levels of item meaningfulness.

If item meaningfulness is related to the differentiation of the item, then we would expect to find less effect of similarity between items for high meaningful material as opposed to low meaningful material. The reasoning here is relatively straightforward. Similarity is conceptualized as the closeness of two items in the cognitive space. If differentiation of the items is weak (e.g., meaningfulness is low), the items will be less resistant to intrusions from very close items. Thus learning will be slower for similar than for nonsimilar material. On the other hand, if differentiation is great, items will be able to resist these intrusion tendencies. In this case, there will be relatively little difference between learning rates for similar and nonsimilar items.

Serial learning studies support the hypothesis of an interaction between meaningfulness and similarity. Underwood and Richardson (1956b, 1958), in two separate studies, employed high- and low-meaningful nonsense syllables at either high or low similarity levels. Similarity proved to be significantly more detrimental to learning of the low meaningfulness lists than of the high meaningfulness lists. In these studies, similarity was defined in terms of the amount of letter duplication among syllables. High similar lists involved reusing the same pool of letters for all items. In the low similar lists there was little duplication of letters among items. Degree of letter overlap was approximately equal for high-meaningful and low-meaningful lists at each similarity level.

Some evidence for an interaction between similarity and meaningfulness can also be found in paired-associates studies. McGehee (1961) found that letter overlap between trigrams increased errors for low-meaningful stimuli but not for high-meaningful stimuli.

In two parallel studies, Underwood (1953a, 1953b) examined the effect of stimulus similarity on the learning of nonsense materials and on the learning of paired adjectives. Similarity produced a sizable and consistent effect on learning of nonsense syllables. For adjectives, the effect of stimulus similarity was also significant but the effect was less regular—medium similarity produced slower learning than low similarity, but also produced slower learning than high similarity.

CONCLUSIONS

We have seen that the meaningfulness of a real word can be conceptualized as being a function of three variables: (a) *The tendency for the word to conserve prior meanings.* Operationally, this has been described as aF/M, in which F is the frequency of occurrence of the word in various other contexts, M is the number of different associations to the word (e.g., Noble's, 1952, m), while a is a parameter relating this variable to learning. (b) *The differentiation of the word.* This is determined by the frequency of experience with the word, and can be operationalized as bF. (c) *The level of abstractness, or amount of imagery evoked by the word* (which appears to be related to the specificity of the word in the cognitive space).

As far as conservation of old meanings and differentiation are concerned, the general relationship between word meaningfulness and the probability of a correct response in new learning can be stated in the following form.

$$\text{Correct } R = C - aF/M - bF$$

The mechanisms involved in level of abstraction are not as well understood, but this variable appears to function in a manner very similar to that of M in the formulation above.

Perhaps the most interesting question arising from this formulation relates to the fact that a and b take on different values when the item is used as a response, as opposed to the values of a and b when the item is a stimulus. Presumably, a or b (or both) are dependent variables related to psychological characteristics stemming from employing an item as a cue to a second item, as opposed to employing the item as a response to some cue. The entire issue of the distinction between stimuli and responses, raised in Chapter 5, thus reappears at this point. However, despite the difference in the specific values of a and b under stimulus versus response conditions, it appears that the *general relationship* stated in the formulation is consistent whether the item functions as a stimulus or a response.

Turning to nonsense words, we find that laboratory manipulation of frequency and number of associations produces essentially the results anticipated from the equation above. Thus, producing meaningfulness in the laboratory appears to be feasible. On the other hand, nonsense material appears to be much more complex, psychologically, than are meaningful words. This is largely because of the great variability in response to a nonsense word, a variability that appears to be both inter- and intra-subject. Not only do subjects differ markedly in the way they encode nonsense material, a given subject is likely not to remember his own encoding. If one subject encodes a nonsense word as a high-frequency real word, for example, and another encodes it as a low-frequency real word, the effects on learning should differ extremely, and great variability in learning will result.

In short, the research reported in this chapter is very consistent in indicating that the crucial variable in determining the rate of learning of nonsense syllables is the extent to which the syllable resembles or reminds the subjects of a real word. Stability of the encoding response to the nonsense syllable appears to be the variable basic to this relationship.

10 | Intention and Strategies in Learning

PRECIS

When confronted with a new learning situation, people often attempt to utilize their previous experiences to facilitate acquisition. In this sense, the learner is not a passive recipient of new information. Instead, he may often be involved in fairly complex thinking behavior. On the other hand, there is no guarantee that such activity will actually facilitate learning. At times, in fact, the opposite is true.

Much of what is known in this area comes from studies of nonintentional ("incidental") learning. A person who does not realize that he is expected to learn is likely to approach materials quite differently than a person who realizes he is engaged in a learning task. Such differences in approach can be examined in relation to the amount of learning which actually occurs.

The evidence indicates that, if the subject attends to the relevant aspects of the material, the primary problem in nonintentional learning is not acquisition; rather, it is retrieval. Further, this is often exhibited as massive retroactive inhibition.

The mechanisms of intentional learning appear to be much more crucial for poorly differentiated materials than for well differentiated materials—in fact, for free recall at least, intention is at times an irrelevant variable when the materials to be learned are very highly differentiated items. Such data suggest the possibility that the mechanisms of intention serve to increase the differentiation of poorly differentiated materials. This could be accomplished by recoding the items into a form that is more differentiated. As shall be seen, such recoding may produce problems of its own.

More recent research has been concerned with studying strategies for learning in a more direct fashion. While very provocative results have been obtained in this area, the topic must be considered in a very early stage of development.

DEMONSTRATION EXPERIMENT

The Problem

Answer the following questions as accurately as you can.
1. What did you have for breakfast this morning?
2. What time did you go to sleep last night?
3. What time did you awaken this morning?
4. What color shirt (or dress) did you wear yesterday?
5. Did it rain today?
6. What did you have for breakfast a month ago last Thursday?
7. What time did you go to sleep on this date last month?
8. What time did you awaken in the morning two months ago today?
9. What color shirt (or dress) did you wear one week ago today?
10. Did it rain a year ago today?

Explanation

The issue of intention in learning has been of interest to psychologists for a long time, though the objectives of this interest have changed markedly with time. Early concern with intention centered on the question of whether such a variable was necessary for learning. Later the question took the form, are there any particular types of responses (e.g., strategies), which subjects use when they intend to learn, that facilitate acquisition and retention?

Let us look at your answers to the questions above, in terms of the first question: Can learning occur without intention? Most persons are able to answer the first five questions, above, with little difficulty. Yet, few people intended to memorize the contents of their breakfast, or the time they went to bed last night, in anticipation of a test for such memories. Thus the demonstration strongly suggests that we may remember things even though we had not intended to learn them.

Now let us consider the second question: Are there types of responses that the learner can make that will facilitate learning and retention? To get some initial, intuitive feeling for this issue, let us compare your answers to questions 1 to 5, above, with your answers to questions 6 to 10. While most of you had little difficulty with questions 1 to 5, few readers could answer questions 6 to 10 with any accuracy. The reason is clearly related to the fact that the latter questions are concerned with events that took place long ago. Presumably, these items were *learned:* This is indicated by the fact that the corresponding information for events of yesterday or today (in questions 1 to 5) could be recalled. Items 6 to 10 can not be answered because you have *forgotten!* You have had so many different breakfasts, for example, over the past month that you do not recall which one of these occurred one month ago last Thursday. Had you known at that time, however, that you would be asked about that specific meal, you could have *tagged it* mentally so that it was distinguishable from the other meals of the month. We shall see that, to a great extent, the problem of recall under conditions of nonintentional learning is not that learning failed to take place; instead, the problem will often prove to be one of inadequate tagging for future recall.

INTENTION AND LEARNING

Intention can influence various aspects of behavior, and psychologists have studied a number of these relationships. It is therefore important that we avoid confusion by being very specific about the focus of the present chapter. We shall be concerned with the presence or absence of intention during the *learning* phase, when the subject is being *presented* with materials. During the *test* phase, when we evaluate learning by determining how much of the material the subjects can remember, all subjects are aware that they are being tested. In other words, lack of intention is a condition during *learning,* but *not during the test.* In Chapter 11 we shall consider studies in which the subjects may not be aware that they are involved in a learning experiment during either learning *or* test phase; these include verbal operant conditioning studies and some of the classical conditioning studies, among others. The issues in this chapter and in Chapter 11 differ in several important respects. For example, a subject may have learned, but if he does not realize that he is being tested he may never emit the relevant response. We have seen before in this book that failure to perform does not guarantee that learning has failed to occur.

How does intention during learning influence later retention? The role of intention has been somewhat obscure, and with the exception of the important work by Saltzman and Postman, relatively few programatic investigations have been conducted in this area. One reason for this appears to be the connotations of "free will" and "indeterminacy" in the term *intention.* Another problem for many psychologists has been that a subject's intention is presumably an internal state of affairs; as such, it is difficult to know what a subject's "real" intention is. As shall be seen, some of these problems have been overcome by relatively recent attempts to operationalize the concept of intention so that it can be dealt with in a reasonably objective manner. In any case, it is clear that powerful factors are at work in this general area and a comprehensive understanding of learning and memory is impossible without taking these factors into account.

A number of questions arise in relation to intention. To a great extent, our consideration of the topic involves examining evidence concerning these questions:

1. Can learning occur in the absence of intention to learn?

2. What are the mechanisms by which intention influences learning? Two of the most frequently mentioned possible mechanisms are that intention increases drive level, and that intention initiates certain types of internal responses (e.g., strategies) which facilitate learning.

3. What aspects of the cognitives system are primarily influenced by intention: association, S or R differentiation, or boundary strength?

Operational Definition of Intention

It is not the purpose of the present section to attempt a precise and comprehensive definition of intention. This would be much too complex a task. Some general observations must be made, however, to avoid misunderstanding and confusion concerning the status of the research we shall discuss.

First, since intention refers to an inferred internal state of the organism, we must clearly recognize that its status in psychological theory must be that of a construct, an intervening variable defined either in terms of stimulus input to the subject or in terms of some response that the subject makes, or to some relationship between these. In the human learning studies to be discussed, the typical operational definition of intention is a stimulus definition: The subject is instructed to learn certain material. The definition of *lack* of intention is somewhat more complex. The subject is presented with some task to perform (the "orienting task") which involves responding to the set of materials for which learning is later to be tested; however, *the orienting task does not imply instructions to learn*. Some commonly used orienting tasks include rating words for familiarity, giving a free association to each of a group of words, pairing words with geometric forms.

In some situations the adequacy of an orienting task may be

questioned. Feldman and Underwood (1957) tested for backward associations after their subjects learned a paired-associates list. Since subjects were not instructed to learn the *A-B* pairs in the *B-A* order, these writers suggest that the learning of backward associations might be considered incidental, rather than intentional learning. Is this a reasonable position? The decision on the acceptability of backward associations as representing cases of nonintentional learning depends on both theoretical and empirical considerations. From a theoretical point of view, if one conceptualizes learning as the formation of a forward association between a stimulus and a response, then the Feldman and Underwood position is very reasonable. If one conceptualizes learning as the formation of a cognitive system involving two or more elements, then people can be thought of as learning the *system* under intentional or nonintentional conditions, and the *B-A* test is simply a test of directionality within a learned system. At this point the reader must make his own decision on the theoretical issue.

As for the empirical considerations, the question becomes, very simply, do backward associations show the same functional relations with other variables that we find for nonintentionally learned material. This issue has simply not been explored in sufficient depth to permit a reasonable answer at present.

Another type of problem in defining lack of intention is typified in a study by Postman and Adams (1956a). In one condition of this study, subjects were presented with two lists successively. Subjects were *instructed to learn the first list; however, they were simply presented the second list without specific instructions to learn.* How satisfactory is a definition which states the second list was learned under nonintentional conditions?

Response definitions of intention are one type of attempt to overcome some of the problems pointed out above. One can simply ask a subject if he intended to learn (or tried to learn, or expected a test of retention). Unfortunately, the interpretation of answers to such questions is sometimes unclear. A subject may indicate intention, after the fact, if it had crossed his mind that he might be tested for retention; or, thinking back, he may believe that perhaps he recalls thinking he might be tested. On the other hand, a subject may deny intention to learn if he feels he has performed poorly. These are, clearly, problems associated with the fact that we have no direct access to a subject's conscious processes. And these are the problems that lead to considering intention as a construct, rather than as a directly observable phenomenon.

Probably the most reasonable attempt to operationalize intention, in the types of learning situations with which we are now concerned, would involve a definition based on the relationship between task and response. Upon completion of the orienting task, control subjects *who have not been tested for retention* could be questioned concerning their expectations during the course of the orienting task. If a sizable number of subjects indicate that they had anticipated a retention test (as is likely in the Postman and Adams condition described above) , the task would be defined as one involving intention to learn.

Postman (1964) has distinguished between two types of incidental learning situations. In one type, the orienting task is one which does not necessitate any learning. Examples include asking subjects to rate items for familiarity or instructing subjects to give their first associate to a given word. In the second type of task, subjects are told to learn something other than the items on which they are to be tested. For example, words embedded in various geometric designs may be presented, with subjects asked to learn the words; a subsequent test of retention for the geometric forms might be considered a test of incidental, nonintentional learning. The test of backward associations also falls into this second type of task. Clearly, when the latter variety of techniques are employed, the sort of operationalization outlined above becomes more crucial.

Can Learning Occur without Intention?

A number of studies suggest that learning *can* occur in the absence of intentions. Only a few of these shall be considered. Postman, Adams, and Phillips (1955) had subjects rate adjectives for familiarity. The nonintentional group was given no instructions concerning a subsequent retention test. The intentional group, like the nonintentional, was instructed to rate the adjectives; in addition, however, they were told to attempt to learn the adjectives. While the intentional group remembered significantly more words than the nonintentional, the nonintentional recalled more than 40% of the adjectives.

Several questions can be raised concerning this type of study. First, is it possible that *some* of the subjects in the nonintentional group actually intended to learn, while some did not? If this were the case, then the nonintentional group as a whole would show some learning, but not as much as the intentional group. A second problem which arises was pointed out by McGeoch (1942, p. 304). McGeoch suggests that the set to learn may arise spontaneously and in a transitory fashion in regard to any material presented to a subject. He appears to suggest that such a set to learn may be relatively unconscious.

A close examination of the Postman, Adams, and Phillips (1955) data suggest that the types of issues raised above are probably without foundation. The relationship between familiarity and recall is particularly relevant. Adjectives with relatively low familiarity ratings showed a substantial effect due to intention while those with high familiarity ratings showed no difference between intentional and nonintentional subjects. If the fact that *some* learning occurred in the nonintentional group were due to a small number of pseudo-nonintentional subjects, the equality of performance at the high familiarity end of the scale would be unlikely. Such equality could, presumably, occur only if the pseudo-nonintentional subjects were much superior in learning ability than the intentional subjects. If the latter were the case, it is difficult to see why the two groups differed at any point in the familiarity scale. The same type of objections arise in regard to McGeoch's notion of transitory learning sets. Here it would be necessary to assume that the set to learn is more likely to occur for familiar than for nonfamiliar words, and that this set occurred for almost all nonintentional subjects upon presentation of these more familiar items.

A study by Postman and Adams (1957) presents similar difficulties for the position that learning cannot occur without intention. In one condition, subjects were presented 14 dissimilar nonsense syllables (*CVC*'s) under the orienting instructions that this was a study of the effects of fatigue on speech. Subjects were asked to spell each syllable as it occurred. In addition to the orienting instructions, the intentional group was told to try to learn the items. The intentional group recalled 6.25 items, the nonintentional recalled 3.96. While this difference is significant, it is clear that learning occurred in the nonintentional group. An examination of the serial position curves for intentional and nonintentioall subjects indicates that the difference in performance between these groups was due to *better retention, by the intentional subjects, of the first three-fourths of the list.* The final portion is recalled equally well by both groups. If one assumed that all the learning in the nonintentional group were due to several pseudo-nonintentional subjects, it would be difficult to account for the fact that the mean performance of the two groups was equal on the last items.

Most of the studies investigating learning under nonintentional conditions have found some degree of incidental learning. This has been true even when subjects have been questioned after the experiment and those who indicated intention were eliminated (e.g., Postman and Phillips, 1954).

Mechanisms of Intention: Motivation versus Strategies

The mechanisms proposed to explain the role of intention on learning can be categorized into two major classes. One category of mechanisms has been characterized as motivational, though, as shall be seen, the term motivation is used in a very broad fashion. The other category is one of specific types of responses (e.g., strategies) which, it is assumed, the subject makes when he intends to learn.

McGeoch (1942, pp. 282–92) has suggested that both of these types of mechanisms operate. In relation to motivation he suggests that intention leads to greater muscular discharge or tension. He then relates these notions of tension to Guthrie's (1935) concept of maintaining stimuli (i.e., stimuli, primarily proprioceptive, which keep a subject in a state of readiness to make certain types of responses). In Hull's (1943) terms, such tension is a drive variable which multiplies existing habits. As tentative evidence for this type of mechanism, McGeoch points to studies which indicate that subjects under no particular instructions to do anything will often slump in their chairs, under states of low muscular tension; on the other hand, under specific instructions to perform some task, the subjects usually sit erect and give indication of increased muscular tension.

This sort of mechanism is difficult to apply to most studies of intention. Most studies involve the subjects performing some specific orienting task, often a demanding one, which would lead to an increase in muscular tension. Despite this, unless the subjects are directed toward learning the specific material to be tested, the retention of this material is impaired. This line of reasoning does not imply that muscular tension is irrelevant to learning or retention. It does suggest that tension is not the basic factor in the performance differential found between intentional and nonintentional learners.

McGeoch indicates that intention also has orienting and directing properties, in addition to the tension inducing functions. By this he appears to mean that the set of responses made to the relevant stimuli is different for subjects who are trying to learn as opposed to those who are not. It is this approach to the problem of intention which has been most fruitful in recent years for our understanding of the processes of intention. To document the importance of differential responses, McGeoch cites studies such as Peterson (1916) and Poppelreuter (1912). Peterson's intentional subjects reported attempting to use mnemonic aids such as associating the experimental items to other words in their vocabulary, while little such activity was reported by the nonintentional subjects. Poppelreuter's intentional subjects spontaneously utilized devices like pronouncing syllables rhythmically, while the nonintentional subjects did not.

The Orienting Task

Saltzman (1953) was probably the first psychologist to deal systematically with the problem of the subject's responses as a crucial factor in intentional learning. Saltzman's greatest contribution was to point out that the orienting task, *per se,* is an important variable in learning. Previous studies had conceived of the orienting task as simply a facade for obscuring the real purpose of the experiment from the nonintentional subjects while forcing these subjects to attend to the material. From ths point of view, there was no need for the intentional learners to perform the orienting task. They were simply presented the material and told to learn it. Saltzman, on the other hand, pointed out that some orienting tasks require subjects to make responses which are similar to those they would make if they intended to learn, while other orienting tasks may actually impede learning. There are several consequences to the Saltzman analysis. One is methodological. If intentional subjects who do not perform the orienting task learn better than nonintentional who do perform the task, the difference cannot unambiguously be attributed to intention; it may be due to characteristics of the orienting task which are detrimental to learning or retention.

The second consequence of the Saltzman position is more important for an understanding of the processes in intention. Saltzman suggests that intention, *per se,* may not be the crucial variable in the difference between intentional and nonintentional learners. If subjects do not intend to learn, but if the orienting task leads them to make the type of responses which are determiners of learning, learning may be as good under nonintentional conditions as under intentional. In other words, the assumption is made that *there exists a class of responses which, if performed upon a set of materials, will lead to the learning of these materials irrespective of the subject's intention or lack of intention to learn.*

As shall be seen, there is strong evidence for Saltzman's position.

POSTMAN'S ANALYSIS OF THE ORIENTING RESPONSE.   In an important paper, Postman (1964) has extended Saltzman's conception of the dimensional characteristics of the orienting task response. Visualize a dimension of orienting tasks arranged from those that interfere most with learning at one end of the dimension to those that *force subjects* to make responses which are *most similar* to the responses which are *necessary for learning* at the other end of the dimension. Postman suggests that intention will have *no differential effect* at either end of this continuum. If the orienting task elicits responses which are extremely similar to those required in learning, the nonintentional subjects will perform as well as the intentional. If the orienting task elicits responses *antagonistic* to learning, intentional subjects performing the orienting task will learn as poorly as the nonintentional. The advantage of intention will appear *between these extremes* on the continuum. Here, the orienting task does not, to any great extent, produce the crucial responses necessary for learning in the nonintentional subjects. On the other hand, it does not interfere greatly with the intentional group. To the extent that evidence supports such a position, Postman suggests, this evidence is counterindicative for a drive theory of intention. A drive theory would presumably predict greater facilitation due to intention at all points along the orienting task continuum.

Several problems exist in regard to Postman's position. The first is that it is difficult to dimensionalize the orienting tasks. One approach might be to present the same material to be learned under a variety of orienting tasks, and to then order the tasks on the basis of their effect on learning. Determining whether these tasks included the two crucial end points of the dimension would be a problem. Postman (1964) has made a suggestion that might help in locating the facilitory end of the dimension. *If intentional subjects who perform the orienting task learn as well as intentional subjects who do not, the orienting task could be thought of as producing responses which are similar to those required for learning.*

A second problem which arises from Postman's analysis is that, conceivably, orienting tasks may arrange themselves along several dimensions in relation to learning, not just the one dimension proposed by Postman. Postman appears to assume that facilitation and inhibition are reciprocal effects along a single dimension. This is not necessarily true. It is possible that a given task will not impede learning (viz., it does not produce responses which interfere with acquisition) , yet this task, in the absence of instructions to learn, will result in little learning. This can be seen in the study by Postman and Adams (1956*b*). The orienting task was to give an association to each of 30 adjectives as it was presented. *Intentional subjects with or without the orienting task did equally well.* Thus this orienting task does not inhibit the learning of adjectives. Despite this, the *intentional subjects remembered significantly more adjectives than the nonintentional.* The orienting task alone was not equivalent to intention in producing retention.

Similar results, reported by Neimark and Saltzman (1953), also indicate that an orienting response may not impede intentional learning, and yet intentional learners perform better than nonintentional.

A study by Mechanic (1962*b*) amplifies the issue. Mechanic compared several orienting tasks in their effect on the learning of the same set of material. In this study, Mechanic presented subjects with a set of cards, each containing two nonsense words. All of the subjects were given one of three different orienting tasks that involved some response to both words, and all of the subjects were also instructed to remember one of the two words on each card. Nonintentional learning was measured by requesting the subjects to recall the words which they were not instructed to remember. Different orienting tasks proved to have sizably different effects on both intentional and nonintentional learning. However, the orienting task which produced the greatest amount of intentional learning did not also produce the greatest amount of nonintentional learning.

The studies reported by Postman and Adams (1956*b*), Neimark and Saltzman (1953) and Mechanic (1962*b*) all point to the same conclusion: The fact that intentional learners recall material well, after performing some particular orienting task on these materials, does not necessarily mean that nonintentional learners who perform this orienting task will recall the material well. Stated simply, *lack of interference in intentional learning is not the same as facilitation of nonintentional learning.* Two separate, though not orthogonal, factors appear to be involved.

RESPONSES NECESSARY FOR LEARNING

We have seen that writers like Saltzman and Postman have taken the position that intention produces responses which are crucial to learning. Implicit in this position is a strategy for research. In order to determine the responses which are necessary for learning to occur, one must develop orienting tasks which eliminate the difference in learning between intentional and nonintentional subjects. Once we have found such orienting tasks and have analyzed them to discover the basic responses which they produce, we shall have a handle on the problem of the responses required for learning.

In the present section of this chapter we shall examine the research undertaken to fulfill this strategy. We shall see that, while the goals of the research program were not completely met, the program taught us a great deal about factors involved in learning and, in some cases, about factors which were *not* involved in the manner that most of us would have anticipated.

Is Attention the Crucial Factor in Intention?

Attention to the relevant aspects of the material is clearly a prerequisite to learning. Most of the tasks used in studies of nonintentional learning were designed to preclude the possibility that the subjects have failed to attend to the material. However, on *a priori* grounds, at least, some tasks are probably much less effective than others in this respect.

WHICH ORIENTING TASKS INSURE ATTENTION? Tasks such as those used by Saltzman (1953) and Neimark and Saltzman (1953) are particularly effective in insuring attention. Saltzman presented a number on a memory drum and instructed subjects to locate and circle this number on a page containing many numbers. In order to locate and circle the correct number, subjects must attend to the relevant stimulus. The data from these studies indicate that the role of intention in learning involves more than assuring attention to the relavant material, since nonintentional subjects often do not recall as well as intentional subjects in these studies (see particularly Neimark and Saltzman, 1953).

Other types of orienting tasks also appear to insure attention to the relevant aspects of the material. Postman and Adams (1956b) instructed subjects to give a meaningful association to each of 30 nonsense syllables or 30 adjectives. It appears reasonable to assume that the subjects must attend to an adjective as a whole word in order to give an association. The case for nonsense syllables is less clear. Saltz and Felton (1968b), for example, found that subjects may use only the first letter of the first two letters of a nonsense syllable as the basis of their associations, particularly for low association level syllables.

Postman, Adams, and Phillips (1955) instructed subjects to *rate* each of 30 adjectives for *familiarity*. Again, in order to perform such ratings, subjects must presumably attend to the words. Another orienting task that appears adequate for directing attention was employed by Mechanic (1962a, 1962b). Mechanic presented two nonsense syllables on a card, one above the other, telling subjects that these were words in two different foreign languages. Subjects were told that words in different languages which have the same meaning often have similar phonetic properties. The subjects were instructed to pronounce each syllable and judge, on the basis of the phonetic properties, which words did indeed have the same meaning.

ATTENTION DOES NOT INSURE LEARNING. All the studies cited above appear to involve adequate attention to relevant cues by nonintentional learners. Yet in all these studies, intention to learn facilitated recall. Thus, while attention may be necessary to learning, it is clearly not sufficient. (Of course, several of the studies involving great likelihood of attention to relevant material have conditions in which there is no advantage for intention. Examples are Saltzman, 1953; Postman, Adams, and Phillips, 1955).

Several studies involve orienting tasks that are doubtful, from the point of view of providing relevant attention. The Postman and Adams (1956b) use of associations with nonsense syllables, mentioned above, is one. Postman, Adams, and Bohm (1956) instructed subjects to match nonsense syllables to geometric figures. Postman and Adams (1958) instructed subjects to guess a number between 1 and 10 for each of 24 nonsense syllables. Postman and Adams (1960) presented words auditorily with the orienting task of rating voice qualities of the speaker. None of these orienting tasks insure attention to the relevant material to be tested for recall. For the most part, these are the studies which show the greatest facilitation due to intention. For the orienting tasks which do not insure attention, intentional and nonintentional subjects recall equally well only in the condition in which there is very little recall for either group (Postman and Adams, 1956b, where the orienting task involved matching nonsense syllables to geometric forms).

DISTRIBUTION OF ATTENTION. Bahrick (1954) reports a study in which increased incentive to learn one set of materials *decreased* the nonintentional learning of a different set of materials. This type of study raises interesting questions concerning the manner in which variables like incentive function. As we shall see, the evidence suggests that in this case, at least, incentive is effective because it produces a change in the subjects' distribution of attention.

Bahrick (1954) presented subjects with geometric forms, each filled with a different color. The subjects were instructed to learn the *serial order in which the forms were presented*. The subjects were then tested to determine if they had learned, nonintentionally, which *color* had been associated with each of the *forms*. Bahrick found that increased monetary reward for correct performance on the serial ordering of forms led to better performance on this task, but poorer performance on the nonintentional association of color and form.

In this type of study, the relevant colors must, presumably, have stimulated the visual receptors. On the other hand, stimulation of the receptors does not guarantee attention. That the effect of incentive in this study is due to manipulation of attention is suggested by results obtained by Mechanic (1962b). Mechanic presented 12 pair of trigrams to subjects, instructing them to say both items of a pair but to remember only the one, designated member of each pair. *In this study, in which subjects were forced to respond to the nonintentional material, incentive had no effect on retention* of either the intentional or nonintentional material. It appears that, when subjects are not forced to respond to the nonintentional material, increased incentive for learning the intentional restricts the distribution of attention. If material is not attended to, it will not interfere with the retention of the material which is attended to.

It should be noted that intentional material was much better learned than nonintentional in Mechanic's study, despite the fact that both types of material were responded to. Thus intention initiated critical responses other than those of attention. It should also be noted that these results are consistent with the general position on motivation taken by Easterbrook (1959). It appears that motivational factors may be conceptualized as reducing the range of competing responses by restricting the distribution of attentional responses to irrelevant, potentially competing stimui.

Practice and Rehearsal

Amount of practice is a basic variable in most learning theories, though the mechanisms whereby it produces its effect are not always conceptualized in the same way. It would seem reasonable, then, to expect that orienting tasks which required repeated practice would result in greater learning by nonintentional subjects.

NUMBER OF TRIALS.   There are two aspects to practice: *number* of trials and the *amount of rehearsal* during any given trial. Let us first examine the evidence concerning number of trials.

The general conclusion can be made that nonintentional learning benefits from repeated practice, but not as much as intentional learning. However, there are important deviations from the generalization.

Atkinson and Saltzman (1954), and Mechanic (1962*a*, 1962*b*) report improvement in nonintentional learning with practice. Atkinson and Saltzman employed an orienting task that required subjects to observe a number, then locate it on a page in which it was embedded in a great many other numbers. A recognition test of memory was used as the index of learning. Their results showed a gradual increment in memory for the nonintentional subjects between 2 and 16 trials. After two trials, intentional and nonintentional performed equally well. However, after 16 trials, the intentional subjects improved by about 3.5 items, while the nonintentional improved by only about one item. The difference between the groups is extremely significant after 16 trials.

The results of the two studies by Mechanic are similar in direction to those of Atkinson and Saltzman. In the studies by Mechanic, nonintentional recall was consistently poorer than intentional at all practice levels. Increased number of trials led to increments in recall of both intentional and nonintentional items, but the effect of practice was much greater for the intentional than the nonintentional items for every condition in these studies.

Failure of nonintentional subjects to show any increment in recall as a function of number of presentations were reported by Postman and Adams (1958). Intentional subjects showed large and consistent increments with practice. Materials were 24 nonsense syllables. The orienting task consisted of guessing a number between 1 and 10 for each syllable. Postman and Adams suggest that this task led to attaching many different syllables to the same numbers over the course of training. This should result in an increase in acquired similarity of items over trials. Apparently, nonintentional learners are less able to resist interference than are intentional learners. It will be seen that a fair amount of data corroborates this hypothesis. In addition, it should be noted that the orienting task did not require the nonintentional subjects to make any specific response to the syllables, *per se*.

Number guessing could be done without even glancing at the syllable. Possibly the lack of imrovement was due to the nonintentional subjects failing to respond to the syllables on successive trials.

REHEARSAL. Why do intentional subjects benefit more from increased number of trials than nonintentional subjects? One possible hypothesis is that subjects rehearse more on each trial under intentional than under nonintentional conditions. There is relatively little evidence, in either intentional or nonintentional learning, concerning the role of rehearsal. Rohrer (1949) reports that instructions to rehearse during the rest period immediately following serial learning resulted in a significant *decrement* in retention as compared to a group that practiced an irrelevant task during this interval. On the other hand, Withey, Buxton, and Elkin (1949) report a tendency toward better retention for subjects instructed to rehearse *following* serial learning. The reason for the difference in results between these studies is not clear. In addition, neither study involved instructing subjects to rehearse during the learning trials, *per se*. In a short-term memory study, Peterson and Peterson (1959) instructed subjects to repeat a nonsense item once or three times before the retention-delay interval. Subjects who repeated the item three times recalled significantly better than those who only repeated the item once.

Evidence against a rehearsal position in nonintentional learning was obtained in an unpublished study by Dr. Richard Wattenmaker, performed in the writer's laboratory. The subjects were told that the study was concerned with the effects of fatigue on handwriting. Subjects were presented 20 nonsense syllables, one at a time at a 6-second rate. Half the subjects were told to write each syllable twice and the other half of the subjects were told to write each syllable six times in the 6-second interval. Wattenmaker had predicted that intentional subjects would recall equally well if they had written the syllables twice or six times, since the effect of intention should be to initiate self-instructions to rehearse. For nonintentional subjects he predicted that those who wrote the syllables six times should recall as well as the intentional subjects, but those who wrote the syllables only twice should recall poorly.

Wattenmaker's results were quite unexpected. He found that both intentional and nonintentional subjects who wrote the syllables six times recalled more *poorly* than the corresponding groups who only wrote the words twice, and this effect was highly significant statistically. Intentional subjects recalled significantly more words than nonintentional subjects. The magnitude of the decrement resulting from increased rehearsal was approximately equal for intentional and nonintentional subjects. In this type of situation, at least, amount of forced rehearsal was clearly detrimental to retention. One hypothesis for the detrimental effect of rehearsal might be that it interfered with the performance of whatever strategies the intentional subjects might ordinarily use to produce retention. This is unlikely, however, since the nonintentional subjects also were hindered in recall by rehearsal, and presumably they were not employing any strategies for learning. A process similar to verbal satiation may be involved in the Wattenmaker study. A number of writers have presented evidence indicating that a number of immediate, successive repetitions of a word leads to the word losing meaning. Kanungo, Lambert, and Mauer (1962) report that paired-associates learning is slower if it is immediately preceded by verbal satiation of the response terms.

At this point it appears that rehearsal, as a strategy for learning, may not necessarily be facilitory. Thus rehearsal cannot be considered a primary factor in the distinction between intentional and nonintentional learning.

Seeking Meaning

It has often been assumed that subjects attempt to implement learning by seeking meaning for the items being learned. This technique is assumed to be particularly effective for nonsense material and relatively unfamiliar words. It might be assumed that if low differentiated items could be recoded into more differentiated words, recall would be facilitated. Surprisingly, the evidence is negative with respect to these assumptions.

Postman and Adams (1956b) investigated this issue in a study involving the learning of nonsense syllables. The orienting task required subjects to give a meaningful association to each syllable. They found that *intentional subjects who performed the orienting task recalled considerably less than intentional subjects who did not.* These results suggest two possibilities. Either the emitted meaningful associations interfered directly with the nonsense syllables, producing forgetting; or emission of the meaningful associations interfered with the performance of more beneficial responses. Further, comparing intentional and nonintentional subjects when both conditions performed the orienting task, we find that nonintentional subjects performed much more poorly.

A study by Underwood and Keppel (1963b), investigating the effects of coding during intentional learning, may be relevant here. These investigators found that coding was facilitory only when decoding was not a problem. For example, given the trigram TFA, recall was facilitated if subjects were encouraged to encode and were permitted to recall the three letters in any order (in which case the item was usually recalled as FAT). However, if the subjects were required to recall the original trigram (TFA), encoding it as FAT was detrimental. Returning to the Postman and Adams (1956b) study, it is possible that the detrimental effect on recall, resulting from emitting a meaningful free associate to a nonsense syllable, may be due to the difficulty in decoding back to the nonsense syllable. As was seen in Chapter 9, the closer the correspondence between the nonsense word and its meaningful associate, the more readily the associate can be decoded back to recover the original nonsense syllable.

Turning to recall of meaningful words, two types of orienting tasks have been used which can be interpreted as seeking meaning. One is the task of emitting an associate. The second is that of rating words for familiarity (presumably, one must respond to the meaning of a word in order to rate it for familiarity). Postman and Adams (1956b) used the orienting task of writing an associate to each adjective. Here intentional subjects who had performed the orienting task recalled as well as intentional subjects who had not. However, nonintentional subjects who had performed the orienting task recalled more poorly than the intentional. It appears reasonable to conclude that giving meaningful associates to adjectives does not interfere with recalling them, but additional mechanisms must also be involved in intentional learning.

Postman, Adams, and Phillips (1955) had subjects rate 30 adjectives for familiarity. Again, intentional subjects recalled better than nonintentional. The greatest difference between intentional and nonintentional subjects occurred for the items which were rated as least familiar. There was very little difference in recall for items rated as very familiar. Apparently, under these circumstances, additional mechanisms are not required for recall of the already well differentiated, highly familiar words. Postman, Adams, and Bohm (1956) used a similar technique and found results consistent with those of Postman, Adams, and Phillips (1955).

One study, Saltzman (1956), reports that inducing associates facilitated recall for both intentional and nonintentional subjects. In this study, subjects were presented numbers and were told to think of some associate (e.g., birthdate) to each. These results suggest that the layman's confidence in seeking meaning, as an aid to memory, may be more than superstition. However, it is not clear why facilitation was found in this study but not in the others in this section. One possibility is that the different types of materials employed in the various studies resulted in different types of meaningful associates. For example, to nonsense syllables, subjects tend to give a word that most closely resembles the syllable (see Chapter 9). If a syllable does not resemble *any* word very closely, sources of interference are clear. To adjectives, a number of different types of associations are possible, such as antonyms, synonyms, or completions (e.g., the response *cheese* to cottage). These may have different characteristics relative to recall, and intentional subjects may differ from nonintentional in their preferences among these types. Finally, numbers appear to elicit words that serve cue functions. Another possible basis for Saltzman's findings could reside in the recognition test employed in his study. (The other studies employed recall.) If perception of the number resulted in reinstating the meaningful associate, the subjects' memory might be facilitated. This issue will be dealt with in the next section of this chapter.

Verbal Cues

Retention of an item is apparently facilitated if the subject makes a verbal response which can serve as a reliable stimulus to the items (e.g., pronounce a nonsense syllable, label a geometric figure, etc.). This is illustrated in a study by Mechanic (1962b). He had subjects perform one of three orienting tasks: (a) cancel certain letters from each pair of nonsense syllables presented; (b) an ESP task in which subjects were to look at each pair of syllables and guess whether the syllable was one which the experimenter had selected, or (c) pronounce each pair silently in order to decide, on the basis of phonetic similarity, if the two syllables in a pair had the same meaning in a foreign language. Subjects were incidentally instructed to remember the top syllable in each pair. They were then tested on recall of the both syllables. Greatest recall of nonintentional items occurred in the orienting task involving pronunciation to determine similarity of meaning; least recall occurred when subjects cancelled letters without regard to the whole syllable.

However, interpretation of this data is made difficult by two facts.

First, note that in this study, none of the orienting tasks was sufficient to overcome the effect of intention: Intentional items were recalled better than nonintentional in all groups. Thus something more than coding material by means of verbal cues is involved in intention.

Note also that Mechanic obtained a perfect inverse relationship between intentional and nonintentional learning over the three conditions. The pronunciation task, which produced the best nonintentional recall, produced the worst intentional recall. Letter cancellation, which produced the worst nonintentional recall, produced the best recall of intentional items. *This inverse relationship is not consistent with the position that orienting tasks which facilitate intentional learning should also facilitate nonintentional learning.* The problem residing in these findings may be primarily methodological. Increasing the learning of nonintentional material may simply increase the amount of interference with the intentional material. The inverse relationship between recall of intentional and nonintentional material could easily be due to the fact that each of Mechanic's subjects was intentional with regard to one word of each pair and unintentional with regard to the other. Had nonintentional subjects performed the orienting tasks with no instructions concerning learning while intentional subjects were instructed to learn *all* the material, the inverse relationship might have disappeared.

Saltzman's (1956) results are also consistent with the importance of verbal cues. Intentional learning was superior to nonintentional when the orienting task consisted of viewing a number in a memory drum and attempting to locate and circle the number on a page containing many other numbers. When this orienting task also involved pronouncing the number aloud as it appeared in the drum, the difference between intentional and nonintentional subjects disappeared. The greater effect of verbalization on nonintentional learning in Saltzman's study than in Mechanic's may be due to any of several differences between their studies. First, Saltzman used a recognition test of retention while Mechanic used a recall test. This could be an important difference since there is some evidence to suggest that intention to learn may be less crucial when specific stimuli are available for the response which is to be remembered. A second difference between the studies is that Mechanic was concerned with the learning of nonsense syllables while Saltzman used numbers as his materials. Decoding a number from verbal to written form is much more unambiguous than decoding a nonsense sound into a written nonsense syllable.

Intention and Task Characteristics

Intention does not appear to be a unitary variable, unrelated to the type of learning task. For example, intention to learn for a free recall test and intention to learn serial order produce somewhat different effects. Postman, Adams, and Bohm (1956) presented 20 nonsense syllables to subjects, using a figure-matching orienting task. Half the intentional subjects were told to learn the order of the items, the other half were told nothing about order. Subjects told to learn the *order* were better able to reproduce the order than subjects who were not, but recalled *fewer individual items*. This relationship held between subgroups who performed the orienting task and between subgroups who did not. Clearly, whatever responses are made in trying to learn the order interfere with the responses made in trying to learn individual items. This indicates that we cannot look for some types of universal implicit learning response or strategy, but must investigate strategies which are specific to the types of learning to be tested. Since most of the studies summarized in previous sections of this chapter were concerned with recall or recognition, one must be conservative in drawing general conclusions from them.

INTENTION AND THE MULTIFACTOR COGNITIVE SYSTEM

In the early chapters of the present book, we analyzed learning in terms of a multifactor cognitive system. The present section will summarize some of the more cogent evidence relating the effects of intention to the elements of the cognitive system, namely: association, item differentiation, and boundary strength of the learned systems. This discussion will throw the issues of intention in a somewhat new perspective and will perhaps enable us to make greater sense of the orienting task data.

We shall see that available evidence suggests that intention may not effect development of associations, *per se*. Instead, the primary effect of intention may be on resistance to interference. From this it might be expected that intention would be least relevant for items which are already highly differentiated. Some evidence exists which supports this expectation. It should be noted that these conclusions are somewhat different from those of Postman (1964). These differences shall be considered as they become relevant to the sections which follow.

Effect of Intention on Association

Postman (1964) has suggested that a primary difference between intentional and nonintentional subjects is that the nonintentional are selective, learning certain words (perhaps because of factors such as vividness of the words) and forming certain associations, but not all, while the intentional subjects attempt to learn all the words. The results of a study by Postman, Adams, and Phillips (1955) provide extremely provocative evidence against this position. This study suggests that, *under certain circumstances at least, learning may be equal for intentional and nonintentional subjects; however, nonintentional subjects may have difficulty recovering the correct responses.*

The orienting task in the Postman, Adams, and Philips (1955) study was that of rating each of 30 adjectives for familiarity. Three of the test procedures were most relevant to the present discussion. In one, subjects were presented with cue words which were closely related to the rated adjectives. Upon presentation of each cue word, subjects were to respond with a word from the list of 30 adjectives rated for familiarity. In a second test procedure, inhibitory cue words were employed, cue words which were only remotely related to the rated adjectives. Upon presentation of each cue word, subjects were to respond with a word from the list of 30 adjectives rated for familiarity. In a second test procedure, inhibitory cue words were employed, cue words which were only remotely related to the rated adjectives; these cue words were expected to elicit competing responses. Two control groups were employed which did not see the 30 adjectives but were merely asked to associate to either the facilitory or inhibitory cues. The results were extremely straightforward. For facilitory cues, *there was no significant difference between intentional and nonintentional* groups. The intentional gave a mean of 17.62 of the adjectives, the nonintentional gave 18.0. The control group which had not been presented the 30 adjectives gave a mean of 9.10 of the adjectives. The difference between the control group and the other two groups was highly significant. Again, for the inhibitory cues, there was no difference between intentional and nonintentional subjects, the respective means being 7.19 and 7.38. Both were significantly superior to the control group which emitted 1.05 of the

30 adjectives. These results should be compared with those of a third set of groups which were presented with the same orienting task, but then required to *free recall* the adjectives. Here, without relevant cues, the intentional subjects recalled 12.62 words and the nonintentional only 9.41, a highly significant difference.

Silver (1967) reports data that are very consistent with those of Postman, Adams, and Phillips. The orienting task was described to subjects as a test of the ease with which pairs of words could be combined in sentences. After subjects had invented a sentence for each of 20 noun-adjective pairs, the subjects were shown the first word of each pair and asked to recall the second word. Nonintentional learners recalled as well as intentional under these circumstances.

These results suggest that when an adequate orienting task is employed (a task which insures attention to the items), the associative factor is *not* influenced by intention. Under appropriate cue conditions, the correct response can be reinstated as well after nonintentional learning as after intentional.

LANGUAGE CUES AND RETENTION. A set of experiments by Postman and Adams (1960) also bears on the issue of cued recall. In the previous section it was seen that nonintentional subjects recall as well as intentional if stimulus cues to the correct response are present. From this, one would expect good recall by nonintentional subjects when meaningful prose is learned. In this study a 214 word paragraph of prose was presented in which 35 words were deleted and replaced by blanks. The orienting task consisted of instructing subjects to fill in the blanks with the words they felt had been deleted. Subjects were then requested to recall the words which they had written into the passage. Intentional subjects recalled 48% of their responses and nonintentional 44%. This difference is not significant when evaluated against a two-tailed hypothesis. Clearly, the effect of intention on recall of English text is markedly reduced when the orienting response involves attention to meaning.

A second study in the Postman and Adams reports anomalous results. Subjects were presented passages of 50 words which differed in the degree of approximation to English. The closest approximation used was actual English text. In more remote approximations, only shorter sequences of words normally went together in English sentences. If sequences of words resembled a sentence, one would expect that previous frequency of usage would make these sequences more resistant to interference. Instead, the results indicated increasing advantage for intentional learners as approximation to English increased. For textual material, intentional subjects recalled about 54% of the items, nonintentional recalled about 27%. Several problems make the interpretation of this experiment difficult. The orienting task was that of rating voice qualities. It is not clear that this task properly forces attention on the words and word sequences. In addition, the passages were read to the subjects in a monotone, as single words not as sentences. This should also obscure the degree of approximation to English for subjects set only to judge voices qualities.

In any case, it appears that intentional learners were able to benefit from the increases in approximation to English, using the syntactically determined sequential cues to facilitate their recall. In this particular study, at least, the nonintentional learners did not benefit as much as the intentional from the syntactic cues.

Resistance to Interference

A great deal of evidence suggests that nonintentional subjects are more susceptible to interference effects, especially retroactive interference, than intentional subjects. Rather consistently, when subjects are presented with a list of items and are then tested for free recall, the nonintentional subjects perform as well as, and sometimes slightly better than, intentional subjects on *the final items* of the list, but nonintentional perform more poorly in recalling the *early and middle* items. Postman and Phillips (1954), Postman and Adams (1957), and Postman and Adams (1960) all report such results. It is particularly important to note that the last few items presented were well recalled by nonintentional subjects even when the subjects received only one trial. Thus they could not know, upon seeing them, that these were the last items in the list. Apparently, *in the absence of succeeding interfering items, intention is not advantageous to recall.* This is true even for nonsense materials. The fact that nonintentional subjects can recall as well as intentional when retroactive interference is minimal is additional support for the contention that association, *per se,* is not influenced by intention.

Apparently resistance to interference is so poor in nonintentional learners (particularly for relatively undifferentiated materials such as nonsense syllables), that increased intralist similarity (Postman and Adams, 1957) or isolation (Postman and Phillips, 1954) will have little additional effect.

The advantage of intention for early items disappears only when the amount of retroactive interference becomes so great that both intentional and nonintentional learners recall only minimally. This can be seen in studies by Postman and Adams (1956b, 1958). For example, Postman and Adams (1958) report data for nonsense syllable lists of 24, 36, and 48 items. While recall by the intentional subjects was superior to that of the nonintentional for the 24-item list, this superiority decreased on the 36-item list and disappeared on the list of 48 items. Apparently, with greater number of items in the list, interference accumulates to produce a drop in percentage of recall for intentional subjects. Nonintentional subjects, on the other hand, recall relatively little (only the last few items and several others) whatever the list length, and so are less affected by length.

Differentiation

It has been seen that when the orienting task requires attention to the relevant material, lack of intention to learn appears to have little effect on the formation of associations but does result in decreased resistance to interference from succeeding materials. Under such circumstances, it would be expected that the difference in recall between intentional and nonintentional subjects should be less for well-differentiated items than for items which are poorly differentiated. This would be expected on the grounds that well-differentiated responses tend to resist interference. (The actual relationship between item differentiation and resistance to interference is a complex one, as was seen in Chapter 6.) Findings to date support this expectation. Postman, Adams, and Phillips (1955) report several relevant sets of data. In one experiment, subjects were presented with nonsense syllables ranging from 0 to 100% association value. Intentional and incidental subjects were run in pairs, the nonintentional subject being told he was the experimenter who must read the items to the other subject who was to learn the list. After a single trial, both the intentional and nonintentional subjects were asked to recall as many syllables as they could remember. The data indicated that intention was a significant factor for low-association syllables. However, intentional and nonintentional subjects did not differ in retention of high-association value syllables.

In a second experiment, reported in the same paper, Postman, Adams, and Phillips used an orienting task which involved rating adjectives for familiarity. Again, intention was a significant factor in recall for the words of low familiarity, but this effect disappeared for words which had been rated as highly famil:ar.

It is interesting to note that high-association nonsense syllables behave more like words which were rated as very familiar than like words which were rated as relatively unfamiliar. Results of the previously cited Saltz and Felton (1968b) study may explain this. Apparently, high-association syllables are easily encoded as high-frequency words.

HOW DOES INTENTION INFLUENCE LEARNING?

Let us now try to pull together the various strands of information concerning intention and learning.

First, we see that, for very well differentiated materials at least, *retrieval* rather than *learning* appears to be the crucial problem for nonintentional learners. If the nonintentional subjects *attend* to the relevant aspects of the material during the original presentation, we find that they will recall as well as the intentional subjects *if they are provided with relevant cues*. In the absence of such cues, recall by the intentional subjects is often significantly superior to that of the nonintentional. These conclusions are consistent with the position taken by Tulvig (1968), described in Chapter 8. Tulvig suggests that retrieval and input problems must be distinguished in the analysis of learning and recall.

The conclusion, as stated above, suggests that one difference between intentional and nonintentional learners may be that the intentional somehow provide themselves with cues for retrieval. How? We clearly do not know how, at this time. However, such a suggestion is very consistent with the observations we made in performing the Demonstration Experiment at the beginning of this chapter. There we saw that we could easily recall if it rained *today,* but had difficulty recalling if it rained *one year ago today.* Presumably we forgot because of interference by the weather conditions of the intervening 364 days. However, had we known one year ago that such a question might arise with regard to *that particular day,* we could have *tagged* the particular information and markedly increased the likelihood of correct recall. Retrieval, not original registration, was clearly the basis for forgetting.

Turning to *poorly differentiated* material we find a consistent superiority for intentional subjects except when the material is so difficult that almost no one is able to remember anything. The Saltzman studies typically used recognition as the test of retention, and recognition is clearly a task involving cued recall; despite this cueing, Saltzman often found that intentional subjects remembered better than nonintentional, using poorly differentiated number sequences as the material to be learned. The influence of retroactive interferences is strikingly high for this type of material.

Such data strongly suggest that the responses made by intentional subjects are instrumental to the differentiation of the poorly differentiated materials. Some of these responses may be concerned with encoding nonsense materials in such a way that they can be retrieved as meaningful words; this, however, would not be sufficient to insure recall of the original nonsense material, since the subject must then decode again to retrieve the original item. The intentional subjects, knowing that this type of decoding will be required, may be in a better position to provide himself with the relevant cues for such decoding.

There is a certain amount of evidence to suggest that intentional subjects may, indeed, develop strategies for decoding. The reader will recall that orienting tasks involving *seeking meaning* for nonsense materials did not erase the differential superiority of intentional over nonintentional learners. If decoding was the problem for the nonintentional subjects then the superiority of the intentional subjects should disappear if decoding is not required. The procedure used by Saltzman (1956) may have accomplished this. Saltzman presented his subjects with numbers and asked them to think of some association to each, such as a birthdate, etc. If the associate produced by a subject were capable of reproducing the number, then no further decoding would be necessary. Saltzman reported that this orienting task facilitated both intentional and nonintentional learners.

Finally, one of the most surprising findings in the present chapter is related to the effects of practice on learning. Increased number of practice trials does not reduce the superiority of intentional learners. Instead it disproportionately facilitates the recall by intentional subjects. Such data sugget that the intentional subjects are profiting from the systematic use of strategies. What is the nature of such possible strategies? This issue will be explored in the following section of this chapter.

STRATEGIES OF LEARNING

One of the more important implications of the research on intentional versus nonintentional learning is that the amount of learning which occurs will be influenced by the types of responses the subjects make to the material. While some work has been done on this issue within the context of intentional learning *per se* (as opposed to comparing intentional and nonintentional learners), much of this work has concentrated on one or two specific types of strategies or coding techniques which appeared particularly appropriate for the material involved in the experiment. The recently reported work by Martin and his associates represents one of the few attempts at a more comprehensive attack on the general issue.

In one of their first studies on this topic, Martin, Boersma, and Cox (1965) attempted to determine the strategies actually used by subjects and then attempted to determine a hierarchy of effectiveness for these strategies. First they had subjects learn a list of paired associates involving low m items from Noble's (1952) list (e.g., a typical pair was MEARDON-ZUMAP). After 10 learning trials, subjects were shown each pair for 60 seconds and were asked to indicate how they attempted to form each association. Table 10–1 indi-

TABLE 10–1. Classification of Associative Strategies

Category Level	Type of Cue Subject Reported Using	Example of Verbal Report
1. No Reported Associations	S was not able to state how he managed to make the association.	Sagrole-Polef: "Don't know how I learned this pair."
2. Repetition	S reported rehearsing the pair.	Volvap-Nares: "Just kept repeating these words to myself."
3. Single Letter Cues	S reported using a single letter in each of the paralogs in making the association.	Tarop-Gojey: "Noticed that each word contained an O."
4. Multiple Letter Cues	S reported using multiple letters in each of the paralogs.	Sagrole-Polef: "Each word contains an OLE."
5. Word Formation	S reported that an actual word was imbedded in one or both of the paralogs and made use of these words in making the association.	Meardon-Zumap: "The word EAR is contained in Meardon and learned that EAR goes with Zumap."
6. Superordinate	S reported selecting elements from each of the two paralogs that had some relationship to each other.	Sagrole-Polef: "Sagrole begins with S and Polef with P, thought of State Police.
7. Syntactical	S reported selecting elements from each of the two paralogs and embedding these elements into a sentence, phrase or clause.	Rennet-Quipson: "Changed Rennet to Bennet and saw Quips in Quipson-thought: Bennet Cerf Quips on TV."

From Martin, Boersma, and Cox, 1965.

cates the categorization of strategies reported by Martin *et al.* This categorization is hypothesized by Martin to represent a continuum with respect to complexity of cues used by the subjects. More complex cues were assumed to signify that a more complex strategy had been used. Based on these verbal reports, a strategy score was calculated for each subject. This score was obtained by assigning to each pair in the list the category level from Table 10–1 which was appropriate in view of the subject's verbal report about the strategy used in learning the pair. These scores were then summed for each subject. E.g., a subject who used a syntactical strategy (weighted 7) on each pair in an 8-pair list received a total score of $7 \times 8 = 56$. A correlation between strategy level and mean number of correct responses yielded a rho of .62, with a relatively linear increase in correct responses as a function of higher strategy levels.

There are, of course, problems in evaluating such findings. Do these results indicate that the ability to utilize more complex cues is an *index* of greater learning ability? Or do the results suggest that the *utilization* of more complex cues *produces* better learning? These alternatives must be tested by insuring, first, that random groups of subjects use different strategies, and then by comparing across these groups. A study by Bulgarella and Martin (1967) did just this. Children were first trained to use either high-level strategies (levels 5 to 7) or low-level strategies (levels 1 to 4). They were then presented with paired-associates lists to learn. The children who were taught to attempt higher-level strategies learned significantly faster than those taught to use lower-level strategies.

The Bulgarella and Martin study is extremely important in that it both indicates that such strategies are trainable and that once trained they can facilitate learning. However, a number of questions remain unanswered. First, of course, the use of two gross strategy levels leaves open the evaluation of the individual strategies within each level. For example, the Wattenmaker data, described earlier in this chapter, suggests that massive rehearsal may be detrimental to recall. If this were the case, Level 2 might be poorer for learning than Level 1. Since Levels 1 to 4 were grouped together in the experiment, this possibility can not be evaluated easily.

Another question yet to be answered concerning Martin's strategy hierarchy is the relationship between the hierarchy and other variables known to influence learning. Martin, Cox, and Boersma (1965), for example, have suggested that the basis for the relationship between m and learning might be that high m words lend themselves to the use of more complex strategies than low m words.

The experimental test of this hypothesis involved having subjects learn one of four lists: *H-H* (high *m* stimuli—high *m* response) , H-L, *L-H,* or *L-L.* Following learning, subjects were requested to report their strategies on each pair and were assigned scores based on the complexity of their strategies. As predicted, high *m* for either the stimulus or responses led to more complex strategies than low *m* items. However stimulus *m* had a greater effect on strategy score than response *m.* This produces some difficulty in interpretation because response *m* had a greater effect on *learning,* in this study, than did stimulus *m;* thus the relationship between strategy and *m* may be primarily correlational, rather than causative.

GENERALITY OF THE MARTIN HIERARCHY.   It can be seen, in examining Table 10–1 that the strategies isolated by Martin *et al.,* are particularly relevant to the learning of paired nonsense material or word pairs in which the pairs are randomly selected words. For a meaningful sentence (or a meaningful pair, such as "dog-run") , *these strategies are largely irrelevant,* since the material already contains the type of organization which the strategies attempt to induce. It should be pointed out that most of the strategies which have been investigated by various researchers are similarly concerned with recoding for meaning.

Many of the strategies reported in the literature fall within Martin's hierarchy. The stimulus selection strategies noted by Underwood (1963) are an interesting example. Underwood (1963) has suggested that the nominal stimulus, in paired-associates learning, may not be the functional stimulus utilized by the subject. For example, given the nonsense syllable DAX as the nominal stimulus, some subjects may simply use the first letter, *D,* as the functional stimulus, and may attach the response to this. This strategy falls at level-5 in the Martin *et al.* schema. Since there is evidence that a single letter can be learned more quickly to a response than a multi-letter nonsense syllable (e.g., Newman, 1963) , subjects who use the single letter as a functional stimulus should learn faster than those who attempt to use the entire nonsense syllable.

The fractionating of a complex stimulus in paired associates has been shown to be facilitating in a number of studies. Brown, Battig, and Pearlstein (1965) had one group learn a list in which each stimulus consisted of three different letters. A second group started with one letter stimuli; after reaching a low criterion of performance a second letter was added; and after a higher criterion was reached the third letter was added. This latter procedure encouraged subjects to fractionate the stimulus, using just a portion (one or two letters) as the functional stimulus. Learning was faster under this condition, as compared with the group which was presented all three letters from the onset of learning. Similarily, Musgrave and Cohen (1964) found that a single word stimulus was more effective in learning than a two word stimulus. If subjects are aware of this strategy of stimulus fractionating, and if the stimulus materials permit its use, it appears to be reasonably effective for the acquisition of unrelated pairs.

A number of other strategies have been suggested, over the years, as mnemonic techniques. Most of these have gone untested. Smith and Noble (1965) have examined one such technique. This technique involves associating a number-letter alphabet with key words which evoke strong images. These images are assumed to provide stable "hooks" onto which new words can be meaningfully connected. When subsequently asked to emit the fifth item, the subject can imagine the key hook word, which then elicits the response to be learned. This memory device is clearly a variant of Martin et al., Level 7. Results indicated little effect on immediate recall, but some effect on later retention. Facilitory effects, when they occurred, were greatest for retention of moderate association syllables which resembled words. Real words of high-association value were not affected; neither were very low association words which are unlikely to remind many subjects of real words. In addition, the technique proved facilitory only for subjects who had great difficulty learning under unaided conditions.

Failure to enhance retention by means of a Level 7 strategy is also reported by Rothkopf (1963). Rothkopf's subjects learned paired associates which consisted of numbers paired with color names (e.g., 1-BROWN). One group simply learned the pairs, while a second group was given mnemonic phrases which served to connect the numbers and colors in a meaningful fashion (e.g., 1 brown penny). Retention was equivalent for the two groups at tests between 0–80 days, though at 120 days the retention of the aided groups was superior to that of the group without the mnemonic phrases.

It is possible, of course, that subjects in such studies tend to use effective strategies even when these are not provided by the experimenter. Another possibility is that strategies may function most beneficially when the subject, himself, initiates the responses critical to the strategy. For example, in the Bulgarella and Martin (1967) study, the children were taught the general type of responses involved in each strategy, but were then required to initiate their own specific strategy responses for each pair to be learned. Under these circumstances, it will be recalled, training on higher level strategies facilitated learning.

Strategies for Recall

Martin's strategy hierarchy is largly oriented toward strategies for learning paired associates. It is not clear how applicable this particular hierarchy might be for other types of learning. In free recall, the crucial issue appears not to be the association of a word to some stimulus, but rather insuring the recall of the word *per se*. Again, much of the research is concerned with strategies for recall of nonsense material.

Underwood and Keppel (1963*b*) and Underwood and Erlebacher (1965) have investigated the specific issue of coding nonsense syllables into meaningful words. Underwood and Keppel presented syllables such as TFA, which could be encoded to the meaningful word FAT. When subjects were instructed to recall the letters of each syllable in any order (e.g., FAT was an acceptable response), these subjects who were instructed concerning the anagram properties of the nonsense syllables recalled significantly more than those who were not so instructed. In other words, encoding facilitated recall, though the absolute effect was only moderate. These results are easily interpreted on the basis of the fact that real words are easier to recall the nonsense syllables. However, when subjects were required to recall the syllables as presented, pointing out the anagram properties of the syllables resulted in a significant *decrement* in subsequent recall. Here, apparently, decoding from the real word back to the nonsense syllable was a severe problem. Similar results occur in the Underwood and Erlebacher study. Only when decoding was extremely easy did encoding facilitate retention. As in the studies by Martin, Underwood and his associates have attempted to facilitate retention of relatively meaningless material by increasing its meaningfulness.

Part-Whole Strategies

When the learning task consists of a long list of items or pairs to be memorized, a strategy which is often mentioned is that of breaking the list of materials into subparts and learning the subparts independently. While it is frequently suggested that subjects may engage in such activity (e.g., first learn the initial three or four words in a serial list, then concentrate on the next subset, etc.), there is little evidence concerning the efficiency of such a procedure. The literature on part versus whole learning is extensive, and the results have been contradictory. Part learning may facilitate learning the parts concentrated on, but this has frequently resulted in poorer learning of the entire material. (See McGeoch and Irion, 1952, for a review of this literature.) In general, differences between the two methods have been small (Postman and Goggin, 1964).

Anecdotally, many subjects report using holistic or partistic strategies, and claim great success for them. It is always possible that individual differences exist between subjects in their ability to use one or the other type of strategy, and these differences obscure group comparisons. It is also possible that self-initiated strategies are more effective than experimenter-initiated strategies.

Despite these qualifications, at present it must be concluded that such strategies have not been proven effective.

Recitation as a Strategy

A study by Gates (1917) is one of the few which have examined strategies for organized, meaningful material. Gates presented short biographies to school children and manipulated amount of time spent in recitation as opposed to merely reading the material. What is "recitation"? After a child had completed reading a biography, the child was instructed to recall as much of it as he could. During this recall, the child was prompted if he left anything out or if he made an error. This is the procedure which Gates referred to as recitation.

Recitation proved to be very facilitory for later recall. Students who recited 90% of the time and read only 10% recalled more than students who read 100% of the time. The optimal ratio of time spent in recitation compared to time spent in reading appeared to differ for different types of material, but 100% reading was consistently a poor strategy.

Forlano (1936) extended the range of materials in which the recitation technique was tested. He found beneficial effects for recitation on all the tasks examined, including learning of nonsense syllables, spelling, and vocabulary.

Recitation appears to be an effective strategy and has the additional virtue of being one of the few strategies examined which is relevant to integrated, meaningful sequences of material. Most other strategies are concerned with aiding the recall of large numbers of discrete items. Because of this, students are told to use the recitation technique in almost every manual on "how to study" which the writer has encountered. The writer knows of manuals in English, Polish, German, Swedish, and Romanian which instruct students in this technique (though the prompting aspect of the technique is often omitted, with unknown consequences). Despite this, very little research has been conducted to determine why the technique works, and to determine the conditions under which it will be optimally effective.

The reader will recall that earlier in this chapter we saw that rehearsal *does not* systematically facilitate retention. Why should rehearsal be less effective than recitation? Procedurally, the distinction appears to be that rehearsal is squeezed in between paced presentations of the material. For example, subjects sometimes rehearse an item several times immediately after seeing it and while waiting for the next item to appear; often this rehearsal is done during the interval in which the subject is, simultaneously, attempting to *anticipate* this next item. At other times, rehearsal is attempted in the interval between presentations of an entire list. For example, the list of items may be shown to a subject at a two-second rate: An item is shown for two seconds, then replaced by another item which is also shown for two seconds, until the subject has seen the entire set of items. The subject may then be given a ten-second rest interval before the entire procedure is repeated. Rehearsal may occur in this ten-second rest interval. Possibly, it is the extreme pacing involved in rehearsal that so often prevents this strategy from being effective.

Possibly, recitation is effective because it permits a student to find his own retrieval cues. Possibly it is effective because it forces the student to organize the material (in which case it should be least effective for material which is inherently unorganized, like nonsense material). Perhaps the effectiveness of recitation really reflects the *ineffectiveness* of repeated reading. Repeated reading of the same passage may lead to a flight of attention. The fact that the material appears so familiar on rereading may give the student the false impression that he knows the material sufficiently well to recall it later when actually he does not know it well at all.

As can be seen, there are many possibilities, but few definite answers. Recitation appears to be effective. It deserves more attention.

MNEMONIC TECHNIQUES: ANECDOTICAL EVIDENCE

No discussion of strategies for learning would be complete without at least mentioning some of the mnemonic devices that have been advocated over the years, but which have largely escaped systematic study. The present section will certainly not attempt to be complete in its coverage. The number of techniques advocated is too immense, and many of the specific techniques are much too complex, to permit more than an abbreviated look at some of the less fantastic appearing procedures. (The reader who is interested in greater detail on this topic should consult the entertaining chapter on mnenomics in the recent book by Norman, 1969.)

PHYSICAL LOCATION AS A CUE.   One of the oldest of the mnemonic devices involves associating the items to be remembered with specific *physical locations*. Norman (1969) notes both ancient Greek and ancient Roman references to this procedure. More recently, the remarkable, modern Russian mnemonist described by Luria (1968), appears to have developed essentially the same technique independently.

The essence of the technique involves forming images of the things which must be remembered and attaching these images to images of physical locations. Thus an ancient Roman rhetorician is described as committing the details of a building to exact memory, so that he can use these details as cues, later, for the material he wishes to memorize for a speech. He will imagine moving from room to room in a predetermined, fixed sequence; in each successive room of his imagination he will plant a cue to remind himself of the next topic (or perhaps clever turn of phrase). At the entrance of a doorway he may imagine placing a plaque with the word "revenge"; further in the room he may plant, in his mind, the body of a Roman soldier spread out on the table; finally, at the end of the room he may plant a chest filled with gold and other treasures. When he later thinks of walking through this room, he will presumably recall each of these images in turn, and these will remind him of the points he wishes to make.

Luria (1968), in a fascinating little book, describes a man whose memory Luria considers, in effect, limitless. No matter how much material Luria presented to the mnemonist (whom he calls S), S could recall it, as long as it was presented in a relatively slow (2 or 3 seconds per item), clear fashion. Further, S was able to recall this material after 10 to 20 years. Physical location as a cue was one of the many techniques used by S to aid his memory. For example, given the names of a series of objects to remember, S might imagine himself walking down a familiar street in Moscow and might imagine himself depositing the objects along this route. At times (though very infrequently) S might forget an item. For example, he forgot the word "egg" in one experiment performed by Luria. In reconstructing the error, he found that he had deposited the egg against a white wall; in his mental retracing of the walk down the street, S had simply passed the white egg without noticing it against the white wall.

Note the two critical components of this technique. One involves the utilization of a *previously established serial sequence* (e.g., the order of the houses along a familiar street) as a set of cues to the order in which the new material is to be recalled. The second component is the use of *images* to facilitate recall. The reader will recall that we discussed the utilization of previously acquired serial sequences in Chapter 8, and the role of imagery in Chapter 9 of this book.

Bower (1970) briefly discusses some preliminary evidence concerning this technique, and appears very enthusiastic about its potentialities as an aid to recall. Winograd, Karchmer, and Tucker (1970) have attempted a more systematic examination of this ancient mnemonic technique, using a walk through a university cafeteria as the vehicle for recall. Preliminary results of the Winograd, *et al.* research suggest that the first use of this set of cues facilitated recall; however, there was evidence for retroactive and proactive inhibition when the same walk was used several times, each time as a vehicle for a different set of materials. Since the anecdotal records appear to deny the likelihood of such interference, Winograd, *et al.* indicate that they will continue exploring this issue in forthcoming research.

SERIAL RHYMING AS A CUE. At this point we should mention a technique, very similar to the one outlined above, which was described by Miller, Galanter, and Pribram (1960). These writers describe training a single subject in the following manner. First they taught their subject a rhyme for each number from 1 to 10 (e.g., one-bun). This ordered set of rhymes was to serve as a mnemonic to aid in the recall of a new set of materials. This new set was the names of ten objects; the subject was told to associate the first of these names with the rhyming word he had previously learned to "one"; the second object was to be associated to the rhyming word for "two," and so forth. Thus the first object, "ashtray," was to be associated with the rhyming word for one—namely, bun. (This might be done, for example, by picturing an ashtray with a bun on it.)

In the final, informal test, they found that if they presented their subject with any number from 1 to 10, he could recall the rhyming word and use this to recall the name of the object that had been associated to this rhyming word. Similarly, given an object name, the subject could remember the appropriate number, and so forth. Miller, Galanter, and Pribram feel that their subject could not have remembered as well had he not used the mnemonic. (Note, however, that the previously cited experiment by Smith and Noble, 1965, *tested* a mnemonic device very similar to that of Miller, Galanter, and Pribram, and found little facilitation of normal memory processes.)

CODING FOR MEANING. The usual claim is that mnemonic devices facilitate recall by transforming material into more meaningful form. Norman (1969) concludes his discussion of mnemonics by stating that nowhere does he find a system that condenses and simplifies; all systems enrich and add to the information in an attempt to force the material into a meaningful organization. Let us consider a simple, common example: The notes of the treble cleft are E G B D F. Music teachers all over the United States provide their students with the following mnemonic to assist in remembering this: Every Good Boy Does Fine.

Yet, the writer has also seen the opposite technique attempted by college students attempting to memorize a sequence of words. A business school student, for example, was told to remember that the effective executive must be decisive, knowledgeable, interested in his subordinates, intelligent, and empathic, in that order of importance. He encoded this as D, K, I, I, E, and claimed that this mnemonic helped him on his course examination. Perhaps it was more important that this student *searched* for a mnemonic than that he found this particular device.

CONCLUSIONS

The basic issues in the present chapter were: (1) Are there specific types of behaviors which, when engaged in, will facilitate learning. (2) If such behaviors are found, by what mechanisms do they achieve their effects.

The importance of specific behaviors (or perhaps strategies) appears greatest for low meaningful, relatively unfamiliar material. For such material, intentional learners retain more than nonintentional with great consistency. At present little is known about the nature of such facilitating behavior. Nonintentional learning can be improved by insuring that the subject respond to the material, during original presentation, in a manner that is similar to the recall responses (e.g., by having him pronounce nonsense syllables). However, typically this merely reduces the advantage of intention, rather than eliminating this advantage.

For very familiar material, on the other hand, intention is much less crucial. Often intentional and nonintentional subjects recall such material equally well. Initial attention to the relevant aspects of the material (e.g., listening to the meaning of words, rather than to the tonal qualities of the voice speaking the words) is essential to this effect.

Given adequate initial attention to the familiar material, *retrieval* rather than *learning* appears to be the central problem for nonintentional subjects. Providing appropriate cues to the material will at times erase any difference between intentional and nonintentional subjects.

Several possible reasons can be suggested for the difference between recall of highly familiar and highly unfamiliar material as a function of intention. One possibility is that, given appropriate conditions of attention, highly familiar words may automatically elicit the responses crucial to recall, even in the absence of intention to learn. A second possibility is that highly familiar material, being well differentiated, may be better able to resist interference than less familiar material. Thus, to the extent that intention acted to reduce interference, intention would be less important for highly familiar material.

Research on strategies has dealt more directly with isolating the particular subject responses which facilitate learning. Most of this research has concentrated on strategies appropriate to nonsense material, or to unrelated real words arbitrarily coupled in a paired-associates task. Typically, these strategies are irrelevant to the learning of real words in meaningful combinations. For example, the highest level of strategy suggested by Martin, Boersma, and Cox (1965) involves combining two words in a syntactic structure (e.g., using the two words in a single sentence). If the subject's task is to learn a sentence, such a strategy is of no assistance. Clearly, the range of situations in which such a strategy can be effective is very limited. With few exceptions, the issue of strategies for retention of organized, meaningful material has been largely ignored.

11 | Awareness and Verbal Control of Behavior

PRECIS

We shall see that evidence at both the human and animal levels strongly supports the position that *awareness* of reinforcement contingencies is not necessary for *learning.* Indeed, learning can occur without the *occurrence* of reinforcement. Contrary conclusions by some recent writers have been based on *performance* measures in a restricted set of situations.

The question of whether *performance* can be systematically modified without the awareness of the reinforcement contingency is not as easily answered. A number of studies have found that performance improved only for the subjects who were aware of the particular responses which the experimenter was reinforcing. Other studies have found moderate improvement in performance in the absence of such awareness. The major difference between these two types of experiments appears to be the presence or absence of systematic hypothesis testing behavior on the part of the subjects. In some situations it appears that systematic hypothesis testing precludes the automatic operation of reinforcement in modifying behavior.

In human subjects, awareness of the reinforcement contingency appears to influence performance by means of verbal control mechanisms. These mechanisms of verbal control have proved to be extremely powerful determiners of behavior. Perhaps the most interesting research to date, in this area, has been concerned with the development of control mechanisms. Such development appears to be gradual and complex in nature. For example, in very young children, the verbal responses necessary for control over behavior are as difficult to attach to appropriate external stimuli as are the overt responses they should control. Later this is no longer true. The verbal responses become attached much more readily than motor responses, and these verbal responses control overt behavior with great effectiveness. *Removal* of the verbal responses leads to collapse of the overt behavior. The mechanisms behind such control are not, as yet, completely understood.

DEMONSTRATION EXPERIMENT

The Problem

Can you resist the influence of old, very well learned habits? We shall soon see. Below you will find sets of very simple arithmetic problems. You are to *reverse* the meanings of the operator signs on these problems so that when you see a sign to add, you will substract; when you see a sign to subtract, you will add.

Set 1: Time yourself on this first set of problems, using a watch or a clock with a second hand. *Work as quickly as you can!*

$63 + 12 =$	$14 - 7 =$	$31 - 11 =$	$19 - 3 =$	$48 + 4 =$
$98 + 2 =$	$79 - 8 =$	$23 - 7 =$	$46 - 9 =$	$57 + 3 =$
$28 + 3 =$	$28 + 13 =$	$28 - 23 =$	$67 + 3 =$	$51 - 11 =$
	$36 + 2 - 15 =$	$82 - 71 + 57 =$		$47 + 23 - 4 =$

(Check your answers at the bottom of this page.)

Set 2: Now try the following set of problems, reversing sign just as you did in the set above. However, on this set, *work as carefully as possible; do not* time yourself.

$19 + 6 =$	$12 - 2 =$	$27 - 17 =$	$2 + 2 =$	$87 - 17 =$
$54 - 50 =$	$32 - 6 =$	$16 + 4 =$	$41 - 1 =$	$76 - 6 =$
	$22 + 3 - 8 =$	$88 - 18 + 4 =$	$62 + 15 - 7 =$	

(Check your answers at the bottom of the page.)

Answers

Set 1:

51	21	42	22	44
96	87	30	55	54
25	15	51	64	62
	49	96	28	

Set 2:

13	14	44	0	104
104	38	12	42	82
	27	102	54	

Explanation of the Experiment

Under conditions of extreme pacing, verbal control is only erratically effective in countering the response tendencies produced by overlearned habits; thus, in Set 1, many subjects find themselves making errors, following the control of old habits and not reversing the signs in performing the arithmetic manipulations. On the other hand, in Set 2, without the pressure of time, most subjects find that they have little difficulty controlling their old, overlearned response tendencies.

For human adults, at least, verbal control is a powerful factor in determining behavior. If such an adult becomes aware that a given stimulus configuration is the basis of correct response in a concept learning problem, he can choose this stimulus consistently, no matter what the reinforcement history of the other stimuli in the problem. Similarly, as we shall see in this chapter, if an adult subject decides to test a particular hypothesis concerning the correct solution to a problem, he will make the relevant testing response with great accuracy—in other words, his behavior is under the control of these factors of awareness and verbal direction, just as your behavior was under your control despite the overlearned tendencies to behave according to the formal meanings of the terms "+" and "−". From this perspective, an important problem to be examined in the present chapter becomes, *is this type of awareness and control essential for learning and performance.*

FOCUS OF THE PRESENT CHAPTER

The emphasis of the preceding chapter was on the role of subject-controlled processes in placing material in *memory storage.* The present chapter turns to the role of subject-controlled processes in *performance.*

The issue of "internal" versus "external" control of behavior has intrigued psychologists over the years. Some have taken the position that behavior is largely determined by the reinforcement contingencies of the environment, with such contingencies operating in an "automatic" fashion to increase the probability of relevant behavior (e.g., Thorndike, 1932). On the other hand, other psychologists have stressed the internal control of behavior; from this point of view external variables, such as reinforcement, affect behavior by means of their information value (e.g., Wallach and Henle, 1941, 1942). Knowing which responses will be reinforced, subjects can presumably increase their emission rates for these responses. This issue is closely related to Hull's (1930) discussion of language as providing "pure stimulus acts" which can direct behavior.

Two related aspects of internal control will be considered in the present chapter. The first is awareness of the reinforcement contingencies. The second is verbal control of behavior. Presumably, if the subject is aware of the reinforcement contingencies, he can exert verbal control over his own behavior to insure that he emits the reinforced response. The following issues will be explored.

1. Is awareness necessary for learning?
2. Is awareness necessary for changes in performance?
3. Is verbal control basic to the mechanisms that related awareness to behavior?
4. How does verbal control develop?

THE ROLE OF AWARENESS IN LEARNING AND PERFORMANCE

Learning and Awareness

Recently, a number of writers have taken the position that learning can not occur unless the person is *aware of the contingency between his behavior and the reinforcement.* In other words, *learning depends upon knowing which responses will be reinforced.* While this position originated in the studies of verbal operant conditioning, some of its proponents have suggested it as a general position for all learning. Let us first, therefore, consider this position in its broadest form: Is awareness of the reinforcement contingency a necessary condition for all learning? The answer to this question is so clearly, "No," that a comprehensive review of the literature is unnecessary. We shall simply examine some of the more obvious lines of research.

NONINTENTIONAL LEARNING. The data from studies of nonintentional learning, summarized in the last chapter, certainly do not support the position that awareness of the reinforcement contingency is necessary for learning. The evidence from these studies indicates that stimulus events may be remembered even if these were originally encountered under conditions in which subjects were unaware that they were to *learn* (to say nothing of being unaware of *what* they were to learn). In fact, these studies suggest that learning can occur even if there is no particular reinforcement present during the original presentation of the material.

LATENT LEARNING. The latent learning studies initiated by Tolman (1932) and his students, which employed animals as subjects, are also relevant here. These studies indicate that, not only can learning occur in the *absence of awareness of the reinforcement contingency,* it can occur in the *absence of reinforcement.*

Let us consider some of the types of latent learning studies that have been reported. In one type of latent learning study, animals were permitted to freely explore a multi-unit maze for a period of time, with no reinforcement in the goal box. Later the animals were introduced into the maze and found food in the goal box. On subsequent trials, these animals learned the maze much more quickly than a control group which had not freely explored the maze prior to the first trial with food in the goal box. One criticism of these studies (see MaCorquodale and Meehl, 1954) has been that animals, during free exploration, may develop anxiety responses to blind alleys. These anxiety responses could lead to avoidance of the blind alleys and a consequent decrease in errors when food is in the endbox of the maze. However, Buxton (1940) found that an initial period of nonreward free exploration was facilitory to subsequent learning even when he placed the food in one of the blind alleys, making this the goal box. Such studies indicate that animals can remember stimulus relationships (e.g., which path leads to a blind alley and which leads to a new segment of the maze) even in the absence of any reinforcement contingencies which might indicate that learning certain of these relationships would later lead to reward. Tolman (1948) has described this type of situation as the learning of a cognitive map.

Seward (1949) has provided a rather dramatic demonstration of latent learning. Rats were permitted to explore a T-maze for 30 minutes a day over a three-day period. Each arm of the T-maze contained a different, distinctive goal box. On the fourth day, the animals were placed directly in one of the two goal boxes, where they found food. Seward then placed the animals in the start box of the T-maze. Of the 32 animals in the experiment, 28 chose the path which led to the goal box in which they had just been fed.

Being fed in a goal box is the equivalent, for the rat, of instructing a person to make a particular response. During the first three days of the Seward study, animals, in effect, were performing without any particular instructions. Since *no particular class of responses was reinforced, no awareness of a response-reinforcement contingency could develop.* Despite this, the animals remembered the position of each goal box, and under appropriate "instructions" the animals could make the appropriate response.

AWARENESS: A LEARNING OR A PERFORMANCE VARIABLE? Clearly, the human and animal research is relatively consistent in indicating that subjects can remember stimuli and relationships between stimuli, even when unaware that any reinforcement was contingent on such memory, since no reinforcement occurred during the acquisition of these memories. Thus *learning can occur* without awareness of reinforcement contingencies. It should be emphasized, of course, that learning does not inevitably occur under conditions of non-awareness. As was seen in the studies of nonintentional learning, the orienting task must, at a minimum, force attention to the relevant cue dimensions.

We shall see that the issue which has been raised in the operant conditioning studies is *not* concerned with the role of awareness on *learning*. Instead, the question becomes, can operant *performance* be modified without awareness of reinforcement contingency. Also, the caution must be raised that the operant conditioning situation is not necessarily a paradigm for all situations in which the relationship between awareness and performance change can be examined.

AWARENESS AND VERBAL OPERANT CONDITIONING

Questions concerning the role of awareness in human behavior are quite old. However, the explorations of this issue in greatest depth are to be found in the context of the verbal operant conditioning studies. Therefore, we shall first, in this section, characterize the nature of these studies.

While there have been many variations on the basic experiment, verbal operant conditioning can be illustrated by a study in which the subject talks freely on any topic, and the experimenter says, "Good," or "um-hum," whenever the subject says "I," or "We." The rate of emission of the critical response can then be measured over successive time intervals. Early studies employing this type of procedure reported that subjects gradually increased the number of critical responses as a function of such verbal reinforcement even when not aware that the experimenter was systematically rewarding these responses. Later experiments have calld these conclusions into doubt, stating that only aware subjects produce increments in operant rate. (Sometimes, as Adams, 1957, points out, subjects may be aware of a reinforcement contingency that is not exactly the same as the one being reinforced by the experimenter, but which is highly correlated with it so that responding on this basis will usually be rewarded.) Operationally, awareness has typically been measured by means of verbal reports by the subjects.

Superficially, it might appear that the question of the role of awareness in operant conditioning is essentially the same as that raised in the nonintentional learning studies discussed earlier. Both are concerned with awareness by the subject that he is to learn some specific response or association. Several crucial differences exist, however, between the two types of studies.

1. AWARENESS DURING LEARNING VERSUS DURING PERFOMANCE. Nonintentional learning experiments present the material to be learned under conditions which disguise the fact that the experimenter is concerned with learning. Thus there is, potentially, lack of awareness during the learning phase. On the other hand, the test for learning (i.e., the performance phase) is conducted under conditions of awareness. The subject, for example, is asked to tell the experimenter the list of words he has just rated for familiarity.

In verbal operant conditioning, both learning and test phases are conducted under conditions of lack of specific instructions concerning the responses being measured.

2. MEMORY VERSUS DISCOVERY. The typical study of nonintentional learning is concerned with memory for a set of materials toward which the subject has made, at a minimum, attentional responses. The typical verbal operant conditioning study is usually a concept attainment task in which the subject must discover the aspects of his responses which are being systematically reinforced. This may prove difficult even when the subjects are instructed concerning the real object of the task. For example, Greenspoon (1955) has subjects emit words without instruction that certain responses were to be emitted more frequently than others. He reinforced certain categories of responses (e.g., plural nouns), and reports learning without awareness. Eriksen (1962) repeated this general procedure, with the modification that subjects were told this was a problem-solving task in which they were to discover the basis for reinforcement. Eriksen reports that only a small number of subjects solved the problem in the number of trials used by Greenspoon. Thus the discovery component of this type of task can not be considered a trivial aspect of the problem.

Even if a subject in an operant conditioning study remembered all the responses he had emitted, he might not know which aspect of these responses was being reinforced. To complicate matters even more, in many verbal operant conditioning studies, the crucial response is just one aspect of a more complex response made by the subject. For example, the subject may be rewarded for using "I" or "we" as one of the words in sentences he emits in free discourse. The other words in the sentence are irrelevant to reinforcement. Here the rewarded response is embedded in a larger response.

3. ORIENTING TASK.   The nonintentional learning studies are characterized by relatively convincing orienting tasks such that the subjects probably do not wonder about the "real" purpose of the experiment. Instead, they work at the particular orienting task (e.g., rate words for meaningfulness). On the other hand the instructions for the verbal operant conditioning studies are typically vague, subjects are often uncertain concerning what they are expected to do, and often there appears to be a good deal of hypothesis testing. There is reason to believe, as we shall presently see, that such hypothesis testing behavior on the part of subjects may actually interfere with the "automatic" operation of reinforcement.

Operant Conditioning under Concept Attainment Orientations

What is the evidence for the position that performance, in verbal operant conditioning, can not be modified in the absence of awareness? The strongest evidence comes from those studies which used rather vague orienting tasks which did not attempt to disguise the nature of the task. As Eriksen (1962) has pointed out, in most of these studies the subjects are aware of the reinforcement, and appear to interpret their task as that of attaining the reinforcement. Thus, the task becomes, essentially, a problem in concept attainment, with the subject attempting to discover the basis for reinforcement. The present section will deal with studies of this sort.

EARLY STUDIES.   The early studies of verbal operant conditioning typically included a brief inquiry, at the end of the experiment, in which the experimenter attempted to assess awareness. These inquiries tended to be nondirective, since, first, the experimenter did not wish to suggest a response which might not have occurred spontaneously to the subject; and second, the typical experimenter appears to have been concerned with giving away the real purpose of the study for fear of test compromise in subsequent subjects. Krasner (1958) reviews a large number of such studies and finds that a great proportion of these report increase in operant rate of reinforced responses for subjects who show no awareness of the correct reinforcement contingencies.

POST-EXPERIMENTAL INQUIRIES.   The first work to seriously challenge the contention that changes in operant rate can occur without awareness comes from Dulany (1961) and Levin (1961). Both these experimenters employed more adequate post-experimental inquiries.

Dulany's initial concern was with correlated hypotheses. The subject might not be aware of the exact basis for reinforcement, but might have some hypothesis which is highly correlated with the correct basis for reinforcement. This is, of course, the issue previously raised by Adams (1957). Dulany requested subjects to emit words *ad libitum* and reinforced plural nouns with "um-humm." Approximately one fourth of the subjects reported, in post-experimental inquiry, that they interpreted the task as one in which they were to give associates, staying within the same category as long as the experimenter said "um-humm," but were to shift categories when the experimenter ceased to reinforce them. This group showed increases in frequency of plural nouns as a function of trials. Control subjects who were never reinforced showed no change in performance. Neither did a group who reported the association hypothesis, but no hypothesis about shifting categories when the experimenter failed to reinforce them. In fact, the performance of this group was indistinguishable from that of the controls.

Dulany presents data which indicates that the associate to a plural noun is likely to produce more plural nouns, and shifting from nonreinforced categories should lead to a greater probability of plural nouns than would occur if subjects continued associating to words that were not plural nouns.

One of the most frequently employed tasks, in the studies of awareness in verbal operant conditioning, was developed by Taffel (1955). In this task, subjects are presented with cards, each of which contains a verb plus the six personal pronouns. The subjects are instructed to construct a sentence containing the verb plus one of the pronouns. Sentences containing "I" or "we" are reinforced. Taffel originally reported increments in reinforced responses for subjects who were not aware of the reinforcement. Subsequent studies have used a more intensive post-experimental interview, developed by Levin (1961), to determine awareness. The conclusion from these studies is that many aware subjects were not identified by Taffel's interview. Using normal subjects, and a variant of Levin's post-experimental inquiry, Spielberger and Levin (1962), Speilberger, Levin, and Shepard (1962), and DeNike (1964), among others have failed to find evidence for increase in operant rate for subjects who were unaware, while aware subjects systematically showed increases in operant rate.

Several of the studies cited above (e.g., Levin, 1961; Spielberger and Levin, 1962) report that some subjects were aware of either the "I" or the "we" contingency, but were not aware that both of these responses were being reinforced. In these cases, increments in performance were specific as to the particular response contingency of which the subject was aware. Such data are certainly consistent with the position that there is no increase in operant rate without awareness of the contingency.

Note that the Taffel (1955) task closely resembles a concept attainment task. The subject is presented card after card, all containing the same six personal pronouns plus a different verb on each card. Reinforcement, he soon discovers, follows some of his sentences, but not others. At this point, many of the subjects appear to engage in systematic hypothesis testing designed to discover the basis for the reinforcements. There are relatively few parameters to this task, and many subjects soon note that the same six personal pronouns appear again and again; therefore, much of the hypothesis testing focuses on aspects of these pronouns. Once subjects find the correct hypothesis, they tend to improve in emission rate for the critical responses. The subjects who fail to discover the correct hypothesis tend not to increase in emission rate for the critical "I" or "we" responses.

DOES AWARENESS GUARANTEE IMPROVEMENT IN PERFORMANCE? One of the more intriguing findings of the verbal operant studies is that many subjects who are aware of the basis for reinforcement simply do not emit the correct response at a high rate. In the studies cited above, the average emission rate for aware subjects was often below 50%. It was this type of consideration that led Dulany (1962, 1968) to stress the importance of the subjects' *intention* to perform, in addition to the subjects' awareness of which response the experimenter will reinforce.

A dramatic example of subject reluctance to respond in an operant conditioning situation is provided in an experiment by Professor Reuben Baron (personal communication). Baron analyzed his data by personality types and found that some subjects showed a marked *drop* in operant rate, virtually to 0% response, *immediately after becoming aware of the basis for reinforcement.* These proved to be negativistic subjects who resented the fact that someone (viz., the experimenter) was trying to manipulate their behavior.

Further evidence on this issue is found in the study by Spielberger and Levin (1962). Using the task developed by Taffel, the role of awareness in operant conditioning was studied as a function of subjects' set, or intentions, concerning the experiment. Some subjects were honestly informed that the study was concerned with their ability to discover which type of sentence was considered good by the experimenter. Other subjects were given the usual, vague instructions to make a sentence by selecting one of the six pronouns and combining it with the verb. These latter subjects were told that the study was concerned with the way sentences are constructed.

Post-experimental inquiry indicated approximately equal numbers of aware subjects in both groups. The aware subjects in both groups showed significant increases in operant rate, while the unaware showed no significant increment as compared to a control group which received no reinforcement. The critical finding concerning learning set was that *aware subjects under a neutral set emitted the reinforced operant less frequency than those under a learning set.* This was a consistent difference that persisted undiminished throughout all blocks of trials. These data suggest that subjects will at least restrain their tendency toward a reinforced response if not instructed specifically that the experimenter wants this response to be emitted. Learning, in the sense that subjects knew which response was rewarded, occurred in the aware subjects with neutral set. Despite this, the performance was less than in the learning set group.

Results reported by Spielberger, Levin, and Shepard (1962) also indicate that under certain conditions operant rate performance is not completely determined by awareness. Following the same type of tasks already described, in which "I" and "we" were reinforced, aware subjects indicated whether they wanted to be reinforced very much, some, or didn't care. The greater the degree of the reported desire for reinforcement, the higher the operant performance level. Again, since all these subjects were aware of the reinforcement contingency, all had learned the correct contingency. Despite this, awareness did not guarantee optimal performance. Similar data are reported by Dulany (1962).

ARE THERE DEGREES OF AWARENESS?   An interesting aspect of the Spielberger, Levin, and Shepard (1962) study is that the amount of probing required to determine awareness was inversely related to performance. Subjects who freely indicated that they had noted the reinforcement and who verbalized the contingency early in the post-experimental inquiry showed the greatest amount of performance increment. Some subjects indicated awareness of the contingency only after being told that there was some contingency and were asked to indicate what the contingency was. These subjects showed less of an increase in operant rate, though they performed significantly better than the control group. Unaware subjects showed no improvement in performance. A more controlled study, by Spielberger (1962), indicated that the poorer performance by the aware subjects who required a more intensive inquiry was not due to unaware subjects to whom the contingency was suggested by the inquiry. Operationally, degree of probing for awareness can be thought of as defining the level of awareness.

AWARENESS AND THE OPERANT CONDITIONING OF A MOTOR RESPONSE. Paul, Eriksen, and Humphreys (1962) attempted to produce operant conditioning without awareness in a situation in which the operant was a motor response. Subjects were placed in a chamber kept at 105°F., 85% humidity. Reinforcement was a draft of cool air. One group was reinforced for a specific hand movement, another for a specific face or mouth movement, and the third group for a foot movement. The orienting task involved telling subjects that the study was concerned with ability to withstand heat in a spaceship; subjects were asked to detect differences between sonar signals, and to work on a peg-board task in the heat chamber. Subjects were considered aware if, during post-experimental inquiry, they could specify the correct reinforcement contingency. All subjects noticed the reinforcement, but only 50% of the subjects could describe the contingency. While the nonaware subjects responded at a somewhat greater rate than the control in each of the three conditions, these differences were far from significant. On the other hand, the aware subjects in two or the three conditions responded at a much higher rate than either the nonaware or the control, and these differences were statistically significant. Apparently, awareness is as crucial in increasing this type of motor operant behavior as in the verbal operant studies reported above.

THE MOMENT OF AWARENESS AND JUST BEFORE. We have seen that, for the verbal operant task with concept attainment features, only the subjects who became aware appear to show systematic increases in operant rate. This, in itself, does not necessarily mean that there was no improvement in operant rate *prior to the moment of awareness.* It is possible, for example, that awareness of the reinforcement contingency *follows,* rather than *precedes,* a subject's increased operant rate. Indeed, one may conceptualize awareness as involving the subject noticing that he is making a particular response relatively frequently.

In terms of the possibility outlined in the paragraph above, Postman and Sassenrath (1961) have proposed that awareness of the reinforcement contingency is a form of learned behavior. As such, its probability of occurrence should increase as a function of reinforcements. Once the awareness has occurred, it can serve as a cue to the operant behavior, increasing its probability of occurrence sharply.

From this type of position, if awareness is just another response which increases in strength with reinforcement, there is no reason to believe that *some* increments in operant performance should not precede awareness. Studies by DeNike (1964) and Spielberger, Bernstein, and Ratliff (1966) have been concerned with whether there is any evidence for an increase in operant performance *before* awareness, in subjects who do eventually exhibit awareness. If one thinks of awareness and operant performance as two different response systems (even if increase in strength one of these systems may influence the strength of the other) an implicit question which is being asked is whether one of these systems is easier to strengthen than the other.

Technically, there are difficult issues involved in attempting to determine if there is an increase in operant rate prior to the increase in awareness. It is difficult to quiz a subject after each trial to determine his awareness without turning the study into a more straightforward concept attainment task in which the subject systematically attempts to discover the basis for reinforcement. To circumvent this problem to some extent, both DeNike (1964) and Spielberger *et al.* (1966) questioned their subjects after each block of 25 responses. The inquiry involved having subjects write their "thoughts" about the experiment. The experimental task in both studies was that of emitting words. Human nouns were reinforced. DeNike found that, on the basis of inquiries, 30% of his subjects became aware. These subjects showed a significant increase in operant performance, compared to a control group, while the nonaware subject did not.

Awareness presumably developed during the block of trials immediately preceding a subject's statement of the correct contingency. DeNike labeled this Block 0, the block immediately preceding it Block -1, and the block following it Block $+1$. On Block -1 there was no indication of any increase in operant rate compared to the control. There was a very large and significant jump in operant performance in Block 0 as compared with Block -1. Subjects then continued to respond at about the same rate as in Block 0, for the remainder of the experiment, so that Blocks 0 and $+1$ do not differ significantly. These data are interpreted by DeNike as supporting the position that an increase in operant behavior does not precede awareness.

However, as DeNike himself indicates, there are problems in interpreting the data in this manner. Awareness presumably developed somewhere in the course of Block 0, since subjects did not give evidence of knowing the contingency prior to this block but did give evidence of awareness immediately following it. From this point of view, the fact that performance is asymptotic at Block 0 is perplexing. If the occurrence of awareness were randomly distributed through the 25 responses of Block 0, mean operant rate on this block should be lower than in subsequent blocks. That operant rate is asymptotic at Block 0 *could* perhaps, indicate that the inquiry immediately preceding Block 0 somehow sensitized subjects so that most became aware very early in Block 0.

Spielberger, Bernstein, and Ratliff (1966) replicated the DeNike study and obtained essentially the same results. One additional finding in the Spielberger, *et al.*, study, however, indicates serious problems in attempting to determine the moment of awareness. These investigators were concerned with the fact that, in DeNike's study, the asymptote for mean number of correct operant responses given by aware subjects was only 7 to 8 responses over blocks of 25 trials—about a 30% emission rate after awareness. Hypothesizing that this low rate was due to lack of incentive, they instructed all subjects after the seventh block of trials that there was a rule for reinforcement, and subjects were to try to receive as many reinforcements as possible. For subjects who had been aware before these added instructions, performance jumped from approximately 30% emission of operants at Block 7 to about 55% at Block 8. A surprising aspect of the data was that some subjects who never indicated awareness, on the basis of their "thoughts" about the experiment which were collected after each block of 25 trials, also showed improvement. These were subjects who, in a post-experimental inquiry, did indicate awareness by the conclusion of the experiment. These data suggest that the instructions to give "thoughts" may be too ambiguous as a means of determining awareness.

Clearly, a major problem in the DeNike and in the Spielberger, *et al.*, studies is that they do not provide a precise enough method of indicating the onset of awareness. Due to this, there is a great deal of ambiguity concerning the significance of Block 0 performance.

Is there a more adequate method for determining whether operant rate can increase, prior to the onset of awareness, in a relatively complex discovery task? It would appear that data from a concept attainment situation might be less ambiguous than data from the more usual operant conditioning task, since the concept task permits more continuous and straightforward probing for awareness. Relevant data from this area will be discussed below.

Awareness and Concept Attainment

There is some evidence from concept attainment studies which suggests that hypothesis testing, on the part of the subjects, may interfere with the "automatic" operation of reinforcement. There are two ways in which such interference may function. It may interfere with *performance* of the correct response, even though no interference occurs with the learning, *per se;* or it may actually interfere with learning. Let us consider these two possibilities separately.

PERFORMANCE EFFECTS.   In Chapter 3 we saw that there are a number of situations in which learning can occur without an immediately concomitant increase in correct performance. This can occur either in animal or in human learning, and can occur even if the subject is being systematically reinforced for the correct response.

What factors can prevent the emergence of the appropriate performance? The animal discrimination-learning studies, examined in Chapter 3, provide an interesting parallel to concept attainment and suggest some possible mechanisms. Animals in a discrimination-learning situation often respond at close to chance levels of success over most of the training trials, and then improve fairly rapidly toward the end of training. Spence (1936) showed that this could occur if there were some extremely strong response tendency that determined behavior on the early trials; position responses, such as always turning right or always turning left, appear to be this strong in the white rat. Consider a rat who has an extremely strong tendency to run to the *left* goal box in a situation where food is always in the *black* goal box. Since the black goal box will be on the left only half the trials (and on the right, the other half), this rat will be reinforced 50% of the trials—viz., he will be correct no more often than would be expected by chance. Despite this, there is evidence that the rat is gradually strengthening his tendency to respond to the black box, during this period of chance performance. (See Chapter 3 for the nature of this evidence.) In short, *learning may occur in situations in which performance is obscured by other, more potent responses.*

What very potent responses could obscure correct performance in a concept attainment task? The writer shall suggest that *hypothesis testing* may serve this function. Because of the strong verbal control we have over our behavior, if we decide to test a particular hypothesis, we shall make the response appropriate to this test. Testing an incorrect hypothesis may insure chance performance on the correct response.

Let us demonstrate this with a hypothetical example. Assume a subject responds on the basis of an incorrect hypothesis (e.g., the hypothesis is that *circles* are correct, when actually red is correct). If the subject says a stimulus is an instance whenever it contains a circle, the number of correct choices will be determined completely by the number of times red and circle coincide on the same stimulus. *If the tendency to respond to red increased as a function of reinforcements, this tendency will be completely hidden.* The increase in responses to red will be evident only on trials in which the subject fails to respond in terms of his hypothesis. From this analysis, it appears that only certain restricted types of concept attainment tasks are likely to permit increments in performance in the absence of awareness concerning the correct contingency. *Such tasks must permit the testing of a specific hypothesis without forcing random behavior in regard to other possible contingencies.*

Saltz (1967b) reports an indirect test of the possibility that incorrect hypotheses interfere with "automatic" increments in concept learning. This test was based on evidence (to be described later in this chapter) that young children have relatively little verbal control over their own behavior. From this it follows that the control effects of incorrect hypotheses should be minimal for such children, and therefore the interfering effects of incorrect hypotheses should be minimal. Saltz compared precriterion performance of four-year-olds with that of eight-year-olds on a simple concept task. The results for the eight-year-olds were essentially the same as that reported above for adult human subjects—performance was at a chance level prior to the criterion block of trials. However, for the four-year-olds, number of correct responses rose steadily across four blocks of Vincentized, precriterion trials.

LEARNING EFFECTS.   Several other studies can be cited which suggest that hypothesis testing can impede the automatic action of reinforcement in concept attainment tasks. In these studies, however, the effect appears to be on learning, rather than being restricted to performance. Rommetveit and Kvale (1965a, 1965b) provide an excellent example of this type of effect. These experimenters had school children play a "game of chance" in which the children put a coin into a slot machine, activating a complex stimulus display. The subject was aware that he had no control over the particular display which would appear, since there was only one slot into which the coin could be placed. Some types of displays were regularly followed by return of a coin of greater value than the one inserted; some were followed by the return of the coin which the subject inserted; some were followed by no coin return—the subject lost his coin. Half the subjects were told that they would be asked to distinguish "good" (rewarding) displays from "bad," half were not. Subjects were tested after long sequences of responses. *Those who had been told that they would be tested did more poorly in indicating the significant distinctions between good and bad displays than those who had not been so instructed.* Analysis of the data indicated that subjects who were set to distinguish between displays tended to analyze the displays into too many irrelevant components that interfered with more naturalistic observation.

Rommetveit and Kvales suggest that premature attempts to verbalize a hypothesis concerning the basis of a concept may actually disrupt the more intuitive processes which are basic to concept attainment. Phelan (1965) reports data which are consistent with this position. Subjects were presented with a two-phase problem. In Phase 1, they sorted complex stimuli until they reached a criterion of errorless sorting. In Phase 2 the subjects were given a new set of stimuli which could be correctly sorted if the subjects used the rules discovered in Phase 1. Two groups were compared on Phase 2 performance; one group, the Verbalizers, were asked to verbalize the rule immediately following Phase 1 and before starting Phase 2. The Nonverbalizers were presented with Phase 2 without instructions to verbalize the rule for Phase 1. In Phase 2, 74% of the Nonverbalizers were successful, only 32% of the Verbalizers. Phelan attributes the difference to the fact that a majority of the Verbalizers gave inadequate hypotheses concerning the solution of Phase 1; after this inadequate verbalization, these subjects acted on the basis of the verbalizations, and thus were unsuccessful in Phase 2. Since the Nonverbalizers did not state hypotheses following Phase 1, we have no data on the adequacy of any hypotheses they may have developed. However, the assumption is made that these subjects would have produced inadequate hypotheses at the same rate as the Verbalizers. It is further assumed that since they were not requested to verbalize, there was less interference in Phase 2 performance due to acting on the basis of incorrect verbalizations.

HOW DOES AWARENESS AFFECT CONCEPT ATTAINMENT? The data examined in this section indicate that, as in the operant conditioning studies of the previous section, there is probably very little evidence for improved *performance* prior to awareness of the reinforcement contingency *in those conditions in which systematic hypothesis testing takes place.* In some cases this appears to represent a masking of learning due to the constraints of the task. In other cases, the systematic hypothesis testing may actually interfere with learning: Under some circumstances, at least, incorrect hypotheses may disrupt learning and interfere with more "intuitive" bases for correct performance.

Operant Conditioning in the Absence of Hypothesis Testing

A few operant conditioning studies have attempted to alter response rates in situations where subjects may be presumed *not* to have engaged in hypothesis testing behavior. Results from these studies suggest that under such circumstances, performance may improve without awareness of the reinforcement contingencies.

Levin (1961), using the Taffel task with hospitalized schizophrenics as subjects, found that his intensive post-experimental inquiry divided his reinforced subjects into three groups. One group was aware of the reinforcement plus the contingency for reinforced. This group showed large and significant increments in operant rate. A second group was aware of the reinforcement, but never discovered what response led to reinforcement. This group showed no significant increment in operant rate. A third group denied even noticing that the experimenter occasionally said "good" during the course of the experiment. This group showed a small but significant increment in operant response despite having no awareness of the reinforcement. It should be noted that studies employing normal subjects do not report subjects who fall in this third category. Thus there is no equivalent normal group against which to evaluate these results.

A possible interpretation of Levin's data is that subjects who are aware of the reinforcement engage in complex hypothesis testing in an effort to determine the reinforcement contingency. This could lead to a great deal of shifting from one response category to another in an attempt to find the contingency, and this behavior could conceivably interfere with the automatic effects of reinforcement.

Levin and Sterner (1966) pursued this possibility by attempting to construct a situation in which the reinforcer was less obviously a signal of correct performances than "good" or "um-hum." The signal they chose was a relatively casual pencil tap. Again using schizophrenics as subjects, the study was conducted in two phases. Phase 1 was a paired-associates task in which the pencil tap was associated with correct anticipations for half the subjects. This phase was conceptualized as inducing secondary reinforcement properties to the tap. Phase 2 was a verbal operant conditioning study similar to that of Levin (1961). However, for all subjects, the casual pencil tap was substituted for the verbal reinforcer. Levin and Sterner report that, on the basis of an intensive post-experimental interview similar to that employed by Levin (1961) in his earlier experiments, most of the subjects proved to be unaware of the tap as a reinforcer. Analyzing data for unaware subjects, a significantly greater number of "I" or "we" responses was emitted by the experimental group for whom the pencil tap had been associated with correct anticipation of paired associates in Phase 1.

Rather serious questions can, obviously, be raised concerning both the Levin (1961) and the Levin and Sterner (1966) papers. Both studies use schizophrenic subjects, and the verbalizations of schizophrenics can not be accepted uncritically. This, of course, is one of the problems which arises in using verbal report as an index (or operational definition) of an internal state. In the Levin study, the critical data are provided by a small group which disclaims having noted that the experimenter had said "good" a number of times during the study. As was noted earlier, normal subjects usually do note this type of behavior on the part of the experimenter. The possibility exists that some of the schizophrenic patients who denied noting the reinforcement had actually been aware of the reinforcement contingency and were behaving negativistically in the inquiry, lying about their awareness. In the Levin and Sterner study, the credibility is greater than subjects could have failed to note the pencil tap as a signal of good performance.

A recent study by Silver (1967) appears to lend strong support to Levin's position. This study employed college students as subjects. Concept attainment orientation (and its hypothesis testing behavior consequences) was minimized by use of an adequate orienting task. Subjects were told that the purpose of the study was to investigate whether word-frequency played a role in the ease of combining words into new ideas. Subjects were presented pairs of words and were asked to make a sentence as quickly as possible using the two words. The experimenter timed subjects with a stop watch. For half of the experimental group, sentences containing past tense verbs were reinforced; for the other half, sentences with present tense verbs were reinforced. The significance of the reinforcement was disguised by telling subjects, "Good, that was very fast for that pair of words." Intensive post-experimental inquiry disclosed no subjects who guessed the actual basis for reinforcement. While some subjects adapted simple strategies to permit the rapid invention of sentences, these did not differ systematically between groups.

In two replications, Silver found that reinforcement of present tense verbs led to significantly more present tense sentences than found in either the control group (which received no reinforcements) or the group which was rewarded for past tense sentences. Silver's study indicates that, in the absence of hypotheses testing behavior, awareness of the reinforcement contingency is not necessary for performance modification.

The effect of reinforcement on operant conditioning, in the absence of awareness of the contingency, does not appear to be strong. It can, apparently, be disrupted fairly easily. However, the effect does appear to exist.

AWARENESS AND THE MOLECULAR RESPONSE

In the sections above, we discussed the role of awareness in situations where a *class* of responses was considered correct, rather than a specific response to a specific stimulus. If reinforcement has an automatic effect on performance, in the absence of awareness concerning the correct basis for reward, we would expect to find such an effect occurring most strongly in situations where a *specific* response to a *specific* stimulus always leads to reward. Classical conditioning and certain of the tasks modeled after the experiments of Thorndike (1932) are relevant to this issue.

Studies in the Thorndike Tradition

Much of the present-day interest in the automatic effect of reinforcement arises from the extensive and historically significant series of studies conducted by Thorndike (e.g., 1932) and his colleagues on the "law of effect." However, while these studies provided us with a great deal of empirical evidence concerning the operation of reinforcement, their import for the relationship between reinforcement and awareness is not clear. Too often, subjects appear to have been questioned in only a superficial manner concerning their awareness. Thorndike's work led to a number of attempts to test the automatic effect of reinforcement; while these did not always probe adequately for awareness, they did employ cover stories that might be expected to reduce the likelihood of awareness.

Wallach and Henle (1941, 1942) developed an ingenious way of testing the Thorndike position that reinforcement automatically leads to the repetition of a response to a given stimulus. Subjects were told that they were to participate in a study of extrasensory-perception (ESP). A list of 20 words was presented, and subjects were to guess which number the experimenter had associated with each word. Subjects were told that they were correct on some guesses, incorrect on others. Then the entire list was presented again, and the subjects were told that the correct response for a word would be randomly changed so that the same response might or might not be correct on the next trial.

If reinforcement automatically increases the tendency to repeat a response to a given stimulus, reinforced responses should be repeated and nonreinforced responses should be less likely to reoccur. The tendency to repeat a response was approximately 10–14%, whether the subjects had been told the response was right or wrong on previous trials. Thus, Wallach and Henle concluded that reinforcement was effective primarily when it *informed* a subject that a given response would be correct if emitted to the stimulus at a later time. This is, of course, a form of the position that performance changes only when the subject is aware that a given response will lead to reinforcement.

Postman and Adams (1955) and Porter (1957) suggested that the Wallach and Henle procedure had several difficulties. First subjects, were given a large number of trials on each stimulus word, with different responses emitted to any given word on different trials. In addition, with 20 stimuli and only 10 possible responses, the same responses were necessarily given to more than one stimulus. Thus response competition was probably great and could have obscured the tendency to repeat reward items. Finally, subjects were often reinforced for giving one response to a stimulus on one trial and for giving a different response to the same stimulus on a different trial. This could lead subjects to change their responses.

Postman and Adams (1955) used the same general task and ESP

orienting instructions employed by Wallach and Henle, but employed only a single trial of 21 stimulus words, in which 3, 10, or 18 of the 21 responses were reinforced. This was followed by a test trial in which subjects were told that the correct responses were being randomly altered so that a response which had been correct on the first trial might or might not be correct on the second trial. No reinforcements were administered during the second trial. Since the responses were the number 1–10, the *a priori* probability of repetition was 10%. The actual repetition of reinforced responses was significantly greater than this *a priori* possibility as was the repetition of punished responses (i.e., responses called "wrong"). These data are somewhat difficult to interpret since it is known that the base rate for particular responses may be greater than the *a priori* probability. However, if it is assumed that the percentage of repetition of punished responses is an index of base rate,[1] and if percentage of repetition of reinforced and punished responses is compared, the reinforced responses were found to significantly exceed the punished in percentage repetition. While the difference between repetition of rewarded and punished responses was relatively small (about 13%), the data support the position that reinforcement increases probability of a molecular response in the absence of awareness.

Porter (1957) attempted to repeat the Postman and Adams study under more controlled conditions. In Postman and Adams, the reinforced responses were from one set of serial positions, while the punished responses were from a different set of serial positions. Since serial position is known to be a relevant variable in many learning situations, Porter counterbalanced this factor. Repetition of reinforced responses was again significantly greater than repetition of responses which had been called "wrong." However, the difference was extremely small, approximately 5%.

Bitterman (1956) in a study based on the Postman and Adams design, found a tendency toward greater repetition of rewarded than punished responses, but, despite a sizable number of subjects, the tendency was not significant.

While the magnitude of the repetition effect, in the ESP studies, is very small, this should be evaluated against the fact that most of these

---

[1] Data reported by Bitterman (1956) support this assumption. Bitterman used the Postman and Adams design, but also tested a control group which had never been told right or wrong for its responses. Response repetition by this group was almost identical with repetition of punished responses in the experimental group when compared over the same stimuli.

employed only a single trial. The administration of multiple trials would be very desirable, in order to examine the phenomenon more closely. Unfortunately, the ESP orienting task does not lend itself easily to multiple trials. In addition, the data might be more persuasive if the effects of reinforcement were compared with nonreinforcement, rather than with punishment.

Conditioning

Somewhat more convincing data on the increase in performance of a molecular response in the absence of awareness come from conditioning. Razran (1936, 1955), investigating salivary conditioning, explained the nature of the study to one group, but told another group that the study was concerned with the effects of work on the digestive processes. In both studies, conditioning was faster for the unaware subjects than the aware. Even more persuasive on this point is the fact that in the second study (1955), informing the unaware subjects concerning the nature of the experiment led to a *decrease* in conditioned response. The superiority of the unaware group is interesting in itself. In addition, it is interesting for the technical reason that it appears to eliminate the possibility that conditioning in the unaware group might be due to the performance of a small number of subjects who "caught on" to the *CS-UCS* contingency despite the instructions.

Related results are reported by Hartman and Grant (1962). Here a double alternation procedure was used, two trials involving *CS-UCS* pairing, the next two involving the *CS*, without the *UCS*, and so forth. One group was informed of the double alternation and was given practice in predicting which *CS* onsets would be followed by a *UCS*. Another group was given no such instructions. Comparing those subjects, in the two groups, whose conditioned responses were of a nonvoluntary type, the subjects who were informed of the double alternation responded on 22% of the appropriate trials; the uninformed responded on 51% of the appropriate trials.

Spence and his students have performed a number of eyelid conditioning studies in which the conditioning aspects of the task were masked; subjects were told that the primary task was that of probability learning under conditions of distraction. On each trial, subjects were asked to guess which of two lights would be lit, with the *CS* and the *UCS* represented as distractors during the guessing. Data reported by Homzie and Weiss (1965) suggest that conditioning may be faster under the masked conditions than when subjects are aware that the critical task is one of conditioning. Spence, Homzie, and Rutledge (1964) report somewhat poorer conditioning for the masked groups than for those with standard instructions. A review of research by Spence (1966) indicates that over a large number of studies the two procedures produce equivalent conditioning rates. It should be noted that the particular masking procedure used involves an increase in stimulus variability from trial to trial (e.g., subjects make distinctive guessing responses which differ across trials). On this basis alone one would anticipate poorer conditioning under the masking instructions.

A study by Chatterjee and Eriken (1962) appears to be relatively unique in indicating the absence of conditioning for unaware subjects. The study involved heart-rate conditioning with words as the CS and shock as UCS. A peculiarity of this study is that subjects were presented with the verbal CS and were asked to free associate to it. After 8.5 seconds, the shock was presented. Saltz and Asdourian (1963) have pointed out that it is difficult to know what the CS is, in this type of situation. An 8.5 second interval between CS and UCS typically produces little conditioning. Therefore it is unlikely that the word presented to the subject is the CS. The last word emitted by the subject, prior to shock, is probably the actual CS. In this case, if presentation of the stimulus word evokes, in the subject, the word which the subject emitted immediately before he was shocked, the conditioning response is likely to occur. Otherwise, there is likely to be little evidence of conditioning.

The "ESP" studies, and particularly the studies of conditioning appear to support the position that reinforcement will increase the performance rate of molecular responses even in the absence of awareness of the reinforcement contingency. The operant conditioning and concept attainment studies suggest that awareness may be more important for an increase in performance of molar responses.

VERBAL CONTROL OF BEHAVIOR

In the studies involving human subjects, the question of awareness has usually implied a concern with verbal control over behavior. Presumably, knowledge of the reinforcement contingency permits a person to direct his own behavior in a manner which will insure reinforcement. Verbal control is certainly a well-accepted fact, though the extent and conditions of such control have been in question. Problems in this area have been studied most extensively under the general topics of "set" and "instructional variables."

The present section will examine the research concerned with the development of verbal control and the range of situations in which it is effective.

Development of Verbal Control

Reacting to the meaning of words appears to be such a pervasive part of human life, that it is difficult to appreciate the fact that such verbal control must have developed gradually. Adults often appear to assume that if a child understands the meaning of words, these meanings must determine behavior. If the child fails to react appropriately to such meanings, he must be "negativistic."

That psychology is not this straightforward and rational is indicated by a very provocative series of experiments reported by the Russian psychologist Luria (1961). Luria suggests that verbal control over behavior develops gradually, and in a very complex manner. For example, if a child under the age of two years is engaged in a particular act, instructions to perform an opposite act will often simply increase the magnitude of the ongoing behavior. Luria reports a study in which a young child, who was in the process of putting on his stockings, was instructed to take the stockings off. The child did not obey the instructions; instead, he intensified the behavior involved in putting on the stockings. As shall be seen, these results are characteristic of a general problem in the development of verbal control. *Initiating* behavior, by means of instructions, develops much earlier than the ability to *inhibit* the performance of a response.

The majority of the experiments reported by Luria involved a deceptively simple situation in which children were merely required to squeeze a rubber bulb upon the onset of some stimulus, or to refrain from squeezing upon the onset (or offset) of some stimulus. In a typical study, young children were told to squeeze the rubber bulb when a light came on. Below the ages of two, the children tended to squeeze erratically whether the light was on or off, despite the fact that they understood the words. Repeated instructions not to squeeze, during the period when the light was off, resulted in either increased tendency to squeeze during this period, or at times, a generalized tendency not to squeeze even when the light was on. Luria attributes these results to the stimulus aspects of the verbal commands. The young children do not react to the instructions, "squeeze" and "don't squeeze" as distinctive commands. If they are set to squeeze, either instruction inhibits the response. From the point of view of the present book, the two-year-old child appears to have difficulty keeping two overlapping systems separate, and tends to be under the control of the strongest of the two systems.

Below two-and-a-half years of age, the child's own verbal responses (i.e., self-instructions) and his motor responses appear to generate parallel and often competing, response systems. Told to say "go," upon the presentation of a light, and then to squeeze the bulb, the typical young child in Luria's experiments had difficulty making both responses. If he said "go," he was likely not to squeeze the bulb, and if he squeezed he was likely not to make the verbal response. Like the motor response, the verbal response was very likely to occur diffusely between onsets of the light.

Luria reports that it was possible to train most two-year-olds to restrict their squeezing responses to the time when the light was on. This was done by training the child to make a specific response which took his hand from the bulb while the light was off. Thus the child was told to squeeze the bulb when the light comes on, but to place his hand on his knee when the light goes off. Gradually the distance between the hand and the bulb was reduced during the "off" period, without recurrence of the incorrect squeezing response. For the young child, at least, it appears that inhibition of a response involves the development of strong tendencies to make competing responses. From the point of view of the present book, the stimulus complex including posture, bulb in hand, etc., is very similar during the light-on and light-off conditions. Prior to Luria's training procedure for developing a specific response to the light-off condition, the child had only a single system involving the squeeze response to light-on. Due to the great stimulus overlap between light-on and light-off the squeeze response occurred to either stimulus. When the child acquired a second system, involving light-off and a hand movement away from the bulb, this second system could acquire resistance to interference from the light-on and squeeze system.

Other procedures which lead to elimination of the diffuse interstimulus squeezing responses are also described by Luria. As shall be seen, a characteristic of these procedures is that they involved establishing distinctive consequences for correct responses. In the first of these procedures, the child was told that if he squeezed the bulb when the light came on, this would turn off the light. Presumably, if the child conceptualized the task as one of turning off a light, he should not squeeze when the light is already off. In a second procedure, the child was told that if he squeezed the bulb when the light came on, a buzzer would sound. Luria reports that under these conditions, accidental responses during the inter-stimulus period completely disappeared for 50% of the children who were between 18 to 24 months of age, and for 75% of the children between 2 to 3 years of age. Details of these studies are not provided, so it is impossible to determine if this effect appeared immediately or developed with practice. Luria does report, however, that removal of these environmental contingencies (e.g., light no longer turns off upon squeeze of bulb) led to a marked return of erratic responses, with only 33% of the 2–3-year-old children continuing to coordinate bulb squeeze to light onset. Finally, a third procedure was employed in a two-light discrimination situation. The child was told to squeeze upon presentation of one light, but to refrain from squeezing upon presentation of a second light. The typical two-year-old could be trained to coordinate his responses to the stimuli by having him say "yes" or "right" after correct responses, and "no" or "wrong" after incorrect. It appears that distinctive consequences of a response can act to isolate a S-R system from interference.

Apparently, then, there are two routes to coordinating a response to a specific stimulus at this age level. One is to build up resistance to interference against the critical response (e.g., bulb squeeze) by incorporating the negative stimulus in a new system. The other is to build up the strength of the critical response to the desired stimulus by reinforcement.

This simple situation, which is also characteristic of much of the animal findings, begins to show some alteration by three years of age. At about this age, verbal responses begin to take on some characteristics which are not found in motor responses. This can be illustrated by turning again to the results reported by Luria. Told to squeeze the bulb upon presentation of the light, the three-year-old child still squeezed in a diffuse fashion even when the light was off. However, told to say "go" and then to squeeze when the light appeared, the verbal response was found to be specific to the onset of the light, and the squeeze accompanied the verbal response. Under these conditions, one trial learning of a single verbal response occurs, the type of learning which is so characteristic of adults. In Chapter 3, it was noted that conditioning and many forms of concept formation are characterized by the correct response becoming attached to irrelevant stimuli. In the two-year-old, the same problem was observed in regard to a single verbal response (e.g., "go") even when the child was specifically instructed concerning the relevant stimulus (the light). By three years of age, the child was found to be capable of isolating the relevant light-word system so that the word "go" did not intrude during the inter-stimulus interval. On the other hand, a corresponding isolation of the light-squeeze system did not occur in the absence of the verbal response to the light. Possibly this is due to the greater differentiation (see Chapters 4 and 5) of the word than the motor response. Once the word is systematically emitted by the light it proves to be an adequate stimulus to the squeeze. Again this could be due to the well-differentiated character of the word for the child. It is interesting to note that if the child was later told not to say the word "go" to the light, the diffuse inter-stimulus squeezing recurred.

These results suggest that one crucial basis for the efficiency of verbal instructions in controlling behavior is that, at some level of development in the child, the words can be more readily attached to external stimuli than can the motor responses; also the words constitute stimuli which can be readily attached to motor responses.

The role of verbal control on motor behavior is not yet at the adult level by three years of age. Luria distinguishes between two aspects of language—the motor aspect and the semantic. Between three and four years of age, the motor aspect still dominates. This is illustrated by telling a child at this age to say "squeeze twice" upon onset of the light. Despite these self-instructions, Luria reports that the child was likely to emit a single prolonged squeeze. On the other hand, if the child was told to say, "go, go" (viz., two motoric speech responses) he was likely to squeeze twice.

A similar effect was found in a choice situation described by Luria. The child was presented with two lights, the instructions being to press a lever upon onset of one of the lights, but not to press upon onset of the other. When tested under conditions in which the child remained *silent,* the response rate to the negative stimulus was 42%. This rate of incorrect response was reduced to approximately 0% by instructing the child to say "press" to the positive stimulus, but to remain silent to the negative. However, if the child said "press" to the positive stimulus and "don't press" to the negative stimulus, the tendency to respond to the negative stimulus jumped to 72%. The children were, apparently, *not* responding to the semantic content of the self-instruction, "Don't press." Luria again suggests that the children were responding to the motoric aspects of their own speech.

Both speech patterns, "press" and "don't press" were stimuli for the response.

Results of a study by Miller, Shelton, and Flavell (1970) contrast in several interesting ways with those of Luria. Like Luria (1961), Miller *et al.* (1970) found that instructing young children to verbal-ize, in a discrimination problem, produced increased errors of omis-sion and commission. Unlike Luria's results, this tendency toward increased errors persisted even to the age of 4 years 11 months. While all types of errors decreased with age, even the oldest children in the Miller *et al.* study were not helped by overt verbal control mecha-nisms. Further, there was a marked tendency, in children at all ages tested, for the motor response to *precede* the verbal. Under such circumstances it would be difficult to defend the notion that the *overt* verbalizations were controlling the motor acts. In the particu-lar situation examined by Miller, Shelton, and Flavell, it appears that the verbal and motor systems tended to be parallel and compet-ing at all age levels tested. On the other hand, it must be pointed out that the children in this study *were* behaving under *some* type of verbal control, since children told to squeeze a bulb to one color light and not to squeeze to a second color were relatively accurate in performing the motor responses *as long as they were not asked to verbalize these instructions aloud.*

Presumably, the differences between the results reported by Luria and those reported by Miller *et al.*, are due to differences in proce-dure. The nature of these procedural differences is unknown since Luria's reports of his studies are extremely sketchy. Indeed, the Miller *et al.* study was originally conceived of as a replication of Luria's work.

Birch (1966) studied the effect of verbal control over behavior in children as a function of time after a verbal instruction. The chil-dren were instructed to press a lever and hold it down. All the children, ranging from two to seven years of age, pressed the lever after the initial instruction, though latency of response was sig-nificantly longer for younger than for older children. However, the younger children stopped responding sooner than the older, and additional verbal commands to continue pressing were less effective for younger children. Since all the children performed the response initially, Birch concludes that the instructions were adequately understood at all age levels and that the subsequent differences in performance must be attributed to motivational factors. This is not necessarily the case. It appears as reasonable to assume that *S-R* systems of younger children are less resistant to interference than the systems of older children. Such a conclusion would fit much of the Luria data, too.

Verbal Control of Instrumental Behavior

Verbal control over many types of responses is clearly established in adults. A demonstration of the influence of verbal control over behavior is provided by Lewin who pitted verbal control against habit. Lewin, in a study described by Hilgard (1956), presented pairs of nonsense syllables repeatedly for hundreds of trials, the subject always saying the second syllable after presentation of the first. He then told his subjects not to give the response upon presentation of the stimulus, and found they could inhibit the learned behavior. Jenkins (1959) reports corroborating data from a free association study. When subjects were presented words and asked to give their first association to each, a large number of the responses were infrequent associates to the stimuli. Instructing subjects to give the most common response to each word increased the frequent associates without altering the reaction time of the responses.

The degree of verbal control over behavior is seen in a concept attainment study by Dulany and O'Connell (1963). Subjects were presented with cards which varied in a great number of dimensions and were required to sort these two into two categories. On each trial, upon being presented each card, but before actually placing it in a category, each subject was requested to verbalize his hypothesis concerning the basis of sorting. Of 3,419 trials, subjects actually placed the card in conformity with their stated hypothesis on 3,408 trials, and performed in a manner inconsistent with their stated hypothesis on only 11 trials. In other words, on only about three trials in a thousand did subjects not behave as they said they would. Of course, as one would expect, the effectiveness of such self-instructions decreases as the self-instruction becomes more complex and the time permitted for the response is shortened (Schwartz, 1966a).

Verbal Control and Problem Solving

We have seen that human beings gradually develop the ability to obey instructions, either their own or those of others, so that adults make relatively few errors in this respect. However, the fact that a subject responds to his own verbal command in a problem-solving situation does not, *a priori,* guarantee that these verbal commands will lead to faster solution of the problem.

First, we must distinguish between continuous emission of hypotheses as opposed to asking the subject to verbalize a hypothesis at one specific point in time. Both Phelan (1965) and Rommetviet and Kvales (1965*a*) present data which suggests that requesting a hypothesis may be detrimental if it occurs after a relatively long series of trials involving no such verbalization. This appears to occur if the subjects have been using some non-verbalizable cues which lead to better than chance performances, while the verbalized guess at the solution is either uncorrelated or negatively correlated with the basis for solution.

Some facilitation in performance is found by Dulany and O'Connell (1963) for subjects who were instructed to emit hypotheses on every trial as opposed to those who were not. The task, described previously in this chapter, involved sorting cards containing many cue dimensions. Cards were to be sorted on the basis of one versus more than one object portrayed on the card. Subjects were told, after each trial, whether they had placed the card correctly. While number of subjects who solved the problem was not significantly different for the two conditions (about 70% of the subjects reached criterion), for the subjects who solved the problem, those instructed to emit hypotheses on every trial reached criterion in a mean of 49 trials; those who were not so instructed required a mean of 104.9 trials to reach criterion. A similar study by Verplanck and Oskamp, summarized by Dulany and O'Connell (1963), found corresponding results, though the differences between groups were not quite as large.

Little systematic work has been done to explore the efficiency of hypothesis formation. Even less has been done to investigate the mechanisms which might mediate such effects. However, some possibilities appear reasonably promising.

1. STIMULUS ISOLATION. Most concept attainment problems are nothing more than complex discrimination problems. Subjects are presented with stimuli that vary in a number of dimensions. The task requirement is that of finding which dimension (or set of dimensions) is relevant, and which values of the dimension require the specific responses which are scored as correct. For example, subjects may be presented with cards containing one or more pictures of objects, the correct responses being *A* for even numbers of objects on a card, *B* for odd numbers of objects. The subject must learn that

color is irrelevant, whether the objects are animate or inanimate is irrelevant, size of the stimuli is irrelevant, only number of objects is crucial. Since all these dimensions vary randomly, any value of any irrelevant dimension will be associated with a critical value of a relevant dimension on some trials. For example, saying A to three animate objects will be rewarded on some trials, strengthening the tendency to say A to animate objects.

One function of verbal hypotheses could be that of isolating a single dimension, permitting the subject to ignore other dimensions. Thus if the subject tests the hypothesis that animate-inanimate is the correct dimension, correlated strengthening of other dimensions can be reduced. Once the verbal responses of "animate" and "inanimate" have been extinguished through hypothesis testing, they may interfere less with responses to other dimensions. There is some tentative evidence for this general possible mechanism. In this chapter we have seen that there is reasonably good evidence that hypothesis testing prevents the automatic reinforcement of the correct response class. As Silver (1967) has shown, when hypothesis testing can be eliminated, the operation of reinforcement can occur in subjects who are unaware of the reinforcement contingency. This strongly suggests that verbal hypotheses may isolate the dimensions which can be influenced by reinforcement.

2. ABSTRACTION OF STIMULI. If the subject verbalizes a dimension of *odd-even,* any occurrence of an odd number of objects will elicit the response *"odd."* This abstraction will be reinforced frequently, whereas any specific odd number will be reinforced much less frequently. In addition, given an instance which contains an odd number not previously encountered in the experiment, the subject still emits the same abstract response, *"odd."* Thus, in addition to permitting the subject to disregard irrelevant dimensions, verbal hypotheses may permit him to give a single, consistent, abstract response to many different instances of a given dimensional value.

3. DIFFERENTIATION OF STIMULI. Since words are highly differentiated, verbal hypotheses can probably be remembered more readily after being attached to stimulus instances.

4. STRATEGY DEVELOPMENT. Bruner, Goodnow, and Austin (1956) have examined various strategies of testing instances in relation to the structure of the correct response whether this response must be conjunctive, disjunctive, etc. This study shows that it may be advantageous to have a verbal plan of the order in which hypotheses are tested. Here the subject follows a set of self-instructions (e.g., test

dimension A, keeping B constant, etc.). The fact that such verbal orders are easily remembered is no doubt an important factor in solving such problems.

Conditioning

Conditioned responses are traditionally thought of as largely beyond verbal control. This is particularly true of those classes of conditioned responses in which the subject can not modify the responses prior to conditioning: *GSR*, heart rate, and other physiological responses fall into this category. Other responses which have been conditioned are under greater verbal control prior to conditioning. Eyelid and finger withdrawal are examples of this type of response. Prior to pairing a *CS* to a puff of air to the eye, a subject can certainly blink upon instruction.

VOLUNTARY VERSUS INVOLUNTARY RESPONSE. Eyelid conditioning is particularly interesting because many experimenters, following Spence and Ross (1959), have distinguished between voluntary and involuntary blinks in terms of the response patterns of the blinks. Some responses occur with very short latency after the presentation of the *CS*, and have a sharp onset. This is the pattern which can be obtained when the subject is simply told to blink. The involuntary conditioned response, on the other hand, has a longer latency and more gradual onset. Subjects who, during conditioning, give voluntary patterns, typically jump to high levels of conditioning in very few trials, while subjects who emit the involuntary conditioned response show more gradual increments. The difference in response patterns leads to the speculation that the voluntary response patterns may be mediated at a cortical level, while the involuntary conditioned response is autonomically mediated. Despite any possible differences in physiological loci, the two types of response often show parallel effects to manipulations of independent variables. For example, Hartman and Grant (1962) compared voluntary and involuntary conditioning in a discrimination conditioning situation (a positive *CS* always followed by the *UCS*, a negative *CS* never followed by the *UCS*). The general level of response was greater for the voluntary than the true conditioning groups; however, the relationship between responses to the two stimuli was the same; and conditions which led to a greater discrimination between positive and negative stimuli for one group had a corresponding effect on the other. In addition, Gormezano and Moore (1962) found that manipulating UCS intensity produced parallel effects in voluntary and involuntary conditioning groups.

On the other hand, some studies have found marked discrepancies between conditioning of voluntary and involuntary CRs. A particularly interesting example of such a difference occurs in a differential eyeblink conditioning study by Cerekwicki, Grant and Porter (1968) which suggests that the voluntary CRs may be mediated in higher brain centers than the involuntary CRs. The procedure in this study consisted of presenting a *single* word to the subject on each trial. If the word was a positive stimulus $(S+)$ it was followed by a puff to the eye; if the word was a negative stimulus $(S-)$ it was not followed by a puff. The critical manipulation was the number of words from a concept category used as $S+$ or $S-$: the $S+$'s might be one, two, three, or four different words from one concept category, while the $S-$'s were a corresponding number of words from a different category. For subjects emitting CRs of the voluntary form, rate of differential conditioning was successively better as number of different words in the $S+$ and $S-$ increased. Clearly, this could only happen if these subjects were reacting to the common meaning of the $S+$ and $S-$ concepts. Results for subjects emitting CRs of the involuntary form were quite different. For these subjects, differential conditioning was best when only a single word was used as $S+$ and a different word as $S-$.

While writers at times appear to assume that voluntary CRs are more characteristic of human conditioning while involuntary CRs are more characteristic of lower organisms, Kimble (1961) presents data which seriously challenge this. Again, the data come from eyelid conditioning where one can, to some extent, distinguish between the two. Characteristically, Kimble reports, the conditioned blink response in dogs and monkeys resembles the voluntary, rather than the involuntary CR. The same appears to be true of human infants. The occurrence of the involuntary type of response in adult human subjects could be due to the fact that such subjects give themselves instructions *not* to make the voluntary response. Indeed, Hilgard (1938) interprets evidence concerning the effects of instructions on conditioning as indicating that the eyeblink is normally conditioned in the presence of inhibitory sets.

THE ROLE OF INSTRUCTIONS ON CONDITIONING. Instructions hava a powerful effect on the performance of the conditioned response, but do not completely control such performance. Hilgard and Humphrey's (1938) report on an eyelid conditioning study in which subjects were first given 100% reinforcement to an $S+$ in Day 1. Days 2 and 3 involved the randon presentation of the $S+$ and a second stimulus, $S-$, which was never followed by the UCS. Days 2 and 3 involved different instructions for various subgroups of subjects. One group was told to respond to the $S+$ but not the $S-$ stimulus. Here responses to the $S+$ occurred on 90% of the trials. A second group was instructed to *refrain* from responding to *either* stimulus. Under these conditions, subjects dropped to only 55% response upon presentation of the $S+$. In other words, some verbal control was exhibited, but it was not nearly perfect. Finally, a third group was instructed to refrain from responding to the $S+$, but to respond to the $S-$. Under these conditions of response competition between the two stimuli, subjects responded on 71% of the positive stimulus presentations. This is almost exactly the rate of responses for a group given *no* instructions concerning responding. In other words, given instructions to respond to *some* stimulus, verbal inhibition of the conditioned response was relatively difficult.

Kimble (1961) describes an unpublished doctoral dissertation by Miller which provides further evidence concerning the effect of instructions on CR suppression. The eyeblink was conditioned to a light. One group was told that the light would be followed by a puff of air to the eye, with no special instructions about responding. This group emitted conditioned responses on 44% of the trials. Another group was told not to wink before feeling the puff. This group was apparently not able to completely suppress the response, and gave conditioned responses on 26% of the trials.

Norris and Grant (1948) also instructed their subjects, under one set of conditions, not to wink before onset of the UCS. The percentage of conditioned responses increased with trials from about 0% on trials 1–5 to about 15% on trials 41–45. In comparison, a group told not to interfere with their natural reactions to the stimuli rose to about 85% response.

In general, these studies show that while instructions can modify the rate of conditioned response, the conditioned response is not under complete verbal control.

Spence (1966) has shown that the rapid extinction of eyelid conditioning, upon cessation of UCS presentations, is apparently due to self-instruction. When the conditioning task is masked as a probability learning task, with the CS and UCS described as "distractors," extinction is very slow.

A study by Wickens (1938) on conditioning of finger withdrawal is very interesting in regard to verbal control over extinction. Subjects were trained to raise a finger upon presentation of a *CS*, using shock as the *UCS*. Most subjects extinguished rapidly upon cessation of shock. Some, however, persisted in responding for many trials. Wickens describes betting one of the slow extinguisher a dollar that he could not refrain from responding. Despite the fact that making the response led to losing the bet, the subject could not refrain from responding.

THE ROLE OF REINFORCEMENT:
A FINAL APPRAISAL

A great number of psychologists have assumed that reinforcement is a critical condition for most, if not all, learning (e.g., Thorndike, 1932; Hull, 1943; Skinner, 1938). Others have suggested that reinforcement is primarily a condition which determines whether previously learned behavior will be *manifested* by the organism; learning, *per se*, does not require reinforcement (e.g., Tolman, 1932; Spence, 1956). This controversy has resulted in tremendous amounts of research. The studies of verbal operant conditioning, cited in this chapter, are only another platform for the enactment of this continuing conflict.

From this point of view, it is interesting to note that the issue of reinforcement was hardly mentioned in the first nine chapters of the present book. The absence of this issue was not a strained piece of perversity on the part of the present writer. Reinforcement is simply not a very relevant issue for most of human learning. Indeed, one must be very ingenious to find a possible source of reinforcement in most studies of short-term memory, paired-associates learning, free-recall learning, etc., etc. Such ingenuity has, in fact, been expended. For the most part it has involved proposing new sets of operational definitions for reinforcement. And, for the most part, these definitions have been so general as to contribute nothing to our capability for predicting when learning would be effective and when it would not. Notions of "self-reinforcement" fall into this category.

Why have so many psychologists insisted on the necessity for reinforcement as a condition for learning? It is the writer's opinion that this instance comes largely from the early emphasis on the study of animal learning. If a psychologist wishes to study the variables relevant to the manner in which a white rat learns a given response, the psychologist must first somehow inveigle the animal into making the response, and then somehow try to make him repeat the response again. How better to do this then by feeding the animal when he makes the response? Skinner (1938), in fact, lures the animal into making the bar-press response by smearing the bar with food. When the animal investigates the food, he accidentally presses the bar; this press is followed immediately by dropping a food pellet to the animal. Skinner refers to this smearing of the bar with food as "shaping" the response.

As other writers have pointed out before, the use of food as a reward is one of the few ways in which we can communicate with most animals concerning what we wish them to learn. Use of human subjects expands our means of communication with our subjects.

The experiments considered in this chapter, and in the one previous, show that reinforcement has little or no effect on memory functions. Silver (1967), for example, found that memory for items was not differentially affected by the verbal reinforcements administered *when subjects thought they were being reinforced for speed of response.* On the other hand, there is some evidence to suggest that reinforcement will lead to an increase in the overt repetition of certain responses, even though the person is unaware that these are the responses which are leading to the reinforcements. In short, then, the human learning evidence appears to be consistent with the positions taken by Tolman (1932) and Spence (1956); Reinforcement is not necessary for learning; however, reinforcement does have an effect on the circumstances under which the person performs the learned response.

CONCLUSIONS

In the present chapter we concentrated on the effects of awareness on *performance,* rather than on learning. We saw that in concept attainment tasks, and in verbal operant tasks that contained large aspects of concept attainment, reinforcement can at times modify behavior of subjects who are not aware of the contingency between their behavior and the reinforcement. However, even when this occurs, the effect appears to be relatively weak.

Does this suggest that failure to show behavior modifications, on the part of unaware subjects in concept attainment and verbal operant conditioning studies, is due to the lack of awareness, *per se?* The data suggest that the answer to this question is, "No." In these studies, it appears that the hypothesis testing behavior, engaged in by the subject in attempting to solve the problem (i.e., in an attempt to "become aware" of the reinforcement contingency) *interferes* with the emergence of relevant behavior modification.

We have seen that a great deal of behavior, in the situations examined, is under the control of verbal processes. This appears to account for the relatively low rate of operant behavior even in aware subjects; despite knowing the basis of reinforcement, many of these subjects simply restrict emission of the responses which the experimenter is trying to elicit.

12 | Effects of Stress
on Learning and Thinking

PRECIS

Stress and anxiety are powerful factors in determining human behavior. Because of this, they have been the focus of a great deal of experimental attention. However, in the laboratory at least, stress has been
conceptualized within the unifactor learning position. The emphasis has
been on stress as a drive state (e.g., a factor that multiplies the strength
of existing habits) and on stress as producing distinctive stimuli which
may become associated with distinctive responses.

The general position, taken in the present book, permits consideration
of a broader set of variables. In the present book, we have distinguished
four basic elements that constitute the learned cognitive system. Of these
four, the evidence to be reviewed suggests that the boundary strength of
the cognitive system is the most sensitive to stress: Stress breaks down
the boundary strength of cognitive systems. Thus, in situations involving
the competition between cognitive systems, stress permits the disruption
of the weaker systems.

Secondly, in previous chapters, we have distinguished between learning
and thinking and have shown how certain variables of thinking (e.g.,
strategy behavior) may operate to facilitate learning. In the present chapter, we shall see that one of the ways in which stress affects learning
appears to be by disrupting strategy behavior. Therefore, concept problems
and learning, involving recoding of material to facilitate recall or involving
the development of cues for retrieval, are particularly hard hit by stress.
This factor also appears to be the basis for the relationship between
attitudes and memory, as we shall see when we examine the research
on attitudes.

The data also show strong individual differences in the reactions to
stress. For example, persons with *low* manifest anxiety scores tend to
show *marked deterioration* in performance under condition of *pain* as
stress, while high-anxious persons are relatively less affected. On the other
hand, *high*-anxious persons react poorly under conditions of *failure* or
threat of failure, while low-anxious persons are less affected by this
stressor.

Finally, the evidence in total is extremely negative with regard to the
position that stress is basically a drive variable. The Hullian position that
stress acts as drive in the $H \times D$ formulation finds very little support in
the learning data.

DEMONSTRATION EXPERIMENT

The Problem

This is a one trial learning study. You will read each of the pairs below, once, then you will be shown the stimuli and will try to recall the response that goes with each stimulus. Pronounce each word distinctly during the learning trial.

BREAD—smile PAINTER—funeral
ORCHID—vomit TROUT—dance
SHIRT—fling   SAUCER—whore

Now cover the learning materials, above, with one hand while you attempt to give the response that belong with each of the stimuli presented below.

TROUT   BREAD
SAUCER PAINTER
ORCHID SHIRT

Explanation

First, it should be noted that we can identify two loci for stress. Stress can be *external* to the system being learned—such as when electric shock is presented during the learning of paired associates—and we are concerned with the manner in which these pairs are learned under these conditions. Or, stress can be *internal* to the system being learned, in which case we may study memory for stress-inducing material. To the extent that words like *vomit, funeral,* and *whore* induce stress, the demonstration above represents an example of stress which is internal to a cognitive system.

Later in this chapter, we shall see that such words did appear to have stressful consequences for groups of college students. This stress had no effect on *learning* rate, when other factors were carefully controlled; however, the stress *did* disrupt later concept acquisition for concepts such as flowers, articles of clothing, or dishes, which had been associated with stressful responses, as compared with concepts which had been associated with neutral responses, in a carefully counterbalanced study.

THE NATURE OF STRESS

What Is Stress?

The term *stress* has been used in a number of ways in psychology. Without going into these various usages in detail, an attempt will be made to delimit the use of the term in the present chapter.

In a preoperational sense, *stress refers to the consequences of noxious stimulation.*

What types of stimulation are noxious? The most straightforward example, perhaps, is a strong electric shock. Shock excites the pain receptors and is therefore a noxious stimulus. However, physical pain has not been the critical factor necessary for categorizing situations as stressful. Psychologists have considered the following as stressful, noxious stimuli:

Telling a subject that he has performed poorly (e.g., failed an I.Q. test).

Pacing: Forcing a subject to respond at such a fast rate that he is likely to make many errors.

Telling a subject that a difficult task which he is performing is a measure of intelligence.

Asking a subject to handle a dead rat (or, in one experiment, asking the subject to decapitate a dead rat).

Presenting a subject with words (or pictures) concerned with death, crude sexual referents, or crude toilet referents.

What do these have in common? Do they really all tap a common psychological variable? Most people feel that they do. And, indeed, we shall see that most of these variables have parallel effects on performance.

RESPONSE DEFINITIONS OF STRESS. At a minimum, most psychologists have considered stress as involving feelings of unpleasantness. Most have also insisted that fear or anxiety must also be involved. Operational definitions of "noxious," "unpleasant," "fear," or "anxiety" are not completely straightforward. Response definitions such as, "a stimulus is noxious if the subject avoids it," runs into difficulty even with pain stimulation, since masochists may actually seek electric shock (e.g., Brown, 1965). Similarly, a person may parachute from an airplane (i.e., show approach behavior toward jumping) despite reports of intense fear (e.g., Epstein and Fenz, 1962). Thus approach behavior can be inconsistent with other indices or criteria of stress.

TENTATIVE CRITERIA. In the present chapter, we shall resolve the problem of defining stress by taking a purely pragmatic course. We shall consider a person to be in a state of stress, if he is presented with stimuli that produce or strongly threaten pain, physical injury, or failure; and stimuli that are associated with strong taboos in the person's culture.

Avoidable versus Nonavoidable Stress

At this point, a distinction must be made between the effects of stress, *per se,* and the effects of escape or avoidance of stress. People often are very adept at learning specific responses which lead to escape or avoidance of noxious stimulation. Under these circumstances, stress *reduction* is presumably the crucial variable, and it tends to operate as an incentive or reinforcer. This specific issue will be touched upon only briefly in the present chapter. This is to be contrasted with the situation in which the person must engage in some task, following the introduction of stress, and his behavior is not directly relevant to the removal of the stress stimulation. Here, presumably, stress initiates a general internal *state* which influences behavior. Such state variables will constitute the primary emphasis of this chapter.

Many of the studies to be considered are confounded by the possibility of stress avoidance, and it is not always easy (or possible) to parcel out this variable. This problem arises, for example, when a subject is informed that he has performed poorly on a task (e.g., failed an I.Q. test), and then is asked to work on a second, similar task. Failure instructions can be considered a noxious, stress stimulus. This subject may attempt to avoid further stress by working harder on the second task. Thus, performance on such a second task must be evaluated with caution. Such considerations are important and, it will be seen, go a long way in permitting more consistent interpretations of the data.

The Hullian Theory of Stress

Research and thinking about stress and its effect on behavior, over the past 30 years, have been dominated by the theory proposed by C. L. Hull (1943) and, more recently, by Spence's extension of the Hullian theory (e.g., Spence, 1958; Spence and Spence, 1966).

Hull (1943) assumed that noxious stimulation has drive properties. Thus the fundamental formulation relating drive (D) to habit strength (H), in the Hullian system, becomes applicable:

$$\text{Performance} = f\ (D \times H).$$

From this, one would expect that stress should facilitate performance. And, indeed, in an early study Taylor (1951) showed that high-anxious subjects conditioned faster than low-anxious subjects. In this study, anxiety was measured by means of a paper and pencil test consisting of a set of items drawn, by Taylor, from the Minnesota Multiphasic Personality Inventory (MMPI); eyelid conditioning was the measure of performance.

The prediction that anxiety should facilitate performance soon proved too simple, since, in many situations, the high-anxious subjects learned *more poorly* than the low-anxious. In order to account for this, Spence suggested that anxiety would be detrimental to performance when the *H* for the *correct* response, in a task, is *lower* than the *H* for the *incorrect* response to the same stimulus. This follows directly from the Hullian formulation. Since *D* multiplies all existing *H*'s, it will increase the relative dominance of whichever *H* is already dominant. Thus, if the incorrect response is dominant, that dominance will be increased. In conditioning, presumably, the *correct* response is the one which is dominant, and therefore anxiety would be expected to facilitate conditioning performance.

Finally, Hull assumed that drives produce distinctive stimuli (S_D). Spence and Spence (1966) have suggested that in some cases such distinctive stimuli, arising from anxiety or stress, may elicit responses which interfere with performance on an experimental task. This notion is, in some ways, an unfortunate addition to the theory, since there appears to be no way of specifying before hand whether competing responses will be elicited by the S_D. Thus, if performance decrements occur for anxious subjects in situations where the theory might otherwise predict facilitation, the S_D can always be invoked to rationalize the data.

A number of writers (e.g., Castaneda, 1956; Chiles, 1958) have extended the Spence theory to noxious stimulation *per se,* predicting that stress (e.g., shock or pacing) will facilitate performance when the correct response is dominant and will be detrimental to performance when an incorrect response is dominant. Much of the research to be examined was originally designed to test this, or related predictions.

SHOCK AS STRESS

Few readers will be surprised to learn that painful electric shock, when used as a stressor, tends to produce systematic decrements in verbal learning and concept attainment. More interesting is the fact that such decrements do not always occur, and, indeed, there is evidence to suggest that under certain conditions verbal learning may actually be facilitated by shock. In addition to examining the circumstances in which shock modifies performance, the succeeding sections will also examine the interaction between shock and certain personality variables.

Verbal Learning

THE EFFECT OF SHOCK ON LEARNING NONSENSE SYLLABLES.   The most consistent effects of shock-induced stress on verbal learning have been found in studies using nonsense syllable materials—this effect is consistently disruptive.

Four studies employing nonsense syllables have been reported in which *making the correct response permitted neither escape nor avoidance of shock*. In three of these, shock produced marked decrements in performance (Deese, Lazarus, and Keenan, 1953; Lazarus and Longo, 1953; Reece, 1954). Only one study, Lazarus, Deese, and Hamilton (1954) found essentially no difference in learning between nonshocked subjects and subjects who received nonavoidable shock during learning. It might be noted that the material in this study was particularly difficult to learn (viz., nonsense syllables with very great intra-list similarity). Even the nonshocked subjects showed very little acquisition.

SHOCK AND THE LEARNING OF MEANINGFUL MATERIALS.   Turning to studies employing meaningful words, we find that the effects of shock are much more erratic. At times shock has been found to produce decrements; at times it has had no effect; and one study has found that shock actually resulted in *facilitated* performance.

Let us first consider the situations in which shock has been found to produce decrements in verbal learning of meaningful words. On the basis of the Hullian drive notion, we would expect such decrements to occur when the correct response was, for some reason, weaker than the incorrect responses. This is certainly not the case in any consistent manner. Besch (1959), for example, reports two paired-associates experiments. In the first of these, intra-pair associations were high (viz., each stimulus and its response were related adjectives), while between pair associations were low. Under these conditions, the dominant response to each stimulus was presumably the correct one, rather than one of the other responses in the list. Therefore, the $H \times D$ formulation would lead one to expect superior performance by the shocked subjects. Instead, the shocked subjects performed significantly more poorly than the nonshocked on this material. (Note that shock was administered *between* trials, so subjects were not attempting to respond while actually being shocked.)

A second experiment, reported by Besch in the same paper, involved some pairs which were highly associated S-R terms and some in which the stimuli and their responses were not highly related. Shocked subjects performed more poorly than nonshocked on both types of materials, though the latter type produced larger decrements than the former.

Lee (1961) used a relatively complex design in which some of her data were consistent with the $H \times D$ formulation while others were not. In Lee's study, subjects learned two paired-associates lists successively, the relationships between these two lists determining whether the correct response was dominant or weak. For example, some of the List 2 pairs consisted of a re-pairing of the stimuli and responses of List 1 (viz., Response 1, which had been learned to Stimulus 1 on the first list was made the correct response to Stimulus 2 during the second list). This is a condition in which the incorrect response to a stimulus is stronger than the correct response at the onset of List 2 learning. Shock was administered between Lists 1 and 2; thus we would expect, on the basis of the Hullian formulation, that shocked subjects should perform more poorly than nonshocked on these pairs. Lee's results were consistent with this prediction.

In another condition in Lee's study, the pairs of List 2 were identical to those of List 1. Here the $H \times D$ formulation would presumably predict superior performance by the shocked subjects, since in List 2 the dominant response to each stimulus was correct. Shocked and nonshocked subjects performed equally well on these materials. Nor did shock produce a consistent effect, during List 2, for those pairs which had not previously occurred on List 1.

Despite the use of relatively large groups of subjects, a study by Saltz (1950) also failed to obtain a difference between shocked and nonshocked subjects in a paired-associates task involving the learning of meaningful words. This study differed from those of Besch (1959) and Lee (1961) in that shock was presented on every trial, *while* the subjects were attempting to anticipate the correct response. Thus shock was potentially both a stressor and a distractor. Subjects can, apparently, adapt surprisingly well under rather adverse conditions.

Only one study, that of Chiles (1958), reported an *increment* in performance with shock. Interestingly enough, from the point of view of Hullian theory, this increment occurred both when the correct response was dominant to its stimulus and when an *incorrect* was dominant.

Since the results of the Chiles study are potentially important, and the procedure is rather unique, we shall describe the experiment briefly. Each subject was presented two responses with each stimulus. The subject was required to choose the one response which he thought was correct. Further, one of these responses was related to the stimulus, the other was not. For half the items, the related word was the correct response; for the other half, the unrelated word was correct. Thus, in Chiles's study the dominant response was correct for some stimuli and incorrect for other stimuli. From the $H \times D$ formulation, one would predict that shock should produce superior performance on the former pairs and inferior performance on the latter. Instead, shock produced significantly *superior* performance for both types of materials, effects being of about equal magnitude.

Concept Performance and Shock

Relatively little research relating concept attainment to stress is reported in the literature. In general, across the various stressors examined, we shall see that stress appears to be more disruptive for concept attainment than for rote learning.

Turning specifically to shock as stressor during concept attainment, Saltz and Riach (1961) report one of the few relevant studies. This study was designed to test the hypothesis that stress breaks down the boundaries between competing systems.

To test this hypothesis, subjects were first trained to distinguish two concepts and then were shocked. The hypothesis that stress leads to a breakdown in boundary strength generated the prediction that concept attainment would be more disrupted by shock if the concepts to be distinguished had many overlapping features than if they had none.

In this study, the concepts were patterns of 3 lights on a panel of 12 lights. On each trial the subjects were shown a pattern of lights and asked to indicate whether it was an instance of Concept *A* or Concept *B*. In the *Nonoverlap* condition, none of the lights used to construct an instance of Concept *A* was ever used to make an instance of Concept *B*, and *vice versa*. In the *Overlap* condition, on the other hand, any of the 12 lights might occur in either the Concept *A* or the Concept *B* pattern.

Subjects were run to a criterion of a minimum of 9 correct responses per block of 12 trials over 2 blocks of trials. Then half the subjects in each condition were shocked 4 times in the next block of 12 trials, and performance over this block of trials was measured.

Results show that, over all subjects, shock had a significantly disruptive effect on concept attainment. Figure 12–1 illustrates the pattern of this effect over the various conditions of the experiment.

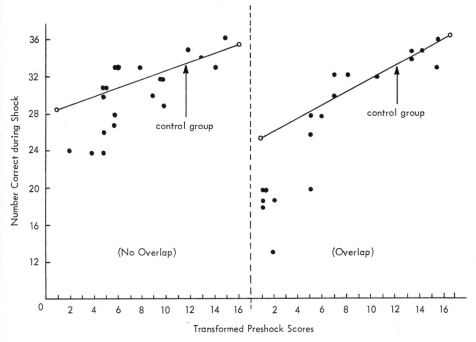

FIGURE 12–1. Effects of Shock on Concept Performance, Plotted as a Function of Pre-Shock Performance. The dots represent the scores of individual subjects after shock. The solid lines represent the scores of the nonshocked control subjects. (Adapted from Saltz and Riach, 1961. Reproduced with permission of the American Psychological Association.)

The solid lines represent the post-criterion performance of the non-shocked control groups in each condition. The dots represent the post-criterion performance of the individual, shocked subjects. In this study, since the subjects were trained to a moderate performance criterion, some subjects exceeded the criterion (e.g., gave 9 correct on 1 criterion block of trials, and 12 correct on the next). The abscissa is an index of the extent to which subjects exceeded the criterion. Presumably, the greater the number of correct responses during the criterion blocks, the greater the resistance to interference developed by a subject.

Comparing shocked and nonshocked subjects, the figure shows that shock produced sizable amounts of disruption in performance for low-criterion subjects. High-criterion subjects exhibited little disruption. Further, the disruption for low-criterion subjects was much greater in the Overlap than in the Nonoverlap condition. Over all subjects, shock was significantly disruptive. The difference between disruptive effects for the Overlap and the Nonoverlap conditions was also significant for the low-criterion subjects.

The results suggest that the degree of disruption accompanying shock is inversely related to the degree of pre-shock resistance to interference developed between relevant competing systems.

Finally, it should be noted that all subjects in this study were trained to the point where the strength of correct responses should be greater than the strength of incorrect responses. From the Hullian $H \times D$ formulation, therefore, increased noxious stimulation should facilitate performance. There was no indication of such a tendency in the data.

Act Regression in Animals

A related set of issues has been studied in animals under the topic heading of "act regression." These studies have been concerned with the fact that, if animals learn two competing responses successively and then are shocked, animals often revert to the first of the responses.

Typically, in such studies, the animals are first trained to run to one arm of a T-maze for food. The food is then placed in the *opposite* arm of the maze so that the first response extinguishes and the animals learn a new response. Electric shock is then introduced at the choice point.

Hamilton and Krechevsky (1933), Kleemeier (1942), Sanders (1937), Martin (1940), and others, have shown that shock tends to disrupt the ongoing (viz., second learned) response, and leads to a "regression" to the first learned response.

Two of these studies are particularly interesting in that they show that the degree of regression is related to the relative amount of pre-shock practice on each of the competing responses (Kleemeier, 1942; Martin, 1940). These results appear to be consistent with the Saltz and Riach (1961) interpretation of the effects of shock on competing systems. *Shock appears to break down the resistance to interference of competing systems, permitting the recurrence of strong, competing responses.*

The Interaction between Shock and Trait-Anxiety

Five of the studies cited above also compared subjects on some personality measure of anxiety. Three of these employed the Taylor Manifest Anxiety Scale; two used the Winnie Scale of Anxiety. Both of these scales are based on items from the MMPI, and the two scales correlate highly.

Taken as a whole, these studies fail to support the Hullian theory of anxiety that has been proposed by Taylor (1956), Spence (1958), and Spence and Spence (1966). Instead, these data strongly suggest that *low-anxious subjects are more susceptible to disruption of learning under conditions of pain or threat of bodily injury than are high-anxious subjects.* (On the other hand, as we shall see in a later section, *high-anxious subjects* are more susceptible to disruption under conditions of *failure* or threat of failure.) Thus, instead of being a drive, as suggested by the Hullian formulation, anxiety appears to be a personality variable that indicates the *type of stressor* to which a person may be susceptible.

Let us now examine the data on which the above conclusions were based.

THE DISRUPTION OF LEARNING BY LOW-ANXIOUS SUBJECTS UNDER CONDITIONS OF SHOCK. Besch (1959) reports data from two experiments. Both are consistent in showing that the low-anxious subjects who were shocked performed more poorly than any other group. In both experiments, this represents a drop in performance compared to the low-anxious subjects who were not shocked. This effect is particularly interesting in her second experiment. Here, under nonshocked conditions the low-anxious were superior to the high-anxious. Under shocked conditions there was a sharp reversal and the low-anxious performed much more *poorly* than the high-anxious. Thus, while shock was detrimental to all groups, its effect was greatest for low-anxious subjects.

Deese, Lazarus, and Keenan (1953) report that nonavoidable shock produced a moderate drop in performance for high-anxious subjects; it produced a sizable drop for low-anxious subjects.

Lee (1961), it will be recalled, had subjects learn two lists successively. On List 2, some of the pairs were new; some were pairs that had appeared previousy in List 1 (i.e., during the learning of List 2, the correct responses were dominant for these pairs); and some were pairs which involved re-pairing of *S-R* items from List 1 (i.e., incorrect responses were dominant). On each of these three types of materials, the *low-anxious* subjects who were *shocked* performed *more poorly* than any other group.

Chiles (1958), in the only verbal learning study which found facilitation due to nonavoidable shock, reports that this facilitation was due primarily to the performance of the *high*-anxious subjects. Low-anxious subjects did not show a consistent facilitation with shock. Again, as in Besch (1959), the low-anxious were superior to the high-anxious under nonshocked conditions, but there was a sharp reversal under shocked conditions.

Only one study, Lazarus, Deese, and Hamilton (1954) failed to show a relative drop in performance for low-anxious subjects under shock. This, it will be remembered, was the one study employing nonsense syllables which failed to show any effect due to shock.

HIGH-ANXIOUS SUBJECTS UNDER SHOCK. We saw in the section above that the results for the low-anxious subjects under shock do not support the Hullian $H \times D$ formulation. The same is true for the high-anxious subjects. Only the data reported by Lee (1961) conform to that theory. Lee found that high-anxious subjects performed better under shock than nonshock conditions when the dominant response was correct and more poorly under shock when the incorrect response was dominant. On the other hand, Besch (1959) found that shock produced *decrements* in the performance of high-anxious subjects when the correct response was dominant. And Chiles (1958) found that high-anxious subjects who were shocked showed equal amounts of facilitation under both conditions, dominant responses correct and dominant responses incorrect.

ANXIETY AND EYELID CONDITIONING. The new perspective on anxiety and pain, suggested in the pages above, permits us to re-examine some of the early research on anxiety that launched the Taylor-Spence theory of anxiety.

In the first of the studies employing the Manifest Anxiety Scale, Taylor (1951) predicted that high-anxious subjects should exhibit faster eyelid conditioning than low-anxious subjects. This is indeed what she found. She interpreted her data as indicating that anxiety is a drive state, that high-anxious subjects are high-drive subjects, and that their faster conditioning was due to their higher D level, in the $H \times D$ formulation, than that of the low-anxious subjects.

We are now able to suggest a different interpretation of the Taylor (1951) data. We have seen that low-anxious subjects show disruption of learning under conditions of physical pain. Note that eyelid conditioning is a defensive reaction to a blow to the eye. The crucial interpretation of Taylor's data may be that *low-anxious perform poorly* under these conditions, not that high-anxious perform well.

It should also be noted that, consistent with the present interpretation of the eyelid conditioning data, conditioning which does not involve a noxious unconditioned stimulus does not result in a difference between performance of high- and low-anxious subjects (Bindra, Peterson, and Strzelecki, 1955).

WHAT IS ANXIETY? The finding that pain is more disruptive for low-anxious than for high-anxious subjects appears puzzling at an intuitive level. However, this inconsistency with intuition may be due, primarily, to the labels which have been used to describe performance on the anxiety scales. Eriksen (1966) summarizes a number of studies which indicate that subjects who attain "high-anxious" scores on the Taylor scale are the "psychasthenics" (i.e., compulsives, obsessives, phobics) as diagnosed on the MMPI. The "low-anxious" tend to be the "hysterics" as diagnosed by this same test. In short, the results of the learning studies may be restated as indicating that psychasthenics are less disrupted by pain than are hysterics.

Conclusions Concerning the Effects of Shock as Stress

To the extent that stress, in the form of nonavoidable shock, is likely to affect the types of performance considered in this section, it appears most likely to result in performance decrements. Such decrements were most consistent in acquisition of nonsense material. The one available concept attainment study also showed sizable decrements due to shock.

DISRUPTION OF STRATEGY BEHAVIOR. The relatively greater probability of decrements for nonsense material than for meaningful material, in verbal learning, poses some interesting problems. As was seen in Chapters 9 and 10, there are several characteristics that distinguish nonsense from meaningful material. First, nonsense items are poorly differentiated. It is possible that stress interferes with the differentiation process, and that this accounts for the obtained results. In addition, however, it was seen that the typical strategies employed in learning nonsense materials (e.g., seeking "meaning") are different from those employed in learning meaning words. In fact, complex strategies appear more likely to be used with nonsense materials. Since stress was found to produce considerable disruption of concept attainment, the hypothesis that strategy behavior is disturbed seems particularly promising. Further support for this suggestion will be found in a later section when the influence of attitudes on retention is discussed.

EVIDENCE CONCERNING SHOCK AS DRIVE. We have noted that, contrary to the Hullian formulation, increments in performance are *not* consistently related to dominance of the correct response, and decrements are not consistently related to dominance of the incorrect response. For example, while Lee (1961) found shock produced a significant decrement in verbal learning performance when the dominant response was incorrect, Chiles (1958) found that shock produced a significant increment under these conditions. Similarly, Besch (1959) found a significant *decrement* when the correct response was a strong associate of the stimulus, while Lee (1961) found that shock had no consistent effect under such conditions, and Chiles (1958) found that shock produced an increment in performance. In other words, both increments and decrements in performance appear for both types of *S-R* relationships. It appears that other variables are more crucial in determining the direction of the effects.

SHOCK AND THE BREAKDOWN OF BOUNDARIES BETWEEN COMPETING SYSTEMS. Turning to the Saltz and Riach (1961) study of concept attainment and the studies of act regression, we find that shock tended to produce greater decrements in performance when the task involved competition between competing *S-R* systems. This conclusion is consistent with Lee's (1961) data. In the condition involving strong competing responses (viz., previously correct response to a given stimulus were made incorrect for that stimulus, but correct to a different stimulus), Lee found that shock produced a decrement in learning. On the other hand, shocked and nonshocked subjects did equally well under uncompetitive response conditions. It must be emphasized, of course, that system overlap is not a necessary condition for shock to produce performance decrements. It appears merely to increase the likelihood and magnitude of such decrements. These data are consistent with the position that stress breaks down the boundaries of *S-R* systems, and permits the occurrence of competing responses.

FAILURE AND I.Q.-ORIENTATION AS STRESS

Effects of Failure: An Overview

We shall see that telling subjects they have failed on a previous task tends to produce decrements in further verbal learning and tends to produce forgetting of the material already learned. Thus, over the population as a whole, failure produces effects which are similar to those obtained with shock as stress.

However, we shall also see that the individual differences in the effects of failure are extremely great. Personality variables, such as are measured by the Taylor Manifest Anxiety Scale, play an even larger role in determining the effects of failure than they played in determining the effects of shock.

In the first sections, below, we shall consider the *general* effects of failure over the population as a whole. Later in the chapter, we shall see that these conclusions may have to be modified for specifiable subgroups in the population.

Failure and Learning

First we shall consider the effects of failure on verbal learning of nonsense syllables.

Four studies have been reported in which subjects were told that they had failed on a previous task, and then were asked to learn a list of nonsense syllables. Two of these studies found significant decrements in rote learning following failure (Sarason, 1956; Taylor, 1958). One study found a nonsignificant tendency toward a decrement (Sarason, 1957a) ; and one study found no general tendency for failure to affect learning (Lucas, 1952).

The Sarason (1956) study, which found decrements with failure instructions, was particularly interesting because it also manipulated the subjects' attitudes toward the significance of failure: Half the subjects were led to believe that the test was related to intelligence while the other half were given "task-oriented" instructions. The task was that of learning a serial list of nonsense syllables. Immediately after Trial 14 of serial learning, half the subjects in each condition were told that their performances had been very poor. All subjects were then given an additional trial. Subjects given failure instructions performed significantly more poorly on Trial 15 than did neutral subjects. In addition, the interaction between I.Q. and failure instructions was significant. *This interaction appears to reflect a smaller drop due to failure, in the I.Q.-instructions condition than in the task-oriented condition.* Possibly subjects try harder after failure if they believe that the task reflects on their intellectual ability. The variable of "trying harder" is one that most psychologists could accept at an intuitive level, but has little operational status at present.

The Taylor (1958) study which found significant decrements with failure instructions involved the successive learning of two paired-associated lists of nonsense syllables. Both intra-list and inter-list competition between the nonsense syllables was kept low. Prior to learning the first list, all subjects were told that the task was related to intelligence. After presentation of the first list, but before presentation of the second, half of the subjects were told that they had performed poorly. Taylor compared List 1 with List 2 performance, and found that failure subjects performed more poorly on List 2 than on List 1, while the reverse was true for subjects who were *not* told they had done poorly on List 1.

Sarason (1957a) reported a tendency for failure to produce decrements, but the results were not significant.

Lucas (1952) found no decrements over all subjects as a function of failure instructions. Subjects learned lists of three consonant nonsense syllables with one trial for each list. Subjects were told that they had done poorly after 0, 1, 2, or 3 of the lists.

Failure and Recall

A number of studies have examined the relationship between failure and a restricted type of recall. Typically in these studies, subjects are presented with a set of tasks, some of which are insoluble. Failure subjects are told this is an I.Q. test. To enhance the feeling of failure, stooges may pretend to finish the tasks quickly while the experimental subjects are still struggling with the items. Subjects in the nonfailure condition, on the other hand, are often told that the tasks are difficult and no mention is made of any relationship between performance and intelligence. At a later time, subjects are asked to recall as many of the *tasks* as possible.

Many of the early studies in this area were analyzed in terms of the difference between recall for completed and noncompleted tasks. As

Glixman (1949) has pointed out, such an analysis obscured the effects of failure on *total level* of recall.

Glixman (1949), reanalyzed the data reported by Alpert (1946) and Rosenzweig (1943), and presented data of his own. In general, these analyses suggest that *failure leads to a reduction in recall.* Both Alpert's data and his own showed that failure produced drops in recall of both completed and noncompleted material compared to the recall of subjects in neutral conditions. The drop was significant for completed material in Alpert and approached significance for the noncompleted material. Glixman's data were significant for noncompleted, but not for completed. Only Rosenzweig's data appear deviant, with failure producing a strong, but not significant *increase* in recall of completed material. Rosenzweig's data for noncompleted material were consistent with that of Alpert and Glixman (i.e., failure produced poorer recall than was found in a control group), but the effect was not significant.

A later study by Caron and Wallach (1957) also found significantly greater forgetting under failure induction than under neutral conditions.

In general, it appears that failure is associated with drops in retention under the conditions described.

THE RELATIVE RECALL OF SUCCESSES VERSUS FAILURES. Given that failure is likely to reduce the general level of recall, we can still ask whether a person is more likely to remember his successes or his failures. Several of the studies cited above were specifically concerned with this issue. As Eriksen (1966) has pointed out, it is not always clear that a completed item represents a success, when the context of the situation indicates to a subject that he has done poorly on the test as a whole. At any rate, studies involving the type of task described above often show that some persons consistently tend to remember more of their successes than their failures, while others consistently tend to remember more of their failures than their successes. Such individual differences have been found to be related to other personality variables. Eriksen (1966) has comprehensively reviewed the data on this topic.

I.Q.-Orientation as Stress

Some psychologists have assumed that stress is produced by telling a subject that the task to be performed is a measure of intelligence. Presumably this assumption would be justified on the grounds that potential failure on an intelligence test can be traumatic. From this point of view, studies that have used this device to produce stress are relevant to the general issue of the effects of failure or threat of failure on learning. On the other hand, however, there is no reason to believe that all subjects expect to do poorly on an intelligence test. As one might expect from such considerations, there are sizable individual differences in the effects of I.Q.-orientation on performance. In this section we shall examine the general effects of this manipulation; the relationship with individual differences will be considered in the succeeding section.

We shall see that, in general, I.Q.-orientation tends to *facilitate* rote learning, but it may have a detrimental effect on tasks involving reasoning and organization.

I.Q.-ORIENTATION AND LEARNING TASKS.   In the Sarason (1956) study, previously cited in regard to failure, I.Q. instructions produced no significant main effects in original learning of a serial list consisting of nonsense syllable, though the I.Q.-orientation group did somewhat better than the neutral group. Nor did these instructions produce a significant main effect on the trial following failure instructions. As previously noted, however, there was a significant interaction between I.Q. instructions and failure. *While failure subjects performed more poorly than nonfailure subjects in both the I.Q.-orientation and task-orientation conditions, this effect was less pronounced in the I.Q.-orientation condition.*

Sarason (1957b) had subjects learn two serial lists of nonsense syllables. Following the first list, subjects were given one of three types of instructions: (a) neutral instructions, (b) instructions to do well as a favor to the experimenter, and (c) instructions to do well since the test measured intelligence. The effects of instructions were significant, with the I.Q.-oriented group doing *better* than the neutral, though more poorly than the groups asked to work hard as a favor to the experimenter.

Sarason and Palola (1960) found that I.Q.-orientation significantly facilitated digit-symbol performance, compared to a task-oriented group. Digit symbols involve some learning, though perceptual speed is also a large component in performance. These results appear to be consistent with the learning data of Sarason's (1957b) study, and aspects of the Sarason (1956) data. *I.Q.-orientation tends to facilitate learning.*

I.Q.-ORIENTATION AND PROBLEM SOLVING.   Several studies have examined the effects of I.Q.-orientation on tasks which are sometimes considered more complex than the rote learning tasks we have been examining above. These studies have not found the general facilitative effects which we have observed in the rote learning studies. Sarason (1961), for example, investigated the effects of I.Q.-orientation on a difficult anagrams task. Anagram problems are often thought of as a variety of problem solving. The subject is presented with a nonsense word, the letters of which can be rearranged to make a real word; the subject must find the real word for each such anagram. Sarason found no effect of I.Q.-orientation on performance in this task.

One conclusion that *is* relatively obvious at this time is that I.Q.-orientation. Gynther (1957) gave subjects questions to answer and rated the answers for communicative efficiency (e.g., tendency to stick to the main topic, etc.). Communicative efficiency scores were significantly lower for subjects who were told that their answers were indicants of intelligence than for subjects given neutral instructions.

At this point it seems fairly clear that I.Q.-orientation will facilitate rote-learning performance. It is less certain that this variable will disrupt more complex, reasoning tasks such as that employed by Gynther; the evidence on this point is simply insufficient at this time.

One conclusion that *is* relatively obvious at this time is that I.Q.-orientation and failure do not have similar effects on behavior. They can not be considered equivalent stressors.

Failure and I.Q.-Orientation: Interactions with Trait-Anxiety

FAILURE AND ANXIETY.   In an earlier section of this chapter, we examined the relationship between shock-induced stress and the personality trait of anxiety as measured by tests such as the Taylor Manifest Anxiety Scale. We saw that shock was much more disruptive for subjects who scored *low-anxious,* on such scales, than subjects who scored *high-anxious.* Failure tends to produce the reverse relationship with anxiety: Failure is more disruptive for subjects who score *high-anxious* on such scales. In fact, some studies find that failure produces *decrements* in the performance of the high-anxious subjects at the same time that it is producing *increments* in the performance of the low-anxious subjects.

A study by Lucas (1952) provides an interesting example of the tendency for high- and low-anxious subjects to show opposite effects under failure conditions. Lucas presented his subjects with several short verbal learning lists in succession so that he could tell them that they had done poorly after 0, 1, 2, or 3 of the tasks. Low-anxious subjects tended to *improve* with successive failures, while high-anxious subjects tended to *drop* in performance under these conditions.

Similarly, on the Koh's Blocks, Mandler and Sarason (1952) report no overall effect of failure; however, failed high-anxious performed significantly more poorly than failed low-anxious. Under neutral conditions the two anxiety levels did not differ significantly. Again, as in Lucas' study, there was a tendency for high-anxious to perform more poorly under failure than under nonfailure, and a reverse tendency for low-anxious, but these effects were not significant.

Sarason (1957a) found no difference between high- and low-anxious subjects in serial learning under neutral conditions. Following failure, high-anxious subjects dropped in performance (compared to a control group of high-anxious subjects who did not fail), while the low-anxious subjects were unaffected by failure.

Two verbal learning studies report that *both* high-anxious and low-anxious subjects performed more poorly under failure conditions than under nonfailure (Sarason, 1956; Taylor, 1958). In both of these studies, the main effects due to failure are significant, while the interactions between failure and anxiety are not significant.

In general, then, it appears that failure has its most consistent detrimental effects for high-anxious subjects. Low-anxious subjects are much less consistent in their reaction to failure, with some studies suggesting that failure may actually lead to improvement in performance, while other studies find decrements.

I.Q.-ORIENTATION AND ANXIETY. It will be recalled that, in general, instructions to the effect that the task is related to intelligence tends to *improve* performance; this is particularly true if subjects are *not* made to believe they are failing the task. Examining these data as a function of anxiety indicates that this effect is not homogeneous across anxiety levels. In the Sarason (1956) study, the *low-* and *medium-anxiety* subjects learned serial lists of nonsense syllables *more rapidly* under I.Q.-orientation than under task-orientation. However, the relationship was reversed for high-anxious subjects: High-anxious subjects learned *more poorly* under I.Q.-orientation. The same interaction was found by Sarason (1957b), also using serial learning of nonsense syllables. Sarason and Palola (1960) tested subjects on a digit-symbol task and found that high-anxious subjects did well in all conditions except the one involving difficult material under I.Q.-orientation. In all three studies cited above, the relevant interaction terms were statistically significant.

Similarly, using a set of difficult anagrams, Sarason (1961) told half his subjects that the task should be easy for anyone of average intelligence, while the other half were told that the task was very difficult. High-anxious subjects performed more poorly under I.Q.-orientation, while medium- and low-anxious subjects performed better under I.Q.-orientation than under task-orientation.

Gynther (1957), it will be recalled, found that communication efficiency was poorer under I.Q.-orientation than under neutral conditions. This effect proved homogeneous for high- and low-anxious subjects.

ARE FAILURE AND I.Q.-ORIENTATION THE SAME VARIABLE FOR HIGH-ANXIOUS SUBJECTS? We have seen that over the population as a whole, failure and I.Q.-orientation often have opposite effects on performance: Failure often depresses performance while there is a tendency for I.Q.-orientation to facilitate performance. This divergence in effects appears less likely to occur in high-anxious subjects. At this point, the data suggest that high-anxious subjects are so concerned about the possibility of failure that I.Q.-orientation is extremely threatening. Over the general population, on the other hand, I.Q.-orientation operates as though it produces an avoidable stress—i.e., hard work will avoid failure.

In this section we have also completed the basis for the assertion made earlier in the chapter about the interaction between trait-anxiety and the various sources of stress: Pain is most likely to produce disruption in the learning exhibited by *low-anxious* subjects; failure or threat of failure is most likely to produce disruption in the learning exhibited by *high-anxious* subjects. In short, there appear to be stable individual differences among people with regard to the types of situations which will produce stress.

Failure and I.Q.-Orientation: Résumé

The data suggest that failure-induced stress will often disrupt learning. Such disruption is least likely under conditions of avoidable stress: If the subject "tried harder" on a subsequent part of the task, he could "undo" previous failure. Such avoidable stress is clearly present in many of the studies employing failure or I.Q.-orientation. It is here that the largest individual differences due to anxiety level appear to occur. The hypothesis can be offered at this point that failure will be most likely to disrupt the performance of both high- and low-anxious subjects when "undoing" is ineffective in removing failure; however, high-anxious subjects are likely to show disruption even when "undoing" is possible.

"Undoing" is least possible in the studies of task-recall, cited above. After the series of tasks is completed, the subjects are merely asked to recall as many of the tasks as they can. The most consistent tendencies toward decrements in performance as a function of failure are found in this set of experiments, where undoing is *not* possible.

At times a tendency toward decrements in performance is also found in the studies which do permit undoing. (Undoing can occur when the subject is told he performed poorly on a learning task; then the subject is then given another trial on the task, or a new list to learn.) The studies involving undoing, which have produced a decrement in List 2 performance, have uniformly used nonsense syllables as materials to be learned. Again, as in the shock studies, there is a tendency for such low differentiated material to be disrupted by stress. Little evidence exists concerning the effects of failure on more highly differentiated meaningful material except for the task-recall studies.

The anxiety data are particularly interesting. These data suggest that high-anxious subjects are more susceptible to failure (or the possibility of failure in the I.Q.-orientation conditions) than are low-anxious subjects. Thus pain as stress (e.g., electric shock) and failure as stress produce completely different interactions with anxiety, since pain had its greatest detrimental effects for *low*-anxious subjects.

PACING AS STRESS

Several studies have assumed that pacing (as opposed, for example, to unlimited time for response) is a stressor. Presumably, the assumption made is that pacing increases difficulty, and difficult material produces more stress than easy material. The majority of these studies find that pacing produces response decrements under conditions of strong competing response systems. In the absence of such competition, paced and nonpaced subjects perform equally well.

The studies to be described in this section were all designed to test the Hullian $H \times D$ formulation. Two predictions were made from this formulation. Performance of paced subjects should be superior to that of nonpaced under conditions in which the dominant response is correct. Pacing should lead to inferior performance, compared to nonpaced, when the dominant response is *incorrect*. All the studies reported below used children as subjects. None of the studies partitioned the subjects by anxiety level.

A study by Castaneda and Palermo (1955) was one of the first reported and is characteristic of the other studies in this area. Subjects learned to push a different button for each of five lights. After initial training, three of the light-button pairs were interchanged (i.e., the button which had previously been associated to one light was now associated with a different light). Thus for these three pair the *incorrect* response was dominant. Two of light-button pairs remained the same as in initial training. Here the *correct* response was dominant. The data indicated that, on the three interchanged pairs, paced subjects performed significantly more poorly than nonpaced. This portion of the data is consistent with the $H \times D$ formulation. However, on the *unchanged* pairs, the mean number of errors was virtually identical for paced and nonpaced subjects. The interaction between change and pacing was highly significant. Thus, as in the shock studies, nonavoidable "stress" could not be shown to facilitate performance.

It should be noted that the interchanged pairs, in the study by Castaneda and Palermo (1955), present the subject with a situation involving great intersystem competition. The *dominant* response to any one of the three stimuli is the *correct* response to a *different* one of the three stimuli. Thus we have three complexly overlapping cognitive systems, with sets of stimuli overlapping at a common response. Based on the Saltz and Riach (1961) hypothesis that stress breaks down the boundaries of systems and permits disruption under conditions of massive system overlap, it is precisely at the interchanged pairs that we would expect to find the greatest decrements in performance upon the introduction of pacing.

The crucial problem for the $H \times D$ formulation was to show that pacing can lead to a significant *facilitation* in performance when the correct response is made dominant. Therefore, Castaneda (1956) designed a second study which was similar to the one by Castaneda and Palermo. Over the 20 criterion trials following initial training, the interaction between change and pacing was significant, as in the first study. A tendency was found for the paced subjects to perform better than the nonpaced on the unchanged pairs, as demanded by the $H \times D$ formulation, but this tendency was not significant. On the interchanged pairs, the paced subjects performed more poorly than the nonpaced; this effect, though considerably larger than the former, also failed to reach significance. By the last eight trials, paced and nonpaced subjects performed equally well on the unchanged items. However, on the interchanged items, the paced subjects were still making more errors than the nonpaced.

A careful examination of the Castaneda data suggests that the most defensible interpretation of the relevant interaction is that paced subjects did much more poorly on interchanged (i.e., competing systems) pairs than on unchanged pairs. Nonpaced subjects, on the other hand, performed only slightly more poorly on the interchanged pairs than on the unchanged. In other words, competing systems were more difficult than noncompeting systems for all subjects, and pacing magnified this difference.

Only one study, that of Castaneda and Lipsitt (1959), reported a significant tendency for pacing to facilitate performance when the *correct* response was dominant, and a significant tendency for pacing to be detrimental when the *incorrect* response was dominant. There are, however, some serious methodological problems in this study. Let us examine these. The stimuli were eight lights which were to be matched with eight lights which were to be matched with eight switches. These were mounted on a panel so that each light had a switch directly below it on the panel. The apparatus is illustrated in Figure 12–2. The arrows indicate which switch was to be pressed for each light. Data from a previous study indicated that subjects have a strong bias toward selecting the switch immediately below an illuminated light. In terms of this bias, the dominant response was correct for half the stimuli, and incorrect for the other half.

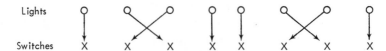

FIGURE 12–2. Diagram of Response Panel used by Castaneda and Lipsitt (1959). Arrows indicate direction lever was to be pulled for response to be considered correct. (Reproduced with permission of the American Psychological Association.)

In the absence of any learning about specific light-switch associations, if the subject always chose the switch under the illuminated light he would be correct half the time. Guessing either the switch to the *right* or the *left* of the light would lead to being correct 25% of the time. Therefore, if the subject had not learned which switch was correct for a particular stimulus, he would be most likely to be correct if he pressed the one immediately below the light which was illuminated. If pacing is detrimental to learning, one would expect a higher degree of guessing and therefore a greater tendency to press the switch immediately below the light, and less tendency to press a switch to the right or left of the light. Thus, if pacing interfered with learning and produced guessing, it should, *by chance,* inflate the number of correct responses for the stimuli to which the correct response is dominant; and it should *by chance* decrease the number of correct responses to stimuli for which the dominant response is incorrect. This is precisely what Castaneda and Lipsitt found.

To some extent, the other pacing studies cited above suffer from the same methodological problems found in Castaneda and Lipsitt. Under pacing, new learning became more difficult. At the same time, the previously learned response to each stimulus proved to be correct a relatively great percentage of the time. To the extent that paced subjects guessed this previously correct response, they would tend to be correct for unchanged pair, but would be systematically in error for changed pair.

Only one of the pacing studies avoided the methodological problems outlined above. Lipsitt and Lolordo (1963) used degree of response competition as a *between*-subjects condition in a situation which appears to have eliminated contamination due to response biases which are correlated with probability of being correct. The task was one of oddity learning. Subjects were presented three stimuli, two of which were same color. The subjects were to learn to choose the stimulus whose color was different from that of the other two stimuli. Half the subjects were given easy problems involving dissimilar, noncompeting colors (red, blue, and green); the other half were given difficult problems involving more similar, competing colors (red, pink, orange). Again, as in the previously cited studies, the interaction between pacing and competition was significant. Pacing had no significant effect on the dissimilar colors, but the paced subjects learned significantly more slowly than the nonpaced on the competing colors. Over the 54 trials employed, the paced subjects showed no learning on the competing materials. By the last block of trials, the paced subjects were correct on less than 30% of the trials for the competing material, while the unpaced were correct on more than 60% of the trials. On the noncompeting materials, paced and nonpaced were responding correctly on over 80% of the trials.

In conclusion, the data of the pacing studies appear to be consistent with the interpretation by Saltz and Riach (1961) concerning the effects of stress. When the correct response tendency is strong, pacing has little effect on performance. Under conditions of strong competing response systems, pacing leads to a disruption of performance.

NATURAL STRESS

Several studies have investigated the effects of nonavoidable naturalistic stress. Again, stress appears to be detrimental to performance.

Beam (1955) tested students immediately prior to a number of stress situations such as taking doctoral qualifying exams, giving oral reports in class, and participating in a dramatic production. The same students were given equivalent tests under neutral conditions.

Beam attempted to test the Taylor-Spence theory by comparing the effects of stress on serial learning with its effects on conditioning the GSR. The basic assumptions, here, were: (1) In serial learning, many of the dominant responses to stimuli must be incorrect, and therefore the drive properties of stress would increase the tendencies to elicit these incorrect responses, impeding learning; (2) in GSR conditioning, the dominant response to the conditioned stimulus must be the correct one, and therefore stress would facilitate conditioning.

The data showed that serial learning was, indeed, significantly poorer under the stress conditions than under neutral. The conditioning data, on the other hand, is difficult to interpret since Beam measured *magnitude* of the GSR, rather than using a probability of response measure. Magnitude of GSR was greater, under stress than under nonstress. However, this could merely indicate that the autonomic system responds more vigorously to electric shock when under stress than when not under stress; the significance of this fact for learning is not clear. This ambiguity concerning the implications of the conditioning data is heightened by the fact that both stress and nonstress conditions led to asymptotic magnitudes of GSR by the second or third conditioning trial, suggesting that the *rate* of conditioning was equal for the two stress conditions.

Capretta and Berkun (1962) found that soldiers crossing an unstable rope bridge over a deep ravine performed more poorly on a digit span task than when tested under nonstress conditions.

Saltz (1961b) examined the effect of natural stress on free associations. Students in introductory psychology were given a very difficult multiple choice midterm examination. After completion of this examination, they were given the Russell and Jenkins group form of the Kent-Rosanoff free-association test while the instructor graded their course examinations; at the end of an hour, they were to receive their grade on the examination. Half the students had taken the free association test a week earlier, under nonstress conditions; and the other half took the test a week later. Compared to the nonstress conditions, stress resulted in a significant, systematic drop in frequency of emission of the most common response to each stimulus word in the free association test. The degree of drop was unrelated to the nonstress frequency of the dominant response.

An interesting aspect of this study was that the data permitted an evaluation of the notion that stress is a stimulus with strong responses associated to it. If this were the basis of the drop in frequent responses, it would be expected that at least some of the emitted responses would be irrelevant to the stimulus presented; these words, presumably, would be related to the stress situation itself. No tendency toward this was found. In virtually every case, when a subject failed to emit the dominant response to a stimulus, his actual response was related to the stimulus word and was to be found among the lower-frequency response obtained by Russell and Jenkins in their study. Similarly, stress and nonstress conditions did not differ in frequency of stress-related responses. In other words, there was no evidence to suggest that the effect of stress was merely that of diverting the subjects from the experimental task.

WITHIN SYSTEM STRESS

The studies reviewed above all involved a source of stress external to the cognitive system being examined. For example, electric shock during learning is a situational stressor which is external and unrelated to the material being learned. Several studies have involved learning traumatic responses (e.g., "dirty" words). Here the stress is internal to the cognitive system being learned. In general, evidence has indicated poorer learning of traumatic than neutral words. A number of objections have been raised to such studies. One problem resides in the fact that such traumatic words tend to be less frequent in the language than the control items against which they are compared. A second problem is that the prior association between the stimulus words and such traumatic items is likely to be less than between the stimuli and the control words. Finally, many subjects may be reluctant to emit the traumatic words.

The best controlled study on this topic was by Kelley (1964). In paired-associates learning, Kelley carefully controlled for frequency of the responses in the language as well as prior associative strength between the stimuli and their traumatic or nontraumatic responses. Under these conditions, Kelley found no difference in the learning of the two types of response.

Saltz and DiLoreto (1965) report one of the few studies concerned with the effects of within system stress on concept attainment. The first phase of the study involved developing stress within specific cognitive systems. This was done by means of a paired-associates task. Instances of some concepts were associated to traumatic responses (e.g., orchid-vomit) while instances of other concepts were associated to neutral responses, using a counterbalanced design. In Phase 2, subjects were presented with a variation of the concept attainment task developed by Rosen (1963). In this phase, none of the specific instances involved in Phase 1 were used. For example, if *flower* was the concept to be attained, then *orchid* was *not* one of the instances used in Phase 2.

Consistent with the Kelley (1964) data, Saltz and DiLoreto found *no differences in phase 1 rote learning* between traumatic and nontraumatic responses. However, *in the concept attainment of Phase 2, large and significant differences were obtained.* Subjects had much more difficulty discovering concepts which, in Phase 1, had been associated to stressors, then in discovering concepts which had been associated to neutral responses. Since the traumatic responses had been associated to concept instances which did not appear in the Phase 2 concept task, the Phase 2 decrements indicate that stress had become internalized into the concept system.

The Saltz and DiLoreto study constitutes part of the evidence for the statement, made at the beginning of this chapter, that stress is more potent in disrupting conceptual behavior than in disrupting rote learning. In this study, the same subjects were presented with the identical set of stress responses in both rote-learning and concept-discovery tasks. Rote learning was unaffected by these stressors. Concept attainment was disrupted.

Personality Factors

Clearly, material which is stressful for one person may not be stressful for another. Rosen (1963) investigated immediate and delayed recall of neutral passages and of passages involving hostile, aggressive acts. These latter passages were eye-witness accounts of Nazi concentration camp atrocities. Recall was related to the gross personality factor of ability to tolerate one's own hostile impulses. Rosen assumed that persons who had difficulty expressing hostility would find the concentration camp stories more traumatic than persons who could express hostility. For the neutral material, no differences in either immediate or delayed (24 hour) recall were obtained as a funcion of ability to express hostility. Thus this personality factor was not related to memory *per se*. However, for the concentration camp descriptions, persons who had difficulty accepting hostile impulses showed a significant decrement in delayed recall, compared to subjects who had little difficulty accepting such impulses. *Immediate* recall was not affected by this personality variable.

A study by Uhlmann and Saltz (1965) also suggests that delayed recall is more susceptible to stress than is immediate recall. These results were obtained in a study based on the hypothesis that stress acts to break down the bondaries of cognitive systems. Thus subjects who, as an individual difference factor, could develop strong boundaries should show less decrement with stress than subjects who developed weak boundaries. On the basis of other evidence, it was suggested that Witkins' field-dependence, field-independence variable (c.f., Witkins, Duk, Paterson, and Karp, 1962) is an individual differences factor which is related to the basic boundary strength variable discussed in Chapter 6. The experiment consisted of presenting a newspaper account of a fire to subjects, and obtaining immediate and delayed (3 hour) recall. Results indicated little drop in retention of nonstressful portions of the story, over time, for either field-dependent or field-independent subjects. However, the more stressful portions of the story showed significant drops in retention with time for the field-dependent (low-boundary strength) subjects, but not for the field-independent (high-boundary strength) subjects.

Attitudinal Effects on Recall

Telling a communist that communism is bad, telling a liberal (during the 1930s) that the New Deal was bad, or telling a die-hard confederate that the Southern cause in the Civil War was bad, may all be considered sources of stress. In effect, then, the numerous studies of recall as a function of attitude fall under the general topic of the present chapter.

A recent study by Wickey (1967) appears promising in regard to resolving some of the conflicting data in this area. Wickey reasoned that recall of a message is related to the extent that a subject can find the basic theme of the message and can organize the material of the message around this theme. In effect, then, comprehension and subsequent recall depends on the concept discovery involved in finding the theme of the message. Wickey's experimental hypothesis was based on the Saltz and DiLoreto (1965) finding that, as far as meaningful material is concerned, stress has its primary effect on concept discovery, rather than rote learning. From this, Wickey hypothesized that attitudinal stress should have its major impact on recall via the disruption of concept behavior involved in discovering the theme of the message. If the theme is sufficiently explicit that no discovery phase is necessary, recall should be unaffected by attitude.

The experimental message was concerned with the Viet Nam war, an issue concerning which the subjects had strong attitudes. Half the material presented to a subject was favorable to the American position in this war, half was unfavorable. In one condition, necessity for theme discovery was eliminated by informing the subjects concerning the bias of each half of the material before actually presenting the material. In a second condition, no such information wae provided. The results were very straightforward. Subjects who agreed with a passage recalled equally well when informed about the theme and when not informed about the theme. Thus the information, *per se,* did not appear to bias the results by providing additional practice. Similarly, subjects who disagreed with a passage, but were informed about the theme, recalled as much as subjects who agreed with the passage. Only the *noninformed* subjects who *disagreed* with the passage showed a significant disruption of recall.

An examination of previous studies suggests that decrements in recall, as a function of attitude, are most likely to occur when theme discovery (or theme ambiguity) is a critical factor. Edwards (1941), for example, used a lengthy message in which half the items were pro–New Deal, half were anti–New Deal. In immediate recall, New Deal advocates remembered more favorable items, while New Deal opponents remembered more of the unfavorable items. Studies by Clark (1940) and Seeleman (1940) also involved messages with ambiguous points of view, and found attitudinal effects on recall.

Fitzgerald and Ausubel (1963), on the other hand, found no attitudinal effects on recall. Here the message was homogeneous in point of view, permitting easy discovery of the theme.

Again, as in the Saltz and DiLoreto study, the data suggest that concept discovery is much more susceptible to disruption under stress conditions than is rote learning.

STRESS AS PUNISHMENT

The main concern of the present chapter has been with the mechanisms involved in nonavoidable stress. We have seen that, if nonavoidable stress has any effect on performance, this effect is likely to be detrimental. Yet, are there not situations in which stress may facilitate performance? The answer to this appears to be, "Yes." But, for the most part, these situations appear to involve factors in addition to nonavoidable stress. Many of the studies in which increased stress led to facilitation of performances involved avoidable, rather than nonavoidable stress. While the complexities introduced by avoidable stress are beyond the scope of the present book, two such types of studies will be briefly described.

Yerkes and Dodson (1908) found that for difficult and moderately difficult discrimination learning tasks, performance was a U-shaped function of intensity of shock administered for making the wrong response. Weak and very strong shock intensities produced poorer learning than moderate intensities. Some writers appear to have interpreted the results of studies in the Yerkes-Dodson tradition as indicating that stress, *per se,* is nonmonotonically related to performance. In terms of the mass of data analyzed in this chapter a more consistent interpretation appears to be that two antagonistic processes are at work. The incentive value of shock avoidance leads to facilitation; however, increasing the shock intensity leads to disruption of competing systems despite the increased incentive involved in avoiding the shock.

In support of this interpretation are the additional findings by Yerkes and Dodson which indicate that the *optimal* degree of stress required to facilitate performance is negatively related to the degree similarity between the stimuli to be discriminated. In other words, the greater the overlap between competing systems, the smaller the intensity of stress required to disrupt performance.

A second type of situation in which stress has often been found to facilitate learning involves using stress as a basis for differentiation. Muenzinger (1934), for example, showed that shock, which was administered just past the choice point for *correct* choices, was almost as effective in reducing errors as shock given for incorrect choices. In this type of situation, shock appears to serve as a context cue, providing an additional basis for differentiating the response alternatives. This mechanism appears to be similar to the color cues employed by Saltz, Whitman, and Paul (1963), discussed in Chapter 3. In the latter study, learning was facilitated if the alley and goal box were in different colors, despite the fact that the animals could not see the goal box while running in the alley. As in the Yerkes-Dodson type studies, Wischner, Fowler, and Kushnick (1963) show that facilitation may occur when the response to be reinforced is followed by moderate shock, but when this response is followed by strong shock, performance is disrupted. The use of shock immediately prior to reinforcement appears to introduce a number of interacting mechanisms whose combined effect is difficult to evaluate. Not only do differentiation and disruption effects occur (the former being positively related to learning while the latter is inversely related), but shock before entering the goal box also introduces complex approach-avoidance gradients in respect to approaching the goal box, *per se.*

CONCLUSIONS

Several issues run through the present chapter. The first is concerned with whether the various stressors are sufficiently similar in effect so that we may consider them as a single variable. A second issue is related to personality factors: Different subjects react to different stimuli as stressors. The third, and most important issue is concerned with the effects of stress on the determinants of behavior.

Stressors

The emphasis, in the present chapter, has been on *nonavoidable* stress. It appears that when the stressor is truly nonavoidable, the following variables all appear to enter into similar functional relations with performance: electric shock, failure, pacing, traumatic associations, and negative attitudes toward a message. Some studies have suggested that failure may, at times, lead to facilitation under conditions where another type of stressor (e.g., shock) would probably produce a decrement in performance. These results appear to occur under conditions where failure may be "undone" by such facilitation. In other words, these are not unambiguously nonavoidance situations. Where failure can not be undone by superior performance on the criterion task, failure operates very much like the other variables mentioned.

Of the variables often considered stressors, I.Q.-orientation functions most dissimilarly from all the others. Here facilitation often occurs in situations where other stressors produce decrements in performance.

Personality Factors

The previous paragraphs were concerned with *general* effects of stress, over all (or most) subjects. Turning to the interactions between personality variables and stress, a strong tendency is found for *low-anxious* subjects to exhibit massive disruption in performance in the face of electric shock, in particular, and probably most situations involving physical pain. *High-anxious* subjects react much less severely to physical pain. On the other hand, high-anxious subjects appear to deteriorate in performance under conditions of failure or even threat of possible failure. The magnitude of this latter effect is particularly apparent in studies which used I.Q.-orientation as stress. Most subjects, told that a task is related to intelligence, will show facilitation in performance; high-anxious subjects do more poorly under these conditions.

Clearly, "low-anxious" refers to a scale score on a particular set of tests, rather than to an immunity to stress effects. Eriksen's (1966) suggestion that high-anxious subjects are those who employ compulsive mechanisms, while low-anxious are those who employ hysteroid mechanisms has some advantage over the unidimensional interpretation of anxiety scale scores.

In addition, there is some evidence to suggest that subjects who develop strong boundaries for cognitive systems are less likely to have these systems disrupted by stress than are subjects whose boundaries are weaker. This conclusion, however, is based on the use of Witkin's field independence measures as an index of boundary strength, and there is some evidence to suggest that field independence is related to compulsive mechanisms while field dependence is related to hysteroid mechanisms. The variables should, somehow, be disentangled before more conclusive interpretations of the data are possible.

Stress Mechanisms

First, it appears that the Hullian $H \times D$ mechanism is not adequate for the prediction of facilitation with stress when the correct response is dominant. As has been seen, with very few exceptions the data is incompatible with this prediction. The first major support for this formulation came from Taylor's (1951) report of superior conditioning for high-anxious compared to low-anxious subjects. In retrospect, this data fits the general pattern of performance *decrement* for *low-anxious* subjects under pain stimulation, rather than indicating performance facilitation for high-anxious subjects.

The great majority of the studies suggest that the obtained data can be more adequately summarized by a *learning ÷ stress* formulation than by *learning × stress*. In general, stress appears to lead to a breakdown of cognitive systems, with the breakdown inversely related to the strength of the system at the time that the stress occurs.

Turning to the problem of isolating the locus of the stress effect, it appears that in verbal learning, stress is more likely to disrupt learning of weakly differentiated materials (e.g., nonsense syllables) than strongly differentiated material (e.g., real words). Little disruption of highly differentiated material is likely to occur except under conditions of extensive system overlap. Here the weakening of system boundaries, under stress, leads to interference between systems and consequent disruption of performance. One study, that of Chiles (1958), suggests that a major locus of disruption is *response* availability or differentiation. In this study, subjects were given a choice of two responses (rather than being required to emit a response), and stress led to performance facilitation. On the other hand, the animal studies of act regression often involve shock in a two choice situation, and shock leads to disruption of the ongoing response, especially if it is the lesser practiced of the two responses.

Stress appears to have a more disruptive effect on concept discovery than on verbal learning. This could suggest that stress breaks down strategy behavior and would be consistent with the greater disruption of nonsense material than of real words.

On the other hand, the more sizable effect of stress on concept discovery may be related to the high degree of system overlap and response ambiguity (e.g., should one respond to color, form, or size) intrinsic to most concept tasks.

The approach of the present book certainly does not answer all the questions which can be raised concerning the effects of stress. On the other hand, it has the interesting virtue of pointing out directions of research which may lead to answers for some of these questions.

INDEXES

Bibliography and Author Index

The numbers in parentheses following each reference give the pages, in this text, in which the paper or book is cited.

A

Abra, J. C. Time changes in the strength of extinguished context and specific association, *Journal of Experimental Psychology,* 1968, 77, 684–686. **(218)**

Adams, J. K. Laboratory studies of learning without awareness. *Psychological Bulletin,* 1957, 54, 383–405. **(386, 389)**

Adams, J. K. *See also* Grant & Adams, 1944.

Adams, P. A. *See* Postman & Adams, 1955, 1956 (a), 1956 (b), 1957, 1958, 1960; Postman, Adams, & Bohm, 1956; Postman, Adams, & Phillips, 1955.

Ager, J. W. *See* Saltz & Ager, 1962, 1968.

Allen, C. K. *See* Wickens, *et al.,* 1963.

Alpert, T. G. Memory for completed and incompleted tasks as a function of personality: An analysis of group data. *Journal of Abnormal and Social Psychology,* 1946, 41, 403–421. **(435)**

Amsel, A. The role of frustrative nonreward in noncontinuous reward situations. *Psychologicial Bulletin,* 1958, 55, 102–119. **(100)**

Amster, H. The effect of variety as a function of task difficulty in the acquisition of word meaning. Unpublished manuscript, 1966. **(58)**

Arbuckle, T. Y. *See* Tulvig & Arbuckle, 1963.

Archer, E. J. A reevaluation of the meaningfulness of all possible CVC trigrams. *Psychological Monographs,* 1960, 74, No. 10 (Whole No. 497). **(331, 334)**

Archer, E. J. *See also* Bulgarella & Archer, 1962.

Archer, J. E. On verbalization and concepts: Comments of Professor Kendler's paper. In A. W. Melton (Ed.) *Categories of human learning,* New York: Academic Press, 1964. **(35, 45, 274)**

Arnoult, M. D. Familiarity and recognition of nonsense shapes. *Journal of Experimental Psychology,* 1956, 51, 269–276. **(142)**

Arnoult, M. D. Stimulus predifferentiation: Some generalizations and hypotheses. *Psychological Bulletin,* 1957, 54, 339–350. **(123)**

Asch, S. E., & Ebenholtz, S. M. The principle of associative symmetry. *Proceedings of the American Philosophical Society,* 1962 (a), 106, 135–163. **(154, 163–65, 181)**

Asch, S. E., & Ebenholtz, S. M. The process of free recall: evidence for non-associative factors in acquisition and retention. *Journal of Psychology,* 1962 (b), 54, 3–31. **(154, 181)**

Asch, S. E., & Lindner, M. A. Note on "strength of association." *Journal of Psychology,* 1963, 55, 199–209. **(154)**

Asdourian, D. *See* Saltz & Asdourian, 1963.

Atkinson, R. C., & Shiffrin, R. M. Human memory: A proposed system and its control processes. In K. W. Spence and J. T. Spence (Eds.), *The psychology of learning and motivation: Advances in research and theory.* Vol. 2, New York: Academic Press, 1968, 88–195. **(238)**

Atkinson, R. L., & Saltzman, I. J. Comparison of incidental and intentional learning after different numbers of stimulus presentations. *American Journal of Psychology,* 1954, 67, 521–524. **(357)**

Attneave, F. Transfer of experience with a class-schema to identification-learning of patterns and shapes. *Journal of Experimental Psychology,* 1957, 54, 81–88. **(119, 128, 136, 138, 140, 141, 180)**

Atwater, S. K. Proactive inhibition and associative facilitation as affected by degree of prior learning. *Journal of Experimental Psychology,* 1953, 46, 400–404. **(209, 214, 217, 225)**

Atwood, D. W. *See* Horowitz, White, & Atwood, 1968.

Austin, G. A. *See* Bruner, *et al.,* 1956.

Ausubel, D. P. *See* Fitzgerald & Ausubel, 1963.

Avant, L. L. *See* Bevan, *et al.,* 1966.

B

Bahrick, H. P. Incidental learning under two incentive conditions. *Journal of Experimental Psychology,* 1954, 47, 170–172. **(355, 356)**

Baker, K. E. *See* Gagne & Baker, 1950.

Barber, T. X., & Calverley, D. S. An experimental study of "hypnotic" (auditory and visual) hallucinations. *Journal of Abnormal and Social Psychology,* 1964, 68, 13–20. **(156)**

Barnes, H., & Saltz, E. Effect of R-pretraining on PAL with unlimited time for response. *Psychonomic Science,* 1970, 18, 81–82. **(174)**

Barnes, J. M., & Underwood, B. J. "Fate" of first list associations in transfer theory. *Journal of Experimental Psychology*, 1959, 58, 97–105. **(180, 209, 286, 287)**

Bartlett, F. C. *Remembering: A study in Experimental and Social Psychology*. Cambridge: Cambridge University Press. 1932. **(275)**

Bastian, J. Associative factors in verbal transfer, *Journal of Experimental Psychology*, 1961, 62, 70–79. **(287, 299, 300)**

Bastian, J. R. Response chaining in verbal transfer. Doctoral dissertation, University of Minnesota, 1956. **(299)**

Battachi, M. W. Organizzazione, atteggiamento e teoria del giudizio nell' apprendimento seriale. *Rivista di Psicologia*, 1958, 3, 211–260. **(267, 269)**

Battig, W. F. *See also* Brown, S. C., *et al.*, 1965; Schild & Battig, 1966.

Battig, W. F., & Koppenaal, R. J. Associative asymmetry in S-R vs R-S recall of double function lists. *Psychological Reports*, 1965, 16, 287–293. **(166, 168)**

Battig, W. F., Williams, J. M., and Williams, J. G. Transfer from verbal-discrimination to paired-associate learning. *Journal of Experimental Psychology*, 1962, 63, 258–268. **(145)**

Beam, J. C. Serial learning and conditioning under real life stress. *Journal of Abnormal and Social Psychology*, 1955, 51, 543–551. **(444)**

Beck, E. C., & Doty, R. W. Conditioned flexion reflexes acquired during combined catalepsy and de-efferentiation. *Journal of Comparative and Physiological Psychology*, 1957, 50, 211–216. **(160)**

Beilin, H. Learning and operational convergence in logical thought development. *Journal of Experimental Child Psychology*, 1965, 2, 317–339. **(73)**

Beilin, H. Cognitive capacities of young children: A replication. *Science,* 1968 (a), 162, 920–921. **(70)**

Beilin, H. Reply to Beve, Mehler, and Epstein. *Science,* 1968 (b), 162, 924. **(70)**

Bensberg, G. J., Jr. Concept learning in mental defectives as a function of appropriate and inappropriate "attention sets." *Journal of Educational Psychology*, 1958, 49, 137–143. **(134)**

Berkun, M. *See* Capretta & Berkun, 1962.

Berlyne, D. E. *Conflict, arousal, and curiosity*. New York: McGraw-Hill, 1960. **(20)**

Berlyne, D. E. Motivational problems raised by exploratory and epistemic behavior. In S. Koch (Ed.) *Psychology: A Study of a Science*. Vol. V. New York: McGraw-Hill, 1963. **(20)**

Bernstein, J. M. *See* Spielberger, *et al.*, 1966.

Bertucco, R. A. *See* Peterson, L. R., *et al.*, 1963.

Besch, N. F. Paired-associates learning as a function of anxiety level and shock. *Journal of Personality,* 1959, 27, 115–123. **(424, 425, 429, 430, 432)**

Bessmer, D. W. *See* Ellis, *et al.,* 1962.

Bevan, W., Dukes, W. F., & Avant, L. L. The effect of variation in specific stimuli on memory for their superordinates, *American Journal of Psychology,* 1966, 79, 250–257. **(303, 304)**

Bever, T. G. *See* Mehler & Bever, 1967, 1968.

Bilodeau, I. M., & Schosberg, H. Similarity in stimulating conditions as a variable in retroactive inhibition. *Journal of Experimental Psychology,* 1951, 41, 199–204. **(164, 191)**

Bindra, D., & Cameron, L. Changes in experimentally produced anxiety with the passage of time. *Journal of Experimental Psychology,* 1953, 45, 197–203. **(229)**

Bindra, D., Paterson, A. L., & Strzelecki, J. On the relation between anxiety and conditioning. *Canadian Journal of Psychology,* 1955, 9, 1–6. **(431)**

Birch, D. Verbal control of nonverbal behavior. *Journal of Experimental Child Psychology,* 1966, 4, 266–275. **(409)**

Bitterman, M. E. Information and effect in incidental learning. *American Journal of Psychology,* 1956, 69, 410–416. **(402)**

Black, A. H. The extinction of avoidance responses under curare-like drugs. *Journal of Comparative and Physiological Psychology,* 1958, 51, 519–522. **(161)**

Blattner, K. C. *See* Peterson, M. J., & Blattner, 1963.

Blockovich, R. N. The learning and scaling of multidimensional stimuli. Ph.D. dissertation, Wayne State University, 1969. **(276)**

Boersma, F. J. *See* Martin C. J., Boersma, & Cox, 1965; Martin, C. J., Cox & Boersma, 1965.

Bohm, A. M. *See* Postman, Adams, & Bohm, 1956.

Born, D. G. *See* Wickens, Born, & Allen, 1963.

Bosley, J. J. *See* DeSoto & Bosley, 1962.

Bourne, L. E., Jr. Long term effects of misinformation feedback on concept identification. *Journal of Experimental Psychology,* 1963, 65, 139–147. **(48)**

Bourne, L. E., Jr. *Human conceptual behavior.* Boston: Allyn & Bacon, 1966. **(45, 47)**

Bourne, L. E., Jr. *See also:* Haygood & Bourne, 1965; Walker & Bourne, 1961.

Bousfield, W. A. *See also* Kincaid, *et al.,* 1962.

Bousfield, W. A., & Cohen, B. H. The occurrence of clustering in the recall of randomly arranged words of different frequencies of usage. *Journal of General Psychology,* 1955, 52, 83–95. **(321)**

Bousfield, W. A., Cohen, B. H., and Whitmarsh, G. A. Associative clustering in the recall of words of different taxonomic frequencies of occurrence. *Psychological Reports,* 1958, 4, 39–44. **(321)**

Bousfield, W. A., Whitmarsh, G. A., and Berkowitz, H. Partial response identities in associative clustering. *Journal of General Psychology,* 1960, 63, 233–238. **(187)**

Bower, G. H. *See also* Trabasso & Bower, 1966.

Bower, G. H. An association model for response and training variables in paired associate learning. *Psychological Review,* 1962, 69, 34–53. **(90, 91)**

Bower, G. H. Analysis of a mnemonic device. *American Scientist,* 1970, 58, 496–510. **(326, 378)**

Bower, G. H., & Trabasso, T. R. Reversals prior to solution in concept identification. *Journal of Experimental Psychology,* 1963, 66, 409–418. **(50)**

Bower, G. H., & Trabasso, T. R. Concept identification. In R. C. Atkinson (Ed.) *Studies in mathematical psychology.* Stanford: Stanford University Press, 1964. **(88, 92)**

Braine, M. D. S., & Shanks, B. L. The development of conservation of size. *Journal of Verbal Learning and Verbal Behavior,* 1965, 4, 227, 242. **(70)**

Brent, S. B. Organizational factors in learning and remembering: Functional unity of the interpolated task as a factor in retractive interference. *American Journal of Psychology,* 1965, 78, 403–413. **(309)**

Brewer, C. L. *See* Peterson, L. R., *et al.,* 1963.

Briggs, G. E. *See also* Wickens & Briggs, 1951.

Briggs, G. E. Acquisition, extinction, and recovery functions in retroactive inhibition. *Journal of Experimental Psychology,* 1954, 47, 285–293. **(217)**

Briggs, G. E. Retroactive inhibition as a function of the degree of original and interpolated learning. *Journal of Experimental Psychology,* 1957, 53, 60–67. **(201, 209, 214, 224, 225)**

Briggs, G. E., Thompson, R. F., & Brogden, W. J. Retention functions in proactive inhibition. *Journal of Experimental Psychology,* 1954, 48, 419–423. **(217)**

Broadbent, D. E. *Perception and Communication.* London: Pergamon Press, 1958. **(236, 238)**

Broadbent, D. E. Flow of information within the organism. *Journal of Verbal Learning and Verbal Behavior,* 1963, 2, 34–39. **(238)**

Brogden, W. J. *See* Briggs, *et al.,* 1954.

Brookshire, K. H., Warren, J. M., & Ball, G. G. Reversal and transfer learning following overtraining in rat and chicken, *Journal of Comparative and Physiological Psychology,* 1961, 54, 98–102. **(234)**

Brown, J. Some tests of the decay theory of immediate memory. *Quarterly Journal of Experimental Psychology,* 1958, 10, 12–24. **(236)**

Brown, J. S. A behavioral analysis of masochism. *Journal of Experimental Research in Personality,* 1965, 1, 65–70. **(421)**

Brown, S. C., Battig, W. F., & Pearlstein, R. Effect of successive addition of stimulus elements on paired associate learning. *Journal of Experimental Psychology,* 1965, 70, 87–93. **(372)**

Brown, Z. M. *See* Horowitz, *et al.,* 1964.

Brownstein, A. J. *See* Marx & Brownstein, 1963.

Bruner, J. S. The course of cognitive growth. *American Psychologist,* 1964, 19, 1–15. **(67)**

Bruner, J. S., Goodnow, J. J., & Austin, G. A. *A study of thinking.* New York: Wiley, 1956. **(42, 48, 55, 87, 412)**

Bruner, J. S., & O'Dowd, D. A note on the informativeness of parts of words. *Language and Speech,* 1958, 1, 98–101. **(259)**

Bugelski, B. R. A remote association explanation of the relative difficulty of learning nonsense syllables in a serial list. *Journal of Experimental Psychology,* 1950, 40, 336–348. **(265, 266, 268)**

Bugelski, B. R., & Cadwallader, T. C. A reappraisal of the transfer and retroaction surfaces. *Journal of Experimental Psychology,* 1956, 52, 360–366. **(212)**

Bulgarella, R., & Archer, E. J. Concept identification of auditory stimuli as a function of amount of relevant and irrelevant information. *Journal of Experimental Psychology,* 1962, 63, 254–257. **(42)**

Bulgarella, R., and Martin, C. J. Conditionability of associative strategies among educable retardates. Paper read at Midwestern Psychological Association, Chicago, 1967. **(371, 373)**

Butler, D. C., & Petersen, D. E. Learning during "extinction" with paired associates. *Journal of Verbal Learning and Verbal Behavior,* 1965, 4, 103–106. **(149)**

Buxton, C. E. *See also* Withey, *et al.,* 1949.

Buxton, C. E. Latent learning and the goal-gradient hypothesis. *Contributions to Psychological Theory,* 1940, 2, No. 2. **(385)**

C

Cadwallader, T. C. *See* Bugelski & Cadwallader, 1956.

Calverley, D. S. *See* Barber & Calverley, 1964.

Cameron, L. *See* Bindra & Cameron, 1953.

Cantor, G. N. Effects of three types of pre-training on discrimination learning in preschool children. *Journal of Experimental Psychology,* 1955, 49, 339–342. **(118, 119, 136, 144)**

Cantor, J. H. Amount of pretraining as a factor in stimulus predifferentiation and performance set. *Journal of Experimental Psychology,* 1955, 50, 180–184. **(119, 142)**

Capretta, P. J., & Berkun, M. Validity and reliability of certain measures of psychological stress. *Psychological Reports*, 1962, 10, 875–878. **(444)**

Carlin, J. E. Word association strength as a variable in paired-associate learning. Doctoral dissertation, University of Minnesota, 1958. **(283)**

Caron, A. J., & Wallach, M. A. Recall of interrupted tasks under stress: A phenomenon of memory or of learning? *Journal of Abnormal and Social Psychology*, 1957, 55, 372–381. **(435)**

Casey, M. *See* Young & Casey, 1964.

Cason, H. Association between the familiar and the unfamiliar. *Journal of Experimental Psychology*, 1933, 16, 295–305. **(332)**

Castaneda, A. Effects of stress on complex learning and performance. *Journal of Experimental Psychology*, 1956, 52, 9–12. **(423, 441, 442)**

Castaneda, A., & Lipsitt, L. P. Relations of stress and differential position habits to performance in motor learning. *Journal of Experimental Psychology*, 1959, 57, 25–30. **(442, 443)**

Castaneda, A., & Palermo, D. S. Psychomotor performance as a function of amount of training and stress. *Journal of Experimental Psychology*, 1955, 50, 175–179. **(441)**

Ceraso, J., & Henderson, A. Unavailability and associative loss in RI and PI *Journal of Experimental Psychology*, 1965, 70, 300–303. **(218)**

Cerekwicki, L. E., Grant, D. A., & Porter, E. C. The effect of number and relatedness of verbal discriminanda upon differential eyelid conditioning. *Journal of Verbal Learning and Verbal Behavior*, 1968, 7, 847–853. **(302–3, 414)**

Chatterjee, B. B., & Eriksen, C. W. Cognitive factors in heart rate conditioning. *Journal of Experimental Psychology*, 1962, 64, 272–279. **(404)**

Chiles, W. D. Effects of shock-induced stress on verbal performance. *Journal of Experimental Psychology*, 1958, 56, 159–166. **(423, 425, 430, 432, 452)**

Cicala, G. A. Running speed in rats as a function of drive level and presence or absence of competing responses. *Journal of Experimental Psychology*, 1961, 62, 329–334. **(101, 103, 105, 106, 107, 198)**

Cieutat, V. J. Group paired-associate learning: stimulus vs. response meaningfulness. *Perceptual and Motor Skills*, 1961, 12, 327–330. **(333)**

Cieutat, V. J., Stockwell, F. E., & Noble, C. E. The interaction of ability and amount of practice with stimulus and response meaningfulness (m, m') in paired associates learning. *Journal of Experimental Psychology*, 1958, 56, 193–202. **(318, 321, 333)**

Clark, J. *See* Young & Clark, 1964.

Clark, K. B. Some factors influencing the remembering of prose material. *Archives of Psychology*, 1940, 36, No. 253. **(448)**

Clark, L. L., Lansford, T. G., & Dallenbach, K. M. Repetition and associative learning. *American Journal of Psychology,* 1960, 73, 22–40. **(88)**

Clark, S. E. *See* Wickens & Clark, 1968.

Cofer, C. N. *See also* Cramer & Cofer, 1960.

Cofer, C. N., & Yarczower, M. Further studies of implicit verbal chaining in paired associate learning. *Psychological Reports,* 1957, 3, 453–456. **(281)**

Cohen, B. H. *See* Bousfield & Cohen, 1955; Bousfield, *et al.,* 1958.

Cohen, J. C. *See* Musgrave & Cohen, 1964.

Coke, E. U. *See* Rothkopf & Coke, 1961.

Cook, S. W. *See* Raskin & Cook, 1937.

Cooper, L. M. Operant behavior as a function of stimulus complexity. *Journal of Comparative and Physiological Psychology,* 1963, 65, 857–862. **(100, 101, 128, 326)**

Coppock, W. J. Preextinction in sensory preconditioning. *Journal of Experimental Psychology,* 1958, 55, 213–219. **(158)**

Corman, C. D., & Wickens, D. D. Retroactive inhibition in short term memory. *Journal of Verbal Learning and Verbal Behavior,* 1968, 7, 16–19 **(247)**

Cotton, J. W. Running time as a function of amount of food deprivation. *Journal of Experimental Psychology,* 1953, 46, 188–198. **(103, 105, 106, 107)**

Cox, D. L. *See* Martin C. J., Boersma, & Cox, 1965; Martin, C. J., Cox, & Boersma, 1965.

Cramer, P., & Cofer, C. N. The role of forward and reverse associations in transfer of training. *American Psychologist,* 1960, 15, 463. **(280, 289)**

Crawford, B. M. *See* Pereboom & Crawford, 1958.

Crespi, L. P. Quantitative variation of incentive and performance in the white rat. *American Journal of Psychology,* 1942, 55, 467–517. **(106)**

Crespi, L. P. Amount of reinforcement and level of performance. *Psychological Review,* 1944, 51, 341–357. **(9)**

Crothers, E. J. *See* Estes, *et al.,* 1960.

Culler, E. A. Recent advances in some concepts of conditioning. *Psychological Review,* 1938, 45, 134–153. **(17)**

D

Dallenbach, K. M. *See* Clark, L. L., *et al.,* 1960.

Dallet, K. M. The transfer surface reexamined. *Journal of Verbal Learning and Verbal Behavior,* 1962, 1, 91–94. **(212–13)**

Dallett, K. M. Proactive and retroactive inhibition in the A-B, A-B′ paradigm. *Journal of Experimental Psychology,* 1964, 68, 190–200. **(218, 286, 306)**

Davitz, J. R. Reinforcement of fear at the beginning and end of shock. *Journal of Comparative Physiological Psychology.* 1955, 48, 152–155. **(162)**

Day, R. S. *See* Horowitz. Day, *et al.,* 1968.

Deese, J. *See also* Lazarus, *et al.,* 1954.

Deese, J. On the structure of association meaning. *Psychological Review,* 1962, 69, 161–175. **(57)**

Deese, J. Meaning and change of meaning. *American Psychologist,* 1967, 22, 641–651. **(57–59)**

Deese, J. Association and memory. In T. R. Dixon & D. L. Horton (Eds.) *Verbal behavior and general behavior theory.* Englewood Cliffs, New Jersey: Prentice-Hall, 1968. **(274, 296)**

Deese, J., Lazarus, R. S., & Keenan, J. Anxiety, anxiety reduction, and stress in learning. *Journal of Experimental Psychology,* 1953, 46, 55–60. **(424, 429)**

Deese, J., & Marder, V. J. The pattern of errors in delayed recall of serial learning after interpolation. *American Journal of Psychology,* 1957, 70, 594–599. **(217)**

Deese, L. *See* Peak & Deese, 1937.

Deffenbacker, K. *See* Wells & Deffenbacker, 1967.

DeNike, L. D. The temporal relationship between awareness and performance in verbal conditioning. *Journal of Experimental Psychology,* 1964, 68, 521–529. **(389, 393–94)**

Denny, M. R. *See* Lippman & Denny, 1964.

De Rivera, J. Some conditions governing the use of the cue-producing response as an explanatory device. *Journal of Experimental Psychology,* 1959, 57, 299–304. **(125, 129–31)**

DeSoto, C. B., & Bosley, J. J. The cognitive structure of a social structure. *Journal of Abnormal and Social Psychology,* 1962, 64, 303–307, **(275)**

Devine, J. V. *See* Ellis, *et al.,* 1962.

DiLoreto, A. *See* Saltz & DiLoreto, 1965.

Diven, K. E. Certain determinants in the conditioning of anxiety reactions. *Journal of Psychology,* 1937, 3, 291–308. **(229)**

Dodson, J. D. *See* Yerkes & Dodson, 1908.

Dollard, J. C. *See* Miller, N. E., & Dollard, 1941.

Doty, R. W. *See* Beck & Doty, 1957.

Draper, D. O. *See* Pollio & Draper, 1966.

Dufort, R. H. *See also* Kimble & Dufort, 1955, 1956; Kimble, *et al.,* 1955.

Dufort, R. H., & Kimble, G. A. Ready signals and the effect of interpolated UCS Presentations in eyelid conditioning. *Journal of Experimental Psychology,* 1958, 56, 1–7. **(98)**

Dukes, W. F. *See* Bevan, *et al.,* 1966.

Dulany, D. E., Jr. Hypotheses and habits in verbal operant conditioning. *Journal of Abnormal and Social Psychology,* 1961, 63, 251–263. **(389)**

Dulany, D. E., Jr. The place of hypotheses and intentions: An analysis of verbal control in verbal conditioning. In C. W. Eriksen (Ed.) *Behavior and awareness..* Durham, North Carolina: Duke University Press, 1962. **(390–91)**

Dulany, D. E. Awareness, rules, and propositional control: A confrontation with S-R behavior theory. In T. R. Dixon & D. L. Horton (Eds.) *Verbal behavior and general behavior theory.* Englewood Cliffs, New Jersey: Prentice-Hall, 1968. **(390)**

Dulany, D. E., Jr., & O'Connel, D. C. Does partial reinforcement dissociate verbal rules and the behavior they might be presumed to control. *Journal of Verbal Learning and Verbal Behavior,* 1963, 2, 361–372. **(410–11)**

Dunlap, R. *See* Leuba & Dunlap, 1951.

Dunning, C. *See* Scott, *et al.,* 1967 (a) , 1967 (b) .

Dyk, R. B. *See* Witkin, *et al.,* 1962.

E

Earhard, B. *See also* Mandler & Earhand, 1964.

Earhard, B., & Mandler, G. Pseudomediation: A reply and more data. *Psychonomic Science,* 1965, 3, 137–138. **(291–92)**

Easterbrook, J. A. The effect of emotion on cue utilization and the organization of behavior. *Psychological Review,* 1959, 66, 183–201. **(101, 356)**

Ebbinghaus, H. *Memory: A contribution to experimental psychology.* (Trans. by H. A. Ruger, & C. E. Bussenius.) New York: Teachers College, Columbia University, 1913. **(263–66, 274)**

Ebenholtz, S. M. *See also* Asch & Ebenholtz, 1962 (a) , 1962 (b) .

Ebenholtz, S. M. The serial position effect of ordered stimulus dimensions in paired associates learning. *Journal of Experimental Psychology,* 1966, 71, 132–137. **(276)**

Edwards, A. L. Political frames of reference as a factor influencing recognition. *Journal of Abnormal and Social Psychology,* 1941, 36, 34–50. **(448)**

Ehrenfreund, D. An experimental test of the continuity theory of discrimination learning with pattern vision. *Journal of Comparative and Physiological Psychology,* 1948, 41, 408–422. **(110, 111, 141, 149)**

Ekstrand, B. R. *See also* Underwood, Ekstrand & Keppel, 1964, 1965.

Ekstrand, B. R. Backward associations. *Psychological Bulletin,* 1966, 65, 50–64. **(168)**

Ekstrand, B. R., & Underwood, B. J. Paced versus unpaced recall in free learning. *Journal of Verbal Learning and Verbal Behavior,* 1963, 2, 288–290. **(187)**

Ekstrand, B. R., & Underwood, B. J. Free learning and recall as a function of unit-sequence and letter-sequence interference. *Journal of Verbal Learning and Verbal Behavior,* 1965, 4, 390–396. **(199, 200, 222–23)**

Elkin, A. *See* Withey, *et al.,* 1949.

Elkind, D. Children's discovery of the conservation of mass, weight, and volume: Piaget replication study II. *Journal of Genetic Psychology,* 1961, 98, 219–227. **(69)**

Elkind, D. Piaget's conservation Problems. *Child Development,* 1967, 38, 15–27. **(68)**

Ellis, H. C., Bessemer, D. W., Devine, J. V., & Trafton, C. L. Recognition of random tactual shapes following predifferentiation training. *Perceptual and Motor Skills,* 1962, 14, 99–102. **(129)**

Ellis, H. C., & Muller, D. G. *Transfer in perceptual learning following* stimulus predifferentiation. *Journal of Experimental Psychology,* 1964, 68, 388–395. **(144)**

Ellson, D. G. Hallucinations produced by sensory conditioning. *Journal of Experimental Psychology,* 1941, 28, 1–20. **(155)**

English, J. M. *See* Runquist & English, 1964.

Epstein, S., & Fenz, W. D. Theory and experiment on the measurement of approach-avoidance conflict. *Journal of Abnormal and Social Psychology,* 1962, 64, 97–112. **(421)**

Epstein, W. The influence of syntactical structure on learning. *American Journal of Psychology,* 1961, 74, 80–85. **(309)**

Epstein, W. A further study of the influence of syntactical structure on learning. *American Journal of Psychology,* 1962, 75, 121–126 **(309)**

Epstein, W. The effect of stimulus and response meaningfulness when response availability is equated. *Journal of Verbal Learning and Verbal Behavior,* 1963, 2, 242–249. **(324)**

Erickson, J. R., & Zajkowski, M. M. Learning several concept-identification problems concurrently: A test of the sampling-with-replacement assumption. *Journal of Experimental Psychology,* 1967, 74, 212–218. **(87)**

Eriksen, C. W. *See also* Chatterjee & Eriksen, 1962; Hake & Eriksen, 1955; Paul, G. I., *et al.,* 1962.

Eriksen, C. W. (Ed.) *Behavior and awareness: A symposium of research and interpretation.* Durham, N.C.: Duke Univ. Press, 1962. **(387–88)**

Eriksen, C. W. Cognitive responses to internally cued anxiety. In C. D. Spielberger (Ed.), *Anxiety and behavior.* New York: Academic Press, 1966. **(431, 435, 451)**

Erlebacher, A. H. *See* Underwood & Erlebacher, 1965.

Ernstein, E. *See* Saltz, Metzen, & Ernstein, 1961.

Ervin, S. M., & Foster, G. The development of meaning in children's descriptive terms. *Journal of Abnormal and Social Psychology,* 1960, 61, 271–275. **(65, 70, 73)**

Estes, W. K. Learning theory and the new "mental chemistry." *Psychological Review,* 1960, 67, 207–225. **(88, 90)**

Estes, W. K., Hopkins, B. L., Crothers, E. J. All-or-none and conservation effects in the learning and retention of paired associates. *Journal of Experimental Psychology,* 1960, 60, 329–339. **(90, 149, 177)**

F

Faterson, H. F. *See* Witkin, *et al.,* 1962.

Feldman, S. M., & Underwood, B. J. Stimulus recall following paired-associate learning. *Journal of Experimental Psychology,* 1957, 53, 11–15. **(163, 347)**

Felton, M. *See* Saltz & Felton, 1968 (a) , 1968 (b) .

Fenz, W. D. *See* Epstein, S., & Fenz, 1962.

Fitch, F. G. *See* Hull, *et al.,* 1940.

Fitzgerald, D., & Ausubel, D. P. Cognitive versus affective factors in the learning and retention of controversial material. *Journal of Educational Psychology,* 1963, 54, 73–84. **(448)**

Fivel, M. W. *See* Osler & Fivel, 1961.

Flavell, J. H. *See* Miller, S. A., *et al.,* 1970.

Forlano, G. School learning with various methods of practice and rewards. *Teachers College Contribution to Education,* 1936, No. 688. **(375)**

Foster, G. *See* Ervin & Foster, 1960.

Fowler, H. *See* Wischner, *et al.,* 1963.

Fraser, J. *See* Postman, Stark, & Fraser, 1968.

Freeman, M. *See* Runquist & Freeman, 1960.

Freibergs, V., & Tulvig, E. The effect of practice on utilization of information from positive and negative instances in concept identification. *Canadian Journal of Psychology,* 1961, 15, 101–106. **(52, 56)**

Friedman, E. A. *See* Miller, G. A., & Friedman, 1957.

G

Gagne, R. M. The acquisition of knowledge. *Psychological Review,* 1962, 69, 355–365. **(308)**

Gagne, R. M. *The conditions of learning.* New York: Holt, Rinehart, Winston, 1965. **(308)**

Gagne, R. M., & Baker, K. E. Stimulus predifferentiation as a factor in transfer of training. *Journal of Experimental Psychology,* 1950, 40, 439–451. **(117–18, 136, 142–43)**

Gagne, R. M., Mayor, J. R., Garstens, H. L., & Paradise, N. E. Factors in acquiring knowledge of a mathematical task. *Psychological Monographs,* 1962, 76, No. 7 (Whole No. 526) . **(308)**

Gagne, R. M., & Paradise, N. E. Abilities and learning sets in knowledge acquistion. *Psychological Monographs,* 1961, 75, No. 14 (Whole No. 518) . **(308)**

Galanter, E. *See* Miller, G. A., *et al.,* 1960.

Gallup, G. G., Jr. *See* Wollen & Gallup, 1968.

Gannon, D. R., & Noble, C. E. Familiarization (*n*) as a factor in paired-associate verbal learning. *Journal of Experimental Psychology,* 1961, 62, 14–23. **(147–48, 330)**

Garstens, H. L. *See* Gagne, *et al.,* 1962.

Gates, A. I. Recitation as a factor in memorizing. *Archives of Psychology,* 1917, 6, No. 40. **(375)**

Gerjuoy, I. R. Discrimination learning as a function of the similarity of the stimulus names. Unpublished doctor's dissertation, State University of Iowa, 1953. **(127, 129)**

Gibson, E. J. *See also* Gibson, J. J. & Gibson, 1955; Walk *et al.,* 1958, 1959.

Gibson, E. J. A systematic of the concepts of generalization and differentiation to verbal learning. *Psychological Review,* 1940, 47, 196–229. **(51, 60, 114–17, 122–24, 130, 132–34, 136–38, 184–85, 260)**

Gibson, E. J., & Walk, R. D. The effect of prolonged exposure to visually presented patterns on learning to discriminate them. *Journal of Comparative and Physiological Psychology,* 1956, 49, 239–242. **(116, 119)**

Gibson, E. J., Walk, R. D., Pick, H. L., Jr., & Tighe, T. J. The effect of prolonged exposure to visual patterns on learning to discriminate similar and different patterns. *Journal of Comparative and Physiological Psychology,* 1958, 51, 584–587. **(120)**

Gibson, J. J., and Gibson, E. J. Perceptual learning: Differentiation or enrichment? *Psychological Review,* 1955, 62, 32–41. **(60)**

Ginsberg, R. A. *See* Suppes & Ginsberg, 1963.

Giovanelli, G., & Tampieri, P. Indagine sul rapporto tra anticipazioni mancate ed errate nell' apprendimento seriale. *Archivio di Scienze Biologiche,* 1964, 48, 30–49. **(267)**

Glanzer, M., & Peters, S. C. Reexamination of the serial position effect. *Journal of Experimental Psychology,* 1962, 64, 258–266. **(269)**

Glaze, J. A. The association value of nonsense syllables, *Journal of Genetic Psychology,* 1928, 35, 255–269. **(274, 330–40)**

Glixman, A. F. Recall of completed and incomplete activities under varying degrees of stress. *Journal of Experimental Psychology,* 1949, 39, 281–295. **(435)**

Goggin, J. *See also* Postman & Goggin, 1964.

Goggin, J. First-list recall as a function of second-list learning method. *Journal of Verbal Learning and Verbal Behavior,* 1967, 6, 423–427. **(211)**

Goggin, J. Retroactive inhibition with different patterns of interpolated lists. *Journal of Experimental Psychology,* 1968, 76, 102–108. **(210–12, 215)**

Goldiamond, I., & Hawkins, W. F. Vexierversuch: The lag relationship between word-frequency and recognition obtained in the absence of stimulus words. *Journal of Experimental Psychology,* 1958, 56, 457–463. **(182, 183, 191)**

Goldstein, N. Saving in the learning of scrambled lists as influenced by degree of familiarity with nonsense syllables. *Journal of General Psychology,* 1950, 42, 87–96. **(263)**

Golin, S. Incubation effect: Role of awareness in an immediate versus delayed test of conditioned emotionality. *Journal of Abnormal and Social Psychology,* 1961, 63, 534–539. **(229)**

Goodnow, J. J. *See also* Bruner, *et al.,* 1956.

Goodnow, J. J., & Postman, L. Probability learning in a problem solving situation. *Journal of Experimental Psychology,* 1955, 49, 16–22. **(48)**

Goodnow, R. E. Utilization of partially valid cues in perceptual identification. Doctoral dissertation, Harvard University, 1954. **(46, 49, 50)**

Goodrich, K. P., Ross, L. E., & Wagner, A. R. Performance in eyelid conditioning following interpolated presentations of the UCS. *Journal of Experimental Psychology,* 1957, 53, 214–217. **(99)**

Goodrich, K. P., Ross, L. E., & Wagner, A. R. Supplementary report: Effect of interpolated UCS trials in eyelid conditioning without a ready signal. *Journal of Experimental Psychology,* 1959, 58, 319–320. **(99)**

Gormezano, I., & Moore, J. W. Effects of instructional set and UCS intensity on the latency, percentage, and form of the eyelid response. *Journal of Experimental Psychology,* 1962, 63, 487–494. **(413)**

Goss, A. E. *See also* Rossman & Goss, 1951.

Goss, A. E. Transfer as a function of type and amount of preliminary experience with the task stimuli. *Journal of Experimental Psychology,* 1953, 46, 419–428. **(144)**

Goss, A. E. A stimulus-response analysis of the interaction of cue producing and instrumental responses. *Psychological Review,* 1955, 62, 20–31. **(121, 122, 124–30)**

Gottschaldt, K. Ueber den Einfluss der Erfahrung auf die Wahrnehmung von Figuren. *Psychologische Forschung,* 1926, 8, 261–317. **(256)**

Goulet, L. R., & Postman, L. An experimental evaluation of the pseudo-mediation hypothesis. *Psychonomic Science,* 1966, 4, 163–164. **(285)**

Grant, D. A. *See also* Cerekwicki, *et al.,* 1968; Hartman & Grant, 1962; Norris & Grant, 1948.

Grant, D. A., & Adams, J. K. Alpha conditioning in the eyelid. *Journal of Experimental Psychology,* 1944, 34, 136–142. **(19)**

Gray, C. W. *See also* Newman, S. E., & Gray, 1964.

Gray, C. W., & Newman, S. E. Associative asymmetry as a function of pronunciability. *Journal of Experimental Psychology,* 1966, 71, 923–924. **(166)**

Greenbaum, K. *See* Katz & Greenbaum, 1968.

Greenbloom, R., & Kimble, G. A. Extinction of R-S association and performance on recall trials without information feedback. *Journal of Verbal Learning and Verbal Behavior,* 1965, 4, 341–347. **(149)**

Greenspoon, J. The reinforcing effect of two responses. *American Journal of Psychology,* 1955, 68, 409–416. **(387)**

Guthrie, E. R. Conditioning as a principle of learning. *Psychological Review,* 1930, 37, 412–428. **(6, 7)**

Guthrie, E. R. *The psychology of learning.* New York: Harper, 1935. **(6, 7, 153, 159, 224, 350)**

Guthrie, E. R. *The psychology of human conflict.* New York: Harper, 1938. **(7)**

Guthrie, E. R., & Horton, G. P. *Cats in a puzzle box.* New York: Rinehart, 1946. **(12)**

Gynther, R. A. The effects of anxiety and of situational stress on communicative efficiency. *Journal of Abnormal and Social Psychology,* 1957, 54, 274–276. **(437–39)**

H

Hake, H. W., & Eriksen, C. W. Effect of number of permissible response categories on learning of a constant number of visual stimuli. *Journal of Experimental Psychology,* 1955, 50, 161–167. **(123, 126, 129–31)**

Hakes, D. T., James, C. T., & Young, R. K. A reexamination of the Ebbinghaus derived-list paradigm. *Journal of Experimental Psychology,* 1964, 68, 508–514. **(264)**

Hall, J. F. Learning as a function of word frequency. *American Journal of Psychology,* 1954, 67, 138–140. **(320)**

Hall, M. *See* Hull, *et al.,* 1940.

Hamilton, H. *See also* Saltz & Hamilton, 1967, 1968, 1969.

Hamilton, H., & Saltz, E. Role of intelligence in precriterion concept attainment by children. *Journal of Experimental Psychology,* 1969, 81, 191–192. **(53)**

Hamilton, J. A., & Krechevsky, I. Studies in the effect of shock on behavior plasticity in the rat. *Journal of Comparative Psychology,* 1933, 16, 237–253. **(428)**

Hamilton, R. *See* Lazarus, *et al.,* 1954.

Harlow, H. F., & Stagner, R. Effect of complete striate muscle paralysis upon the learning process. *Journal of Experimental Psychology,* 1933, 16, 283–294. **(160)**

Hartman, R. R. *See* Horton and Hartman, 1963.

Hartman, T. F., & Grant, D. A. Effects of pattern of reinforcement and verbal information on acquisition, extinction, and spontaneous recovery of the eyelid. *Journal of Experimental Psychology,* 1962, 63, 217–226. **(403, 413)**

Hawkins, W. F. *See* Goldiamond & Hawkins, 1958.

Haygood, R. C., & Bourne, L. E., Jr. Attribute-and-rule learning aspects of conceptual behavior. *Psychological Review,* 1965, 72, 175–195. **(86, 87)**

Heaslet, G. *See* Martin, J. G., *et al.,* 1963.

Heath, R. M. *See* McClelland and Heath, 1943.

Hebb, D. O. Distinctive features of learning in the higher animal. In J. F. Delafresnaye (Ed.) *Brain mechanisms and learning.* New York: Oxford University Press, 1961. **(239, 240)**

Hefferline, R., & Perera, T. Proprioceptive discrimination of a covert operant without its observation by the subject, *Science,* 1963, 139, 834–835. **(155)**

Heinemann, S. H. *See* Mandler & Heinemann, 1956.

Hellyer, S. Supplementary report: Frequency of stimulus presentation and short term decrement in recall. *Journal of Experimental Psychology,* 1962, 64, 650. **(81, 82, 143, 237, 246)**

Henderson, A. *See* Ceraso & Henderson, 1965.

Henle, M. *See* Wallach, H., & Henle, 1941, 1942.

Henschel, D. *See* Postman, Stark, & Henschel, 1969.

Hilgard, E. R. *See also* Umemoto & Hilgard, 1961.

Hilgard, E. R. An algebraic analysis of conditioned discrimination in man. *Psychological Review,* 1938, 45, 472–496. **(414)**

Hilgard, E. R. *Theories of learning.* New York: Appleton-Century-Crofts, 1956. **(410)**

Hilgard, E. R., & Humphreys, L. G. The effects of supporting and antagonistic voluntary instructions on conditioned discriminations. *Journal of Experimental Psychology,* 1938, 22, 291–304. **(414)**

Hilgard, E. R., & Marquis, D. G. *Conditioning and learning.* New York: Appleton-Century-Crofts, 1940. **(17)**

Hilner, K. *See* Peterson, L. R., *et al.,* 1962.

Hintzman, D. L. Articulatory coding in short term memory. *Journal of Verbal Learning and Verbal Behavior,* 1967, 6, 312–316. **(239)**

Hockett, C. F. Chinese versus English: An exploration of the Whorfian thesis. In H. Hoijer (Ed.), *Language in culture.* Chicago: University of Chicago Press, 1954. **(31)**

Hoffman, H. N. A study in an aspect of concept formation with subnormal, average, and superior adolescents. *Genetic Psychology Monographs,* 1955, 52, 191–239. **(53)**

Holstein, S. B., & Premack, D. On the different effect of random reinforcement and presolution reversal on human concept identification. *Journal of Experimental Psychology,* 1965, 70, 335–337. **(93)**

Hom, G. *See* Martin, J. G., *et al.,* 1963.

Homzie, M. J. *See* Spence, K. W., Homzie & Rutledge, 1964.

Homzie, M. J., & Weiss, G. UCS intensity and the associative strength of the eyelid CR with a masked conditioning procedure. *Journal of Experimental Psychology*, 1965, 69, 101–103. **(403)**

Hooper, F. H. An exploration of vocabulary processes. Master's thesis, Wayne State University, 1964. **(59)**

Hooper, F. H. Piaget's conservation tasks: The logical and developmental priority of identity conservation, Ph.D. dissertation, Wayne State University, 1967. **(67)**

Hopkins, B. L. *See* Estes, *et al.*, 1960.

Hopkins, R. H. *See* Weaver, *et al.*, 1968.

Hopkins, R. H., & Schulz, R. W. The A-B, B-C, A-C mediation paradigm: Recall of A-B following varying numbers of trials of A-C learning. *Psychonomic Science*, 1967, 9, 235–236. **(291)**

Horowitz, L. M. Free recall and ordering of trigrams. *Journal of Experimental Psychology*, 1961, 62, 51–57. **(187, 188)**

Horowitz, L. M. Sequential learning, associative symmetry and thought. In J. F. Voss (Ed.), *Approaches to thought,* Columbus, Ohio: C. E. Merrill, 1969. **(258)**

Horowitz, L. M., Brown, Z. M., & Weissbluth, S. Availability and the direction of association. *Journal of Experimental Psychology*, 1964, 68, 541–549. **(165)**

Horowitz, L. M., Day, R. S., Light, L. L., & White, M. A. Availability growth and latent verbal learning. *Journal of General Psychology*, 1968, 78, 65–83. **(178)**

Horowitz, L. M., & Izawa, C. A. Comparison of serial and paired-associate learning. *Journal of Experimental Psychology*, 1963, 65, 352–361. **(261)**

Horowitz, L. M., & Larsen, S. R. Response interference in paired-associate learning. *Journal of Experimental Psychology*, 1963, 65, 225–232. **(175, 177, 180, 181)**

Horowitz, L. M., Lippman, L. G., Norman, S. A., & McConkie, G. W. Compound stimuli in paired-associate learning. *Journal of Experimental Psychology*, 1964, 67, 132–141. **(146)**

Horowitz, L. M., White, M. A., & Atwood, D. W. Word fragments as aids to recall: The organization of a word. *Journal of Experimental Psychology*, 1968, 76, 219–226. **(259)**

Horton, D. L., & Hartman, R. R. Verbal mediation as a function of associative directionality and exposure frequency. *Journal of Verbal Learning and Verbal Behavior*, 1963, 1, 361–364. **(279, 280, 283)**

Horton, D. L., & Kjeldergaard, P. M. An experimental analysis of associative factors in mediated generalization. *Psychological Monographs,* 1961, 75, No. 11 (Whole No. 515). **(279–81, 289)**

Horton, D. L., & Wiley, R. E. The effect of mediation on the retention and strength of previously formed associations. *Journal of Verbal Learning and Verbal Behavior,* 1967 (a), 6, 36–41. **(285)**

Horton, D. L., & Wiley, R. E. Mediated association: Facilitation and interference. *Journal of Experimental Psychology,* 1967 (b) , 73, 636–638. **(283, 291)**

Horton, G. P. *See* Guthrie & Horton, 1946.

Houston, J. P. Short-term retention of verbal units with equated degrees of learning. *Journal of Experimental Psychology,* 1965, 70, 75–78. **(248)**

Houston, J. P. First-list retention and time and method of recall. *Journal of Experimental Psychology,* 1966, 71, 839–843. **(218)**

Hovland, C. I. *See also* Hull, *et al.,* 1940.

Hovland, C. I., & Weiss, W. Transmission of information concerning concepts through positive and negative instances. *Journal of Experimental Psychology,* 1953, 45, 165–182. **(52, 56)**

Howes, D. On the relationship between the probability of a word as an association and in general linguistic usage. *Journal of Abnormal and Social Psychology,* 1957, 54, 75–85. **(182, 191)**

Howes, D. H., & Solomon, R. L. Visual duration threshold as a function of word-probability. *Journal of Experimental Psychology,* 1951, 41, 401–410. **(183)**

Hull, C. L. Quantitative aspects of the evolution of concepts. *Psychological Monographs,* 1920, 28, No. 1 (Whole No. 123) . **(40, 51)**

Hull, C. L. Knowledge and purpose as habit mechanisms. *Psychological Review,* 1930, 37, 511–525. **(383)**

Hull, C. L. The conflicting psychologies of learning—a way out. *Psychological Review,* 1935 (a) , 42, 491–516. **(163)**

Hull, C. L. The mechanism of assembly of behavior segments in novel combinations suitable for problem solution. *Psychological Review,* 1935 (b) , 42, 219–245. **(278)**

Hull, C. L. *Principles of behavior.* New York: Appleton-Century-Crofts, 1943. **(6, 7, 96, 97, 104, 153, 159, 350, 416, 422)**

Hull, C. L. *Essentials of behavior,* New Haven: Yale University Press, 1951. **(7)**

Hull, C. L. A behavior system: *An introduction to behavior theory concerning the individual organism.* New Haven: Yale University Press, 1952. **(7)**

Hull, C. L., Hovland, C. I., Ross, R. T., Hall, M., Perkins, D. T., & Fitch, F. G. *Mathematico-deductive theory of rote learning.* New Haven: Yale University Press, 1940. **(163, 268)**

Humphreys, L. G. *See* Hilgard and Humphreys, 1938; Paul, G. I., *et al.,* 1962.

Hunt, E. B. *Concept learning: An information processing problem.* New York: Wiley, 1962. **(35, 50)**

Hunt, R. G. Meaningfulness and articulation of stimulus and response in paired associates learning and stimulus recall. *Journal of Experimental Psychology,* 1959, 57, 262–267. **(318, 322)**

Huttenlocher, J. Effects of manipulation of attributes on efficiency of concept formation. *Psychological Reports,* 1962, 10, 509–516. **(55)**

I

Inhelder, B. *See also* Piaget & Inhelder, 1962.

Inhelder, B., & Piaget, J. *The growth of logical thinking from childhood to adolescence.* New York: Basic Books, 1958. **(71)**

Irion, A. L. *See* McGeoch & Irion, 1952.

Irwin, J. M. *See* Melton & Irwin, 1940.

Iscoe, I. *See also* Semler & Iscoe, 1963.

Iscoe, I., & Semler, I. Paired associate learning in normal and mentally retarded children as a function of four experimental conditions. *Journal of Comparative and Physiological Psychology,* 1964, 59, 387–392. **(326, 327)**

Izawa, C. A. *See* Horowitz & Izawa, 1963.

J

Jacobs, A. Formation of new associations to words selected on the basis of reaction-time-GSR combinations. *Journal of Abnormal and Social Psychology,* 1955, 51, 371–377. **(322)**

James, C. T. *See* Hakes, *et al.,* 1964.

Jenkins, J. J. *See also* Russell & Jenkins, 1954.

Jenkins, J. J. Effects on word-association of the set to give popular responses. *Psychological Reports,* 1959, 5, 94. **(410)**

Jenkins, J. J. Mediated associations: Paradigms and situations. In C. N. Cofer & B. S. Musgrave (Eds.) *Verbal behavior and learning: Problems and processes,* New York: McGraw-Hill, 1963. **(281, 283, 286–89, 293–95, 299, 300)**

Jensen, A. R. How much can we boost IQ and scholastic achievement? *Harvard Educational Review,* 1969, 39, 1–123. **(13)**

Jensen, A. R., & Rohwer, W. D., Jr. What is learned in serial learning? *Journal of Verbal Learning and Verbal Behavior,* 1965, 4, 62–72. **(260)**

Johnson, D. M. Word association and word-frequency. *American Journal of Psychology,* 1956, 69, 125–126. **(182, 191)**

Johnson, N. F. Sequential verbal behavior. In T. R. Dixon & D. L. Horton (Eds.) *Verbal behavior and general behavior theory.* Englewood Cliffs, New Jersey: Prentice-Hall, 1968. **(309)**

Jones, F. N., & Jones, M. H. Vividness as a factor in learning lists of nonsense syllables. *American Journal of Psychology,* 1942, 55, 96–101. **(184)**

Jones, J. E. Contiguity and reinforcement in relation to cs-ucs intervals in classical average conditioning. *Psychological Review*, 1962, 69, 176–186. **(162)**

Jones, M. H. *See* Jones, F. N., & Jones, 1942.

Jung, J. Transfer of training as a function of degree of first-list learning. *Journal of Verbal Learning and Verbal Behavior*, 1962, 1, 197–199. **(212)**

Jung, J. A cumulative method of paired associate and serial learning. *Journal of Verbal Learning and Verbal Behavior*, 1964, 3, 290–299. **(83, 84)**

Jung, J. Comments on Mandler's "From association to structure." *Psychological Review*, 1965, 72, 318–322. **(235)**

K

Kagan, J., Moss, H. A., & Sigel, I. E. Psychological significance of styles of conceptualization. In J. C. Wright and J. Kagan (Eds.) Basic cognitive processes in children. *Monograph of the Society for Research in Child Development*, 1963, 28, No. 2 (Serial No. 86). **(54)**

Kantrowitz, M. H. Concept conservation in children; some theoretical formulations. M.A. thesis, Wayne State University, 1969. **(32)**

Kanungo, R. N., Lambert, W. E., & Mauer, S. M. Semantic satiation and paired-associates learning. *Journal of Experimental Psychology*, 1962, 64, 600–607. **(359)**

Kaplan, E. *See* Werner & Kaplan, 1950.

Karp, S. A. *See* Witkin, *et al.*, 1962.

Katz, P. A. Effects of labels on children's perception of discrimination learning. *Journal of Experimental Psychology*, 1963, 66, 423–428. **(119, 126, 127, 129)**

Katz, S., & Greenbaum, K. Chained paired associate errors and method of rehearsal. *Journal of Verbal Learning and Verbal Behavior*, 1968, 7, 133–136. **(169)**

Keenan, J. *See* Deese, *et al.*, 1953.

Kelley, E. L. An experimental attempt to produce artificial chromaesthesia by the technique of the conditioned response. *Journal of Experimental Psychology*, 1934, 17, 315–341. **(156)**

Kelley, R. J. The learning and recall of emotional and neutral words in a negative transfer situation as a function of differentiation. Doctoral dissertation, Wayne State University, 1964. **(446)**

Kendler, H. H. "What is learned?"—A theoretical blind alley. *Psychological Review*, 1952, 59, 269–277. **(23)**

Kendler, H. H. *Basic Psychology* (Second edition). New York: Appleton-Century-Crofts, 1968. **(50)**

Kendler, H. H., & Kendler, T. S. Vertical and horizontal processes in problem solving. *Psychological Review*, 1962, 69, 1–16. **(51, 73)**

Kendler, T. S. *See* Kendler, H.H., & Kendler, 1962.

Kendler, T. S. Concept formation. *Annual Review of Psychology,* 1961, 13, 447–472. **(35, 45)**

Keppel, G. *See also* Postman, Keppel, & Stark, 1965; Shuell & Keppel, 1967; Underwood, Ekstrand, & Keppel, 1964, 1965; Underwood & Keppel, 1962, 1963 (a), 1963 (b), 1963 (c) ; Underwood, Rehula, & Keppel, 1962.

Keppel, G., & Rauch, D. S. Unlearning as a function of second-list error rate. *Journal of Verbal Learning and Verbal Behavior.* 1966, 5, 50–58. **(209, 211, 216)**

Keppel, G., & Underwood, B. J. Proactive inhibition in short-term retention of single items. *Journal of Verbal Learning and Verbal Behavior,* 1962 (a) , 1, 153–161. **(79–81, 240, 241, 245)**

Keppel, G., & Underwood, B. J. Retroactive inhibition of R-S associations. *Journal of Experimental Psychology,* 1962 (b) , 64, 400–404. **(212, 213)**

Kimble, G. A. *See also* Dufort & Kimble, 1958; Greenbloom & Kimble, 1965.

Kimble, G. A. *Hilgard and Marquis' Conditioning and learning.* New York: Appleton-Century-Crofts, 1961. **(18, 111, 121, 159, 414, 415)**

Kimble, G. A., & Dufort, R. H. Meaningfulness and isolation as factors in verbal learning. *Journal of Experimental Psychology,* 1955, 50, 361–368. **(184, 318)**

Kimble, G. A., & Dufort, R. H. The associative factor in eyelid conditioning. *Journal of Experimental Psychology,* 1956, 52, 386–391. **(98, 99)**

Kimble, G. A., Mann, L. J., & Dufort, R. H. Classical and instrumental eyelid conditioning. *Journal of Experimental Psychology,* 1955, 49, 407–417. **(98)**

Kimble, G. A., & Ost, J. W. P. A conditioned inhibitory process in eyelid conditionary. *Journal of Experimental Psychology,* 1961, 61, 150–156. **(19)**

Kincaid, W. D., Bousfield, W. A., & Whitmarsh, G. A. The parasitic reinforcement of verbal associative responses. *Journal of Experimental Psychology,* 1962, 64, 572–579. **(282, 283, 300)**

King, R. A. The effects of training and motivation on the components of a learned instrumental response. Doctoral dissertation, Duke University, 1959. **(105, 106)**

King, R. A. The effects of training and motivation on the components of a learned instrumental response. In G. A. Kimble (Ed.) *Foundations of conditioning and learning.* New York: Appleton-Century-Crofts, 1967. **(103, 105, 107)**

Kjeldergaard, P. M. *See* Horton & Kjeldergaard, 1961.

Kleemeier, R. W. Fixation and regression in the rat. *Psychological Monographs,* 1942, 54, No. 4 (Whole No. 246). **(428)**

Kohler, I. The formation and transformation of the perceptual world. *Psychological Issues,* 1963, 3, No. 4 (Whole No. 12). **(255, 256)**

Köhler, W. *The mentality of apes.* New York: Harcourt, Brace, 1925. **(11)**

Koppenaal, R. J. *See also* Battig & Koppenaal, 1965.

Koppenaal, R. J. Time changes in the strengths of A-B, A-C Lists; Spontaneous recovery? *Journal of Verbal Learning and Verbal Behavior,* 1963, 2, 310–319. **(217, 218, 224)**

Krasner, L. Studies of the conditioning of verbal behavior, *Psychological Bulletin,* 1958, 55, 148–171. **(388)**

Krechevsky, I. *See also* Hamilton, J. A., & Krechevsky, 1933.

Krechevsky, I. "Hypotheses" in rats. *Psychological Review,* 1932, 39, 516–532. **(109)**

Krechevsky, I. A study of the continuity of the problem-solving process. *Psychological Review,* 1938, 45, 107–133. **(109–11)**

Kressel, K. *See* Winnick & Kressel, 1965.

Krueger, W. C. F. The effect of overlearning on retention. *Journal of Experimental Psychology,* 1929, 12, 71–78. **(199)**

Krueger, W. C. F. The relative difficulty of nonsense syllables. *Journal of Experimental Psychology,* 1934, 17, 145–153. **(331)**

Kuiken, D., & Schulz, R. W. Response familiarization and the associative phase of paired associate learning. *Journal of Verbal Learning and Verbal Behavior,* 1968, 7, 106–109. **(177)**

Kurtz, K. H. Discrimination of complex stimuli: the relationship of training and test stimuli in transfer of discrimination. *Journal of Experimental Psychology,* 1955, 50, 283–292. **(119, 134–36, 138, 141)**

Kushnik, S. A. *See* Wischner, *et al.,* 1963.

Kvale, S. *See* Rommetveit & Kvale, 1965 (a), 1965 (b).

L

L'Abate, L. Manifest anxiety and the learning of syllables with different association values. *American Journal of Psychology,* 1959, 72, 107–110. **(333)**

Lambert, W. E. *See* Kanungo, *et al.,* 1962.

Land, V. *See* Peterson, L. R., *et al.,* 1962.

Lansford, T. G. *See* Clark, L. L., *et al.,* 1960.

Larsen, S. R. *See* Horowitz & Larsen, 1963.

Lashley, K. The problem of serial order in behavior. In L. Jeffress (Ed.) *Cerebral mechanisms in behavior.* New York: Wiley, 1951. **(259)**

Lashley, K. S. *Brain mechanisms and intelligence.* Chicago: University of Chicago Press, 1929. **(109)**

Lawrence, D. H. Acquired distinctiveness of cues: 1. Transfer between discriminations on the basis of familiarity with the stimuli. *Journal of Experimental Psychology*, 1949, 39, 770–784. **(123, 131–33, 141, 149)**

Lawrence, D. H. Acquired distinctiveness of cues: II. Selective association in a constant stimulus situation. *Journal of Experimental Psychology*, 1950, 40, 175–188. **(131, 133, 134)**

Lazarus, R. S. *See* Deese, et al., 1953.

Lazarus, R. S., Deese, J., & Hamilton, R. Anxiety and stress in learning: The role of intraserial duplication. *Journal of Experimental Psychology*, 1954, 47, 111–114. **(424, 430)**

Lazarus, R. S., & Longo, N. The consistency of psychological defense against threat. *Journal of Abnormal and Social Psychology*, 1953, 48, 495–499. **(424)**

Lee, L. C. The effects of anxiety level and shock on a paired-associate verbal task. *Journal of Experimental Psychology*, 1961, 61, 213–217. **(425, 429, 430, 432)**

Leeper, R. W. A study of a neglected portion of the field of learning: The development of sensory organization. *Journal of Genetic Psychology*, 1935, 46, 41–75. **(254)**

Leuba, C. Images as conditioned sensations. *Journal of Experimental Psychology*, 1940, 26, 345–351. **(155)**

Leuba, C., & Dunlap, R. Conditioning imagery. *Journal of Experimental Psychology*, 1951, 4, 352–355. **(155)**

Levin, H. *See* Marchbanks & Levin, 1965.

Levin, S. M. *See also* Spielberger & Levin, 1962; Spielberger, *et al.*, 1962.

Levin, S. M. The effects of awareness on verbal conditioning. *Journal of Experimental Psychology*, 1961, 61, 67–75. **(389, 390, 398, 399)**

Levin, S. M., & Sterner, K. The acquisition of positive secondary reinforcement in human subjects. *Psychonomic Science*, 1966, 6, 47–48. **(399)**

Levine, M. Cue neutralization: The effects of random reinforcement upon discrimination learning. *Journal of Experimental Psychology*, 1962, 63, 438–443. **(93, 94)**

Levine, M. Hypothesis behavior by humans during discrimination learning. *Journal of Experimental Psychology*, 1966, 71, 331–338. **(94)**

Levy, B. A., & Murdock, B. B., Jr. The effects of delayed auditory feedback and intra-list similarity in short-term memory. *Journal of Verbal Learning and Verbal Behavior*, 1968, 7, 887–894. **(239)**

Lewin, K. Field theory and learning. *Yearbook of the National Society for Study of Education*, 1942, 41, Part II, 215–242. **(17)**

Light, L. L. *See* Horowitz, Day, *et al.*, 1968.

Lindley, R. H. Association value and familiarity in serial verbal learning. *Journal of Experimental Psychology*, 1960, 59, 366–370. **(332, 336)**

Lindley, R. H. Association value, familiarity, and pronunciability ratings as predictors of serial verbal learning. *Journal of Experimental Psychology,* 1963, 65, 347–351. **(334–36)**

Lindner, M. A. *See* Asch & Lindner, 1963.

Lippman, L. G. *See also* Horowitz, Lippman, *et al.,* 1964.

Lippman, L. G., & Denny, M. R. Serial position effect as a function of intertrial interval. *Journal of Verbal Learning and Verbal Behavior,* 1964, 3, 496–501. **(269)**

Lipsitt, L. P. *See also* Castaneda & Lipsitt, 1959.

Lipsitt, L. P., & Lolordo, V. M. Interaction effect of stress and stimulus generalization on children's oddity learning. *Journal of Experimental Psychology,* 1963, 66, 210–214. **(443)**

Loess, H. Proactive inhibition in short-term memory. *Journal of Verbal Learning and Verbal Behavior,* 1964, 3, 362–368. **(80, 241, 247)**

Logan, F. A. A micromolar approach to behavior theory. *Psychological Review,* 1956, 63, 63–73. **(17)**

Lolordo, V. M. *See* Lipsitt & Lolordo, 1963.

Longo, N. *See* Lazarus & Longo, 1953.

Lorge, I. *See also* Thorndike & Lorge, 1944.

Lorge, I. *The Semantic Count of the 570 Commonest English Words.* New York: Bureau of Publication. Teachers College, Columbia University, 1949. **(329)**

Lowe, R. C. See Wohlwill & Lowe, 1962.

Lucas, J. D. The interaction effects of anxiety, failure, and intraserial duplication. *American Journal of Psychology,* 1952, 65, 59–66. **(433, 434, 437)**

Lumsdaine, A. A. Conditioned eyelid responses as mediating generalized finger reactions. *Psychological Bulletin,* 1939, 36, 650. **(277)**

Luria, A. R. *The role of speech in the regulation of normal and abnormal behavior.* New York: Liveright, 1961. **(405–410)**

Luria, A. R. *The mind of a mnemonist.* New York: Basic Books, 1968. **(377, 378)**

M

MacDonald, A. The effect of adaptation to the unconditioned stimulus upon the formation of conditioned avoidance responses. *Journal of Experimental Psychology,* 1946, 36, 1–12. **(99)**

Macorquodale, K., & Meehl, P. E. "Edward C. Tolman." In W. K. Estes, *et al. Modern learning theory.* New York: Appleton-Century-Crofts, 1954. **(385)**

Madigan, S. A. *See* Paivio & Madigan, 1968.

Maltzman, I. Thinking from a behavioristic point of view. *Psychological Review,* 1955, 62, 275–286. **(278)**

Mandler, G. *See also* Earhard & Mandler, 1965; Segal & Mandler, 1967.

Mandler, G. Response factors in human learning. *Psychological Review,* 1954, 61, 235–244. **(122, 182)**

Mandler, G. From association to structure. *Psychological Review,* 1962, 69, 415–427. **(232, 235)**

Mandler, G. Subjects do think: A reply to Jung's comments, *Psychological Review,* 1965, 72, 323–326. **(232, 235)**

Mandler, G. Organization and memory. In K. W. Spence & J. T. Spence (Eds.) *The psychology of learning and motivation.* Vol I. New York: Academic Press, 1967. **(304–7)**

Mandler, G., & Earhard, B. Pseudomediation: Is chaining an artifact? *Psychonomic Science,* 1964, 1, 247–248. **(285)**

Mandler, G., & Heinemann, S. H. Effect of overlearning of a verbal response on transfer of training. *Journal of Experimental Psychology,* 1956, 51, 39–46. **(235)**

Mandler, G., & Sarason, S. B. A study of anxiety and learning. *Journal of Abnormal and Social Psychology,* 1952, 47, 166–173. **(438)**

Mann, L. J. *See* Kimble, et al., 1955.

Marchbanks, G., & Levin, H. Cues by which children recognize words. *Journal of Educational Psychology,* 1965, 56–57–61. **(259)**

Marder, V. J. *See* Deese & Marder, 1957.

Marks, L., & Miller, G. A. The role of semantic and syntactic constraints in the memorization of English sentences. *Journal of Verbal Learning and Verbal Behavior,* 1964, 3, 1–5. **(309, 310)**

Marquis, D. G. *See* Hilgard & Marquis, 1940.

Martin, C. J. *See also* Bulgarella & Martin, 1967.

Martin, C. J. Association and differentiation variables in all-or-none learning. *Journal of Experimental Psychology,* 1965, 69, 308–11, **(89, 91, 109, 119, 148, 330)**

Martin, C. J., Boersma, F. J., & Cox, D. L. A classification of associative strategies in paired-associate learning. *Psychonomic Science,* 1965, 3, 455–456. **(370–74, 380)**

Martin, C. J., Cox, D. L., & Boersma, F. J. The role of associative strategies in the acquisition of P-A material: An alternative approach to meaningfulness. *Psychonomic Science,* 1965, 3, 463–464. **(371)**

Martin, C. J., & Saltz, E. Serial versus random presentation of paired-associates. *Journal of Experimental Psychology,* 1963, 65, 609–615. **(266)**

Martin, J. G., Oliver, M., Hom, G., & Heaslet, G. Repetition and Task in mediating response acquisition. *Journal of Experimental Psychology,* 1963, 66, 12–16. **(281, 310)**

Martin, R. F. "Native" traits and regression in the rat. *Journal of Comparative Psychology,* 1940, 30, 1–16. **(428)**

Marx, M. H., & Brownstein, A. J. Effects of incentive magnitude on running speeds without competing responses in acquisition and extinction. *Journal of Experimental Psychology,* 1963, 65, 182–189. **(103, 106, 107)**

Mateer, F. *Child behavior, a critical and experimental study of young children by the method of conditioned reflexes.* Boston: Badger, 1918. **(17, 18)**

Mauer, S. M. *See* Kanungo, et al., 1962.

Mayor, J. R. *See* Gagne, et al., 1962.

McAllister, D. E. *See* McAllister, W. R., & McAllister, 1962.

McAllister, W. R., & McAllister, D. E. Postconditioning delay and intensity of shock as factors in the measurement of acquired fear. *Journal of Experimental Psychology,* 1962, 64, 110–116. **(231)**

McClelland, D. C., & Heath, R. M. Retroactive inhibition as a function of degree of association of original and interpolated activities. *Journal of Experimental Psychology,* 1943, 33, 420–430. **(299)**

McConkie, G. W. *See* Horowitz, Lippman, *et al.,* 1964.

McCulloch, T. L., & Pratt, J. G. A study of the presolution period in weight discrimination by white rats. *Journal of Comparative Psychology,* 1934, 18, 271–290. **(109)**

McGee, R. K. *See* Meier & McGee, 1959.

McGehee, N. Stimulus meaningfulness, interstimulus similarity and associative learning. Doctoral dissertation, Northwestern University, 1961. **(339)**

McGehee, N. E., & Schulz, R. W. Mediation and paired-associates learning. *Journal of Experimental Psychology,* 1961, 62, 568–570. **(281)**

McGeoch, J. A. The influence of degree of learning upon retroactive inhibition. *American Journal of Psychology,* 1929, 41, 252–262. **(201)**

McGeoch, J. A. The influence of association value upon the difficulty of non-sense-syllable lists. *Journal of Genetic Psychology,* 1930, 37, 421–426. **(332)**

McGeoch, J. A. The direction and extent of intra-serial associations at recall. *American Journal of Psychology,* 1936 (a), 48, 221–245. **(163, 263, 264)**

McGeoch, J. A. Studies in retroactive inhibition VII. Retroactive inhibition as a function of the length and frequency of the interpolated lists. *Journal of Experimental Psychology,* 1936 (b), 19, 674–693. **(223)**

McGeoch, J. A. *The psychology of human learning.* New York: Longmans, Green & Company, 1942. **(268, 349–51)**

McGeoch, J. A., & Irion, A. L. *The psychology of human learning.* New York: Longmans, Green, 1952. **(268, 375)**

McGovern, J. B. Extinction of associations in four transfer paradigms. *Psychological Monographs,* 1964, 78, No. 16 (Whole No. 593). **(212, 213)**

McNealy, D. A. *See* Noble & McNealy, 1957.

Mechanic, A. The distribution of recalled items in intentional and incidental learning. *Journal of Experimental Psychology,* 1962 (a), 63, 593–600. **(355, 357)**

Mechanic, A. Effects of orienting task, practice, and incentive on simultaneous incidental and intentional learning. *Journal of Experimental Psychology,* 1962 (b), 64, 393–399. **(353, 355–57, 361, 362)**

Mednick, M. T. Mediated generalizations and the incubation effect as a function of manifest anxiety. *Journal of Abnormal and Social Psychology,* 1957, 55, 315–321. **(229)**

Meehl, P. E. *See* Macorquodale & Meehl, 1954.

Mehler, J., & Bever, T. G. Cognitive capacity of very young children. *Science,* 1967, 158, 141–142. **(70)**

Mehler, J., & Bever, T. G. Reply by J. Mehler and T. G. Bever. *Science,* 1968, 162, 979–981. **(70)**

Meier, G., & McGee, R. K. A reevaluation of the effect of early perceptual experience on discrimination performance during adulthood. *Journal of Comparative and Physiological Psychology,* 1959, 51, 390–395. **(120)**

Melton, A. W. Implications of short-term memory for a general theory of memory. *Journal of Verbal Learning and Verbal Behavior,* 1963, 2, 1–21. **(80, 81, 239–41)**

Melton, A. W., & Irwin, J. M. The influence of degree of interpolated learning on retroactive inhibition and the overt transfer of specific responses. *American Journal of Psychology,* 1940, 53, 173–203. **(208, 209, 226)**

Mermelstein, E., Carr, E., Mills, D., & Schwartz, J. The effect of various training techniques on the acquisition of the concept of conservation of substance. Unpublished manuscript, 1967. **(73)**

Merryman, C. T. *See* Merryman, S. S., & Merryman, 1968.

Merryman, S. S., & Merryman, C. T. Differential recall of stimuli and responses following paired-associates learning. *Journal of Experimental Psychology,* 1968, 77, 345–346. **(165)**

Messick, S. J. *See* Solley & Messick, 1957.

Metzen, J. D. *See* Saltz, Metzen, & Ernstein, 1961.

Meyers, D. R. *See* Silver, C. A., & Meyers, 1954.

Miller, G. A. *See also* Marks & Miller, 1964.

Miller, G. A., & Friedman, E. A. The reconstruction of mutilated English texts. *Information Control,* 1957, 1, 38–55. **(259)**

Miller, G. A., Galanter, E., & Pribram, K. *Plans and the structure of behavior.* New York: Holt, Rinehart and Winston, 1960. **(378)**

Miller, N. E., & Dollard, J. C. *Social learning and imitation.* New Haven: Yale University Press, 1941. **(121, 122, 124–30)**

Miller, S. A., Shelton, J., & Flavell, J. H. A test of Luria's hypotheses concerning the development of verbal self-regulation. *Child Development,* 1970, 41, 651–665. **(409)**

Milner, B. Amnesia following operation on the temporal lobes. In C. W. M. Witty & O. L. Zangwill (Eds.) *Amnesia.* London: Butterworths, 1966. **(239)**

Mink, W. D. *Semantic generalization as related to word association..* Doctoral dissertation, University of Minnesota, 1957. **(293–95)**

Mink, W. D. Semantic generalization as related to word association. *Psychological Reports,* 1963, 12, 59–67. **(293–95)**

Modigliani, V. *See also* Saltz & Modigliani, 1967, 1968.

Modigliani, V. Concept conservation as a function of stimulus boundedness and age. Doctoral dissertation, Wayne State University, 1969. **(63, 64)**

Modigliani, V., & Saltz, E. Evaluation of a model relating Thorndike-Lorge frequency and *m* to learning. *Journal of Experimental Psychology,* 1969, 82, 584–586. **(319, 320, 323)**

Moore, J. W. *See* Gormezano & Moore, 1962.

Moss, H. A. *See* Kagan, *et al.,* 1963.

Mowrer, O. H. *Learning theory and behavior.* New York: Wiley, 1960. **(18)**

Muenzinger, K. F. Motivation in learning: II. The function of electric shock for right and wrong responses in human subjects. *Journal of Experimental Psychology,* 1934, 17, 439–448. **(449)**

Muller, D. G. *See* Ellis & Muller, 1964.

Murdock, B. B., Jr. *See also* Levy & Murdock, 1968.

Murdock, B. B., Jr. "Backword" associations in transfer and learning. *Journal of Experimental Psychology,* 1958 (a), 55, 111–114. **(168, 169, 285)**

Murdock, B. B., Jr. Intralist generalization in paired-associate learning. *Psychological Review,* 1958 (b), 306–314. **(143)**

Murdock, B. B., Jr. The effects of task difficulty, stimulus similarity, and type of response on stimulus predifferentiation. *Journal of Experimental Psychology,* 1958 (c), 55, 167–172. **(136, 137, 140, 141)**

Murdock, B. B., Jr. The immediate retention of unrelated words. *Journal of Experimental Psychology,* 1960, 60, 222–234. **(321)**

Murdock, B. B., Jr. The retention of individual items. *Journal of Experimental Psychology,* 1961, 62, 618–625. **(79–81, 237, 238)**

Murdock, B. B., Jr. Short-term retention of single paired-associates. *Journal of Experimental Psychology,* 1963, 65, 433–443. **(81, 242, 243)**

Murdock, B. B., Jr., & vom Saal, W. Transpositions in short-term memory. *Journal of Experimental Psychology*, 1967, 73, 137–143. **(239)**

Murphy, D. B., & Myers, T. I. The occurrence, measurement, and experimental manipulation of visual 'hallucinations.' *Perceptual and Motor Skills*, 1962, 15, 47–54. **(156)**

Murray, D. J. Vocalization-at-present and immediate recall with varying presentation rates. *Quarterly Journal of Experimental Psychology*, 1965, 17, 47–56. **(239)**

Murray, D. J. The role of speech responses in short-term memory. *Canadian Journal of Psychology*, 1967, 21, 263–276. **(239)**

Musgrave, B. S., & Cohen, J. C. Effects of two-word stimuli on recall and learning in a paired-associate task. *Journal of Experimental Psychology*, 1964, 68, 161–166. **(373)**

Myers, T. I. *See* Murphy & Myers, 1962.

N

Neimark, E., & Saltzman, I. J. Intentional and incidental learning with different rates of stimulus presentation. *American Journal of Psychology*, 1953, 66, 618–621. **(353, 354)**

Newman, S. E. *See also* Gray & Newman, 1966; Saltz & Newman, 1959.

Newman, S. E. Performance during paired-associate training as a function of number of elements comprising the stimulus term. Office of Naval Research (Contact Nonr 486–08) Technical Report No. 4, 1963. **(146, 372)**

Newman, S. E. A replication of paired-associate learning as a function of S-R similarity. *Journal of Experimental Psychology*, 1964, 67, 592–594. **(168)**

Newman, S. E., & Gray, C. W. S-R vs. R-S recall and R-term vs. S-term recall following paired-associate training. *American Journal of Psychology*, 1964, 77, 444–450. **(166)**

Newman, S. E., & Saltz, E. Isolation effects: Stimulus and response generalization as explanatory concepts. *Journal of Experimental Psychology*, 1958, 55, 467–472. **(184, 266)**

Newman, S. E. and Saltz, E. Effects of contextual cues on learning from connected discourse. *American Journal of Psychology*, 1960, 73, 587–592. **(129)**

Newton, J. M., & Wickens, D. D. Retroactive inhibition as a function of the temporal position of the interpolated learning. *Journal of Experimental Psychology*, 1956, 51, 149–154. **(219, 220, 227)**

Nieuwenhuyse, B. *See* Zajonc & Nieuwenhuyse, 1964.

Noble, C. E. *See also* Cieutat, *et al.*, 1958; Gannon & Noble, 1961; Smith, R. K., & Noble, 1965.

Noble, C. E. An analysis of meaning. *Psychological Review*, 1952, 59, 421–430. **(315, 319, 340, 370)**

Noble, C. E. The effect of familiarization upon serial verbal learning. *Journal of Experimental Psychology,* 1955, 49, 333–338. **(178)**

Noble, C. E. Measurements of Association value (*a*), rated associations (*a'*) and scaled meaningfulness (*m'*) for the 2100 CVC combinations of the English alphabet. *Psychological Reports,* 1961, 8, 487–521. (Monograph Supplement 3-V8). **(331, 334)**

Noble, C. E., & McNealy, D. A. The role of meaningfulness (*m*) in paired-associate learning. *Journal of Experimental Psychology,* 1957, 53, 16–22. **(318)**

Norman, D. A. *See also* Waugh & Norman, 1965.

Norman, D. A. *Memory and attention.* New York: Wiley, 1969. **(377, 379)**

Norman, S. A. *See* Horowitz, Lippman, *et al.,* 1964.

Norris, E. B., & Grant, D. A. Eyelid conditioning as affected by verbally induced inhibitory set and counter reinforcement. *American Journal of Psychology,* 1948, 61, 37–49. **(415)**

O

O'Connel, D. C. *See* Dulany & O'Connel, 1963.

O'Dowd, D. *See* Bruner & O'Dowd, 1958.

Oliver, M. *See* Martin, J. G., *et al.,* 1963.

Osgood, C. E. The nature and measurement of meaning. *Psychological Bulletin,* 1952, 49, 197–237. **(36)**

Osgood, C. E. *Method and theory in experimental psychology.* New York: Oxford University Press, 1953. **(18, 36, 278)**

Osgood, C. E. Comments on Professor Bousfield's paper. In C. N. Cofer (Ed.) *Verbal learning and verbal behavior.* New York: McGraw-Hill, 1961. **(300)**

Osgood, C. E., Suci, G. J., & Tannenbaum, P. H. *The measurement of meaning.* Urbana, Ill.: University of Illinois Press, 1957. **(32)**

Osler, S. F., & Fivel, M. W. Concept attainment: I. The role of age and intelligence in concept attainment by induction. *Journal of Experimental Psychology,* 1961, 62, 1–8. **(53)**

Osler, S. F., & Trautman, G. E. Concept attainment: II. Effect of stimulus complexity upon concept attainment at two levels of intelligence. *Journal of Experimental Psychology,* 1961, 62, 9–13. **(53)**

Ost, J. W. P. *See* Kimble & Ost, 1961.

P

Paivio, A. *See also* Yarmey & Paivio, 1965.

Paivio, A. Abstractness, imagery, and meaningfulness in paired-associate learning. *Journal of Verbal Learning and Verbal Behavior,* 1965, 4, 32–38. **(325, 326)**

Paivio, A. Paired-associate learning and free recall of nouns as a function of concreteness, specificity, imagery, and meaningfulness. *Psychological Reports,* 1967, 20, 239–245. **(325)**

Paivio, A. A factor-analytic study of word attributes and verbal learning. *Journal of Verbal Learning and Verbal Behavior,* 1968, 7, 41–49. **(325)**

Paivio, A., & Madigan, S. A. Imagery and association value in paired-associate learning. *Journal of Experimental Psychology,* 1968, 76, 35–39. **(325)**

Palermo, D. S. *See* Castaneda & Palermo, 1955.

Palola, E. G. *See* Sarason, I. G., & Palola, 1960.

Paradise, N. E. *See* Gagne, *et al.,* 1962; Gagne & Paradise, 1961.

Paterson, A. L. *See* Bindra, *et al.,* 1955.

Paul, C. *See also* Saltz, Whitman, & Paul, 1963.

Paul, C. Effects of overlearning upon single habit reversal in rats. *Psychological Bulletin,* 1965, 63, 65–72. **(235)**

Paul, C., & Silverstein, A. Relation of experimentally produced interlist intrusions to unlearning and retroactive inhibition. *Journal of Experimental Psychology,* 1968, 76, 480–485. **(210–12, 216)**

Paul, G. I., Eriksen, C. W., & Humphreys, L. G. Use of temperature stress with cool air reinforcement for human operant conditioning. *Journal of Experimental Psychology,* 1962, 64, 325–335. **(392)**

Paul, H. Proactive inhibition in short-term memory. Doctoral dissertation, Wayne State University, 1966. **(80, 241, 245, 247)**

Peak, H., & Deese, L. Experimental extinction of verbal material. *Journal of Experimental Psychology,* 1937, 20, 244–261. **(244)**

Pearlstein, R. *See* Brown, S. C., *et al.,* 1965.

Pearlstone, Z. *See* Tulvig & Pearlstone, 1966.

Pereboom, A. C., and Crawford, B. M. Instrumental and competing behavior as a function of trials and reward magnitude. *Journal of Experimental Psychology,* 1958, 56, 82–85. **(102–4, 106, 198)**

Perera, T. *See* Hefferline & Perera, 1963.

Perkins, C. C., Jr., & Weyant, R. C. The interval between training and test trials as a determiner of the slope of generalization gradients. *Journal of Comparative Physiological Psychology,* 1958, 51, 596–600. **(231)**

Perkins, D. T. *See* Hull, *et al.,* 1940.

Peters, H. N. The relationship between familiarity of words and their memory value. *American Journal of Psychology,* 1936, 48, 572–584. **(321)**

Peters, S. C. *See* Glanzer & Peters, 1962.

Petersen, D. E. *See* Butler & Petersen, 1965.

Peterson, J. The effect of attitude on immediate and delayed reproduction: a class experiment. *Journal of Educational Psychology,* 1916, 7, 523–532. **(351)**

Peterson, L. R. Short-term memory. *Scientific American,* 1966, 215, 90–95. (236)

Peterson, L. R., Brewer, C. L., & Bertucco, R. A. A guessing strategy with the anticipation technique. *Journal of Experimental Psychology,* 1963, 65, 258–264. (265)

Peterson, L. R., & Peterson, M. J. Short-term retention of individual verbal items. *Journal of Experimental Psychology,* 1959, 58, 193–198. (78–80, 236, 237, 240, 358)

Peterson, L. R., & Peterson, M. J. Minimal paired-associate learning. *Journal of Experimental Psychology,* 1962, 63, 521–527. (245)

Peterson, L. R., Saltzman, D., Hillner, K., & Land, V. Recency and frequency in paired-associates learning. *Journal of Experimental Psychology,* 1962, 63, 396–403. (81, 243)

Peterson, M. J. *See also* Peterson, L. R., & Peterson, 1959, 1962.

Peterson, M. J. Cue trials, frequency of presentation, and mediating responses. *Journal of Experimental Psychology,* 1964, 67, 432–438. (283)

Peterson, M. J., & Blattner, K. C. Development of a verbal mediator. *Journal of Experimental Psychology,* 1963, 66, 72–77. (283)

Pfafflin, S. M. Stimulus meaning in stimulus predifferentiation. *Journal of Experimental Psychology,* 1960, 59, 269–274. (144, 145)

Phelan, J. B. A replication of a study on the effects of attempts to verbalize on the process of concept attainment. *Journal of Psychology,* 1965, 59, 283–293. (397, 411)

Phillips, L. W. *See* Postman, Adams, & Phillips, 1955; Postman & Phillips, 1954.

Piaget, J. *See also* Inhelder & Piaget, 1958.

Piaget, J. *The psychology of intelligence.* London: Routledge and Kegan Paul, 1950. (66, 71)

Piaget, J. *Logic and psychology.* New York: Basic Books, 1957. (66, 71)

Piaget, J. Quantification, conservation, and nativism. *Science,* 1968, 162, 976–979. (70)

Piaget, J., & Inhelder, B. *La development des quantites physiques chez l'enfant.* (2nd ed.) Pares: DeLachaux et Niestle, 1962. (67)

Pick, H. L., Jr. *See* Gibson, E. J., *et al.,* 1958; Walk, *et al.,* 1958, 1959.

Pishkin, V. Effects of probability of misinformation and number of irrelevant dimensions upon concept identification. *Journal of Experimental Psychology,* 1960, 59, 371–378. (48)

Pollio, H. R. Associative structure and verbal behavior. In T. R. Dixon & D. L. Horton (Eds.) *Verbal behavior and general behavior theory.* Englewood Cliffs, New Jersey: Prentice-Hall, 1968. (276)

Pollio, H. R., & Draper, D. O. The effect of a serial cognitive structure on paired-associates learning. *Journal of Verbal Learning and Verbal Behavior,* 1966, 5, 301–308. (276)

Poppelreuter, W. Nachweis der Unzweckmässigkeit die gebräuchlichen Assoziations-experimente mit sinnlosen Silben nach dem Erlernungs- und Trefferverfahren zur exakten Gewinnung elementarer Reproduktionsgesetze zu verwenden. *Zeitschrift für Psychologie,* 1912, 61, 1–24. (351)

Porter, E. C. *See also* Cerekwicki, *et al.,* 1968.

Porter, L. W. The effect of "right" in a modified Thorndikian situation. *American Journal of Psychology,* 1957, 70, 219–236. (401, 402)

Postman, L. *See also* Goodnow & Postman, 1955; Goulet & Postman, 1966; Solomon & Postman, 1952; Underwood & Postman, 1960.

Postman, L. Extra-experimental interference and the retention of word. *Journal of Experimental Psychology,* 1961, 61, 97–110. (222)

Postman, L. Repetition and paired-associate learning. *American Journal of Psychology,* 1962 (a) , 75, 372–389. (89)

Postman, L. Retention of first-list associations as a function of conditions of transfer. *Journal of Experimental Psychology,* 1962 (b) , 64, 380–387. (212)

Postman, L. The effects of language habits on the acquisition and retention of verbal associates. *Journal of Experimental Psychology,* 1962 (c) , 64, 7–19. (222, 315–17, 319, 322)

Postman, L. The temporal course of proactive inhibition for serial lists. *Journal of Experimental Psychology,* 1962 (d) , 63, 361–369. (222)

Postman, L. Transfer of training as a function of experimental paradigm and degree of first-list learning. *Journal of Verbal Learning and Verbal Behavior,* 1962 (e) , 1, 109–118. (212, 287)

Postman, L. Short-term memory and incidental learning. In A. W. Melton (Ed.) *Categories of human learning.* New York: Academic Press, 1964. (348, 352, 363, 364)

Postman, L. Unlearning as a function of successive interpolation. *Journal of Experimental Psychology,* 1965, 70, 237–245. (210, 215)

Postman, L., & Adams, P. A. "Isolation" and the law of effect. *American Journal of Psychology,* 1955, 68, 96–105. (401, 402)

Postman, L., & Adams, P. A. Studies in incidental learning: III. Interserial interference. *Journal of Experimental Psychology,* 1956 (a) , 51, 323–328. (347)

Postman, L., & Adams, P. A. Studies in incidental learning: IV. The interaction of orienting tasks and stimulus materials. *Journal of Experimental Psychology,* 1956 (b) , 51, 329–333. (352–55, 359, 360, 367)

Postman, L., & Adams, P. A. Studies in incidental learning: VI. Intralist interference. *Journal of Experimental Psychology,* 1957, 54, 153–167. (349, 366)

Postman, L., and Adams, P. A. Studies in incidental learning: VII. Effects of frequency of exercise and length of list. *Journal of Experimental Psychology,* 1958, 56, 86–93. (355, 357, 367)

Postman, L., & Adams, P. A. Studies in incidental learning: VIII. The effects of contextual determination. *Journal of Experimental Psychology,* 1960, 59, 153–164. **(355, 365, 366)**

Postman, L., Adams, P. A., & Bohm, A. M. Studies in incidental learning: V. Recall for order and associative clustering. *Journal of Experimental Psychology,* 1956, 51, 334–342. **(355, 360, 363)**

Postman, L., Adams, P. A., & Phillips, L. W. Studies in incidental learning: II. The effects of association value and of the method of testing. *Journal of Experimental Psychology,* 1955, 49, 1–10. **(348, 349, 355, 360, 364, 365, 367)**

Postman, L., & Goggin, J. Whole versus part learning of serial lists as a function of meaningfulness and intralist similarity. *Journal of Experimental Psychology,* 1964, 68, 140–150. **(375)**

Postman, L., Keppel, G., & Stark, K. Unlearning as a function of the relationship between successive response classes. *Journal of Experimental Psychology,* 1965, 69, 111–118. **(211, 213)**

Postman, L., and Phillips, L. W. Studies in incidental learning: I. The effects of crowding and isolation. *Journal of Experimental Psychology,* 1954, 48, 48–56. **(350, 366)**

Postman, L., & Sassenrath, J. The automatic action of verbal rewards and punishments. *Journal of General Psychology,* 1961, 65, 109–136. **(392)**

Postman, L., & Stark, K. Studies of learning to learn: IV. Transfer from serial to paired-associate learning. *Journal of Verbal Learning and Verbal Behavior,* 1967, 6, 339–353. **(261)**

Postman, L., Stark, K., & Fraser, J. Temporal changes in interference. *Journal of Verbal Learning and Verbal Behavior,* 1968, 7, 672–694. **(218, 219)**

Postman, L., Stark, K., & Henschel, D. Conditions of recovery after unlearning. *Journal of Experimental Psychology Monograph,* 1969, 82, No. 1, Part 2. **(218, 219, 227, 228)**

Pratt, J. G. *See* McCulloch & Pratt, 1934.

Premack, D. *See* Holstein & Premack, 1965.

Pribram, K. *See* Miller, G. A., *et al.,* 1960.

Primoff, E. Backward and forward associations as an organizing act in serial and paired-associate learning. *Journal of Psychology,* 1938, 5, 374–395. **(168, 261)**

Pubols, B. H., Jr. The facilitation of visual and spatial discrimination reversal by overlearning. *Journal of Comparative and Physiological Psychology,* 1956, 49, 243–248. **(232)**

R

Raskin, E., & Cook, S. W. The strength and direction of associations formed in the learning of nonsense syllables. *Journal of Experimental Psychology,* 1937, 20, 381–395. **(264, 265)**

Ratliff, R. G. *See* Spielberger, *et al.,* 1966.

Rauch, D. S. *See* Keppel & Rauch, 1966.

Razran, G. Attitudinal control of human conditioning. *Journal of Psychology,* 1936, 2, 327–337. **(403)**

Razran, G. Semantic and phonetographic generalizations of salivary conditioning to verbal stimuli. *Journal of Experimental Psychology,* 1949, 39, 642–652. **(294, 295)**

Razran, G. A direct laboratory comparison of Pavlovian conditioning and traditional association learning. *Journal of Abnormal and Social Psychology,* 1955, 51, 649–652. **(403)**

Razran, G. Backward conditioning. *Psychological Bulletin,* 1956, 53, 55–69. **(162)**

Razran, G. The observable unconscious and the inferable conscious in current Russian Psycho-physiology. *Psychological Review,* 1961, 68, 81–147. **(19)**

Reece, M. M. The effect of shock on recognition thresholds. *Journal of Abnormal and Social Psychology,* 1954, 49, 165–172. **(424)**

Reed, J. C., & Riach, W. The role of repetition and set in paired-associate learning. *American Journal of Psychology,* 1960, 53, 608–611. **(89)**

Rehula, R. *See* Underwood, Rehula, & Keppel, 1962.

Reid, L. S. The development of noncontinuity behavior through continuity learning. *Journal of Experimental Psychology,* 1953, 46, 107–112. **(232, 234)**

Restle, F. The selection of strategies in cue learning. *Psychological Review,* 1962, 69, 329–343. **(50, 88, 92–94)**

Riach, W. *See* Reed & Riach, 1960; Saltz & Riach, 1961.

Richardson, B. J. *See* Underwood & Richardson, 1956 (a) , 1956 (b) , 1958.

Richardson, D. H. *See* Rosen, *et al.,* 1962.

Richter, M. Memory, choice, and stimulus sequence in human discrimination learning. Doctoral dissertation, Indiana University, 1965. **(94)**

Robinson, J. S. The effect of learning verbal labels for stimuli on their later discriminations. *Journal of Experimental Psychology,* 1955, 49, 112–115. **(125, 126, 129, 143)**

Rock, I. The role of repetition in associative learning. *American Journal of Psychology,* 1957, 70, 186–193. **(88–92, 109)**

Rohrer, J. H. Factors influencing the occurrence of reminiscence. Attempted formal rehearsal during the interpolated period. *Journal of Experimental Psychology,* 1949, 39, 484–491. **(358)**

Rohwer, W. D. *See* Jensen & Rohwer, 1965.

Rommetveit, R., & Kvale, S. Stages in concept formation: III. Further inquiries into the effects of an extra intention to verbalize. *Scandinavian Journal of Psychology,* 1965 (a) , 6, 65–74. **(396, 397, 411)**

Rommetviet, R., & Kvale, S. Stages in concept formation: IV. A temporal analysis of effects of an extra intention to verbalize. *Scandinavian Journal of Psychology,* 1965 (b) , 6, 75–79. **(396, 397)**

Rosen, H. Recall as a function of differentiation and hostility. Doctoral dissertation, Wayne State University, 1963. **(446, 447)**

Rosen, H., Richardson, D. H., & Saltz, E. Supplementary report: Meaningfulness as a differentiation variable in the von Restorff effect. *Journal of Experimental Psychology,* 1962, 64, 327–328. **(186, 188)**

Rosenzweig, S. An experimental study of "repression" with special reference to need persistive and ego-defensive reactions to frustration. *Journal of Experimental Psychology,* 1943, 32, 64–74. **(435)**

Roskind, W. *See* Sigel, *et al.,* 1967.

Ross, L. E. *See* Goodrich, *et al.,* 1957, 1959; Spence & Ross, 1959.

Ross, R. T. *See* Hull, *et al.,* 1940.

Rossman, I. L., & Goss, A. E. The acquired distinctiveness of cues: the role of discriminative verbal responses in facilitating the acquisition of discriminative motor responses. *Journal of Experimental Psychology,* 1951, 42, 173–182. **(142, 143)**

Rothkopf, E. Z. A deduction from an excitation-inhibition account of retractive inhibition. *Journal of Experimental Psychology,* 1957, 53, 207–213. **(219, 224)**

Rothkopf, E. Z. Programmed self-instructional booklets, mnemonic phrases, and unguided study in the acquistion of equivalences. *Journal of Programmed Instruction,* 1963, 1, 19–28. **(373)**

Rothkopf, E. Z., & Coke, E. U. "The Prediction of Free Recall from Word Association Measures." *Journal of Experimental Psychology,* 1961, 62, 433–438. **(187)**

Runquist, W. N. *See also* Underwood, Runquist, & Schulz, 1959.

Runquist, W. N., & English, J. M. Response pretraining and forced availability in paired-associate verbal learning. *Psychonomic Science,* 1964, 1, 121–122. **(174)**

Runquist, W. N., & Freeman, M. Roles of association value and syllable familiarization in verbal discrimination learning. *Journal of Experimental Psychology,* 1960, 59, 396–401. **(173, 174, 324)**

Russell, W. A., & Jenkins, J. J. The complete Minnesota norms for responses to 100 words from the Kent-Rosanoff word association test. *U.S. Navy Office of Naval Research Tech Report,* 1954 (Contract No. N8, Report 11) . **(282)**

Russell, W. A., & Storms, L. H. Implicit verbal chaining in paired associates learning. *Journal of Experimental Psychology,* 1955, 49, 287–293. **(281, 289)**

Rutledge, E. F. *See* Spence, K. W., *et al.,* 1964.

Ryan, J. J., III. Comparison of verbal response transfer mediated by meaningfully similar and associated stimuli. *Journal of Experimental Psychology,* 1960, 60, 408–415. **(287, 299, 300)**

S

Saltz, E. *See also* Barnes, H., & Saltz, 1970; Hamilton, H., & Saltz, 1969; Martin, C. J., Saltz, 1963; Modigliani & Saltz, 1969; Newman, S. E., & Saltz, 1958, 1960; Rosen, *et al.,* 1962; Sigel, *et al.,* 1967; Uhlmann & Saltz, 1965.

Saltz, E. Effect of shock on performance in a paired-associate learning task. *Proceedings of the Iowa Academy of Science,* 1950, 57, 429–433. **(425)**

Saltz, E. Response pretraining: Differentiation or availability? *Journal of Experimental Psychology,* 1961 (a) , 62, 538–587. **(174–77, 179, 188–90)**

Saltz, E. The effect of induced stress on free associations. *Journal of Abnormal and Social Psychology,* 1961 (b) , 62, 161–164. **(81, 444, 445)**

Saltz, E. Compound stimuli in verbal learning: Cognitive and sensory differentiation vs. stimulus selection. *Journal of Experimental Psychology,* 1963, 66, 1–5. **(128, 139, 326)**

Saltz, E. The precriterion phase in verbal discrimination learning. *Journal of Verbal Learning and Verbal Behavior,* 1964, 3, 166–170. **(91)**

Saltz, E. Spontaneous recovery of letter-sequence habits. *Journal of Experimental Psychology,* 1965, 69, 304–307. **(244)**

Saltz, E. Thorndike-Lorge frequency and m of stimuli as separate factors in paired-associate learning. *Journal of Experimental Psychology,* 1967 (a) , 73, 473–478. **(318–20)**

Saltz, E. Verbal control, hypothesis testing, and the course of concept attainment. Paper read at meetings of the Psychonomic Society, Chicago, 1967 (b) . **(396)**

Saltz, E., & Ager, J. W. Issues in scaling meaningfulness: Noble's revised CVC norms. *Psychological Reports,* 1962, 10, 25–26. **(334)**

Saltz, E., & Ager, J. W. Role of context cues in learning: Reply to Greeno. *Psychological Reports,* 1968, 22, 351–354. **(128)**

Saltz, E., & Asdourian, D. Incubation of anxiety as a function of cognitive differentiation. *Journal of Experimental Psychology,* 1963, 66, 17–22. **(227–32, 404)**

Saltz, E., & DiLoreto, A. "Defense" against traumatic concepts. *Journal of Abnormal Psychology,* 1965, 1, 281–284. **(446, 448)**

Saltz, E., & Felton, M. Response pretraining and subsequent paired-associate learning. *Journal of Experimental Psychology,* 1968 (a) , 77, 258–262. **(174, 175, 189, 306, 330)**

Saltz, E., & Felton, M. Encoding of nonsense syllables for meaning. *Psychological Reports,* 1968 (b) , 23, 1087–1093. **(337, 338, 354, 368)**

Saltz, E., & Hamilton, H. W. Spontaneous recovery of List 1 responses in the A-B, A-C paradigm. *Journal of Experimental Psychology,* 1967, 75, 267–273. **(219, 224)**

Saltz, E., & Hamilton, H. W. Concept conservation under positively and negatively evaluated transformations. *Journal of Experimental Child Psychology,* 1968, 6, 44–51. **(32, 62, 67, 71)**

Saltz, E., & Hamilton, H. Do lower IQ children attain concepts more slowly than children of higher IQ? *Psychonomic Science,* 1969, 17, 210–211. **(53)**

Saltz, E., Metzen, J. D., & Ernstein, E. Predifferentiation of verbal stimuli in children. *Psychological Reports,* 1961, 9, 127–132. **(146)**

Saltz, E., & Modigliani, V. Response meaningfulness in paired-associates: T-L frequency, *m,* and number of meaning *(dm)* . *Journal of Experimental Psychology,* 1967, 75, 318–320. **(316–18, 323)**

Saltz, E., & Modigliani, V. Conservation of meaning as a factor in forgetting new associations. *Journal of Experimental Psychology,* 1968, 80, 322–325. **(302, 304)**

Saltz, E., & Newman, S. E. The von Restorff isolation effect: Test of the intralist association assumption. *Journal of Experimental Psychology,* 1959, 58, 445–451. **(184, 185, 266)**

Saltz, E., & Riach, W. J. The effect of stress on stimulus differentiation. *Journal of Experimental Psychology,* 1961, 62, 585–593. **(426–28, 432, 441, 444)**

Saltz, E., & Sigel, I. E. Concept overdiscrimination in children. *Journal of Experimental Psychology,* 1967, 73, 1–8. **(57, 61)**

Saltz, E., Whitman, R. N., & Paul, C. Performance in the runway as a function of stimulus differentiation. *American Journal of Psychology,* 1963, 76, 124–127. **(99–101, 107, 230, 450)**

Saltz, E., & Wickey, J. Resolutions of the liberal dilemma in the assassination of President Kennedy. *Journal of Personality,* 1965, 33, 636–648. **(39, 66)**

Saltz, E., & Wickey, J. Further evidence for differentiation effects of context stimuli: A reply to Birnbaum. *Psychological Reports,* 1967, 20, 835–838. **(128)**

Saltz, E., and Youssef, Z. I. The role of response differentiation in forgetting. *Journal of Experimental Psychology,* 1964, 68, 307–311. **(177, 191)**

Saltzman, D. *See* Peterson, L. R., *et al.,* 1962.

Saltzman, I. J. *See also* Atkinson, R. L., & Saltzman, 1954; Neimark & Saltzman, 1953.

Saltzman, I. J. The orienting task in incidental and intentional learning. *American Journal of Psychology,* 1953, 66, 593–597. **(351, 354, 355)**

Saltzman, I. J. Comparison of incidental and intentional learning with different orienting tasks. *American Journal of Psychology,* 1956, 69, 274–277. **(360, 362, 369)**

Sanders, M. J. An experimental demonstration in regression in the rat. *Journal of Experimental Psychology,* 1937, 21, 493–510. **(428)**

Sarason, I. G. Effect of anxiety, motivational instructions, and failure on serial learning. *Journal of Experimental Psychology,* 1956, 51, 253–260. **(433, 434, 436, 438)**

Sarason, I. G. The effect of anxiety and two kinds of failure on serial learning. *Journal of Personality,* 1957 (a), 25, 383–392. **(433, 434, 438)**

Sarason, I. G. Effect of anxiety and two kinds of motivating instructions on verbal learning. *Journal of Abnormal and Social Psychology,* 1957 (b), 54, 166–171. **(436, 438)**

Sarason, I. G. The effects of anxiety and threat on the solution of a difficult task. *Journal of Abnormal and Social Psychology,* 1961, 62, 165–168. **(437, 439)**

Sarason, I. G., & Palola, E. G. The relationship of test and general anxiety, difficulty of task, and experimental instructions to performance. *Journal of Experimental Psychology,* 1960, 59, 185–191. **(436, 438)**

Sarason, S. B. *See* Mandler & Sarason, 1952.

Sassenrath, J. *See* Postman & Sassenrath, 1961.

Schild, M. E., & Battig, W. F. Directionality in paired-associate learning. *Journal of Verbal Learning and Verbal Behavior,* 1966, 5, 42–49. **(167)**

Schlosberg, H. *See* Bilodeau & Schlosberg, 1951; White & Schlosberg, 1952.

Schulz, R. W. *See* Staats, *et al.,* 1962.

Schulz, R. W. *See also* Hopkins & Schulz, 1967; Kuiken & Schulz, 1968; McGehee & Schulz, 1961; Underwood, Runquist & Schulz, 1959; Underwood & Schulz, 1960; Weaver, *et al.,* 1968; Weaver, & Schulz, 1968.

Schulz, R. W., & Tucker, I. F. Stimulus familiarization and length of the anticipation interval in paired-associates learning. *Psychological Record,* 1962 (a), 12, 341–344. **(147)**

Schulz, R. W., & Tucker, I. F. Supplementary report: Stimulus familiarization in paired-associates learning. *Journal of Experimental Psychology,* 1962 (b), 64, 549–550. **(147)**

Schulz, R. W., & Weaver, G. E. The A-B, B-C, A-C mediation paradigm: The effects of variation in A-C study—and test—interval lengths and strength of A-B or B-C. *Journal of Experimental Psychology,* 1968, 76, 303–311. **(283, 300)**

Schwartz, S. H. A paradigm for the investigation of antecedent processes in concept attainment. Doctoral dissertation, University of Illinois, 1966 (a). **(55, 410)**

Schwartz, S. H. Trial-by-trial analysis of processes in simple and disjunctive concept-attainment tasks. *Journal of Experimental Psychology,* 1966 (b) , 72, 456–465. **(55)**

Schwenn, E., & Underwood, B. J. Simulated similarity and mediation time in transfer. *Journal of Verbal Learning and Verbal Behavior,* 1965, 4, 476–483. **(283)**

Scott, K. G., Whimbey, A. E., & Dunning, C. A functional differentiation of STM and LTM. *Psychonomic Science,* 1967 (a) , 7, 143–144. **(248)**

Scott, K. G., Whimbey, A. E., & Dunning, C. Separate LTM and STM systems? *Psychonomic Science,* 1967 (b) , 7, 55–56, **(248)**

Seeleman, V. The influence of attitude upon the remembering of pictoral material. *Archives of Psychology,* 1940, 36, No. 258. **(448)**

Segal, M. A., & Mandler, G. Bidirectionality and organizational processes in paired-associate learning. *Journal of Experimental Psychology,* 1967, 74, 305–312. **(167, 168)**

Semler, I. *See also* Iscoe & Semler, 1964.

Semler, I., & Iscoe, I. Comparative and developmental study of learning ability of Negro and white children under four conditions. *Journal of Educational Psychology,* 1963, 54, 38–44. **(326, 327)**

Seward, J. P. An experimental analysis of latent learning. *Journal of Experimental Psychology,* 1949, 39, 177–186. **(385)**

Shanks, B. L. *See* Braine & Shanks, 1965.

Shantz, C. U., & Sigel, I. E. Logical operations and concepts of conservation in children: A training study. Final Report, Office of Education, Bureau of Research, June, 1967. **(71–73)**

Sheffield, F. D. The role of meaningfulness of stimulus and response in verbal learning. Doctoral dissertation, Yale University, 1946. **(332, 338)**

Shelton, J. *See* Miller, S. A., *et al.,* 1970.

Shepard, M. C. *See* Spielberger, *et al.,* 1962.

Shiffrin, R. M. *See* Atkinson, R. C., & Shiffrin, 1968.

Shipley, W. C. An apparent transfer of conditioning. *Journal of General Psychology,* 1933, 8, 382–391. **(277)**

Shipley, W. C. Indirect conditioning. *Journal of General Psychology,* 1935, 12, 337–357. **(288)**

Shuell, T. J., & Keppel, G. A further test of the chaining hypothesis of serial learning. *Journal of Verbal Learning and Verbal Behavior,* 1967, 6, 439–445. **(262)**

Sigel, I. E. *See also* Kagan, *et al.,* 1963; Saltz & Sigel, 1967; Shantz & Sigel, 1967.

Sigel, I. E., Saltz, E., & Roskind, W. Variables determining concept conservation in children. *Journal of Experimental Psychology,* 1967, 74, 471–475. **(62, 67, 71)**

Silver, C. A., & Meyers, D. R. Temporal factors in sensory preconditioning. *Journal of Comparative and Physiological Psychology,* 1954, 47, 57–59. (157, 158)

Silver, D. The role of awareness in learning and operant performance in the verbal operant situation. M. A. Thesis, Wayne State University, 1967. (365, 399, 400, 412, 417)

Silverstein, A. *See* Paul, C., & Silverstein, 1968.

Sisson, E. D. Retroactive inhibition: The influence of degree of associative value of original and interpolated lists. *Journal of Experimental Psychology,* 1938, 22, 573–580. (332)

Skinner, B. F. *The behavior of organisms: an experimental analysis.* New York: Appleton-Century, 1938. (181, 416, 417)

Slamecka, N. J. An inquiry into the doctrine of remote associations. *Psychological Review,* 1964, 71, 61–76. (263–65)

Smith, M. H., Jr., & Stearns, E. G. The influence of isolation on surrounding materials. *American Journal of Psychology,* 1949, 62, 369–381. (184)

Smith, R. K., & Noble, C. E. Effects of a mnemonic technique applied to verbal learning and memory. *Perceptual and Motor Skills,* 1965, 21, 123–134. (373, 378)

Smoke, K. L. An objective study of concept formation. *Psychological Monographs,* 1932, 42, No. 191. (42)

Sokolov, Ye.N. *Perception and the conditioned reflex.* London: Pergamon Press, 1963, (19)

Solley, C. M., & Messick, S. J. Probability, learning, the statistical structure of concepts, and the measurement of meaning. *American Journal of Psychology,* 1957, 70, 161–173. (47–50)

Solomon, R. L. *See* Howes & Solomon, 1951.

Solomon, R. L., and Postman, L. Frequency of usage as a determinant of recognition thresholds for words. *Journal of Experimental Psychology,* 1952, 43, 195–201. (183)

Solomon, R. L., & Turner, L. H. Discriminative classical conditioning in dogs paralyzed by curare can later control discriminative avoidance responses in the normal state. *Psychological Review,* 1962, 69, 202–219. (161)

Sonstroem, A. M. On the conservation of solids. In J. S. Bruner, R. R. Olver, & P. M. Greenfield (Eds.), *Studies in cognitive growth.* New York: Wiley, 1966. (73)

Spence, J. T., & Spence, K. W. The motivational component of manifest anxiety: Drive and drive stimuli. In C. D. Spielberger (Ed.), *Anxiety and behavior,* New York: Academic Press, 1966. (422, 423, 429)

Spence, K. W. *See also* Spence, J. T., & Spence, 1966.

Spence, K. W. The nature of discrimination learning in animals. *Psychological Review,* 1936, 43, 427–449. (395)

Spence, K. W. Continuous versus noncontinuous interpretations of discrimination learning. *Psychological Review,* 1940, 47, 271–288 **(110)**

Spence, K. W. An experimental test of the continuity and non-continuity theories of discrimination learning. *Journal of Experimental Psychology,* 1945, 35, 253–266. **(109, 110)**

Spence, K. W. *Behavior theory and conditioning.* New Haven: Yale University Press, 1956. **(14–16, 20, 96, 97, 108, 416, 417)**

Spence, K. W. A theory of emotionally based drive (D) and its relation to performance in simple learning situations. *American Psychologist,* 1958, 13, 131–141. **(422, 429)**

Spence, K. W. Cognitive and drive factors in the extinction of the conditioned eye blink in human subjects. *Psychological Review,* 1966, 73, 445–458. **(404, 415)**

Spence, K. W., Homzie, M. J., & Rutledge, E. F. Extinction of the human eyelid CR as a function of the discriminability of the change from acquisition to extinction. *Journal of Experimental Psychology,* 1964, 67, 545–552. **(404)**

Spence, K. W., & Ross, L. E. A methodological study of the form and latency of eyelid response in conditioning. *Journal of Experimental Psychology,* 1959, 58, 376–381. **(413)**

Spielberger, C. D. The role of awareness in verbal conditioning. In C. W. Eriksen (Ed.) *Behavior and awareness,* Durham, N.C.: Duke University Press, 1962. **(392)**

Speilberger, C. D., Bernstein, J. M., & Ratliff, R. G. Information and incentive value of the conditioning stimulus in verbal conditioning. *Journal of Experimental Psychology,* 1966, 71, 26–31. **(393, 394)**

Spielberger, C. D., & Levin, S. M. What is learned in verbal conditioning. *Journal of Verbal Learning and Verbal Behavior,* 1962, 1, 125–132. **(389–91)**

Spielberger, C. D., Levin, S. M., & Shepard, M. C. The effects of awareness and attitude toward the reinforcement on the operant conditioning of verbal behavior. *Journal of Personality,* 1962, 30, 106–120. **(389, 391)**

Sprott, R. L. *See* Wallach, L., & Sprott, 1964.

Staats, A. W. *See* Staats, C. K., *et al.,* 1962.

Staats, C. K., Staats, A. W., and Schulz, R. L. The effects of discriminative pretraining on textual behavior. *Journal of Educational Psychology,* 1962, 53, 32–37. **(145)**

Stagner, R. *See* Harlow & Stagner, 1933.

Stark, K. *See also* Postman, Keppel, & Stark, 1965; Postman & Stark, 1967; Postman, Stark, & Fraser, 1968; Postman, Stark, & Henschel, 1969.

Stark, K. Transfer from serial to paired-associate learning: A reappraisal. *Journal of Verbal Learning and Verbal Behavior,* 1968, 7, 20–30. **(261)**

Stearns, E. G. *See* Smith, M. H., & Stearns, 1949.

Sterner, K. *See* Levin & Sterner, 1966.

Stockwell, F. E. *See* Cieutat, *et al.*, 1958.

Storms, L. H. *See* Russell & Storms, 1955.

Strzelecki, J. *See* Bindra, *et al.*, 1955.

Suci, G. J. *See* Osgood, *et al.*, 1957.

Suppes, P., & Ginsberg, R. A fundamental property of all-or-none models, binomial distribution of responses prior to conditioning with application to concept formation in children. *Psychological Review*, 1963, 70, 139–161. **(65, 91)**

T

Taffel, C. Anxiety and the conditioning of verbal behavior. *Journal of Abnormal and Social Psychology*, 1955, 51, 496–501. **(389, 390)**

Tampieri, P. *See* Giovanelli & Tampieri, 1964.

Tannenbaum, P. H. *See* Osgood, *et al.*, 1957.

Taylor, J. A. The relationship of anxiety to the conditioned eyelid response. *Journal of Experimental Psychology*, 1951, 41, 81–92. **(422, 430, 431, 452)**

Taylor, J. A. Drive theory and manifest anxiety. *Psychological Bulletin*, 1956, 53, 303–320. **(429)**

Taylor, J. A. The effects of anxiety level and psychological stress on verbal learning. *Journal of Abnormal and Social Psychology*, 1958, 57, 55–60. **(433, 434, 438)**

Thompson, R. F. *See* Briggs, *et al.*, 1954.

Thorndike, E. L. Animal intelligence. *Psychological Review, Monograph Supplement*, 1898, 2, No. 8. **(12)**

Thorndike, E. L. *The fundamentals of learning.* New York: Bureau of Publications, Teachers College, Columbia University, 1932. **(383, 400, 416)**

Thorndike, E. L., and Lorge, I. *The teacher's word book of 30,000 words.* New York: Teachers College, Columbia University, 1944. **(182, 222, 319)**

Thune, L. E., & Underwood, B. J. Retroactive inhibition as a function of degree of interpolated learning. *Journal of Experimental Psychology*, 1943, 32, 185–200. **(209, 214, 225)**

Tighe, T. J. *See* Gibson, E. J., *et al.*, 1958; Walk, *et al.*, 1958, 1959.

Tolman, E. C. *Purposive behavior in animals and men.* New York: Appleton-Century-Crofts, 1932. **(7, 384, 416, 417)**

Tolman, E. C. Cognitive maps in rats and men. *Psychological Review*, 1948, 55, 189–208. **(7, 385)**

Trabasso, T. R. *See also* Bower & Trabasso, 1963; Bower & Trabasso, 1964.

Trabasso, T. R., & Bower, G. H. Presolution dimensional shifts in concept identification: A test of the sampling with replacement axiom in all-or-none models. *Journal of Mathematical Psychology,* 1966, *3,* 163–173. **(94, 95)**

Trautman, G. E. *See* Osler & Trautman, 1961.

Tucker, I. F. *See* Schulz & Tucker, 1962 (a) , 1962 (b) .

Tulvig, E. *See also* Freibergs & Tulvig, 1961.

Tulvig, E. Theoretical issues in free recall. In T. R. Dixon & D. L. Horton (Eds.) *Verbal behavior and general behavior theory.* Englewood Cliffs, New Jersey: Prentice Hall, 1968. **(305–7, 368)**

Tulvig, E., & Arbuckle, T. Y. Sources of intratrial interference in immediate recall of paired-associates. *Journal of Verbal Learning and Verbal Behavior,* 1963, 1, 321–334. **(243)**

Tulvig, E., & Pearlstone, Z. Availability versus accessibility of information in memory for words. *Journal of Verbal Learning and Verbal Behavior,* 1966, 5, 381–391. **(305)**

Turner, L. H. *See* Solomon & Turner, 1962.

Twedt, H. M., & Underwood, B. J. Mixed vs. unmixed lists in transfer studies. *Journal of Experimental Psychology,* 1959, 58, 111–116. **(212, 213)**

U

Uhlmann, F. W., & Saltz, E. Retention of anxiety material as a function of cognitive differentiation. *Journal of Personality and Social Psychology,* 1965, 1, 55–62. **(447)**

Umemoto, T., & Hilgard, E. R. Paired-associates learning as a function of similarity: Common stimulus and response items within the list. *Journal of Experimental Psychology,* 1961, 62, 97–104. **(167, 168)**

Underwood, B. J. *See also* Barnes, J. M., & Underwood, 1959; Ekstrand & Underwood, 1963, 1965; Feldman & Underwood, 1957; Jantz & Underwood, 1958; Keppel & Underwood, 1962 (a) , 1962 (b) ; Schwenn & Underwood, 1965; Thune & Underwood, 1943; Twedt & Underwood, 1959.

Underwood, B. J. The effect of successive interpolations on retroactive and proactive inhibition. *Psychological Monographs,* 1945, 59, No. 3 (Whole No. 273) . **(214, 215, 330)**

Underwood, B. J. Retroactive and proactive inhibition after five and forty-eight hours. *Journal of Experimental Psychology,* 1948 (a) , 38, 29–38. **(217)**

Underwood, B. J. "Spontaneous recovery" of verbal associations. *Journal of Experimental Psychology,* 1948 (b) , 38, 429–439. **(217, 218)**

Underwood, B. J. Proactive inhibition as a function of time and degree of prior learning. *Journal of Experimental Psychology,* 1949, 39, 24–34. **(217, 226)**

Underwood, B. J. Proactive inhibition with increased recall-time. *American Journal of Psychology,* 1950 (a) , 63, 594–599. **(217)**

Underwood, B. J. Retroactive inhibition with increased recall time. *American Journal of Psychology,* 1950 (b) , 63, 67–77. **(226)**

Underwood, B. J. Studies of distributed practice: VIII. Learning and retention of paired nonsense syllables as a function of intralist similarity. *Journal of Experimental Psychology,* 1953 (a) , 45, 133–142. **(301, 339)**

Underwood, B. J. Studies of distributed practice: IX. Learning and retention of paired adjectives as a function of intralist similarity. *Journal of Experimental Psychology,* 1953 (b) , 45, 143–149. **(301, 339)**

Underwood, B. J. Interference and forgetting. *Psychological Review,* 1957, 64, 49–60. **(221)**

Underwood, B. J. Stimulus selection in verbal learning. In C. Cofer (Ed.) *Verbal behavior and learning: Problems and processes.* New York: McGraw-Hill, 1963. **(146, 338, 372)**

Underwood, B. J. Degree of learning and the measurement of forgetting. *Journal of Verbal Learning and Verbal Behavior,* 1964, 3, 112–129. **(200, 247, 248)**

Underwood, B. J., Ekstrand, B. R., & Keppel, G. Studies of distributed practice: XXIII. Variations in response term interference. *Journal of Experimental Psychology,* 1964, 68, 201–212. **(187, 188)**

Underwood, B. J., Ekstrand, B. R., & Keppel, G. An analysis of intralist similarity in verbal learning with experiments on conceptual similarity. *Journal of Verbal Learning and Verbal Behavior,* 1965, 4, 447–462. **(189, 190)**

Underwood, B. J., & Erlebacher, A. H. Studies of coding in verbal learning. *Psychological Monographs,* 1965, 79, No. 13 (Whole No. 606) . **(374)**

Underwood, B. J., & Keppel, G. One trial learning? *Journal of Verbal Learning and Verbal Behavior,* 1962, 1, 1–13. **(90)**

Underwood, B. J., & Keppel, G. Bidirectional paired-associate learning. *American Journal of Psychology,* 1963 (a) , 76, 470–474. **(167)**

Underwood, B. J., & Keppel, G. Coding processes in verbal learning. *Journal of Verbal Learning and Verbal Behavior,* 1963 (b) , 1, 250–257. **(360, 374)**

Underwood, B. J., & Keppel, G. Retention as a function of degree of learning and letter-sequence interference. *Psychological Monographs,* 1963 (c) , 77, Whole No. 567. **(223)**

Underwood, B. J., & Postman, L. Extra-experimental sources of interference in forgetting. *Psychological Review,* 1960, 67, 73–95. **(221, 223, 243)**

Underwood, B. J., Rehula, R., & Keppel, G. Item selection in paired-associate learning. *American Journal of Psychology,* 1962, 75, 353–371. (89)

Underwood, B. J., & Richardson, J. Some verbal materials for the study of concept formation. *Psychological Bulletin,* 1956 (a), 53, 84–95. (41)

Underwood, B. J., & Richardson, J. The influence of meaningfulness, intralist similarity, and serial position on retention. *Journal of Experimental Psychology,* 1956 (b), 52, 119–126. (339)

Underwood, B. J., & Richardson, J. Studies in distributed practice: XVIII. The influence of meaningfulness and intralist similarity of serial nonsense lists. *Journal of Experimental Psychology,* 1958, 56, 213–219. (339)

Underwood, B. J., Runquist, W. N., & Schulz, R. W. Response learning in paired-associate lists as a function of intralist similarity. *Journal of Experimental Psychology,* 1959, 58, 70–78. (171, 174, 179, 180, 187–90)

Underwood, B. J., & Schulz, R. W. *Meaningfulness and verbal learning.* Chicago: J. B. Lippincott, 1960, (145, 172, 191, 258, 315–17, 332, 334, 336)

V

Voeks, V. W. Acquisition of S-R connections: A test of Hull's and Guthrie's theories. *Journal of Experimental Psychology,* 1954, 47, 137–147. (18, 95–98)

Voeks, V. W. Gradual strengthening of S-R connections or increasing number of S-R connections. *Journal of Psychology,* 1955, 39, 289–299. (95–98)

vom Saal, W. *See* Murdock & vom Saal, 1967.

von Restorff, H. Über die Wirkung von Bereichsbildungen im Spuren-feld. In W. Kohler and H. von Restorff, Analyse von Vorgängen im Spurenfeld. I. *Psychologische Forschung,* 1933, 18, 299–342. (183)

von Senden, M. *Space and sight.* Glencoe, Ill.: Free Press, 1960. (41, 255)

Voss, J. F. Effect of pairing directionality and anticipatory cue in paired-associate learning. *Journal of Experimental Psychology,* 1965, 69, 490–495. (167)

W

Wagner, A. R. *See* Goodrich, *et al.,* 1957, 1959.

Walk, R. D. *See also* Gibson, E. J., & Walk, 1956; Gibson, E. J., *et al.,* 1958.

Walk, R. D., Gibson, E. J., Pick, H. L., & Tighe, T. J. Further experiments on prolonged exposure to visual forms: The effect of single stimuli and prior reinforcement. *Journal of Comparative and Physiological Psychology,* 1958, 51, 483–487. (120, 136, 140, 141)

Walk, R. D., Gibson, E. J., Pick, H. L., Jr., & Tighe, T. J. The effectiveness of prolonged exposure to cutouts vs. painted patterns for facilitation of discrimination. *Journal of Comparative and Physiological Psychology*, 1959, 52, 519–521. **(120)**

Walker, C. M., & Bourne, L. E., Jr. Concept identification as a function of amount of relevant and irrelevant information. *American Journal of Psychology*, 1961, 74, 410–417. **(42)**

Wallach, H., & Henle, M. An experimental analysis of the law of effect. *Journal of Experimental Psychology*, 1941, 28, 340–349. **(383, 401, 402)**

Wallach, H., & Henle, M. A further study of the function of reward. *Journal of Experimental Psychology*, 1942, 30, 147–160. **(383, 401, 402)**

Wallach, L., & Sprott, R. L. Inducing number conservation in children. *Child Development*, 1964, 35, 1057–1071. **(73)**

Wallach, M. A. *See* Caron & Wallach, 1957.

Warren, J. M. *See* Brookshire, *et al.*, 1961.

Wattenmaker, R. Effects of practice on incidental learning. Unpublished paper, 1965. **(358, 371)**

Waugh, N., & Norman, D. A. Primary memory. *Psychological Review*, 1965, 72, 89–104. **(238)**

Weaver, G. E. *See also* Schulz & Weaver, 1968.

Weaver, G. E., Hopkins, R. H., & Schulz, R. W. The A-B, B-C, A-C mediation paradigm: A-C performance in the absence of study trials. *Journal of Experimental Psychology*, 1968, 77, 670–675. **(283)**

Weaver, G. E., & Schulz, R. W. A-B, B-C, A-C mediation paradigm: Recall of A-B following varying numbers of trials of A-C learning. *Journal of Experimental Psychology*, 1968, 78, 113–119. **(285)**

Wechsler, D. *The measurement of adult intelligence.* (3rd ed.) Baltimore: Williams & Wilkins, 1944. **(38)**

Wegner, N., & Zeaman, D. Strength of cardiac CR's with varying unconditioned stimulus durations. *Psychological Review*, 1958, 65, 238–241. **(162)**

Weiss, G. *See* Homzie & Weiss, 1965.

Weiss, W. *See* Hovland & Weiss, 1953.

Weissbluth, S. *See* Horowitz, *et al.*, 1964.

Wells, H., & Deffenbacker, K. Conjunctive and disjunctive concept learning in humans and squirrel monkeys. *Canadian Journal of Psychology*, 1967, 21, 301–308. **(45)**

Wendt, G. R. An interpretation of inhibition of conditioned reflexes as competition between reaction systems. *Psychological Review*, 1936, 43, 258–281. **(223)**

Werner, H., & Kaplan, E. Development of word meaning through verbal context: An experimental study. *Journal of Psychology,* 1950, 29, 251–257. **(57)**

Weyant, R. C. *See* Perkins & Weyant, 1958.

Whimbey, A. E. *See* Scott, *et al.,* 1967 (a) , 1967 (b) .

White, C. T., & Schlosberg, H. Degree of conditioning of the GSR as a function of the period of delay. *Journal of Experimental Psychology,* 1952, 43, 357–362. **(161)**

White, M. A. *See* Horowitz, Day, *et al.,* 1968; Horowitz, White, & Atwood, 1968.

Whitman, R. N. *See also* Saltz, Whitman, Paul, 1963.

Whitman, R. N. Concept attainment as a function of intelligence and cognitive style. Doctoral dissertation, Wayne State University, 1966. **(54)**

Whitmarsh, G. A. *See* Bousfield, *et al.,* 1958; Bousfield, *et al.,* 1960; Kincaid, *et al.,* 1962.

Wickens, D. D. *See also* Corman & Wickens, 1968; Newton & Wickens, 1956.

Wickens, D. D. The transference of conditioned excitation and conditioned inhibition from one muscle group to the antagonistic muscle group. *Journal of Experimental Psychology,* 1938, 22, 101–123. **(415)**

Wickens, D. D. Encoding categories of words: an empirical approach to meaning. *Psychological Review,* 1970, 77, 1–15. **(239)**

Wickens, D. D., Born, D. G., & Allen, C. K. Proactive inhibition and item similarity in short-term memory. *Journal of Verbal Learning and Verbal Behavior,* 1963, 2, 440–445. **(80, 241, 242, 245)**

Wickens, D. D., & Briggs, G. E. Mediated stimulus generalization as a factor in sensory pre-conditioning. *Journal of Experimental Psychology,* 1951, 42, 197–200. **(288)**

Wickens, D. D., & Clark, S. E. Osgood dimensions as an encoding class in short-term memory. *Journal of Experimental Psychology,* 1968, 78, 599–604. **(242)**

Wickey, J. *See also* Saltz & Wickey, 1965, 1967.

Wickey, J. Cognitive factors in the immediate and delayed recall of attitudinal materials. Doctoral dissertation, Wayne State University, 1967. **(447, 448)**

Wiley, R. E. *See* Horton & Wiley, 1967 (a) , 1967 (b) .

Williams, J. G. *See* Battig, *et al.,* 1962.

Williams, J. J. *See* Battig, *et al.,* 1962.

Winnick, W. A., & Kressel, K. Tachistoscopic recognition thresholds, paired-associates learning, and free recall as a function of abstractness-concreteness and word frequency. *Journal of Experimental Psychology,* 1965, 70, 163–168. **(318, 321, 322)**

Winograd, E., Karchmer, M. A., & Tucker, R. Strolling down memory lane with the method of locations. Paper read at meeting of the Psychonomics Society, San Antonio, Texas, 1970. **(378)**

Wischner, G. J., Fowler, H., & Kushnik, S. A. Effect of strength of punishment for "correct" or "incorrect" responses on visual discrimination performance. *Journal of Experimental Psychology,* 1963, 65, 131–138. **(450)**

Withey, S., Buxton, C. E., & Elkin, A. Control of rest interval activities in experiments on reminiscence in serial verbal learning. *Journal of Experimental Psychology,* 1949, 39, 173–176. **(358)**

Witkin, H. A., Dyk, R. B., Faterson, H. F., & Karp, S. A. *Psychological differentiation.* New York: Wiley, 1962. **(447)**

Wohwill, J. F., & Lowe, R. C. Experimental analysis of the development of the conservation of number. *Child Development,* 1962, 33, 153–167. **(69, 72)**

Wolff, J. L. Concept attainment, intelligence, and stimulus complexity: An attempt to replicate Osler and Trautman (1961). *Journal of Experimental Psychology,* 1967, 73, 488–490. **(54)**

Wollen, K. A. One-trial versus incremental-paired associates learning. *Journal of Verbal Learning and Verbal Behavior,* 1962, 1, 14–21. **(90)**

Wollen, K. A., & Gallup, G. G., Jr. R-S recall as a function of presence or absence of successive pair repetitions in S-R learning. *Journal of Verbal Learning and Verbal Behavior,* 1968, 7, 77–80. **(169)**

Wyckoff, L. B., Jr. The role of observing responses in discrimination learning. Part I. *Psychological Review,* 1952, 59, 431–442. **(121, 123, 141)**

Y

Yarczower, M. *See* Cofer & Yarczower, 1957.

Yarmey, A. D., & Paivio, A. Further evidence on the effects of word abstractness and meaningfulness in paired-associate learning, *Psychonomic Science,* 1965, 2, 307–308. **(325)**

Yerkes, R. M., & Dodson, J. D. The relation of strength of stimulus to rapidity of habit-formation. *Journal of Comparative Neurology and Psychology,* 1908, 18, 459–482. **(449)**

Young, R. K. *See also* Hakes, *et al.,* 1964.

Young, R. K. A comparison of two methods of learning serial associations. *American Journal of Psychology,* 1959, 72, 554–559. **(262)**

Young, R. K. Paired-associates learning when the same items occur as stimuli and responses. *Journal of Experimental Psychology,* 1961, 61, 315–318. **(168, 261)**

Young, R. K. Tests of three hypotheses about the effective stimulus in serial learning. *Journal of Experimental Psychology,* 1962, 63, 307–313. **(261)**

Young, R. K., & Casey, M. Transfer from serial to paired-associates learning. *Journal of Experimental Psychology,* 1964, 67, 594–595. **(261)**

Young, R. K., & Clark, J. Compound-stimulus hypothesis in serial learning. *Journal of Experimental Psychology,* 1964, 67, 301–302. **(261)**

Youssef, Z. I. *See also* Saltz & Youssef, 1964.

Youssef, Z. I. Association and integration in serial learning. Doctoral dissertation, Wayne State University, 1964. **(260–66)**

Youssef, Z. I. Association and integration in serial learning. *American Journal of Psychology,* 1967, 80, 355–362. **(260–66)**

Z

Zajkowski, M. M. *See* Erikson & Zajkowski, 1967.

Zajonc, R. B., & Nieuwenhuyse, B. Relationship between word frequency and recognition: Perceptual process or response bias? *Journal of Experimental Psychology,* 1964, 67, 276–285. **(183)**

Zeaman, D. *See* Wegner & Zeaman, 1958.

Subject Index

505

This book has been set in 11 and 10 point Baskerville, leaded 2 points. Part titles and chapter titles are set in 14 point Craw Modern. Chapter numbers are in 10 point Helvetica and 18 point Craw Modern. The size of the type page is 27 by 46 picas.

71 72 73 74 75 8 7 6 5 4 3 2 1